Doing Good Qualitative Research

Doing Good Qualitative Research

Edited by
Jennifer Cyr and Sara Wallace Goodman

OXFORD
UNIVERSITY PRESS

OXFORD
UNIVERSITY PRESS

Oxford University Press is a department of the University of Oxford. It furthers
the University's objective of excellence in research, scholarship, and education
by publishing worldwide. Oxford is a registered trade mark of Oxford University
Press in the UK and certain other countries.

Published in the United States of America by Oxford University Press
198 Madison Avenue, New York, NY 10016, United States of America.

© Oxford University Press 2024

All rights reserved. No part of this publication may be reproduced, stored in
a retrieval system, or transmitted, in any form or by any means, without the
prior permission in writing of Oxford University Press, or as expressly permitted
by law, by license, or under terms agreed with the appropriate reproduction
rights organization. Inquiries concerning reproduction outside the scope of the
above should be sent to the Rights Department, Oxford University Press, at the
address above.

You must not circulate this work in any other form
and you must impose this same condition on any acquirer.

Library of Congress Cataloging-in-Publication Data
Names: Cyr, Jennifer, 1978– editor. | Goodman, Sara Wallace, 1979– editor.
Title: Doing good qualitative research / [edited by Jennifer Cyr, Sara Wallace Goodman].
Description: New York, NY : Oxford University Press, [2024] |
Includes bibliographical references and index.
Identifiers: LCCN 2023056771 (print) | LCCN 2023056772 (ebook) |
ISBN 9780197633144 (paperback) | ISBN 9780197633137 (hardback) |
ISBN 9780197633168 (epub) | ISBN 9780197633151 (PDF) | ISBN 9780197633175 (online)
Subjects: LCSH: Qualitative research—Methodology. | Social sciences—Methodology.
Classification: LCC H62 .D639 2024 (print) | LCC H62 (ebook) |
DDC 001.4/2—dc23/eng/20240119
LC record available at https://lccn.loc.gov/2023056771
LC ebook record available at https://lccn.loc.gov/2023056772

DOI: 10.1093/oso/9780197633137.001.0001

Paperback printed by Marquis Book Printing, Canada
Hardback printed by Bridgeport National Bindery, Inc., United States of America

Contents

List of Tables and Figures ix
Acknowledgments xi
List of Contributors xiii

1 Introduction 1
  Jennifer Cyr and Sara Wallace Goodman

PART I SETTING UP A RESEARCH PROJECT

2 Choosing a Research Question 13
  Julia Lynch

3 The Researcher's Gaze: Positionality and Reflexivity 23
  Lahoma Thomas

4 Theorization and Causality 37
  Cathie Jo Martin

5 The Construction of Knowledge 49
  Jooyoun Lee

6 Case Study and Selection 61
  Sara Wallace Goodman

7 The Potential of Mixed Methods for Qualitative Research 72
  Thalia Gerzso and Rachel Beatty Riedl

8 Preparing a Causal Research Design 85
  Jody LaPorte

9 Preparing an Interpretive Research Design 96
  Tanya B. Schwarz and Carrie Reiling

PART II PREPARING FOR THE FIELD

10 Preparing for the Field: The Nuts and Bolts 111
   Hannah Lebovits

11 Sampling Hard-to-Reach Populations 122
   Rana B. Khoury

12 Power Dynamics between Researcher and Subject 132
   Rachel Ayrton

13 Developing a Flexible Data-Collection Plan 145
   Lindsay Mayka and Jessica A. J. Rich

14	Considering Collaboration as Part of Your Research Design Mneesha Gellman	156
15	A Plan for Managing and Storing Your Data Verónica Pérez Bentancur	166

PART III COLLECTING QUALITATIVE DATA

16	Interviewing Elites Lantian Li	183
17	Interviewing and Listening to Ordinary People Katherine J. Cramer	195
18	Interviewing Vulnerable Populations Wendy Pearlman	208
19	Focus Groups Jennifer Cyr	222
20	Ethnography Jessica Pisano	233
21	Supplementing Qualitative Work with Surveys, and Vice Versa Emily Thorson and Emily M. Farris	245
22	Locating and Working with Historical Data Diana S. Kim	255
23	Fieldwork in Fragile Contexts and with High-Risk Populations: Ethics, Relationships, and Rapport Julie Chernov Hwang	265
24	Studying Indigenous Peoples' Politics: Recommendations for Non-Indigenous Researchers Tulia G. Falleti	275
25	Qualitative Research as a Minoritized Scholar Robin L. Turner	286
26	Mental Health, Identity, and Fieldwork Dana El Kurd and Calla Hummel	299
27	Navigating Ethical Issues and Choices in the Field Lauren Duquette-Rury	308
28	Digital Fieldwork: Opportunities and Challenges Diana Kapiszewski, Lauren MacLean, and Lahra Smith	323

PART IV ANALYZING QUALITATIVE DATA

29 **Reading Closely** *Antje Ellermann*	339
30 **The Role of Description** *Deborah Avant*	349
31 **Content Analysis** *Zawadi Rucks-Ahidiana*	361
32 **Qualitative Social Network Analysis** *Jennifer Spindel*	373
33 **Process Tracing** *Amy H. Liu*	386
34 **Comparative Historical Analysis** *Prerna Singh*	397
35 **Discourse Analysis** *Tania Islas Weinstein*	410
36 **Qualitative Comparative Analysis** *Ioana-Elena Oana*	422

PART V PUBLISHING QUALITATIVE RESEARCH

37 **Research Transparency in Qualitative Inquiry** *Diana Kapiszewski*	435
38 **Ethics of Transparency and Data Sharing** *Samantha Majic*	446
39 **Strategizing Fit and Legibility** *Shantel Gabrieal Buggs and Jennifer Patrice Sims*	456
40 **Publishing Qualitative Research** *Sara Wallace Goodman and Jennifer Cyr*	467
Index	479

List of Tables and Figures

Tables

Table 7.1	Summary of the Promises and Pitfalls of Each Methodological Tool Used in Political Science Scholarship	77
Table 12.1	Behaviours Indicative of Shifting Power in Research Encounters	136
Table 15.1	Example of Data Requirements in a Qualitatitative DMP	169
Table 27.1	A Flexibility Strategy and Consideration for an Ethics of Care Qualitative Practice	314
Table 31.1	Race Search Terms	364
Table 31.2	Actor Codes	367
Table 33.1	Types of Evidence	391
Table 33.2	Finding Evidence for Hypothesis 1	393
Table 33.3	Finding Evidence for Rival Hypothesis	393
Table 40.1	Identifying Similarities and Differences in Review Evaluation, by Journal	473

Figures

Figure 4.1	Frequency of Society Words in Education Snippets (Goals of Public System)	43
Figure 6.1	Criteria for Case Selection	65
Figure 15.1	Main Phases in a Research Project's Data Cycle That Guide the Design of a Qualitative DMP	168
Figure 15.2	Summary of Main Elements in a Qualitative DMP	174
Figure 19.1	Basic Questions about Focus Groups	225
Figure 22.1	The Myanmar National Archives Building in Yangon	256
Figure 22.2	Entrance to the Archives of the Kowloon branch of HSBC in Hong Kong	256
Figure 22.3	Index for Colonial Office Records, Series Number 273 (CO 273).	259
Figure 31.1	Sample Article	365
Figure 31.2	Search Results for Asian Search Terms in MaxQDA	369
Figure 32.1	Networks Showing Weight and Types of Ties	375
Figure 32.2	Friendship and Rivalry Ties, Indian Subcontinent, 1950s–1965	378
Figure 33.1	The Checklist	387
Figure 33.2	Example of a Timeline	389
Figure 33.3	Example of a Causal Graph	389
Figure 40.1	Qualitative Submissions by Journal Type	470

Acknowledgments

Jen wishes to thank her family. Our life is lovely and chaotic. I wouldn't have it any other way. I am also incredibly thankful for my coeditor, Sara, whose "hairbrained" idea (her word, not mine) was the impetus for all 500 of these pages. You are a force of nature—what a joy to be your co-pilot on this crazy multi-year ride. It feels impossible, but we *still* have not yet met in person. And so, I give a final word of thanks to social media, for bringing us together in a COVID-induced blur of direct messaging, despite thousands of miles of distance and mandatory quarantines.

And Sara wishes to thank her coeditor, Jen, for putting up with my ruthless efficiency and compulsive email habits, and for teaching me how to use WhatsApp. And thank you for agreeing to my hairbrained idea of assembling a comprehensive volume, with over 40 contributors, on qualitative methods in the middle of pandemic when it looked like no one would ever be able to collect qualitative data again. I wasn't looking for more work, but I just really wanted this type of volume to exist in the world, so that anyone who wants to do qualitative work has an accessible resource for getting started. Thank you for being a fantastic coeditor, thoughtful methodologist, inspiring human, and model academic for us all. Thank you also to my family, who didn't even know about this edited volume, because if they found out I was working on *another* book they'd probably yell at me and tell me to find a hobby.

Last, both of us wish to thank our contributors. This book exists thanks to the brilliant scholars whose wisdom and experience fill these pages. We are grateful to each of you and feel privileged to amplify your voices here. Your generosity and expertise will help so many scholars who wish to do good qualitative research. And with that, *we dedicate this book to the next generation of social science scholars, who we hope will lead their fields toward inclusive excellence.*

Contributors

Deborah Avant is the Sié Chéou-Kang Chair for International Security and Diplomacy at the Josef Korbel School of International Studies, University of Denver.

Rachel Ayrton is a Leverhulme Early Career Fellow in the Institute for Research into Superdiversity, University of Birmingham.

Verónica Pérez Bentancur is Assistant Professor in the Department of Political Science, Universidad de la República, Uruguay.

Shantel Gabrieal Buggs is Assistant Professor of Sociology, Florida State University.

Katherine J. Cramer is the Virginia Sapiro Professor of Political Science and the Natalie C. Holton Chair of Letters & Science, University of Wisconsin–Madison.

Jennifer Cyr is Associate Professor of Political Science at Universidad Torcuato Di Tella in Buenos Aires.

Lauren Duquette-Rury is Associate Professor of Sociology, Wayne State University.

Dana El Kurd is Assistant Professor of Political Science, University of Richmond.

Antje Ellermann is Professor of Political Science and founding Director, UBC Centre for Migration Studies, University of British Columbia.

Tulia G. Falleti is the Class of 1965 Endowed Term Professor of Political Science and Director of the Center for Latin American and Latinx Studies, University of Pennsylvania.

Emily M. Farris is Associate Professor of Political Science, Texas Christian University.

Mneesha Gellman is Associate Professor of Political Science in the Marlboro Institute for Liberal Arts and Interdisciplinary Studies, Emerson College.

Thalia Gerzso is a Postdoctoral Fellow in the Department of Government at the London School of Economics.

Sara Wallace Goodman is Chancellor's Fellow and Dean's Professor of Political Science, University of California, Irvine.

Calla Hummel is Associate Professor of Political Science, University of Miami.

Julie Chernov Hwang is Associate Professor in the Department of Political Science and International Relations, Goucher College.

Tania Islas Weinstein is Assistant Professor of Political Science, McGill University.

Diana Kapiszewski is the Provost's Distinguished Associate Professor of Government, Georgetown University.

Rana B. Khoury is Assistant Professor of Political Science, University of Illinois at Urbana-Champaign.

Diana S. Kim is Assistant Professor at Georgetown University in the Edmund A. Walsh School of Foreign Service.

Jody LaPorte is the Gonticas Fellow in Politics and International Relations and Director of Studies for PPE, Lincoln College, University of Oxford.

Hannah Lebovits is Assistant Professor of Public Affairs, University of Texas–Arlington.

Jooyoun Lee is Professor of Global Studies and Political Science, St. Edward's University.

Lantian Li is a UX Researcher at Google with a PhD in Sociology from Northwestern University.

Amy H. Liu is Professor in the Department of Government, University of Texas at Austin.

Julia Lynch is Professor of Political Science, University of Pennsylvania.

Lauren MacLean is the Arthur F. Bentley Chair and Professor of Political Science, Indiana University.

Samantha Majic is Professor of Political Science, John Jay College of Criminal Justice.

Cathie Jo Martin is Professor of Political Science, Boston University.

Lindsay Mayka is Associate Professor of Government, Colby College.

Ioana-Elena Oana is a Research Fellow in the Department of Political and Social Sciences at the European University Institute.

Wendy Pearlman is Professor of Political Science, Northwestern University, where she also holds the Charles Deering McCormick Professorship of Teaching Excellence.

Jessica Pisano is Professor of Politics at The New School for Social Research.

Carrie Reiling is Assistant Professor of Political Science and International Studies, Washington College.

Jessica A. J. Rich is Associate Professor in the Department of Political Science and Codirector of the Marquette Democracy Project, Marquette University.

Rachel Beatty Riedl is the John S. Knight Professor of International Studies in the Department of Government and Director of the Einaudi Center, Cornell University.

Zawadi Rucks-Ahidiana is Assistant Professor of Sociology, University at Albany, State University of New York.

Tanya B. Schwarz is an independent researcher and Executive Director at Pi Sigma Alpha, the National Political Science Honor Society.

Jennifer Patrice Sims is Associate Professor of Sociology, University of Alabama in Huntsville.

Prerna Singh is the Mahatma Gandhi Associate Professor of Political Science and International Studies, Brown University.

Lahra Smith is Associate Professor in the Department of Government and Director of the African Studies Program, Georgetown University.

Jennifer Spindel is Assistant Professor of Political Science, University of New Hampshire.

Lahoma Thomas is Assistant Professor in the Criminal Justice Department, Toronto Metropolitan University.

Emily Thorson is Assistant Professor of Political Science, Syracuse University.

Robin L. Turner is Associate Professor of Political Science, Butler University and an international research associate at the Society, Work, and Politics Institute, University of Witwatersrand.

1
Introduction

Jennifer Cyr and Sara Wallace Goodman

Qualitative Research? In This Environment?

This is a book about doing good qualitative research. It's about how qualitative methods, insights, and practices can provide rich, causal stories about social and political events. It's about how qualitative methods are sometimes the only way to interpret certain types of evidence. And it's about how anyone—regardless of institution or training or background—can carefully implement a qualitative research design.

Qualitative research can help us answer some of the most important research questions of our time. And yet it has never been more unpopular in political science. Only a fraction of published work in top journals employ qualitative methods. In looking at the methods used in a random sample of articles from top-10 political science journals between 2000 and 2009, researchers found only 16.9% of single-method articles employ qualitative methods (inclusive of both small-N analysis and interpretive approaches). Between 2010 and 2018 this figure dropped to 9.4%.[1] Qualitative methods are much more prevalent in sociology, but as a "low-consensus" field, some journals (e.g., *Social Science Research*, *European Sociological Review*) end up predominantly publishing quantitative work, while others (e.g., *British Journal of Sociology*, *Sociological Forum*) are more qualitative-friendly outlets.[2]

Not only is qualitative research disproportionately underpublished in political science, but evidence also shows it is submitted to journals at lower rates than quantitative work. In the discipline's flagship journal, *American Political Science Review*, submission rates of qualitative work are far lower than those for quantitative work. Looking at 2020 data, 50% of all submissions used "statistical-observational" methods, with another 18.6% employing "experimental (lab, survey, or field)" methods. All other kinds of methodological approaches pale in comparison, such as "case study/small N," at 5.2%.[3] To wit, even with the "return of the single-country study"—once the comparative political scientist's bread and butter—these studies mostly consist of experiments or study of statistical analyses of national administrative data.[4]

How did we get here? We can identify several factors that have hindered qualitative research in political science. Intellectually, for example, we can trace this disadvantage to the "behavioral turn" in the mid-20th century, which emphasized a more quantitative approach to explaining social and political behavior and marked a change in how social scientists conducted empirical research. For instance, the landmark volume *The Civic Culture* showed not only that social scientists could feasibly survey individuals in large numbers (and across countries), but it also reflected the novelty that individual behavior and attitudes were things political scientists could study at all, as opposed to, say, comparing constitutions and laws. The behavioral turn also promoted the idea that the study of politics could (and should) be value-free, rigorous, and objective.[5] Today we understand that this purported neutrality is a myth. The goal of making the social sciences more "scientific" has nevertheless endured, as does the idea that more quantitative evidence reduces bias.[6]

The consequences of the behavioral turn is most concrete in graduate student training. Finding statistically significant relationships came to be valued more than description. Consequently, graduate programs evolved to privilege quantitative methods courses and incorporate specialists in the growing subfield of political methodology, which frequently implies *quantitative* or experimental political methodology. Indeed, many graduate programs, as they work to include courses on the new methodological gold standard of the day, however defined, offer sequences that range from basic statistics and experiments to formal models and Bayesian inference. But they often neglect to include any qualitative data collection or analysis in their methods sequence.[7] So even though political science may have "gone further than any other social science in developing a rigorous field of study devoted to qualitative methods,"[8] few are trained in advanced or even basic qualitative techniques.[9] This means fewer scholars are *producing* qualitative work, and fewer scholars can subsequently *evaluate* qualitative work, for instance, as a peer reviewer. Consequently, new PhDs have only certain tools at their disposal when they begin to carry out their research or evaluate others' research. Inevitably, these trends influence citation practices.

There are also larger, structural trends at play that favor quantitative work: the increasing popularity of the lab model of research, methodological faddism of data science, and the rewards of "fast science" over the often slow work of data collection by talking to people or combing through archives. Diminishing opportunities to invest in and learn qualitative skills are endogenous to declining incentives and timelines to produce qualitative research.

We've begun this book by describing a big, seemingly insurmountable problem. And yet—*and yet!*—here we are, presenting an edited volume with 40 chapters on producing good qualitative research, from picking a topic to publishing results. Why? Because qualitative methods are worth the trouble. Concept formation, decisions about measurement, case study work, causal process tracing, even reading closely and systematically are all skills that are indispensable for all research designs. In their classic text *Rethinking Social Inquiry*, Brady and Collier[10] persuasively demonstrate that exemplary qualitative research looks quite different from exemplary quantitative work. Simply put, broad training in qualitative methods helps scholars make all kinds of arguments, becoming better producers, reviewers, and consumers of social science research. Even if you work outside of qualitative research communities, it is likely that you will review—or want to cite—qualitative research in your own work. We believe qualitative research is not only worth protecting but is indispensable to understanding the political and social world.

To be sure, we are not the first to identify the critical decline in qualitative research, nor the first to offer up an intervention to reverse this decline. The past few decades have seen near-heroic efforts to redress the systemic hurdles that qualitative research faces. *Rethinking Social Inquiry* is one of many texts that take seriously the theoretical rigor that underpins qualitative work. See also, for example, Gary Goertz's book on concepts,[11] James Mahoney and Dietrich Rueschemeyer's book on comparative historical analysis,[12] and Dvora Yanow and Peregrine Schwartz-Shea's edited volume on the interpretive turn in political science.[13] These works helped us to engage with and understand different types of qualitative research in a meaningful way. The Institute for Qualitative and Multi-Methods Research provides intensive courses on a plethora of different qualitative data collection and analytical methods. The Qualitative and Multi-Methods Research section of the American Political Science

Association has served as a venue for sharing and engaging with qualitative work. The research publication that this section spawned (*Qualitative and Multimethod Research*)[14] offers a place for researchers to write about qualitative methods. The Southwest Workshop on Mixed Methods Research is a venue where scholars can rigorously consider how qualitative methods might best combine with other methods of data collection and analysis. In sum, qualitative methods are arguably discussed and debated now more than ever. Nevertheless, and perhaps paradoxically, the research lag remains, as does the tendency against including it in our graduate courses.

While one book cannot overturn long-standing trends in the social sciences, we do think this book provides a comprehensive take that can make much of the actual "doing" of qualitative data collection and analysis more understandable, more accessible, more feasible, and therefore more likely. Our goal with this volume is to provide *practical* advice on carrying out a qualitative research project, from start (i.e., finding the research question) to finish (i.e., finding a publishing venue). Toward that end, it includes actionable advice from over 40 experts who have honed their craft by *doing good qualitative research* and who seek to help train the next generation by contributing their experiences and insights to this volume.

The chapters, as you will see, are short, easy to consume, and engaging to read. The objective is to present practical, comprehensive information about qualitative methods within your research. You will receive a first-person account of how to do a particular step in the research process, and you will also find honest advice about the expected and unexpected challenges associated with doing qualitative research. Each chapter is both accessible and rigorous. The chapters combine "real talk" with serious theoretical and practical knowledge. Our goal is to make qualitative research more "knowable" for those social science scholars who seek this knowledge. As a consequence, we hope to open qualitative methods to a wider research community.

Our audience is everyone. We recognize that, unless one is at a handful of schools with access to a handful of scholars, early-career researchers will not generally receive training in producing qualitative research. For researchers who haven't received such training, this volume serves as an introduction to the full gamut of qualitative research considerations. For students lucky enough to receive training in qualitative methods, we recognize that access to advanced techniques is still limited. Did your advisor tell you, "Go do interviews," and you don't know where to start? Are you preparing for the field and feel totally overwhelmed? Do you think your data might be appropriate for qualitative comparative analysis (QCA) but aren't sure how to proceed? Are you concerned about positionality in your data collection or analysis? Or maybe you want to supplement an observational, large-N study with process tracing? Or archives? This book is for you. It will help you find your coordinates as a qualitative scholar and provide the tools to allow you to navigate a project on your own.

Let us introduce one caveat before diving into the work of doing good qualitative research. This volume brings together dozens of scholars with years of experience in the art and science of undertaking qualitative methods. These scholars have a wealth of knowledge to impart, and you will walk away from this text a better qualitative methodologist—and, therefore, a better scholar—as a result. Yet we emphasize that the chapters present one way to carry out each step in the qualitative research process. No chapter purports to explain *the only* way to carry out that step—and, indeed, some steps in the research process are hotly debated. Consequently, the authors in this volume look beyond their own experiences to provide references to other perspectives and approaches to undertaking qualitative research—sometimes explicitly in the text or by referencing suggested readings at the end of each chapter. There is no single way to do good qualitative research; nevertheless, we think it is worthwhile to compile a set of strategies that takes you from the initial stage of finding a research question to the final stage of seeking a publication venue. Our knowledge about qualitative methods, as with all knowledge, is cumulative. This volume stands upon the shoulders of the qualitative methodologists who came before us, and we hope it inspires more work in the future.

What Is *Good* Qualitative Research?

Before we can provide a roadmap to doing good qualitative research, we first need to establish some definitions. (We'd be remiss if we didn't note that qualitative scholars tend to excel at conceptualization.) First, what is qualitative research? Some define it as "case-based," "small-N," or non-numeric. These are helpful in distinguishing qualitative work from quantitative work but do not elucidate its full panoply of characteristics (e.g., features) and epistemologies (i.e., approaches to and understanding of knowledge). Therefore, we suggest that qualitative research generally involves building explanations or constructing meaning through the careful, nuanced analysis or interpretation of data collected via a range of sources: for example, talking to people, collecting primary documents and artifacts, and participating in and observing social practices.

Qualitative research can be descriptive, causal, or interpretive. In this volume, we distinguish positivist from interpretivist qualitative research, since these two approaches vary in terms of their epistemological foundations. A positivist approach to qualitative methods sees phenomena of interest in the social world as "knowable" objects of study, the conclusions about which we can apply to other, similar phenomena. An interpretivist approach, by contrast, sees that one's claims about the world are inextricable from one's own interaction with that world. The researcher's perspective inevitably shapes the conclusions that they make. Knowledge, as a consequence, is constructed through the interaction of phenomena of study and the researcher. Who is doing the research, and what and whom we access as researchers, will shape our understanding of the world around us.

In practice, then, the body of research that we include under the banner of qualitative research encompasses two distinct epistemologies. It also includes different data collection methods and analytical approaches. So how, then, do we define *good* qualitative research, given the diversity of qualitative methods and its capacity to change over time? We identify five goals that should serve as benchmarks:

1. *Rigorous:* Good qualitative research, we suggest, requires rigor and honesty. These standards may exist in practice in other methods, but they are indispensable to qualitative work.
2. *Aligned:* It aligns method with motivation: the methodological choices made should be appropriate and feasible for the research question and data at hand.
3. *Flexible:* Good qualitative research is supported by a flexible research design that allows for the frequently used practice of iteration and nonlinear progression between data and analysis.
4. *Ethical:* It is also ethical and respects distinct boundaries by centering considerations like positionality and community or subject vulnerability.

5. *Inclusive:* Finally, good qualitative research should embody (or perhaps even pioneer) the best practices in the social sciences, such as inclusion and accessibility.

We discuss each of these goals in turn.

Rigor: Good qualitative research should be rigorous in its execution and transparent in its presentation. The first point speaks to a commitment to carry out qualitative methods systematically, that is, with a conscious, dedicated effort to abide by the norms and practices underpinning each qualitative method and approach. This may involve devising and adhering to a data management plan (see Chapter 15, "A Plan for Managing and Storing Your Data"), but it can also mean taking detailed notes of the iterative-recursive process that unfolds as one undertakes research (see Chapter 9, "Preparing an Interpretivist Research Design").

Transparency, for its part, can refer to making explicit how one gathers and analyzes information as well as making that information accessible to others (see Chapter 37, "Research Transparency in Qualitative Inquiry"). More generally, however, good qualitative research involves fully explaining one's position, approach, and process. In other words, transparency *may* refer to data availability, but it certainly demands fidelity of process and—especially critical to interpretive work—of positionality. What kind of discourse analysis (Chapter 35) does one intend to undertake? What was the potential impact of doing half of one's interviews (Chapters 16–18) in person and the other half online? How did personal or contextual circumstances impact your initial research question (Chapter 2) or your choice of case selection (Chapter 6)? Rigor and transparency are fundamental to doing compelling, persuasive, honest qualitative research. They are also crucial for assessing qualitative work and situating it in the broader literature.

Alignment: Good qualitative research properly aligns one's methodological choices with the final goals of the research project. Proper methodological alignment entails making smart choices when it comes to data collection methods. When, for example, does it make sense to use focus groups (Chapter 19) rather than interviews? What data collection strategies are most appropriate for a particularly vulnerable community (Chapter 18) or in a violent context (Chapter 23)? Finally, good methodological alignment can mean bucking current methodological trends in terms of what counts as "valuable" research. For example, a more recent shift away from single-method research designs may compel a scholar to adopt a mixed-method strategy (Chapter 7), even though their research question would be best served by utilizing one method in an innovative or particularly in-depth way.

Flexible: To be sure, good qualitative research is not just about the final product. It is also about the *process* of doing research. Good qualitative research, for example, is often iterative. A qualitative researcher understands that "getting it right" (however defined) will likely involve revising a theory or interpretation and revisiting a research site. The importance of iteration for qualitative work cannot be overstated. It underpins the abductive process that initiates interpretivist work (see, e.g., Chapter 5, "The Construction of Knowledge"). It also is vital for tracing an argument from an outcome of interest back to a purported cause. The chapter on process tracing (Chapter 33) reinforces this point. The sequencing of process tracing is rarely respected in practice. The best qualitative researchers circle back and start over after new information is uncovered. This makes qualitative research particularly distinct from disciplinary trends in experimental and observational analysis, which emphasize preregistration.

Ethical: Good qualitative research contemplates—and indeed foregrounds—the potential impact of data collection on participants and also on oneself. All good qualitative research must be ethically bounded. This means, on the one hand, privileging the security and safety of the data source (be it a person or an artifact), even if this means forgoing the information they may provide. In her chapter on ethical issues in the field (Chapter 27), Lauren Duquette-Rury describes a particular research site in Mexico whose government had come under the threat of organized crime. Once she saw that her "conspicuous presence was contributing to locals' anxiety" and that speaking with her might put them in danger, she decided to leave rather than continue collecting data.

On the other hand, an ethical and bounded approach involves being reflective and reflexive with respect to our positionality vis-à-vis the people with whom we wish to speak and the places we hope to visit. Good qualitative research should not be extractive. We should reconstruct people's stories thoughtfully and in a way that acknowledges power asymmetries and historical context (see Chapters 3 and 12). Where applicable, we may even wish to collaborate with our interlocutors on the ground to build a research project that responds to their needs as much as ours (see Chapter 14).

Ethically bounded qualitative research also takes into account the researcher's own health and state of mind during the data collection and analysis process. Doing research can be taxing, both physically and mentally. The pressures to "get the answer right" may compel us to pursue an interview even though we are exhausted or the participant makes us feel unsafe. Similar pressures may push us to forgo a meal or three as a way to maximize our time in the archives (see Chapter 22 on archival research). In other words, our pursuit of knowledge may lead us to neglect to take care of ourselves. The impacts of our choices when we are in the field can be potentially devastating for our physical and mental well-being (see, e.g., Chapter 26 on fieldwork and mental health). Good qualitative research involves being ethical, mindful, and careful. We must not forget, as Duquette-Rury tells us in her chapter, that researchers are human first.

Inclusive: Finally, good qualitative research should be available and accessible to all. Good qualitative research involves multiple viewpoints and perspectives. It challenges established theories, uncovers historical inequalities, and considers the ramifications of those inequalities on how we see and know the world. This last point remains largely aspirational; to challenge established understandings and forge new ones, we need a greater diversity of perspectives in how we conduct research. Meanwhile, the *study* of qualitative methods (as opposed to the *practice* of qualitative methods) has historically been dominated by white men. Thus, you may have noticed that this 40-chapter volume features only contributions by women and nonbinary/genderqueer individuals. This was a conscious choice on our part. In doing this, we do not discount the experiences and expertise of our male colleagues, mentors, and friends. We are grateful for their contributions, and they are cited extensively throughout this volume, as they should be.

However, here we center and elevate to authority other individuals—women, nonbinary, genderqueer—from different ranks, fields, institutions, countries, and backgrounds. A roster inclusive of underrepresented experiences and marginalized scholars brings to light under-discussed insights about power dynamics, safety, access, and positionality. This arguably enriches the field with new considerations, tools, and perspectives. Inevitably these practices make social science better and enable more individuals to do good qualitative research. And if one goal of this volume is to elevate underrepresented voices to enrich methodological practices with experiences, a second is to bring those insights together. Our hope is that presenting a "one-stop shop" for the range of considerations and practices of doing good qualitative research may invite a reader to meander through its pages and "stumble" upon a chapter they may not think is relevant to them at first glance. It is important to stress that while these chapters reflect experiences and best practices *of* women, nonbinary/genderqueer individuals, and minoritized scholars from a variety of backgrounds, their content will be useful to anyone who wants to do good qualitative research. Quality is not gendered: everyone should care about rigor, alignment, flexibility, ethics, and inclusion in producing qualitative research. To repeat, *this is a volume for everyone*.

Book Outline

Our aim is that this volume will provide a comprehensive introduction to the application of qualitative methods—from formulating the initial research question to seeking out publication of the final product and everything in between, including case selection, fieldwork/data collection, and data analysis. Through its structure, accessible writing style, and multitude of considerations, we hope this text can be a useful primer for a person who wants to carry out a qualitative research-based project from start to finish. By weaving together these different aspects of qualitative research, we also hope to simplify and demystify qualitative research methods and open it up to a wider research community.

The chapters that follow share a number of features. They are relatively short in length and provide a balance between theory and practical advice. They are structured similarly. Each begins with a general overview of the topic, in which the author introduces concepts, defines terms, and lays out positions of a debate and, where relevant, positionality considerations. The next section is an overview of the state of practice. Here, authors often draw on their research experience as well as other examples from their field. This is the "doing" of the method. The next section is an overview of remaining issues, including potential pitfalls, trade-offs, and insights. Each chapter concludes with recommended readings. No chapter intends to be the final word or the definitive account on any one aspect of qualitative work. Think of each as a meaningful introduction to the method, type of data, or consideration. The reader should then be able to deduce at the end of, for example, the chapter on working with historical data (Chapter 22) if this type of data is "right" for their project. If yes, the chapter provides recommendations on where to find out more.

Given this structure, the book is designed to allow a reader to "dip in and out" of sections and chapters as desired. Each is self-contained and can be read on its own or in any order. It could also, however, be read from beginning to end to provide cohesive, stepwise guidance to conducting qualitative research.

Chapters are gathered into five sections to capture the various stages of pre-field, field, and post-field work. Part I ("Setting Up a Research Project") covers crucial first steps in setting up a research design project that collects and analyzes qualitative data. It considers how you choose an executable research question (Chapter 2), answers questions of researcher positionality when it comes to selecting an executable research design (Chapter 3), and offers chapters on theorization and knowledge construction (Chapters 4 and 5) and case selection strategies (Chapter 6). In principle, these chapters are for any type of data collection or analysis, as they reflect critical considerations for research design in general. This section ends with considerations for when your research may necessitate multimethods (Chapter 7) as well as a how-to for preparing a research design for both positivist (Chapter 8) and interpretivist (Chapter 9) approaches. This research design could serve as the basis of a dissertation prospectus, a pre-analysis plan, or a best practice guide for even experienced researchers.

Once a research design is in place, anticipating data needs from "the field" involves crucial steps from the researcher before they start collecting data. Part II ("Preparing for the Field: The Nuts and Bolts") invites the reader to think through these preparatory considerations, building on the steps taken to devise a research design in Part I. It begins with practical steps in preparing for fieldwork (Chapter 10), including factors for reaching remote populations (Chapter 11) and taking into account power dynamics (Chapter 12). It also invites the reader to anticipate multiple uses for data (Chapter 13), collaborative methodology (Chapter 14), and data management a priori (Chapter 15).

Part III ("Collecting Qualitative Data") contains several chapters that deal with the practicalities of being in the field and different strategies for data collection. It goes over distinct interview considerations for different human subject groups, including elites, ordinary people, and vulnerable populations (Chapters 16, 17, 18). It also covers focus groups (Chapter 19), ethnography (Chapter 20), the use of surveys to obtain qualitative material (Chapter 21), as well as locating historical data in archives (Chapter 22). It considers the importance of context, such as when working with high-risk and Indigenous populations (Chapters 23 and 24), and ethical and positional considerations that apply to researcher and subject, including undertaking fieldwork as a minoritized scholar (Chapter 25), mental health (Chapter 26), and community and organization ethics (Chapter 27). Part III concludes with a chapter on best practices for digital fieldwork (Chapter 28), a distinct field site in its own right but also a site of new opportunities for travel-restricted researchers and subjects.

Once a researcher has collected qualitative data, Part IV ("Analyzing Qualitative Data") walks through the different potential qualitative methods for analyzing that data. This part kicks off with an important chapter on best practices for systematic and close reading—a skill that is required for good research but rarely taught (Chapter 29). Other methods covered include description (Chapter 30), content analysis (Chapter 31), social network analysis (Chapter 32), process tracing (Chapter 33), comparative historical analysis (Chapter 34, discourse analysis (Chapter 35) and QCA (Chapter 36). We are not purists; some of these approaches pair qualitative and quantitative methods, such as QCA and content analysis. We maintain that sometimes a mixed-method approach—including analyzing qualitative data with quantitative methods—is appropriate to answer a given research question. Several chapters (e.g., Chapters 7, 21, 32, 36) highlight synergies with multimethod approaches. Consequently, we believe that broad knowledge—where readers gain competence and confidence in both quantitative and qualitative approaches—only strengthens such approaches. Again, *this book is for everyone.*

Last, much of the publication process is part of what's called the "hidden curriculum," or aspects of research and publishing to which many students without strong networks do not have access. We seek to demystify the publishing process here. We start from a position that recognizes there are unique difficulties in publishing qualitative research, particularly in high-impact outlets. Moreover, issues of legibility and fit may arise when one's work transcends the boundaries of a single discipline. We also acknowledge there are evolving standards for data transparency that require attention. Part V ("Publishing Qualitative Research") takes the reader through these issues, including transparency considerations

(Chapters 37 and 38) and strategizing fit (Chapter 39), and concludes with an overview of how political science journal editors evaluate—and see reviewers evaluate—qualitative submissions (Chapter 40), which informs a set of recommendations for publishing qualitative research.

These chapters represent, we think, a fruitful roadmap for any producer, consumer, teacher, or student interested in good qualitative research. While they cannot describe or anticipate every potential challenge, opportunity, and question that may arise, nor can they emphasize every potential way of doing qualitative work, the chapters should nevertheless be especially helpful for a new researcher to make confident choices as they navigate the road to publication. We know that, as with any kind of research, doing good qualitative research can be difficult and frustrating. It should not, however, be a mystery to those who wish to engage with it or, perhaps even worse, a secret club to which only a select few have access. Everyone and anyone can do good qualitative research.

Notes

1. Jacobs, "Letter from the Section President," ii. Mixed-method work that includes qualitative methods at 5.5%.
2. Schwemmer and Wieczorek, "The Methodological Divide of Sociology."
3. Hayward, Kadera, and Novkov, "*American Political Science Review* Editorial Report."
4. Pepinsky, "The Return of the Single-Country Study."
5. Hamati-Ataya, "Behavioralism."
6. Grossmann, *How Social Science Got Better*.
7. Emmons and Moravcsik, "Graduate Qualitative Methods Training in Political Science."
8. Gerring, "Qualitative Methods," p. 16.
9. To be sure, some graduate programs adopt a more pluralist approach to their methodological sequence. For the sake of transparency, both editors received training in qualitative methods (but not data collection) as doctoral students (at Northwestern University [Cyr] and Georgetown University [Goodman]). But this is one of the premises of the volume: access to comprehensive qualitative methods should not depend on where you get your degree or what faculty populate a given department.
10. Brady and Collier, *Rethinking Social Inquiry*.
11. Goertz, *Social Science Concepts*.
12. Mahoney and Rueschemeyer, *Comparative Historical Analysis in the Social Sciences*.
13. Yanow and Schwartz-Shea, *Interpretation and Method*.
14. https://www.qmmrpublication.com/.

References

Almond, Gabriel, and Sidney Verba. *The Civic Culture: Political Attitudes and Democracy in Five Nations*. Princeton, NJ: Princeton University Press, 1963.

Brady, Henry E., and David Collier. *Rethinking Social Inquiry: Diverse Tools, Shared Standards*. Lanham, MD: Rowman & Littlefield, 2004.

Emmons, Cassandra V., and Andrew M. Moravcsik. "Graduate Qualitative Methods Training in Political Science: A Disciplinary Crisis." *PS: Political Science & Politics* 53, no. 2 (2020): 258–264.

Gerring, John. "Qualitative Methods." *Annual Review of Political Science* 20, no. 1 (2017): 15–36.

Goertz, Gary. *Social Science Concepts: A User's Guide.* Princeton, NJ: Princeton University Press, 2006.

Grossmann, Matt. *How Social Science Got Better: Overcoming Bias with More Evidence, Diversity, and Self-Reflection.* Oxford: Oxford University Press, 2021.

Hamati-Ataya, Inanna. "Behavioralism." In *Oxford Research Encyclopedia of International Studies.* New York: Oxford University Press, 2019. https://oxfordre.com/internationalstudies/

Hayward, Clarissa, Kelly Kadera, and Julie Novkov. "*American Political Science Review* Editorial Report: Executive Summary (Spring 2021)." *Political Science Today* 1, no. 3 (August 2021): 46–53. https://www.cambridge.org/core/journals/political-science-today/article/american-political-science-review-editorial-report-executive-summary-spring-2021/76D67845C65DCC5785C9F4DFF89C6E8E.

Jacobs, Alan. "Letter from the Section President." *Qualitative and Multi-Method Research* 19, no. 2 (Fall 2021–Spring 2022): ii–iv.

Mahoney, James, and Dietrich Rueschemeyer, eds. *Comparative Historical Analysis in the Social Sciences.* Cambridge: Cambridge University Press, 2003.

Pepinsky, Thomas B. "The Return of the Single-Country Study." *Annual Review of Political Science* 22, no. 1 (2019): 187–203.

Schwemmer, Carsten, and Oliver Wieczorek. "The Methodological Divide of Sociology: Evidence from Two Decades of Journal Publications." *Sociology* 54, no. 1 (2020): 3–21.

Yanow, Dvora, and Peregine Schwartz-Shea. *Interpretation and Method: Empirical Research Methods and the Interpretive Turn.* Armonk, NY: M. E. Sharpe, 2006.

PART I
SETTING UP A RESEARCH PROJECT

2
Choosing a Research Question

Julia Lynch

This chapter is about how to choose a research question. It is directed at younger scholars choosing a dissertation question,[1] but the issues it raises will be useful for anyone at the start of a career or of a new major research agenda. Some 20 years into my own career as a professor of political science, I apply many of the same decision rules when I am beginning a new project. Experience turns out to be an excellent teacher when it comes to choosing a research question. It helps us learn about ourselves as researchers and writers, which is critical because *the questions that best fit our own unique preferences, skills, and behaviors are the best questions.*

If you are lucky, then, by the time you have passed your qualifying exams and advanced to candidacy for the PhD, you will have taken more than a class or two in graduate school, college, or high school that asked you to choose your own topic to research. If you haven't and there is still time, seek out one of those classes now! If you have, you will likely have already encountered some of the trade-offs that come up in this chapter. You may have already internalized a checklist for choosing a research question. (Is it a question? Does it generate an answer that we need in the world? Has it already been answered? Do I care enough about it to keep working on it? Does it speak to other literature? Can I figure out a series of steps I can take to answer it?) And you may have some ideas about the types of research questions that seem to work well for you, given your interests and proclivities as a researcher.

In this chapter, I share my thoughts on the conventional wisdom about choosing a research question, and some of what I've learned from my own experience about selecting research questions that work for me. Each of the main types of research questions I discuss—gap-filling, problem-driven, methods-driven, passion-driven, ambitious, cautious—have pros and cons. The best research question *for you* is likely to be the one that meets your specific needs as a scholar and as a person. However, all good research questions share a characteristic that I discuss in the final section of the chapter: they provide enough analytic *leverage* to be worth pursuing.

Research Topics or Research Questions?

You may have heard people use the terms "research topic" and "research question" interchangeably. In my view, these are actually quite different. A research *topic* is a general area of inquiry. It's what you might tell a curious seatmate on an airplane flight when they ask what your research is about: "I work on environmental policy in Latin American countries" or "My research is about what citizenship means in multiethnic societies." It could be somewhat more specific: "I'm studying how people think about the fairness of different kinds of inequalities, such as inequalities in health versus income inequalities." But a research topic is broad enough to be the inspiration for more than one research product: several articles, a dissertation plus other articles, a dissertation book plus another book, and more. A topic always contains multiple possible research questions.

A research *question* is the specific problem that we are trying to shed light on through the inquiry we conduct for a specific product (paper, thesis, article, book). A research question generally starts with *Who, What, When, Where, Why,* or *How* and ends with a question mark. Beyond that, there are many different kinds of research questions. A research question may be descriptive (What are the characteristics of the parties that have developed in the world's postcommunist states?), causal (Why do certain types of parties tend to emerge when formerly communist regimes democratize in certain ways?), constitutive[2] (What is a postcommunist party system?), or normative (Are the party systems that come after communism better at securing human thriving than the regimes that preceded them?). If it is causal, it may be focused on the causes of effects (What causes the underprovision of collective goods in societies with high levels of ethnic conflict?) or on the effects of causes (When collective goods are underprovided, what are the consequences for ethnic divisions?).[3]

When we ask research questions, we may be motivated mainly by questions about the world, as in the previous paragraph: What is the world really like? Why or how did it come to be that way? Or we may at heart be asking about ourselves, as researchers or disciplines: Why are our expectations confounded in this instance? Why did we not see this before? What do we need to do, or to think, about this? For example, we might seek to explain why a particular country that we would predict would do a poor job containing the spread of infectious diseases due to its low state capacity in fact prevented the early spread of COVID-19—and in so doing, learn something important about our conceptualization of state capacity. We might revise our theories to include factors like social cohesion that we might not have previously considered relevant or question how our own biases about the African continent may have affected our expectations of which governments would be effective in the early phases of the pandemic.

Finally, it is worth noting that when using methods such as ethnography or grounded theory[4] or when researching in the field of political theory, it is not unusual to begin working on a topic without a specific research question. In this case, rather than starting with a question, one might start with a theoretically informed hunch that a particular setting, event, case, or body of text, if examined more closely, might reveal something interesting and worth knowing. In other words, we are starting with a relationship between concepts that we are interested in exploring rather than with a question per se. For example, political scientist Adnan Naseemullah reports in the preface to his recent book *Development after Statism* that his research question—How can industrialization occur in developing countries despite liberalizing reforms in the 1980s and 1990s that left governments less able to shape markets?—arose "inductively ... from fourteen months of interview-based field research."[5]

Gap-Filling versus Problem-Driven Research Questions

I began working on this chapter by asking a nonrepresentative, convenience sample of graduate students, colleagues, and people on Twitter about the best and worst advice they had been given about choosing a research question. The advice cited by those people who had been trained in a different tradition, a different subfield of political science, or in a different discipline altogether often diverged substantially from my own notions of what constitutes a good question and how to choose one. In fact, my questioning yielded responses that were divided on a number of important issues.

One issue was whether researchers ought to choose questions that fill gaps in the literature or that are motivated by real-world problems. Advocates of the former advise researchers to *identify a reasonably small question left open in the existing literature*. Seeking out a question by looking for gaps in the existing literature has real advantages: it makes a question easier to find (one need only "read conclusions of just published work and get inspired by the 'further research should...' section," advised one commenter on Twitter) and can result in identifying problems that are narrowly enough circumscribed to be answerable in a reasonable period of time. Gap-filling projects are also likely to be of interest to other researchers who have already published in areas proximate to the gap, making it more likely to find champions and to get one's own work published.

Those who find motivation in thinking outside the existing box or breaking new theoretical ground may feel stifled by this advice, however. The incremental progress over the existing research landscape promised by gap-filling "normal science"[6] may feel like insufficient payoff for the blood, sweat, and tears that go into a dissertation. Moreover, some gaps in the literature are there for a reason, and trying to fill these "much-needed gaps"[7] may result in research questions that are excessively narrow, unimportant, and/or impossible to answer. For such researchers, a second major approach to finding a research question—*focusing on a substantive issue in the world that is important*—may be more appealing. "Center your research on the world, and not the literature," advised one advocate of this approach on Twitter. "[D]on't get your question from the literature," counseled another. Instead, "[g]et it from something interesting in the real world then use the literature to help you answer the question. The most important thing in your office isn't the books. It's the window."

The strategy of "focusing on what matters in the world" can ensure that your dissertation, with which you will likely be identified for the early phase of your career, generates some important insights that you can claim as your own, rather than the narrow "salami slices" or "minimum publishable units" typically yielded by gap-filling research questions.[8] This advice holds that the contribution of your work to solving real-world problems says more to the job market about your potential as a scholar than would a few early journal articles that make minor advances over the existing literature. But a graduate student anxious about running out of funding or wasting time chasing impossible answers will easily recognize potential drawbacks to this second, problem-driven approach: how can we know ahead of time whether the answer to a question will help solve a real-world problem? And aren't most truly important questions just too big for a graduate student to take on?

In my view many of the trade-offs we perceive between choosing topics that are gap-filling versus substantively important, or taking on projects that are too small versus too big, can be resolved by keeping our eye on the ball of *leverage*—a topic to which we shall return after discussing a two additional sets of trade-offs.

Skills, Methods, and the Market

A second decision when choosing a research question is to determine how much one's choice of question ought to depend on methods and skills. On the one hand, aspiring scholars are frequently advised to *choose research questions that you can answer using the skills you have*. Given the limited time on your PhD-funding or tenure clock, it makes sense to choose questions that require only those skills in which you have already invested. Working with skills obtained early in your trajectory as a political scientist makes it possible to publish more, sooner. Additionally, in light of the tendency for PhD programs to emphasize (albeit sometimes with a lag) training in those skills that are rewarded in a discipline, choosing a topic that you are well-trained to carry out is also likely to make your research more marketable. However, some political scientists who responded to my Twitter inquiry offered the following advice with tongue planted firmly in cheek: "Study a topic that might be of interest to your future employer. You've got a hammer (method), find a nail"; "Focus on causal inference; only ask questions where you can get 'clean identification' of a causal effect. Prioritize cleverness.... And most of all: be sure that your topic will be acceptable to big-name scholars in your field."

In the background of this skepticism and snark lurks a concern that the market for skills is constantly changing, so it can be hard to predict what will be hot or not in several years' time. One scholar who counseled pursuing "[q]uestions foundational to a lifetime of inquiry (and hopefully funding) in a nationally prioritized area of interest," followed that advice with a rueful "Unless a pandemic dries up higher ed jobs. Live for today. Choose something interesting. Learn methods you can apply widely." To this second set of advisors, it is less important to please current disciplinary gatekeepers than to choose a question that matters to you, and then learn whatever skills you need to answer that question well. Of course, it must be possible to acquire the necessary skills in an appropriate time frame—but PhD researchers are, above all, well-trained to learn new things quickly. (We throw relatively inexperienced graduate students into the classroom as teaching assistants, for example, not because they are experts on the topics covered in most large undergraduate lecture courses, but because we trust them to be able to learn unfamiliar material more efficiently than the undergraduates they teach.) In this view, it is unnecessary to choose a research question that is aligned with the methods or skills you already have: if you need a new skill, you can learn it. What matters more is to *choose a question that ignites passion*.

Passion Projects

Indeed, it is striking how contrary most advice about choosing a research question is to the caricatured view of science as a dispassionate enterprise, done without affect that could prejudice rational investigation. To be sure, many would warn against taking on a question that our moral or political commitments dictate ought to be answered in a particular way, lest our desire to produce the "right" answer compromise our methodological or analytic rigor. Yet some of the most productive scholars base their research on questions about topics that concern them deeply. For example, the late, great political scientist Guillermo O'Donnell was transparent about the important role that his political commitments played in generating passion for his research. O'Donnell chose to work on "the kinds of real-world problems that deeply bother me when I am shaving," many of which derived from his "obsession" with "the political misadventures of my country, Argentina."[9]

It doesn't take a radical constructivist to see that our preconceptions are very likely to affect the way we interpret the world even when we aren't aware that we are invested in one answer versus another—so a thoroughly dispassionate approach to social science research is unlikely to be achievable in any event. This being the case, working on a project animated by deep commitment can make answering the research question a matter of personal urgency, and mustering the energy to complete it that much easier. Most advisors know from their own experience that a key to success when launching a new research agenda is the ability to sustain passionate interest and enthusiasm over a long enough period of time to see it through to final publication—typically at least five years. As one sociologist put it on my Twitter thread, a research topic "has to get you out of bed in the morning, or you're going to lose your mind and no therapist can help."

But passion can be excited by many forms of affect, positive or negative: curiosity or fascination, a desire to set the record straight, even spite, as several scholars reported on Twitter. One of my colleagues urges students to begin looking for a dissertation question by focusing on "what pisses you off." Some of my favorite advice on the topic of passion comes from Barbara Geddes: "The standard advice on how to choose a research topic leaves out the role of such emotions as commitment, irritation, and obsession in the choice.... Contrary to the advice about looking for holes in the literature, the initial stages of good research in the comparative field often begin either with an intense but unfocused curiosity about why some event or process has happened or with a sputtering sense of indignation at the patent idiocy of some particular argument advanced in the literature."[10]

Puzzles

A final piece of advice regarding choosing a research question that scholars often hear concerns puzzles. Many advisors suggest harnessing passionate curiosity by *framing a research question as a puzzle*. "I always say at the beginning it starts with an observation and a 'what's up with that?'" said one Twitter commenter. "My approach is to find something and then be able to explain it to someone and end by saying, 'Isn't that WEIRD??'" wrote another scholar. "Mine are always the result of going 'wait, how does THAT work/happen?!'" volunteered a third. One exceptionally well-published mid-career scholar advises, "A good research question is something that genuinely puzzles you and starts with why, what, how or when and ends with a question mark." A puzzle, then, involves some empirical observation that is unexpected in light of existing theories in your own discipline and/or closely related disciplines.

The search for a research question that is a puzzle involves, first, identifying an empirical phenomenon of interest (e.g., something that varies across cases or units such as countries, time periods, institutions, or individuals); second, learning about and/or accurately measuring an outcome's variation across cases; and third, having read widely enough in the literature that could potentially explain the phenomenon to be able to tell what is predicted by existing theory versus what is truly puzzling. Answering a research question framed as a puzzle thus involves explaining why something occurs and takes the form it does, despite our best predictions to the contrary. By fruitfully joining a specific empirical question to a question about our scholarly understanding, this type of question allows us to shed light on issues that have the potential to be important in both a real-world sense and in the sense of significantly advancing theory. This, I suspect, is what gives the advice to search out puzzle questions its staying power: I was advised this way as a graduate student, and I continue to advise many of the PhD students who work with me to frame their dissertation questions as puzzles.

However, the reality is that today's early-career researchers in political science and other social sciences may find this advice more difficult to follow than it was in an earlier era. They are as likely to have done undergraduate degrees in fields like economics or mathematics as in political science or area studies, and their graduate coursework generally allocates more time to studying methods and reading recently published articles than to learning about the deep body of empirical or theoretical knowledge gathered in a particular area by successive generations of scholars. As a result, identifying variation and determining whether it is puzzling become possible only *after* a student has already settled on a (potential) dissertation topic and begun to read extensively and research independently in that area. A good research question, as distinct from a topic, may still take the form of a puzzle—but the advice to *begin* the dissertation work by looking for a puzzle may be difficult to follow unless students have already written a few papers on the general topic. (The astute reader may well observe that this is another good reason to take classes in graduate school that require you to write research papers.)

This review of the conventional wisdom about choosing a research question reveals that there are in fact multiple conventional wisdoms and multiple viable types of research questions. Each of these bits of wisdom is valuable and likely to be truly helpful to some subset of researchers. Given that, how on earth are we to decide which advice to follow and which to ignore? In what remains of this chapter, I offer my own advice for charting your own path through the conventional wisdom (as well as some less-conventional advice) in order to choose a research question that will work for you.

Gaining Leverage

The distinctions between gap-filling or problem-driven, methods-driven or passion-driven, ambitious or cautious research questions can help us think about their pros and cons in different circumstances and to different scholars. But all good research questions share a common feature: *leverage*. Leverage is the ratio between the size of the question and the amount of knowledge that it allows us to generate. A question that is small enough to be tractable, but that has a big impact, will always be more satisfying to me than a small question that advances understanding in a small way, or a massive project that has a big impact but requires decades to complete or asks a reader to wade through thousands of pages in order to understand the punch line.

Leverage may seem like a slippery concept: how can we know if a research question is going to have leverage, when we don't know until we answer the question what knowledge it is going to generate? And isn't leverage something inherently subjective, something that we know when we see it but have trouble defining in the abstract? Both are fair questions. But in my experience, questions that are likely to have high leverage:

- Have answers that fill a gap in more than one literature within your discipline or across disciplines.
- Have answers that can be generalized to empirical settings beyond the one examined in the research.
- Can be cast as instances of a broader class of questions.
- Generate interest or excitement among many people for different reasons.

For example, my dissertation project, which became *Age in the Welfare State,* came out of the causal question "Why do some countries allocate most of their social policy spending to programs benefiting the elderly, while others spend more on children and working-age people?" This was a puzzle because neither existing typologies of welfare states nor theories about the causes of variation in how welfare states allocated resources to groups other than age groups explained the empirical variation that I had discovered in the age orientation of social spending.

I had a hunch that this was a question that would have a fairly big payoff, if I could answer it, because it:

- Spanned the disciplines of social policy, political economy, demography, and distributive justice.
- Seemed likely to be answerable in a way that would generalize to at least the set of rich democracies with advanced welfare states.
- Was an instance of two broader sets of questions: about the causes of variation in social spending on different groups, and about the treatment through various policy means of different age groups in the population.
- Seemed to excite enthusiastic ad hoc hypothesizing from nearly everyone I spoke to about my question, from my family members to policy makers to other political scientists.

My question was gap-filling in the sense that the comparative social policy literature had not addressed the issue of how welfare states distributed resources by age. But it was also a puzzle, because the existing theories that might have spoken to the question did not do a good job explaining the variation I had observed. It was clearly a big question, requiring studying multiple policy areas in multiple countries over time. But it seemed likely to me to have a big payoff because at the time, the challenge posed by aging populations for welfare states was beginning to enter policy debates in multiple countries, and not only scholars in many other disciplines but also ordinary people seemed interested in both the question and its possible answers. And the combination of the theoretical puzzle with obvious policy relevance and consequences for the lives of ordinary people made me excited to work on the project.

Much of the advice that early-career scholars receive about the need to choose a specific kind of research question (whether it be gap-filling or problem-driven, methods-driven or passion-driven, etc.) seems to me to be motivated, often implicitly, by the goal of finding questions that have leverage. But unfortunately there is no clear relationship between leverage and the types of questions identified in the conventional wisdom. A narrow, gap-filling question can have a great deal of leverage if it fills a gap that advances the literature in significant ways or points to avenues for research that have not yet been explored. Problem-driven research can have low leverage if it provides a good answer to a problem that is of limited concern to most people. Bringing new or unusual skills to bear in pursuit of the answer to a question is no guarantee that the question itself will have leverage; by the same token, focusing on methods that are fashionable or "cutting-edge" can just as easily produce results that do little to move knowledge forward. All other things being equal, puzzle-driven questions may be more likely than other types of questions to reliably generate leverage, because framing a question as an empirical observation that is unexplained by existing theory generates answers that have both empirical and theoretical impact. Even so, if either the empirical or the theoretical contribution of solving a puzzle is limited, a puzzle question may have low leverage.

Where, then, ought we look for questions that have leverage? While it may not always be possible to know before you have started researching whether or not your research question fulfills one or more of these criteria, it can often be intuited relatively quickly by reading broadly in the theoretical and empirical literature; by thinking systematically and creatively about what your research is a "case" of;[11] and by talking with a broad range of scholars and nonscholars about your proposed research to hear how they react to your questions.

Know Thyself

The conventional wisdom to work on a research question that you are passionate about strikes me as useful to just about any researcher in choosing a research *topic*. Attempting to pursue market trends by working on a topic because it is on the front page of the newspaper or the cover page of the top journals in the discipline almost inevitably leads to disappointment as the news cycle or the field moves on while you struggle to publish your first results. Working on a topic that your gut tells you matters even if few others are talking about it has a much higher potential upside.[12] Choosing a topic because it's what your advisor thinks is interesting or because it's somehow typical of work in your field or because it's what funders want to fund at the moment presents similar pitfalls. Those of us who have the privilege to choose what to work on (as many in the lab sciences, for example, may not) surely owe it to ourselves and to our discipline to choose a topic that we are truly excited by.

But once we have done that, we still need to decide on a specific research question, and the choice can be bewildering. This is where asking more specific questions about yourself can be very helpful. What kinds of research do you actually *like* doing, as opposed to simply tolerate? Does the thrill of finding a "smoking gun" document in an archive get you going? Or do you loathe the prospect of spending hours in a musty, poorly lit storage room? Do you love talking to people and finding out about their lives, or would you rather observe from a distance? Are you more excited by the prospect of generating new data or of finding the secrets hidden in an existing data set? Be sure to choose a research question that will involve doing much of what you love, and little to none of what you loathe.

What kind of research question makes your heart sing when you see other people answer it? Ask yourself what it is about the work that you are drawn to that you find so appealing. Is it a clever identification strategy? A persuasive argument about how the subject impacts ordinary people? An accumulation of empirical material about a fascinating place or time? A way of engaging with the human subjects of the research that empowers them? The use that will be made of the knowledge?[13] Reading broadly and paying attention to how your own affect is related to the style of research questions that others ask can help guide you to the kind of research question that will make you want to keep going.[14]

Self-knowledge goes beyond techniques and methods, though. How much patience do you have? Some kinds of projects take longer than others because they are bigger, require a lot of data collection, or employ methods that are inherently time-intensive. Do you prefer feeling like you are participating in a shared research enterprise to build a wall brick by brick, or are you a lone wolf or someone who prefers to break boxes rather than fill them in? How risk-averse are you? The answers to these questions about yourself can help guide you to which of the strategies presented in the "conventional wisdom" section are likely to lead you to the kind of research question that is best for *you* rather than some other researcher.

Notes

1. In writing this chapter, I have imagined my audience as a PhD student in a political science program in the United States and have used the terminology that will be most familiar to that audience.
2. Wendt, "On Constitution and Causation in International Relations."
3. Goertz and Mahoney, "Causes-of-Effects versus Effects-of-Causes."
4. Glaser and Strauss, *The Discovery of Grounded Theory*.
5. Naseemullah, "Preface," n.p.
6. Kuhn, *The Structure of Scientific Revolutions*.
7. O'Toole, "Phrase."
8. Menon and Muraleedharan, "Salami Slicing of Data Sets."
9. Quoted in Munck and Snyder, *Passion, Craft, and Method in Comparative Politics*, 297.
10. Geddes, *Paradigms and Sand Castles*, 28–29.
11. Soss, "On Casing a Study versus Studying a Case."
12. The job market for PhD researchers is in reality many markets: academic, nonacademic, policy, private sector, arts and sciences versus professional school, and more. As a result, unless you know up front that you have a very strong preference for one market outcome versus another, it may be hard to predict which of those markets you will be in, and what kind of research questions the "buyers" in that market will prefer.
13. One of the commenters on my Twitter thread, a geographer, reported that her choice of research questions involves asking "a) what social relations are engendered in the act of knowing/seeking to know; b) what work do I think this knowledge will do in the world; and c) who wants to know and why?" On this point, see Derickson, "Disrupting Displacements."
14. On affect and choosing a research question, see Andrew Gibson, "The Affective Researcher," unpublished manuscript.

Recommended Readings

Geddes, Barbara. *Paradigms and Sand Castles: Theory Building and Research Design in Comparative Politics*. Ann Arbor: University of Michigan Press, 2003.
    In addition to the wonderful quote on choosing a topic that I cited earlier in this chapter, Geddes offers advice on how to turn large, "compound" questions into smaller, more tractable ones, using the example of transitions from authoritarian to democratic rule.

Munck, Gerardo L., and Richard Snyder. *Passion, Craft, and Method in Comparative Politics*. Baltimore: Johns Hopkins University Press, 2007.
    Based on in-depth interviews conducted by the authors in the early 2000s with some of the most prominent scholars of comparative politics in the United States, this book offers unparalleled insights into the research process of actual people (albeit very influential ones)—including how these scholars chose what to study, and why.

Ruggieri, Andrea, and Adam McCauley. "From Questions and Puzzles to Research Project." In *The Sage Handbook of Research Methods in Political Science and International Relations*, edited by Luigi Curini and Robert Franzese, 2022. https://doi.org/10.4135/9781526486387.

This chapter is part of a comprehensive methods handbook and offers a broad overview of issues surrounding choosing a topic, in addition to treating many of the issues that I touch on only briefly in this chapter.

Soss, Joe. "On Casing a Study versus Studying a Case." In *Rethinking Comparison: Innovative Methods for Qualitative Political Inquiry*, edited by Erica S. Simmons and Nicholas Rush Smith, 84–106. Cambridge: Cambridge University Press, 2021.

In this compelling chapter, Soss argues that figuring out what you are actually studying (i.e., what your research is a case of) often comes after you think you have chosen a research question—and that "casing" can itself be an act of intellectual interpretation and a site of creativity.

References

Derickson, Kate Driscoll. "Disrupting Displacements: Making Knowledges for Futures Otherwise in Gullah/Geechee Nation." *Annals of the American Association of Geographers*, January 24, 2022, 1–9.

Geddes, Barbara. *Paradigms and Sand Castles: Theory Building and Research Design in Comparative Politics*. Ann Arbor: University of Michigan Press, 2003.

Glaser, Barney, and Anselm Strauss. *The Discovery of Grounded Theory: Strategies for Qualitative Research*. New Brunswick, NJ: Routledge, 1999.

Goertz, Gary, and James Mahoney. "Causes-of-Effects versus Effects-of-Causes." In *A Tale of Two Cultures: Qualitative and Quantitative Research in the Social Sciences*, edited by Gary Goertz and James Mahoney, 37–44. Princeton, NJ: Princeton University Press, 2012. ProQuest Ebook Central. https://ebookcentral-proquest-com.proxy.library.upenn.edu/lib/upenn-ebooks/detail.action?docID=980043.

Kuhn, Thomas S. *The Structure of Scientific Revolutions*. 3rd ed. Chicago: University of Chicago Press, 1996.

Lynch, Julia. *Age in the Welfare State: The Origins of Social Spending on Pensioners, Workers, and Children*. Cambridge: Cambridge University Press, 2006.

Menon, Vikas, and Aparna Muraleedharan. "Salami Slicing of Data Sets: What the Young Researcher Needs to Know." *Indian Journal of Psychological Medicine* 38, no. 6 (November 1, 2016): 577–578.

Munck, Gerardo L., and Richard Snyder. *Passion, Craft, and Method in Comparative Politics*. Baltimore: Johns Hopkins University Press, 2007.

Naseemullah, Adnan, ed. "Preface." In *Development after Statism: Industrial Firms and the Political Economy of South Asia*, ix–xiv. Cambridge: Cambridge University Press, 2016.

O'Toole, Garson. "Phrase: Fills a Much-Needed Gap (Joke 1950) (Non-Joke 1857)." Listserv.Linguistics.Org, May 4, 2010. http://listserv.linguistlist.org/pipermail/ads-l/2010-May/098911.html.

Soss, Joe. "On Casing a Study versus Studying a Case." In *Rethinking Comparison: Innovative Methods for Qualitative Political Inquiry*, edited by Erica S. Simmons and Nicholas Rush Smith, 84–106. Cambridge: Cambridge University Press, 2021.

Wendt, Alexander. "On Constitution and Causation in International Relations." *Review of International Studies* 24 (1998): 101–117.

3
The Researcher's Gaze
Positionality and Reflexivity

Lahoma Thomas

Introduction

> Girlie, take good care of yourself.
> Hold the talk. These are our stories.
> Ma-Ma loves you.[1]

That is the advice my "Ma-Ma" (grandmother) wrote in a notebook she slipped into my suitcase before I left for fieldwork in 2014. Her message astutely gestured toward notions of subjectivity and power, and I readily understood the meaning. She was instructing me, a Black woman grandchild, to hold—which I recognized also meant to honor and protect—the stories of other Black women whom I was setting off to interview in the Caribbean. In addition, her use of "our" evoked the belief that the stories would become part of Black women's collective stories. For me, this note succinctly captures the idea that our subjectivities inform so much of our work by influencing the scholarship we undertake and how we conduct research. My grandmother understood that I, like all other researchers, was not entering the field as a neutral or objective instrument in the research process.[2] Rather, I was going into the field as a Black woman, as someone connected to the region, bringing along with me my own history and what it meant to me to return to the region to do this kind of work. The narratives we bring forth in our scholarship—as well as those we omit—and the manner in which we present those narratives do not occur by happenstance. My grandmother's note remains the most instructive piece of advice I have received as a scholar.

This type of insight was absent from my doctoral training for fieldwork in political science. For most doctoral students, such training mainly concerns logistical procedures (i.e., securing ethical approval from one's institution, establishing institutional and personal contacts in the field, and developing a strategy for scheduling and conducting interviews).[3] While this instruction is helpful in guiding graduate students to be ready for fieldwork, it inadequately prepares them for the "doing" of fieldwork, which is very much shaped by who we are.

Similarly, my review of the literature about methodology in political science revealed inattentiveness to the ways in which social location and subjectivities inform the research process. That is, in the literature about research methodology in political science, the researcher is elided, assumed to be distinct from the process.[4] Positioning the researcher in this way stems from the strong push for a positivist research model in political science, which emphasizes the importance of the neutral researcher and controlling the research environment to minimize factors that may impede an objective research process. This is a challenging perspective to uphold because all research emanates from a particular ideological viewpoint.

Knowledge acquired through a positivist research method does not escape the fact that the researcher can never be seen as neutral. Consider research results that emerge from computerized data analysis. It would be inaccurate to presume that the results are devoid of the researcher's subjective influences because the conception, collection, and interpretation of the findings still come from the researcher. Thus, even positivist methods stand to benefit from a discussion about where, why, how, and by whom the project was conceived and the data collected in order to make transparent the positionality of the researcher, thereby strengthening the credibility of the research process.[5]

Research by Ryan and Golden shows that the use of reflexivity in a mixed-methods study "adds a necessary insight into the complex dynamics that do exist between researchers and participants in quantitative research."[6] While conducting a quantitative study to investigate depression among Irish-born migrants living in London, Ryan and Golden found that their own distinct accents signaled to potential research participants their identities as Irish-born women. The authors write about how the initial phone conversation to set up interviews required important reflection on how the participants could detect their accents and make reasonable guesses about their ethnicity. The respondents frequently commented on the Irishness of the researchers and inquired as to which county in Ireland they came from.[7] Respondents placed "the researchers within a localized Irish context," which the researchers observed "underlined its relevance to the relationship between us, as researchers, and the respondents."[8] The authors' reflection on how their Irishness may have facilitated recruitment for the study reveals how the positionality of the researcher can play an important role in the research process, even in quantitative studies.

Recently, there has been an important push within political science methodology toward the practice of reflexivity—the process of turning one's lens back on oneself to examine how one's subjectivities and positionality inform processes of knowledge construction. The concept of reflexivity operates from the premise that knowledge is constructed rather than revealed, thereby requiring us to consider the ways in which power and privilege can either be reinscribed or reconfigured through the knowledge-making process that researchers engage in.[9] (For more on the construction of knowledge, see Chapter 5.) However, the literature often conflates reflexivity with other concepts, such as reflectivity, critical reflection, or self-reflection, even though these similar concepts entail very different processes. Consequently, the methodological interventions currently framed as reflexivity involve a reflective (not reflexive) exercise about the researcher's own experience. This dilutes the transformative work that reflexivity can do if one incorporates it into one's research practice.

In this chapter, I discuss how reflexivity emerged in the social sciences to address the ways in which the connection between the researcher's subjectivities and the actual research process has been rendered absent. I then consider the shortcomings of reflexivity as a practice in qualitative research. As an intervention, I introduce a concept from Black feminist genealogy called relational reflexivity, which connects reflexivity and relationality. Connecting these two concepts helps us focus on the structural basis of identity formation, positionality, power, and wider social relations, which renders explicit the co-constitutive relationship between the researcher and the research. The practice of relational reflexivity can lead to important insights. I use my grandmother's note to me as the landscape through which I illustrate such insights and show the relevance of relational reflexivity as a methodological tool. The chapter concludes with some suggestions for researchers who want to incorporate relational reflexivity into their own practice.

Reflexivity in the Social Sciences

The concept of reflexivity has been discussed increasingly within social science research, particularly qualitative and ethnographic research. Reflexivity refers to a "self-critical approach that questions how knowledge is generated and, further, how relations of power operate in this process."[10] It requires deep critical thinking about how one's own social location informs not only the ways one sees and makes sense of the world, but also the processes in which one engages to produce knowledge. The praxis of reflexivity within the social sciences, however, often collapses or interchanges other, similar but different processes—namely, reflectivity, critical reflection, and self-reflection. For D'Cruz and Jones, the conceptual merging of reflectivity, critical reflection, and reflexivity signals the relative newness of these concepts within the social sciences.[11] While there is certainly some cross-pollination among these three practices, reflexivity is distinctive from the former two, as I will discuss shortly.

Scholars in disciplines such as education, sociology, anthropology, geography, and social and political thought have actively engaged with these issues, leading the discussion on positionality and subjectivity as they relate to fieldwork[12] and knowledge production.[13] Their work has not only shaped scholars' cognitive approach to research in their respective fields but also illuminated the assumptions embedded in different disciplines about the nature of being and the organization of power and social relations.[14]

By far the most notable challenge to the notion of the "neutral" and "objective" researcher has come from anticolonial and Black feminist scholars who highlighted how existing research practices reinforce relations of power.[15] Scholarship emerging from the positions of the colonized and the formerly enslaved has long challenged the social and natural sciences for reproducing the relations of power between the colonizer and the colonized, or the researcher and the researched.[16] The critique has always come from the position of denaturalizing the dialectic between the colonized and the colonizer, or the civilized and the "Other." The call for reflexivity within the machinery of epistemology and knowledge production derives from the self-reflexive understanding among postcolonial and Black radical scholars that their very skin positions them as a subject that is always both the site and the subject of research.

These critical challenges and calls for introspection have spurred a movement to orient research practices toward those who bring positionality and biases into consciousness. Further, there has been a move to examine the effects of identity politics in the conception of research, fieldwork experience, and knowledge production more generally. In so doing, those at the forefront have signaled that interrogating one's positionality in the production of knowledge, recognizing it as a site of power, is a task that all scholars should undertake. The concept of reflexivity has thus been proposed as a methodological corrective insofar as it could provide transparency about the researcher's subjectivity and relative power in the research process. The project of incorporating reflexivity into research practices offers an alternative way of producing knowledge.

As a discipline, political science has moved at a glacial pace in tackling themes of identity and the researcher's positionality in qualitative research, which is symptomatic of the neglect of larger issues of race and diversity in this field.[17] Graduate training and the literature on research methodology within political science provide little in the way of analyzing the implications of the researcher's identity or positionality in formulating, planning, and conducting fieldwork. Political scientist Erica Townsend-Bell attributes this to the discipline having assumed that "the subject to whom advice is given is simply a political scientist, with no other salient identities that might intercede."[18] Having been cast into a state of "racelessness," the researcher assumes the default subject position: whiteness.[19] This whiteness is simultaneously assigned objectivity. The lack of scholarly attention to this matter preserves the myth about the neutrality of the researcher, and it leaves unchallenged the practice of separating subjectivity and epistemology from structures of power in society.

The concept of reflexivity is relatively new within the political science literature about methodology, with few scholars seeking to incorporate reflexive analysis in their work.[20] Although reflexivity is lauded as a transformative research intervention, there is a lack of clarity about what it is, how it should be executed, and how it is distinct from writing in a journal about anxiety regarding one's own identity. There is no clear articulation of what makes reflexivity transformational, distinct from other exercises of reform. Merely thinking about how one is privileged vis-à-vis the communities with which one has chosen to engage in one's research pursuits is not enough. That sort of performative reflection is abstracted—it does not require one to engage in or with the structural and material antagonisms of the social world in which we operate. Indeed, this type of reflection constitutes another form of possessive individualism that gets marketed as critical transformative thought. In reality, transformative thought has to be accompanied by transformative modes of action—it must engage with the structures that determine how thought is produced in order to change the material conditions of living. Lacking this intention to transform material conditions that manifest unstated assumptions and structural inequities, scholars have readily written about their experience in the field without even asking if what they are engaging in constitutes reflexivity. A broad reading of reflexivity within the social sciences reveals that authors often interchange or intertwine the concept with differing notions of reflectivity, critical reflection, and self-reflection.[21] While there is overlap on certain key points, the concepts are distinct—they mean different things.

The concepts of reflectivity and critical reflection are part of a self-evaluating practice emerging out of professions like social work and nursing.[22] Reflectivity is a model for thinking about and improving professional practice—it is "designed to assist professionals to become aware of the theory or assumptions involved in their practice, with the purpose of closing the gap between what is espoused and what is enacted."[23] Critical reflection is an extension of reflectivity that remains concerned with the experience of practitioners, but it also seeks to identify more complex dimensions of their subjectivities in order to illuminate the assumptions implicit in their practice—critical reflection becomes a project of the self.[24] Similarly, the concept of self-reflection refers to the analysis of one's own experience in fieldwork as singular, discrete.

In other words, reflexivity becomes individualized. However, an individualistic approach to reflexivity ignores the structural basis of identity formation, positionality, power, and social relationships.[25] Reflexivity practiced in this manner results in the researcher recentering themselves, reifying their own power, and limiting their analysis of how the self is involved in the research process. Blurring the distinction between reflexivity and self-reflection also provides the false sense that identifying one's privilege is sufficient to counter issues of power asymmetries in the research process, writ large.

The misapplication of the term "reflexivity" to what has been practiced in methodological scholarship has led scholars to become suspicious of reflexivity.[26] Similar skepticism has been articulated by anticolonial and antiracist scholar-activists who characterize reflexivity as performative, having observed its shortcomings in antiracist settings and organizations and, more generally, in liberatory and antiracist discourses. Several scholars have drawn parallels between reflexivity as conventionally practiced and the confessional tale in which one owns up to one's privileges.[27] As a "move to innocence," the practice of reflexivity as confession attempts to delink the researcher from systems of power and domination.[28] For Mawhinney, "the role of storytelling and self-confession—which serves to equate stories of personal exclusion with stories of structural racism and exclusion[—makes use of] strategies to remove involvement in and culpability for systems of domination."[29] Similarly, for Ahmed, confessing one's privilege presents a "fantasy of transcendence," whereby articulating an awareness of racism is a maneuver to position oneself as being unimplicated in its effects.[30] The confession then becomes a stand-in for the political project rather than leading to any concrete action that would disrupt the structures of power enabling one's privilege.[31] For Pillow, self-reflexivity has also been used to situate oneself closer to the subject in order to find similarities and absolve oneself of guilt.[32]

Although these critiques attend to the limitations of reflexivity as practiced in antiracist activist spaces, these insights can be applied to any area of research. For instance, the anthropological project requires that researchers recenter themselves as the authority on the nature and condition of the Black, Indigenous, and colonized peoples they study. Spivak is critical of this objectification and fetishization in her discussion of the native informant.[33] For Spivak, it is an exercise in economic imperialism, the anthropological project being inherently about the reification of colonial difference and the expansion of global capital through the codification, monetization, and valuation of academic works. Moreover, the researcher, despite any well-meaning attempt to complicate their relationship to dispossession, restructures the colonial project through spatial and temporal differences. The researcher cannot escape the structures of coloniality without engaging them materially, and the political-ethical subjectivity of researchers as "progressive" and "critically reflexive" requires othering and is constituted through alterity.[34]

The trend of using the reflexive method as a mode of confession works against what it had been intended for: disrupting the power of the researcher. Instead, the practice of reflexive writing to record the researcher's experience of fieldwork rearticulates Eurocentric epistemologies and methodologies, whereby the researcher's subjectivities are centralized and explored through the relations of power that construct difference vis-à-vis the researcher and the community. The methodological turn to incorporate reflexivity does not fix the problematics of research as a site of power and privilege, nor does it aim to trouble and disrupt those structures of epistemic domination. Rather, it undermines our responsibilities as knowledge producers to transform the material relations that predetermine our locations within colonial and racial divisions of labor. And it subserves the same goal as Eurocentric epistemologies—identified by decolonial scholars in the Latin American context, postcolonial and international relations scholars, and feminist and Indigenous theorists—sustaining Western knowledge and cosmologies at the apex of epistemic hierarchies. These scholars have documented the ways in which being networked within capitalist-colonial global systems of power lies at the heart of producing subjectivity in the interests of modernity and empire.[35]

A relational reflexivity, one that centers power in our relations with others, addresses the critique leveled against the confessional tale. The emphasis on relationality moves us beyond reflexivity of the self toward a critical examination of how power operates in our relations with others and within the structural social systems in which we are embedded.

Relational Reflexivity

My proposed method of relational reflexivity draws from the Black feminist standpoint, the intellectual legacy of Black women activists and scholars who have long grounded their methodological and epistemological practices in reflexivity and relationality to account for the ways in which race, gender, class, and sexuality, among other identities of social differentiation, wield power. Relational reflexivity impacts what it is that we know as researchers and how we come to know it.

Relational reflexivity emphasizes the relational nature of social categories and social divisions. Where one stands with respect to power is determined by one's subject position within the shifting network of relationships.[36] Power, in other words, is relational. Relational reflexivity is attuned to how power is reinforced through particular subjectivities and relational dynamics, and it highlights the complexity and fluidity of positionality. Power dynamics in the field are often in flux because power develops and changes according to the types of relationships we build, the types of interactions we share, and our location within those relationships.[37]

The inclusion of relational reflexivity as a methodological tool allows for consideration of how our relationships (personal, interpersonal, and to our scholarship) are shaped and sustained by our lived experiences, the experiential embodiment produced through racialization, gendering, sexualization, and other forms of identity classification.[38] To recognize the power embedded in our social location is not simply to focus on ourselves as individuals but to address and see ourselves, our social location, and our privilege on a larger relational level. By this I mean that it is not just about how we, as researchers (with our interlocking subject positions), move through the world; it is also about understanding how subjectivity is structured by social location, which implicates forms of domination that are beyond our individual day-to-day experience. We may be individuals, but we are individuals moving through histories, societal assumptions, and practices that are embedded, sometimes involuntarily, based on our identities. Pragmatically, making use of relational reflexivity can mean taking on forms of intellectual, institutional, and grassroots labor that require moving beyond the traditions of one's own disciplinary training and practices. Methodologically, practicing relational reflexivity involves constant negotiation, as one needs to take seriously the scholarship and praxis of the communities with which one is dialectically engaged.

Relational Reflexivity as a Black Feminist Praxis

Fundamentally, Black feminist praxis is reflexive and relational. It offers a broader understanding of reflexivity that recognizes the self cannot be divorced from the network of relations in which it is embedded. Black feminist scholars have long problematized the traditional distinction not only between subjectivity and objectivity but also between perception and fact. Understanding the connection between knowledge and power relations, Black feminist epistemologies have always advanced the practice of reflexivity.[39] Black feminist scholarly practice draws on reflexivity to better understand structural oppression, using the empirical realities of Black women's lives as a site of important knowledge, as a "talking back"[40] and challenge to existing hegemonic systems of oppression, social theory, policies, and practices.[41] Given that knowledge is situated and positioned,[42] as researchers we must grapple with how our biographies influence how we engage in the research process—for instance, whose stories we tell or do not tell, how we construct those stories, what questions we ask or do not ask, and how we ask those questions. Put plainly, all aspects of who we are influence the ways in which we research and create knowledge. Black feminist epistemologies articulate a critical politics that does not accept the implicit claim that researchers are separate from both the research process and the knowledge they produce.

Black feminist epistemologies also provide a critical framework for understanding notions of relationality. A relational approach puts relationships at the center of the understanding of the self, desire, motivation, and politics.[43] The self is conceived of as an "actor-in-relations," embedded in overlapping relational circles of various types.[44] By centering relationships, we can focus on how people and behaviors are shaped by relationships throughout their lives—from relational norms embedded in economic institutions to relational norms about interactions with neighbors—without reducing the direction of influence to one particular level. A Black feminist framework challenges the idea that the individual is separate from the social world. Black feminist epistemologies and methodologies understand that the individual is embedded within a system of relations and that social identities—such as race, gender, class, sexuality, and ability (and their adjacent processes)—are interrelated not only at the individual and interpersonal levels but also at the level of social structure.[45] Thus, processes to classify and categorize are significant mechanisms that shape all aspects of the relationships in our lives: our political, public lives; our social, private lives; our individual, experiential, internal lives; and our interactions with social structures. Black feminist epistemologies helpfully demonstrate the ways in which race, gender, class, sexuality, geography, and other categories of difference simultaneously animate hierarchies of power, domination, and oppression.

Relational Reflexivity in Practice

My own biography illustrates how one practices relational reflexivity. As I am a Black Canadian woman of Caribbean descent who has professional experience as a Black feminist social worker (specifically as a trauma counselor), my conceptualization of research projects and my development of methodological practices are influenced by these positionalities—in the questions I ask and how I ask them; in my interactions with others; in my collection of data; in my recounting and interpretation of research informants' experiences; and in my decisions about what to publish and what to omit. Understanding my own research process requires moving beyond recounting my individual experiences to focus on the relational, institutional, and structural conditions out of which the research emerges. Thus, I will next delve into a discussion of my research in Jamaica and the realities to which my grandmother referred in her note to me.

In Jamaica, relations and systems of power are situated within the historical, social, cultural, material, and spiritual contexts in which Black people live—conditions constituted through the experiences of slavery, displacement, exile, state violence, and struggle.[46] This not only describes the historical and cultural contexts I entered for my research in 2014, but also the relational contexts of my own biography. In fact, these are the realities my grandmother evoked when she spoke of "our stories." She intuitively understood the existence of a level of relational connectivity between myself and the Black women whose stories she instructed me to hold. For my grandmother, who is Bajan, it did not matter that I was going to another island in the Caribbean; she still perceived these Black women's stories as our stories. My intention here is not to flatten the concept of Blackness in the Caribbean but rather to identify that there is an embodied Black political subjectivity[47] that emerges from the histories of enslavement and colonialism in the Americas.

My research in Jamaica was done in urban areas largely controlled not by agents of the state but by dons, leaders of criminal organizations who had complex relations with the state. I am relationally reflexive about the unintended impacts of my research, particularly in terms of further pathologizing and reinforcing existing tropes about the Black community's acceptance of and susceptibility to criminality. As a Black woman scholar coming from a marginalized community, I am critical of contributing to the disempowerment and oppression of the Black community because I am far too aware of the impact of knowledge power structures on the lived realities of its members. Thus, my research methodology—relational reflexive practice—does not come from the realm of confessional tales about how I experienced the research or speculations about how the community experienced me vis-à-vis my set of privileges, nor does it simply rest in the abstract realm of contemplation about a researcher's intellectual responsibility to convey empirical truths (small t).

Conclusion

I invite researchers interested in the practice of relational reflexivity to think about the power structures shaping knowledge production when deciding how to engage in the research process. Drawing on the methodological discussions by Black and Indigenous feminist scholars,[48] all of whom contributed to my own reflexive practice, I propose—as a preliminary step to engage in relational reflexivity—that researchers ask themselves the following questions:

Relation to self and others:
1. What is the purpose of the research? What are the researcher's intentions personally, intellectually, and sociopolitically?
2. Who conceived of the research? For whom? And why?
3. Who designed the research? Who is asking the questions? Who is executing the research?
4. Who owns the research?

Relation to epistemological regimes and the academic industrial complex:
1. What questions are being asked?
2. What methods are employed?
3. How is the data being interpreted? By whom?
4. Who decides which results are disseminated?
5. How will the results be disseminated?
6. What disruptions to the practice of social inquiry that fetishizes the "Other" as a subject of curiosity are being made?

Relation to empire: patriarchal, white supremacist, imperialist logics
1. Whose histories are centered?
2. Whose identities are reified?
3. Whose interests benefit from the research? Who and what does it serve?

4. What is the relationship of the research to principles of social justice and notions of freedom?
5. Is the research a barrier to or in service of liberatory practices?

These questions can act as a guide for scholars to develop their own practice of relational reflexivity. Because relational reflexivity recognizes the distinct positionality of researchers within global structures of power and violence, individual approaches to research will be diverse. Entering this space of reflection with a set of critical queries will allow researchers to develop their own modes of transformative relation.

Notes

1. Thelma Roberts, personal notebook, 2014.
2. Henderson, "We Thought You Would Be White"; Townsend-Bell, "Being True and Being You"; Pezalla, Pettigrew, and Miller-Day, "Researching the Researcher-as-Instrument"; Davenport, "Researching While Black"; Bouka, "Researching Violence in Africa"; Fisher, "Positionality, Subjectivity, and Race"; Fujii, "The Real Problem of Diversity"; Bond, "Reflexivity and Revelation"; Thomas, "Dear Political Science"; Thomas, "Unmasking."
3. Hertel, Singer, and Van Cott, "Field Research in Developing Countries"; Kapiszewski, MacLean, and Read, *Field Research in Political Science*; Townsend-Bell, "Being True and Being You."
4. Brady, "Causation and Explanation in Social Science"; Bartels and Brady, "The State of Quantitative Political Methodology"; Fearon, "Counterfactuals and Hypothesis Testing in Political Science"; Kellstedt and Whitten, *The Fundamentals of Political Science Research*.
5. Ryan and Golden, "Tick the Box Please."
6. Ryan and Golden, "Tick the Box Please," 1193–1194.
7. Ryan and Golden, "Tick the Box Please," 1195.
8. Ryan and Golden, "Tick the Box Please," 1195.
9. Taylor and White, "Knowledge, Truth and Reflexivity"; D'Cruz and Jones, *Social Work Research*; D'Cruz, Gillingham, and Melendez, "Reflexivity, Its Meanings and Relevance for Social Work."
10. D'Cruz, Gillingham, and Melendez, "Reflexivity, Its Meanings and Relevance for Social Work," 2.
11. D'Cruz and Jones, *Social Work Research*.
12. Ortbals and Rincker, "Fieldwork, Identities, and Intersectionality"; Mullings, "Insider or Outsider, Both or Neither"; Moss, "Focus."
13. Spivak, *In Other Worlds*; Collins, "Reflections on the Outsider Within"; Collins, "Learning from the Outsider Within"; Banks, "The Lives and Values of Researchers"; Mohanty, "Under Western Eyes."
14. For more on these distinctions, see Shilliam, *Decolonizing Politics*.
15. Davis, *Women, Race, and Class*; hooks, *Ain't I a Woman*; hooks, *Talking Back*; Collins, "Learning from the Outsider Within"; Collins, *Black Feminist Thought*; Collins, "Reflections on the Outsider Within."
16. For more on this discussion, see Said, *Culture and Imperialism*; Spivak, *In Other Worlds*; Mohanty, "Under Western Eyes."; Collins, "Learning from the Outsider Within"; Collins, "Reflections on the Outsider Within"; hooks, *Talking Back*.
17. Smith, "The Puzzling Place of Race in American Political Science"; Bouka, "Researching Violence in Africa as a Black Woman"; Fujii, "The Real Problem of Diversity in Political Science."
18. Townsend-Bell, "Being True and Being You"; Mazzei and O'Brien, "You Got It, So When Do You Flaunt It?"; Hertel, Singer, and Van Cott, "Field Research in Developing Countries," (311).
19. Hendrix, "Did Being Black Introduce Bias Into Your Study?"

20. Neufeld, "Reflexivity and International Relations Theory"; Madsen, "Reflexivity and the Construction of the International Object"; Berling and Bueger, "Practical Reflexivity and Political Science"; Soedirgo and Glas, "Toward Active Reflexivity."
21. D'Cruz, Gillingham, and Melendez, "Reflexivity, Its Meanings and Relevance for Social Work."
22. Schön, *Educating the Critically Reflective Practitioner*; Schön, *The Reflective Practitioner*; Fook and Gardner, *Practising Critical Reflection*.
23. Fook and Gardner, *Practising Critical Reflection*, 24.
24. Elliott, *Concepts of the Self*; D'Cruz and Jones, *Social Work Research*; D'Cruz, Gillingham, and Melendez, "Reflexivity, Its Meanings and Relevance for Social Work."
25. Elliott, *Concepts of the Self*.
26. Visweswaran, *Fictions of Feminist Ethnography*; Pillow, "Confession, Catharsis, or Cure?"
27. Mawhinney, "Giving Up the Ghost"; Elliott, *Concepts of the Self*; Ahmed, *Strange Encounters*; Ahmed, "The Non-Performativity of Anti-Racism"; Tuck and Yang, "Decolonization Is Not a Metaphor"; Bonnett, "Constructions of Whiteness in European and American Anti-Racism"; Amos, "Playing with Shadows."
28. Mawhinney, "Giving Up the Ghost," 17, cited in Tuck and Yang, "Decolonization Is Not a Metaphor," 9; Fellows and Razack, "The Race to Innocence"; Tuck and Yang, "Decolonization Is Not a Metaphor."
29. Mawhinney, "Giving Up the Ghost," 17, cited in Tuck and Yang, "Decolonization Is Not a Metaphor," 9.
30. Ahmed, "Declarations of Whiteness," para. 54.
31. Ahmed, "Declarations of Whiteness"; Ahmed, "The Non-Performativity of Anti-Racism"; Tuck and Yang, "Decolonization Is Not a Metaphor."
32. Pillow, "Confession, Catharsis, or Cure?"
33. Spivak, *In Other Worlds*.
34. Fraser, "Epistemologies of Imperial Feminism(s)"; Birla, "Postcolonial Studies."
35. For more discussion on this, see Fabian, *Time and the Other*; Anibal, "Coloniality of Power, Ethnocentrism, and Latin America"; Mohanram, *Black Body*; Wynter, "Unsettling the Coloniality of Being/Power/Truth/Freedom"; Wai, *Epistemologies of African Conflicts*; Spivak, "Imperialism and Sexual Difference"; Smith, *Decolonizing Methodologies*; Simpson, *Mohawk Interruptus*; hooks, *Feminist Theory*; Collins, *Black Feminist Thought*.
36. Takacs, "Positionality, Epistemology, and Social Justice in the Classroom."
37. Takacs, "Positionality, Epistemology, and Social Justice in the Classroom."
38. Thomas, "Dear Political Science"; Thomas, "Unmasking."
39. Combahee River Collective, "The Combahee River Collective Statement"; Davis, *Women, Race, and Class*; Lorde, *Sister Outsider*; hooks, *Talking Back*; Collins, *Black Feminist Thought*.
40. hooks, *Talking Back*.
41. Collins, *Black Feminist Thought*; hooks, *Ain't I a Woman*; Crenshaw, "Demarginalizing the Intersection of Race and Sex"; Crenshaw, "Mapping the Margins."
42. Collins, *Black Feminist Thought*.
43. Nedelsky, *Law's Relations*; Qin, "Relational Theory of World Politics."
44. Qin, "Relational Theory of World Politics."
45. Davis, *Women, Race, and Class*; Crenshaw, "Mapping the Margins"; Winker and Degele, "Intersectionality as Multi-Level Analysis,"; Nash, *Black Feminism Reimagined after Intersectionality*.
46. Thomas, "Seeing from Da Yaad."
47. Thomas, "Seeing from Da Yaad."
48. Smith, *Decolonizing Methodologies*; James, *Resisting State Violence*; Brand, *A Map to the Door of No Return*; Collins, "Learning from the Outsider Within"; Collins, *Black Feminist Thought*; Hartman, *Scenes of Subjection*; hooks, *Feminist Theory*; Sharpe, *In the Wake*; Wynter, "Unsettling the Coloniality of Being/Power/Truth/Freedom."

Recommended Readings

Hartman, Saidiya. 2007. Lose Your Mother. New York: Farrar-Straus-Giroux.
Alexander M Jacqui. 2006. Pedagogies of Crossing: Meditations on Feminism, Sexual Politics, Memory, and the Sacred. Durham, NC: Duke Univ. Press

References

Agathangelou, Anna M., Dana M. Olwan, Tamara Lea Spira, and Heather M. Turcotte. "Sexual Divestments from Empire: Women's Studies, Institutional Feelings, and the 'Odious' Machine." *Feminist Formations* 27, no. 3 (2015): 139–167. https://www.jstor.org/stable/43860818.
Ahmed, Sara. "Declarations of Whiteness: The Non-Performativity of Anti-Racism." *Borderlands* 3, no. 2 (2004).
Ahmed, Sara. "The Non-Performativity of Anti-Racism." *Meridians* 7, no. 1 (2006): 104–126. http://www.jstor.org/stable/40338719.
Ahmed, Sara. *Strange Encounters: Embodied Others in Postcoloniality*. New York: Routledge, 2000.
Amos, Yukari Takimoto. "Playing with Shadows: White Academics' Rituals of Goodness." *International Journal of Qualitative Studies in Education* 36, no. 8 (2023): 1459–1465. https://doi.org/10.1080/09518398.2022.2025479.
Anibal, Quijano, and Michael Ennis. "Coloniality of Power, Ethnocentrism, and Latin America." *Nepantla: Views from South* 1, no. 3 (2000): 533–580. https://muse.jhu.edu/journal/140.
Banks, James A. "The Lives and Values of Researchers: Implications for Educating Citizens in a Multicultural Society." *Educational Researcher* 27, no. 7 (1998): 4–17. https://doi.org/10.3102/0013189X02700.
Bartels, Larry M., and Henry E. Brady. "The State of Quantitative Political Methodology." In *Political Science: The State of the Discipline II*, edited by Ada W. Finifter, 121–159. Washington, DC: American Political Science Association, 1993.
Berling, Trine Villumsen, and Christian Bueger. "Practical Reflexivity and Political Science: Strategies for Relating Scholarship and Political Practice." *PS: Political Science & Politics* 46, no. 1 (2013): 115–119. doi:10.1017/S1049096512001278.
Birla, Ritu. "Postcolonial Studies: Now That's History." In *Can the Subaltern Speak? Reflections on the History of an Idea*, edited by Rosalind C. Morris, 87–99. New York: Columbia University Press, 2010.
Bond, Kanisha D. "Reflexivity and Revelation." *Qualitative and Multi-Method Research* 16, no. 1 (2018): 45–47. doi.org/10.5281/zenodo.2562284.
Bonnett, Alastair. "Constructions of Whiteness in European and American Anti-Racism." In *Debating Cultural Hybridity: Multicultural Identities and the Politics of Anti-Racism*, edited by Pnina Werbner and Tariq Modood, 173–192. London: Zed Books, 2015.
Bouka, Yolande. "Researching Violence in Africa as a Black Woman: Notes from Rwanda." *Research in Difficult Settings* (blog), May 2015. http://conflictfieldresearch.colgate.edu/wp-content/uploads/2015/05/Bouka_WorkingPaper-May2015.pdf.
Brady, Henry, E. "Causation and Explanation in Social Science." In *The Oxford Handbooks of Political Science*, edited by Janet M. Box-Steffensmeier, Henry E. Brady, and David Collier, 1054–1107. New York: Oxford University Press, 2008.
Brah, Avtar, and Ann Phoenix. "Ain't I a Woman? Revisiting Intersectionality." *Journal of International Women's Studies* 5, no. 3 (2004): 75–86. https://vc.bridgew.edu/jiws/vol5/iss3/8.
Brand, Dionne. *A Map to the Door of No Return*. Toronto: Vintage Canada, 2002.
Collins, Patricia Hill. *Black Feminist Thought: Knowledge, Consciousness, and the Politics of Empowerment*. New York: Routledge, 1990.
Collins, Patricia, Hill. "Learning from the Outsider Within: The Sociological Significance of Black Feminist Thought." *Social Problems* 33, no. 6,1 (1986): S14–S32. https://doi.org/10.2307/800672.

Collins, Patricia Hill. "Reflections on the Outsider Within." *Journal of Career Development* 26, no. 1 (1999): 85–88. doi.org/10.1177/089484539902600.

Combahee River Collective. "The Combahee River Collective Statement." 1977. https://www.blackpast.org/african-american-history/combahee-river-collective-statement-1977/.

Crenshaw, Kimberlé W. "Demarginalizing the Intersection of Race and Sex: A Black Feminist Critique of Antidiscrimination Doctrine, Feminist Theory and Antiracist Politics." *University of Chicago Legal Forum* 140 (1989): 139–167. https://chicagounbound.uchicago.edu/uclf/vol1989/iss1/8.

Crenshaw, Kimberlé. "Mapping the Margins: Intersectionality, Identity Politics, and Violence against Women of Color." *Stanford Law Review* 43, no. 6 (1991): pp. 1241–1299.

Davenport, Christian. "Researching While Black: Why Conflict Research Needs More African Americans (Maybe)." Political Violence at a Glance, April 10, 2013. https://politicalviolenceataglance.org/2013/04/10/researching-while-black-why-conflict-research-needs-more-african-americans-maybe/.

Davis, Angela Y. *Women, Race, and Class*. New York: Random House, 1981.

D'Cruz, Heather. "Social Work Research as Knowledge/Power in Practice." *Sociological Research Online* 5, no. 1 (2000): 5–19. doi.org/10.5153%2Fsro.421.

D'Cruz, Heather, Phillip Gillingham, and Sebastien Melendez. "Reflexivity, Its Meanings and Relevance for Social Work: A Critical Review of the Literature." *British Journal of Social Work* 37 (2007): 73–90. doi.org/10.1093/bjsw/bcl001.

D'Cruz, Heather, and Martyn Jones. *Social Work Research: Ethical and Political Contexts*. London: Sage, 2004.

Elliott, Anthony. *Concepts of the Self*. Cambridge, UK: Polity Press, 2001.

Fabian, Johannes. *Time and the Other: How Anthropology Makes Its Object*. New York: Columbia University Press, 1983.

Fearon, James D. "Counterfactuals and Hypothesis Testing in Political Science." *World Politics* 43 (1991): 169–195. doi.org/10.2307/2010470.

Fellows, Mary Louise, and Sherene Razack. "The Race to Innocence: Confronting Hierarchical Relations among Women." *Journal of Gender, Race & Justice* 1 (1998): 335–352. https://scholarship.law.umn.edu/faculty_articles/274.

Fisher, Karen, T. "Positionality, Subjectivity, and Race in Transnational and Transcultural Geographical Research." *Gender, Place and Culture* 22, no. 4 (2015): 456–473. doi.org/10.1080/0966369X.2013.879097.

Fook, Jan, and Fiona Gardner. *Practising Critical Reflection: A Resource Handbook*. New York: Open University Press, 2007.

Fraser, Faye. "Epistemologies of Imperial Feminism(s): Violence, Colonization, and Sexual (Re)Inscriptions of Empire." PhD diss., York University, 2022.

Fujii, Lee Ann. "The Real Problem of Diversity in Political Science." Duck of Minerva, April 4, 2017. http://duckofminerva.com/2017/04/the-real-problem-with-diversity-in-political-science.html.

Gayatri, Chakravorty Spivak. "Imperialism and Sexual Difference." *Oxford Literary Review* 8, no. 1 (1986): 225–240. https://www.jstor.org/stable/43964608.

Hartman, Saidiya. *Scenes of Subjection: Terror, Slavery, and Self-Making in Nineteenth-Century America*. New York: Oxford University Press, 1997.

Henderson, Frances B. "'We Thought You Would Be White': Race and Gender in Fieldwork." *Political Science and Politics* 42, no. 2 (2009): 291–294. doi.org/10.1017/S1049096509090581.

Hendrix, Katherine Grace. "'Did Being Black Introduce Bias into Your Study?': Attempting to Mute the Race-Related Research of Black Scholars." *Howard Journal of Communications* 13 (2002): 153–171. doi.org/10.1080/10646170290089935.

Hertel, Shareen, Matthew M. Singer, and Donna Lee Van Cott. "Field Research in Developing Countries: Hitting the Road Running." *PS: Political Science and Politics* 42, no. 2 (2009): 305–309. https://www.jstor.org/stable/40647531.

hooks, bell. *Ain't I a Woman: Black Women and Feminism*. Boston: South End Press, 1981.

hooks, bell. *Feminist Theory: From Margin to Center*. London: Pluto Press, 1984.

hooks, bell. *Talking Back: Thinking Feminist, Thinking Black*. Boston: South End Press, 1989.

James, Joy. *Resisting State Violence: Radicalism, Gender, and Race in the US Culture*. Minneapolis: University of Minnesota Press, 1996.

Kapiszewski, Diana, Lauren M. MacLean, and Benjamin L. Read. *Field Research in Political Science: Practice and Principles.* Cambridge: Cambridge University Press, 2015.

Kellstedt, Paul M., and Guy D. Whitten. *The Fundamentals of Political Science Research.* Cambridge: Cambridge University Press, 2018.

Lorde, Audre. *Sister Outsider.* Trumansburg, NY: Crossing Press, 1984.

Madsen, Mikael Rask. "Reflexivity and the Construction of the International Object: The Case of Human Rights." *International Political Sociology* 5, no. 3 (September 2011): 259–275. https://doi.org/10.1111/j.1749-5687.2011.00133. x.

Mawhinney, Janet. "'Giving Up the Ghost': Disrupting the (Re)Production of White Privilege in Anti-Racist Pedagogy and Organizational Change." Master's thesis, Ontario Institute for Studies in Education, University of Toronto, 1998. http://www.collectionscanada.gc.ca/obj/s4/f2/dsk2/tape15/PQDD_0008/MQ33991.pdf.

Mazzei, Julie, and Erin E. O'Brien. "You Got It, So When Do You Flaunt It? Building Rapport, Intersectionality, and the Strategic Deployment of Gender in the Field." *Journal of Contemporary Ethnography* 38, no. 1 (2009): 358–383. doi.org/10.1177/089124160833.

Mohanram, Radhika. *Black Body: Women, Colonialism and Space.* Minneapolis: University of Minnesota Press, 1999.

Mohanty, Chandra T. "Under Western Eyes: Feminist Scholarship and Colonial Discourse." In *Third World Women and the Politics of Feminism,* edited by Chandra T. Mohanty, Ann Russo, and Lourdes Torres, 51–80. Bloomington: Indiana University Press, 1991.

Moss, Pamela. "Focus: Feminism as Method." *Canadian Geographer* 37, no. 1 (1993): 48–61. doi.org/10.1111/j.1541-0064.1993.tb01540.x.

Mullings, Beverley. 1999. "Insider or Outsider, Both or Neither: Some Dilemmas of Interviewing in a Cross-Cultural Setting." *Geoforum* 30 (1999): 337–350. https://doi.org/10.1016/S0016-7185(99)00025-1.

Nash, Jennifer C. *Black Feminism Reimagined after Intersectionality.* Durham, NC: Duke University Press, 2019.

Nedelsky, Jennifer. *Law's Relations: A Relational Theory of Self, Autonomy, and Law.* New York: Oxford University Press, 2011.

Neufeld, Mark. "Reflexivity and International Relations Theory." *Millennium* 22, no. 1 (March 1993): 53–76. doi.org/10.1177/03058298930220010.

Ortbals, Candice D., and Meg E. Rincker. "Fieldwork, Identities, and Intersectionality: Negotiating Gender, Race, Class, Religion, Nationality, and Age in the Research Field Abroad: Editors' Introduction." *PS: Political Science and Politics* 42, no. 2 (April 2009): 287–290.

Pezalla, Anne E., Jonathan Pettigrew, and Michelle Miller-Day. "Researching the Researcher-as-Instrument: An Exercise in Interviewer Self-Reflexivity." *Qualitative Research* 12, no. 2 (2012): 165–185. doi:10.1177/1487941111422107.

Pillow, Wanda S. "Confession, Catharsis, or Cure? Rethinking the Uses of Reflexivity as Methodological Power in Qualitative Research." *International Journal of Qualitative Studies in Education* 16 (2003): 175–196. doi:10.1080/0951839032000060635.

Qin, Yaqing. "Relational Theory of World Politics." *International Studies Review* 18 (2016): 33–47. doi.org/10.1093/isr/viv031.

Ryan, Louise, and Anne Golden. "'Tick the Box Please': A Reflexive Approach to Doing Quantitative Social Research." *Sociology* 40, no. 6 (2006): 1191–1200.

Said, Edward. *Culture and Imperialism.* London: Chatto & Windus, 1993.

Schön, Donald A. *Educating the Critically Reflective Practitioner: Toward a New Design for Teaching and Learning in the Professions.* San Francisco: Jossey-Bass, 1987.

Schön, Donald A. *The Reflective Practitioner: How Professionals Think in Action.* New York: Routledge, 1992.

Sharpe, Cristina. *In the Wake: On Blackness and Being.* Durham, NC: Duke University Press, 2016.

Shilliam, Robbie. *Decolonizing Politics: An Introduction.* Medford, MA: Polity Press, 2021.

Simpson, Audra. *Mohawk Interruptus: Political Life across the Borders of Settler States.* Durham, NC: Duke University Press, 2014.

Smith, Linda Tuhiwai. *Decolonizing Methodologies: Research and Indigenous Peoples*. London: Zed Books, 2012.

Smith, Rogers M. "The Puzzling Place of Race in American Political Science." *PS: Political Science and Politics* 37, no.1 (2004): 41–45. https://www.jstor.org/stable/4488760.

Soedirgo, Jessica, and Aarie Glas. 2020. "Toward Active Reflexivity: Positionality and Practice in the Production of Knowledge." *PS: Political Science & Politics* 53, no. 3 (2020): 527–531. doi:10.1017/S1049096519002233.

Spivak, Gayatri Chakravorty. "Imperialism and Sexual Difference." *Oxford Literary Review* 8, no. 1 (1986): 225–240. https://www.jstor.org/stable/43964608.

Spivak, Gayatri Chakravorty. *In Other Worlds: Essays in Cultural Politics*. London: Routledge, 1987.

Takacs, David. "Positionality, Epistemology, and Social Justice in the Classroom." *Social Justice* 29, no. 4 (2002): 168–181.

Taylor, Carolyn, and Susan White. "Knowledge, Truth and Reflexivity: The Problem of Judgement in Social Work." *Journal of Social Work* 1, no. 1 (2001): 37–59. doi.org/10.1177/1468017301001001.

Thomas, Lahoma. "Dear Political Science, It Is Time for a SELF-REFLEXIVE Turn!" *Duck of Minerva* (blog), December 12, 2018. https://www.duckofminerva.com/2018/12/dear-political-science-it-is-time-for-a-self-reflexive-turn.html.

Thomas, Lahoma. "Unmasking: The Role of Reflexivity in Political Science." *Qualitative and Multi-Method Research* 16, no. 1 (2019): 42–44. doi.org/10.5281/zenodo.2562282.

Thomas, Lahoma. "Seeing from Da Yaad: Black Women and the Politics of Respect." PhD diss., University of Toronto, 2021.

Townsend-Bell, Erica. "Being True and Being You: Race, Gender, Class, and the Fieldwork Experience." *Political Science and Politics* 42, no. 2 (2009): 311–314. doi.org/10.1017/S1049096509090623.

Tuck, Eve, and K. Wayne Yang. 2012. "Decolonization Is Not a Metaphor." *Decolonization: Indigeneity, Education & Society* 1, no. 1 (2012): 1–40.

Visweswaran, Kamala. *Fictions of Feminist Ethnography*. Minneapolis: University of Minnesota Press, 1994.

Wai, Zubairu. *Epistemologies of African Conflicts: Violence, Evolutionism, and the War in Sierra Leone*. New York: Palgrave Macmillan, 2012.

Winker, Gabriele, and Nina Degele. "Intersectionality as Multi-Level Analysis: Dealing with Social Inequality." *European Journal of Women's Studies* 18, no. 1 (2011): 51–66. doi:10.1177/1350506810386084.

Wynter, Sylvia. "Unsettling the Coloniality of Being/Power/Truth/Freedom: Towards the Human, after Man, Its Overrepresentation—An Argument." *CR: The New Centennial Review* 3, no. 3 (2003): 257–337. doi:10.1353/ncr.2004.0015.

4
Theorization and Causality

Cathie Jo Martin

Introduction

Qualitative research requires being a good listener. You ask your sources—people or texts—to tell you their stories. You listen quietly to understand their truths. The process is not so much about mastery and imposing one's will on the narrative; rather, the object is to grasp the realities—cognitive frames, motivations, and perceived constraints—of the protagonists. With attention, care, and active listening to sources, qualitative research helps us to create theories about political problems and processes. It helps us (1) to define research questions and theory, (2) to identify causal mechanisms and propose hypotheses, and (3) to evaluate how these causal factors operate and whether they operate as expected. These research activities contribute to more realistic and robust theories about the workings of the political world.

Allow me to illustrate this by example, one drawn from personal experience. I have recently journeyed into the long 19th century in Denmark and Britain to understand early, path-defining choices in education system development. Denmark, a small, agricultural country on the periphery of Europe, created the second-earliest, mass public education system in the world in 1814. Britain, leader of the industrial revolution, left schooling to church societies until 1870, when a public system was finally put into place. Agricultural Denmark developed expansive vocational education programs for workers as part of its secondary education system reforms in 1892 and 1903; industrial Britain chose to limit secondary education to humanistic studies for elites in 1902.[1] Scholars offer many excellent (albeit somewhat contradictory) theories about education system development having to do with state-building, industrialization, and conflict between the church and state.

I suspected, however, that cultural differences underlay these battles over education and that cultural assumptions influenced the goals of and ideas about reform, the interests of the antagonists, and the institutional rules of the game. This required me to seek out and listen to firsthand accounts that illustrated cultural differences and to comprehend how policymakers and the chattering classes viewed schools, the working classes, society, and state. For this, I turned to the experts in cultural production—historical fiction writers—and investigated cultural depictions of education. This process entailed contemplating the stories in their novels, reading their letters in archives, and using computational linguistics methods to analyze their words.[2]

This chapter uses this illustration as a running example of how qualitative methods help us to perform important tasks of research, from design and theoretical development to assessments of causality. And while research designs may require employing a variety of qualitative and quantitative methods (for more, see Chapter 7), scholars keen on rigorous explanation of social, political, and economic phenomena may leverage the unique strengths and opportunities offered by a qualitative approach.

Defining Terms

At the outset, we should define a few terms, such as "theory development," "hypothesis," and "causal mechanism." Maybe you have heard these terms, or maybe this is your introduction to them, so let us consider what these terms mean, what they do in a research project, and why qualitative methods are uniquely positioned to carry out these tasks.

Eckstein defines "theory" as a "mental construct that orders phenomena or inquiry."[3] Theoretical constructs may take many forms; for example, classificatory schema that sort phenomena have a different purpose from analytic arguments positing causal relationships among phenomena, yet both suggest stylized patterns between empirical observations.

A "hypothesis" is derived from a theory and predicts a relationship between variables that may be generalized to a broad set of cases. Hypotheses provide a bridge between theory and empirical phenomena, as they are "operationalized" in a way that makes them observable in the empirical world. Hypotheses are falsifiable, in the sense that one may evaluate evidence in order to determine whether hypotheses correctly predict relationships.[4] For example, power resources theory suggests that high levels of welfare state provision develop in societies with a strong working class. One specific hypothesis is that countries with high levels of unionization are more likely to develop expansive unemployment benefits than countries with low levels of unionization.[5]

A "causal mechanism" provides an account of how a factor has its intended effect. For example, Thelen suggests that a process of conversion may underlie processes of incremental institutional change in vocational training programs. Even when the programs on the surface remain largely intact, they may lose their capacities to provide skills to marginal workers. Competing factions struggle to gain control over the programs, and in this way the programs are converted to new purposes.[6] Thus, causal mechanisms constitute the black box of cause and effect. If a hypothesis suggests that factor A causes phenomenon B, the causal mechanism specifies how this is done.

The Uses of Qualitative Research to Explain Political Outcomes

Constructing Theory

Qualitative research helps us to shed light on political outcomes in several ways. First, qualitative research helps us to develop theory: to identify the research question, the parameters of a problem, and the likely factors contributing to its resolution. The process of theory development entails using specific observations to posit broader patterned relationships among phenomena. Scholars consider alternative narratives about how phenomena interact in specific cases; they then theorize more enduring relationships among these phenomena.[7] The process is inductive, as we often stumble on compelling narratives that seem true to broader experience.[8] Bates suggests that the "soak and poke" phase of research requires immersion in the local culture and the intuition to let the facts speak for themselves. Inductive data-gathering helps one to move outside of the deep tracks of existing debates and eases the discovery of missing or underexplored factors in the empirical story.[9] Although inductive investigations may sometimes feel like wandering in the wilderness, we may avoid premature theories that close down alternative lines of research.

Bates describes his own process of growing awareness in his search to understand why farmers in East Africa failed to grow as much coffee as they were able to produce. His initial insights about coffee producers gradually developed into a theory about government interventions. While Bates was initially drawn to a cultural argument, he came to realize that farmers' fears about additional taxation partly drove their reticence to produce more. He then recognized a relationship between changing fiscal policies and variations in production; building on this realization, he articulated a cross-national, comparative theory about the relationship between state policies and the strategic choices of coffee producers. The cross-national comparison led him to consider how variations in government types—and particularly in levels of authoritarianism and party systems—affected fiscal policies and farmers' strategies.[10] His inductive and intuition-driven research gave him the freedom to find unexpected factors in his stories about economic choices and political change.

My research on the early development of education systems exemplifies how qualitative research may be used to define the research problem. Other authors have convincingly argued that cross-national variations in education system development reflect state-building, class struggle, and differences in church-state relations.[11] Yet by lingering with the literature of the 18th and early 19th centuries, I discovered a meaningful cross-national difference in the overarching *goals* of education, and I surmised that these differences in goals also had an impact on education system trajectories.

British and Danish authors held to vastly different cultural views of educational goals: Danish writers sought education reforms to strengthen society; British authors favored education to nurture individual self-development. Danish bureaucrats and authors drew strong connections among education, economic growth, and social stability; they offered this package deal as a formula to build a strong society. The father of Danish literature, Ludvig Holberg, laid out the logic of how education contributed to a well-ordered society in his 1741 international best-seller, *Niels Klim's Journey under the Earth* (which was written in Latin). Niels Klim travels to the subterranean utopia of Pontu, where schools enable each citizen to acquire skills to contribute to society: "[S]tudents are employed in solving complicated and difficult questions.... No one studies more than one science, and thus each gets a full knowledge of his peculiar subject."[12] Similarly, poet-priest Nicholai Frederik Severin Grundtvig believed that peasants should be both literate and educated about Danish history in order to participate fully in Danish society.[13]

For British authors, education was a means to perfect the individual and to contribute to self-actualization (largely for the upper and middle classes). British contemporaries of Holberg barely mention education, other than to ridicule the stereotypical bumbling tutor; thus, Daniel Defoe's protagonist in *Robinson Crusoe* (1719) readily admits that formal schooling holds no allure; only on the desert island does he learn to create products, but without the benefits of skills training.[14] Samuel Taylor Coleridge later frames learning as a path for individual self-discovery: he warns that "a man ... unblest with a liberal education, should act without attention to the habits, and feelings, of his fellow citizens"; education famously stimulates the heart to love.[15] Matthew Arnold explains, "The best man is he who most tries to perfect himself, and the happiest man is he who most feels that he is perfecting himself."[16]

One's "raw materials" may not be literature, but this example illustrates how research questions can come out of qualitative research (see Chapter 2), drive a researcher to new sources of data (see Chapter 13), and enable maximally inductive, curious exploration of outcomes—institutional and behavioral alike. As in this case, a qualitative research project may point to or open up a new source of data. For example, political scientists typically do not work with literature, but fiction provides an excellent source for assessing historical, cross-national differences in cultural attitudes and public opinion (or at least views of the bourgeois intelligentsia). Fiction allows us to understand respondents' thought processes in real time and to avoid reading history backward.[17]

Identifying Causal Mechanisms

Second, qualitative research helps us to identify hypotheses and to elaborate the causal mechanisms that underlie theoretical predictions about relationships among phenomena. Qualitative research helps to advance our collective understanding of political issues by unveiling theoretical gaps in extant work that stem from understudied or poorly understood causal mechanisms. Qualitative research uniquely contributes to theory-building by demonstrating the mechanisms by which variables operate. Large-N quantitative studies may verify strong correlations among factors, but we cannot always be certain that these correlations accurately capture causal relationships, and the findings cannot show definitively that the model driving the quantitative tests is correct. Even if a statistical model sets forth the explanatory factors that matter, it is less well suited for identifying the reasons why they matter. Causal inference cannot be assumed from observational data; these data simply do not provide sufficient information about processes to justify causal claims.[18] Articulating concepts is a crucial component of research design; however, this stage is often neglected in research methods. Moreover, qualitative observations may be used to refine hypotheses, as scholars glean expanding insights into the nature of political phenomena.[19] Thus, qualitative research is an important tool for strengthening the validity of causal inference.[20]

For example, while cultural influences are often cited in political science, the mechanisms by which cultural factors have bearing on political phenomena are less well established. The lack of precise descriptions of causal mechanisms was particularly problematic in cultural claims about the superiority of American political institutions, especially because these claims were associated with a distinct international political agenda.[21] In recent decades, scholars have used survey research to assess cross-national distinctions in cultural values, and these more objective and less value-laden approaches have contributed much to our understanding of cross-national differences in religious values and comparative attitudes toward the welfare state and more.[22] Yet big-N studies of public opinion do not capture the full complexity of how public opinion matters to political outcomes or why altering words in opinion surveys may change respondents' answers.

Qualitative research offers a means for exploring cultural views in a more intimate fashion; in particular, literature offers us a relatively autonomous venue for soaking and poking in the worldviews of centuries past. The qualitative study of literature enables us to listen to the data in an inductive fashion and to avoid interviewer error that may occur when posing questions to respondents. In this way, we may use qualitative data to refine our theoretical hypotheses.

Qualitative research also may uncover omitted and missing variables that are critical to a story, and that may even set the context for the operation of the causal mechanisms. Falleti and Lynch refer to this as the "context conditionality" of causal mechanisms, where contextual factors mediate the mechanisms by which a cause has an effect.[23]

My work shows how the neglected variable of culture provides context for the operation of another variable, working-class power. Scholars widely accept that working-class power contributes to social reforms, including the educational attainment of the working class.[24] Yet the specific relationship is a bit unclear, as scholars hold different views of how norms of cooperation and conflict enter into this process. Some authors suggest that countries with the most militant unions developed extensive welfare state benefits because well-organized labor wrested concessions from the capitalist class.[25] Others believe that social benefits were more likely to develop in countries with strong historical norms of cooperation and muted class antagonisms.[26]

I find that culture provides the context for the exercise of power of organized labor and for the content of elite and working-class demands. At least as early as the 1700s, British and Danish authors presented radically different views of farmers and workers. The cultural tropes wielded by literary writers stipulate the context for the class struggles and compromises that shaped trajectories of education, social, and labor policies.

British authors, for example, were largely suspicious of the working man. During the French Revolution, many intellectuals feared that working-class literacy would be accompanied by social instability.[27] For Thomas Malthus, the working class constituted a drag on the British economy, because population would increase with a rise in the means of subsistence.[28] Victorian British social reformers such as Charles Dickens and Elizabeth Gaskell deplored class injustices and were sympathetic to the plight of the poor, yet even they worried about Malthusian overpopulation and the culture of poverty afflicting workers.[29] Gaskell drew unions as fatally flawed institutions that contributed to workers' misery: "[O]nce banded together, yo've no more pity for a man than a wild hunger-maddened wolf."[30] George Gissing stressed the cruelty of the urban poor in *The Netherworld*, as when he wrote about one character, "[T]his lust of hers for sanguinary domination was the natural enough issue of the brutalizing serfdom of her predecessors in the family line."[31] The Fabian socialist H. G. Wells feared cultural degradation associated with mass culture and described the "extravagant swarm of new births" as the "essential disaster of the nineteenth century."[32]

Danish authors held to a significantly more positive view of the "small people" than did British writers: they considered industrialization to be an important collective project and sought education of workers to further collective goals of building society, national strength, and economic prosperity. Unlike in Malthusian Britain, farmers and workers were celebrated as the backbone of Danish society at the dawn of the 19th century; educated workers were viewed as essential to cultivating useful citizens for the nation-building and the industrializing projects. In *Montanus den Yngre*, Thomasine Gyllembourg connected social solidarity and investment in workers' skills to economic productivity and industrialization. Her forward-thinking protagonist wrote a treatise on foreign technology, connected prosperity to the freedom of working men, and argued for skills training to offset unemployment related to mechanization.[33]

These strong cultural differences about labor resonated in the expression of preferences for education reform by leaders on the left in late 19th-century Britain and Denmark. While some British authors, socialists, and labor leaders supported technical education for the working classes, many argued for one-track upper secondary schools so that workers would not receive a two-tiered education. The Independent Labour Party sought universal, free secular education at all levels, and Wells believed that technical education was suitable only for substandard jobs.[34]

Danish activists across the political spectrum sought secondary education for all as a way to build society ("sambundets udbytte") and ascribed to a wide range of educational interventions.[35] Educator and politician Vilhelm Rasmussen argued that Denmark's greatest asset was its human resources; a good education would make young people committed to improving their life circumstances and would bolster cultural development and democracy. Rasmussen sought appropriate schools for students of all abilities and supported examinations to place students properly, as these could identify students' innate capacities, initiative, and ingenuity.[36]

This example helps us to understand the role of qualitative research in articulating causal mechanisms and shedding light on how variables such as culture provide context for the interpretation of interests in episodes of class struggle. Without qualitative research, we might miss the crucial lesson of this story: literary depictions contribute to the characterizations of the working class in the 19th century, and these characterizations provides important context for understanding policy reforms. The claim is not that cultural calculations were *the* defining factor in cross-national variations in education systems; however, the data suggest that cultural depictions delimit the possibilities of reform. In this way, qualitative observations allow us to tease out causal mechanisms and to redefine theory.

Testing Causal Mechanisms

Third, qualitative research helps us to evaluate claims about causal mechanisms: at this testing stage, qualitative research is particularly adept at assessing competing causal claims (when both receive support from quantitative tests) and coping with causal complexity. Process tracing methods enable us to assess conflicting arguments about processes of change and are particularly invaluable in scholarly debates that highlight contrasting causal mechanisms. Context becomes particularly important under conditions of multicausality, context conditionality, and endogeneity.[37] Moreover, a factor may be relevant without being causal, as it may set the context for the factors that drive the outcome.[38]

Several types of qualitative methods allow us to assess the validity of our hypotheses and causal inference: these include process tracing, within-case analyses, and attention to most-likely and least-likely cases and looking at outliers, to name but a few.[39] Qualitative process tracing allows us to track the impacts of a factor or occurrence on subsequent events (see Chapter 34); in this way, we can ensure that the observed relationship between a causal variable and its effect is not fallacious. Qualitative case studies are particularly rich sources in the process of identifying and ruling out causal mechanisms, because their thick descriptions provide narratives about how phenomena interact.[40]

Bayesian inference is an important mechanism for assessing the validity of a causal inference. This technique entails estimating uncertainty in situations and then evaluating whether the independent variables fit with the hypotheses. If one discovers an independent variable in a situation in which one does not expect to find it, or does not find an expected variable, one may reasonably question whether the variable is indeed important to the finding. This technique helps us to make inferences from a small number of observations and incorporate contextual knowledge into our analyses.[41]

Qualitative and quantitative approaches may be strengthened through the use of mixed methods; indeed, a good "rule of thumb" is to bring as much evidence to bear as possible (see Chapter 7). A multimethod research design combining correlational (cross-case) and process-level (within-case) observations improves the estimation of causal effects.[42] Yet it is important to stop and observe the difference between quantitative and qualitative methods of analysis. Quantitative methods give us a general idea of relationship among explanatory factors. Qualitative analyses—comparative historical analysis, process tracing, and thick description—offer novel tools for identifying and following causal mechanisms.

My study of education reform relies on both qualitative and quantitative data to develop hypotheses about the role of culture in cross-national differences in education system development. I use quantitative data to observe long-term differences in British and Danish corpora of literature to document cross-national distinctions in views toward education. Computational text analyses allow one to test systematically observable differences in the frequencies of words in corpora of British (622) and Danish (521) novels, poems, and plays between 1700 and 1920 (after which copyright laws limit access). I hypothesize that if countries have distinctive cultural narratives, these should be readily apparent in their large national corpora of literature, should exhibit sharp cross-national differences, and should persist for generations or even centuries. I use both supervised and unsupervised learning models to compare word frequencies and topics across countries. (For more on these methods, see Chapter 32.) The analysis finds statistically significant differences between Danish and British corpora over two centuries, as cultural depictions of society, individuals, the working class, and the state in literary references to education differ wildly in the two countries (Figure 4.1).

But this evidence establishes only a correlation or a pattern in the relationship between cultural depictions of education and trajectories of education system development. Therefore, I complement this large-N finding with qualitative research to tease out *why* the

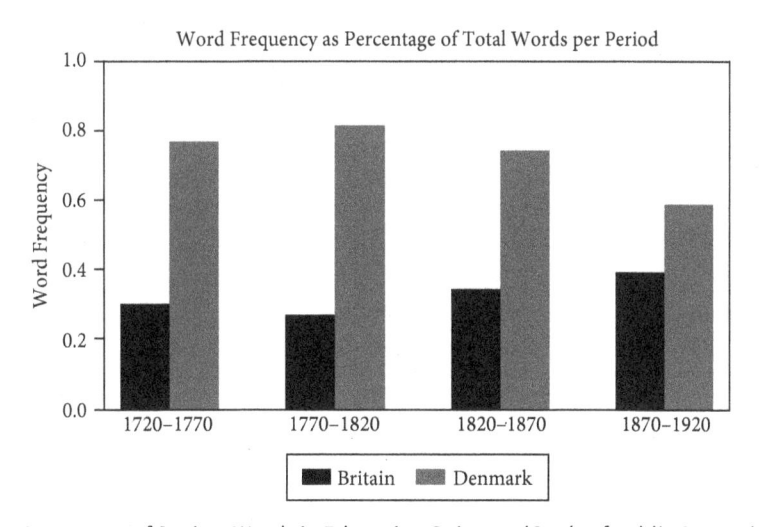

Figure 4.1 Frequency of Society Words in Education Snippets (Goals of Public System). Words are *England, English, Britain, country, folk, people, collective, communal, custom, social, mutual.*

observed pattern exists and *how* this comes to be. I obtain my qualitative observations with a close reading of texts and archival material to explore precisely what authors think about education and how they become involved in specific struggles over education reform. A close reading of texts, such as the authors cited above, shows that British and Danish authors think about education in the ways suggested by the quantitative data. (See Chapter 30 for a further discussion of these methods.)

Furthermore, with archival investigations, I can place authors at the scene of the crime. As it turns out, writers were extremely important but undervalued political actors in reform movements of the 18th and 19th centuries, as they provided a venue for transmitting views of the (largely middle-class) people up to state rulers in predemocratic regimes.[43] Authors had a comparative advantage in framing policy problems. Thus, Benjamin Disraeli admits that he wrote *Sybil* (1844) to draw attention to dysfunctional party politics and to the troubles of the working man.[44] Writers made emotional appeals to readers, and their depictions of heroes and villains helped to politicize or demobilize aggrieved groups. Rudyard Kipling recognizes the power of the national corpus when he writes, "The magic of Literature lies in the words, and not in any man.... [A] bare half-hundred words breathed upon by some man in his agony, or in his exaltation, or in his idleness, ten generations ago, can still lead whole nations into and out of captivity."[45]

Authors also placed an explicit role providing legitimacy to political movements, and they explicitly they used their works to mobilize elite and popular opinion in support of particular political agendas. For example, Danish authors formed a faction of the Left Party in the late 19th century and joined forces with the farmers' wing of the party to struggle for political change. Christian Berg, the head of the farmer's wing, viewed the authors as making a huge contribution to the Left Party cause. According to Berg, the authors' Literary Left faction allowed the party to wage "war with culture" instead of with more materialistic means. The authors constituted "our poets, our professors, our jurists, journalists.... Like manna from heaven, the literary Left came down into this desert.... [W]e had what we lacked."[46]

The combination of quantitative text analysis, a close reading of texts, and process tracing of authors' involvement with education reform struggles provides considerable evidence in support of the causal claim that nationally specific views about education set the context for educational system outcomes. Authors were not the most significant agents of change, yet they played specific and recognized roles in providing ideology for the movements. Qualitative and quantitative evidence work together here to verify cross-national differences in cultural depictions of political problems and demonstrate their correspondence with cross-national variations in institutional solutions.

The process by which I arrived at these insights also exemplifies the joy of revelation often produced by qualitative research. Reading novels made me aware of stark cultural differences and brought me to look more closely at authors as political actors; in the process, I discovered an arena of political action that I hitherto knew little about and that has been largely overlooked in our field.

Pitfalls and Drawbacks

All this is not to say that qualitative research does not have drawbacks—it does! For one thing, scholars who do qualitative research report having difficulty getting their work accepted by leading political science journals. Scholars may face a high hurdle in convincing editors and reviewers that a qualitative approach has merit, particularly when one looks beyond traditional variables such as interests and institutions. Yet a careful and explicit presentation of methods is a scholar's best friend in such endeavors, and mixed methods also help to overcome this hurdle.

Qualitative case studies are also limited in their generalizability, although strategies such as within-case analyses and attention to most-likely and least-likely cases can help to offset the problems posed by a small N. My solution to this problem is to utilize a blend of qualitative and quantitative methods and to be very clear about what each approach offers to the study of institutional and policy change. Quantitative text analysis allows me to identify empirical patterns in large corpora of literature over time. We may assess—from the proverbial bird's eye view—how authors over generations collectively work with nationally distinctive structures of symbols and narratives in their literary works. Authors inherit symbols and narratives from their literary ancestors, rework and apply these cultural tropes to the issues of the day, and pass along collective truths of their national corpora to future generations.[47] Qualitative analyses—a close reading of texts and process tracing using primary and secondary sources—allows me to identify causal mechanisms and further test my hypotheses. With qualitative text analyses, we can discover how authors thought about education in real time and trace how authors became activists in political struggles over education reform. Both tasks are important, yet at the end of the day, qualitative methods are necessary to grasp actors' motivations and experiences.

Adventures in Qualitative Research

Qualitative research methods provide a powerful tool for theorizing political puzzles and for navigating the maze of meaning through which protagonists and antagonists travel toward their policy accords. Before we can test hypotheses (using either qualitative or quantitative methods), we must construct plausible stories about the who, what, when, where, and how of politics. Qualitative research helps us to formulate research questions that are consistent with the worldviews of the actors involved. Qualitative research offers insights into the dynamics of causal processes and the specific ways that causal variables have their intended effect. Finally, qualitative research helps us to test hypotheses and provides a reality check about the validity of suggested causal mechanisms.

Capturing the meaning underlying causal processes may be particularly important in our contemporary world, when vicious culture wars inform material interests, define class cleavages, and rip apart democratic institutions. Political science as an exercise in prediction and explication—whether applied to election outcomes, public opinion polls, or social movement uprisings—seems to be an increasingly futile undertaking. Culture is more frequently the stuff that politics is made of, and only by listening closely to the cries and whispers of the mobilized masses can we hope to make sense of this topsy-turvy world.

Notes

1. Gjerløff and Jacobsen, *Da skolen bliv sat I system*; Green, *Education and State Formation*.
2. Martin, "Imagine All the People"; Martin, *Education for All*.
3. Eckstein, "Case Study and Theory in Political Science," 125.

4. Eckstein, "Case Study and Theory in Political Science," 125.
5. Korpi, "Social Policy and Distributional Conflict in the Capitalist Democracies," 298.
6. Thelen, *How Institutions Evolve*, 7–8; Palier and Thelen, "Institutionalizing Dualism," 119–120.
7. Eckstein, "Case Study and Theory in Political Science," 125.
8. Laitin, "Comparative Politics," 631.
9. Bates, "From Case Studies to Social Science," 178.
10. Bates, "From Case Studies to Social Science," 178–180.
11. Ansell and Lindvall, "The Political Origins of Primary Education Systems," 505–506.
12. Holberg, *Niels Klim's Journey under the Ground*, 491.
13. Grundtvig, "Skolen for Livet og akademiet i Soer."
14. Defoe, *Robinson Crusoe*, 4.
15. Coleridge, "The Watchman," 128.
16. Arnold, *Culture and Anarchy*, 46.
17. Ahmed, "Reading History Forward," 1059.
18. Collier and Brady, *Rethinking Social Inquiry*.
19. Gerring, "What Is a Case Study and What Is It Good for?," 348; Thomas, "The Qualitative Foundations of Political Science Methodology."
20. Collier and Brady, *Rethinking Social Inquiry*.
21. Huntington, *The Clash of Civilizations*.
22. Norris and Inglehart, *Sacred and Secular*; Svallfors, "Worlds of Welfare and Attitudes to Redistribution."
23. Falleti and Lynch; "Context and Causal Mechanisms in Political Analysis," 1143.
24. Stephens, *The Transition from Capitalism to Socialism*; Korpi, "Social Policy and Distributional Conflict in the Capitalist Democracies."
25. Lipset, "Radicalism or Reformism," 1–2.
26. Cusack, Iversen, and Soskice, "Economic Interests and the Origins of Electoral Systems"; Martin and Swank, *The Political Construction of Business Interests*; Martin, Nijhuis, and Olsson, "Cultural Images of Labor Conflict and Cooperation."
27. Brantlinger, *The Reading Lesson*.
28. Malthus, *An Essay on the Principle of Population*, 27–28.
29. Steinlight, *Populating the Novel*.
30. Gaskell, *Mary Barton*, 180.
31. Gissing, *The Essential George Gissing*, Loc 95.
32. Carey, *The Intellectuals and the Masses*, 1.
33. Gyllembourg, *Montanus den Yngre*.
34. Wells, *Experiment in Autobiography*, 93.
35. Skovgaard-Petersen, *Dannelse og Demokrati*, 178, 138.
36. Nørr, *Det Højere skolevæsen og kirken*, 197–198.
37. Denk and Lehtinen, "Contextual Analyses with QCA-Methods."
38. Mahoney and Goertz, "Tale of Two Cultures."
39. Collier and Brady, *Rethinking Social Inquiry*.
40. Gerring, "What Is a Case Study and What Is It Good for?," 350.
41. Collier and Brady, *Rethinking Social Inquiry*; Fearon, "Counterfactuals and Hypothesis Testing in Political Science," 173.
42. Beland and Cox, "Introduction," 6; Humphreys and Jacobs, "Mixing Methods," 653.
43. Keen, *The Crisis of Literature in the 1790s*, 29–33.
44. Disraeli, *Sybil*, 454.
45. Kipling, *Book of Words*, 6.
46. Hvidt, *Edvard Brandes*, 127–128.
47. Martin and Chevalier, "What We Talk About," 809; Martin, *Education for All*; Williams, *Culture and Society*.

Recommended Readings

Maxwell, Joseph A. "Why qualitative methods are necessary for generalization." Qualitative Psychology 8.1 (2021): 111.
   Psychologist Joseph Maxwell distinguishes between internal generalization (which extends observed findings to others within the group or population) and external generalization (which applies insights to other settings, groups or populations). Sampling is more important to internal than to external generalization, Qualitative methods are particularly important to external generalization, because these help us to view the mental constructs and context that make observed causal processes transferable to other settings.
Skarbek, David. "Qualitative research methods for institutional analysis." Journal of Institutional Economics 16.4 (2020): 409–422.
   Political scientist David Skarbek investigates how economists study institutions with qualitative methods and applies these insights to his own investigations into criminal organizations.

References

Ahmed, Amel. "Reading History Forward: The Origins of Electoral Systems in European Democracies." *Comparative Political Studies* 43, no. 8 (2010): 1059–1088.
Ansell, Ben, and Johannes Lindvall. "The Political Origins of Primary Education Systems." *American Political Science Review* 107, no. 3 (August 2013): 505–522.
Arnold, Matthew. *Culture and Anarchy* (1867–1868) 2001. Blackmask Online. http://public-library.uk/ebooks/25/79.pdf.
Bates, Robert. "From Case Studies to Social Science: A Strategy for Political Research." In *Oxford Handbook of Comparative Politics*, edited by Carles Boix and Susan Stokes, 172–185. Oxford: Oxford University Press, 2008.
Béland, Daniel, and Robert Henry Cox. "Introduction." In *Ideas and Politics in Social Science Research*, edited by D. Béland and H. Cox, 3–20. Oxford: Oxford University Press, 2011.
Carey, John. *The Intellectuals and the Masses: Pride and Prejudice amongst the Literary Intelligentsia, 1880–1939*. London: Faber & Faber, 1992.
Collier, David, and Henry Brady. *Rethinking Social Inquiry*. Lanham, MD: Rowman and Littlefield, 2004.
Brantlinger, Patrick. *The Reading Lesson*. Bloomington: Indiana University Press, 1998.
Coleridge, Samuel Taylor. "The Watchman," part 4. March 25, 1796. doi: https://doi.org/10.1017/S0003055407070384
Cusack, Thomas, Torben Iversen, and David Soskice. "Economic Interests and the Origins of Electoral Systems." *American Political Science Review* 101, no. 3 (2007): 373–391.
Defoe, Daniel. *Robinson Crusoe* (1719). Classic e-book.
Denk, Thomas, and Sarah Lehtinen. "Contextual Analyses with QCA-Methods." *Quality & Quantity: International Journal of Methodology* 48, no. 6 (November 2014): 3475–3487.
Disraeli, Benjamin. *Sybil* (1845). London: UK Bureau Books, 2020.
Eckstein, Harry. "Case Study and Theory in Political Science." In *Case Study Method: Key Issues, Key Texts*, edited by Roger Gomm, Martyn Hammersley, and Peter Foster, 119–164. Thousand Oaks, California: Sage, 2000.
Falleti, Tulia, and Julia Lynch. "Context and Causal Mechanisms in Political Analysis." *Comparative Political Studies* 42, no. 9 (2009): 1143–1166.
Fearon, James. "Counterfactuals and Hypothesis Testing in Political Science." *World Politics* 43, no. 2 (1991): 169–195.
Gaskell, Elizabeth. *Mary Barton* (1848). Ware, UK: Wordsworth Classic, 2012.
Gerring, John. "What Is a Case Study and What Is It Good for?" *American Political Science Review* 98, no. 2 (May 2004): 341–354.
Gissing, George. *The Essential George Gissing*. Halcyon Classics Series. 1889. Kindle.
Gjerløff, Anne Katrine, and Annette Faye Jacobsen. *Da skolen bliv sat I system 1850–1920*. Aarhus: Aarhus Universitet Forlag, 2014.

Green, Andy. *Education and State Formation*. London, UK: Palgrave Macmillan, 1990.
Gyllembourg, Thomasine. *Montanus den Yngre* (1837). Copenhagen: Lindhardt og Ringholf, 2019.
Holberg, Ludvig. *Niels Klim's Journey under the Ground* (1741). Translated by John Gierlow. Boston: Saxton, Peirce, 1845.
Humphreys, Macartan, and Alan M. Jacobs. "Mixing Methods: A Bayesian Approach." *American Political Science Review* 109, no. 4 (2015): 653–673.
Huntington, Samuel. *The Clash of Civilizations*. New York: Simon and Schuster, 1996.
Hvidt, Kristian. *Edvard Brandes, Portræt af en radikal blæksprutte*. Copenhagen: Gyldendal, 2017.
Keen, Paul. *The Crisis of Literature in the 1790s*. Cambridge: Cambridge University Press, 1999.
Kipling, Rudyard. *A Book of Words*. New York: Charles Scribner's Sons, 1928.
Korpi, Walter. "Social Policy and Distributional Conflict in the Capitalist Democracies," *West European Politics* 3, no. 3 (1980): 296–316.
Laitin, David. "Comparative Politics: The State of the Subdiscipline." In *Political Science: The State of the Discipline*, edited by Helen Milner and Ira Katznelson, 630–659. New York: Norton, 2002.
Lipset, Seymour Martin. "Radicalism or Reformism." *American Political Science Association* 77, no. 1 (March 1983): 1–18.
Mahoney, James, and Gary Goertz. "Tale of Two Cultures—Contrasting Qualitative and Quantitative." *Political Analysis* 14, no. 3 (Summer 2006): 227–249.
Mahoney, James, and Dietrich Rueschmeyer. "Comparative Historical Analysis." In *Comparative Historical Analysis in the Social Sciences*, edited by James Mahoney and Dietrich Rueschemeyer, 3–40. New York: Cambridge University Press, 2003.
Malthus, Thomas. *An Essay on the Principle of Population*. Vol. 1 (1797). Washington City: Roger Chew Wrightman, 1809.
Martin, Cathie Jo. *Education for All: Authors, Culture and Education Development in Britain and Denmark*. New York: Cambridge University Press, 2023.
Martin, Cathie Jo. "Imagine All the People: Literature, Society and Cross-national Variation in Education Systems." *World Politics* 70, no. 3 (2018): 398–442.
Martin, Cathie Jo, and Tom Chevalier. "What We Talk About When We Talk About Poverty: Culture and Welfare State Development in Britain, Denmark and France." *British Journal of Political Science* (2021): 805–828.
Martin, Cathie Jo, Dennie Oude Nijhuis, and Erik Olsson. "Cultural Images of Labor Conflict and Cooperation: Literature and the Evolution of Industrial Relations Systems." *European Journal of Sociology* 62, no. 3 (2021): 381–419.
Martin, Cathie Jo, and Duane Swank. *The Political Construction of Business Interests*. New York: Cambridge University Press, 2012.
Norris, Pippa, and Ronald Ingelhart. *Sacred and Secular*. Cambridge, MA: Harvard University Press, 2012.
Nørr, Erik. *Det Højere skolevæsen og kirken*. Aarhus: Akademisk Forlag, 1979.
Palier, Bruno, and Kathleen Thelen. "Institutionalizing Dualism: Complementarities and Change in France and Germany." *Politics and Society* 38, no. 1 (2010): 119–148.
Skovgaard-Petersen, Vagn. *Dannelse og Demokrati: Fra latin- til almenskole* (1976). Lov om højere almenskoler 24. Copenhagen: Gyldendals pædagoiske bibliotek, 1903.
Steinlight, Emily. *Populating the Novel*. Ithaca, NY: Cornell University Press, 2018.
Stephens, John. *The Transition from Capitalism to Socialism*. London: Palgrave Macmillan, 1979.
Svallfors, Stefan. "Worlds of Welfare and Attitudes to Redistribution." *European Sociological Review* 13 (1997): 283–304.
Thelen, Kathleen. *How Institutions Evolve*. New York: Cambridge University Press, 2004.
Thomas, George. "The Qualitative Foundations of Political Science Methodology." *Perspectives on Politics* 3, no. 4 (December 2005): 855–866.
Wells, H. G. *Experiment in Autobiography*. Vol. 1. New York: Macmillan, 1934.
Williams, Raymond. *Culture and Society*. New York: Columbia University Press, 1963.

5
The Construction of Knowledge

Jooyoun Lee

Introduction

We, the researchers, engage in research activity to obtain knowledge about the world, our community, and our surroundings, in an attempt to gain a better understanding of how they work. The way that we understand our world in the field of the social sciences has been heavily influenced by the practices of research in the natural sciences, which posits that knowledge can and must be obtained scientifically. At the heart of the idea of scientific knowledge lies the assumption that knowledge is objective, meaning that it exists independent of humans and that we can obtain knowledge in an impartial and value-neutral way. Such a view is grounded in the idea of essentialism, a belief that the members or instances of a given category possess "hidden properties called *essences* that make them members of the category and that endow them with a certain nature."[1] Social science researchers tend to adopt this essentialist orientation, which is "an innate bias," when they seek to understand the external world.[2] However, as James Mahoney argues, such an essentialist orientation is "not appropriate for the *scientific* study of social reality."[3] The first section of this chapter interrogates the conviction that knowledge is objective by critiquing the ontological and epistemological assumptions of objective knowledge and providing an overview of how the concept of the construction of knowledge has been developed by introducing key pioneering scholars and the status of this line of research. The second section presents the state of practice regarding how to practically conduct research involving the construction of knowledge. The third section discusses potential problems and some tips to help researchers overcome those issues.

The Construction of Knowledge, Power, and the Multiplicity of Human Experience

Revisiting Ontological and Epistemological Assumptions of Objective Knowledge

The idea of scientific research is typically rooted in the following ontological and epistemological assumptions. First, ontologically, there is an emphasis on the belief that the world exists "out there" in an objective way; "facts" and the objects of knowledge exist independent of knowers and remain separate and isolated throughout the process of research.[4] According to this perspective, the reality of the world, or "truth," has been preserved timelessly, untouched by human activity, in a single way, so as to provide universally applicable general laws.

However, social order is the product of human activity, and it "exists only and insofar as human activity continues to produce it," instead of being derived from the "laws of nature."[5] According to Friedrich Nietzsche, "truth" is an "illusion,"[6] and knowledge is an "invention" of humans. History did not happen the way that history has been made.[7] There is much discrepancy between knowledge and the world to be known. Nietzsche states, "In some remote corner of the universe, bathed in the fires of innumerable solar systems, there once was a planet where clever animals invented knowledge. That was the grandest and most mendacious minute of 'universal history.'"[8] "Clever animals" refers to humans, who are responsible for "inventing" knowledge. Rather than being detached from researchers and humans, reality is constantly being constituted and impacted by human actions through a dialectic between "subjectively meaningful action (the meaning of 'doings') and socially crystallized meanings (the meaning of 'dones')."[9]

Second, and relatedly, the belief in "empirical observation" is rooted in the epistemological conviction that "truth" can be discovered and obtained empirically in an unbiased manner.[10] In this view, the researcher is endowed with the ability to observe and discover the reality and the regularities of the world. This view holds that our way of knowing the reality can be achieved in an objective, neutral, and value-free way. Objectivity can be achieved and maximized by the researcher's detached stance of observing the object under carefully controlled conditions.[11] This also entails the idea that knowers have the intrinsic ability to distance themselves from the objects to be known, or "reality," and to discover general laws in a value-neutral way by unfailingly maintaining distance between themselves and the reality of the world. Objectivity and value-neutrality have been treated as synonymous, in the sense that "objective knowledge is declared value-neutral and presented as a collection of impartial and wholly disinterested facts or truths."[12]

However, the "objectivity" and "value-neutrality" of knowledge is not given or predetermined, as epistemological assumptions are not natural or neutral. The researcher's perception of the objects is heavily influenced by social contexts and the cultural norms of a given society. The researcher and the researcher's productions cannot be completely detached and separated from the social context and circumstantial environment. For example, the rise of a particular conception of race and race relations was socially constructed in the historical context of European modernization, when the undertaking of the European Enlightenment in the 18th century relied heavily on the ascendancy of the idea of human rationality and "scientific" progress.[13] Such reliance was never neutral or value-free, as the use of "science" was carried out to justify European imperial projects and colonize vast parts of the world. In fact, ideas of race and race relations have been subject to change in the context of changing norms and specific historical contexts of national and global politics.[14] Knowledge is historically contingent and socially constructed and contested. In this sense, conceptions of knowledge are "historically variable and contentious."[15]

Moreover, "the house of knowledge has many mansions," and there are multiple types of knowledge.[16] Instead of existing in a single, objective way, "reality" exists in multiple ways through multiple representations of it. The reality that we conceive as reality is a representation of reality rather than objective reality itself.[17] Typically, a widely accepted idea of reality reflects collective understandings of societies of individuals embedded in particular places and times, but even shared understandings, such as revolutions and acts of discrimination, are subject to "spatiotemporal instability" and are open to change.[18] What we know about the society, the community, and the world is a mediated conception that has been constituted by human actions deeply embedded in relations of power, which in turn inform human perceptions and behaviors in a constantly interactive way. Knowledge is constructed and always in the process of construction, rather than being objective and reified.

Power, Mutual Constitution, and the Status of Research

Knowledge does not and cannot spring up naturally or autonomously on its own, independent of human agency or human action. This subsection introduces how the idea of the construction of knowledge has developed by looking at the notion of power and key pioneering scholars who advocated this view and the way that the researcher and the external world are mutually constituted and providing an overview of the status of this line of research.

Nietzsche is one of the founding scholars who articulated the idea that knowledge is constructed by humans. He notes that "there is not a nature of knowledge, an essence of knowledge, of the universal conditions of knowledge"; rather "knowledge is always the historical and circumstantial result of conditions outside the domain of knowledge."[19] At the root of knowledge lie struggles and power relations, and humans are deeply involved in this condition. Developing Nietzsche's idea of the invented nature of knowledge by humans and an attention to power, Michel Foucault brings light to the nexus of power and knowledge.[20] For Foucault, knowledge comes out of conflict, combat, and the outcome of conflict, and, in this light, knowledge reflects a process of battles and struggles and their results. Power gives rise to knowledge by making things "true." If we truly wish to know what knowledge is and to understand it at its root, we need to understand what the relations of struggle and power are. Particular types of subjects and domains of knowledge are formed in the context of political and economic conditions and struggles.[21] Analyzing power inherently entails an analysis of power relations rather than power itself, which involves power relations between individuals or between groups, as well as the relations of the production and circulation of signs and elements of meaning.[22]

The process of knowing involves who the knower is and what the knower wants to know. The knower is the product of, and is constantly situated in, a process of socialization that has been informed by a set of particular social norms and power relations which constitute a meaning system in a given society at a certain point of time of history. The position of the knower is significantly affected by this process and impacts the process and the result of knowledge; this is epistemologically significant, since the specific circumstances of knowers operate as a subjective factor that conditions the "nature, possibility, and/or justification of knowledge."[23]

Equally important is the idea that uniform experience shared by all people is impossible.[24] Depending on their political, social, cultural, and economic positions, humans have diverse experiences, and their experiences are historically conditioned. Our values formed from these diverse experiences and "enter into all our descriptions of the social world."[25] Mediated by political, cultural, economic, and historical conditions and by their own positionality, humans are integrally involved in the process of *interpreting* the world and *constructing* knowledge, instead of being value-neutral and detached from knowledge in such a way as to discover it. As Edward Said notes, no device has yet been created to detach the researcher from social, cultural, and political circumstances, nor from their engagement with a class, a social position, and a membership in a society.[26] The researcher and the external world are mutually constituted.

Drawing on the idea that knowledge is socially constructed, as articulated by Nietzsche and Foucault, the research on the construction of knowledge has significantly expanded in the field of international relations. For this line of work, researchers interrogate the workings of norms, ideas, beliefs, meanings, and power. Diverse groups of scholars in the field, including constructivist, critical, feminist, and postcolonial researchers, are increasingly engaged with the research on the numerous modes of knowledge production taking place historically or contemporarily in various areas, including but not limited to international security, international political economy, peace studies, foreign policy analysis, international organizations, and nonstate actors and transnational activism. For example, John M. Hobson uses a postcolonial lens to problematize the conventional wisdom that the West and non-West have been historically separated in the workings of the global economy, arguing that this view produces and perpetuates a Eurocentric perspective that the West was the origin and the center of the liberal global economy.[27] He refutes this idea by revealing the way that the West and non-West have been intimately intertwined in the production and process of the global economy throughout history, challenging the West-centric practices of knowledge production in international relations ingrained in the nexus of power and denying agency to the non-West. The following section describes the practice of doing research on the construction of knowledge by drawing on explorations of the production and circulation of meanings.

"Doing" the Construction of Knowledge

Representation, Discourse, and Subjectivity

Researchers can take multiple avenues in examining how a particular meaning system is constructed and disseminated in social relations, how certain ideas become accepted as legitimate knowledge, and how power is involved in this process. Facts, events, and incidents do not speak for themselves. Social understandings of certain topics or objects are conveyed through language. In light of this, it is crucial to recognize that knowledge is discursively constructed through language. A discourse is a set of statements that embody a way of representing and discussing a particular topic or subject.[28] Knowledge is produced by discursive practice—the practice of producing meaning.[29] The way that certain events, people, countries, institutions, and experiences are known is constructed by language through the process of naming, narrating, and interpreting them. For example, language creates the reality of who is a terrorist as opposed to a freedom fighter, and the language practice is heavily influenced by subject position. For example, the British celebrated the Malayan People's Anti-Japanese Army during World War II even though it targeted civilian collaborators. The same groups were labeled terrorists by the British when they attacked the British colonial authority in Malaya after the war.[30] Concepts structure thinking and produce a particular meaning associated with the concepts and naming.

Language employs diverse devices to articulate, signify, and communicate messages and information; thus, discourses circulated in a given society entail representations rather than "truth" or objective reality.[31] This process is not value-free or neutral, however. It involves diverse kinds of power, and through the establishment and the process of power relations, things are made "true" as knowledge about reality.[32] For example, the term "the North Korea problem" creates a particular reality that necessitates a certain course of actions to punish North Korea. This prompts researchers to examine North Korea with a particular focus, such as Pyongyang's nuclear weapons program, in a way to perpetuate the idea that North Korea is a "rogue state." This discursive practice underpins the interests of great powers that construct the idea of Korea's intractable conflict, artificially normalizing the status quo of its division as the optimal balance, although such division, in reality, perpetuates the abnormality of the Korean body.[33] If North Korea is not referred to as "the North Korea problem," different ways of analyzing the country will be possible, and this will open up different policy implications which entail different possibilities for interacting with the country. In fact, in 2018, before a historic summit between North Korea and the United States, American media portrayed Kim Jong-un as the "chairman" of the country rather than a "dictator." This was a significant shift in language practice because Kim was primarily referred to as a "dictator." A shift of this language practice paved the way for a summit between Kim and President Donald Trump to occur.

Equally important is attention to the role of agency in the process of knowledge production. While human perceptions and actions are shaped by mainstream discourses, the continuation of dominant discursive practices is carried out by humans. The reproduction of dominant discursive practices, which leads to the breeding of mainstream knowledge, cannot be executed automatically in a vacuum. This process entails ways in which dominant forms of discursive practices are adopted and consumed by diverse actors. Moreover, without the role of an agent that reinterprets the world differently, any meaningful change in discursive practices will not be enacted. In this sense, narratives become "a form of political action."[34]

The point of the questions when the researcher sets up a research project is to consider whose subjectivity enters into a dominant form of interpretation and produces a mode of knowledge that ultimately becomes a mainstream meaning system. Understanding the way that a particular mode of knowledge is formed and constructed requires an examination of the political and social relations of a given society. Researchers can investigate the way that a particular form of knowledge is constructed in a specific social context, considering power relations at a certain point in time, and investigate in what way a particular construction of knowledge has the constitutive power to shape societal norms, group identities, and courses of actions.

Examples of Practical Application

To "do" the construction of knowledge researchers first can look for particular words or terms to tease out specific meanings produced by language. Then they can analyze texts and discourses and their interplay with larger social, political, and historical circumstances. The researchers can also tease out discrepancies between what we know about the world in the form of knowledge and the world to be known, and the implications of gaps. Said's *Orientalism* is arguably one of the most widely acknowledged and prominent examples of knowledge construction; he focuses on how knowledge about the "Orient" and "Orientals" is constructed by the Anglo-French-American experience of Arabs at the intersection of power, knowledge, and discourse. Orientalism represents a mode of discourse about the

"Orient" and the "Orientals," and this representation produces knowledge which is taken as "truth." Said found that the constructed image of the "Orient" as "backward" and "uncivilized" is widely and systematically circulated in popular and literary statements and in the languages of various venues. These statements and discourses about the "Orient" and the "Orientals" are not based on objective observation or on innocent "discovery," however. The process is politically charged and laden with political, intellectual, cultural, and moral dimensions of power.

This is how Orientalism is not just an idea or a structure of ideas. Rather, it is more a system of ideas integrally supported and disseminated by a set of materials, involving the power of institutions, culture, and the state, and their various mechanisms. Said emphasizes that the phenomenon of Orientalism is "*willed human work*," a human invention, and the process of inventing a collection of representations about the "Orient" is heavily influenced by and dependent on "the alliance between cultural work, political tendencies, the state, and the specific realities of domination."[35] This idea is not random or sporadic but appears systematically and regularly in a consistent way, and this cannot be fully understood without the alliance of various forms of power and their configurations. Ultimately, the "Orient" is a European invention, and Orientalism embodies a Western desire to dominate and exercise authority over the "Orient" in order to assert the Western self as "civilized" and "advanced," as opposed to the "barbaric" and "backward" "Orient." Relative degrees of power between East and West enable the discursive relationship between the "Orient" and the "Occident." The construction of knowledge and its endurance involves extensive forms of power with political motives and consequences. In sum, Said defies the idea that "true" knowledge is objective and innocent by uncovering the political nature of knowledge construction.

Once knowledge about a particular topic or object is produced and accepted, the meaning associated with the knowledge has social consequences, since policies and actions are formulated by acting upon that knowledge. Power makes something emerge, and knowledge is intertwined with operations of power. Simultaneously, representations and discourses have performative power. The nexus of power-discourse-knowledge becomes crucial.[36] In other words, the construction of knowledge cannot be completely understood without the politics of discursive production and discursive practices ingrained in power and power relations. For example, David Campbell explores the production and reproduction of the discourse of danger as a necessary representation of others, in order to construct the state identity of the United States of America as an imagined community.[37] He argues that the crisis arising from international Cold War politics was deeply grounded in the crisis of representation of communism and the Soviet Union and in the inscribing of boundaries between the "civilized" and the "barbaric," and the "normal" and the "pathological." The discourses of danger pertaining to communism and the Soviet Union produce meaning about "what to fear" by drawing on a variety of intensive forms of power. This has been fundamental to fixing who "we" are as a source of foreign policy.[38] These examples indicate the "weaponization of knowledge"[39] in terms of how the production, reproduction, and circulation of knowledge are politically charged. Even after the end of the Cold War, the U.S. diplomatic community continuously used the old language of threat and counterthreat, perpetuating the "convenient truths" to justify military expenditures of $1.2 trillion over the next five years.[40]

A more detailed example of "doing" the construction of knowledge can be drawn from my own work on historical memory, in which I explored how knowledge about the past is a social construction by focusing on representations of Japan's past modern wars, including

World War II, exhibited in Japan's war and peace museums.[41] My research questions included how war and peace are imagined, remembered, and communicated to the present generation in Japanese museums, what role museums play in constructing a nation's historical memory and identity, and what implications it may have for Japan's relations with Asia. The work was developed as part of my broad research project on Japanese historical memory, identity construction, and foreign relations. I conducted fieldwork at the Yasukuni Shrine's war museum, known as the Yūshūkan, and at the Hiroshima Peace Memorial Museum in order to analyze the artifacts displayed in the two museums, including personal stories, photographs, belongings of the deceased, and the panels that describe these artifacts. My aim was to examine their visual and discursive messages in order to analyze what kinds of events were exhibited, how these events were narrated in the panels, and whose stories and photographs were shown, in an attempt to explore what is remembered, what is forgotten, what is emphasized, and what is omitted. This analysis allowed me to excavate what is known about the past war and what kind of knowledge about the nation's past is constructed as a crucial source of the constructions of national identity.

I found that the Yūshūkan's artifacts and narratives convey meanings that justify, honor, and rationalize Japan's war as a heroic national enterprise. In the Yūshūkan, imperial Japan's military actions, which inflicted atrocities and suffering on other Asian nations, were completely omitted. Moreover, no visual artifacts relating to the atomic bombings in Japan were exhibited, erasing how the war led to suffering on the part of ordinary Japanese people as well. These omissions not only sanitize Japan's war but also construct heroic representations of the war and the nation's history. In contrast, the artifacts and the narratives displayed in the Hiroshima Peace Memorial Museum highlight the devastation and destruction caused by the war in the national infrastructure and institutions, as well as in terms of human suffering, and describe how innocent people suffered from the evil effects of the war, producing the meaning of national trauma. Selective remembering and forgetting entail markedly contrasting interpretations of the war and of how the nation's past is made known to the contemporary generation, indicating that knowledge of Japan's war is never objective. Rather, the exhibits in the two museums are the results of the intense struggles and power involving various stakeholders, including interest groups, such as the Japanese War Bereaved Families Association, state and local institutions and politicians, and museums as socially constituted institutions. As Said notes, history is man-made, and what people know about their nation's history is what they themselves have made.[42] The divergent knowledge about the past war constructed in the two different museums suggests different avenues for possible actions regarding how to promote peace.

As Foucault emphasized, power relations involve the production and circulation of signs and meanings. Researchers can examine the production of meaning as a form of knowledge by analyzing particular sites or ways in which certain understandings about topics and objects are constructed, shared, and disseminated through language and symbolic practices. Researchers can also explore political relations in a given society, locations of power, the conditions under which a particular form of knowledge can be produced, accepted, and contested. Instead of accepting knowledge as objective, researchers can question mainstream knowledge about reality and the way that reality is known. It is important to be aware that systems of statements that operate as rules and structures of knowledge are not objective. The task of the analyst interested in uncovering the politics of knowledge is to "identify and expose the real, but obscured, nomological order that subtends and epistemologically governs the production of systems of actual statements."[43] By doing so, scholars can articulate gaps between dominant knowledge and what is omitted. This process will contribute to illuminating a different type of knowledge production. The researcher needs to ask whose view is inscribed as knowledge and whose knowledge is deemed significant and accepted in a given society.

Potential Problems

Acknowledging that knowledge is constructed requires researchers to interrogate existing forms of knowledge as inventions. One of the ways to explore how certain forms of knowledge are constructed and what kinds of meaning are created as structures of knowledge is to investigate practices of language and discourse. Analysts need to decide what sorts of texts to examine and how extensively they want to explore to gain a systematic representation of certain topics or objects. This sometimes poses a challenge because the researcher has to figure out when to stop analyzing texts; for instance, one can decide to stop looking at more data when one fails to uncover any new pattern of discourse. Also, some crucially important historical texts might not be available, or texts written in a foreign language could be difficult to analyze.

In addition, selecting which texts to examine and determining the scope of the exploration requires constant interactions between a researcher's subjectivity and the analysis of existing literature. For example, when I was working on Japan's war and peace museums, I had to make a decision on how many war and peace museums I wanted to explore for the project. I looked at previous research and found that studies comparing the Yūshūkan and the Hiroshima Peace Memorial Museum were lacking despite the fact that each of these museums received wide scholarly attention as an iconic memory site for Japan's war experience. The realization of this gap in the literature convinced me to focus on these two museums instead of expanding the number of museums, because I believed that the comparison of these two memory sites would yield meaningful implications. In my monograph that I am currently working on, however, I am examining multiple sites in a chapter on Japanese war and peace museums in order to provide "new" findings regarding knowledge production about Japan's past war.

It is important to recognize that analyzing the way knowledge is constructed through language does not necessarily yield a complete understanding of reality. Analytical categorization valorizes certain actors while marginalizing others. For example, in analyzing the narrative of leaders' actions in state-centric diplomatic history, focusing on men as leaders reinforces a state-centric view, while other analytical categories, such as gender, can uncover the role of women and alternative types of subjectivity, values, and actions.[44] The issue here is whose agency is constructed and contextualized in understanding reality.[45] Similarly, a focus on empire in terms of nation-states has closed off the categories of gender, ethnicity, and religion.[46]

Knowledge and interpretation are inseparable, given that all knowledge is an interpretation.[47] Scholars should be mindful that the act of interpretations is value-laden. The selection of a particular theoretical framework and analytical categorization reflects the researcher's worldviews and values and is reflexively entrenched in ideological assumptions, since an analyst cannot be completely dissociated or exempt from the socialization process of knowing the world through cultural processes and the analyst's evolving positionality. This limitation can be offset by engaging additional methods, such as surveys and content analysis.[48] Incorporating other methods opens up an opportunity for scholars who have not been engaged in the research on the construction of knowledge but are inclined to undertake this line of research. For example, researchers who are familiar with using surveys on climate change or immigration can identify some changes or stability in public opinion on a given issue over time and analyze specific texts, such as newspapers and speeches of key individuals, as well as political and social conditions, to trace whether there have been any changes and continuity in language practices regarding how the issue was talked about. As addressed earlier, which texts to select for analysis involves a researcher's subjectivity. Equally important is that the act of conducting research is a way of constructing knowledge, which has an effect on what is knowable.[49]

Gaining access to and documenting available texts, data, and voices from the marginalized can pose a challenge as well, since the perspectives of the weak have been systematically marginalized by systems of knowledge that control what is to be known. A lack of available data could lead the researcher to sideline analytical categories that highlight the marginalized or the weaker. For example, the views and voices of ordinary people in North Korea are not easily captured due to difficulties going inside the country, and thus challenges obtaining texts about them and conducting interviews with them. These practical challenges could prompt the researcher to focus on other aspects of North Korea, such as its nuclear weapons program. This could perpetuate the people's marginalization by determining whose views are incorporated into the process of knowledge production. It is important for the researcher to be curious about whose views are neglected in the literature in terms of understanding the world and how such a gap can be addressed. Researchers should be mindful of the potential consequences of the analytical categorization in producing, reinforcing, or challenging dominant knowledge; analysts should be aware of their potential to create an alternative form of knowledge.

Notes

1. Mahoney, *The Logic of Social Science*, 23.
2. Mahoney, *The Logic of Social Science*, 1.
3. Mahoney, *The Logic of Social Science*, emphasis in original.
4. Ben-Ari and Enosh, *Dialectics, Power, and Knowledge Construction in Qualitative Research*; Code, *What Can We Know?*, 31–32; Mahoney, *The Logic of Social Science*.
5. Pfadenhauer, "The Cultural Dimension of Social Constructions," 66–67, quoted in Berger and Luckmann, *The Social Construction of Reality*, 52.
6. Heidegger, *Nietzsche*.
7. Foucault, *Power*, 9.
8. Quoted in Foucault, *Power*, 7–8.
9. Pfadenhauer, "The Cultural Dimension of Social Constructions," 67.
10. See George, *Discourses of Global Politics* for the evolution of a dichotomy between a domain of empiricist "fact" and a realm of "theorized" knowledge in the positivism/empiricism of the period since the Enlightenment of the 18th century in terms of Western philosophical images of truth, rationality, and reality.
11. Code, *What Can We Know?*, 34.

12. Code, *What Can We Know?*, 31.
13. See Fester and Carey, "Introduction" for the pluralized and revised account of the Enlightenment.
14. See Klotz, *Norms in International Relations*.
15. Hawkesworth, *Feminist Inquiry*, 62.
16. Rosenberg, *Philosophy of Social Science*, 213.
17. Ben-Ari and Enosh, *Dialectics, Power, and Knowledge Construction in Qualitative Research*.
18. Mahoney, *The Logic of Social Science*, 17.
19. Foucault, *Power*, 12–13.
20. He seeks to defy a sharp separation between ontology and epistemology in approaching the philosophy of knowledge. See Mader, "Knowledge," 234.
21. Foucault, *Power*, 14–15.
22. Foucault, *Power*, 337–338.
23. Code, *What Can We Know?*, 27.
24. Hawkesworth, *Feminist Inquiry*, 62.
25. Hall, *Essential Essays*, 157.
26. Said, *Orientalism*, 10.
27. Hobson, *Multicultural Origins of the Global Economy*.
28. See Chapter 31 of this volume on content analysis for further detail of discourse analysis.
29. Hall, *Essential Essays*, 155.
30. Bayly and Harper, *Forgotten Armies*.
31. Said, *Orientalism*, 21.
32. Foucault, *Power*; Hall, *Essential Essays*, 157.
33. Lee, "Healing an Abnormalised Body."
34. Klotz and Lynch, *Strategies for Research in Constructivist International Relations*, 51.
35. Said, *Orientalism*, 15, emphasis added.
36. Foucault, *Power*; Said, *Orientalism*.
37. Campbell, *Writing Security*.
38. Campbell, *Writing Security*, 169–170.
39. Price, *Weaponizing Anthropology*.
40. Lapham, "Apes and Butterflies."
41. Lee, "Yasukuni and Hiroshima in Clash?"
42. To Said, geographical and cultural entities, such as localities, regions, and geographical sectors, can also be man-made as the "Orient" and the "Occident."
43. Mader, "Knowledge," 229.
44. Klotz and Lynch, *Strategies for Research in Constructivist International Relations*, 46–48.
45. Klotz and Lynch, *Strategies for Research in Constructivist International Relations*, 51.
46. Fester and Carey, "Introduction," 24.
47. May, *Between Genealogy and Epistemology*, 76.
48. See Chapter 21 on surveys and Chapter 31 on content analysis in this volume.
49. Mahoney notes that human "kinds have *reality-creating effects* for human beings" (*The Logic of Social Science*, 18, emphasis in original).

Recommended Readings

Doty, Roxanne Lynn. "Foreign Policy as Social Construction: A Post-Positivist Analysis of U.S. Counterinsurgency Policy in the Philippines." *International Studies Quarterly* 37, no. 3 (1993): 279–320.
    An excellent work on how discourse creates a particular reality that generates certain possibilities regarding U.S. foreign policy in the nexus of power-knowledge-discourse.

George, Jim. *Discourses of Global Politics*. Boulder, CO: Lynne Rienner, 1994.
>An excellent work on how we "know" our world and how we apply that knowledge through global politics in a historical and philosophical context.

Hobson, John M. *Multicultural Origins of the Global Economy: Beyond the Western-Centric Frontier*. Cambridge: Cambridge University Press, 2021.
>An excellent work on how knowledge about the West as the origin of the global economy can be defied.

Manchanda, Nivi. *Imagining Afghanistan: The History and Politics of Imperial Knowledge*. Cambridge: Cambridge University Press, 2020.
>An excellent work on how Afghanistan has been represented in terms of knowledge production and as acts of power.

Polkinghorne, Donald E. *Narrative Knowing and the Human Sciences*. Albany, NY: State University of New York Press, 1988.
>Provides a comprehensive overview of the role of language, narrative, and discourse in the human and social sciences.

References

Bayly, Christopher Alan, and Timothy Norman Harper. *Forgotten Armies: The Fall of British Asia, 1941–1945*. Cambridge, MA: Belknap Press, 2004.

Ben-Ari, Adital, and Guy Enosh. *Dialectics, Power, and Knowledge Construction in Qualitative Research: Beyond Dichotomy*. New York: Routledge, 2020.

Berger, Peter L., and Thomas Luckmann. *The Social Construction of Reality*. New York: Anchor Books, 1967.

Campbell, David. *Writing Security: United States Foreign Policy and the Politics of Identity*. Minneapolis, MN: University of Minnesota Press, 1998.

Code, Lorraine. *What Can We Know? Feminist Theory and the Construction of Knowledge*. Ithaca, NY: Cornell University Press, 1991.

Fester, Lynn, and Daniel Carey. "Introduction: Some Answers to the Question: 'What Is Postcolonial Enlightenment?'" In *The Postcolonial Enlightenment: Eighteenth-Century Colonialism and Postcolonial Theory*, edited by Daniel Carey and Lynn Festa, 1–34. Oxford: Oxford University Press, 2009.

Foucault, Michel. *Power: Essential Works of Foucault 1954–1984*. Edited by James D. Faubion. New York: New Press, 2000.

George, Jim. *Discourses of Global Politics*. Boulder, CO: Lynne Rienner, 1994.

Hall, Stuart. *Essential Essays*. Vol. 2: *Identity and Diaspora*. Edited by David Morley. Durham, NC: Duke University Press, 2019.

Hawkesworth, Mary. *Feminist Inquiry: From Political Conviction to Methodological Innovation*. New Brunswick, NJ: Rutgers University Press, 2006.

Heidegger, Martin. *Nietzsche*. Vol. 3: *The Will to Power as Knowledge and as Metaphysics*. New York: Harper & Row, 1987.

Hobson, John M. *Multicultural Origins of the Global Economy: Beyond the Western-Centric Frontier*. Cambridge: Cambridge University Press, 2021.

Klotz, Audie. *Norms in International Relations: The Struggle against Apartheid*. Ithaca, NY: Cornell University Press, 1995.

Klotz, Audie, and Cecelia Lynch. *Strategies for Research in Constructivist International Relations*. New York: M. E. Sharpe, 2007.

Lapham, Lewis H. "Apes and Butterflies." *Harper's*, May 1992, 8–12.

Lee, Jooyoun. "Healing an Abnormalised Body: Bringing the Agency of Unseen People Back to the Inter-Korean Border." *Third World Quarterly*, 2021, advance online publication. https://www.tandfonline.com/doi/full/10.1080/01436597.2021.1928488?src=.

Lee, Jooyoun. "Yasukuni and Hiroshima in Clash? War and Peace Museums in Contemporary Japan." *Pacific Focus* 33, no. 1 (2018): 5–33.

Mader, Mary Beth. "Knowledge." In *The Cambridge Foucault Lexicon*, edited by Leonard Lawlor and John Nale, 226–235. New York: Cambridge University Press, 2014.

Mahoney, James. *The Logic of Social Science*. Princeton, NJ: Princeton University Press, 2021.

May, Todd. *Between Genealogy and Epistemology*. University Park: Pennsylvania State University Press, 1992.

Pfadenhauer, Michaela. "The Cultural Dimension of Social Constructions." In *Social Constructivism as Paradigm? The Legacy of the Social Construction of Reality*, edited by Michaela Pfadenhauer and Hubert Knoblauch, 65–74. London: Routledge, 2019.

Price, David H. *Weaponizing Anthropology: Social Science in Service of the Militarized State*. Oakland, CA: AK Press, 2011.

Rosenberg, Alexander. *Philosophy of Social Science*. Boulder, CO: Westview, 1988.

Said, Edward. *Orientalism*. New York: Vintage Books, 1979.

6
Case Study and Selection

Sara Wallace Goodman

This chapter presents and critically examines best practices for case study research and case selection. Prominent case selection heuristics reflect objective research design needs (what I term "appropriateness"), but I argue that overlooked considerations of feasibility (including positionality, resources, and skills) and interest play equally important roles when justifying the cases we select and study. I conclude by arguing for an iterative process of research design, one that equally weighs pragmatic considerations and academic concerns of best fit. This strategy hopes to make qualitative research more accessible and to diversify the types of cases we study and questions we ask.

Overview

To identify useful strategies for selecting cases, we begin by defining what we're selecting: cases. A case is a representative illustration of the thing you are studying. There is an often-cited edict by Adam Przeworski and Henry Teune that we should "replace proper nouns" with conceptual variables,[1] and I think that's a useful place to start in thinking about cases. We study concepts, and the places and people where those concepts appear are cases. The "thing you're studying" might be civil war, monarchy, migration, conflict, or discrimination. The cases, then, might be 18th-century France, Imperial Japan, the U.S.-Mexico border, or a London Underground train station, respectively. As Erica Simmons and Nicholas Rush Smith note, cases may reflect not only a "focus on time or geography" but also "political processes (how things happen), practices (what people do), meanings (how people interact with symbolic systems), and concepts (how people order that world)."[2]

How do we study a case? A case study, according to John Gerring, is "an intensive study of a single case or a small number of cases that promises to shed light on a larger population of cases."[3] Alexander George and Andrew Bennett offer a similar view, but emphasize instead a structured, focused purpose, where "cases should be undertaken with a specific researcher objective in mind and a theoretical focus appropriate for that objective."[4]

As case studies are intensive, (Gerring), as well as structured and focused (George and Bennett) they are necessarily small. We do not have a firm heuristic for what constitutes "small" other than an N size that is manageable for a researcher. Looking at canonical texts in comparative politics, where states are the unit of analysis, Barrington Moore's *Social Origins of Dictatorship and Democracy* looked intensively at seven countries (England, France, United States, Germany, Japan, China, and Russia); Theda Skocpol's *States and Social Revolutions* provided a comparative analysis of France, Russia, and China; and Robert Putnam's *Making Democracy: Civic Traditions in Modern Italy* arguably had only one, Italy, as a case of democratic governance. This is a contested point because the "case study" in Putnam's analysis of why democratic governments succeed or fail is not Italy per se but the regions in which we observe factors (social capital) that enable (North) or hinder (South) democratic institutional performance. But data on performance is collected and analyzed at the administrative level—that is, across Italy's 20 regional governments.

The first challenge of case study selection is identifying *what the case is*. It is where you observe the outcome of your study. A case study, then, is the story of the relevant factors that produced that outcome (and often also include those factors that didn't and why). Moreover, the case is not only *where* the phenomenon is happening but *at what level*. The unit of analysis might be a region (northern versus southern Italy), a country (e.g., the United States), an international organization (e.g., the International Monetary Fund, the European Union), an institution (the U.S. Supreme Court), a bureaucracy (the British Home Office), or a policy area (e.g., immigration, healthcare). Cases may also be more than one thing at the same time, comprising what Thea Riofrancos describes as "constitutive multiplicity." They are defined by what she describes as "siting," wherein observable, salient, and contested events are not selected but "sited" within global processes and "co-constitutive of a broader process of interest."[5] Cases (or sites) need to observable, but this does not mean they are self-evident. Cases may be identified and selected from established practices in one's intellectual discipline of study ("studying a case"), where they are deduced from a well-specified universe of cases and disciplinary norms, or they may be created through ongoing, theoretically motivated research activity ("casing a study").[6]

The second part of Gerring's case study definition—"to shed light on a larger population of cases"—implies a case's singular purpose: inferential utility. Elsewhere, Gerring elucidates that a case "comprises the type of phenomenon that an inference attempts to explain."[7] It is a focused story about a phenomenon, not merely the context or country in which the phenomenon takes place. Some inferences are descriptive—like single-outcome studies, where the objective is to describe one case well[8]—and some are causal, which necessarily employ within-unit, temporal variation. If variation is studied across units, it becomes a case comparison. But single-unit studies must represent the object of analysis and *in its representativeness* teach us about a phenomenon and be comparable to other cases that exhibit that phenomenon as well. So, for example, an intensive study about immigrant integration in Paris should tell us about the phenomenon of immigrant integration in other major French cities or other European capitals, or about the process of integration more generally. The degree to which a case study has representativeness depends on a clear understanding of its scope conditions, which are the subset of cases to which a theory applies, defining where we can and cannot apply lessons from the case—the parameters of its "representiveness." The extent to which one can generalize from a single case is a highly contested subject of debate at the center of case study research.[9]

Discerning reach and representativeness can be difficult and places a heavy burden on area and subject expertise. How do you know the case you are studying is the appropriate and correct one for analysis? On what criteria? Small-N studies use purposive sampling, unlike large-N studies, which exclusively use—or start out with—a universe of random observations. Small-N researchers need prior knowledge about the "population" of cases they are examining to identify which are representative of that phenomenon. That presents a significant entry barrier to cross-regional studies, for instance, where language skills necessarily limit the number of cases of which one can have sufficient knowledge. For this reason, Gerring[10] and, elsewhere, Seawright and Gerring[11] suggest pairing the enterprise of case study research with large-N studies, especially if you can use the latter as a first step to identify how cases are situated within a larger sample, and then using this for selecting cases that are, say, typical or deviant.

This heuristic is certainly useful but not always possible. While we do not have space here to adjudicate between the unique insights and comparative advantages of case studies compared to quantitative approaches,[12] suffice it to say that they do different things. Case studies explain how things work and are produced. This means they identify the processes for *how* the explanation produces the outcome of interest, that is, the causal mechanism. To do so, qualitative scholars typically employ methods like process tracing or narratives that draw on archives or interviews to map a causal argument. This is a different enterprise from large-N studies, which aim to estimate average effects across many observations. Given this distinction, we can see how their pairing would make for a formidable research design, but we should avoid adopting the view that casework is in service to or legitimately representative only when contextualized by large-N analysis. Case studies have distinct advantages in their own right: hypothesis testing (through, for example, process tracing), but also theory building, assessing scope conditions, historical explanation, mapping complexity, and contributing to conceptual validity and measurement.[13]

State of Practice

How do we choose which cases to study? All studies require case selection justification. The first chapter of every book includes one. It appears in every article's introduction or methodology section. Even quantitative, large-N studies need to justify what they are a case *of* in order to produce appropriate generalizations or cumulation or make claims of external validity. And justification is more important than ever, as the past decade has seen a resurgence of single-country studies in political science,[14] though many are not intensive studies but theory-testing field experiments. The number of cases you can study *intensively* is necessarily limited by the availability of resources, as well as the time and energy of the researcher. So if you can choose only one or two, you want to choose correctly.

The challenge of choosing cases is intimately tied to how cases are studied. The predominant approach to small-N qualitative study is cross-case comparison. Its lineage dates to the mid-19th century and John Stuart Mill's system of comparative logic. In brief, Mill characterizes comparisons by their outcomes: a method of similarity observes most-different systems producing a similar outcome, while a method of difference observes most-similar systems producing a different outcome from one another, due to one or more items of variance. These strategies are grounded in an idea that cross-case control can be established through selection procedures, which mitigates the likelihood of compound treatment effects and enables the elimination of alternative explanations.

In the 1970s, there began a growing interest in the study of case study types. Przeworski and Teune "updated" Mill's paired comparison, characterizing most-similar and most-different comparisons based not on effects or outcomes (dependent variables) but causes (independent variables),[15] and it is this terminological updating that is more widely used in the social sciences today. Arend Lijphart presents a departure from this explicit case comparison to describe case types not by their relation but by their utility, proposing case study types such as "hypothesis-generating," "theory-confirming," and "theory-infirming." (Others include atheoretical, interpretative, and deviant.)[16] Harry Eckstein saw case studies as better suited for testing hypotheses than for theory building, advancing the concept of a "crucial" case study. (Other case types include configurative-idiographic, disciplined-configurative, heuristic, and plausibility probe.)[17]

The next big advances in case type theorizing appear across the work of John Gerring and Jason Seawright,[18] who consolidate previous insights and propose a variety of techniques for case selection, most recently extreme, index, deviant, most-similar, and diverse.[19] Around this point, we see a lot of contributions seeking to build and specify within this space,[20] including multimethod strategies for case selection,[21] defenses of the analytic leverage of controlled comparisons,[22] and typologies of case selection strategies, organized by study purpose. These include Gerring and Cojocaru's distinction between examining outcomes—descriptive or causal—and hypotheses, be they exploratory, estimating, or diagnostic,[23] and Blatter and Haverland's classification, based on whether your study is one of covariation, causality, congruence, or a combination therein, with mixed purpose.[24]

Indeed, a mixed-method approach often requires multiple selection techniques. And many of these justifications come from a situation in which a large-N data set is available a priori, enabling the researcher to use matching techniques[25] or to observe which cases are on-the-line/typical or off-the-line/deviant. Here, quantitative scholars can rely on random sampling and large-N data sets to situate cases as influential or crucial. For instance, Lamis Abdelaaty's *Discrimination and Delegation* examines how states balance international and domestic pressures in crafting refugee policies. She first identifies patterns of state behavior by examining refugee admissions in a global data set. From this analysis of cross-national trends, she then selects three most-different cases for in-depth case study: Egypt (a typical case), Turkey (an outlier), and Kenya (a crucial case).

But what happens when a researcher doesn't have a global data set to start from? How do you know which cases to use? A standard research design that many qualitative studies employ today is to select on the independent variables, such that you have sufficient variation to support your theory and eliminate rivals. This is, essentially, a most-similar design, where the researcher establishes as much control as possible, save for the study variable, which exhibits variance. For example, Abigail Williamson, in investigating local immigrant incorporation in new immigrant destinations, selects four similar-size cities "not because of the nature of their responses to immigrants, but because of their demographic change," that is, when they received immigration. She goes on to describe a careful selection strategy of choosing cities that exhibit rapid demographic change, and then employs a matching strategy for additional comparison cases.[26] Alisha Holland specifies this research design-motivated strategy directly in her study of Latin American cities, writing that they "vary along the principal independent variables under both my theory and competing state-capacity-based explanations."[27]

Of course, adopting a most-similar design still does not tell a researcher which cases to choose, but it points you in the right direction, narrowing the field of possible cases by homing in on the most theoretically important point of variance. The literature offers many tools and techniques, accommodating the oftentimes idiosyncratic nature of selection. In addition to matching strategies, researchers may also rely on procedures like explanatory typologies to drive case selection,[28] in which different combinations of variables produce different theoretical possibilities, each occupying a distinct property space, and the research slots in cases-of-best-fit based on background knowledge and area expertise. Herron and Quinn, for instance, advise that "sampling from the largest cell of a 2x2 table is competitive with other, more complicated, case selection methods."[29]

And while Gerring is authoritative on matters of case selection techniques, we must treat his nine ideal case types as such—ideal. In reality, cases may follow more than one logic of case selection, such that a case can be both crucial and typical. In recognizing that cases can fulfill more than one purpose, one must not forget the golden rule: cases used for theory development should not then be used for theory testing. This can be tricky, as the research process is inherently iterative as one increases precision, clarity, and parsimony of a theory. A good example of keeping these different objectives explicit is found in Evan Lieberman's *Boundaries of Contagion*. In explaining the role of race politics in shaping government responses to AIDS, Lieberman described the selection of South Africa and Brazil as critical to theory development, where they exhibit strong and weak institutionalized categories of race, respectively, while India was a case of theory testing, which he conducted through process tracing.[30]

In the ideal world, one has perfect knowledge of all the cases that possibly support a given research design and chooses from among them the one that best fits. Indeed, Gary Goertz famously recommends to his students that before selecting a case they first write a list of the universe of possible cases—as a way to force them to think through scope conditions before utilizing other criteria (prior knowledge, etc.). But in the real world, appropriateness is secondary to a series of other considerations about *feasibility* (which includes positionality, cost, skill, access) and *interest*. These fall into a category Gerring describes as "pragmatic/logical issues" that often affect case selection,[31] even as they are very much treated as a residual set of concerns. But let's not hand-wave or relegate them to afterthoughts, as they are often the criteria that drive our decision-making. Figure 6.1 presents these three criteria in relation to one another, illustrating that they need to overlap to sustain an implementable research design. The order in which these criteria are considered is less important than that the process remains iterative—that the researcher toggles between research design needs and pragmatic concerns. As you consider which cases are *appropriate*, that is, crucial, influential, most likely, and so on, you should also and simultaneously assess which cases are *feasible* and *interesting* or sustainable for the course of a research project. As the previous section already reviewed voluminous contributions to the conversation of appropriateness, I will focus on the remaining criteria here.

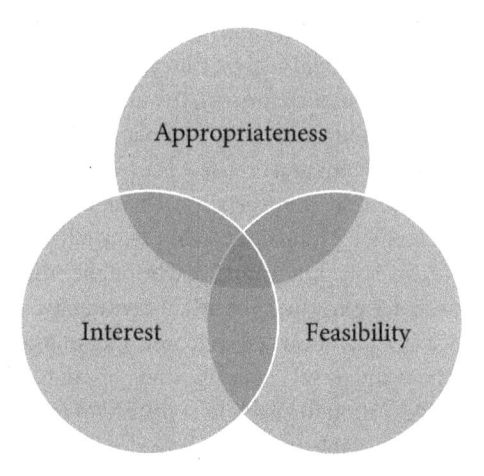

Figure 6.1 Criteria for Case Selection.

Feasibility is first and foremost shaped by positionality. Race, gender, accent, resources, phenotype, class, and so on are all factors that enable or hinder access to specific communities. For instance, if you need a translator to speak to immigrants, you may not be able to ascertain certain types of information or ask sensitive questions because you are communicating through a third-party interlocutor. If you are Black, you may be unable to gather reliable data from White nationalists. If you are not a citizen of a certain country or affiliated with institutions in that country, you may be unable to access certain data sets or obtain a research visa. All these considerations fall under the ambit of positionality (see Chapter 3). If the perfect research design cannot be implemented *by* you, then it is not a perfect design *for* you. The best research design is an implementable one. That said, one is by no means relegated to studying *only* where they have the most positional access or advantage. Rather, I am suggesting we approach considerations of case selection with an active and ongoing eye toward appropriateness, interest, and feasibility.

Related, research costs money. If the ideal case study could be designed in a lab, someone would still have to pay for that lab. Accessing field sites, per diems for food and accommodation, transportation, translators, transcribers, research assistants, software, hardware—these are all costs associated with doing research. The best-case scenario is one where your project is fully funded—by a university, foundation grant, research lab, or other source. But many of us fall short of this ideal, and resource considerations play a role in determining where we can collect data, for how long we can collect data, and how many people we can employ to collect and analyze data. These considerations necessarily inform the kinds of cases that *could* fit a research design—a designation that is helpful to make before determining the cases that *should* (i.e., appropriateness).

I would also slot into resource considerations a perennial question: How many? How many cases do you need versus how many cases can you reasonably investigate? In almost every case selection type, the appropriate number of cases is one or two. A crucial case necessarily examines at least one, and a case comparison usually requires at least two (but can include diachronic analysis of a single case over time). One sees many examples of comparisons with three or more cases. One can always add a case to increase analytical leverage or to increase breadth or scope, but the trade-off is almost always at the cost of intensity. In *Immigration and Membership Politics in Western Europe*, I ended up studying six cases to answer the question "Why do states adopt language and country knowledge requirements for citizenship acquisition (as well as related legal statuses like entry and permanent residence)?"[32] But by structuring them as three paired comparisons, I could analyze the cases around different causes: restrictive policy context (comparing Austria and Denmark), the influential role of right-wing governments (Germany and the United Kingdom), and the policymaking process itself (comparing most-different cases of the Netherlands and France). The trade-off was comparability and parsimony for intensity. More cases mean more theoretical breadth, while intense studies of fewer cases yield more empirical depth, looking not just at policy adoption and adaption but also content analysis of tests, outcomes by groups, and maybe public attitudes.

Again, in an ideal research design, four cases might accurately capture all the variation of, say, welfare policy in order to study a certain outcome, like marginalization or healthcare. But a researcher may not have the travel expenses, time, or contacts to study all four cases. Can you restate the research question to justify two, instead of four, cases? Can you limit the scope conditions on the study variable to make a scaled-back design both appropriate and manageable?

The third consideration of feasibility has to do with one's skills. If you plan on doing an in-depth case study that relies on fieldwork—interviewing elites, reading archives, and so on—you need to speak the language or hire and train an assistant to do the work for you. Again, if we were to paint a best-case scenario, you would start graduate school knowing you want to study a certain social or political phenomenon in a specific country and already speak that language. The reality, however, is that as you progress through your training—or along the path of research design precision—you may see that a different case is better suited for analysis, or the research question changes so that you find yourself looking at cases you may be unfamiliar with. Again, qualitative researchers often do not start with large-N data sets, and so they may not even be aware of the full universe of possible cases. You might speak Spanish as a second language but then later discover that Brazil or Israel is the crucial case for your project. This requires pragmatic adjustments to the research design, which may involve learning a new language, hiring research assistants, or perhaps forging research partnerships with host country institutions. It may also involve adjusting the scope conditions of your study. Without full knowledge of the universe of cases, one does not have full confidence that one is selecting appropriately representative cases. But there are some constraints that are insurmountable—like full knowledge of the documents in the lost library of Alexandria, making this a problem that is important but ultimately one that a researcher cannot fix. This need not be a definitive impediment but can be an opportunity to narrow scope conditions.

In the example of *Immigration and Membership Politics*, I did have an understanding of the full universe of cases—states that adopted language and country knowledge requirements for immigration, settlement, and citizenship in Western Europe. This was possible because it was a new policy for Europe; the temporal and geographic bounds of states that introduced cultural requirements were finite and mappable. With full knowledge, I could select cases with variation on my explanatory variables of interest, prior citizenship policy context (liberal, restrictive) and government orientation (left, right), as well as study causal processes of policy adoption and adaptation in two most different cases (defined by variation in the explanatory variables), France and the Netherlands. Without full knowledge, I probably would have selected the "big and shiny" cases. Those are the cases that frequently make the (English-language) news, have large populations, and may even be referred to as containing "intrinsic importance." They are the cases that are typically studied: Great Britain, France, Germany. These cases are undoubtedly important. They would make for a fine study as well, but I would be limited in the types of inferences I could draw without key cases like the Netherlands and Denmark (smaller states that typically lose out to their flashy neighbors).

The last criterion of case selection is that it must be interesting—not interesting to the field in that it is intrinsically important or a crucial case, but interesting to *you*. You are the one who must carry out the data collection, analysis, and write-up. You took up the research question for a reason—you must be motivated and interested enough to complete it. It should sustain you as a researcher; you should enjoy your work and want to know more. Remember: research is elective.

You may have stumbled upon what looks like the perfect case, but it may not be the perfect case for you. Here, I recognize that case selection sounds an awful lot like dating advice, but sometimes cases that look good on paper are not good for you for reasons beyond traditional case selection criteria. If the goal of your research is to complete your research, pragmatic considerations like feasibility and interest are critical case selection criteria. (If, on the other hand, the goal of your research is pure erudition, and you live the life of a bon vivant, without considerations for funding, employment, and rent—ignore my advice.) If this means sidelining research questions you do not have the resources or ability to answer at this time, then pick another research question or retool it to fit your parameters. Regardless of how one prioritizes the different criteria of case selection, one should be clear and transparent about the reasons—be they interest, skills, funding, or something else—for choosing one case over another.

Continuing Issues

An unintended consequence of an argument for pragmatism is that it may undercut efforts for more diversity in social science casework. Prioritizing feasibility may inadvertently limit the scope of available countries and communities for analysis and increase the number of studies in easily accessible sites and cases. It may lead researchers to self-select out of doing qualitative casework altogether, opting instead for large-N quantitative pursuits, where data sets are available for download from the convenience of one's computer. Neither of these outcomes is desirable, nor my objective. In advocating for equal and early consideration of pragmatism, I aim to frontload practicalities of research and habituate a practice of precising a research question by iterating between fit and feasibility.

Speaking of disciplinary incentives, there is a second critique worth engaging, that arguments derived from small-N qualitative cross-case comparison do not support causal inference or carry external validity. While many maintain the view that they do,[33] Seawright makes the case for why they may not but are still worth pursuing in any case, where they "sharpen conceptualizations and measurement; allow exploration of the prevalence of causal capacities; and provide raw materials for the construction of theories of causal moderation."[34] Put simply, case studies perform vital tasks for understanding the world around us.

My hope here is that grounding the idiosyncratic, often large-N-reliant heuristics of case selection in considerations of practicality and interest may encourage researchers to see the skills and resources at their disposal not as limitations but as opportunities. As academia increases its commitment to inclusive excellence, it also portends more inclusivity in the types of research we value, the types of questions we ask, and therefore the types of cases we study.

Notes

1. Przeworski and Teune, *The Logic of Comparative Social Inquiry*.
2. Simmons and Smith, *Rethinking Comparison*, 3.
3. Gerring, "What Is a Case Study and What Is It Good For?," 342.
4. George and Bennett, *Case Studies and Theory Development in the Social Sciences*, 70.
5. Riofrancos, "From Cases to Sites," 109.
6. Soss, "On Casing a Study Versus Studying a Case."
7. Gerring, "What Is a Case Study and What Is It Good For?," 9.
8. Gerring, "Single-Outcome Studies."
9. Flyvbjerg, "Five Misunderstandings about Case-Study Research."
10. Gerring, *Case Study Research*.
11. Seawright and Gerring, "Case Selection Techniques in Case Study Research."

12. See, for example, Goertz and Mahoney, *A Tale of Two Cultures*.
13. For more, see Gerring, "What Is a Case Study and What Is It Good For?"
14. Pepinsky, "The Return of the Single-Country Study."
15. Przeworski and Teune, *The Logic of Comparative Social Inquiry*.
16. Lijphart, "Comparative Politics and the Comparative Method."
17. Eckstein, "Case Study and Theory in Political Science."
18. Gerring, *Case Study Research*.
19. Gerring and Seawright, *Finding Your Social Science* Project. Previous iterations also included typical, influential, crucial, pathway, and most-different. See Seawright and Gerring, "Case Selection Techniques in Case Study Research."
20. Levy, "Case Studies"; Rohlfing, *Case Studies and Causal Inference*.
21. Seawright, *Multi-Method Social Science*.
22. Slater and Ziblatt, "The Enduring Indispensability of the Controlled Comparison."
23. Gerring and Cojocaru, "Selecting Cases for Intensive Analysis."
24. Blatter and Haverland, *Designing Case Studies*.
25. Nielsen, "Case Selection via Matching."
26. Williamson, *Welcoming New Americans?*, 17.
27. Holland, *Forbearance as Redistribution*, 3.
28. Elman, "Explanatory Typologies in Qualitative Studies of International Politics."
29. Herron and Quinn, "A Careful Look at Modern Case Selection Methods," 458.
30. Lieberman, *Boundaries of Contagion*, 22.
31. Gerring, "Case Selection for Case-Study Analysis," 679.
32. Goodman, *Immigration and Membership Politics in Western European*.
33. Slater and Ziblatt, "The Enduring Indispensability of the Controlled Comparison."
34. Seawright, "Beyond Mill," 12.

Recommended Readings

Gerring, John. "What Is a Case Study and What Is It Good For?" *American Political Science Review* 98, no. 2 (2004): 341–354.
  Influential text defining the utility of a case study.
Seawright, Jason, and John Gerring. "Case Selection Techniques in Case Study Research: A Menu of Qualitative and Quantitative Options." *Political Research Quarterly* 61, no. 2 (2008): 294–308.
  A detailed menu of considerations (including mixed methods) for selecting cases.
Simmons, E. S., and N. R. Smith, eds. *Rethinking Comparison*. New York: Cambridge University Press, 2021.
  An updated, authoritative text on a variety of comparison strategies and heuristics across several epistemologies.
Small, Mario Luis. "How Many Cases Do I Need? On Science and the Logic of Case Selection in Field-Based Research." *Ethnography* 10, no. 1 (2009): 5–38.
  While this is for ethnographic work, it helps the reader think through case values and the research process more generally and the logic of design.

References

Abdelaaty, Lamis Elmy. *Discrimination and Delegation: Explaining State Responses to Refugees*. New York: Oxford University Press, 2021.
Blatter, Joachim, and Markus Haverland. Designing Case Studies: Explanatory Approaches in Small-N Research. Palgrave Macmillan, 2012.

Eckstein, Harry. "Case Study and Theory in Political Science." In *Handbook of Political Science: Strategies of inquiry*, edited by Fred I. Greenstein and Nelson W. Polsby, 79–137. Reading, PA: Addison-Wesley, 1975.

Elman, Colin. "Explanatory Typologies in Qualitative Studies of International Politics." *International Organization* 59, no. 2 (2005): 293–326.

Flyvbjerg, Bent. "Five Misunderstandings about Case-Study Research." *Qualitative Inquiry* 12, no. 2 (2006): 219–245.

George, Alexander L., and Andrew Bennett. *Case Studies and Theory Development in the Social Sciences*. Cambridge, MA: MIT Press, 2005.

Gerring, John. "Case Selection for Case-Study Analysis: Qualitative and Quantitative Techniques." In *The Oxford Handbook of Political Methodology*, edited by Janet Box-Steffensmeier, 645–684. Oxford: Oxford University Press, 2008.

Gerring, John. *Case Study Research: Principles and Practices*. New York: Cambridge University Press, 2006.

Gerring, John. *Case Study Research: Principles and Practices*. New York: Cambridge University Press, 2007.

Gerring, John. "Single-Outcome Studies: A Methodological Primer." *International Sociology* 21, no. 5 (2006): 707–734.

Gerring, John. "What Is a Case Study and What Is It Good For?" *American Political Science Review* 98, no. 2 (2004): 341–354.

Gerring, John, and Lee Cojocaru. "Selecting Cases for Intensive Analysis: A Diversity of Goals and Methods." *Sociological Methods & Research* 45, no. 3 (2016): 392–423.

Gerring, John, and Jason Seawright. *Finding Your Social Science Project*. New York: Cambridge University Press, 2023.

Goertz, Gary, and James Mahoney. *A Tale of Two Cultures: Qualitative and Quantitative Research in the Social Sciences*. Princeton, NJ: Princeton University Press, 2012.

Goodman, Sara Wallace. *Immigration and Membership Politics in Western European*. New York: Cambridge University Press, 2014.

Herron, Michael C., and Kevin M. Quinn. "A Careful Look at Modern Case Selection Methods." *Sociological Methods & Research* 45, no. 3 (2016): 458–492.

Holland, Alisha C. *Forbearance as Redistribution: The Politics of Informal Welfare in Latin America*. New York: Cambridge University Press, 2017.

Levy, Jack S. "Case Studies: Types, Designs, and Logics of Inference." *Conflict Management and Peace Science* 25, no. 1 (2008): 1–18.

Lieberman, Evan. *Boundaries of Contagion*. Princeton, NJ: Princeton University Press, 2009.

Lijphart, Arend. "Comparative Politics and the Comparative Method." *American Political Science Review* 65, no. 3 (1971): 682–693.

Moore, Barrington. *Social Origins of Dictatorship and Democracy: Lord and Peasant in the Making of the Modern World*. Vol. 268. Boston: Beacon Press, 1993.

Nielsen, Richard A. "Case Selection via Matching." *Sociological Methods & Research* 45, no. 3 (2016): 569–597.

Pepinsky, Thomas B. "The Return of the Single-Country Study." *Annual Review of Political Science* 22, no. 1 (2019): 187–203.

Przeworski, Adam and Henry Teune. *The Logic of Comparative Social Inquiry*. New York: John Wiley and Sons, 1970.

Putnam, Robert D. *Making Democracy Work: Civic Traditions in Modern Italy*. Princeton, NJ: Princeton University Press, 1993.

Riofrancos, Thea. "From Cases to Sites." In *Rethinking Comparison: Innovative Methods for Qualitative Political Inquiry*, edited by Erica S. Simmons and Nicholas Rush Smith, 107–126. New York: Cambridge University Press, 2021.

Rohlfing, Ingo. *Case Studies and Causal Inference: An Integrative Framework*. London: Palgrave Macmillan, 2012.

Seawright, Jason. "Beyond Mill: Why Cross-Case Qualitative Causal Inference Is Weak, and Why We Should Still Compare." *Qualitative and Multi-Method Research* 16, no. 1 (2018): 8–14.

Seawright, Jason. *Multi-Method Social Science: Combining Qualitative and Quantitative Tools.* New York: Cambridge University Press, 2016.

Seawright, Jason, and John Gerring. "Case Selection Techniques in Case Study Research: A Menu of Qualitative and Quantitative Options." *Political Research Quarterly* 61, no. 2 (2008): 294–308.

Simmons, Erica S., and Nicholas Rush Smith. *Rethinking Comparison: Innovative Methods for Qualitative Political Inquiry.* New York: Cambridge University Press, 2021.

Skocpol, Theda. *States and Social Revolutions: A Comparative Analysis of France, Russia and China.* New York: Cambridge University Press, 1979.

Slater, Dan, and Daniel Ziblatt. "The Enduring Indispensability of the Controlled Comparison." *Comparative Political Studies* 46, no. 10 (2013): 1301–1327.

Soss, Joe. "On Casing a Study versus Studying a Case." In *Rethinking Comparison: Innovative Methods for Qualitative Political Inquiry*, edited by Erica S. Simmons and Nicholas Rush Smith, 84–106. New York: Cambridge University Press, 2021.

Williamson, Abigail Fisher. *Welcoming New Americans? Local Governments and Immigrant Incorporation.* Chicago: University of Chicago Press, 2018.

7
The Potential of Mixed Methods for Qualitative Research

Thalia Gerzso and Rachel Beatty Riedl

Introduction

Over the past decades, research designs using a mixed-method approach have become more interesting, rigorous, and systematic,[1] with particular attention to identifying the ways that different methods allow different types of observations, claims, and identification strategies. Defined as the combination of "data gathering and analyzing techniques from two or more methodological traditions," the scope of mixed-method research has extended beyond the traditional combination of regression analysis and case studies.[2] Scholars have increasingly used qualitative research to strengthen experimental and formal analyses by creating new descriptive data in which divergence needs to be explained, by identifying puzzles that do not conform to existing theories, and by buttressing the experimental and formal analyses with comparative case studies to demonstrate external validity under a variety of contexts and conditions.

Combining different methods allows researchers to do more: to triangulate different types of data sources,[3] to demonstrate compatibility in micro and macro levels of an overarching argument, to test assumptions that cannot be tested in single-method research,[4] to trace the causal process in a particular place and time while representing the general logic in a formal model or broader patterns through statistical analysis.[5]

This expansion is possible because the methods are not simple substitutes for one another. Rather than telling the same story in different languages, mixed methods tell distinctively different perspectives of a story, making the overall understanding of the phenomenon in question richer and more complex yet also more precise. Thus, mixed-method research offers many advantages to both qualitative and quantitative scholars, contributing to knowledge production and generalizability. These benefits have been driving the adoption of mixed methods across the social sciences, and the benefit to qualitative researchers is particularly acute.[6] Mixed methods allow qualitative researchers a variety of tools to gather and test different forms of empirical observations to link together evidence of complex arguments, at multiple levels of analysis, across time and space. In doing so, mixed methods allow qualitative researchers to strengthen the breadth and depth of the empirical approach, offering greater precision on the causal mechanisms while simultaneously increasing understanding of the generalizability of the argument.

In sequence, qualitative research can identify the questions and hypotheses, shape realistic treatments or data-gathering strategies, and inform the preanalysis plan and overall experimental design, statistical model, or assumptions of the formal model. It can also, last or concurrently with other methodological approaches, observe the causal effect in real life, in varied settings, and provide further evidence of external validity, or home in on the observable evidence of causal mechanisms linking X to Y.

Despite these benefits, a mixed-method approach is not the panacea for all methodological issues researchers can face when designing their empirical strategy. While two methodological approaches can complement one another, multimethod research cannot always reduce all errors or validate exact findings.[7] Furthermore, adopting a mixed-method approach requires a solid understanding of each of the methodological tools used, as they often rely on a different set of assumptions or levels of analysis. A consequence of this is that mixed-method research is often time-consuming and requires resources that are not always available, especially to young scholars.[8] Ambitious mixed-methods research designs will potentially take more time, resources, and coordination (research assistants; coauthors with distinct complementary skills; access to data sources, research labs, and participant pools; language capacity and translators; etc.) to do more than scratch the surface. Finally, it is not always easy to conciliate the constraints imposed by journals and the ambitious designs of a mixed-method approach. Like any other scholars, mixed-method researchers must justify their research design and discuss at length their findings, but they must do it for each methodological tool they employ. This exercise is not always easy to achieve within an article's word limit, which pushes multimethod research design into long-term book projects more often than journal articles. Further, when authors attempt to carve out a single empirical component of an integrated, rigorous multimethod design, it is often unsatisfying because it was not fully meant to stand alone.

For all these reasons, adopting a mixed-method approach can be daunting for some scholars. This chapter seeks to facilitate the process by providing a typology of combinations available to political scientists, in addition to their value and shortcomings. More specifically, we aim to identify the key characteristics of different methodological tools to better understand what they make visible, what they obscure, and what they need to be complemented by.

This chapter is divided into two sections. First, we discuss the benefits and limitations of common methodological tools used in political science scholarship to, second, outline the potential and pitfalls of particular multimethod combinations and sequences.

Overview: Understanding the Benefits and Limitations of Methodological Tools in Political Science

In order to combine different research approaches, it is essential for researchers to be familiar with the goals, assumptions, and limitations of the tools they plan to deploy. The goal is to try to identify what can be combined *and* the conditions under which methods can be associated.

Instead of attempting to determine which methodological approach is superior, we seek to show that each method can help us observe political phenomena from different angles. In other words, each methodological tool makes some phenomena more visible and obscures others. The purpose of a mixed-method approach is to select combinations that will enhance the breadth and depth of understanding of the topic of inquiry and the reliability of the findings as a whole.

We proceed by discussing the most common methodological approaches in political science research, identifying the main goals of methodological tools, and identifying what can help us observe and what remains unobservable. This intellectual exercise is key as it's crucial to understand the assumptions, purposes, and limits of each method in order to best combine them.

Experimental work is extremely useful for establishing the existence—or absence—of a causal relationship between two variables at a micro level. For these reasons, research designs using an experimental setup are particularly useful for scholars of political behavior. In *From Pews to Politics*, McClendon and Riedl demonstrate that religious teachings communicated in sermons can influence both the degree and the form of citizens' political participation.[9] By providing different content (religious or secular; emphasizing individual agency or structural/institutional constraints), treatments isolate specific ideas communicated through sermons and break apart the multiple bundled aspects that make cultural phenomena so difficult to study with precision. Experiments allow a variety of treatments to be evaluated in direct comparison with one another and require assumptions and hypotheses to be prespecified. Although experiments allow researchers to precisely estimate the causal effect of X on Y, it can be difficult to understand the causal mechanism at play. Because of their design, experiments also often raise external validity issues.

The value of the experiment holds all other factors constant, but it also constrains our observation and measurement of the true effect of the cause in interaction with the complex social and political world it is embedded in; religion is a prime example. A measurement of the effects of religious messaging in a controlled lab environment, devoid of the communal practices of hearing such a message in a shared religious service, delivered with the authority of a trusted leader, surely underestimates the actual impact. Qualitative research, particularly ethnographic observation, is essential to understanding the potential interactions and over- and underestimations from such separation from context in any setting.

Qualitative research can attend to the limitations of experimental studies by *informing* the initial experimental design (ethnographic work and context-specific data gathering to identify interesting questions, design realistic treatments, and produce meaningful measures of expected outcomes), *exploring* the causal mechanism through focus groups, interviews, archival records, and more, and *expanding* observations to macro-level implications of political behavior, to best understand what broader impact such individual reactions can catalyze. McClendon and Riedl demonstrated this trio by constructing a new database of sermon content to map out the real-world variation in religious messaging and constructing the experimental treatments based on this empirical mapping, to maximize external validity.[10] Focus groups illuminated the individual and group mindset tying religious primes to specific types of reactions based on ideas of individual empowerment, and comparative historical analysis allowed a broader examination of the extent to which these differences in religious messaging matter for political outcomes at the national level across time and space.

Observational studies are a second methodological approach commonly used in political science scholarship. Depending on the type of data (i.e., micro or macro level) and regression models, researchers can identify associations between variables at different levels of analysis. In "Rape during Civil War," Cohen exploits a cross-sectional data set of wartime rape during civil wars that took place from 1980 to 2012 to determine whether there are substantial variations that can be leveraged to develop a theory about the causes of rape during interstate conflict.[11] This methodological approach also allows her to establish whether significant associations between variables exist in her universe of cases. If cross-sectional statistical analysis is helpful in highlighting interesting variations or correlations, it's essential to be aware of what this methodological approach obscures. For instance, researchers cannot identify the direction of the causal arrow or make causal claims. In other words, regression analyses fail to tell us how and why the explanatory variable has an effect on the outcome of interest. Furthermore, these statistical analyses often raise endogeneity concerns because of the absence of randomization as it's not always easy to identify potential confounders.

To address these limitations, Cohen uses qualitative data on combatants' and civilians' experiences with violence during intrastate conflicts. By doing so, she is able to trace the main mechanisms of competing arguments at the micro level. Defined by assumptions of rationality and strategic reasoning, formal models allow researchers to study dynamic interactions by modeling abstract representations of real-life situations. This methodological approach has several benefits. First, these models can identify testable hypotheses regarding the causal relationship between the explanatory variable and the outcome of interest. Second, formal models are particularly useful for identifying the conditions under which political phenomena occur. Finally, as opposed to other methodological tools that can observe outcomes at a specific level of analysis, formal models allow researchers to study strategic interactions at different levels of analysis.

While international relations scholars have extensively relied on formal models to understand the causes of war,[12] formal models have also helped scholars theorize relations between different sets of formal institutions.[13] At a micro level, scholars have used formal models to explain behavior and relations between political elites. For example, in *Constraining Dictatorship*, Meng uses a formal model to show how autocrats use institutions to facilitate elite bargaining. Although formal models have proven to be an effective methodological tool in political science scholarship, researchers must be aware of their challenges. First, formal modeling relies on deductive logic, whereas most empirical instruments are based on inductive logic. This difference can lead formal modelers to identify behaviors that are nonobservable for scholars using conventional data.[14] Because formal models rely on deductive reasoning, theories and hypotheses generated from the model are often dependent on the specifications and assumptions of the model.[15]

But it is precisely where these methodological tools are limited that qualitative tools find their strengths. For instance, observational and experimental approaches tend to obscure the causal mechanism at play, while scholarship using qualitative methods allows researchers to better understand the motivations of political actors and the sequence of events. By approaching the research question from a different angle, researchers are able to obtain granular data about the subjects they study, and thus are able to comprehend their behavior. We focus on three approaches here: ethnography, case study, and comparative historical analysis.

Ethnographic research allows individuals to determine whether previous generalizations made about a political phenomenon can apply to a specific case.[16] In his seminal work, Scott uses ethnography to study why peasants' revolutions are so rare.[17] Scott spent several years living in a village in the Philippines to observe the relationship between landlords and peasants. This ethnographic work allowed Scott to witness extremely subtle forms of peasants' resistance and rebut existing assumptions about class relationships. The method was key to this conceptual and theoretical innovation, because the resistance itself was designed and executed precisely to be undetected. Scott's work supplements and informs existing work on resistance in all its forms, because it calls attention to what is often unobservable, and in doing so, builds beyond data sets like ACLED and the Banks Protest data/CNTS Data Archive that count instances of riot, strike, demonstration, and protest that are observable enough to be recorded in local news media. By layering these multiple forms of observation, one can theorize and test the conditions that might lead resistance to evolve from "everyday" to street protest and armed conflict.

In a second example, case study research offers several contributions. The in-depth study of one or several cases can be used to (1) describe a phenomenon, (2) build a theory and generate hypotheses, and (3) test the observable implications of one's theory.[18] For example, while attending town hall meetings in the countryside of France, Patana[19] heard many residents express frustration regarding the lack of local opportunities and services. These observations allowed her to inductively build a theory that links residential constraints to support for the far-right parties in France.

Because of the level of observation required by ethnography and case study methodology, these tools are most helpful for scholars focusing on phenomena that can be observed at the micro level. Indeed, neither tool is designed to make generalizations. Therefore, when adopting ethnography or case study to implement their research design, researchers must think about the external validity implications of their claims. It is also important to note that ethnographic work and case study methodology can rely on different assumptions than other methodological tools (i.e., interpretivism vs. positivism; see Chapter 5). Hence, it is important to take this into account when seeking to combine methodological approaches.

Comparative historical analysis is a case study methodology characterized by the use of systematic comparison and the analysis of processes over time to explain large-scale, substantively important outcomes across a well-defined set of national cases.[20] It offers tools for causal and descriptive inference, including testing hypotheses about necessary and sufficient causes, and analyzing complex temporal processes, including path-dependent sequences. In descriptive inference, the comparative historical approach offers tools for concept analysis and achieving measurement validity. Collier and Collier's classic example,[21] *Shaping the Political Arena*, demonstrates how and why state party responses to the emergence of an organized working class then shaped the resulting political coalitions, party systems, regime dynamics, and patterns of stability or conflict across Latin America. Comparative historical analysis combines well with experimental, formal, statistical, and ethnographic or single-case study inductive methods because the small number of cases creates a disciplined configurative approach,[22] avoids problems of conceptual stretching,[23] achieves analytic depth, and reduces the number of variables in conjunction with using stronger theory.[24]

By describing and comparing the different methods used in political science scholarship, we are able to identify the key points researchers need to think about when elaborating a research design using a mixed-method approach. First, we must ask ourselves what variation or phenomenon we are trying to explain. This is a crucial step as it helps us identify the level of analysis we need to focus on. By doing so, we can choose methodological tools that are best suited to shed light on the outcome we seek to explain.

Second, we need to clearly define the purpose of our research agenda. Is the piece about theory-building or generating hypotheses, constructing new empirical observations to map variation, testing alternative propositions, or all of the above? Different methods can help us achieve our goals at different stages of the research process. For instance, formal modeling or Directed Acyclic Graphing can help us map the different outcomes and counterfactuals.

Table 7.1 Summary of the Promises and Pitfalls of Each Methodological Tool Used in Political Science Scholarship

Method	Level of analysis	Purpose	Challenges (What can be complemented)
Experiments	Micro	Establish causal effect, internal validity; Evaluate specific treatments	External validity; Understanding how the mechanism works; Linking micro/political behavior to group outcomes or macro change
Regression/Observational Studies	Micro and macro	Identify variations and correlation between the dependent and independent variables	Endogeneity concerns; Cannot identify the direction of the causal arrow
Formal Modeling/Game Theory	Micro and macro	Model central processes/logic of political behavior or systems; Produces empirically testable propositions; Deductive reasoning and precision of argument and assumptions	Different logic than most empirical tools; Does not empirically prove the validity of a theory
Ethnography	Micro	Identify motivations	Different assumption (interpretivism); External validity
Case Study	Micro and macro	Establish mechanisms and sequence of events	Generalizability; Extent/degree of causal effect; Can be based on interpretivist logic
Comparative Historical Analysis	Macro	Establish mechanisms, sequence of events; Inductive theory building and/or test of deductive propositions	Generalizability/extent of scope conditions; Extent/degree of causal effect

Observational studies can identify patterns and cases to test our hypotheses, while comparative historical analysis and case studies can explore the sequence of events. Finally, once we have selected the methodological tools we want to use, we need to be aware of their assumptions and limitations. The combination of two methodological approaches relying on very different assumptions (e.g., interpretivism vs. positivism or inductive vs. deductive logic) can create challenges in integrating disparate pieces into an encompassing and coherent argument.

These steps are key as they allow researchers to determine the goals of each methodological tool employed and how to combine them effectively. Our approach suggests that there is no one-size-fits-all recipe for mixed-method research. Qualitative methods should not be construed as a mere supplement for quantitative research. Depending on the research question, qualitative tools can help identify patterns and sequences of events or assess the internal validity of observable implications. Mixed-method research is an iterative process that is shaped by the research question.

Multimethod Combinations and Sequences: Practices and Pitfalls

In this section, we outline a selection of combinations available for political scientists. Although this list is not exhaustive, we selected these combinations as they appear to be the most useful in current practice in political science. This list, however, should not prevent researchers from exploring other combinations using the resources we outlined in Table 7.1. Our goal is to understand how these combinations can uncover what was unobservable when using a single-method approach. In addition to highlighting the benefits of each combination, we draw attention to potential pitfalls.

Ethnography and Experiment

Social scientists asking important and socially meaningful questions often rely on a kind of ethnography—careful observations of the world around us, informing which questions we ask and how we ask them. But a deeper merging of ethnographic methods and experimental research design has the potential to serve as a tool to combine the logic of average effects of randomized controlled trials (and therefore a comparison to what did *not* happen) with a logic of causation through chronological narrative, a before-and-after comparison of individual processes through ethnography. Because they both operate at the level of the individual and are fundamentally about what is observable human behavior, they can inform one another. "Building ethnographic methods into the separate branches of randomized controlled trials could substantially increase the range of conclusions that can be produced by experimental research designs, as well as by ethnographic methods. Experimental designs offer greater internal validity for learning *what* the effects of a social program are, and ethnographic methods offer greater insight into *why* the effects were produced. The prospects for such integration depend on the capacity of two different communities within social science to work together for the common goal of discovering the truth."[25] Ethnography can be conducted prior to experimental design to understand and map the differences within the population and hypothesize the relevant comparisons and how various treatments might have heterogeneous effects. Ethnography can also be assigned posttreatment and therefore can say something systematically about the sampling frame and the specific category of people in the experiment's universe of eligible cases.[26] When the ethnographic sample can be based on treatment evaluation, it offers a clear basis for sampling on theoretical grounds based on early differences in experience. In this symbiotic merger, the experimental research design is enriched with ethnographic knowledge at the outset, and the ethnographer flushes out the meaning of treatment effects by following subsamples throughout the experimental process and subsequently.

Observational Studies and Case Study, including Comparative Historical Analysis

Combining statistical analysis and case studies or comparative historical analysis is probably the most common form of mixed-method research used in political science scholarship.[27]

This popularity might be explained by its capacity to address the limitations of both methods. In fact, each method can address specific issues at several stages of the research process. If descriptive statistics can help researchers identify sources of variation of relevant variables for their models,[28] qualitative evidence can be as efficient at the theory-building stage. By conducting 300 interviews with political and traditional Senegalese elites, Wilfarht[29] found a variation in redistributive policies that is linked to the existence of precolonial African kingdoms.

After building the theory and identifying its observable implications, statistical analysis can be used by qualitative researchers for two main purposes. First, because there is a certain limit to the number of people one can interview or how much time one can spend in the field, statistical analysis can help researchers to test the validity of their hypotheses on a bigger sample, thus limiting the risk of biases. Despite an impressive sample of 300 interviews, Wilfhart[30] used quantitative data to determine whether the existence of a precolonial kingdom explains distributional patterns and tested for alternative explanations. Second, statistical regressions can help scholars identify outliers but also cases where variation on the dependent and independent variables can be observed. Using descriptive statistics for the case selection thus allows researchers to justify their case selection and prevent accusations of arbitrariness. This practice is also most helpful in identifying counterfactual cases that could strengthen the qualitative analysis.

Finally, another strength of this combination is its ability to highlight the causal mechanisms at play.[31] Whereas observational studies allow researchers to determine whether X is associated with Y, case studies can help us understand how the explanatory variable affects the outcome of interest. To understand what is driving the proclivity toward legislative expansion in sub-Saharan Africa, the authors conducted three case studies using process tracing to uncover the motivation behind these institutional reforms.[32] By selecting cases that exploit variation on the dependent variable, the authors were able to retrace the sequence of events. They found that legislative size tends to increase before elections or important constitutional reforms. The case study also allowed the authors to identify the motivations (e.g., patronage, intraparty cohesion, weakening the legislature) behind this institutional engineering.

Despite its ability to help scholars strengthen their research design at each step of the way, one must be wary of the numerous pitfalls one can encounter when combining observational studies with case studies or comparative historical analysis (for more, see Chapter 34). First, one must be wary of "mismatched concepts."[33] Whereas operationalizing and measuring multidimensional concepts tend to be easier in qualitative research, those concepts tend to be harder to measure quantitatively. This discrepancy can be problematic if researchers are oblivious to it. Hence, when combining both methods, we must, if we can, (1) measure multicomponent independent variables quantitatively and qualitatively and (2) ensure that the quantitative measure chosen captures the different dimensions we use in the qualitative analysis.

Second, because statistical models exploit sources of variation in the outcome and explanatory variable to determine if there is a relationship between the two, researchers need to be consistent and identify the entire universe of outcomes before selecting their cases. Many studies using regression and case studies tend to select cases where both the outcome of interest and the explanatory variable can be observed.[34] Although these cases are important for outlining the causal mechanism, they're insufficient. Regression analysis allows us to identify other cases that can either strengthen or falsify our theory. It's therefore important to study cases where both the independent and dependent variables are observed ($X = 1, Y = 1$), where no instances occur ($X = 0, Y = 0$), and where only one variable is observed ($X = 1$ and $Y = 0$ or $X = 0$ and $Y = 1$).[35] This step is crucial, as the first two can help us identify the causal mechanisms and counterfactual cases, and the last one can falsify our hypotheses.

Comparative Historical Analysis and Experiments

Combining comparative historical analysis and experiments provides a strong claim to internal *and* external validity. An interesting experimental study may suggest an innovative finding about human responses to a particular treatment. The natural next question is: So what? Do the individual patterns aggregate to macro-level implications, catalyzing regime change, human development, and well-being, revolution, migration, or other significant outcomes? To answer those questions, researchers can turn to an examination of macro-political outcomes to explore whether the aggregate patterns are consistent with individual political behavior in response to specific, isolated treatments.

The challenge of this merger is operating at different levels of analysis—connecting individual political behavior to national-level divergent outcomes across time—making it difficult to align discrete parts of the overarching argument and design a methodology that makes this link visible across comparative cases. Because comparative historical analysis requires attention to temporal processes and sequence, relevant data include interviews based on historical memory, archives, and institutional records. Very few of these types of sources identify "the average individual," and fewer still will provide sufficient identifying information on the masses to be able to differentiate them by treatment, according to the hypotheses driving the experiment. So there will naturally be a disconnect between the types of analysis and what is observable, and there are many possible threats to inference in trying to demonstrate such relationships. But the value of the comparative case study does not have to be based on its strong claims about causal relationships. Instead, it can add external validity and substantive import to the experimental findings by providing descriptive data of historical and contemporary examples of the aggregate impact in the political sphere across countries, *consistent* with the individual-level patterns identified in the experimental studies.

Returning to the example of McClendon and Riedl,[36] and building on the experimental approach, we posited that if exposure to religious *ideas* helps to shape forms of political participation, then aggregate forms of religious participation should, at the very least, vary across the religious denominations that take up these messages, and that there should be general consistency in denominations' forms of mobilization across different strategic contexts. Across three cases and seven distinct historical periods, even though relationships of various religious denominations to the state are different across countries and have changed within countries over time, core forms of political engagement strategies have remained similar. The overall approach expands the significance and impact of the experimental findings and allows comparative-historical analysis to take up new types of explanatory variables, decentering focus away from elites and making individual behavior and the aggregate role of regular individuals more visible in macro-level outcomes.

Formal Modeling and Case Study

At first glance, the combination of case studies and formal modeling can appear antithetical. While formal models rely on inductive logic and seek to elaborate parsimonious models, a case study aims to exploit an abundance of empirical evidence to explore causal mechanisms and counterfactual scenarios. Furthermore, both tools seek to improve our understanding of mechanisms. Hence, one may wonder: Can they complement each other? We argue that such combinations offer many benefits to both qualitative researchers and formal modelers.

First, such an approach can help scholars articulate a parsimonious theory. If case studies can help researchers trace the process that leads to the phenomenon of interest, the richness of archival records or qualitative evidence can lead to the identification of myriad confounders, potentially making theory-building quite daunting. By using formal modeling, researchers can map the different processes and outcomes available under different specifications.[37] Second, this combination can be beneficial for game theorists as it allows them to verify the validity of the models' assumptions.[38] Indeed, because the assumptions on which models rely tend to oversimplify the world, they are often seen as the main weakness of this methodological approach. Using case studies to show how these assumptions are empirically grounded can help researchers strengthen their models. Finally, this combination can help researchers translate how the modeled sequence works empirically.[39] It can be hard to comprehend how the sequence outlined in several models (e.g., repeated games, games where the decision process is made mentally) would function in the real world. In this instance, case studies can show how the mechanisms would work empirically. For instance, to illustrate his formal model Spaniel[40] conducted a case study of the Soviet Union's decision to engage in arms proliferation instead of suspending its weapons program.

Despite these benefits, this combination has its challenges. Because scholarship exploiting formal models can focus on a specific set of actors or phenomena, researchers seeking to adopt a mixed-method approach must be cautious about the data they rely on. When evaluating the model's assumptions, researchers must triangulate data sources to make sure they do not introduce systemic bias.[41] Furthermore, in some instances, case studies cannot always help us uncover what formal modeling obscures. For instance, understanding the psychology and/or the rationale of strategic actors is not always possible since the mental process remains unobservable.

Conclusion

In sum, a rigorous and practical approach to mixed methods can enhance research by compensating for limitations in any single approach and expanding the complexity as well as precision of our understanding of political phenomena. And keeping in mind the challenges or incompatibilities can assist in the actual planning and implementation, as well as in the description of what can realistically be accomplished through any combination. Certainly, not every combination is right for every research topic, and it is our view that the question should drive the method selection: How can we best observe, understand, empirically test, and build enduring, generalizable theories about important political processes and outcomes? This chapter endeavors to provide ways of thinking about the potential and pitfalls, with a goal of maximizing knowledge accumulation across the discipline.

Notes

1. Lieberman, "Nested Analysis as a Mixed-Method Strategy for Comparative Research"; King, Keohane, and Verba, *Designing Social Inquiry*.
2. Goertz, "Multimethod Research"; Seawright, "Better Multimethod Design."
3. Tarrow, "Bridging the Quantitative-Qualitative Divide in Political Science."
4. Seawright, "Better Multimethod Design."
5. Goertz, "Multimethod Research."
6. Seawright, "Better Multimethod Design."
7. Ahmed and Sil, "When Multi-Method Research Subverts Methodological Pluralism."
8. Verghese, "Multi-method Fieldwork in Practice."
9. McClendon and Riedl, *From Pews to Politics*.
10. McClendon and Riedl, *From Pews to Politics*.
11. Cohen, *Rape during Civil War*.
12. For example, Fearon, "Signaling versus the Balance of Power and Interests."
13. For example, Tsebelis, "Decision Making in Political Systems."
14. Monroe et al., "No!"
15. Kuehn, "Combining Game Theory Models and Process Tracing."
16. Wedeen, "Reflections on Ethnographic Work in Political Science."
17. Scott, *Weapons of the Weak*.
18. Schwandt and Gates, "Case Study Methodology."
19. Patana, "Residential Constraints and the Political Geography of the Populist Radical Right."
20. Mahoney, "Comparative-Historical Methodology"; Collier, "Comparative-Historical Analysis."
21. Collier and Collier, *Shaping the Political Arena*.
22. Lijphart, "Comparative Politics and the Comparative Method."
23. Sartori, "Concept Misformation in Comparative Politics."
24. Collier, "The Comparative Method."
25. Sherman and Strang, "Experimental Ethnography."
26. Boruch, *Randomized Experiments for Planning and Evaluation*.
27. Seawright, "Better Multimethod Design."
28. Goertz, "Multimethod Research."
29. Wilfahrt, "Precolonial Legacies and Institutional Congruence in Public Goods Delivery."
30. Wilfahrt, "Precolonial Legacies and Institutional Congruence in Public Goods Delivery."
31. Goertz, "Multimethod Research."
32. Gerzso and van de Walle, "The Politics of Legislative Expansion in Africa."
33. Coppedge, "Speedbumps on the Road to Multi-Method Consensus in Comparative Politics."
34. Goertz, "Multimethod Research."
35. Goertz, "Multimethod Research."
36. McClendon and Riedl, *From Pews to Politics*.
37. Goemans, "Qualitative Methods as an Essential Component to Quantitative Methods."
38. Kuehn, "Combining Game Theory Models and Process Tracing."
39. Kuehn, "Combining Game Theory Models and Process Tracing."
40. Spaniel, "Arms Negotiation, War Exhaustion, and the Credibility of Preventive War."
41. Ahmed and Sil, "When Multi-Method Research Subverts Methodological Pluralism."

Recommended Readings

Meng, Anne. *Constraining Dictatorship: From Personalized Rule to Institutionalized Regimes.* New York: Cambridge University Press, 2020.
>Combining game theory, descriptive statistics, observational study, and case study, Meng investigates why some African incumbents have decided to institutionalize their regime.

McClendon, Gwyneth, and Riedl, Rachel Beatty. *From Pews to Politics: Religious Sermons and Political Participation in Africa.* New York: Cambridge University Press, 2019.
>Documents the current diversity of sermon content in contemporary Christian houses of worship and then uses a combination of laboratory experiments, observational survey data, focus groups, and case comparisons in Zambia, Uganda, and Kenya to interrogate the impact of sermon exposure on political participation and the longevity of that impact. The book leverages the pluralism of sermons in sub-Saharan Africa to gain insight into the content of cultural influences and their consequences for how ordinary citizens participate in politics.

Wilfahrt, Martha. "Precolonial Legacies and Institutional Congruence in Public Goods Delivery: Evidence from Decentralized West Africa." *World Politics* 70, no. 2 (2018): 239–274.
>Combining regression analysis and case study of Senegal, Wilfahrt determines whether the existence of a precolonial kingdom explains distributional patterns

References

Ahmed, Amel, and Rudra Sil. "When Multi-Method Research Subverts Methodological Pluralism— or, Why We Still Need Single-Method Research." *Perspectives on Politics* 10, no. 4 (December 2012): 935–953. https://doi.org/10.1017/S1537592712002836.

Boruch, Robert F. *Randomized Experiments for Planning and Evaluation: A Practical Guide.* Thousand Oaks, CA: Sage, 1997.

Cohen, Dara Kay. *Rape during Civil War.* Ithaca, NY: Cornell University Press, 2016. https://www.jstor.org/stable/10.7591/j.ctt20d8b3j.

Collier, David. "Comparative-Historical Analysis: Where Do We Stand?" SSRN Scholarly Paper, June 1, 1998. https://papers.ssrn.com/abstract=1757222.

Collier, David. "The comparative method in Political Science: The State of the Discipline II", ed. A Finifter, Washington, DC: *American Political Science Association* (1993): 105–19.

Collier, Ruth Berins, and David Collier. *Shaping the Political Arena: Critical Junctures, the Labor Movement, and Regime Dynamics in Latin America.* Notre Dame, IN: University of Notre Dame Press, 2002. https://doi.org/10.2307/j.ctvpj74pj

Coppedge, Michael. "Speedbumps on the Road to Multi-Method Consensus in Comparative Politics." *Qualitative and Multi-Method Research* 7, no. 2 (2009): 15–17.

Fearon, James D. "Signaling versus the Balance of Power and Interests: An Empirical Test of a Crisis Bargaining Model." *Journal of Conflict Resolution* 38, no. 2 (1994): 236–269.

Gerzso, Thalia, and Nicolas van de Walle. "The Politics of Legislative Expansion in Africa." *Comparative Political Studies* 55, no. 14 (December 1, 2022): 2315–2348. https://doi.org/10.1177/00104140221074277.

Goemans, Hein. "Qualitative Methods as an Essential Component to Quantitative Methods." *Newsletter of the APSA Organized Section on Qualitative Methods* 5, no. 1 (2007): 11–13.

Goertz, Gary. "Multimethod Research." *Security Studies* 25, no. 1 (January 2, 2016): 3–24. https://doi.org/10.1080/09636412.2016.1134016.

King, Gary, Robert O. Keohane, and Sidney Verba. *Designing Social Inquiry: Scientific Inference in Qualitative Research.* STU-Student edition. Princeton, NJ: Princeton University Press, 1994. https://www.jstor.org/stable/j.ctt7sfxj.

Kuehn, David. "Combining Game Theory Models and Process Tracing: Potential and Limits." *European Political Science* 12, no. 1 (March 2013): 52–63. https://doi.org/10.1057/eps.2012.9.

Lieberman, Evan S. "Nested Analysis as a Mixed-Method Strategy for Comparative Research." *American Political Science Review* 99, no. 3 (August 2005): 435–452. https://doi.org/10.1017/S00030 55405051762.

Lijphart, Arend. "Comparative Politics and the Comparative Method." *American Political Science Review* 65, no. 3 (1971): 682–693.

Mahoney, James. "Comparative-Historical Methodology." *Annual Review of Sociology* 30, no. 1 (2004): 81–101. https://doi.org/10.1146/annurev.soc.30.012703.110507.

McClendon, Gwyneth H., and Rachel Beatty Riedl. *From Pews to Politics: Religious Sermons and Political Participation in Africa*. Cambridge Studies in Comparative Politics. Cambridge: Cambridge University Press, 2019. https://doi.org/10.1017/9781108761208.

Meng, Anne. *Constraining Dictatorship: From Personalized Rule to Institutionalized Regimes*. Cambridge: Cambridge University Press, 2020.

Monroe, Burt L., Jennifer Pan, Margaret E. Roberts, Maya Sen, and Betsy Sinclair. "No! Formal Theory, Causal Inference, and Big Data Are Not Contradictory Trends in Political Science." *PS: Political Science & Politics* 48, no. 1 (January 2015): 71–74. https://doi.org/10.1017/S1049096514001760.

Patana, Pauliina. "Residential Constraints and the Political Geography of the Populist Radical Right: Evidence from France." *Perspectives on Politics* 20, no. 3 (September 2022): 842–859. https://doi.org/10.1017/S153759272100219X.

Sartori, Giovanni. "Concept Misformation in Comparative Politics." *American Political Science Review* 64, no. 4 (1970): 1033–1053.

Schwandt, Thomas A., and Emily F. Gates. "Case Study Methodology." In *The Sage Handbook of Qualitative Research*, edited by Norman K Denzin and Yvonna S Lincoln 341–358. Thousand Oaks, CA: Sage, 2017.

Scott, James C. *Weapons of the Weak: Everyday Forms of Peasant Resistance*. New Haven, CT: Yale University Press, 1985.

Seawright, Jason. "Better Multimethod Design: The Promise of Integrative Multimethod Research." *Security Studies* 25, no. 1 (January 2, 2016): 42–49. https://doi.org/10.1080/09636412.2016.1134187.

Sherman, Lawrence W., and Heather Strang. "Experimental Ethnography: The Marriage of Qualitative and Quantitative Research." *Annals of the American Academy of Political and Social Science* 595, no. 1 (September 1, 2004): 204–222. https://doi.org/10.1177/0002716204267481.

Spaniel, William. "Arms Negotiation, War Exhaustion, and the Credibility of Preventive War." *International Interactions* 41, no. 5 (October 20, 2015): 832–856. https://doi.org/10.1080/03050 629.2015.1051225.

Tarrow, Sidney. "Bridging the Quantitative-Qualitative Divide in Political Science." Ed. Gary King, Robert O. Keohane, and Sidney Verba. *American Political Science Review* 89, no. 2 (1995): 471–474. https://doi.org/10.2307/2082444.

Tsebelis, George. "Decision Making in Political Systems: Veto Players in Presidentialism, Parliamentarism, Multicameralism and Multipartyism." *British Journal of Political Science* 25, no. 3 (1995): 289–325.

Verghese, Ajay. "Multi-method fieldwork in practice: Colonial legacies and ethnic conflict in India." *Qualitative & Multi-Method Research* 10, no. 4 (2012): 41–44.

Wedeen, Lisa. "Reflections on Ethnographic Work in Political Science." *Annual Review of Political Science* 13, no. 1 (2010): 255–272. https://doi.org/10.1146/annurev.polisci.11.052706.123951.

Wilfahrt, Martha. "Precolonial Legacies and Institutional Congruence in Public Goods Delivery: Evidence from Decentralized West Africa." *World Politics* 70, no. 2 (April 2018): 239–274. https://doi.org/10.1017/S0043887117000363.

8
Preparing a Causal Research Design

Jody LaPorte

Descriptive Overview

Preparing a research design is an important step in any project. For graduate students, it can be a rite of passage marking the transition from coursework to writing a dissertation. For more advanced scholars, formulating a proposal can be necessary for developing a new research agenda, pursuing funding opportunities, or securing institutional support.

This chapter considers what constitutes good design when the goal is to uncover and document causal relationships. A causal research project may seek to examine the underlying factors that brought about a given phenomenon, or it might probe whether that phenomenon influences other outcomes. The purpose of a causal research design is to investigate these relationships by establishing—through either empirical observation or counterfactual reasoning—that a different value of the hypothesized independent variable(s) would result in a different outcome. Yet, a key point about causal relationships is that we cannot observe causality directly; we must *infer* it. Thus, the goal of a good research design is to devise ways to discern that a causal relationship exists, and to provide evidence that will be convincing to others, without being able to directly witness the causal forces at work.

The approach to preparing a causal research design that is laid out in this chapter involves creating a plan that allows the researcher to formulate their causal argument and then to compare the observable implications of this theory against empirical data. To be sure, as the chapter discusses, preparing and conducting research projects rarely proceeds in a neatly deductive or even unilinear way. The next section guides qualitative researchers through this process and identifies the core components of a causal research design. The section after that addresses potential challenges that researchers may encounter and offers some practical steps to avoid and alleviate these problems. Throughout the discussion, I use a running example of my own experience of developing a research design for my doctoral dissertation on the politics of nondemocratic regimes in post-Soviet Eurasia.

State of Practice

A research design can be thought of as a blueprint that outlines the central question and hypothesis that you want to investigate, as well as a plan for how you intend to do that. This section argues that successful causal research designs will fulfill certain criteria that, taken together, create a rigorous and structured analytical inquiry.

Poses a Causal Research Question

A good causal research design opens with a clearly stated question that will be investigated in the project. Qualitative researchers, in particular, tend to be motivated by a certain set of empirical events and take as their starting place a desire to understand those events better. It can therefore be tempting to center the project around establishing, conceptualizing, or classifying the existence of a phenomenon. On their own, these are questions of description. While descriptive research is valuable in its own right, it is fundamentally different from causal inquiry.[1]

Causal research questions are those that investigate the causes or consequences of a given event or phenomenon. We often investigate why—or in some cases, how—a given outcome occurred. This is a "causes of effects" approach, in which the project is designed to explain a particular political event or to account for divergence or convergence across a specified set of cases.[2] Equally valid, though less common in qualitative research, analysts may pursue an "effects of causes" approach that seeks to identify the consequences of a given phenomenon. Questions in this vein ask what effect a set of events had on other outcomes of interest.

Most research questions operate at the intersection of empirical and theoretical interests. For example, when I started planning my doctoral dissertation in the mid-2000s, the major empirical events in my region of interest were the Color Revolutions. These were mass protests against fraudulent elections that had ousted autocrats in Georgia, Ukraine, and Kyrgyzstan. While that was my starting point, it was clear that more advanced researchers were already on the ground doing fieldwork, and some were already publishing their arguments. One principal explanation suggested that the success or failure of these protests depended, at least in part, on the government's willingness to repress protesters.[3] I decided to problematize this question in a broader set of cases, asking: Why do some autocrats repress protests, while others do not?

Identifies What Is at Stake

Having posed a causal research question, it is important to articulate what is at stake in finding an answer. What will this project tell us that we did not know already, and (crucially) why is that worth knowing? Keep in mind that your audience may include colleagues who spend their time immersed in other questions, regions, or theoretical frameworks and have not given your topic very much thought. Your goal is to convince them, as well as experts in your field, that this project is worth pursuing.

You will want to demonstrate that this research question is not satisfactorily answered in the existing literature. Doing so inevitably requires you to critically review the related scholarship on this topic. The point is not simply to summarize related books and articles, but rather to "situate your proposed project in relation to existing knowledge."[4] What do we know about this topic, and how is your project different from that? The literature review identifies the precise theoretical debate or specific gap in the existing theories that your project will fill.

Often this involves working at a higher level of abstraction than you might expect. For example, in my dissertation proposal, I referenced the Color Revolutions, but I also noted that most research on post-Soviet regimes until then had focused on the creation and consolidation of democracy. Overlooked in these studies was the fact that many postcommunist countries did not democratize at all. Thus, by studying repression the project would address the disparity between our theories of democratization and the realities of authoritarian persistence in Eurasia.

Besides demonstrating that there is a gap in our knowledge, it is important to show that we *should* find an answer to this question. Why is the answer worth knowing? This task can be straightforward when the issue affects large numbers of people—which can occur, for example, when studying macro-level events in populous countries such as China, India, and Brazil. Population size notwithstanding, your topic may generalize to a larger category of cases, including certain regime settings, economic or regional contexts, or in countries with similar historical legacies. You can articulate how focusing on one or a handful of in-depth cases will help us to understand this broader phenomenon. Furthermore, most outcomes of interest to political scientists have important downstream consequences on political outcomes, such as the quality of democracy, institutional stability, or prospects for peace or conflict. Or the question be of interest to policymakers if, for example, by answering this question, we may be able to better understand critical allies or adversaries or design more effective policy solutions.

Specifying the practical consequences of your research can help to justify why it is worth investing time and money in this project. In my case, besides the theoretical implications, I stressed the geostrategic significance of the cases under study. It included countries such as Azerbaijan and Kazakhstan, which have extensive oil and gas reserves and had received huge amounts of foreign investment. Some of the regimes also maintained close ties with Russia, a country of central importance to foreign policymakers which itself was becoming increasingly authoritarian.

Research designs are often motivated by multiple considerations, and a good research design will engage many different rationales. The key point is that this is an opportunity for you to insert your voice into this discussion. You are pursuing this project because it has implications for things that you care about. Articulating the research puzzle, as you see it, allows you to convey what matters to you, as well as the theoretical and empirical impact that you would like to see this project bring about.

Describes the Core Concepts and Variables

You should provide an accurate and rigorous account of the core concept and variables. In a "causes of effects" inquiry, this core concept will be the outcome to be explained. Decades ago, Przeworski and Teune exhorted scholars to replace proper names with variables.[5] Slater and Ziblatt note that this maxim applies to qualitative work as much as it does to quantitative analysis. Qualitative research "should not be taken to mean that researchers who know their cases well care *only* about explaining those particular cases" but rather is predicated on "using those cases to elaborate more general, portable theoretical claims."[6]

This is not simply a matter of identifying the phenomenon or summarizing empirical events—though it may well include a good deal of that. It also requires shifting from concrete facts to abstract concepts and variables by considering such questions as: What larger category of phenomenon is this an instance of?[7] What are the necessary and sufficient properties of this phenomenon through which we would identify other cases? How does this variable vary? Are you interested in explaining this phenomenon's presence versus absence, or variation in type, or variation in degree?[8] Even if you are studying a single case, it is helpful to communicate how the outcome fits within the range of possible scores on this variable and what the "negative case" might be, even if it is not directly observed.[9] All projects draw on prior concepts to some degree. Explicitly referencing how and why you do so can help to place your work within the existing scholarship and increase the internal and external validity of your findings.

In preparing my dissertation proposal, I needed to define which events qualified as protests—including whether they needed to exhibit certain activities, meet a certain size threshold, or involve a high level of public visibility. I also needed to conceptualize what repression meant in this context and how it varied. Working within theories of collective mobilization from political science and sociology, I decided to focus on street protests as my unit of analysis and to measure repression based on whether such events were legally sanctioned by local officials and/or dispersed in practice by police.

Offers a Causal Hypothesis

You need to offer a hypothesis—that is, a tentative argument that offers an answer to the research question. You are likely to have a hunch about what might be going on. This may be developed from your prior case knowledge or preliminary research, but it also could be derived from the existing literature. That is particularly true if you believe that a theory developed in one setting might also apply (perhaps with some modifications) to the new conditions, context, or phenomenon under study.

A causal hypothesis has two core components. It should specify the independent variable(s) that you think contribute to producing this outcome. As above, these causal factors should be rigorously conceptualized, with thought given to their core properties, how they vary, and how their presence might be measured or observed. Qualitative researchers are often interested in the impact of combinations of variables. An argument that identifies multiple independent variables will also hypothesize about how those variables interact and what it is about the conjunction of these factors that produce the outcome. In addition, it should hypothesize about the causal mechanism, which, broadly speaking, refers to the energy that propels the causal story forward.[10] Qualitative analyses frequently derive some analytical leverage from cross-case analysis, but they place particular emphasis on within-case analysis and unpacking the causal processes at work. What generates the forward momentum in this theory? What motivates the actors to do things? What effect did their actions have, and why?

In my research, I developed a hypothesis focused on rulers' desire to gather information about their citizens and sources of discontent. Previous scholars had argued that information-seeking could explain repression versus toleration of protests in China.[11] I hypothesized that this argument may apply more widely to post-Soviet autocracies. My research design proposed that limited toleration of dissent provides benefits, especially information on citizens' policy preferences, the level of popular support for the regime, and the identity of opposition activists. I identified three independent variables that shaped rulers' incentives to pursue this strategy: (1) international factors, (2) incumbents' preferences, and (3) domestic opposition.

Both the causal variables and the mechanism need to be articulated as falsifiable claims that can be tested. What evidence would be confirmatory versus disconfirmatory for your claims? This is often posed in the language of observable implications: If this argument is correct, then what would you expect to find in the data? Likewise, theorizing about the causal mechanism may include developing process tracing tests to systematically evaluate whether the empirical evidence supports your hypothesis.[12]

Accounts for Competing Explanations

A good causal research design accounts for competing explanations. You should acknowledge the most plausible rival hypotheses and discuss what steps will be taken to rule them out. Some rival hypotheses may stem from common knowledge or received wisdom among observers or participants in these dynamics, but most competing explanations are derived from the related scholarly literature. What explanations have previous scholars put forth to explain either this instance or similar outcomes in other places and times? You are likely to compile a long list of possible competing explanations; ultimately, you will want to focus on the most prominent and most plausible ones. It is important to engage these competing hypotheses and to *show* that they are invalid.

The goal is to design your research in a way that eliminates these potential threats to your causal argument. Qualitative researchers often address this point, at least in part, through their case selection. As Chapter 6 elaborated, Mill's Methods advise researchers to select cases with an eye toward controlling for rival hypotheses, thereby eliminating them as plausible explanations. By choosing cases that display contrasting outcomes despite similar scores on rival hypotheses (in the Method of Difference) or similar outcomes despite variation across the competing hypotheses (in the Method of Agreement), the researcher can demonstrate that these alternative explanations cannot systematically account for the outcome.

In my project, the most prominent competing explanations for variation in repression focused on regime openness and state capacity. To address this, I chose three country cases—Azerbaijan, Belarus, and Kazakhstan—with relatively similar scores on both of those variables. I also tried to narrow the time period under study in order to find periods when these cases were most similar. This design invoked the logic of Mill's Method of Difference, as the cases also exhibited significant variation across both the outcome and my hypothesized explanatory variables.

It is worth noting that some scholars have expressed skepticism about our ability to rule out alternative explanations using Mill's Methods.[13] Others have pointed out that comparative work can offer valuable inferential leverage even when the case studies are not "structured" to be perfectly compatible.[14] Researchers may wish to consider these perspectives when developing their research designs. In my view, these critiques remind us of two underlying principles that underpin good qualitative causal research. On one hand, it is crucial to articulate the logic of your research design. This includes decisions about case selection and what you are (and are not) hoping to achieve with it. On the other hand, we cannot rely on case selection alone to investigate causal hypotheses. Mill's Methods need to be paired with further data collection, process tracing, and causal process observations in order to draw rigorous conclusions.[15]

Moreover, not all rival hypotheses can be ruled out through careful case selection. If the project focuses on a single case study, there will not be contrasting cases. Even when doing comparative research, case selection alone is rarely strong enough to rule out the full range of possibilities. For example, the three country cases in my study varied in terms of their reliance on oil and hydrocarbon wealth, which was another important alternative explanation. It may be impossible to control for all rival explanations, in which case you will need to specify your plans for gathering further data to adjudicate between these competing explanations and your hypothesized argument.

Outlines Plans for Data Collection and Analysis

Having laid out the analytical components, it is time to discuss your concrete plans. What steps will you take in order to test your hypothesis and to adjudicate between competing explanations? What data will be collected? How will it be obtained, and what methods will you use to analyze it?

It can be helpful to distinguish between the *data* that you are hoping to collect—that is, the empirical observations and information to be gathered—and the *sources* that you will pursue to find this data. Thus, one aspect of this concerns the actual material that will be relied upon. Which sources will be used, and why? You may intend to use existing materials—such as data compiled by national governments or international organizations—for at least a portion of your analysis. What are the potential biases of these sources, and how will that be mitigated? Similarly, if you will rely on newspapers or archival material, you should reflect on the likely "silences" in these sources. Whose voice is and is not captured in this record? How might that affect your conclusions? Similar questions arise in the conduct of personal interviews. It is worth carefully elaborating who will be interviewed, how they will be contacted, and what interview questions will be asked. In my case, I sought out sources that represented both government and opposition perspectives to make sure that my conclusions were not skewed by one side or the other. Equally important, you might consider what pieces of information interviewees might disclose, as well as which topics they may be reticent to discuss.

Causal research rests on an assumption that the social world exists as an impartial "fact," separate from our subjective understanding of it. Although all data sources are likely to have biases and blind spots, we assume there is an objective truth that we are trying to infer. Consequently, it is crucial to acknowledge any potential partiality, corroborate across different points of view, and triangulate across multiple data sources. It often requires both pragmatism and transparency, in equal parts, to discuss the strengths and weaknesses of your empirical strategy and to outline the measures you will take to avoid potential sources of bias in your findings.

Across all of these materials, researchers should outline their plans for obtaining and analyzing data from these sources. It is not enough to state that you will read the government reports, search the newspaper articles, or transcribe the interviews. What evidence are you looking for in this material, and what will you do with it? Reference to specific observable implications, intervening variables, and process tracing tests can help to structure this discussion. As readers, we expect to see how the evidence that is found will be used to adjudicate between different arguments. Without prejudging the conclusion, you can identify the techniques that will be used to aggregate individual data points into systematic measures of the variables under study. For example, I proposed using news articles to construct an original data set of protest events, which would be used to analyze the major trends cross-nationally and over time in each country.

All of these points should be accompanied by a timeline or schedule for completion. While necessarily tentative, an overview of the project schedule—outlining how long each part of the data collection and analysis will take, as well as the overall temporal scope of the project—can help to make these plans more tractable.

Plans for Contingencies

Things rarely go entirely according to plan, and so a good causal research design also plans for contingencies. Problems can arise unexpectedly. The COVID-19 pandemic quickly rendered certain types of projects unfeasible, as borders shut, restrictions were imposed, and travel became impossible. Russia's invasion of Ukraine in February 2022 illustrates how rapidly situations on the ground can change. Even absent major world events, researchers may encounter visa delays, closed archives, funding problems, and personal or family emergencies that delay or interrupt your plans for data collection.

Research designs outline a plan for data collection, but they must also be pragmatic and flexible. It is important to consider how you will handle possible analytical and logistical setbacks. Admittedly, this is something I failed to do sufficiently in my research design, as I describe below. But Kapiszewski, MacLean, and Read correctly suggest that this is an essential part of preparing a causal research design: "[S]cholars can identify in their research designs critical choice points, sketch out a logic for making the relevant decisions, list options for consideration and specific criteria for choosing among them, and discuss a plan for obtaining the required information. It may be useful to develop one or more alternative strategies (addressing different types of contingencies) for key aspects of a project."[16]

Whether to make these contingency plans explicit in your research design will depend on your advisors' preferences, the expectation of funding agencies, and the norms for your discipline. Some reviewers prefer to see that you are thinking ahead, while others believe that this undermines the clarity of the research design. It is worth inquiring in advance and soliciting feedback on drafts to gauge how much detail is appropriate. Even if you do not need to include an extensive written discussion, thinking through these scenarios can help to prepare for a prospectus defense or grant interview and for the practicalities of data collection.

Discusses Why You Are the Right Person to Do This Research

The final component of a good research design is a convincing argument about why you are the perfect person to undertake this research. If the previous sections are about selling the project, here is where you get to promote yourself. What makes you the best person for the job? You can emphasize the preliminary research that you have carried out, your research methods training, and any initial field research you have conducted. In my proposal, I underscored my advanced Russian-language skills, as well as previous trips to the region and existing networks of contacts. We want to know that you are poised to succeed in carrying out this research, so don't be shy!

Potential Challenges and Solutions

Preparing a research design requires you to think several steps ahead and to articulate confidently how the project will unfold, even as you may be unsure what the data might reveal. It can feel like you are being asked to anticipate arguments and evidence before you have done the research. Further, the different sections of the research design are interdependent. The correct case selection techniques arise from how the question is formulated, how the outcome is conceptualized, and which alternative hypotheses are specified. But pinpointing the most salient aspects of variation in the outcome to be explained may depend on the cases under study. It can seem as if you need to solve multiple puzzles simultaneously.

It can help to focus on one aspect of the research design that you are most excited by or invested in. This might be a certain set of cases that you are confident you want to include in the study. Or you might be motivated by a certain research question or a particular outcome, but less sure about the precise cases. In either scenario, it can be useful to start with a non-negotiable part of the project and then build up the rest of the research design around that decision.

Another challenge can arise during the execution of the research project. Sometimes the situation on the ground changes between preparing the research design and beginning data collection. You may find that your initial hypothesis is not entirely supported by evidence, or unanticipated findings may open a new line of inquiry. Even the tightest research design can fall apart in the face of unexpected results. Strict adherence to the scientific method would mean rejecting this new information in order to "stick to the plan." But as Yom points out, "real-world research seldom follows [the] elegant deductive procedures" and linear processes associated with the scientific method. Indeed, researchers who use qualitative and fieldwork-based methods frequently *need* to revise their projects while conducting research because they "pose questions about geographic, substantive, or theoretical terrain that is relatively unexplored in existing scholarship; and because fieldwork is commonly shaped by unexpected events and challenges."[17]

Yom proposes that scholars approach their work through the lens of "inductive iteration." In this approach the initial hypothesis is developed "with the understanding that new insights from data and cases could well show it to be incomplete, and so in need of revision."[18] Conducting research then becomes a matter of continuously refining your causal arguments to accurately capture the empirical reality. Kapiszewski, MacLean, and Read similarly suggest that researchers view "collecting data and analyzing data as processes that move forward simultaneously and in parallel."[19] By analyzing the data on an ongoing basis—using memos, fieldwork journals, and descriptive summaries about major events—you can quickly identify new lines of inquiry, assess whether to pursue them, and gather the appropriate evidence to support your reformulated claims.

A more complicated scenario arises when the data casts doubt on your conceptualization of the dependent variable or your case selection criteria. I refer to these situations as "crises of research design" because they require not just rethinking the argument but reworking core elements of the design. This happened to me. During fieldwork for my dissertation, I realized that my tightly controlled design was not aligned with empirical realities. I broadened the scope of analysis—moving from explaining state response to protests to how autocrats treat opposition groups more generally. I also shifted my case selection.[20] While this was the right route for me, these are significant decisions that may increase the time and funding necessary to complete the project. You should consult with your advisors, colleagues, and funding agencies before making major changes, though ultimately it is your decision how to proceed.

What, then, is the value of preparing a causal research design? First, it creates a plan of action; even if revisions need to be made later, it offers a framework for getting started. Second, even if tweaks become necessary, most analyses remain within a similar area of inquiry. Having prepared a research design, you will already have reviewed the literature and digested the core theories and concepts. Consequently, you will be better prepared to recognize analytical opportunities when they arise and to theoretically situate the end result. Third, it demonstrates that you know how to design a research project, which means that you can do it again if necessary. Preparing a good research design offers confidence that any further adjustments will be made without losing sight of the principles of rigorous research.

Conclusion

This chapter has argued that successful causal research designs share several core features. The eight criteria laid out here are each important on their own, but they are also interlinked. Developing a good causal research design requires taking a bird's-eye view across the individual components and considering how each part of the design contributes to the larger goal of drawing valid causal inferences.

Notes

1. Gerring, "Mere Description," 722.
2. Mahoney and Goertz, "A Tale of Two Cultures."
3. Way, "The Real Causes of the Color Revolutions."
4. Knopf, "Doing a Literature Review," 127.
5. Przeworski and Teune, *The Logic of Comparative Social Inquiry*.
6. Slater and Ziblatt, "The Enduring Indispensability of the Controlled Comparison," 1311.
7. Sartori, "Concept Misformation in Comparative Politics"; Collier and Levitsky, "Democracy with Adjectives."
8. Collier, LaPorte, and Seawright, "Putting Typologies to Work."
9. Mahoney and Goertz, "The Possibility Principle."
10. Bennett and Checkel, *Process Tracing*; Gerring, "The Mechanismic Worldview"; Gerring, "Causal Mechanisms"; Beach and Pedersen, *Process-Tracing Methods*.
11. Lorentzen, "Regularizing Rioting."
12. Collier, "Understanding Process Tracing"; Waldner, "What Makes Process Tracing Good?"
13. Seawright, "Beyond Mill."
14. Simmons and Rush Smith, *Rethinking Comparison*.
15. Brady, Collier, and Seawright, "Toward a Pluralistic Vision of Methodology."
16. Kapiszewski, MacLean, and Read, "Dynamic Research Design," 15.
17. Kapiszewski, MacLean, and Read, "Dynamic Research Design," 3.
18. Yom, "From Methodology to Practice," 626.
19. Kapiszewski, MacLean, and Read, *Field Research in Political Science*, 335.
20. LaPorte, "Confronting a Crisis of Research Design"; LaPorte, "Foreign versus Domestic Bribery."

Recommended Readings

George, Alexander, and Andrew Bennett. *Case Studies and Theory Development in the Social Sciences.* Cambridge, MA: MIT Press, 2005.
> This book focuses on designing and executing qualitative projects, including the deeper philosophy of social science principles that underpin the case study approach.

Gerring, John. *Case Study Research: Principles and Practices*, 2nd ed. New York: Cambridge University Press, 2019.
> This updated book presents a comprehensive and accessible introduction to designing case study and qualitative research, covering concepts, case selection, and internal and external validity.

Gonzalez-Ocantos, Ezequiel. "Designing Qualitative Research Projects: Notes on Theory Building, Case Selection and Field Research." In *Sage Handbook of Research Methods in Political Science and International Relations*, edited by L. Curini and R. Franzese Jr. Thousand Oaks, CA: SAGE, 2019. https://doi.org/10.4135/9781526486387
> This chapter offers an in-depth look at causal mechanisms and advises researchers on how to develop a causal hypothesis.

Mahoney, James and Gary Goertz. *A Tale of Two Cultures: Qualitative and Quantitative Research in the Social Sciences*. Princeton, NJ: Princeton University Press, 2012.
> This book compares and contrasts the logic of causal inference across qualitative and quantitative approaches; in doing so, it elaborates the rationale for many of the principles and practices of qualitative research design in greater depth.

Van Evera, Stephen. *Guide to Methods for Students of Political Science*. Ithaca, NY: Cornell University Press, 2016.
> This short volume contains straightforward advice for planning qualitative research projects, starting from the initial idea through the research design to presenting the final product.

References

Beach, Derek, and Rasmus Brun Pedersen. *Process-Tracing Methods: Foundations and Guidelines*. Ann Arbor: University of Michigan Press, 2013.

Bennett, Andrew, and Jeffrey T. Checkel, eds. *Process Tracing: From Metaphor to Analytic Tool.* Cambridge: Cambridge University Press, 2014.

Brady, Henry E., David Collier, and Jason Seawright. "Toward a Pluralistic Vision of Methodology." *Political Analysis* 14, no. 3 (2006): 353–368. https://doi.org/10.1093/pan/mpj021.

Collier, David. "Understanding Process Tracing." *PS: Political Science and Politics* 44, no. 4 (2011): 823–830.

Collier, David, Jody LaPorte, and Jason Seawright. "Putting Typologies to Work: Concept Formation, Measurement, and Analytic Rigor." *Political Research Quarterly* 65, no. 1 (March 1, 2012): 217–232. https://doi.org/10.1177/1065912912437162.

Collier, David, and Steven Levitsky. "Democracy with Adjectives: Conceptual Innovation in Comparative Research." *World Politics* 49, no. 3 (1997): 430–451.

Gerring, John. "Causal Mechanisms: Yes, But ..." *Comparative Political Studies* 43, no. 11 (2010): 1499–1526. https://doi.org/10.1177/0010414010376911.

Gerring, John. "The Mechanismic Worldview: Thinking Inside the Box." *British Journal of Political Science* 38, no. 1 (2008): 161–179.

Gerring, John. "Mere Description." *British Journal of Political Science* 42, no. 4 (October 2012): 721–746. https://doi.org/10.1017/S0007123412000130.

Kapiszewski, Diana, Lauren M. MacLean, and Benjamin L. Read. "Dynamic Research Design: Iteration in Field-Based Inquiry." *Comparative Politics* 54, no. 4 (2022): 645–670. https://doi.org/10.5129/001041522X16352603126875.

Kapiszewski, Diana, Lauren M. MacLean, and Benjamin L. Read. *Field Research in Political Science: Practices and Principles*. Strategies for Social Inquiry. Cambridge: Cambridge University Press, 2015. https://doi.org/10.1017/CBO9780511794551.

Knopf, Jeffrey W. "Doing a Literature Review." *PS: Political Science & Politics* 39, no. 1 (January 2006): 127–132. https://doi.org/10.1017/S1049096506060264.

LaPorte, Jody. "Confronting a Crisis of Research Design." *PS: Political Science & Politics* 47, no. 2 (April 2014): 414–417. https://doi.org/10.1017/S1049096514000328.

LaPorte, Jody. "Foreign versus Domestic Bribery: Explaining Repression in Kleptocratic Regimes." *Comparative Politics* 50, no. 1 (2017): 83–102.

Lorentzen, Peter L. "Regularizing Rioting: Permitting Public Protest in an Authoritarian Regime." *Quarterly Journal of Political Science* 8, no. 2 (February 24, 2013): 127–158. https://doi.org/10.1561/100.00012051.

Mahoney, James, and Gary Goertz. "A Tale of Two Cultures: Contrasting Quantitative and Qualitative Research." *Political Analysis* 14, no. 3 (2006): 227–249. https://doi.org/10.1093/pan/mpj017.

Mahoney, James, and Gary Goertz. "The Possibility Principle: Choosing Negative Cases in Comparative Research." *American Political Science Review* 98, no. 4 (2004): 653–669.

Przeworski, Adam, and Henry Teune. *The Logic of Comparative Social Inquiry*. New York: Wiley-Interscience, 1970.

Sartori, Giovanni. "Concept Misformation in Comparative Politics." *American Political Science Review* 64, no. 4 (1970): 1033–1053. https://doi.org/10.2307/1958356.

Seawright, Jason. "Beyond Mill: Why Cross-Case Qualitative Causal Inference Is Weak, and Why We Should Still Compare." In *Rethinking Comparison: Innovative Methods for Qualitative Political Inquiry*, edited by Erica S. Simmons and Nicholas Rush Smith, 31–46. Cambridge: Cambridge University Press, 2021. https://doi.org/10.1017/9781108966009.002.

Simmons, Erica S., and Nicholas Rush Smith, eds. *Rethinking Comparison: Innovative Methods for Qualitative Political Inquiry*. Cambridge: Cambridge University Press, 2021. https://doi.org/10.1017/9781108966009.

Slater, Dan, and Daniel Ziblatt. "The Enduring Indispensability of the Controlled Comparison." *Comparative Political Studies* 46, no. 10 (October 2013): 1301–1327. https://doi.org/10.1177/0010414012472469.

Waldner, David. "What Makes Process Tracing Good? Causal Mechanisms, Causal Inference, and the Completeness Standard in Comparative Politics." In *Process Tracing: From Metaphor to Analytic Tool*, edited by Andrew Bennett and Jeffrey T. Checkel, 126–152. New York: Cambridge University Press, 2015.

Way, Lucan. "The Real Causes of the Color Revolutions." *Journal of Democracy* 19, no. 3 (July 2008): 55–69. https://doi.org/10.1353/jod.0.0010.

Yom, Sean. "From Methodology to Practice: Inductive Iteration in Comparative Research." *Comparative Political Studies* 48, no. 5 (April 2015): 616–644. https://doi.org/10.1177/0010414014554685.

9
Preparing an Interpretive Research Design

Tanya B. Schwarz and Carrie Reiling

What Is Interpretive Research?

How does one go about preparing an interpretive research design? In what ways might an interpretive design differ from other qualitative projects? In this chapter, we engage with these questions and offer some suggestions for researchers interested in pursuing interpretive research. In this first section, we summarize some of the unique features of interpretivism. The following two sections detail how to prepare an interpretive research design and the potential challenges faced when doing so. We draw on our own research experiences conducting ethnographic and interview-based fieldwork to highlight how interpretivists navigate this process—Schwarz with faith-based peacebuilding organizations[1] and Reiling with local women's peace and security organizations in West Africa.[2]

Qualitative researchers should begin the task of research design by first understanding why they would choose to use interpretive methodologies (also see Chapter 5). Interpretivists are chiefly concerned with meaning-making practices and how that meaning-making results in political and social behavior. While interpretive research generally analyzes the meaning of language and how language shapes our social world, not all interpretive approaches are the same. We focus here on critical and feminist interpretivisms, though interpretive research can draw on a multitude of theoretical traditions from the social sciences and humanities. Critical interpretivism "emphasizes that language cannot be a perfect representation of the world itself" and is socially constructed, context-dependent, and shaped by power.[3] Interpretive does not mean "impressionistic," however.[4] Interpretive research tends to be highly analytic in order to carefully demonstrate how the meanings came to be and why they matter. Roxanne Doty uses the terminology of *how-possible* instead of *why-possible* to address questions of power in creating certain possibilities and precluding others.[5] Feminist interpretive approaches incorporate these same critical understandings but emphasize reflexivity in the research process and an attention to the power relations between the researcher and the research participants.[6] In short, interpretive research is different from other forms of qualitative research because it emphasizes the fluidity of meanings as mutually constitutive and shaped by power. These epistemological foundations result in a unique approach to the research process.

For example, interpretivists employ an abductive logic of inquiry, which does not test existing theories or try to generalize from observations. Instead, the task of abductive reasoning is focused on sense-making, wherein the researcher looks for evidence that would provide greater understanding of a specific phenomenon.[7] As one would expect, this leads to a unique relationship with causality as well. In particular, interpretivists rely on "expanded notions of causality" that often center on constitutive causality.[8] Though not all interpretivists eschew positivist notions of causality,[9] most interpretivist scholars want to know not only *how* their research participants understand themselves and their environment but also *why* they do what they do. They view the research space as a broader contextual environment where "evidence can never prove without a doubt that a given social or political event emanates from a single cause"[10] and causality operates in multiple directions. Thus, "constitutive causality" refers to the ways in which humans' understandings influence their actions by "mak[ing] possible or impossible the interactions they pursue."[11] Such an understanding of causality does not and cannot employ explanations of events that focus on a discrete set of variables or one-way causality.

Moreover, because interpretivism emphasizes the role of the researcher in the construction of knowledge, interpretivist scholars must reflect on their own positionality, a term used to describe a researcher's ascribed identity as well as the power relations that shape identities in the research process.[12] Interpretivist research projects require a reflexive approach (see Chapter 3) that acknowledges the role of power that "infuses every aspect of the research enterprise" and the role of the researcher in that enterprise.[13] The researcher's own experiences, identities, and social communities affect the research that will be produced because of issues like access, but also because of the researcher's choices throughout the research process, choices that might include whether to use a translator, what time of year the research takes place, or how to ethically interact with one's research participants, plus any number of events outside the researcher's control. This even extends to the writing phase. Because the interpretivist views language as producing rather than reflecting social reality, the act of writing is enfolded within the broader data collection and analysis process.[14]

Schwarz's research experiences highlight the ways that a reflexive approach can shape how the researcher experiences and interprets their fieldwork. For instance, some of the NGO representatives Schwarz interviewed, after hearing about her evangelical upbringing, assumed that she still identified as an evangelical Christian. Schwarz noticed how the individuals who assumed this shared identity spoke about religion, prayer, and proselytism differently than those who did not make these assumptions. Schwarz's research participants opened up to her and trusted her when they believed she shared their perspectives and beliefs—not only providing Schwarz with unique access to specific narratives and perspectives but also providing critical information about how these research participants' views of religious insiders and outsiders shaped their behavior.[15] Thus, interpretive researchers not only include an attention to power relations between the researcher and the research participants, but they also privilege such interactions in their analysis.

In the rest of this chapter, we delve into how an abductive logic of inquiry that views causality as constitutive and meanings as fluid shape an interpretive research design and the key considerations that interpretivists must grapple with during the design process. We draw on our own experiences as interpretive researchers to elucidate some of the key features of interpretive research and to emphasize common challenges and solutions in interpretive research designs.

Preparing the Research Design for an Interpretive Project

Research designs require a few key features, including, but not limited to, a research question, an explanation of what or who the researcher is studying, a discussion about which specific concepts and methods the researcher will employ and why, and a research timeline. Like other research projects, an interpretive research design should include all these components. Interpretivists, however, engage with these design components in distinct ways due to the use of an abductive logic of inquiry, explained further in this section.

While *deductive* reasoning tests existing theories and *inductive* reasoning seeks to generalize from observations, *abductive* reasoning strives to make sense of phenomena that do not make sense. To do this, the interpretivist engages in a "puzzling-out process" during which they engage in a kind of investigative journey, moving through various empirical texts and observations in search of evidence that would provide greater *understanding* of the phenomenon in question.[16] In practice, the use of abductive reasoning results in three key implications for an interpretive research design: (1) the researcher does not use hypotheses for testing or analysis, (2) the researcher must incorporate conceptual flexibility into the design, and (3) the researcher employs unique criteria for evaluating the strength of the research.

For instance, when beginning her research, Schwarz wanted to understand the role of religion in transnational peacebuilding. She thought there might be a disconnection between how scholars portrayed religion in their work and how religious actors understand themselves. To investigate further, Schwarz's research[17] asked (1) How do faith-based transnational peacebuilding organizations understand their own identities, practices, and values? and (2) How do these understandings inform the peacebuilding work of these organizations? The first question focuses on *how* faith-based organizations understand themselves and give meaning to their worlds, while the second asks *why* these organizations act in certain ways. What did Schwarz expect to find when exploring these questions?

As noted, the interpretivist abductive researcher does not employ hypotheses or evoke similarly rigid expectations, though they should still have some ideas about what they might find, based on their examination of the existing literature and preliminary research on the subject. Moreover, the researcher must build some conceptual and theoretical flexibility into their project to account for the yet unknown encounters and resources. Rather than engaging in a unidirectional process, where the researcher tests a hypothesis or uncovers truths that can then be generalized, interpretivists understand research to be an "iterative-recursive" process of going back and forth between the research question and the possible explanations for it.[18] Thus, Schwarz's initial expectations for her research did not include hypotheses to test, but instead her general expectations for what she might find (based on the literature and her previous research), while also allowing and preparing for the unexpected. For instance, as relates to prayer in particular, Schwarz expected many of the organizations to employ prayer in their work to further their peacebuilding and human rights causes; however, she noted that those forms of prayer, and how the different groups might refer to "prayer" or prayer-like practices, might vary widely.

Relatedly, Reiling's research experiences highlight the importance of allowing for the unexpected in the field. For example, in her initial research design, she asked: As women navigate postconflict politics and peacebuilding in Côte d'Ivoire, do they prioritize their security and empowerment goals the same way these have been defined by the international community? Furthermore, how do women's organizations respond to the priorities and pressures of the international community, their national governments, and transnational donors and women's organizations? As she conducted her research, though, she found that asking women working for civil society organizations how they understood and employed the concept of "security" was not producing data that could lead to theoretical or empirical conclusions.

Midway through the research process, Reiling was writing a grant report and reflecting on the interviews, when she caught how several of the interview participants shifted their definitions of security midway through the conversation. Through an iterative-recursive process, she began to listen to what the women were describing rather than the actual terminology itself, and more precise, relevant answers to her questions emerged. Specifically, their answers illustrated how women used the language of security to speak to some audiences and the discourses of peace or development to speak to others, all around the same practices.[19] As she continued her research, Reiling adapted her research design and research questions to ask about the meanings of "security." She also added more opportunities for participant observation to understand how practices and the language to describe them were shaped.

In addition to building analytical flexibility into the research design, the interpretivist must also consider how their research will be evaluated and design their research accordingly. How do interpretive researchers know that their research is accurate? Rather than relying on positivist notions of validity, reliability, or generalizability, interpretivists focus on trustworthiness. Trustworthiness refers to the extent to which the research results can be seen to reflect broader intersubjective understandings among the researcher and the research participants, rather than simply "'proving' what he [sic] already 'knows.'"[20] Ensuring the trustworthiness of interpretive research usually includes at least three components: (1) a discussion of how to engage in reflexive practices to account for the researcher's own role in the coproduction of research results; (2) a discussion of the methods the researcher will use and why, often with a specific focus on the use of "thick description"; and (3) a plan to share their findings with their research participants to make sure that they align with the participants' own understandings.[21]

To ensure the trustworthiness of our research, both authors wrestled with our own identities and experiences and how they would shape our research findings while writing our research designs. For example, a large part of Schwarz's research on faith-based organizations focused on these organizations' understandings and use of prayer in their political work. From early in the project, Schwarz debated whether she should use the concept of prayer, given that her Christian upbringing had strongly shaped the way she understood the term. Her reflexive approach required her to grapple with the possibility that using such a concept might shape her research outcomes. For Schwarz, taking a reflexive and bottom-up approach to the concept of prayer meant both grappling with her own understandings of the term (shaped by a variety of individual, familial, societal, and disciplinary contexts) and allowing for differing, plural, and perhaps contradictory or unexpected meanings of the term to arise during her fieldwork. In her research design, Schwarz decided to move forward with using the term "prayer," specifically because it is a term that international relations scholars often assume to be religious, and it was these kinds of assumptions she wanted to interrogate. However, she allowed for the possibility that prayer would not mean the same thing to those she interviewed, so she decided to follow the lead of her interviewees and the organizations she studied. If other terms were used in initial discussions or organizational materials, she relied on those instead. For instance, some representatives preferred to use the term "worship" or "meditation" rather than "prayer." In those instances, Schwarz interrogated the meaning of the terms used by the organizational representatives and how they were used in the organizations' work.

Meanwhile, Reiling, a white researcher from the United States, was quite obviously from outside the communities she was studying in multiple African countries. She knew that her observable identity would certainly shape all her interactions, so she built into her research design the fact that her research participants regularly engaged with donors from the United States and Europe to describe their work. Rather than asking them about their "true beliefs," she designed her project to ask them about their work and then analyzed the language they used to describe it. Instead of reporting her research through the lens of an objective researcher, Reiling acknowledged to readers the outsider status of her nationality and race but also noted that she was sympathetic to the activists' goal of achieving peace and security for themselves and their communities. She also used multiple methods of data collection and analysis—interviews, participant observation, and policy and document analysis—to further bolster the trustworthiness of her interpretations.

An interpretive research design employs bottom-up concept formation[22] or elucidation[23] that comes from, in part, the identity of the researcher. Because the interpretivist views language as intersubjective and socially constructed rather than reflective of an objective reality, interpretive research treats concepts as fluid and lived, marked by disjunctures in meaning. Concept formation happens *throughout* the research process. In fact, one might say that the whole point of an interpretive project is to understand these kinds of disjunctures and why and how the research participants give meaning to certain concepts and their social worlds. Yanow points out that interpretive data is less about being collected, gathered, or accessed by the researcher than about being generated by the researcher and the researched.[24]

The second component that an interpretivist researcher must provide to ensure the trustworthiness of their research is an in-depth discussion of what methods they will use and why. This will usually include a discussion about why the use of "thick description" is so important in many interpretive projects. The inclusion of a methods section is not unique to an interpretivist research design, of course; any strong research design will explain why the methods used are the best for answering the specific research question under investigation, as well as the opportunities and limitations of using such methods. Because interpretive research is grounded in the assumption that knowledge is socially constructed and context-dependent, it precludes the possibility of wholesale generalizability for interpretive research. This does not mean that findings from interpretive research cannot be useful in other contexts. It simply means that such usefulness depends on the context and which findings one is talking about. As Schwartz-Shea and Yanow point out with regard to generalizability, interpretive research is unique in that it "shifts responsibility for the applicability of research learning to other research settings from the researchers to the readers of the research."[25] In other words, it is up to the reader to determine which aspects of a particular research project, if any, are applicable to other contexts. However, for a reader to make this assessment, a researcher must "describe their research contexts in sufficiently 'thick' ways ... contributing all manner of historical, demographic, economic, geographic, and cultural nuances."[26] A strong interpretive research design, then, will include a methodological plan that incorporates the chance to collect the necessary data needed to provide a thick description to the reader.[27]

Reiling's research illustrates both the necessity for thick description and how the knowledge from one context can be appropriately incorporated into other contexts. Her dissertation's research design focused on the fact that her case study was different from the other African countries where research on the lives of women was often conducted; Côte d'Ivoire is a French-speaking country with a lesser-known civil war. It was, in fact, the issues with generalizability that Reiling wanted to highlight in her research: the problem of developing global policies about women who live in radically different historical, political, and cultural contexts. Thick description, then, worked on two levels, by adding trustworthiness to her findings and by illustrating the problems of repeatedly relying on the same contexts to develop policy. After this initial research, with the benefit of additional research funding, Reiling was able to add two additional countries to her study: Guinea and Mali. In the amended research design, the findings from Côte d'Ivoire guided the subsequent research, and in turn, the new research bolstered the trustworthiness overall and contributed to extensive thick description of why context matters in determining global policies about women.

The third step toward trustworthiness of interpretive research findings is sharing the written materials with the research participants. Some qualitative researchers (interpretivist or positivist) share transcripts of their interviews with their interviewees to ensure the accuracy of the document or to allow the interviewee to clarify specific points, if applicable. This is often referred to as "member checking." However, from an interpretivist perspective, the point of sharing our research materials is less about making sure our accounts are objectively correct and more about providing a mechanism to capture local vocabularies and tacit knowledge—allowing for the back-and-forth of interpretive research to uncover complex and situated meanings.[28]

A feminist or critical interpretive approach goes even further with the practice of sharing research. Because the goal of critical feminist research is emancipatory[29] rather than objective knowledge-making, some interpretivists may see research sharing as an essential practice of research ethics. For instance, Reiling integrated a feminist methodological principle of "sharing knowledge and mobilizing collectively"[30] in her research project with West African local women's organizations. She emphasized her role as a coproducer of knowledge with her research participants and also included an explicit research goal of sharing her findings with her research participants to help them better understand best practices in policy implementation and how national-level government institutions could support these organizations. Thus, for Reiling, sharing her research results with her research participants not only helped her to refine her findings and analysis but also served as an important ethical practice that was central to her own impetus for doing the research in the first place.

The burden of building an interpretive iterative-recursive process to ensure trustworthiness as part of the research design necessitates a logistical plan that is more fluid than most. Obviously, most research projects have finite budgets and timelines, but an interpretive project must allow room for the unexpected. The researcher will often need to tweak their project plan to follow the clues as they work their way through the puzzling-out process.

In this section we have summarized some of the components of an interpretive research design, which are fundamentally different from other research designs due to the unique criteria reviewers use to evaluate interpretive work, as well as the interpretivist's use of an abductive logic of inquiry. In the next section, we delve further into the interpretivist research design to highlight some potential challenges and provide advice on how to tackle them.

The Challenges of an Interpretive Research Design and How to Mitigate Them

In an ideal world, creating a research design would be easy and straightforward: the researcher could simply plug in the required elements and call it a day. Unfortunately, research designs are more complicated and can vary greatly depending on the researcher's approach.

Interpretivists, in particular, must carefully but directly grapple with a range of epistemological, logistical, and ethical issues when determining how to craft a strong research project. Often, interpretivists also have to be prepared to respond to those who might not understand interpretive approaches or who expect all research to conform to the norms of positivist research. We address some of the challenges related to these issues here and provide some suggestions on how to mitigate these difficulties.

The adherence to an abductive logic of inquiry and its resulting implications for the research process leads to several challenges that are not necessarily specific to interpretive research but are certainly more visible. For instance, a bottom-up approach to concept formation requires the researcher to create and re-create their approach throughout the research process. However, it is simply impossible to even begin to think about a research question before choosing those concepts that are central to one's research question. This seemingly contradictory state of affairs can lead to significant frustration, especially when writing a research design. To put it more directly, *how can a researcher formulate a research question without settling on certain key concepts from the start?* At various stages of the research process, and particularly at the design stage, the researcher must simply choose those concepts they want to use *for now*. This does require the researcher to specifically explain why they have settled on these concepts and articulate how they will grapple with the difficulties of employing such concepts during the research process.

Furthermore, though researchers must preselect some concepts during the design phase, they should also plan for and encourage concept fluidity during their data coproduction phase. The abductive logic of inquiry employed by interpretivist researchers requires a researcher to move back and forth between potential explanations and their research question. While noninterpretive projects may also be iterative, interpretivist approaches are unique in that the researcher is more likely to privilege *meaning*, thus necessitating changes to the core concepts of the original research design. For instance, in her interviews with Ivorian women, Reiling asked the first questions but then "allow[ed] them to steer the conversation."[31] By choosing to conduct her interviews in this way, Reiling allowed her research participants more linguistic space, thus revealing what concepts and perspectives were more familiar to them. Reiling still had to provide a conversational structure to guide her participants, but when possible, she simply listened. This changed over time as she and her research participants became more comfortable with one another and as Reiling learned their conceptual language and was able to engage in knowledge sharing. However, her approach to interviewing prioritized the terms, concepts, and language of her research participants, when possible, and even resulted in her changing her own use of the term "NGO" when she learned that her research participants referred to their own groups as "local women's organizations" and differentiated themselves from "transnational NGOs."[32] By building conceptual flexibility into her research design, Reiling was able to open herself up to the different understandings of her research participants, which actually resulted in a key research finding about how West African women's organizations defined themselves as distinct from transnational NGOs based outside the African continent, even when working on the same global peacebuilding activities.[33]

In addition to an attention to conceptual fluidity, using an abductive approach may result in a complete overhaul of the research question itself or the methods the researcher employs. However, as the example from Reiling's research shows, these challenges, which some may view as "bugs in the system," are actually central to good interpretive research. The real difficulty lies in how to communicate these processes and perspectives in the research design when one does not have a good sense of how much one's initial concepts, questions, or methods might change during the research. In general, we suggest trying to maintain a balance of firmness and fluidity. That is, one cannot begin a research project without boundaries. It is still necessary for the interpretivist researcher to propose a research question, employ specific concepts, and choose their methods. In addition, the researcher must have a good reason for each of these choices. However, those reasons should conform to interpretivist evaluation criteria rather than criteria used for positivist research designs, which can present another challenge in the research design review stage.

It is perhaps not too controversial to say that the disciplines of political science and international relations in the United States are dominated by positivist methodologies that emphasize research incorporating unidirectional causal explanations, hypothesis testing, and/or decontextualized knowledge.[34] Of course, there are vast differences in research approaches, both qualitative and quantitative, so we do not mean to paint with too broad a brush. Generally speaking, however, graduate students entering these disciplines are taught how to conduct and evaluate positivist research but are rarely exposed to interpretive research—though this fact is contingent on the graduate program a student chooses. Depending on the student's previous training, this may not necessarily hinder their ability to evaluate interpretivist research. For instance, prior to graduate school, Reiling hailed from a humanities undergraduate program where interpretive approaches were the norm. However, Schwarz's research training trajectory was quite different. Until her second year in graduate school, she was altogether unaware of interpretivist research and thus had no way to evaluate it. Similarly, many scholars in our fields have not been trained in conducting or evaluating interpretive work. This can present significant roadblocks during the research design review process if the reviewer is not properly acquainted with interpretive approaches.

Researchers who adopt an interpretive approach in their research design can tackle the challenge of being methodologically outnumbered by employing a few strategies. The primary one is to be as clear as possible—to explain quite plainly and explicitly the foundations of the research, why the question is important, what the implications are, and how they will conduct the research. Furthermore, interpretivists should anticipate objections to the methodology, though without defensiveness. Interpretive research has made some inroads in political science, and so citing interpretive methodology texts and examples can illustrate the analytical usefulness of an interpretive approach.

In some circumstances, interpretive researchers can also adopt some of the structure and language of positivist research without misleading the reader or sacrificing the epistemological foundations of the project. Reiling successfully used this approach in writing grant applications for scientific foundations. She used a model from a successful quantitative project to translate her own project so that it could be more easily read as "legitimate" science while remaining faithful to interpretivism. Borrowing a grant proposal structure and signposting from positivist work helped Reiling (who was more used to writing in a humanistic style) explain her theoretical foundations and analytic choices so that abduction and reflexivity were legible to an audience unfamiliar with the concepts and in fact became part of the trustworthiness of her research.

One additional challenge we want to address is that of logistical fluidity. A strong interpretivist research design will plan for flexibility and fluidity throughout the process, and this must also extend to the logistical aspects of research. Changes to research questions, concepts, or methods during the research process not only affect the intellectual trajectory of a project; they also may result in unforeseen logistical difficulties. In many cases, the tweaks to a research plan are relatively minor—adding a few interviews or analyses of historical works the researcher did not anticipate. However, in some cases, more significant or even drastic changes may need to be made.

For example, when she began her fieldwork in West Africa, Reiling assumed her French-language skills were up to the task, but quickly realized that was not the case; she did not have the fluency or local knowledge needed to fully engage in formal conversations with her research participants.[35] Because meaning and local knowledge are central to an interpretivist approach, Reiling needed to quickly address her language issue to continue with her research. Taking the advice of some of her research participants, she hired a local tutor, who not only helped improve her French skills but also provided her with information about Côte d'Ivoire that she would not have accessed otherwise. Luckily, early in the research design phase, Reiling had budgeted for unexpected costs like these and also allowed extra time during her fieldwork for unplanned events and encounters. As she found later in her research, her nonfluency lent itself to surprising encounters. She obviously was not French, and therefore no one aligned her with the colonizing country. Her language mistakes actually endeared her to some who were not native French speakers and also provided space for research participants to explain themselves to ensure common understanding; the participants themselves provided the thick description Reiling was seeking. A strong interpretivist research design will strive to build flexibility into the design to mitigate challenges that arise. Such flexibility is even more important today, given the additional challenges to fieldwork due to COVID-19 and the impacts of climate change.

Conclusion

In this chapter we have summarized some of the central components of interpretive research, highlighted how these components shape a related research design, and articulated some of the challenges one may confront when creating a research design for interpretive research. Creating an interpretive research design undoubtedly comes with challenges—some of which a researcher might not encounter if employing other approaches. However, we argue that interpretive research and the resultant findings are critical for understanding political phenomena around the world. Thus, we believe the challenges an interpretivist faces during the design process are valuable and necessary.

Notes

1. Schwarz, "Challenging the Ontological Boundaries of Religious Practices in International Relations Scholarship"; Schwarz, *Faith-Based Organizations in Transnational Peacebuilding*.
2. Reiling, "Pragmatic Scepticism in Implementing the Women, Peace, and Security Agenda"; Reiling, "The Planning and Practice of Feminist Fieldwork Methodologies in Conflict and Post-Conflict Contexts".

3. Scauso, Schwarz, and Lynch, "Training in Critical Interpretivism," 485.
4. Schwartz-Shea and Yanow, *Interpretive Research Design*, 70.
5. Doty, "Foreign Policy as Social Construction," 298.
6. Ackerly, Stern, and True, *Feminist Methodologies for International Relations*.
7. Schwartz-Shea and Yanow, *Interpretive Research Design*, 27–28.
8. Lynch, *Interpreting International Politics*, 22.
9. Wedeen, "Conceptualizing Culture."
10. Lynch, *Interpreting International Politics*, 13.
11. Schwartz-Shea and Yanow, *Interpretive Research Design*, 52.
12. Schwartz-Shea and Yanow, *Interpretive Research Design*.
13. Turner, "Remembering Lee Ann in South Africa," 49.
14. Richardson and St. Pierre, "Writing," 970.
15. Also see N. Brown, "Negotiating the Insider/Outsider Status."
16. Schwartz-Shea and Yanow, *Interpretive Research Design*, 27–28.
17. Schwarz, "Challenging the Ontological Boundaries"; Schwarz, *Faith-Based Organizations*.
18. Schwartz-Shea and Yanow, *Interpretive Research Design*, 27.
19. Reiling, "Pragmatic Scepticism."
20. Yanow, "Neither Rigorous nor Objective?," 109.
21. Schwartz-Shea and Yanow, *Interpretive Research Design*, ch. 6.
22. Schwartz-Shea and Yanow, *Interpretive Research Design*, 49.
23. Shaffer, *Elucidating Social Science Concepts*, 6–10.
24. Yanow, "Neither Rigorous nor Objective," 115.
25. Schwartz-Shea and Yanow, *Interpretive Research Design*, 48.
26. Schwartz-Shea and Yanow, *Interpretive Research Design*, 48, relying on Lincoln and Guba, *Naturalistic Inquiry*.
27. Schwartz-Shea and Yanow, *Interpretive Research Design*, 49.
28. Schwartz-Shea and Yanow, *Interpretive Research Design*, 106.
29. Tickner, "Feminism Meets International Relations," 28–29.
30. Reiling, "Feminist Fieldwork Methodologies," 5.
31. Reiling, "Feminist Fieldwork Methodologies," 8.
32. Reiling, "Feminist Fieldwork Methodologies," 9.
33. Reiling, "Pragmatic Scepticism."
34. Scauso, Schwarz, and Lynch, "Training in Critical Interpretivism," 484.
35. Reiling, "Feminist Fieldwork Methodologies," 6–8.

Recommended Readings

Ackerly, Brooke A., and Jacqui True. *Doing Feminist Research in Political and Social Science*, 2nd ed. London: Red Globe Press, 2020.
    Rich with examples, *Doing Feminist Research* describes feminist, predominantly interpretivist, methodologies in a guidebook to the research process, from ethics to research design to the research process to publication.

American Political Science Association. "Interpretive Methodologies and Methods." Accessed August 16, 2023. https://connect.apsanet.org/interpretationandmethod/.
    A "related group" within the American Political Science Association, the Interpretive Methodologies and Methods website and its accompanying email list is a locus for recent scholarship and ongoing discussions of how to do interpretive research, both conceptually and practically.

Routledge Book Series on Interpretive Methods. Accessed August 16, 2023. https://www.routledge.com/Routledge-Series-on-Interpretive-Methods/book-series/RSIM.

Comprising several slim books, this series from Routledge covers approaches to a variety of interpretive issues, including specific methods, political science subfields, and, yes, research design.

Smith, Linda Tuhiwai. *Decolonizing Methodologies: Research and Indigenous Peoples*, 2nd ed. London: Zed Books, 2012.

Rather than a how-to on researching indigenous communities, Smith foregrounds indigenous researchers to unpack Western forms of knowledge, research, and disciplines. While not explicitly interpretivist, this book unsettles the "voice of authority" and guides scholars toward "getting the story right, telling the story well."

Yanow, Dvora, and Peregrine Schwartz-Shea, eds. *Interpretation and Method: Empirical Research Methods and the Interpretive Turn*, 2nd ed. New York: Routledge, 2015.

Interpretation and Method can be considered *the* encyclopedia for interpretivist methodologies in the social sciences. Each chapter provides insight into research design and methods of data collection and analysis, all with examples from contributors' own research experiences.

References

Ackerly, Brooke A., Maria Stern, and Jacqui True, eds. *Feminist Methodologies for International Relations*. Cambridge: Cambridge University Press, 2006.

Brown, Nadia E. "Negotiating the Insider/Outsider Status: Black Feminist Ethnography and Legislative Studies." *Journal of Feminist Scholarship* 3 (Fall 2012): 19–34.

Doty, Roxanne Lynn. "Foreign Policy as Social Construction: A Post-Positivist Analysis of U.S. Counterinsurgency Policy in the Philippines." *International Studies Quarterly* 37, no. 3 (1993): 297–320. https://doi.org/10.2307/2600810.

Lincoln, Yvonna S., and Egon G. Guba. *Naturalistic Inquiry*. Thousand Oaks, CA: Sage, 1985.

Lynch, Cecelia. *Interpreting International Politics*. New York: Routledge, 2014.

Lynch, Cecelia. "Reflexivity in Research in Civil Society: Constructivist Perspectives." *International Studies Review* 10, no. 4 (2008): 708–721.

Reiling, Carrie. "The Planning and Practice of Feminist Fieldwork Methodologies in Conflict and Post-Conflict Contexts." In *SAGE Research Methods Cases*, 1–12. London: SAGE, 2020. https://methods.sagepub.com/case/planning-practice-feminist-fieldwork-methodologies-conflict-post-conflict

Reiling, Carrie. "Pragmatic Scepticism in Implementing the Women, Peace, and Security Agenda." *Global Affairs* 3, nos. 4–5 (2017): 469–481.

Richardson, Laura, and Elizabeth Adams St. Pierre. "Writing: A Method of Inquiry." In *The SAGE Handbook of Qualitative Research*, 3rd. ed., edited by Norman K. Denzin and Yvonna S. Lincoln, 959–978. London: SAGE, 2005.

Scauso, Marcos, Tanya Schwarz, and Cecelia Lynch. "Training in Critical Interpretivism: Within and Beyond the Academy." In *The SAGE Handbook of History, Philosophy, and Sociology of International Relations*, edited by Andrea Gofas, Inanna Hamati-Ataya, and Nicholas Onuf, 483–497. London: SAGE, 2018.

Schwarz, Tanya B. "Challenging the Ontological Boundaries of Religious Practices in International Relations Scholarship." *International Studies Review* 20, no. 1 (2018): 30–54.

Schwarz, Tanya B. *Faith-Based Organizations in Transnational Peacebuilding*. London: Rowman & Littlefield International, 2018.

Schwartz-Shea, Peregrine, and Dvora Yanow. *Interpretive Research Design: Concepts and Processes*. New York: Routledge, 2012.

Shaffer, Frederic Charles. *Elucidating Social Science Concepts: An Interpretivist Guide*. New York: Routledge, 2016.

Tickner, J. Ann. "Feminism Meets International Relations: Some Methodological Issues." In *Feminist Methodologies for International Relations*, edited by Brooke A. Ackerly, Maria Stern, and Jacqui True, 19–41. Cambridge: Cambridge University Press, 2006.

Turner, Robin L. "Remembering Lee Ann in South Africa: Meta-data and Reflexive Research Practice." *Qualitative and Multi-Method Research* 16, no. 1 (2018): 48–50.

Wedeen, Lisa. "Conceptualizing Culture: Possibilities for Political Science." *American Political Science Review* 96, no. 4 (2002): 713–728.

Yanow, Dvora. "Neither Rigorous nor Objective? Interrogating Criteria for Knowledge Claims in Interpretive Science." In *Interpretation and Method: Empirical Research Methods and the Interpretive Turn,* 2nd ed., edited by Dvora Yanow and Peregrine Schwartz-Shea, 97–119. Abingdon: Routledge, 2015.

PART II
PREPARING FOR THE FIELD

10
Preparing for the Field
The Nuts and Bolts

Hannah Lebovits

Introduction

Before entering the field, researchers prepare themselves and their study for the immersive experience. The field is a dynamic place, and without the right preparations you might miss out on the rich data collection experience, severely impacting the quality and rigor of your work and potentially harming the populations with whom you come in contact. If that sounds stressful and daunting, I'm here to tell you that that's the right feeling to have—for now. However, while we will approach the field with caution and care, this chapter will help reduce your stress level by providing some clear instructions for field preparations. However, because field preparations can vary significantly depending on one's study, this should not be seen as the authoritative text on the matter but rather a starting point from which to begin thinking about the basics of field preparations.

Positionality is important, especially when discussing field research, so I'll present mine here (also see Chapter 3). I'm an interpretivist (see Chapter 5), a woman, and a social scientist who seeks to identify, track, and analyze the ways that people make sense of the world around them—to determine how those meaning-making activities explain larger community development dynamics. My epistemological leanings prompt me to believe that the best way to understand a social phenomenon is to collect and analyze textured, thick, and multilayered data. In line with that approach, my data sets consist of participant observations, direct interviews, oral histories, recorded events, and documents. Because I assume that these items inform each other, my methodological approach is abductive, meaning that I often enter into the research process expecting to find surprising, unpredictable results that fit somewhat into existing literatures and theories but that also generate new theoretical insights.

Over the course of my academic career, I have transitioned from mostly conceptual and content analysis work to more immersive, personal, and intimate research settings for data collection and analysis. I've studied neighborhood political activity in New York City, third spaces in Jewish communities across the United States, adjustments in top-down and bottom-up governance in struggling suburbs in Ohio and Pennsylvania, and the public management of homelessness in Dallas, Texas. On an average day I might engage in some observations, review some documents, interview a few people, and then review old transcripts of interviews to see if there are any new themes or errors. While I do this, I take a lot of notes and write memos to myself about what I've done, said, thought, and anything else that might give me additional insight.

Most of my research is "field-oriented," meaning it occurs within a specific space that contains its own norms and requires entry and exit. As a social constructivist, I consider the dynamic nature of the field site to be a part of the research process as well, noting the socially created meaning of specific spaces and their cultures. But what exactly is "the field," and how can we maximize the value, rigor, and quality of fieldwork? Before we discuss preparing for the field, we must define it, in both traditional and emerging senses.

Defining the Field

Fieldwork differs from other forms of data gathering in three important ways: spatial, relational, and temporal.[1] First, the field involves a physical space. A researcher engages in fieldwork only when they expect that being embedded within a specific context is important to their data collection and analysis processes. They believe, based on their own intuition as well as prior studies of the topic they wish to explore, that being deeply embedded in this physical landscape is somehow necessary to answer their research question. Second, the field is relational. It involves give and take, seeking and finding, and a social contract. It requires the researcher to engage directly with the data they are collecting to make sense of it. Third, the field is bound by time. It operates differently at various times, and accessibility can be limited or expanded at different hours. It shifts over time, with different phenomena occurring as time progresses. The researcher who enters the field must be aware of the temporal shifts in order to best answer their research question.

Throughout the stages of research, the field might include a variety of sublocations as you navigate leads and gain a better understanding of the phenomena you are studying. I refer to these variations as "field sites"; they include all immersive locations in which data is collected. Sometimes I visit one field site prior to a research project to gain a better understanding of the dynamics at play and which specific elements of a broader phenomenon might be relevant to my research question. For you, this might be appropriate at the predissertation stage and might include observations at a meeting, document retrieval at an archive, and/or preliminary interviews. It may also comprise what researchers describe as "soaking and poking,"[2] the period during which researchers lightly observe and investigate a phenomenon before engaging in an intensive research endeavor.

At times, being in the field is the main method to collect data for an entire study, such as when I documented storefront images from various ethnic neighborhoods in Brooklyn.[3] At other times, the field is a place I might visit for insight but is not the location of my primary data collection. For instance, I have spent time at resource centers for homeless LGBTQ youth to gain a sense of which services these youth require, thus setting the stage for the immersive research effort that asks why these services do not often appear on local policy agendas. Or I might visit a field site during analysis or after a research project is complete to add or compare new data to my emerging findings, as I did in an old schoolhouse in Maple Heights, Ohio.[4]

At some field sites, the connection between the researcher and the subject of the research is physically close, relationally deep, and often long-lasting. These sites are the traditional ethnographic field sites that provide a setting for anthropology studies, where a scholar might live with or consistently keep up with people in the cultural group for years at a time to understand the nuances of the group. Other forms of field site visits are significantly less intense, including only a quick observation, a short interview with someone you don't know well, and/or just a few field notes. In some cases, these short visits involve rapid ethnographic assessment procedures, a common field tactic to capture a quick review of a culture, region, or experience.[5] When using a Rapid Ethnographic Assessment Procedure (REAP) approach, the scholar often comes to the site with significant existing knowledge but is time bound and seeks only to illustrate a singular point. Following a REAP approach can enable researchers to capture a succinct understanding of the phenomenon without long-term engagement. Another short field visit might involve retrieving what I call "framing data." These short site visits are not extensive data collection experiences but provide important opportunities to capture information that will be incredibly helpful as you sift through and build your research.

Though most of this chapter will discuss traditional field sites, there are several that are unique and require distinct preparation methods. Before discussing preparations for standard approaches, I would like to turn your attention to some of these nontraditional field sites, which involve processes that are not often discussed in many qualitative research courses. The first is the *digital* field site: areas of interactive social activity that change over time and rest within a fixed place (often a web page/blog, social media platform, or other interactive web-based medium; see also Chapter 28). Digital field sites are a growing area of interest for many qualitative scholars, especially since the global COVID-19 pandemic has made some kinds of physical field research more difficult. There are several complicating factors to the digital field, not the least of which is the limited scope/sight the researcher can capture at any time. Though we cannot discuss the complexities of the digital field here, it is important to note that preparations for the digital field do look different from those in a traditional field setting.[6] Prior to entering the digital field, the researcher should consider outlining those differences and revising the upcoming list accordingly.

Another nontraditional field site is the *participatory action research* (PAR) site, a place where the researcher intends to take part in an effort to cultivate change. In most field sites, our approach as researchers is to minimize the degree of impact we have on the environment. In a participatory action site, however, the researcher is intentionally manipulating the environment, along with others.[7] Material and personal preparations might stay the same, but preparing for social interactions with participants will differ significantly. Especially when the PAR effort is intended to enhance justice for the participants or the populations they represent, the field site can be necessarily tense and more difficult to navigate relationally. Additionally, the PAR strategy reduces the distance between the scholar and participants, which can invite potential boundary concerns for both parties. The participants might forget that they are still being studied, and the researcher may allow their closeness to the phenomenon to complicate their study by losing the distinct thread of the research effort. A researcher who engages in this form of fieldwork will have to adapt the social/relational preparations to better suit the realities they will face.

Last, the *autoethnographic field*, a space in which the researcher is engaged in a scholarly review of a phenomenon they too experience, will require a different set of preparations from the ones outlined here. Autoethnographic efforts are often intentionally draining on the scholar, who is expected to be both distant from their own experiences and living through them, so the relational, personal, and entry/exit preparations will be different.[8] The researcher might also bring into their study other participants who are also autoethnographers of the same phenomenon, which will necessitate two sets of preparation materials. Additionally, the autoethnographic field might require the scholar to mine their own experiences and personal items to identify important data points which require their own set of physical, material, and psychological preparations.

Preparing to Enter a Traditional Field Site

Before preparing to enter the field, researchers should consider several things. First, they should determine whether the field is the primary data collection site and, if so, which fields they will need to access. For example, a researcher who wants to better understand developmental politics to conceptualize the ways parks might be redeveloped for more affluent and largely white populations has several field and nonfield options. They might decide to review city council meeting minutes, interview local leaders over the phone, and review design plans, making their work less field-oriented and more content-collection- and analysis-driven.

Alternatively, the researcher might decide they need to engage in an immersive archival experience to study the historical development and redevelopment of a specific park in the city. The archival field site can certainly be considered a "field" according to our definition, but the process of extracting data from the field site is not intensive. As yet another option, the researcher might decide their research question is best answered by spending long periods of time sitting near park areas and observing a park redevelopment in real time to acquire an intimate view of the process as it occurs. Only in this final plan will they be engaging in a high-intensity field endeavor. So, while all three options are valuable, they vary in their engagement with field sites.

Second, researchers should consider whether their study involves human subjects and requires institutional review board (IRB) oversight. As university IRBs vary in their practices, it is best to meet with your university's IRB coordinator directly to confirm whether the study requires approval. In preparing for this meeting, you might consider whether the field is the primary research site. When the field is not the primary research site, this fieldwork might not require review, as it is not a data collection site for your study directly and, thus, does not constitute "research" in the formal sense. Additionally, if the field site is the core data collection landscape but the research does not involve contact with people or the data collection process is not intended to produce a generalizable data set, the fieldwork might not require IRB approval. Keep in mind that the IRB process can take between several weeks and more than six months, depending on the complexity of your research project and the norms of your academic institution. If your research requires IRB approval, you will likely have to submit an interview protocol, informed consent forms, and other documentation. An approved IRB form can often be amended should your research shift while you are in the field, but if you are concerned that your project might require approval, recognize that this might shift your timeline as well. Again, it is best to reach out to your local IRB coordinator to ensure you are in compliance with the expectations of your institution.

Third, the researcher must identify whether there will be one field site or a variety of fields to traverse over the course of the study. At the onset of the study, considerations are often guided by case selection (Chapter 6) and a variety of research design needs. Similarly, you will have to decide the degree of relational intensity and the amount of time you will or can commit to the field. And you will have to consider entry and exit strategies to ensure you do indeed have access to the field and will be able to leave it when the research endeavor is complete. Entry strategies will involve identifying key gatekeepers—the individuals who provide and restrict access to your subject matter[9]—and securing their support as well as access to the location. Gatekeepers sit at the boundary between your unfettered access to the data collection process and your existing state as someone interested in but not yet deeply connected to the field. There are many types of gatekeepers you will meet over the course of your research efforts.[10] Some of them will already be in the field, while others might be in your institution or somewhere between your institution and your participants. During my digital fieldwork studying responses to COVID-19 in Jewish third spaces,[11] for example, I was exposed to several gatekeepers who presented themselves as knowledge holders yet used their social media accounts to make false claims about specific Jewish populations. Identifying these gatekeepers prior to navigating and preparing for the field helped me to recognize their limits and find ways to access secondary data collection processes.

Exit strategies will include plans to disengage from the field and those who are within it, logistical strategies to leave the physical location, and a plan to ensure that you have not negatively impacted the field site. Prior to entering the field, it is best to decide how you plan to leave it—keeping in mind that changes that occur over the course of your research might necessitate changes to the exit strategy as well. Exit strategies should align with the level of intensity and intimacy necessary to perform your research and may range from saying goodbye to the librarian or determining a follow-up date for any additional, last-minute data collection to packing up an entire apartment abroad, attending a goodbye party, or deleting top-secret location data from your electronic devices. Simply leaving the field because you have extracted enough data is an abrupt approach that will not give you enough time to process your experiences and will likely negatively affect those who remain there after you leave. Additionally, your exit from the field can impact your data collection and analysis, as the last interactions you have with your gatekeepers might include some significant new data point. Do not confuse your exit strategy with your saturation signal, to be discussed shortly.

Once these initial stages are complete, the researcher is ready to actively prepare for the field. There are four key categories to focus on: general preparations, physical and material preparations, social/relational preparations, and personal/psychological preparations. This might seem like a lot—because it is! The field is a dynamic and ever-changing environment. You won't stop preparing for it—or reflecting on your preparations—until you leave. As long as you continue to document your progress and make notes about what you do and how you do it, you will retain the integrity, rigor, and high quality of your research, even as your field, you, and your research adapt.

General Preparations for Field Research

The Game Plan: In my early years as a scholar, I believed that stepping into a field without any expectations was the ideal way to learn to navigate the things I would encounter. As a result of that perspective, I often ended up with insufficient and poor-quality data that led me nowhere specific because I lacked guidance. Since then, I've used a strategy I call "The Game Plan," which helps me maintain a strong understanding of the research goal and remain focused, even if/when the field changes. Ideally, this plan would be written out and editable so that if you need to shift in your approach, you can add additional notes along the way. The game plan might look like a dissertation proposal, a grant proposal, and/or a personal memo. Mine include a purpose statement clearly outlining what I seek to accomplish in the field, a preliminary expectation of when I believe I will hit a data saturation point, a data management plan, and a clear set of research limitations. The purpose statement will be clearly connected to your research study and is a valuable tool to always keep with you, so that you can explain the study and its components to important actors. Presenting this purpose statement can allow an archivist to show you the exact location of a much-needed document. It might give a gatekeeper a sense of who exactly you need to meet. And it might even be the first few sentences of your methodology section, describing for the reader exactly what you came to the field to do.

The preliminary saturation point, something I refer to as the "saturation signal," will serve as your initial goal while in the field. Positivist, grounded theory scholars define saturation as the point at which the researcher has accessed so much data they are unlikely to find anything new even if they spend more time in the field.[12] However, in my research I prefer to use the social constructivist idea of "warranted assertibility"[13] to discuss saturation. In this framework, the saturation signal is the point in an ongoing information-processing effort at which the scholar can assert some findings with confidence. This might be achieved after you collect a number of interviews, cover a specific distance, locate a list of documents, complete an initial exploration of a geographic area, or complete an initial network map. This preliminary saturation point is often based on prior studies and your own intuition and might shift as you collect data in the field and notice new trends or causal lines that need to be explored. As a loose measure, I tend to feel I've hit this point when I can comfortably speak to other scholars who study the same topic or practitioners who are deeply involved in the issue I'm studying, and watch their heads nod when I make claims.

The last two sections of the game plan will likely be more standardized than the first two. The data management plan will include replicable details of how you will collect, preserve, and track your data (see also Chapter 15, "A Plan for Managing and Storing Your Data," and Chapter 13, "Developing a Flexible Data-Collection Plan"). The limitations section will remind you of where your research boundaries are vis-à-vis scheduling, financial capacity, and accessibility. These elements of the plan can follow a traditional data and limitations section format.

Physical and Material Preparations

Basic Needs: Do not forget that you will need to take care of your basic needs while engaging in field research. Clothing, lodging, transit, food/drink, laptop charger and power converter, vaccines/medical supplies, identifying documents, and specific travel items that help you focus will all be necessary. You will need to consider the requirements of the field and the limitations in your Game Plan when deciding which options to choose from. For example, if you are traveling to a field site that is culturally different from your norm, you might have to pack specific items that allow you to integrate into the field without harming or offending those who are indigenous to it. These preparations will require you to research the location and its norms, as well as speak to scholars who have visited similar fields before.

Data storage devices: If you will need certain documentation to enter and exit the field, if you plan to scan documents, and if you will be taking notes, you will need tools to store this information and retrieve it quickly. These types of supplies generally include pens, notebooks, an image-capturing device, an audio-capturing device, a physical storage container (binder or folder), an electronic storage container (internal or external hard drive), and an electronic word-processing system. Most of these tasks can be performed by a single device, but it is wise to have backups and paper copies available, in case of any malfunction or theft.

Communication devices and pathways: Fieldwork might require that you communicate with others in the field as well as those outside of it. You will need to secure phone/internet access prior to entering the field and might even need to get it approved by several people within the field. Keep in mind that some communication networks are more heavily monitored than others, and your field might have its own norms.

Geographic layout: Prior to entering the field, it is important that you know the mapped layout of the field and how you might traverse it. This is true for both physical and digital fieldwork, as the latter involves crossing social networks and pathways and will require flexibility and navigation skills. If your fieldwork is archival in nature, knowing where the resources are within the archival area will significantly improve your productivity and reduce the amount of time you waste searching (on archival work, see also Chapter 22). Many archives now come with digital catalogs, so consider looking through those and keeping a log of which boxes you might need before entering the site.

Social and Relational Preparations

Developing relationships: Field sites always include direct human interactions, whether you are specifically studying those interactions or not. When visiting an old schoolhouse in Ohio to retrieve archival documents,[14] for example, I had to create and navigate a relationship with the volunteer archivist to ensure that the documents I needed were there, to determine appropriate behavior in the space, and to follow up when I had additional needs. Preparing for these interactions is vital to your pre-field game plan and requires a consideration of the ways race, gender, class, and other specific identity markers may enable or harm your ability to build solid relationships.[15] Casual conversations can help build trust and establish relational bonds, so come prepared with things to discuss and share. On the other hand, you should also be prepared to just listen and follow instructions.

When your fieldwork involves direct interactions with participants as well as gatekeepers, it is important that you have answers to fieldwork-specific questions prepared. Common questions are: What are you doing? Why? Why do you think I'm important? Where will my words/experiences be shared with the public? What will you say about me? Preparing answers beforehand as well as practicing them with others who share identity traits with the population you seek to learn from will help you address their concerns head-on. Once participants agree to join a study, topics of discussion outside of the explicit goals of the fieldwork endeavor—such as music, travel, food, and hobbies—can be useful icebreakers and help participants feel more comfortable. Location, time, dress, and recording strategies will all need to be perfected to maximize the efficacy of these interactions. Culture barriers can also impact your ability to build relationships and should be explored in tandem with each other, to make sure that your words accurately convey your sentiments. Many interactions in the field *cannot* be scripted prior to entering, but for those that can, remember to prepare, practice, and perform.

It is also important, while preparing for the field, to consider the lives of those you will interact with and your importance within that framework. Remember that you are inconsequential to most people with whom you interact and are therefore likely to be forgotten, even when people want to speak with and help you. You may need to gently remind people of your appointment/meeting. For research with marginalized persons (see also Chapter 18), you will have considered the ethics of your fieldwork in your IRB application, but you will now also have to consider how important you might become to someone with a limited resource network—and what you will do about that once in the field. Setting down limits before entering the field—such as "I will freely share food but not my phone number"—can vastly improve the likelihood that you will retain those boundaries.

In preparing for the relational aspect of your fieldwork, don't forget to prepare and pack your interview protocol, participant observation templates, and any other tools you've created or acquired to assist you in your systematic collection of data.

Know your norms: Every field comes with its own rules and norms—including the rights of visitors to the field. Before entering, make sure that you are aware of your rights and responsibilities, especially when they differ from those in your regular spaces. For example, when researching democratic socialist activity in suburban and rural areas,[16] I learned about "progressive stack," a practice that gives the most marginalized members in a group the chance to speak before others. I had to be more aware of my own positionality as well as the impact of this norm on the organizational practices. Even in digital spaces, there are rights that may vary, particularly as different countries monitor and regulate social media differently.

Ethical considerations: As scientists, it is important that the work we do does not harm the environments in which we do it. The nature of the field is such that your presence will impact human behavior, so you will have to critically consider your ethical obligations to those with whom you interact, as well as the space you take up. In my experience, one frequently overlooked ethical consideration to address is the degree to which marginalized individuals will be protected from harm and retain power over their narratives. Depending on the level of vulnerability of the research participant, threats to their power and safety can be felt even through your language, dress, and actions.[17] You will have to enter the field with a plan to protect this power and safety.[18]

Accountability mechanisms: Building on the other elements of social/relational preparations, setting up an accountability strategy, such as a reflexivity notebook or frequent check-ins with mentors, before entering the field can help ensure better alignment with your game plan and the social/relational commitments. Other strategies might include using social media to document your activities and reviewing best practices regularly. You can also share this strategy with your colleagues, coauthors, and research participants as an additional check. This is not a conclusive list. What matters is that you create and abide by a strategy that works best for you. No one can force you to consistently behave in accordance with the logistical, relational, and ethical standards you've set for yourself, so you will have to choose to do so and stick with it.

Personal and Psychological Preparations

Obligations: Now that you've thought through your game plan, the material items you need, and the social/relational strategy you'll pursue, it's time to consider how much of yourself you can realistically give to the field. Your personal obligations, such as caregiving, volunteering/

communal activities, and public scholarship, along with your professional obligations, like teaching and administrative work, should be considered.

Financial constraints: Research costs money and can sometimes be funded through internal grants or other forms of funding. However, field research efforts can also be a strain on your personal finances. You might have to pay for basic needs that come up as the field changes; you might be expected to lay out money and then be reimbursed; and you might have to pay for some things on your own (such as childcare/family care). Before heading to the field, consider the personal financial costs and create a personal budget, with a fair amount of flexibility.

Psychological and physiological impact: Fieldwork can be physically, emotionally, and intellectually taxing. Regardless of the environment, the nature of data extraction from an ever changing and dynamic environment makes fieldwork exhausting. It is important to prepare for this reality before going to the field (see also Chapter 26 for more on mental health while in the field). Will you need to regularly connect with a mental health professional? Will you be able to bring along a few items to help center you? To what degree will you allow the field to disrupt your daily routines, such as sleep and exercise? Going to the field with these questions answered will not only reduce the personal difficulties you will face; it will enhance the rigor of your research endeavor as attention to your physical and mental health will strengthen your focus.

***

Fieldwork can be daunting. Field researchers are given a chance to get closer to a phenomenon—and the individuals, institutions, and mechanisms that create and shape it—than others have before us, and we should not take the responsibilities that come with this opportunity lightly. The spatial, relational, and temporal elements of the field make it significantly more dynamic than other sites of data collection and analysis.[19] The field preparations discussed in this chapter will provide a solid basis for good fieldwork and are worth investing in. Trust me, your future self will appreciate it.

Notes

1. Hall, *City, Street and Citizen.*
2. Fenno, *Home Style.*
3. Lebovits, "From Shtetl Streets to Council Seats."
4. Lebovits. "Restorative Revitalization in Inner Ring Suburban Communities."
5. See, for example, Taplin, Scheld, and Low, "Rapid Ethnographic Assessment in Urban Parks."
6. Gabrys, "The Forest That Walks."
7. Kemmis, McTaggart, and Nixon, *The Action Research Planner.*
8. Adams, Ellis, and Holman Jones, "Autoethnography."
9. Andoh-Arthur, *Gatekeepers in Qualitative Research.*
10. Broadhead and Rist, "Gatekeepers and the Social Control of Social Research."
11. Lebovits. "Stop the Spread."
12. For more on this, see Bowen. "Naturalistic Inquiry and the Saturation Concept."
13. Dewey. "Propositions, Warranted Assertibility, and Truth."
14. Lebovits, "Restorative Revitalization in Inner Ring Suburban Communities."
15. Mazzei and O'Brien, "You Got It, So When Do You Flaunt It?"
16. Lebovits, "People, Place, Process."

17. Liamputtong, *Researching the Vulnerable*.
18. Liamputtong, *Researching the Vulnerable*.
19. Rubin, *Rocking Qualitative Social Science*.

Recommended Readings

Rubin, A. T. *Rocking Qualitative Social Science: An Irreverent Guide to Rigorous Research*. Stanford, CA: Stanford University Press, 2021.
> This text is highly accessible and casts a wide fieldwork net. Rubin encourages social science researchers to become familiar with the standardized approaches to doing high-quality research as well as learn to trust their instincts.

Huffman, T. "Pragmatic Fieldwork: Qualitative Research for Creative Democracy and Social Action." *Journal of Social Justice* 3 (2013): 1–24.
> I found this article to be incredibly helpful in my conceptualizations of the field research to which I am increasingly drawn. I think that many scholars engage in this form of research without fully understanding it. Hoffman's text is a must-read for anyone interested in justice-oriented fieldwork.

Sieber, J. E., ed. *The Ethics of Social Research: Fieldwork, Regulation, and Publication*. New York: Springer Science & Business Media, 2012.
> At first glance, this volume might not seem to be relevant for political science, policy, and sociology researchers. However, I have found the chapters to be deeply relatable in their understanding of the relational aspects of the field and believe you will be surprised by how much you learn.

References

Adams, Tony E., Carolyn Ellis, and Stacy Holman Jones. "Autoethnography." In *The International Encyclopedia of Communication Research Methods*, edited by Jörg Matthes, 1–11. Hoboken, NJ: John Wiley & Sons, 2017.

Andoh-Arthur, J. *Gatekeepers in Qualitative Research*. New York: Sage, 2020.

Bowen, G. A. "Naturalistic Inquiry and the Saturation Concept: A Research Note." *Qualitative Research* 8, no. 1 (2008): 137–152.

Broadhead, R. S., and R. C. Rist. "Gatekeepers and the Social Control of Social Research." *Social Problems* 23, no. 3 (1976): 325–336.

Dewey, J. "Propositions, Warranted Assertibility, and Truth." *Journal of Philosophy* 38, no. 7 (1941): 169–186.

Fenno, R. F., Jr. *Home Style: House Members in Their Districts*. Boston: Little, Brown, 1978.

Gabrys, J. "The Forest That Walks: Digital Fieldwork and Distributions of Site." *Qualitative Inquiry* 28, no. 2 (2022), 228–235.

Hall, S. *City, Street and Citizen: The Measure of the Ordinary*. Milton Park, Abingdon, Oxfordshire: Routledge, 2012.

Kemmis, S., R. McTaggart, and R. Nixon. *The Action Research Planner: Doing Critical Participatory Action Research*. Singapore: Springer, 2014.

Lebovits, Hannah. "From Shtetl Streets to Council Seats: What Neighborhood Commercial Areas Teach Us about Urban Politics in Orthodox Jewish Neighborhoods and Why It Matters." Invited lecture, Julis-Rabinowitz Program on Jewish and Israeli Law, Harvard Law School, Spring 2022.

Lebovits, Hannah. "People, Place, Process: Unpacking Local Efforts to Produce Social Sustainability." PhD diss., Cleveland State University, 2021.

Lebovits, Hannah. "Restorative Revitalization in Inner Ring Suburban Communities: Lessons from Maple Heights, OH." *Urban Affairs Review* 59, no. 5 (2023): 1470–1495.

Lebovits, Hannah. "Stop the Spread: Learning from Synagogue Responses to COVID-19." Paper presented at Association for Jewish Studies Conference, Chicago, December 2021.

Liamputtong, P. *Researching the Vulnerable: A Guide to Sensitive Research Methods*. New York: Sage, 2007.

Mazzei, J., and E. E. O'Brien. "You Got It, So When Do You Flaunt It? Building Rapport, Intersectionality, and the Strategic Deployment of Gender in the Field." *Journal of Contemporary Ethnography* 38, no. 3 (2009): 358–383.

Rubin, A. T. *Rocking Qualitative Social Science: An Irreverent Guide to Rigorous Research*. Stanford, CA: Stanford University Press, 2021.

Taplin, D. H., S. Scheld, and S. M. Low. "Rapid Ethnographic Assessment in Urban Parks: A Case Study of Independence National Historical Park." *Human Organization* 61, no. 1 (2002): 80–93.

11
Sampling Hard-to-Reach Populations

Rana B. Khoury

Descriptive Overview

You have considered the "nuts and bolts" of carrying out your fieldwork. Now it is time to think seriously about who you will speak to when you arrive in the field. Political scientists conduct research on a wide range of politically salient populations, including first-movers of protests, undocumented migrants, left- and right-wing activists, rebels, the superrich, refugees, and prisoners. These groups may seem disparate, but they share something in common: they are all hard to reach. What makes a population hard to reach? How do we access them? Should we? I explore answers to each of these questions in the three sections of this chapter.

Researchers use the term "hard-to-reach," often interchangeably with "hidden," to reference (1) a population's characteristics and/or (2) a researcher's access to that population.[1] Though formulated for quantitative researchers, Tourangeau's classification of "hard-to-survey" populations comprehensively captures the first notion: the characteristics of a population that make it hard to study. These populations are:

1. Hard to reach: a label often applied to all such populations, but which can specifically refer to those that are mobile and difficult to contact.
2. Hard to sample: not found on population lists and rare in the general population.
3. Hard to identify or "hidden": their behavior is risky or sensitive.
4. Hard to persuade: unwilling to engage.
5. Hard to interview: lack physical, mental, linguistic, or other abilities to participate.[2]

Some populations might be characterized by multiple such traits, such as undocumented migrants who are absent from formal sampling frames like voter registration lists, whose visibility is purposefully low to avoid risks to their well-being, and who might lack permanent or formal contact information.

A second approach to conceptualizing hard-to-reach populations attends to the position of the researcher and their ability to achieve access to a target population. In particular, the population's "boundaries, characteristics, and distribution" are hard for a researcher to know due to challenges of access.[3] These challenges can result from institutional gatekeepers that erect barriers to researchers, the "structural precarity" of a population such as their lack of transportation, or other limitations to the "access points of researchers."[4]

These dual notions—population characteristics and researcher access—are not mutually exclusive, nor do they necessarily mean vulnerability. The superrich, for instance, are hard to identify because of their own desires to keep their income and wealth private. They also pose challenges to access because of institutional gatekeepers like the Internal Revenue Service that do not share lists with private researchers.[5] The wealthy are *not* difficult for researchers to access because of their precarity, however—hard-to-reach often overlaps, but does not equate, with vulnerability.

In some settings, *entire* populations may be difficult to study because of generalized challenges of access and vulnerability.[6] Under authoritarianism, interviewees are often suspicious, mistrustful, and nervous about speaking to researchers for fear of political repercussions.[7] In conflict environments, difficulties of recruiting interviewees include a "lack of contact information, a lack of system information, cultural differences, legal, political, and ideological constraints, technical accessibility, and, most important, an atmosphere of distrust."[8] Within those broad populations, too, are marginalized groups that are even more precarious and challenging to reach. The obstacles can stack up quickly. Do not despair!

Giving up on talking to people in these challenging contexts is not an ideal option, even if it *is* sometimes a necessary one. In many of these same contexts, quantitative data is "simply not there, or not credible, for politically sensitive issues."[9] As well, if researchers avoid these contexts altogether, there are likely significant knowledge losses on the most pressing of political topics. Finally, hard-to-reach populations often want their voices and stories to be heard,[10] or they risk being silenced by powerful actors.

Fortunately, qualitative field researchers are well-positioned to think about how we might overcome sampling challenges, whether it is ethical to do so, and if so doing is pertinent to our research goals. They often emphasize building trustful relations with people in their research sites in order to understand their lived political experiences. In this chapter, I emphasize their insights, practices, and debates. But before diving in, let's briefly orient ourselves to quantitative approaches to sampling; comparison can help us better understand our own enterprise.

Survey researchers begin with a population universe, say, the United States, and then define their "target" population, such as Americans in the 48 contiguous states. They then obtain a "sampling frame"—a comprehensive and accessible list that represents the target population—from which they randomly sample individuals so that each has a known, nonzero, and equal probability of inclusion in the sample in order for us to make claims about the larger population. When those ideal sampling frames do not exist, especially for hard-to-reach populations, survey researchers deploy a variety of alternatives.[11]

As a qualitative researcher, you are not bound to the strictures of random sampling. Yet some of the ideas underlying probabilistic reasoning might be important for us, too. Often, we want to think about how well the folks we talk to represent the population in which we are interested. Do the research participants whom we manage to reach systematically differ from those we do not? If so, a survey researcher would call that a problem of "selection bias." Relatedly, do the people we do not reach systematically differ from those we do, resulting in "nonresponse bias"? Qualitative researchers are often attentive to these biases, as I will explain below.

At other times, quantitative reasoning is far less pertinent. If we are interested in interpreting the meaning-making, language, power relations, and symbols of actors in a community, the people we talk to need not represent a larger population. These research objectives characterize the work of ethnographers and interpretivist scholars, who enjoy unique access to the hard-to-reach, as the next section shows.

For scholars deploying any of these methods, ethics is an "ongoing responsibility," as Fujii puts it. Ethics is not just a procedural hurdle to overcome at the doors of the institutional review board (IRB) of your institution.[12] Sustained attention to the "dilemma of power," or the "power imbalance between researcher and researched," is necessary.[13] That power imbalance is likely to be asymmetrical in the study of hard-to-reach populations, particularly when they are vulnerable (see also Chapter 18).

Now that we have established basic concepts related to who is hard to reach, let's dive into *how* we might reach them.

State of Practice

How do qualitative researchers access populations that are hard to reach? In this section, I describe a particularly ubiquitous method—snowball sampling—and explain its advantages and drawbacks. I then introduce ethnography.

Snowball sampling, simply put, "consists of identifying respondents who are then used to refer researchers on to other respondents."[14] This simple definition belies a more multifaceted approach, elaborated by Cohen and Arieli. First, researchers use snowball sampling to *locate* a hard-to-reach population. Second, they use the method to *access* members of that population through trustful relations. Third, they *involve* them in the data collection process by using their ties with current and past research participants to gain cooperation from new ones.[15] I address each of these three steps in turn.

First, *locating* the target population entails connecting to the figurative first snowflakes from which snowballs will grow. A researcher can attempt to locate their target population from above, as from the assessments of key informants, elite sources, and records, but these sources may not proffer accurate accounts of populations engaged in grassroots or illicit processes.[16] Hard-to-reach populations should (also) be accessed from below. Qualitative researchers report beginning their snowball samples by showing up at community events, connecting to nongovernmental organizations and community leaders, through the contacts of other researchers or journalists, by sending cold emails, and chatting with folks on the streets.[17]

Second, a researcher cultivates trust in order to gain and sustain *access* to their target populations. What is trust? Norman identifies three interrelated dimensions of trust that are relevant for researchers, especially in contexts of difficult access.[18] "Cognitive trust" relates to rational and knowledge-based trust; this often takes procedural forms promoted by IRBs, including clear explanations of research objectives and protocols for data protection, and obtaining consent. "Emotional trust" is based on personal relations, including those between a researcher and their participants and between participants. "Behavioral trust" is that obtained on the basis of observed actions that develop over time, as a researcher's relationship with their community evolves throughout the research process.[19]

Third, snowball sampling *involves* participants in the research process, as participants connect a researcher to other members of the target population. Participants are likely to recruit participants more proficiently than a researcher could by targeting individual snowflakes without building on the relations of each to others. That's because snowballing leverages relations between participants who have greater knowledge about, access to, and influence over their own community. For example, Pearlman explains the aptness of snowball sampling in her study of "protest cascades" in Syria, the research population for which was Syrian refugees. "Prior field research," she writes, "especially on sensitive topics related to protest, violence, and personal suffering in conflict, convinced me of the value of being introduced to potential interviewees through someone whom they knew and trusted."[20]

As noted in the descriptive overview, populations are hard to reach not (just) because of their own characteristics but also because of the institutional and structural barriers around those populations. Snowball sampling is suitable under both conditions. Indeed, its value is evident when other methods are simply not up to the task of overcoming barriers and accessing hard-to-reach populations. In a survey that intended to deploy probability sampling to reach foreign nationals in South Africa, potential respondents feared identifying themselves to the study team's formal organizational partner; the team ultimately relied on the foreign nationals themselves to snowball them to their desired sample size.[21]

I myself terminated a quantitative survey due to a sudden drop in successful recruitment of respondents in Turkey, one of my field sites. Following a national referendum, the government assumed an apparent mandate to enforce regulations on international nongovernmental organizations operating from its territory. My Syrian respondents, many of whom were employed by those INGOs, became reluctant to participate in the survey despite its multiple protocols intended to protect respondents and gain their "cognitive" trust. All the while, however, my qualitative interview research with the same population, which relied on snowball sampling, was largely unaffected by events. Snowball sampling continued to serve me well because it involved personal relations between me and the participants, and between participants who connected me to one another, garnering me "emotional" and "behavioral" trust throughout my time in the field.

Snowball sampling does have disadvantages. It tends to favor individuals with large networks, resulting in selection bias and a lack of representativeness that can extend through multiple waves of one prosocial individual's acquaintances.[22] Yet snowballing's advantages to researchers studying difficult populations in challenging contexts are so significant that its use "may make the difference between research conducted under constrained circumstances and research not conducted at all."[23] And researchers can proactively minimize its biases. For example, in their study of army deserters in civil war, Koehler, Ohl, and Albrecht varied their "entry points," that is, the individuals at the start of a snowball chain, "in order to minimize the danger of network bias."[24]

Snowball sampling is not the sole sampling method available to qualitative researchers. Purposive sampling instructs a researcher to select participants based on the researcher's own aims and judgments, as opposed to the references that drive snowballing. In institutional sampling, a researcher achieves access to members of an organization associated with the target population. Yet both methods are incomplete ways to access a hard-to-reach population. Purposive sampling implies that potential participants are not hidden from a researcher, who ostensibly enjoys knowledge of and access to them. Institutional sampling is a useful vehicle for gaining access to members of an organization, but they may be systematically different from the wider population of interest. Still, these sampling methods can be useful starting points from which to initiate a snowball sample—or an ethnography.

Ethnography, Bayard de Volo and Schatz contend, can be "the most reliable and practical means of collecting data" in challenging contexts.[25] Ethnography is much more than a sampling method; it is a multifaceted method for both data collection and analysis. Yet insofar as ethnography generally "involves immersion in the place and lives of people under study,"[26] the method is aptly suited to establishing trustful relations with the subjects of our research.

In establishing those relations, ethnographers are purposeful in approaching the question of access.

Pachirat explains that different modes of access differently structure the "line of vision" of a researcher.[27] "Proxy access" is what interview researchers achieve, for example via snowball sampling; it can put us in direct conversation with research participants, but not in direct immersion into their everyday lives. In contrast, "direct access," achievable through participant observation, can offer rich access to relationships and to "rhythms" in the everyday setting of a population of interest.

Pachirat also warns that no form of access is complete. Direct access, Pachirat cautions, necessarily limits a researcher's view of processes not only "from above," but also from other "belows," some of which are in contestation with each other.[28] Such reflexivity regarding how well ethnographers can "approximate" the experiences of a population should be recognizable to quantitative researchers concerned with sampling biases. Pachirat's ethical concern to avoid "silencing" some parts of a population should be noted by all researchers interested in hidden populations.

In the next section, we'll listen to some silences—and shouts too.

Potential Problems

The previous two sections described *who* constitutes a hidden population and *how* qualitative researchers go about reaching them. Now we turn to the question of whether we *should* try to do so. Studying hard-to-reach populations can be, simply put, hard. In the process, researchers will necessarily navigate a series of ethical, methodological, and practical issues, and they will be pressed to make trade-offs along the way. In this final section, I consider some of these issues including limitations on and saturation of data, and the ethics of attempting to reach the hard-to-reach.

To illustrate, I draw on examples from my own study of the Syrian conflict. Specifically, my research has sought to explain how the international humanitarian system affected trajectories of Syrians' nonviolent activism—especially in rebel-held territory and in refugee host states. My fieldwork was based in countries neighboring Syria, primarily Turkey and Jordan, which hosted two of the largest populations of Syrian refugees. Although my project also makes claims about processes that occurred inside Syria, I never ventured into the country's rebel-held regions. This was a simple calculation for me: the risks of physical insecurity and retribution that would have resulted from my presence inside the country—to my interlocutors and myself—were immensely high. The trade-off I made to avoid those risks, however, was one of data limitations.

Other sources of information on actions and events inside the country have been accessible, including through interlocutors in refuge connected to those areas, social media applications, and the extensive gray literature of international aid organizations. Yet I am certain that important knowledge is lost, that we have yet to grasp the localized complexities of the conflict, and that the stories and voices of people on the ground have been overshadowed by powerful military actors and master narratives. My choice not to venture into the conflict zone may or may not fit into a growing trend of "research-related risk aversion" within northern universities, as identified by Duffield. This aversion, Duffield contends, has contributed to "growing remoteness" and a shift to computational methodologies in international and area studies. With these trends, Duffield laments, "ground truth" is lost.[29]

In any case, entering rebel-held territory would have necessitated illicit border crossing—a presumable nonstarter for IRBs. IRBs, notably, are no longer the only university bodies that can draw red lines around human subject research. The kinds of institutional barriers to access that I identified at the start of this chapter are, according to some, growing. As Sluka observes, "safety in the field is increasingly being officially defined as a university controlled and sanctioned affair ... as new or additional committees designed to specifically handle what are deemed risky or dangerous research proposals" are created.[30] These developments are, in his view, regrettable, and represent the securitization of research by powerful institutional actors in the Global North that divorce their ostensible "ethical" judgments from researchers' political imperatives to produce critical studies of state terror, violence, and oppression.

While rebel-held territory was, in my assessment, too hard to reach, a contrasting problem of access arose at the start of my first trip to the field in Jordan. I found myself quite easily accessing the country's largest camp for Syrian refugees, Zaatari Camp. For a time, Zaatari was the center of a great deal of journalistic, academic, donor, organizational, and popular interest. Once I found myself inside the camp, I could easily move from one tent (or caravan) to another, interviewing a larger number of people than I ever have in one day of research. I quickly learned a lesson identified by reflective scholars of displacement: vulnerable populations, like refugees, are not necessarily hard to reach. At this point, I encountered the inverse of the problem identified above: an oversaturation of data.

Some groups of refugees—widely considered vulnerable populations—are relatively easy to reach and "overresearched." Omata explains that refugees associated with "policy relevant" camps, migration routes, conflicts, or other phenomena are often subject to repeated research by academics, aid organizations, and journalists.[31] In such "popular" research destinations, local industries have emerged populated by firms—with widely varying credentials and sometimes questionable practices—to field surveys for outside researchers who step in and out of "exotic" settings as though they are tourists.[32]

The data collected on such overresearched populations may well be biased. One such pathway for bias, identified by Parkinson, occurs when research participants, who have been interviewed repeatedly by nonacademic actors, such as humanitarian workers, regurgitate a narrative to an academic researcher that they have learned is valuable to outsiders.[33] In such settings, accessing a vulnerable population might be relatively easy in practical terms, but the oversaturation of data holds consequences for the analysis.

A third problem—one of ethics—is at play as well. Human subject researchers are implored to *do no harm* to their study participants. One way to avoid harm is to adhere to such IRB protocols as the procedural process of obtaining consent. However, the "dilemma of power" can distort the very meaning of consent.[34] As Masterson and Mourad explain, "even with [a researcher's] best attempts to disclose their intentions and affiliations," extremely vulnerable participants may still believe that refusal to participate could adversely affect their obtainment of benefits, and thus they "may not be able to offer meaningful consent for a research project." Often, these research participants are left frustrated, disappointed, retraumatized, or fatigued, even while researchers benefit professionally from their suffering.[35] These outcomes do not align with a *do no harm* approach.

Ethical questions matter in contending with data limitations as well. Is your access to a hard-to-reach population important enough to put your life, or the lives of others, at risk?

The answer may seem to be an obvious no, as it was for me when I refrained from entering Syria to conduct my dissertation research. But in fact, there can be professional incentives to conduct "extreme" field research.[36] For those researchers who decide to enter conflict zones or other challenging contexts in order to study the hard-to-reach, the kind of reflexivity promoted by Pachirat is necessary. They might find, for instance, that the dilemma of power sometimes tips in the other direction.[37]

How did I proceed with my project in the face of data limitations, saturation, and ethical challenges? That first time I went to Zaatari Camp was also my last time. I adopted an ethnographic sensibility and approached a smaller number of interlocutors in the non-camp settings in which most Syrians resided. I immersed with a refugee family, staying as a guest in their rented apartment for parts of my yearly trips to the field, from where I observed and participated in the rhythms of everyday life in displacement. At the same time, I snowballed through interviewees engaged in political or social activism, who were a small fraction of the overall refugee population often engaged in informal endeavors. As well, I turned my analytical lens on the organizations that structured those activists' potential: international aid organizations. I learned that expatriate humanitarian workers could be quite protective and guarded against academic researchers; they were hard to reach because they were engaged in sensitive field operations, often in competition with other organizations over projects and grants. But as holders of powerful passports and decision-making power over the lives of their beneficiaries and local implementing partners, they were not vulnerable.

These methods were a good fit for my purposes, which included closely tracing the processes that gave shape to Syrians' activism, interpreting the meaning-making of the individuals engaged in it, and grappling with the everyday routines of humanitarian organizations that shaped the livelihoods of large refugee populations through complex institutional mechanisms.

There is knowledge to be gained from your research. I urge you to keep reading to learn how to protect, interview, and analyze the experiences of populations that are hard to reach or vulnerable.

Notes

1. Singer, "Studying Hidden Populations."
2. Tourangeau, "Defining Hard-to-Survey Populations."
3. Singer, "Studying Hidden Populations."
4. Ellis, "What Do We Mean by a 'Hard-to-Reach' Population?"
5. Page, Bartels, and Seawright, "Democracy and the Policy Preferences of Wealthy Americans."
6. Cohen and Arieli, "Field Research in Conflict Environments"; Firchow and Mac Ginty, "Including Hard-to-Access Populations Using Mobile Phone Surveys and Participatory Indicators."
7. Clark, "Field Research Methods in the Middle East."
8. Cohen and Arieli, "Field Research in Conflict Environments."
9. Romano, "Conducting Research in the Middle East's Conflict Zones," 441.
10. Wood, "The Ethical Challenges of Field Research in Conflict Zones."
11. Khoury, "Hard-to-Survey Populations and Respondent-Driven Sampling."
12. Fujii, "Research Ethics 101."
13. Fujii, "Research Ethics 101."
14. Atkinson and Flint, "Accessing Hidden and Hard-to-Reach Populations."

15. Cohen and Arieli, "Field Research in Conflict Environments."
16. Wood, *Insurgent Collective Action and Civil War in El Salvador*.
17. Rana B. Khoury (@rbkhoury), "Folks Who Use Snowball Sampling in Qual Research...," tweet, *Twitter*, April 19, 2022, https://twitter.com/rbkhoury/status/1516466109850873856.
18. Norman, "Got Trust?"
19. Norman, "Got Trust?"
20. Pearlman, "Methods Note for 'Moral Identity and Protest Cascades in Syria.'"
21. Misago and Landau, "Gutters, Gates, and Gangs."
22. Van Meter, "Methodological and Design Issues."
23. Cohen and Arieli, "Field Research in Conflict Environments," 433.
24. Koehler, Ohl, and Albrecht, "From Disaffection to Desertion," 441.
25. Bayard de Volo and Schatz, "From the Inside Out," 269.
26. Wedeen, "Reflections on Ethnographic Work in Political Science," 257.
27. Pachirat, "The Political in Political Ethnography."
28. Pachirat, "The Political in Political Ethnography."
29. Duffield, "From Immersion to Simulation."
30. Sluka, "Too Dangerous for Fieldwork?"
31. Omata, "'Over-Researched' and 'Under-Researched' Refugee Groups."
32. Ghosn and Parkinson, "'Finding' Sectarianism and Strife in Lebanon."
33. Parkinson, "(Dis)Courtesy Bias."
34. Fujii, "Research Ethics 101."
35. Masterson and Mourad, "The Ethical Challenges of Field Research in the Syrian Refugee Crisis," 3. See also Nayal, "Palestinian Refugees Are Not at Your Service."
36. Driscoll and Schuster, "Spies Like Us."
37. Malejacq and Mukhopadhyay, "The 'Tribal Politics' of Field Research."

Recommended Readings

Lake, Milli, Samantha Majic, and Rahsaan Maxwell. "Research on Vulnerable and Marginalized Populations: Final Report of QTD Working Group IV.3." Marginalized Populations (February 13, 2019). American Political Science Association Organized Section for Qualitative and Multi-Method Research, Qualitative Transparency Deliberations, Working Group Final Reports, Report IV.3, 2018. http://dx.doi.org/10.2139/ssrn.3333511

    An essay on the populations that may be considered vulnerable in political science research, which differ from those identified by IRBs, and how we can simultaneously protect them and our data, maintain high ethical standards, and navigate imperatives of research transparency.

Cronin-Furman, Kate, and Milli Lake. "Ethics Abroad: Fieldwork in Fragile and Violent Contexts." *PS: Political Science & Politics* 51, no. 3 (2018): 607–14. https://doi.org/doi:10.1017/S1049096518000379

    A reflection on how conflict-affected contexts can constitute permissive environments in which researchers access, intervene, and (perhaps inadvertently) exploit local populations, and a set of guidelines on how to avoid so doing.

Arjona, Ana, Zachariah Mampilly, and Wendy Pearlman. "Research in Violent or Post-Conflict Political Settings: Final Report of QTD Working Group IV.2." American Political Science Association Organized Section for Qualitative and Multi-Method Research, Qualitative Transparency Deliberations, Working Group Final Reports, Report IV.2, 2018.

    An essay on how researchers can ethically navigate contexts of political violence, protect their data, and contend with three types of research transparency: (1) transparency toward their research subjects, (2) data transparency related to the sharing of evidence, and (3) analytical transparency regarding how that evidence is assessed.

Driscoll, Jesse, and Caroline Schuster. "Spies Like Us." *Ethnography* 19, no. 3 (2017): 411–430.
> A provocative reflection on how ethnographic methods, in combination with incentives for junior scholars to undertake "extreme fieldwork," can combine to resemble—in the eyes of observant locals—spycraft conducted on behalf of a national security state.

Jacobsen, Karen, and Loren B. Landau. "The Dual Imperative in Refugee Research: Some Methodological and Ethical Considerations in Social Science Research on Forced Migration." *Disasters* 27, no. 3 (2003): 185–206.
> A review of methodological practices common in research on refugees, and a call for adopting more transparent and rigorous social science practices in order to make sound descriptive and causal inferences about displacement.

Rodgers, Graeme. "'Hanging Out' with Forced Migrants: Methodological and Ethical Challenges." *Forced Migration Review* 21 (2004): 48–49.
> A rebuttal to Jacobsen and Landau's apparent dismissal of participatory and immersive research practices.

References

Atkinson, Rowland, and John Flint. "Accessing Hidden and Hard-to-Reach Populations: Snowball Research Designs." *Social Research Update* 33 (2001).

Bayard de Volo, Lorraine, and Edward Schatz. "From the Inside Out: Ethnographic Methods in Political Research." *PS: Political Science & Politics* 37, no. 2 (2004): 267–271.

Clark, Janine A. "Field Research Methods in the Middle East." *PS: Political Science & Politics* 39, no. 3 (2006): 417–424.

Cohen, Nissim, and Tamar Arieli. "Field Research in Conflict Environments: Methodological Challenges and Snowball Sampling." *Journal of Peace Research* 48, no. 4 (2011): 423–435.

Driscoll, Jesse, and Caroline Schuster. "Spies Like Us." *Ethnography* 19, no. 3 (2017): 411–430.

Duffield, Mark. "From Immersion to Simulation: Remote Methodologies and the Decline of Area Studies." *Review of African Political Economy* 41, no. S1 (2014): S75–S94.

Ellis, Rachel. "What Do We Mean by a 'Hard-to-Reach' Population? Legitimacy versus Precarity as Barriers to Access." *Sociological Methods & Research*, March 9, 2021, 0049124121995536.

Firchow, Pamina, and Roger Mac Ginty. "Including Hard-to-Access Populations Using Mobile Phone Surveys and Participatory Indicators." *Sociological Methods and Research* 49, no. 1 (2020): 133–60.

Fujii, Lee Ann. "Research Ethics 101: Dilemmas and Responsibilities." *PS: Political Science & Politics* 45, no. 4 (October 2012): 717–723. https://doi.org/10.1017/S1049096512000819.

Ghosn, Faten, and Sarah E. Parkinson. "'Finding' Sectarianism and Strife in Lebanon." *PS: Political Science & Politics* 52, no. 3 (July 2019): 494–497. https://doi.org/10.1017/S1049096519000143.

Khoury, Rana B. "Hard-to-Survey Populations and Respondent-Driven Sampling: Expanding the Political Science Toolbox." *Perspectives on Politics* 18, no. 2 (2020): 509–526.

Koehler, Kevin, Dorothy Ohl, and Holger Albrecht. "From Disaffection to Desertion: How Networks Facilitate Military Insubordination in Civil Conflict." *Comparative Politics* 48, no. 4 (2016): 439–457.

Kubik, Jan. "Ethnography of Politics: Foundations, Applications, Prospects." In *Political Ethnography: What Immersion Contributes to the Study of Power*, edited by Edward Schatz, 25–52. Chicago: University of Chicago Press, 2009.

Malejacq, Romain, and Dipali Mukhopadhyay. "The 'Tribal Politics' of Field Research: A Reflection on Power and Partiality in 21st-Century Warzones." *Perspectives on Politics* 14, no. 4 (2016): 1011–1028.

Masterson, Daniel, and Lama Mourad. "The Ethical Challenges of Field Research in the Syrian Refugee Crisis." *APSA MENA Politics Section Newsletter* 2, no. 1 (2019): 1–5.

Misago, Jean-Pierre, and Loren B. Landau. "Gutters, Gates, and Gangs: Collaborative Sampling in 'Post-Violence' Johannesburg." *Journal of Refugee Studies* 26, no. 1 (2013): 116–125.

Nayal, Moe Ali. "Palestinian Refugees Are Not at Your Service." *Electronic Intifada*, May 17, 2013. https://electronicintifada.net/content/palestinian-refugees-are-not-your-service/12464.

Norman, Julie. "Got Trust? The Challenge of Gaining Access in Conflict Zones." In *Surviving Field Research*, edited by Chandra Lekha Sriram, John C. King, Julie A. Mertus, Olga Martin-Ortega, and Johanna Herman. New York: Routledge, 2009.

Omata, Naohiko. "'Over-Researched' and 'Under-Researched' Refugee Groups: Exploring the Phenomena, Causes and Consequences." *Journal of Human Rights Practice* 12, no. 3 (November 1, 2020): 681–695. https://doi.org/10.1093/jhuman/huaa049.

Pachirat, Timothy. "The Political in Political Ethnography: Dispatches from the Kill Floor." In *Political Ethnography: What Immersion Contributes to the Study of Power*, edited by Edward Schatz, 143–162. Chicago: University of Chicago Press, 2009.

Page, Benjamin I., Larry M. Bartels, and Jason Seawright. "Democracy and the Policy Preferences of Wealthy Americans." *Perspectives on Politics* 11, no. 1 (2013): 51–73.

Parkinson, Sarah E. "(Dis)Courtesy Bias: 'Methodological Cognates,' Data Validity, and Ethics in Violence-Adjacent Research." *Comparative Political Studies*, July 11, 2021, 00104140211024309. https://doi.org/10.1177/00104140211024309.

Pearlman, Wendy. "Methods Note for 'Moral Identity and Protest Cascades in Syria.'" Harvard Dataverse, 2016. https://doi.org/10.7910/DVN/LDUGW0.

Romano, David. "Conducting Research in the Middle East's Conflict Zones." *PS: Political Science & Politics* 39, no. 3 (2006): 439–441.

Singer, Merrill. "Studying Hidden Populations." In *Mapping Social Networks, Spatial Data, and Hidden Populations*, edited by Jean J. Schensul et al., vol. 4, *Ethnographer's Toolkit*, 125–192. Walnut Creek CA: AltaMira Press, 1999.

Sluka, Jeffrey Alan. "Too Dangerous for Fieldwork? The Challenge of Institutional Risk-Management in Primary Research on Conflict, Violence and 'Terrorism.'" *Contemporary Social Science* 15, no. 2 (2020): 241–257. https://doi.org/10.1080/21582041.2018.1498534.

Tourangeau, Roger. "Defining Hard-to-Survey Populations." In *Hard-to-Survey Populations*, edited by Roger Tourangeau, Brad Edwards, Timothy P. Johnson, Kirk M. Wolter, and Nancy Bates, 3–20. Cambridge: Cambridge University Press, 2014.

van Meter, Karl M. "Methodological and Design Issues: Techniques for Assessing the Representatives of Snowball Samples." *NIDA Research Monograph* 98 (1990): 31–43.

Wedeen, Lisa. "Reflections on Ethnographic Work in Political Science." *Annual Review of Political Science* 13 (2010): 255–272.

Wood, Elisabeth Jean. "The Ethical Challenges of Field Research in Conflict Zones." *Qualitative Sociology* 29 (2006): 373–386.

Wood, Elisabeth Jean. *Insurgent Collective Action and Civil War in El Salvador*. Cambridge: Cambridge University Press, 2003.

12
Power Dynamics between Researcher and Subject

Rachel Ayrton

Descriptive Overview

Researchers are a powerful presence in the knowledge they produce. This is particularly apparent in qualitative research, where the self is an instrument in the generation of knowledge.[1] Qualitative research is also a *social* phenomenon: it is through relationships and interactions with research subjects, or participants, that we co-construct knowledge. Into these relationships researchers and participants bring all the baggage of their social positioning, roles, expectations, bodies, and emotions—in other words, their whole selves.[2] That is part of what makes qualitative research so challenging, and so exciting.[3] The dynamics of power that operate in the wider social world enter into research through the social agents who produce it.

Power is one of the most important concepts in social research. Many qualitative researchers approach their work with a democratizing agenda—seeking to create a more just social world—and see the pursuit of more equal research relationships as part of this practice. For those without this normative macro-ethical concern, awareness of power remains important to the localized ethics of professional conduct and beneficence toward participants. It also bears on the quality of research and the data that it produces.

In order to cultivate an awareness of power in qualitative research practice it is first crucial to understand what power is and how it operates. There are numerous theories of power, including Steven Lukes's three-dimensional approach, John Gaventa's account of empowerment, Michel Foucault's theory of disciplinary power, and Pierre Bourdieu's notion of fields of power.[4] I draw on these texts to outline four misplaced assumptions, or myths, about power, which exist in popular wisdom. These provide the way into a working understanding of power and how it manifests in researcher-subject relations to produce research that is of good quality, ethical, and sometimes transformative.

The first myth is that power is something people "have" or possess, and therefore can choose to hoard or share. Instead, theorists of power suggest that it circulates everywhere and can be *exercised*, not possessed. Foucault asserts, "[Power] is the moving substrate of force relations.... [P]ower is everywhere; not because it embraces everything but because it comes from everywhere."[5] Power is complex, always shifting, and features in everyday encounters—including research relations.[6] The question then is not "Who has power?" but "How is power operating in this setting?"

The second myth is that power is invested in certain kinds of people and not others—the "powerful" or the "powerless." Foucault argues that everyone is subject to power—it "comes from below,"[7] facilitating and constraining social action for everyone.[8] Clearly, however, not everyone has access to the same choices or opportunities; there are evident material inequalities in the world. Bourdieu explains the *appearance* that power is located in certain people in his theory of fields of power. Social agents, he suggests, hold positions in social space based on the social, cultural, or economic resources ("capitals") at their disposal. These positions are relative to each other and explain how, although power circulates, people are unequally positioned in relation to it.[9]

The third myth is that people compete over power and exercise it for their own gain. In fact, power is used positively ("power to") as well as to dominate ("power over") and is vital for achieving social goods.[10] Far from competing over power, in my research I have observed participants exercising power to include others, to promote someone else's position or knowledge, or to sideline their own.[11]

The final assumption relates specifically to qualitative research practice: that power is a problem causing bias, so we should strive to eliminate it. However, it becomes clear that power is an inescapable aspect of human existence and affects all relationships, including those between researchers and research subjects.[12] Further, power is deeply relevant to many of the topics that qualitative researchers study. By accepting that power is inevitable and not *necessarily* a bad thing, we open up the possibility of observing its operation as an aspect of knowledge-production and working with it toward social good in the immediate settings of our research and in the wider world.

In response to these observations, I am cultivating in my own practice an approach which I term *power-conscious* research. Power-consciousness involves acting *attentively* and *ethically* toward power in researcher-subject relations. It is being attentive to power through observing its effects in the microdynamics of research relations and using these observations to enhance research findings. In other words, power-consciousness improves the quality and rigor of research. It is ethical in that it seeks to cultivate reciprocal relationships with research participants.[13] This contributes to the localized, internal ethics of research. Further, power-consciousness can have macro-ethical implications. By enlarging spaces for participants as well as researchers to exercise power and extend the boundaries of what is possible,[14] ultimately power-conscious research aims toward greater epistemic justice. In this chapter, I will unpack these ideas and what they mean in practice.

State of Practice

Power relations between researcher and subject/participant shift throughout the course of the research process.[15] I therefore consider the practice of power-conscious research in three stages: preparation; data collection; and analysis, writing, and dissemination. I will draw frequently on examples from my doctoral and postdoctoral research on national identity and belonging among the South Sudanese diaspora in the United Kingdom, which uses focus groups involving photo elicitation and interviews.[16] Qualitative research requires substantial intellectual, practical, physical, and emotional effort from its practitioners, and all these faculties are needed to pursue power-conscious research.[17]

Preparation

Prior to entering the field, a researcher can anticipate and prepare for the power dynamics that may affect their relationships with research subjects. They begin by reflexively evaluating their own positionality and that of their intended participants according to two dimensions: understanding social locations, or "ontological differences,"[18] and understanding positions in knowledge construction, or "epistemological differences."[19] Researchers can then evaluate the way research encounters are designed and structured with a view to enabling negotiation and choice for participants.

Positionality refers to the ways people view themselves and are viewed by others, while the practice of reflexivity involves deconstructing positionality to produce a more honest account of research.[20] Reflexivity is an essential qualitative research practice for considering how power relations may affect the project (for more, see Chapter 3). Reflexively considering the social locations of oneself and potential participants involves thinking *intersectionally*. Intersectionality is one of feminism's most important, and most exported, theoretical contributions. It involves understanding how social agents are subject to multiple categories of social differentiation. These are experienced simultaneously and are mutually co-constitutive, shaping specific experiences.[21] As Nira Yuval-Davis summarizes, intersectionality describes how "multiple axes of social power constitute particular (shifting and contested) social positionings, identifications and normative values."[22] These positionings include social, economic, political, and personal inequalities, which affect the ways of being in the world available to social agents.

Attending to the personal and social characteristics affecting researchers and participants/subjects enables the researcher to anticipate and prepare for the dynamics of power in the research encounter itself, and the research more broadly. When I began my research with the South Sudanese diaspora in the United Kingdom, I considered how age, gender, educational background, and racialized colonial legacies might affect power dynamics. South Sudanese society is traditionally patriarchal and respectful of elders. I anticipated being younger than most participants, and as a married woman in my 30s I did not meet gendered expectations in relation to childbearing. However, my educational position as a doctoral student conferred authority due to the status of education in South Sudanese and British cultures. Further, I was conscious of Britain's role in the colonization of Sudan and the historical racialized differentiation between myself (a white British citizen) and participants along these lines; however, I was unsure whether this would function as a source of privilege or contempt. I entered the field conscious of these tensions and alert to how the dimensions of positionality I had reflexively identified may shape nascent research relationships.

In addition to personal and social characteristics, parties in research may have (or have had) particular roles that imply power differences. For example, Su Jung Um interviewed teachers whom she had previously instructed as part of their training. In one case, she inadvertently slipped into her former instructor role of evaluating teachers' practice. One participant interpreted this as "advice" and reflected on her need to improve aspects of her teaching. Um had not intended to prompt self-critique and points to how formal roles can shape the dynamics of power in interactions.[23] These examples show how contextual and comparative the reflexive process is. It involves identifying the aspects of social differentiation that are likely to be the most pertinent given who the researcher is, who the intended participants are, and what the topic of research is.

The researcher and participant also occupy *epistemological* locations—that is, roles in the production of knowledge.[24] Being a researcher or research participant is itself an identity position with implications for power relations between them. These roles structure a kind of "formal power" into the research encounter and can be exercised in practice to reinforce, adapt, or breach expectations.[25] The implications of epistemological location depend on the context of the inquiry, the institutional setting, and the motivations of the researcher and participant.[26] Different social and cultural contexts shape the attitudes and behaviors that "researcher" and "research participant" roles induce, depending on how these parties are constructed as "experts" and with what consequences. The institution(s) the research is situated within—*which* university, public body, or voluntary sector organization—and how it is perceived can have a material impact. Finally, while researchers and research participants often share a commitment to creating knowledge on the topic, people conduct or take part in research for many reasons, and it is important to reflexively consider how this too will feed into power dynamics and the knowledge produced.

Importantly, intersectional facets of positionality—both personal and social characteristics and epistemological roles—are *co-constitutive*: they do not exist in isolation or act alone. Instead, it is the *interplay* of these categories that produces unique consequences for the power dynamics of research.[27] The way this works in practice is often ambiguous and unpredictable: it is impossible to fully anticipate which aspects of social positioning will be relevant and how these will be mobilized in practice. Nevertheless, reflexivity provides a baseline understanding of the unequal contexts in which the research is taking place. A useful first step is to write down potential sources of differentiation in a table or mind map, detailing possible impacts on the research relationship and implications for the research design and its expression on an ethics application form. This reflexive discipline equips the power-conscious qualitative researcher to observe, and analyze, the operation of power in practice.

During Data Collection

In data collection, hypothetical power relations are actualized in real relationships. The guiding principle for the power-conscious researcher in this phase is to use the resources at their disposal to create as expansive a space as possible for the participant to exercise power—as Clarissa Hayward puts it, freedom to shape the limits of what is possible.[28] Epistemological locations tend to give the researcher a monopoly on the exercise of power. At the extreme, this can result in an extractive and oppressive relationship. By managing the conditions of research to enable participants to exercise power too, research can proceed in more democratic spaces (an ethical practice), enabling the researcher to observe how participants use power, enriching the data. In practice, this means cultivating a deep respect for participants' autonomy and expertise, attentive listening, and adapting to offer flexibility and choice.

Data collection begins by recruiting participants and negotiating the terms of their involvement. The researcher's role is to identify and describe aspects of the study most relevant to the participant. I investigate national identity—a politically sensitive topic—and therefore discuss data management and possible limits to anonymity with particular care. Research encounters are not natural: the researcher designs them. Understanding this opens up scope for negotiation according to participants' preferences. Such choices may include the location, duration, or format of the research encounter. In recent interviews I have, at participants' request, enabled joint rather than individual interviews, shared interview questions before seeking consent, and accepted written responses in light of concerns over audio recording. Introducing variety into the forms of data production increases the analytical workload; however, when participants are comfortable with the terms of their involvement, they relax and share more freely. Further, through this negotiation we have established mutually respectful relationships, which boosts the immediate ethics of the project and my longer-term work with this community. A willingness to subject one's plans to a participant's preferences reflects a commitment to reciprocity in researcher-subject relations, "doing research 'with' instead of 'on.'"[29] It establishes a flexible power arrangement,[30] which is likely to carry over into data collection.

In the research encounter itself, the researcher needs to be attentive to power—how the potential scenarios appraised in advance manifest in practice. As Um has observed, interviews (and other qualitative techniques) are not fully conscious dialogs—people bring their baggage with them.[31] It is not always possible from moment to moment to evaluate what is going on in the constantly shifting power relations and to make considered responses. Nevertheless, remaining attuned to the mobilities of power is a skill that can be cultivated through preparation and practice.

Orit Karnieli-Miller, Roni Strier, and Liat Pessach have suggested that, in the research encounter, participants exercise considerable power as they hold the knowledge and experiences that the researcher needs.[32] However, Katja Vähäsantanen and Jaana Saarinen have instead described the interaction between researchers and participants as a "dance,"[33] where power is constantly in motion as both parties respond to each other and the topic, which sets the tune. Drawing on their interview-based study and my focus group research,[34] Table 12.1 lists some strategies or behaviors[35] that researchers and participants enact in research encounters, often unconsciously, which are indicative of shifting power.

Being attuned to ways power shifts within research encounters can help the researcher know how to respond with respect for participants' boundaries. Ethics is also about self-care and consideration of third parties (e.g., in focus group discussions or where a research assistant is involved). Although the modus operandi of power-conscious research is to

Table 12.1 Behaviours Indicative of Shifting Power in Research Encounters

Emphasizing similarities or differences with the other
Mitigating similarities or differences with the other
Drawing boundaries around identity groups to include/exclude the other
Self-disclosure (e.g., personal story or revealing expertise)
Offering or ascribing a position to oneself or the other
Accepting or rejecting a position offered
Overt negotiations over control (e.g., topic of conversation, timekeeping)
Asking questions
Changing the subject
Silence
Minimizing (short answers)
Maximizing (long answers, possibly evading the question)
Testing or instructing
Defending or contesting the "rules" of the interaction (e.g., turn-taking)
Self-deprecation or aggrandizement

Sources: Drawn from Vähäsantanen and Saarinen, "The Power Dance in the Research Interview"; Ayrton, "The Micro-dynamics of Power and Performance in Focus Groups."

acknowledge and observe power dynamics from a nondominatory stance, the researcher may need to be assertive to safeguard the space for all who occupy it in exceptional situations where someone's behavior adversely affects the well-being of others. In focus groups with the South Sudanese diaspora, I usually take a low-key approach to facilitation, responding to groups' self-moderation. However, I once mobilized my role as "chair" when one participant was persistently ignoring others' feedback that he was dominating the discussion, to their growing exasperation. On other occasions, I have shifted the topic or initiated an activity following the discussion of harrowing events because I perceived the emotional repercussions for others and myself.

To nurture awareness of power dynamics, it can be useful to keep a research diary or (where there are research assistants or co-researchers) undertake verbal collective reflexivity immediately after the encounter. In either format, one can note what felt easy, what felt difficult, and how to account for what happened.[36] These valuable observations can help shape future interactions with participants. They can also assist in the transition to analysis.

Analysis, Writing, Dissemination

In data analysis, the researcher has time to assess how power operated in research encounters, what implications this has for the knowledge created, and what to do about this. This builds on the groundwork undertaken so far by analyzing the microdynamics of power alongside cultures of silence and considering the ethics of representation in writing and dissemination.

During analysis, it is possible to identify which categories of power differentiation were in fact salient to participants and how this manifested. For example, in my early research with the South Sudanese diaspora, I found that in their comments participants juxtaposed my status as a nonmigrant and representative of the cultural majority in the United Kingdom with their experiences of displacement and exclusion to strengthen their arguments.[37] More recently, I interviewed participants while pregnant. My embodied fulfillment of gendered cultural norms evoked warmth, compassion, and a sense of solidarity, including attention to my comfort and offering friendly advice. My epistemological role as a researcher was tempered by my embodied personal and social role as an expectant mother—a more benign and vulnerable presence, in their eyes—which helped to establish trust early in the interview. Which categories come to the fore, which do not, and how these positions are used are significant aspects of interpreting data once the interplay between power and knowledge generation is acknowledged. The microdynamics of power are evident when participants uphold, contest, or abandon the "rules" of the encounter; in what resources they draw on to confer (or relinquish) authority to their contributions; and how they redraw boundaries to include or exclude others.[38] While these momentary, everyday movements of power might seem insignificant, they echo how power relations in the wider world are structured, which is often relevant to the topic of research and adds an additional dimension to the analysis.

Beyond expressions of power in talk and action, what is *not* said can be revealing. Paulo Freire argued that cultures of silence emerge when oppressed peoples internalize the image and guidelines of the oppressor and lack the consciousness of their position necessary for resistance.[39] As Foucault observed, "[T]he perfection of power should tend to render its actual exercise unnecessary";[40] or, in Bourdieu's terminology, symbolic violence involves both domination and complicity.[41] Submissive silence can be expressed through resignation, excessive fatalism, self-deprecation, apathy, or inability to conceive of alternatives.[42] In a previous study of mothers' experiences of medical care in South Sudan,[43] a number of participants expressed distrust in the health system, a severely underresourced sector that prevented medical professionals from fulfilling their duty of care to patients. Faced with no alternative, some mothers expressed the resigned and fatalistic viewpoint "We just hope."

Power-consciousness continues into the writing and dissemination of research. At this juncture the researcher becomes the storyteller: they wrest control and ownership of the story from participants.[44] The "politics of the gaze" becomes paramount—considering who benefits from our representations and how the "other" is invented through our writings.[45] Locally, research participants (or those like them) may be left feeling a sense of injury, misrepresentation, or exploitation. Globally, research is not necessarily benign—it feeds into the construction and re-creation of modernity. Modernity is colonial, and thus built on systematic racism and sexism.[46] In knowledge-generation, "epistemic violence" can occur when certain groups' right to speak is marginalized and their knowledges disappear due to the dominance of other (usually Western) ways of knowing.[47] This involves "eliminating knowledge, damaging a given group's ability to speak, being listened to and being heard, and unequally distributing intelligibility."[48] Conversely, research can support "epistemic justice," which works against these trends and is the quest of those seeking to decolonize knowledge.[49] Power-conscious researchers consider carefully the moral weight of representing the other.

This hefty ethical burden becomes lighter by inviting participants into the analysis and presentation of research.[50] Institutional constraints (particularly for those pursuing a qualification) or the limits of a participant's availability and interest can restrict involvement. It can also cause practical and ethical complications.[51] Nevertheless, researchers can offer participants access to their transcripts, invite comments on emerging themes, or share drafts of outputs. In my current postdoctoral research I collaborate with a South Sudanese advisory group to steer and direct the research. I share transcripts with interviewees (and will edit them if asked), and I hope to engage in participatory analysis and collaborative writing with advisory group members. Others have found that participants continue to be "present" and influence the researcher during the writing process, even when they are not directly involved.[52] By whatever means, the implications of research outputs for both local ethics and wider structures of oppression deserve consideration. As Claudia Brunner asserts, "It is high time we started to unlearn privileges of geopolitical location, race, class, gender, sexuality, ability, and other categories that circumscribe who and where we are in the academic field. Understanding epistemic violence is a prerequisite for initiating this process, both for the marginalized and for the privileged voices in the field, and for all of those who, along different categories, potentially happen to find themselves in both groups."[53]

Potential Problems

The approach to power between researcher and subject that I have outlined presents a number of issues. First, this flexible approach involving negotiation with participants around how research is conducted can make gaining ethical consent challenging. Empirical work usually requires approval from an institutional review board in a university or public institution. This involves presenting a detailed description of what the research is about and how it will be conducted. In my experience this is an invaluable process—the more I put into it, the more I get out of it. However, the ethics process requires the researcher to commit to a certain research design before engaging with participants. How, then, can flexibility be achieved?

As both an applicant to and a former member of a faculty research ethics committee, I find reviewers have fewer "red lines" as to what is allowable than we might think. By providing a detailed description of the intended participants, considering in advance possible alternative approaches, and making the case for this range of options, it is possible to gain agreement to flexibility. Involving potential participants in early research design can help to anticipate participants' preferences—for example, codesigning topic guides and sampling strategies and reviewing ethics forms together. It can also be helpful when stating, for example, the number of participants or the duration of research encounters to offer a range, rather than committing to a figure absolutely. Beyond that, it is a judgment call whether a change emerging in data collection is within the parameters of the ethics permission granted (e.g., sharing a question schedule with a participant in advance of an interview) or whether it exceeds those parameters (e.g., undertaking observation instead of or in addition to interviews) and therefore requires the submission of a revision. Flexibility adds an additional administrative burden on the researcher, but the benefits to the research relationship are significant.

Second, the question of power in research relationships relates to debates over the relative merits of being an "insider" or "outsider" to participants' identity communities. Commonly, insider status is viewed as an advantage: some have found that when the researcher shares experiences or identities with participants they feel more comfortable and share more authentically.[54] Alternatively, interpreters or research assistants who match participants' language and/or culture can act as cultural mediators or brokers.[55] However, being an outsider also has advantages, as participants are less likely to take knowledge for granted and may offer deeper explanations.[56] As we have seen, differences and disagreements can be productive.[57] What should be clear from the approach outlined above is that "insider" and "outsider" are *relative* and *negotiable* categories.[58] Researchers (and research assistants) are often both insiders and outsiders simultaneously,[59] depending on what facet of social or cultural positioning is in focus. An intersectional approach enables the researcher to consider where commonalities and differences lie, how these shape power relations, and, ultimately, the knowledge that is produced.

Finally, it is worth revisiting the question of whether the researcher should try to reduce power differentials. On one hand, I have argued that power inevitably circulates in research and it is neither necessary nor desirable to eliminate it. On the other hand, I have suggested creating spaces where participants as well as researchers may exercise power, which seems to suggest some degree of "leveling up." Practitioners of culturally responsive research value acknowledging social and cultural positions and consider how to minimize distance between researchers and participants.[60] This is a natural aspect of relationship-building which will feature in nascent research relationships. Care is needed, however, to avoid a mismatch between a sense of informality and equality in the research relationship and the way the data is ultimately used, which could reinforce or exacerbate the very inequalities that have been superficially mitigated when gathering data.[61] Ben-Ari and Enosh have helpfully offered a third way between the aspiration to equity and the alternative of exploitation. By approaching research relationships through the lens of reciprocity, we can view knowledge production as a "joint venture."[62] In this way, differences are acknowledged and power continues to circulate, but within the context of a relationship founded on mutual recognition and respect.

In this chapter I have argued for a conception of power as something that people exercise but do not possess, that everyone is subject to (although people may be unequally positioned in relation to it), and that is not only used to dominate but also directed toward social goods. Power is ever-present in social relationships and is not something we can eliminate from research. Nor should we want to: attending to the dynamics of power adds a rich seam to the knowledge we generate. Power-conscious research involves *attending* to power and acting *ethically* in relation to it—resisting domination and drawing out the potential for good, both within the immediate context of the research and through its broader implications for society. Cultivating reciprocal relationships and opening up spaces that allow both researcher and participant to shape the limits of what is possible provide a foundation on which stones of epistemic justice can be laid.

Notes

1. Cannella, "Qualitative Research as Living Within/Transforming Complex Power Relations."
2. Hordge-Freeman, "'Bringing Your Whole Self to Research.'"
3. Mason, *Qualitative Researching*.
4. Foucault, *The History of Sexuality*; Gaventa, *Power and Powerlessness*; Bourdieu, "Social Space and Symbolic Power"; Sadan, *Empowerment and Community Planning*.
5. Foucault, *The History of Sexuality*, 93.
6. Um, "The Chimera."
7. Foucault, *The History of Sexuality*, 94.
8. Hayward, "De-facing Power," 12.
9. See Bourdieu, "The Forms of Capital"; Bourdieu, "Social Space and Symbolic Power"; Swartz, *Culture and Power*, ch. 6; Ayrton, "The Micro-dynamics of Power and Performance in Focus Groups."
10. Gaventa and Cornwall, "Power and Knowledge"; Hayward, "De-facing Power."
11. Ayrton, "The Micro-dynamics of Power and Performance in Focus Groups."
12. Foucault, *Discipline and Punish*; Paechter, "Power, Knowledge and the Confessional in Qualitative Research"; Hayward, "De-facing Power"; Gaventa and Cornwall, "Power and Knowledge."
13. Ben-Ari and Enosh, "Power Relations and Reciprocity."
14. Hayward, "De-facing Power."
15. Karnieli-Miller, Strier, and Pessach, "Power Relations in Qualitative Research"; Edwards and Alexander, "Researching with Peer/Community Researchers"; Ozano and Khatri, "Reflexivity, Positionality and Power in Cross-Cultural Participatory Action Research with Research Assistants in Rural Cambodia."
16. Ayrton, "The Micro-dynamics of Power and Performance in Focus Groups."
17. Mason, *Qualitative Researching*.
18. Ben-Ari and Enosh, "Power Relations and Reciprocity."
19. Ben-Ari and Enosh, "Power Relations and Reciprocity."
20. Ozano and Khatri, "Reflexivity, Positionality and Power in Cross-Cultural Participatory Action Research with Research Assistants in Rural Cambodia."
21. Lutz, Herrera Vivar, and Supik, "Framing Intersectionality."
22. Yuval-Davis, "Situated Intersectionality and Social Inequality," 96.
23. Um, "The Chimera."
24. Karnieli-Miller, Strier, and Pessach, "Power Relations in Qualitative Research."
25. Vähäsantanen and Saarinen, "The Power Dance in the Research Interview."

26. Karnieli-Miller, Strier, and Pessach, "Power Relations in Qualitative Research."
27. Vähäsantanen and Saarinen, "The Power Dance in the Research Interview.
28. Hayward, "De-facing Power."
29. Pillow, "Confession, Catharsis, or Cure?," 179; Ben-Ari and Enosh, "Power Relations and Reciprocity." For more on this, see Chapter 14, on collaborative research designs.
30. Ozano and Khatri, "Reflexivity, Positionality and Power in Cross-Cultural Participatory Action Research with Research Assistants in Rural Cambodia."
31. Um, "The Chimera."
32. Karnieli-Miller, Strier, and Pessach, "Power Relations in Qualitative Research."
33. Vähäsantanen and Saarinen, "The Power Dance in the Research Interview."
34. Ayrton, "The Micro-dynamics of Power and Performance in Focus Groups."
35. Vähäsantanen and Saarinen, "The Power Dance in the Research Interview" use the term "tactics," which I find problematic because it implies a competitive style of relationship whereby someone will ultimately "win." Power-conscious research involves fostering reciprocal relationships where researcher and researched collaborate in as equitable a way as possible to achieve a shared interest: the production of knowledge on a particular topic.
36. Pillow, "Confession, Catharsis, or Cure?"; Ozano and Khatri, "Reflexivity, Positionality and Power in Cross-Cultural Participatory Action Research with Research Assistants in Rural Cambodia."
37. Ayrton, "The Micro-dynamics of Power and Performance in Focus Groups."
38. See Ayrton, "The Micro-dynamics of Power and Performance in Focus Groups" for a detailed analysis drawing on Bourdieu's theory of fields of power.
39. Freire, *Pedagogy of the Oppressed*; Freire, *Cultural Action for Freedom*.
40. Foucault, *Discipline and Punish,* 201; cited in Paechter, "Power, Knowledge and the Confessional in Qualitative Research," 79.
41. Ganuza, Karlander, and Salö, "A Weave of Symbolic Violence."
42. Freire, *Pedagogy of the Oppressed*; Freire, *Cultural Action for Freedom*; Gaventa, *Power and Powerlessness*.
43. Ayrton, "Putting Her Life in Their Hands."
44. Karnieli-Miller, Strier, and Pessach, "Power Relations in Qualitative Research."
45. Pillow, "Confession, Catharsis, or Cure?," 175; Castro-Gómez, "The Social Sciences, Epistemic Violence, and the Problem of the Invention of the Other."
46. Bhambra, *Rethinking Modernity*; Brunner, "Conceptualizing Epistemic Violence."
47. Spivak, "Can the Subaltern Speak?"; Dotson, "Tracking Epistemic Violence, Tracking Practices of Silencing."
48. Brunner, "Conceptualizing Epistemic Violence," 202.
49. Meghji, *Decolonizing Sociology*.
50. Rodriguez et al., "Culturally Responsive Focus Groups."
51. See Karnieli-Miller, Strier, and Pessach, "Power Relations in Qualitative Research," 283–284 for a discussion of the issues surrounding involving participants in the validation of research findings.
52. Um, "The Chimera."
53. Brunner, "Conceptualizing Epistemic Violence," 208–209.
54. Fallon and Brown, "Focusing on Focus Groups"; Rodriguez et al., "Culturally Responsive Focus Groups."
55. Ayrton, "Putting Her Life in Their Hands"; Stapleton, Murphy, and Kildea, "Insiders as Outsiders."
56. Jok, "Power Dynamics and the Politics of Fieldwork under Sudan's Prolonged Conflicts"; Ayrton, "The Micro-dynamics of Power and Performance in Focus Groups."
57. Ben-Ari and Enosh, "Power Relations and Reciprocity"; Vähäsantanen and Saarinen, "The Power Dance in the Research Interview."
58. Ayrton, "The Micro-dynamics of Power and Performance in Focus Groups."

59. Edwards, "A Critical Examination of the Use of Interpreters in the Qualitative Research Process"; Edwards and Alexander, "Researching with Peer/Community Researchers"; Ozano and Khatri, "Reflexivity, Positionality and Power in Cross-Cultural Participatory Action Research with Research Assistants in Rural Cambodia."
60. Rodriguez et al., "Culturally Responsive Focus Groups."
61. Karnieli-Miller, Strier, and Pessach, "Power Relations in Qualitative Research."
62. Ben-Ari and Enosh, "Power Relations and Reciprocity," 427.

Recommended Readings

Sadan, Elisheva. *Empowerment and Community Planning*. Translated by Richard Flantz. Self-published, 2004. http://www.mpow.org/elisheva_sadan_empowerment.pdfChapter 1 "Theories of Power" provides an accessible and thorough introduction to a range of theories of power.

Foucault, Michel. *The History of Sexuality, Volume 1*. Translated by Robert Hurley. New York: Pantheon Books, 1978.
   See especially chapter 2, "Method."

Bourdieu, Pierre. "Social Space and Symbolic Power." *Sociological Theory* 7, no. 1 (1989): 14–25.
   A concise introduction to Bourdieu's theory of fields of power. For an overview, see Swartz's *Culture and Power*, ch. 6; for an application, see Ayrton, "The Micro-dynamics of Power."

Karnieli-Miller, Orit, Roni Strier, and Liat Pessach. "Power Relations in Qualitative Research." *Qualitative Health Research* 19, no. 2 (2009): 279–289.
   This useful article takes a developmental approach to power relations in research and combines the desire to democratize qualitative research with consideration of the methodological and ethical challenges this brings.

Ben-Ari, Adital, and Guy Enosh. "Power Relations and Reciprocity: Dialectics of Knowledge Construction." *Qualitative Health Research* 23, no. 3 (2012): 422–429.
   Gives a good overview of approaches to power in researcher-subject/participant relations in different research paradigms. The authors draw on dialectical thinking to value the role of differences in knowledge-creation and the norm of reciprocity in research relations.

References

Ayrton, Rachel. "The Micro-dynamics of Power and Performance in Focus Groups: An Example from Discussions on National Identity with the South Sudanese Diaspora in the UK." *Qualitative Research* 19, no. 3 (2019): 323–339.

Ayrton, Rachel. "Putting Her Life in Their Hands: A Methodological and Substantive Exploration of Factors Affecting South Sudanese Mothers' Trust in Medical Professionals Responsible for Their Family's Care" (MSc diss., University of Southampton, 2012).

Ben-Ari, Adital, and Guy Enosh. "Power Relations and Reciprocity: Dialectics of Knowledge Construction." *Qualitative Health Research* 23, no. 3 (2012): 422–429.

Bhambra, Gurminder. *Rethinking Modernity: Postcolonialism and the Sociological Imagination*. Basingstoke: Palgrave Macmillan, 2007.

Bourdieu, Pierre. "The Forms of Capital." In *Handbook of Theory and Research for the Sociology of Education*, edited by J. Richardson, 241–258. Westport, CT: Greenwood, 1986.

Bourdieu, Pierre. "Social Space and Symbolic Power." *Sociological Theory* 7, no. 1 (1989): 14–25.

Brunner, Claudia. "Conceptualizing Epistemic Violence: An Interdisciplinary Assemblage for IR." *International Politics Reviews* 9 (2021): 193–212.

Cannella, Gaile S. "Qualitative Research as Living Within/Transforming Complex Power Relations." *Qualitative Inquiry* 21, no. 7 (2015): 594–598.

Castro-Gomez, Santiago. "The Social Sciences, Epistemic Violence, and the Problem of the Invention of the Other." *Nepantla* 3, no. 2 (2002): 269–285.

Dotson, Kristie. "Tracking Epistemic Violence, Tracking Practices of Silencing." *Hypatia* 26, no. 2 (2011): 236–257.

Edwards, Rosalind. "A Critical Examination of the Use of Interpreters in the Qualitative Research Process." *Journal of Ethnic and Migration Studies* 24, no. 1 (1998): 197–208.

Edwards, Rosalind, and Claire Alexander. "Researching with Peer/Community Researchers: Ambivalences and Tensions." In *The Sage Handbook of Innovation in Social Research Methods*, edited by Malcolm Williams and William Paul Vogt, 269–292. Los Angeles: Sage, 2011.

Fallon, Grahame, and Reva Berman Brown. "Focusing on Focus Groups: Lessons from a Research Project Involving a Bangladeshi Community." *Qualitative Research* 2, no. 2 (2002): 195–208.

Fanon, Frantz. *The Wretched of the Earth* (1965). Translated by Constance Farrington. London: Penguin Books, 2001.

Foucault, Michel. *Discipline and Punish: The Birth of the Prison*. Translated by Alan Sheridan. New York: Vintage Books, 1977.

Foucault, Michel. *The History of Sexuality, Volume 1*. Translated by Robert Hurley. New York: Pantheon Books, 1978.

Freire, Paulo. *Cultural Action for Freedom*. Harmondsworth: Penguin Books, 1972.

Freire, Paulo. *Pedagogy of the Oppressed* (1970). Translated by Myra Bergman Ramos. London: Penguin, 2017.

Ganuza, Natalia, David Karlander, and Linus Salö. "A Weave of Symbolic Violence: Dominance and Complicity in Sociolinguistic Research on Multilingualism." *Multilingua* 39, no. 4 (2019): 451–473.

Gaventa, John. *Power and Powerlessness: Quiescence and Rebellion in an Appalachian Valley*. Urbana: University of Illinois Press, 1980.

Gaventa, John, and Andrea Cornwall. "Power and Knowledge." In *Handbook of Action Research: Participative Inquiry and Practice*, edited by Peter Reason and Hilary Bradbury, 70–80. London: Sage, 2001.

Hayward, Clarissa Rile. "De-facing Power." *Polity* 31, no. 1 (1998): 1–22.

Hordge-Freeman, Elizabeth. "'Bringing Your Whole Self to Research': The Power of the Researcher's Body, Emotions, and Identities in Ethnography." *International Journal of Qualitative Methods* 17, no. 1 (2018): 1–9.

Jok, Jok Madut. "Power Dynamics and the Politics of Fieldwork under Sudan's Prolonged Conflicts." In *Research Methods in Conflict Settings: A View from Below*, edited by Dyan Mazurana, Karen Jacobsen, and Lacey Andrews Gale, 149–165. Cambridge: Cambridge University Press, 2013.

Karnieli-Miller, Orit, Roni Strier, and Liat Pessach. "Power Relations in Qualitative Research." *Qualitative Health Research* 19, no. 2 (2009): 279–289.

Lutz, Helma, Maria Teresa Herrera Vivar, and Linda Supik. "Framing Intersectionality: An Introduction." In *Framing Intersectionality: Debates on a Multi-faceted Concept in Gender Studies*, edited by Helma Lutz, Maria Teresa Herrera Vivar, and Linda Supik, 1–22. Farnham: Ashgate, 2011.

Mason, Jennifer. *Qualitative Researching*. 2nd ed. London: Sage, 2002.

Meghji, Ali. *Decolonizing Sociology: An Introduction*. Cambridge, UK: Polity Press, 2021.

Ozano, Kim, and Rose Khatri. "Reflexivity, Positionality and Power in Cross-Cultural Participatory Action Research with Research Assistants in Rural Cambodia." *Educational Action Research* 26, no. 2 (2018): 190–204.

Paechter, Carrie. "Power, Knowledge and the Confessional in Qualitative Research." *Discourse: Studies in the Cultural Politics of Education* 17, no. 1 (1996): 75–84.

Pillow, Wanda. "Confession, Catharsis, or Cure? Rethinking the Uses of Reflexivity as Methodological Power in Qualitative Research." *International Journal of Qualitative Studies in Education* 16, no. 2 (2003): 175–196.

Rodriguez, Katrina L., Jana L. Schwartz, Maria K. E. Lahman, and Monica R. Geist. "Culturally Responsive Focus Groups: Reframing the Research Experience to Focus on Participants." *International Journal of Qualitative Methods* 10, no. 4 (2011): 400–417.

Sadan, Elisheva. *Empowerment and Community Planning*. Translated by Richard Flantz. Self-published, 2004. http://www.mpow.org/elisheva_sadan_empowerment.pdf.

Spivak, G. C. "Can the Subaltern Speak?" In *Marxism and the Interpretation of Culture*, edited by N. Carry and L. Grossberg, 271–313. Urbana: University of Illinois Press, 1988.

Stapleton, Helen M., Rebecca Murphy, and Sue V. Kildea. "Insiders as Outsiders: Bicultural Research Assistants Describe Their Participation in the Evaluation of an Antenatal Clinic for Women from Refugee Backgrounds." *Qualitative Social Work* 14, no. 2 (2015): 275–292.

Swartz, David. *Culture and Power: The Sociology of Pierre Bourdieu*. Chicago: University of Chicago Press, 1997.

Um, Su Jung. "The Chimera: Multiple Selves, Conflicting Desires, and Fluctuating Power Relations in Qualitative Research." *Qualitative Report* 26, no. 5 (2021): 1693–1704.

Vähäsantanen, Katja, and Jaana Saarinen. "The Power Dance in the Research Interview: Manifesting Power and Powerlessness." *Qualitative Research* 13, no. 5 (2012): 493–510.

Yuval-Davis, Nira. "Situated Intersectionality and Social Inequality." *Raisons Politiques* 58, no. 2 (2015): 91–100.

13
Developing a Flexible Data-Collection Plan

Lindsay Mayka and Jessica A. J. Rich

Overview

Qualitative researchers generate a lot of data as they read, interview, interpret, and/or observe. One challenge is determining what data to collect and how to collect it. Another challenge is deciding how to use that data. Before the data-collection process even begins, scholars should consider the different analytical purposes that their data may serve throughout the research process. Scholars should then develop strategies to collect data that best serve those purposes. Scholars should also be open to iteration in their research designs and data-collection strategies, because we often face unanticipated challenges or make new discoveries along the way that may take our research in fortuitous directions.[1]

This chapter considers three key questions that researchers confront as they develop and update their data-collection plan. First, what are my objectives and priorities in data collection? We argue that the key to success in data collection is making your objectives explicit and learning how to prioritize among them. Second, how should I combine sources of data to strengthen my claims? We discuss the need for scholars to triangulate different sorts of data and ways to know when to *stop* collecting additional data. Finally, how can I make my data useful for multiple projects? We identify strategies to structure and document interviews that will make data modular. In this chapter, we provide practical tips for how to approach each question, drawing on concrete examples from our own research projects.

Question 1: What Are My Objectives in Data Collection?

One of the most fundamental tasks in preparing to collect data is setting your core objectives. For any given project, we face a potentially overwhelming number of data-collection goals—particularly for those doing field research. Potential goals of data collection include developing a research question, understanding context, developing concepts and measures, selecting cases, developing hypotheses, testing hypotheses, and understanding causal processes.[2] In a survey of 1,142 political scientists reporting on 1,468 discrete projects, 76% of the surveyed fieldwork projects described included at least four of these analytic tasks.[3] In the majority of projects included in the survey, fieldwork helped researchers accomplish over *seven* analytic tasks.[4] In our experience, the key to fieldwork success is not paring down your objectives but, rather, making them explicit (see Chapter 10) and learning how to prioritize.

Which objectives you prioritize will likely depend on your current stage of the research process. In early stages of research, we find that we are often most interested in learning something new and surprising from our data. In later stages of research, we may be primarily interested in using data to substantiate a claim in which we are already confident or to defend it from critique. Often, we occupy the middle ground: wanting to learn more about our cases but also seeking evidence to support specific claims. As we gather more information, we gradually transition from a heavier emphasis on learning to a primary focus on substantiating.

As your objectives change, you may want to update your data-collection process by seeking out new types of data sources. While you are in the research-design stage, you may start by collecting news and policy reports written for lay audiences to gain necessary context. You may also want to talk to other academics, who can be both a source of information and a guide in making decisions about data-collection strategies. With academics, we can float our initial hypotheses to ensure they are not off-base, ask about key information we may be missing, and discuss case-selection strategies. These early conversations also help us develop new contacts and make sense of documents (e.g., policy reports or news items) that seem inaccessible or impenetrable without a stronger base of knowledge. While it may seem daunting to contact an academic expert to discuss your undeveloped project, we find that most scholars are happy to help fellow academics. To facilitate the introduction, we sometimes ask academic friends or mentors to send an initial email on our behalf, but we have also reached out with "cold" emails that briefly introduce ourselves and our projects before requesting a quick chat. Academic conferences are particularly useful spaces for these conversations, as conference attendees have already decided to spend those several days discussing scholarly ideas.

This initial groundwork can set up the more formal phase of data collection. You might begin by scheduling preliminary interviews with people who have knowledge about the historical development of your topic or who can provide basic descriptive information. In our own research, preliminary interviews with journalists, academics, people working in think tanks, and midlevel bureaucrats have provided invaluable information. While you should do some homework before your first official interviews, such as reading background documents, know that you will likely never feel fully prepared for interviews. These early conversations help you to start making sense of the story, and they can help you with important research tasks, such as refining your research question, selecting cases, and developing hypotheses.

Once you have built a descriptive picture of what is happening (or has happened), you will turn your focus toward more advanced analytical tasks, such as concept development, hypothesis testing, interpretive analysis, and/or the identification of causal processes. At this point, you may pivot to data sources that can offer evidence to support (or reject) already developed hypotheses or that can fill specific gaps in your evidence. By now, you should have a deeper base of knowledge that allows you to understand documents written for insiders, opening up the possibility of working with new kinds of documents as data sources. You should be able to glean more nuanced information from interview subjects who use jargon or veiled language—people who can provide key evidence that is hard for us to discern before we are familiar with the context surrounding our research topic.[5] In later stages of a project, you are also better positioned to grapple with contradictions that emerge from your data by making sense of the context, perspectives, and motivations of interview subjects, for example. In practice, the different phases of the data-collection process often overlap. We are simply suggesting that your *focus* in collecting data will shift over time.

You may also want to adjust your plans in light of new discoveries you make as you advance in your fieldwork—a process that Kapiszewski, MacLean, and Read refer to as iteration.[6] Sometimes we have tightly focused "to-do" and "to-get" lists of data to collect.[7] However, this typically happens later in the life of a project. More often, we do not entirely know where we are going, and data helps us find our way. We may even discover that our original question was off-base: that while we were originally focused on X, the really interesting thing going on is Y. We caution against using to-do and to-get lists too rigidly, because doing so can close us off to adjustments along the way.

The genesis of Rich's first book, *State-Sponsored Activism: Bureaucrats and Social Movements in Democratic Brazil* (2019), demonstrates the value of adjusting research plans in light of new discoveries. Initially, she set out to test hypotheses about how partisan politics and civil-society strength affect levels of grassroots participation. Because Brazil is a highly decentralized country, she expected these factors to vary mostly at the state level, and so her research design centered on a subnational comparison of four Brazilian states that differed in partisan leadership and levels of civil-society strength.

Through the preliminary observational and interview data she collected, however, Rich made two discoveries that ultimately led her to a new puzzle. First, she discovered that, while there certainly was *some* subnational variation in grassroots participation, the degree of variation was strikingly less than she had expected. Second, she discovered that partisan politics was less important in determining such variation than she had expected. Instead, national-level bureaucrats—an actor she had not previously considered—appeared to be more directly involved in grassroots participation than politicians. Moreover, Rich found that national-level bureaucrats actively encouraged local grassroots participation across the country, despite Brazil's ostensibly high levels of political and administrative decentralization. Through this iterative research process, Rich gained a better descriptive understanding of the phenomenon, which led her to reject her initial hypotheses and identify a new independent variable—activist bureaucrats—which became the centerpiece of her book.

In response, Rich shifted her data-collection focus to answering the new puzzle of why grassroots participation was surprisingly strong across the country, even in states with weak civil society and/or obstructive governors. Her answer focused on national bureaucrats, who encouraged the spread of grassroots mobilization into new states and cities because they depended on a strong and mobilized civil society to combat elite opposition to their policy objectives at the state and local levels.[8]

By extension, a completely "efficient" or linear approach to fieldwork is, in our experience, impossible, and even in direct opposition to the objectives of fieldwork experience. We remember worrying when we were graduate students that any fieldwork time we spent "just hanging around" was inefficient—a waste of precious resources. Yet, for many of us, "soaking and poking"[9] is essential to learn what is actually happening on the ground that is interesting and surprising. Often, we head into the field with hunches, and we use soaking-and-poking observations to refine our research questions and select our cases. For example, for both coauthors of this chapter, the first two months of our dissertation fieldwork were not spent "collecting data" in the traditional sense but learning about the universe of cases related to our research topics in the language of our case studies (Spanish and Portuguese), given that virtually nothing on our topics was available in English or at our home institutions. We then used this information to refine our questions and case selection—a process that occurred *during* field research, long after the prospectus stage. Without the discoveries we made through "inefficient" soaking and poking, we both would have produced drastically different, and ultimately less interesting, books.

This is not to say it is essential, or even desirable, for qualitative researchers to spend endless months on soaking-and-poking fieldwork. Time and resource constraints will limit the amount of time most of us can spend in the field, as we discuss later in this chapter. Rather, our point is to encourage the qualitative researcher to take an inclusive approach to measuring their progress in the field. Interviews and archival material can be important data for your project, but "just hanging around" can also be important if you are learning new things along the way.

Question 2: How Should I Combine Different Sources of Data?

In planning their data-collection strategies, researchers should think about how different sources of data can complement one another to strengthen our claims. Just about anything can serve as useful data in qualitative analysis: social media posts, campaign memorabilia, or outdated maps, to list a few examples. In her work on commercial sexual exploitation of children in Colombia, Mayka has collected children's puzzles and day planners that were created by the government to disseminate its interpretation of children's rights to different audiences. We encourage scholars to think beyond the more obvious sources, such as interviews and archival documents, to discover data that offers new angles missing from the written record or verbal accounts.

Qualitative data is often messy and full of contradictions. Interview respondents interpret an event through their singular perspectives, which may conflict with the viewpoints of others. Interview respondents may misremember or intentionally misrepresent the facts of an event. Written records selectively include certain stories and details, while omitting others. Given the messiness of qualitative data, we should weigh various pieces of evidence against each other to sort through discrepancies and areas of confusion.[10] This process is called data triangulation, a "research procedure that employs empirical evidence derived from more than one method or from more than one type of data."[11]

Data triangulation is especially useful to make sense of data sources that yield contradictions and ambiguities—particularly for claims at the crux of their argument that might draw the attention of skeptical reviewers or critics. Moreover, these contradictions and ambiguities can themselves reveal important ideas about sources of bias in the data or the political "work" being done when individuals recount events in divergent ways. These insights can generate new questions, concepts, and arguments that might be missed the first time around.

Data triangulation can involve leveraging either data produced through different methods or different pieces of data produced through the same method to evaluate a claim.[12] Scholars can engage in data triangulation by combining quantitative and qualitative data, or with qualitative data alone. Scholars may triangulate data at any stage of the research process described above, depending on their needs.[13] To decide when triangulation is needed, scholars should think about the gaps, biases, and shortcomings of their initial sources of data, and how they can counterbalance those limitations with other pieces of data.

A paper coauthored by Mayka and González shows how triangulation can address concerns about interpretation and generalizability.[14] This paper argues that participatory institutions, which are designed to deepen democracy, can in some contexts contract, rather than expand, the citizenship rights of marginalized groups. The spark for the paper came out of González's ethnographic observations of São Paulo's community security councils (CONSEGs). González noticed that during CONSEG meetings, participants frequently depicted marginalized groups as dangerous security threats that must be controlled through police violence, rather than as rights-bearing citizens. Mayka and González used triangulation to address two concerns about these initial findings.

First, Mayka and González addressed potential critics who might question González's interpretation based solely on ethnographic observations that participants demanded repression. The researchers conducted interviews with stakeholders across different positionalities, including police commanders, CONSEG participants, and activists defending the rights of marginalized groups—in other words, groups with starkly different views about the appropriate role for police in the city. These interviews confirmed González's interpretations. Several key CONSEG participants expressed views that repressive policing was essential for democratic citizenship. Moreover, a variety of respondents described incidents of hostility toward marginalized groups at CONSEG meetings, albeit with different interpretations about whether hostility was merited or not.

Second, the researchers addressed questions about whether these observations reflected broader patterns throughout São Paulo. A skeptic might wonder if the same processes observed in the six CONSEGs chosen for in-depth observation arise in the other 87 CONSEGs in the city.[15] How widespread is this phenomenon of using participatory institutions to demand repression?[16] While Mayka and González believed that these patterns applied in diverse neighborhoods throughout the city, ethnographic and interview data alone was insufficient to back up this impression. To assess the generalizability of these patterns, Mayka and González coded the 2011 meeting minutes for all CONSEGs throughout the city of São Paulo. This content analysis of the minutes revealed striking consistency in the demands for repression of marginalized groups at CONSEGs, in wealthy and low-income communities alike.

While triangulation can be useful to make better sense of qualitative data, researchers should avoid collecting additional data that simply replicates the limitations of the initial data source. For example, conducting many interviews with various members of the ruling government can be useful to better understand perspectives and decision-making within the government—yet it still captures only a limited slice of the political process. Unless the researcher is specifically interested in understanding the dynamics of the ruling government, they may instead want to speak to actors occupying a broader range of positionalities in the political process, beyond those in the ruling government—particularly those who have conflicting incentives.[17] This process will likely yield new interpretations of what "really" happened, opening the door for the researcher to make sense of areas of convergence and divergence. Likewise, combining these interviews with evidence from policy documents from that same government, or news accounts from a newspaper sympathetic to the ruling government, can deepen understanding in some ways but will likely replicate the biases and limited perspectives. It is more important for a researcher to think about what gaps need to be addressed rather than simply gathering more and more data.

How can a researcher know when to *stop* collecting data and to begin analysis and writing? Focusing on your priorities and objectives in data collection is crucial to know when enough is enough. Often, qualitative researchers feel compelled to mimic the data-collection language and practices of quantitative researchers by pursuing a "sampling logic" approach to data collection,[18] striving to achieve unbiased or representative samples by collecting larger and larger numbers of interview subjects, focus groups, events to observe, and so on. However, if your core objective is to reveal causal mechanisms and processes, then you should approach data collection using a "case study logic."[19] The goal of a "case study logic" approach to data collection is not representativeness but, rather, saturation—when new data points cease to provide new or surprising information that is relevant to the question.[20] Using the example above, interviewing dozens of minor players involved in passing difficult policy reform may be less useful than gaining the trust of a handful of central figures who can spend longer periods of time hashing out the details of the reform process and their political calculations along the way.

While there are always loose ends, eventually researchers reach a point of diminishing returns. Beyond these epistemic guidelines, practical considerations also constrain the urge to gather more and more data. Hard deadlines, especially those that come from having a return ticket from the field, force the researcher to focus on the top priorities in data collection.

Question 3: How Can I Make My Data Useful for Multiple Projects?

While gathering data, researchers generally stumble upon interesting and puzzling discoveries that are not central to the initial research project. One benefit that comes from collecting extensive qualitative data is that you can use this data for side projects or future papers. In other words, qualitative data can be modular, used in different ways to address the objectives of distinct research projects. Below, we offer examples to illustrate some practical strategies to collect modular data that is useful for multiple research projects. We draw primarily on our experience using interview data, but these principles could be applied to a range of qualitative methodologies.

One example comes from Mayka's research on civic participation in the Colombian health policy sector. Mayka's first book, *Building Participatory Institutions in Latin America*, analyzed the construction of participatory institutions across different policy sectors in Brazil and Colombia.[21] For this project, Colombia's participatory health committees served as a negative case: this participatory institution never underwent the process of institution building and existed only on paper. Facing the problem of "the dog that didn't bark," Mayka had to find creative ways to explain the *absence* of a participatory institution. She interviewed diverse stakeholders in the health sector—including those who had never even heard of the health committees—to map out alternative modes of participation in health, given that it did not happen through participatory institutions. These interviews revealed the importance of participatory judicial processes to advance claims-making in health. A few years later, Mayka returned to these interviews for a paper coauthored with Herrera that examined the promise of legal strategies for participation in Colombia.[22] Mayka contributed case material to analyze legal strategies in health, while Herrera drew on her research on the environmental sector.

Another example comes from Rich's research on highly capable government bureaucracies. For Rich's book, she conducted several interviews in which bureaucrats described in detail how they used technical cooperation agreements with United Nations organizations in a subversive way: to avoid government rules on who they could hire and how they could spend their money. These interviews revealed how accountability initiatives, intended to reduce corruption, can actually hinder the development of capable government agencies by making it harder for directors to recruit experts and spend their budgets. The interviews further highlighted a common way public servants escape the accountability rules that limit their effectiveness: outsourcing bureaucracies to nonstate organizations. These comments were not direct answers to her questions about the different ways these bureaucrats supported activists—the central theme of her book—yet they provided her with insights about international organizations that led her to write a separate paper about the subject, once she finished the book.[23] This example highlights how respondents who share stories and insights that seem like tangents may in fact offer data that is useful for a future paper.

Of course, not all tangents will be fruitful, and researchers should not necessarily abandon their original interview questions altogether. However, being open to new lines of questioning may reveal puzzling insights that seed future work. A practical implication here is that researchers should build in flex time when scheduling interviews. Otherwise, they may have to cut short a fascinating interview to rush to the next appointment—an unfortunate situation that both coauthors of this chapter have experienced.

If possible, given ethical and practical constraints, we recommend recording interviews, participant observation sessions, and focus groups. Listening to recordings at a later time often reveals valuable insights that can spark new ideas or serve as evidence to substantiate claims for future work.

Trade-offs in Data Collection: Time and Money

Time and money serve as perhaps the most important constraints that shape trade-offs about how much data to collect. Knowing these trade-offs before entering the field or accessing a data source can help a researcher set realistic expectations, streamline a (flexible) to-do list for project completion, and design efficient avenues to reach saturation. Setting priorities given these trade-offs is often an iterative process, occurring both during the initial research design and repeatedly throughout the data-collection process.

The official wisdom of research design says you should start with your research question and hypotheses, and then develop the best research design and data-collection strategy to address this question. Yet in practice, the research questions we pursue are conditioned by the data-collection strategies that are feasible given our time and resource constraints. Some graduate students do not receive funding at all for field research and must conduct projects based on text sources, quantitative data, or digital fieldwork. During graduate school, both authors of this chapter had limited research funding but comparatively more time, which enabled extended field research trips that are conducive to soaking and poking (along with a side of financial stress). At this stage in our careers, as professors with the stability of tenure but with more complicated family and professional obligations, leisurely trips that involve extensive exploration with unclear results are not always possible. For recent projects, we have both undertaken short, one- to two-week research trips that consist of intense workdays that include three to four interviews each day.[24]

Researchers can complement short fieldwork stints with text-based data that is accessible from their universities. For example, Mayka has hired undergraduate research assistants to build and code newspaper archives for a recent project about governments' use of human-rights discourses to justify repressive policing of skid-row zones.[25] Her decision to focus on how the issue is framed in public statements and the media stemmed at least in part from greater access to funding for undergraduate RAs who could build and help code a news archive, compared to a more limited ability to travel to the field. An alternative approach to the project might have focused more on ethnographic observation of the skid-row zones subject to repressive police interventions, but that project would require extensive time commitments that are not feasible at this point. We urge scholars to be realistic and forthright about how time and funding constraints can shape what is and is not feasible in data collection, and to pursue research projects that best capitalize on their comparative advantages in these resources.

Another decision that involves a time and money trade-off is whether you will invest in interview transcriptions (for recorded interviews) or simply write up careful notes after your interviews. While transcriptions capture a more complete record of the interview, they can be expensive.[26] Typing detailed notes after each interview costs the researcher less money than hiring a transcriber yet demands greater time and energy of the researcher. There is another hidden cost associated with only writing detailed summaries of interviews in lieu of transcriptions: the researcher cannot do as many interviews in a single day, given the need to type up notes immediately afterward. Particularly for researchers doing brief but intense fieldwork trips, there are barely enough hours in the day to recuperate between interviews, much less write interview summaries. Moreover, during fieldwork, each additional day involves extra expenses in food and lodging, and sometimes childcare or eldercare costs back home. In this context, it might actually be *less* expensive to hire transcribers. Still, for those who can spare the time, typing up notes after your interviews has benefits that get lost with a reliance on transcription: taking detailed notes can reveal new insights that are overlooked when just reading the interview results on the page. Researchers who have limited fieldwork time may also do this from home by carefully relistening to their interview recordings.

In practice, many researchers will use a combination of typed summaries and interview transcriptions. Rather than thinking of the two methods of recording interviews as dichotomous alternatives, we suggest you focus on your preferred balance between the two options: whether you want to rely more on your own labor or on external costs.

Conclusion

This chapter provides guidance for researchers who are planning (and in the middle of) qualitative data collection to help them think through the varied objectives, challenges, and trade-offs involved. We contend that researchers should be reflective and flexible in their data-collection plan, which may shift at different stages of the research process as the project evolves over time. Moreover, we highlight ways that researchers can and should triangulate different sources of data with one another as a way to acknowledge and even embrace the contradictions of qualitative data. Maintaining flexible plans and keeping careful records can help researchers collect the data that is most useful for their current purposes, while also setting them up for future research projects.

Notes

1. Kapiszewski, MacLean, and Read, "Dynamic Research Design."
2. Kapiszewski, MacLean, and Read, *Field Research in Political Science*, 74–75.

3. Kapiszewski, MacLean, and Read, *Field Research in Political Science*, 74–75.
4. Kapiszewski, MacLean, and Read, *Field Research in Political Science*, 74.
5. Sometimes we encounter such documents and interviewees early in our research, before we can fully make sense of them. For this reason, detailed notes are essential–and recordings advisable when possible—so that you can return to this data later in your project. We revisit the importance of keeping detailed notes later in this chapter.
6. Kapiszewski, MacLean, and Read, "Dynamic Research Design."
7. For useful examples, see Kapiszewski, MacLean, and Read, *Field Research in Political Science*, 88–89.
8. Rich, *State-Sponsored Activism*.
9. Fenno, *Home Style*.
10. Mosley, "'Just Talk to People,'" 21–22.
11. Seawright and Collier, "Glossary," 356.
12. Ayoub, Wallace, and Zepeda-Millán, "Triangulation in Social Movement Research," 68.
13. Ayoub, Wallace, and Zepeda-Millán, "Triangulation in Social Movement Research," 68.
14. González and Mayka, "Policing, Democratic Participation, and the Reproduction of Asymmetric Citizenship."
15. González used criteria for case selection to capture São Paulo's diversity. The selected CONSEGs varied along demographic variables (socioeconomic and racial composition), region within São Paulo, and levels of crime.
16. To be clear, we do not claim that these six cases are "representative" of CONSEGs throughout the city; on the fallacies of the concept of "representativeness" in ethnographic research, see Small, "'How Many Cases Do I Need?'" Nevertheless, the existence of this phenomenon throughout the city of São Paulo reveals the mechanisms by which marginalized groups themselves can replicate deep-seated inequalities seen in policing.
17. Tansey, "Process Tracing and Elite Interviewing."
18. Collier, Brady, and Seawright, "Sources of Leverage in Causal Inference"; Small, "'How Many Cases Do I Need?'" Note that the sampling logic approach can be good for asking descriptive questions about a population.
19. Small, "'How Many Cases Do I Need?,'" 24–25.
20. Bleich and Pekkanen, "How to Report Interview Data," 91.
21. Mayka, *Building Participatory Institutions in Latin America*.
22. Herrera and Mayka, "How Do Legal Strategies Advance Social Accountability?"
23. Rich, "Outsourcing Bureaucracy to Evade Accountability."
24. Scheduling many interviews in a day also involves a trade-off between efficiency in the field and flexibility to pursue new leads and conduct hours-long interviews. As we describe earlier, this flexibility in interviewing can yield valuable new information for future or side projects.
25. Mayka, "The Power of Human Rights Frames in Urban Security."
26. In theory, a researcher might transcribe their own interviews, but we would not recommend this strategy: transcribing is very time-consuming, and a researcher's time is usually better spent elsewhere. New AI-based transcription software options are an economical alternative to manual transcriptions.

Recommended Readings

Ayoub, Phillip, Sophia Wallace, and Chris Zepeda-Millán. "Triangulation in Social Movement Research." In *Methodological Practices in Social Movement Research*, edited by Donnatella della Porta, 67–96. New York: Oxford University Press, 2014.
    This chapter provides an overview of data triangulation, with a focus on applications to the study of social movements.

Brady, Henry, and David Collier, eds. *Rethinking Social Inquiry*. 2nd ed. Lanham, MD: Rowman & Littlefield, 2010.
> This edited volume argues that qualitative researchers are primarily focused on gathering data about "causal-process observations," a logic which is helpful for researchers to think about the types of data that they may need to substantiate their claims.

González-Ocantos, Ezequiel, and Jody LaPorte. "Process Tracing and the Problem of Missing Data." *Sociological Methods and Research* 50, no. 3 (2019): 1407–1435.
> This article addresses the problem of missing data, a common challenge among researchers who conduct process tracing.

Kapiszewski, Diana, Lauren MacLean, and Benjamin Read. "Dynamic Research Design: Iteration in Field-Based Inquiry." *Comparative Politics* 54, no. 4 (2022): 654–670.
> The article by Kapiszewski, MacLean, and Read identifies advantages, challenges, and practical tips for scholars who iterate their fieldwork-based research designs as they gain new information.

Small, Mario. "'How Many Cases Do I Need?' On Science and the Logic of Case Selection in Field Based Research." *Ethnography* 10, no. 1 (2009): 5–38.
> Small argues for the need for "saturation" in many qualitative studies, rather than "representativeness"—a model more appropriately used in quantitative studies. Small also presents two strategies for sampling in data collection to achieve saturation.

Tansey, Oisin. 2007. "Process Tracing and Elite Interviewing: A Case for Non-probability Sampling." *PS: Political Science & Politics* 40, no. 4 (2007): 765–772.
> Tansey argues that non-probability sampling techniques are best for process-tracing and suggests researchers use a combination of reputational and positional criteria when selecting interview subjects.

References

Ayoub, Phillip, Sophia Wallace, and Chris Zepeda-Millán. "Triangulation in Social Movement Research." In *Methodological Practices in Social Movement Research*, edited by Donatella della Porta, 67–96. New York: Oxford University Press, 2014.

Bleich, Erik, and Robert Pekkanen. "How to Report Interview Data." In *Interview Research in Political Science*, edited by Layna Mosley, 84–105. Ithaca, NY: Cornell University Press, 2013.

Collier, David, Henry Brady, and Jason Seawright. "Sources of Leverage in Causal Inference: Toward an Alternative View of Methodology." In *Rethinking Social Inquiry: Diverse Tools, Shared Standards*, edited by Henry Brady and David Collier, 161–199. Lanham, MD: Rowman & Littlefield, 2010.

Fenno, Richard. *Home Style: Representatives in Their Districts*. Boston: Little, Brown, 1978.

González, Yanilda, and Lindsay Mayka. "Policing, Democratic Participation, and the Reproduction of Asymmetric Citizenship." *American Political Science Review*, forthcoming.

Herrera, Veronica, and Lindsay Mayka. "How Do Legal Strategies Advance Social Accountability? Evaluating Mechanisms in Colombia." *Journal of Development Studies* 56, no. 8 (2020): 1437–1454.

Kapiszewski, Diana, Lauren MacLean, and Benjamin Read. "Dynamic Research Design: Iteration in Field-Based Inquiry." *Comparative Politics* 54, no. 4 (2022) 645–670.

Kapiszewski, Diana, Lauren MacLean, and Benjamin Read. *Field Research in Political Science: Practices and Principles*. New York: Cambridge University Press, 2015.

Mayka, Lindsay. *Building Participatory Institutions in Latin America: Reform Coalitions and Institutional Change*. Cambridge: Cambridge University Press, 2019.

Mayka, Lindsay. "The Power of Human Rights Frames in Urban Security: Lessons from Bogotá." *Comparative Politics* 54, no. 1 (2021): 1–25.

Mosley, Layna. "'Just Talk to People'? Interviews in Contemporary Political Science." In *Interview Research in Political Science*, edited by Layna Mosley, 1–28. Ithaca, NY: Cornell University Press, 2013.

Rich, Jessica A. J. "Outsourcing Bureaucracy to Evade Accountability: How Public Servants Build Shadow State Capacity," *American Political Science Review* 117, no. 3 (2023): 835–850.

Rich, Jessica A. J. *State-Sponsored Activism: Bureaucrats and Social Movements in Democratic Brazil.* New York: Cambridge University Press, 2019.

Seawright, Jason, and David Collier. "Glossary." In *Rethinking Social Inquiry: Diverse Tools, Shared Standards*, edited by Henry Brady and David Collier, 313–359. Lanham, MD: Rowman & Littlefield 2010.

Small, Mario. "'How Many Cases Do I Need?' On Science and the Logic of Case Selection in Field Based Research." *Ethnography* 10, no. 1 (2009): 5–38.

Tansey, Oisin. "Process Tracing and Elite Interviewing: A Case for Non-probability Sampling." *PS: Political Science and Politics* 4, no. 4 (2007): 765–772.

14
Considering Collaboration as Part of Your Research Design

Mneesha Gellman

Collaborative Methodology: An Introduction

Collaborative methodology (CM) offers a path forward for researchers who want to work with, rather than on, people impacted by research topics.[1] It is a framework for the philosophical and practical process of sharing ownership of the research process with people affected by the research themes. This means intentionally designing and implementing projects as a joint effort by parties traditionally referred to as the researcher and the subject. In CM, people typically referred to as research subjects are treated as stakeholders, or people who live the reality of the research topic and are therefore invested in its study. Principal investigators, or external researchers, are also stakeholders. For both roles, CM establishes a roadmap to enable partnership in the research process.

Fundamentally, CM acknowledges and seeks to realign the operation of power in social science research in favor of those affected by study themes. The CM framework essentially upends standard social science power paradigms by inviting those usually named "subjects"—because they are subjected to the research design of an external investigator—to instead be agents or co-creators of a research design, and active members in carrying it out. This transformation—from envisioning people as subjects to engaging them as co-creating stakeholders—is crucial to CM's success. While such a shift can be disorienting for researchers trained in traditional extractive research, CM is an essential tool, particularly when working with historically and contemporarily marginalized communities—meaning people who have been or continue to be oppressed, stigmatized, or impacted by structural injustice in some way as a group.

At the base level, collaboration means working together, and there is little additional proscription of roles in any universal fashion. Who works with whom, and how such working together should take place, is open for interpretation and definition in case-by-case contexts. My definition of CM includes researchers laboring with stakeholders to generate each stage of the research puzzle, from creating the guiding questions to determining methods[2] to collect data, developing data instruments, and making decisions about communicating findings.

CM, Visibility, and Transparency

CM implies a theoretical and practical commitment to mutually derived and consensual knowledge frameworks, processes, and products used by both community stakeholders and external researchers. Reimagining the research design process as something open to full participation by those usually labeled "subjects" is not easy terrain for political scientists. Concerns about objectivity and neutrality are some of the standard interjections against CM. Yet, at a time when traditional power holders are being defrocked in a range of arenas, from policing to politicians, it seems timely to push against such concerns.

Is objectivity a screen behind which the White[3] male armchair research-driven process hides? Is neutrality an excuse to be disconnected or disinvested in the outcome of research that has high stakes for people who have less social capital than researchers? The sociopolitical reckoning with power and privilege globally in the 2020s surely allows for resistance to disciplinary mandates that have long set the terms of research design.

"Reflexive openness" lays out best practices for how positionality should be addressed in writing up research—transparently and directly[4]—and CM extends this to advocate for such reflexivity in early stages of research design as well. Thus, CM can play a role in promoting "methodological rigor"[5] by demanding a deep level of stakeholder accountability that comes from intense scrutiny over research accuracy. While this accountability may appear different from some techniques discussed in the Data Access and Research Transparency standards,[6] CM can meet the needs of researchers by providing a roadmap for how to be deeply transparent in both research design and implementation. CM helps make visible the assumptions connected to power and positionality that may otherwise be invisible. It is thus poised to be part of best practices of research methodology for maximum transparency, especially when working with marginalized communities.

What CM Is Not

CM means working together, where participant and observer are both stakeholders; CM is not the same as activist scholarship. CM shares some of the attributes of participatory action research (PAR) and feminist methodology in that it strives to undo power hierarchies and prioritizes stakeholder inclusion. These approaches, taken across multiple disciplines in an array of project types, are used by scholars seeking to connect their research to direct action that may benefit communities. In fact, PAR's three central tenets are (1) breaking down power hierarchies within research, (2) engaging traditionally subjected subjects as stakeholders with integral rights in the research process, and (3) deriving action from research.[7] Feminist methodology explicitly aims to amplify female-identified voices, sharing a concern with CM to make research more inclusive and subvert power hierarchies.[8]

But CM differs from these two methodologies in important ways. Centrally, CM does not require a responsive action plan to be implemented based on the results of the research—something that is normal in PAR. Nor does CM explicitly center female-identified voices. It is entirely possible that communities may take action based on study findings, or that researchers may advocate for things based on study outcomes, or that female-identified voices may be centered in CM projects. But these attributes are not built into CM itself. Instead, these elements may stem from characteristics of individual researchers, communities, or research designs. CM maintains a focus on stakeholder inclusion and strives to undo power hierarchies in research design. It leaves open how each CM-driven project is customized by its co-creators.

CM, alongside PAR and feminist methodology, rejects the position that social science research is neutral. Old debates such as when to code countries as democratic show that our personal biases are frequently at play, whether coding indicators or labeling regimes.[9] At the same time, CM does not share with PAR the requirement that research be "explicitly political, socially engaged, and democratic."[10] It very well might be, but collaboration with stakeholders varies tremendously, as seen in the 2021 Profession Symposium on Quantitative and Qualitative Collaborative Methodologies in *PS: Political Science and Politics*.[11]

Identity, Positionality, and CM

There is growing discussion of power and positionality in political science. Contributors to a 2018 Profession Symposium on Engaged Research in *PS: Political Science and Politics*,[12] alongside scholars such as Timothy Pachirat[13] and Katherine Cramer,[14] speak to relationships that highlight power dynamics. In my own work, I discuss positionality up front at each step of the research process and have detailed this in recent work.[15] Fundamentally, being open about one's own identity in relation to the people one hopes to learn about allows power dynamics to be more evident and open for discussion.

For example, I know that my privileged employment as a professor with a flexible schedule and living-wage salary means that I should be the one to travel for meetings with stakeholders, and they know that too. It makes scheduling more straightforward if we all agree that I work around their schedules and not the other way around. In my own research, I am also clear that as the outsider asking to study Native American issues and spaces, I have to ask for permission not just from my institutional review board (IRB), but first from the multiple layers of Tribal authority that manage Native sovereign governance.[16]

Depending on who the stakeholders are and how they want to be involved, as well as the contours and basic premise of the research puzzle, CM can take many forms. Explicit power and positionality analysis, along with stakeholder inclusion, can be compatible with a range of social science approaches. Moreover, CM addresses issues of transparency and positionality head-on. In this way, CM is poised to offer advantages over extractive research, in addition to being an ethical imperative (for more, see Chapter 28) in research that involves power differentials (e.g., Chapters 11 and 18).

Doing Collaborative Methodology

There is no one script for doing CM. But there are two basic tenets that can make the quality implementation of CM more viable. The design of CM at the early stages of a study and the inclusion of stakeholder needs and perspectives both set CM projects up for success. I discuss each in turn, along with a caveat for comparative researchers.

The first critical tenet of robust CM is that it needs to be built into the research process from the beginning of a project. If researchers wait until the collecting, analyzing, or publishing of data to address collaboration, it is less likely that CM will be successful. Before being able to design research together, researchers need to build relationships with stakeholders. This could develop from cold-calling an organization of interest and finding interested interlocutors, volunteering in a given community to first build social relationships, or going back to an organization or community where you worked before.

Once relationships have been formed, then researchers and stakeholders can work together to collaboratively create the research puzzle by identifying the questions, hypotheses, and arguments of interest. For example, only after several meetings with the Yurok Tribe's Education Department did we hash out details of the research landscape. In general, IRB approval should be sought after the puzzle has been agreed on but before data collection takes place. Some researchers may get IRB approval before beginning any CM discussions and may then need to file IRB modification applications or apply for a new study, depending on how much the study changes through CM.

A second tenet of CM is that it should be rooted in an intention to include stakeholders' needs and perspectives rather than to extract information. This need not compromise neutrality or objectivity, but instead requires a researcher's humility in recognizing that their own professional goals are not the sole goals of the project. Particularly when working with historically and contemporarily marginalized communities, information extraction belies ongoing neocolonization that scholars perpetuate on people they want to take information from while offering little of use in return.

The following example shows how I have navigated this tension in my own work. My comfort zone as a researcher is as a political ethnographer. In early conversations with the Yurok Tribe's Education Department, they expressed interest in quantitative data because Tribal funding applications and other necessities are often linked to quantitative data. Though I proffered interviews, focus groups, and field observations as data collection methods, I also agreed to conduct a student survey as a quantitative component.

In practice, having never studied survey methods beyond cursory training in graduate school, I spent quite a bit of time reading up on how to design and conduct them. Then I spent an inordinate amount of time working out problems in data visualization in Excel, Google Forms, and Tableau, and finally analyzing the results. It was time-consuming, but I did it with enthusiasm, recognizing that the methods repertoire requested was both my obligation to honor and a chance to expand my own skill set. In addition, it allowed for a type of data triangulation that arguably provided another layer of evidence in the research. This is a clear illustration of the difference between CM and other research designs: if the purpose of CM is to involve stakeholders in each step of the research design, this will include researchers being open to the methods preferences of others.

To provide one example in more detail, collaboration on the survey instrument draft itself was a testament to the importance of CM. Watching my draft survey questions get critiqued by Yurok elders and language-keepers[17] was one of the most humbling and gratifying moments of the project. During breaks in an intensive Yurok language workshop in the summer of 2017, I shared a draft of the survey with Yurok language teachers and the students they work with, along with other community members. In their reactions to my draft questions, I saw the way I got the concepts right but the wording sometimes embarrassingly wrong. After reading the questions out loud and dissecting them, language-keepers helped translate my academic-speak into everyday language that the target population—high-schoolers ages 14–18—could relate to. In addition to pragmatic issues of stakeholder resonance, the editing of the survey in a collaborative way also strengthened the measurement and concept validity within the project.

I am profoundly grateful for the CM process in creating a framework to collaborate with the Yurok Tribe's Education Department. The experience workshopping the survey draft pushed me to be more reflective on how academic language itself can be exclusionary, and how CM may necessitate code-switching by researchers who are speaking to stakeholder as well as academic communities. Learning to use a vernacular that resonates with stakeholders should perhaps be part of any research toolkit, but CM includes a built-in language-review process.

Potential Trade-offs

There are numerous trade-offs in doing CM in social science research. I discuss five: (1) CM in comparative work, (2) CM in particular stakeholder contexts, (3) CM as risky for new junior scholars, (4) resource distribution in CM, and (5) CM as a burden for stakeholders. First, while CM can be compatible with many kinds of research methods, I have found it challenging but not impossible to apply in comparative work. For example, I developed a research framework based on one case study site and then applied it to another case study. I worked extensively with the Yurok Tribe in Northern California to design a CM-based project looking at the politics of Indigenous language access in a public high school curriculum. I wanted to look comparatively at this phenomenon in Oaxaca, Mexico, which I had included as a case study in my first book. Although I had strong networks from earlier research, ultimately the transfer of research questions, along with interview, focus group, and survey instruments from the California case studies to the Oaxacan ones, meant there was less space for collaboration in Mexico.

While I did utilize CM principles in both locations, including consultation with community leaders before data collection commenced, it was not an equally collaborative project across both sites. Though I did take numerous steps to make the research more relevant locally, including adding several interview and focus group questions that led to a few tangent projects,[18] ultimately the results show two different experiences of CM. Many decisions about research design were made in California with Yurok interlocutors before being applied in Mexico. In California, the project fell on the deeply collaborative end of the continuum, while in Mexico, it fell more in the middle. Future comparative collaborative methodologists may continue to fine-tune how to hold both practices together more equitably.

Second, CM may not be a research imperative for everyone. There are many kinds of research that may not work with collaboration, and others where it simply isn't necessary. Conflict researchers may find the potential to become mouthpieces for a given actor too dangerous, making collaboration undesirable. Work with elites, for example, may be ethically exempt from requiring CM because the power dynamics are not set up for an external researcher to have power over elites. In fact, just the opposite may be the case, where extracting information from elites may be one of the only ways researchers can claim power.

Work in authoritarian contexts may also be ill-suited for CM if, by collaborating with outside researchers, community members place themselves in significant danger through such an alliance. Researchers in any of these situations can consider what it would mean to collaborate methodologically and then decide not to do it, whether because of ethics, power dynamics, or risk to participants. However, even philosophically considering collaboration as one of many potential approaches pushes researchers to identify when they are choosing an extractivist research model for a strategic reason. Arguably, such a process increases transparency in the discipline as a whole.

Third, there are numerous structural barriers to mainstreaming CM for junior scholars. Graduate training itself at top universities in the United States is generally neither democratic nor socially engaged. Typically, social science programs train students to engage canonical works in ways that maximize their edge in the job market. Pressures of time, mostly based on funding clocks, compound the directive to design and carry out research independently and as efficiently as possible, without engaging stakeholders.

Thus, for researchers, risks from using CM center on concerns about career benchmarks, including completing dissertations, gaining an academic position, tenure and promotion, and publishing. The merits of CM are smaller because standard social science career benchmarks do not usually include reference to work impact beyond the scholarly field. In other words, the discipline prioritizes citation statistics over tangible community or policy impact. While the time needed for and commitment to a research site may not be possible for every researcher, addressing career benchmarks and incentives is one way that senior scholars and other leaders can work to make CM research more viable.

Fourth, researchers engaging in CM face challenges of resource distribution, particularly time and money. It takes longer to carry out CM research because there are multiple stakeholders to engage with at various steps. Exactly how long depends on the characteristics of each project. My collaborative work with the Yurok Tribe has taken longer than if I did the research on my own, because I take time to meet with stakeholders at regular intervals, discuss their ideas, integrate them, and revise in iterations. My position as a privileged academic with tenure made this timeline possible, albeit still stressful.

But it is important to note that the research might not have been permitted at all if I hadn't taken the time to utilize CM, and this may hold true for researchers in other Indigenous contexts. The Yurok Tribe has the ability to permit or deny any research that has to do with the Tribe. My interest in using CM hand in hand with the Yurok Tribe's Education Department meant that I had local partners with whom to navigate the levels of Tribal review necessary to obtain permission to perform research and to review any drafts of possible publications (including this one). Had I designed an extractive research project, it is doubtful that such a project would have been approved, whether by the Office of the Tribal Attorney, Education Department staff, or even the superintendents and principals of the districts and schools where I did data collection. All of them asked if I had Tribal approval to do the study, and the approval was connected to carrying out a research design that shared power with stakeholders.

Fifth, researchers do not carry the burdens of CM alone. The participation of community stakeholders can entail trade-offs. Collaboration takes time, something that many people in marginalized communities are short on if they are hustling to make ends meet. Interlocutors may work for small amounts of money and have lengthy to-do lists. Participating in research might take time away from paid work. For many people, the luxury of a few hours here and there to meet and discuss ideas with a researcher may undermine their ability to support themselves. Ultimately, research-related emails or phone calls may not be as important to someone's survival as other commitments. In practice, this means that CM projects do not follow researcher timelines but those of community stakeholders.

An additional risk for community members in collaboration is that they legitimize the project by participating in it. Community members risk their reputations if a study negatively portrays their network or somehow fails. It is imperative that CM researchers are thoughtful and transparent about how to address these concerns early on in conversations about what collaborative research could look like. For example, I spoke to the Yurok Tribal Council about how, if there were findings showing a negative outcome for Yurok-language access by youth in the high schools, I would talk to the Tribe about it before publishing the results. Ultimately that was not a concern because the data overwhelmingly showed positive benefits to all students enrolled in Yurok courses, but it was important to establish protocols with Yurok leaders for a variety of scenarios in advance. Any CM researcher should do the same, reaching consensus with stakeholders about how negative findings should be handled prior to arriving at that scenario.

Despite many trade-offs, the benefits of CM are also real. For example, "Benefits for Participants" is frequently a throw-away section in many IRB applications. Researchers (including me in earlier work) tend to proclaim a general benefit to human knowledge that may be insufficient for CM. A strength of CM is that it makes researchers be as concrete as possible about the research benefits, grounding it in reality.

In my recent work, benefits from the research include the creation of citable publications that document the impact of Yurok-language access on young people. The Yurok Tribe may choose to use the evidence in my publications in grant-seeking efforts for Yurok-language instruction, as well as in petitions to expand Yurok-language access in the pre-K through college formal curriculum. In Oaxaca, a benefit is that teachers and school directors can use the research findings to design interventions to better support Indigenous student success, as well as account for them in data collection documents.

In sum, there are numerous trade-offs inevitable in engaging CM, and researchers should be well aware of these issues so that they may navigate them with sensitivity.

Conclusion

My goal in this chapter is not to make a case that everyone should do CM, but rather to assert the place of CM as a legitimate social science methodology that can be one of the frameworks researchers consider in conceptualizing their work. However, for the subset of researchers who work with historically or contemporarily marginalized communities, some form of CM is imperative for ethical research. This is because extractive research with such communities continues neocolonial relationships based on taking resources away to benefit the more powerful. In contrast, CM promotes collaboration in ways that address the needs of both researchers and community members.

By changing the framework of how we view the purpose of research, CM is one concrete way in which researchers can be less extractivist, especially when working in the context of structural inequality. CM can encompass a wide range of methods, spanning the qualitative and quantitative as well as the positivist and interpretivist spectrums. In addition, there are creative ways to bring CM into discussions of research transparency and reliability. CM mandates a highly transparent research process that centers positionality, reflexive openness, and community accountability. Decolonization of the discipline is a necessary step, and arguably also makes for better research. Pushing researchers to address both the purpose and the audience of research, CM is a process of research accountability that centers the very people it purports to affect.

Notes

1. I thank the Yurok Tribal Council, Yurok Education Department, Yurok Language Program, and the Office of the Tribal Attorney for their permission for and participation in the research discussed here. I also thank Jennifer Cyr and Sara Wallace Goodman for comments on earlier drafts, and Joshua Dankoff, Annika Falconer, Lauren Holt, and Abigail Lange for editing assistance. Any errors remain my own.
2. Though many people erroneously use the terms interchangeably, "methodology" and "methods" are not the same thing. "Methodology" describes a system of principles or a philosophical approach governing a research framework, while "methods" refer to concrete tools of data collection.
3. For more on why capitalizing "White" is important, see MacArthur Foundation, "Capitalizing Black and White."
4. See MacLean et al., "Research Ethics and Human Subjects"; Thomson, "Reflexive Openness as Ethical Research Practice."
5. See Firchow and Gellman, "Collaborative Methodologies," 525.
6. See https://www.dartstatement.org/. DA-RT efforts have included the Journal Editors' Transparency Statement, for example, which requires researchers to make their raw data available to all or else to defend why sharing is not possible. Such efforts have been questioned by many, including political ethnographers and others who do qualitative and interpretive work; Jacobs et. al., "The Qualitative Transparency Deliberations," 171–208.
7. Baum, MacDougall, and Smith, "Participatory Action Research," 854–856; Kemmis, McTaggart, and Nixon, *The Action Research Planner*, 3.
8. Bardzell and Bardzell, "Towards a Feminist HCI Methodology," 3; Campbell and Wasco, "Feminist Approaches to Social Science," 773–774; Harding, *Whose Science?*
9. Doorenspleet, "Reassessing the Three Waves of Democratization."
10. Brydon-Miller, Greenwood, and Maguire, "Why Action Research?," 13.
11. Firchow et al. "Quantitative and Qualitative Collaborative Methodologies."
12. See, among others, Bleck, Dendere, and Sangaré, "Making North-South Research Collaborations Work," 554; Thachil and Vaishnav "The Strategic and Moral Imperatives of Local Engagement: Reflections on India," 546.
13. Pachirat, *Among Wolves*, 56.
14. Cramer, "Transparent Explanations, Yes."
15. Gellman, "Collaborative Methodology with Indigenous Communities"; Gellman, *Indigenous Language Politics in the Schoolroom*.
16. Gellman, *Indigenous Language Politics in the Schoolroom*.
17. Yurok language-keepers are people who have the best ability to speak the Yurok language, and also have an implied duty to pass the language on to others. There are roughly a dozen language-keepers in the Yurok Tribe today, a number the Tribe hopes will grow with the increased availability of Yurok-language classes in schools. Note that this process is related to but not the same as member-checking (Schwartz-Shea "Member-Checking: Not a Panacea, Sometimes a Quagmire" (2020): 39–46).
18. Gellman, "'No nos importaba a nadie.'"

Recommended Readings

Lara-Cooper, Kishan, and Walter J. Lara Sr., eds. *Ka'm-t'em: A Journey toward Healing*. Pechanga, CA: Great Oak Press, 2019.

This book gives voice to Indigenous leaders in the far north of California who are at the forefront of identity reclamation work, foregrounding their worldviews on cultural survival.

Tuhiwai Smith, Linda. *Decolonizing Methodologies: Research and Indigenous Peoples*. London: Zed Books, 2012.

This book is a foundational text for anyone interested in understanding the role that research plays in colonization and how it can be redirected.

Wilson, Shawn. *Research Is Ceremony: Indigenous Research Methods*. Halifax: Fernwood, 2008.

Wilson describes how research with and by Indigenous peoples entails a process of accountability within relationship, a very different model than much social science research.

References

Bardzell, Shaowen, and Jeffrey Bardzell. "Towards a Feminist HCI Methodology: Social Science, Feminism, and HCI." Paper presented at the Proceedings of the SIGCHI Conference on Human Factors in Computing Systems, Vancouver, 2011.

Baum, Fran, Colin MacDougall, and Danielle Smith. "Participatory Action Research." *Journal of Epidemiology and Community Health* 60, no. 10 (2006): 854–857. doi:10.1136/jech.2004.028662.

Bleck, Jaimie, Chipo Dendere, and Boukary Sangaré. "Making North-South Research Collaborations Work." *PS: Political Science and Politics* 51, no. 3 (2018): 554–558.

Brydon-Miller, Mary, Davydd Greenwood, and Patricia Maguire. "Why Action Research?" *Action Research* 1, no. 1 (2003): 9–28.

Campbell, Rebecca, and Sharon M. Wasco. "Feminist Approaches to Social Science: Epistemological and Methodological Tenets." *American Journal of Community Psychology* 28, no. 6 (2000): 773–791.

Cramer, Katherine. "Transparent Explanations, Yes. Public Transcripts and Fieldnotes, No. Ethnographic Research on Public Opinion." *Newsletter of the American Political Science Association, Organized Section for Qualitative and Multi-Method Research* 13, no. 1 (2015): 17–20.

Doorenspleet, Renske. "Reassessing the Three Waves of Democratization." *World Politics* 52 (2000): 384–406.

Firchow, Pamina, and Mneesha Gellman. "Collaborative Methodologies: Why, How, and for Whom?" *PS: Political Science & Politics* 54, no. 3 (2021): 525–529. doi:10.1017/S1049096521000330.

Firchow, Pamina, Mneesha Gellman, eds. "Quantitative and Qualitative Collaborative Methodologies." *PS: Political Science and Politics* 54, no. 3 (2021): 525–564. doi:10.1017/S1049096521000299.

Gellman, Mneesha. "Collaborative Methodology with Indigenous Communities: A Framework for Addressing Power Inequalities." *PS: Political Science and Politics* 54, no. 3 (2021): 535–538. doi:10.1017/S1049096521000299.

Gellman, Mneesha. *Indigenous Language Politics in the Schoolroom: Cultural Survival in Mexico and the United States*. Philadelphia: University of Pennsylvania Press, 2023.

Gellman, Mneesha. "'No nos importaba a nadie': Navegando en la búsqueda del éxito académico en Oaxaca, México." *Polis: Revista Latinoamericana* 20 (2021): 59–78. doi:http://dx.doi.org/10.32735/S0718-6568/2021-N59-1588.

Harding, Sandra. *Whose Science? Whose Knowledge? Thinking from Women's Lives*. Ithaca, NY: Cornell University Press, 2016.

Alan M. Jacobs and Tim Büthe with Ana Arjona, Leonardo R. Arriola, Eva Bellin, Andrew Bennett, Lisa Björkman, Erik Bleich, Zachary Elkins, Tasha Fairfield, Nikhar Gaikwad, Sheena Chestnut Greitens, Mary Hawkesworth, Veronica Herrera, Yoshiko M. Herrera, Kimberley S. Johnson, Ekrem Karakoç, Kendra Koivu, Marcus Kreuzer, Milli Lake, Timothy W. Luke, Lauren M. MacLean, Samantha Majic, Rahsaan Maxwell, Zachariah Mampilly, Robert Mickey, Kimberly J. Morgan, Sarah E.Parkinson, Craig Parsons, Wendy Pearlman, Mark A. Pollack, Elliot Posner, Rachel Beatty Riedl, Edward Schatz, Carsten Q. Schneider, Jillian Schwedler, Anastasia Shesterinina, Erica S. Simmons, Diane Singerman, Hillel David Soifer, Nicholas Rush Smith, Scott Spitzer, Jonas Tallberg, Susan Thomson, Antonio Y. Vázquez-Arroyo, Barbara Vis, Lisa Wedeen, Juliet A. Williams, Elisabeth Jean Wood and Deborah J. Yashar. "The Qualitative Transparency Deliberations: Insights and Implications." *Perspectives on Politics* 19, no. 1 (2021): 171–208.

Kemmis, Stephen, Robin McTaggart, and Rhonda Nixon. *The Action Research Planner: Doing Critical Participatory Action Research*. Singapore: Springer Science & Business Media, 2014.

MacArthur Foundation. "Capitalizing Black and White: Grammatical Justice and Equity." 2020. https://www.macfound.org/press/perspectives/capitalizing-black-and-white-grammatical-justice-and-equity.

MacLean, Lauren M., Elliot Posner, Susan Thomson, and Elisabeth Jean Wood. "Research Ethics and Human Subjects: A Reflexive Openness Approach." *Perspectives on Politics* 19, no. 1 (2021): 188–189.

Pachirat, Timothy. *Among Wolves: Ethnography and the Immersive Study of Power*. New York: Routledge, 2018.

Schwartz-Shea, Peregrine. "Member-Checking: Not a Panacea, Sometimes a Quagmire." *Qualitative and Multi-Method Research* 1, nos. 17–18 (2020): 39–46.

Thachil, Tariq, and Milan Vaishnav. "The Strategic and Moral Imperatives of Local Engagement: Reflections on India." *PS: Political Science and Politics* 51, no. 3 (2018): 546–549.

Thomson, Susan. "Reflexive Openness as Ethical Research Practice." *PS: Political Science & Politics* 54, no. 3 (2021): 530–534.

15
A Plan for Managing and Storing Your Data

Verónica Pérez Bentancur

Overview

In recent decades, qualitative social scientists increasingly have proposed standards to promote good research practices and advance understanding of social life dynamics. These efforts have focused on improving research designs and data analysis strategies.[1] However, good qualitative research also depends on gathering good data and specifying the decisions made during a project's data lifecycle. This chapter discusses the use of documentation through data management plans (DMPs) as a practice that might help scholars create and administer the large and diverse volume of information qualitative research projects commonly yield and, simultaneously, helps make this information more accessible to other researchers.

Qualitative scholars typically rely on in-depth case analysis, comparisons of a few cases, or ethnographic methods to test or generate dense theories and understand their cases in detail.[2] In doing so, they normally devote time to fieldwork activities that employ a variety of tools to collect information: in-depth interviews, direct observation, focus groups, systematic review of press articles, historical documents, and verbatim records, among others.[3] The data produced in such studies differs greatly from data generated by quantitative or experimental researchers. Whereas quantitative data tends to be organized into data sets, qualitative data most often cannot be reduced to a matrix.[4] For instance, qualitative data may consist of quotes from interviews, excerpts from documents, notes derived from direct observation activities, images, or any combination of empirical materials collected from two or more sources during fieldwork.[5]

The advantages of qualitative fieldwork for scientific inquiry have been widely acknowledged.[6] As Robert Bates stated in the Munck and Snyder volume *Passion, Craft and Methods*, "Fieldwork is the cure for bullshit. When you do fieldwork, you take your research problems from reality."[7] Nevertheless, qualitative research can also pose a daunting challenge.[8] First, analyzing and organizing qualitative information may be frustrating and time-consuming. Second, researchers might fail to gather the relevant data needed, or end up collecting a considerable amount of irrelevant information.[9] Third, due to the amount and diversity of data qualitative researchers typically produce, they may end up with massive volumes of disorganized information after their fieldwork.[10] On top of this, the nature of qualitative data could make this information very difficult to organize for dissemination and eventual reuse.

To overcome these difficulties, previous authors have recommended several practices to manage data in different phases of a qualitative research project.[11] Building on these prior efforts, this chapter discusses the use of data management plans in qualitative research as a useful way to deal with qualitative data systematically, during an ongoing research process and once it is completed.

Verónica Pérez Bentancur, *A Plan for Managing and Storing Your Data* In: *Doing Good Qualitative Research*. Edited by: Jennifer Cyr and Sara Wallace Goodman, Oxford University Press. © Oxford University Press 2024. DOI: 10.1093/oso/9780197633137.003.0015

A DMP is a pre-fieldwork written document that can be amended both during fieldwork and afterward in which a scholar records the main decisions made during the data cycle of a research project. This document differs from a research project but should be aligned with it, particularly with its methodological strategy. A DMP should describe the data to be gathered during the project and also the ways in which data will be processed, analyzed, and stored, as well as how it will be shared and preserved after the investigation ends. DMP design implies moving beyond a research proposal to carefully ponder the "micro-level" decisions scholars should make regarding data during the research process.[12]

Some research or grant-making agencies include DMP as part of their requirements to apply for funding, often providing DMP design templates. Yet these guidelines are often too general and are frequently designed to address quantitative research data, which limits their usefulness for qualitative scholars.[13] Instead, this chapter discusses the use of DMP in qualitative research and provides concrete guidelines to develop a DMP as a systematic approach to data in qualitative inquiry. This chapter may prove particularly useful for those who have based their research on a positivist approach.

The chapter argues that the design of DMP documents offers many advantages for qualitative studies. First, through rigorous consideration of a project's data requirements, a DMP allows for more efficient data collection during fieldwork. When scholars design a DMP, they are better prepared for fieldwork. Second, by establishing clear standards to deal with data during the study, DMPs may guide the work of assistants. Third, by documenting the main decisions involved in the data cycle of a research project, a DMP makes it easier for researchers to revisit a project and gain an understanding of what was done many months or even years before. Finally, a DMP helps scholars to make explicit the data management procedures followed during the research. Thus, the design of data management plans can be considered an aspect of recent efforts to produce tools that improve transparency and replicability in qualitative studies.[14]

State of Practice

How is a qualitative DMP produced? What are its necessary elements? There are multiple checklists that guide the creation of a DMP; however, these guidelines generally are designed with "quantitative language," which could limit their usefulness for qualitative scholars.[15] An exception is the "Data Management Plan (DMP) Checklist" developed by the Qualitative Data Repository (QDR) of the Center of Qualitative and Multimethod Inquiry at Syracuse University.[16] Building on this specific antecedent, this section provides detailed procedures to develop a qualitative DMP, specifying the main elements these documents should include.

A DMP ought to always be aligned with the research proposal, but the concrete elements a DMP should contain are guided by a project's data cycle, which begins with the creation of data and ends with its dissemination and eventual reuse. Figure 15.1 illustrates this cycle. In a DMP, a scholar should specify how they will manage their data in each of these phases. Although there is no consensus on how a DMP template must be designed, its main sections may follow the structure of the data cycle in Figure 15.1.

As mentioned, scholars ideally ought to write a DMP in the pre-fieldwork stage, after writing their research proposals. Yet a DMP is a "living document";[17] it may be amended in

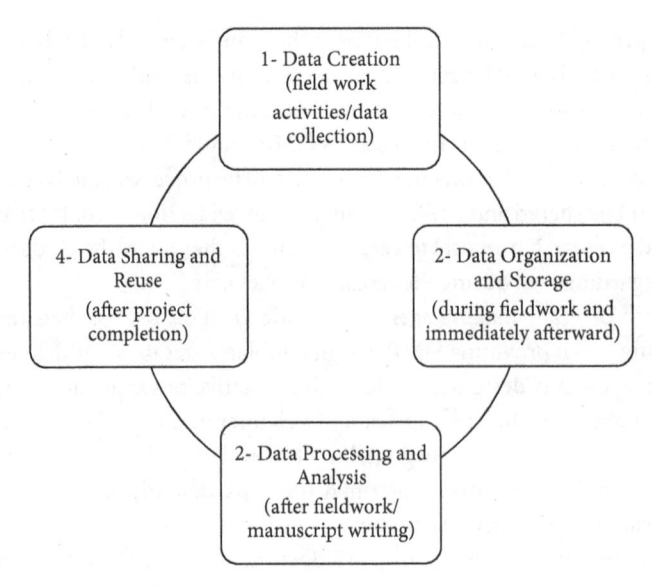

```
                    ┌─────────────────┐
                    │ 1- Data Creation│
                    │   (field work   │
                    │ activities/data │
                    │   collection)   │
                    └─────────────────┘
   ┌──────────────┐                    ┌──────────────────────┐
   │ 4- Data Sharing and│              │ 2- Data Organization │
   │     Reuse    │                    │      and Storage     │
   │ (after project│                   │ (during fieldwork and│
   │  completion) │                    │ immediately afterward)│
   └──────────────┘                    └──────────────────────┘
                    ┌─────────────────┐
                    │2- Data Processing and│
                    │     Analysis    │
                    │ (after fieldwork/│
                    │ manuscript writing)│
                    └─────────────────┘
```

Figure 15.1 Main Phases in a Research Project's Data Cycle That Guide the Design of a Qualitative DMP.

any phase of the project to record any changes to the original plan that might occur during the ongoing investigation.

Step 1: Data Creation

The first step in a DMP concerns the data creation process. In this phase, based on the project's theory and hypothesis, a researcher ought to describe with as much detail as possible the data they will require to support their hypotheses and how they plan to collect it. This is a critical stage in a DMP. Good research mainly relies on the development of good theories and suitable methodological strategies.[18] Yet it also depends on the collection of good data and on the specification of the procedures followed to do so.[19] Scholars should dedicate time to develop a plan for how they will generate their evidence.[20] Prior work has highlighted the importance of carefully designing a "to-get list"[21] or "data collection plans."[22]

When it comes to doing extensive qualitative fieldwork, a critical element is thinking through the kinds of evidence needed to test a given hypothesis or argument. In this step, for each of the project's hypotheses—descriptive or causal—researchers should ask themselves: What kind of evidence should I find during fieldwork if my hypotheses are true? Which pieces of evidence would confirm my main hypothesis, and which would rule out the alternative ones? Which of the available sources would provide direct evidence to support my hypothesis, and which would provide less direct evidence? In my experience with in-depth case analysis designs, carefully recording the data requirements for testing the hypotheses before fieldwork confers several advantages, including an efficiency improvement of fieldwork, focusing the attention on what is most relevant, facilitating the collection of more reliable data.[23] More specifically, this first step of the process enables researchers to improve the design of their interview protocols, better aligning the questions with the information needed to support a project's hypotheses. It also allows one to better design the lists of prospective interviewees to contact, and of possible documents to review or to guide the systematic review of press articles.

Table 15.1 shows an example of this exercise based on my book *How Party Activism Survives: Uruguay's Frente Amplio*, coauthored with Rafael Piñeiro Rodríguez and Fernando Rosenblatt.[24] The book analyzes how political activism is sustained over time in Uruguay's Frente Amplio (FA, Broad Font), a political party born in 1971 as a mass-based organization. The volume highlights that the FA is a deviant case because of its resistance to the external and internal pressures parties often face, which push them to become professional electoral organizations. While other parties that similarly originated as leftist mass-based organizations, such as the Partido dos Trabalhadores in Brazil, have lost their grassroots structures, the FA retains its activists, who play a significant role within the party to this day.

The book's methodological strategy combined an online survey to party grassroots with process tracing analysis based on extensive fieldwork with the purpose of tracing the process of reproduction of the party's structure. Six descriptive and causal hypotheses guided our book project; we also specified a set of alternative hypotheses. As part of our planning for fieldwork, we registered the data requirements to support each hypothesis and we identified the sources that could provide evidence: press articles, documents, and in-depth interviews, among others. We used "process tracing language" to specify the probative value of the evidence needed. (Table 15.1 shows this exercise for the project's Hypothesis 1.) After these steps, we designed the in-depth interview protocols and created a list of potential interviewees who could provide evidence to test our hypotheses. We also developed a list of documents to review. We attached to our DMP the interview protocols, the list of interviewees, and the list of documents to review.[25]

An important consideration in qualitative work is that the kinds of evidence that might help support a hypothesis are multiple and may come from several sources. Still, not all of

Table 15.1 Example of Data Requirements in a Qualitatitative DMP

Hypothesis 1 (descriptive inference—FA's origin): Since its formation, the FA has been a mass-organic leftist party (Levitsky and Roberts, 13). To classify the FA as this type of party since its inception, one should observe the following attributes: (1) strong local branches; (2) active grassroots membership; (3) close ties to labor unions and other organized social constituencies; (4) widespread labor-intensive mobilization of grassroots partisan and social networks.

Required evidence to support the hypothesis (i.e., pieces of evidence showing):

1. The bases (FA's base committees) were granted a significant political role in the party's decision-making structure (attributes 1 and 2).
2. An organizational structure that acknowledges the territorial organizations of grassroots activists beyond those of the electoral factions that compose the party (attributes 1 and 2).
3. Dual membership of leaders and activists (they are also members of labor unions or social movements).
4. Labor-intensive campaign activities in the 1971 election.

The joint presence of the four pieces of evidence constitute doubly decisive evidence of the FA as a mass-organic leftist party.

Sources: foundational documents, public speeches by Gral. Líber Seregni (the first presidential candidate and leader of the FA), press articles, interviews with activists (see list of already available interviews in Appendix A), secondary sources (see list of secondary references in Appendix B).

Source: Piñeiro, Pérez and Fernando Rosenblatt (2016).

them will have the same probative value for the hypothesis; while some pieces of information may represent strong evidence (straightforward and unbiased), others may be weak. In the example in Table 15.1, we used process tracing tests to assess the probative value of our potential evidence since our methodological strategy was based on process tracing analysis. Nonetheless, alternative ways to evaluate beforehand your potential sources' probative value can also be valid. For instance, de Vries and Glawion,[26] in the context of qualitative fieldwork using interviews, highlighted the importance of carefully considering how close interviewees are to the outcome of interest. While evidence emerging from interviews may always be biased,[27] the proximity of a given interviewee to the outcome of interest is critical to ponder how reliable your data may be. Accordingly, a typical question a researcher should ask themselves when planning fieldwork is: What kind of data sources (e.g., what interviewees) are most likely to provide the most direct evidence concerning my outcome of interest? Or what kind of data sources are most likely to provide "smoking gun" tests?

In my experience, once in the field, recording the initial data requirements to test the hypotheses, as well as the potential probative value of the proposed evidence, allowed me to better track progress in the field, informing my decision about when to cease fieldwork activities. Additionally, by previously identifying the types and volume of the data to be collected, I was better prepared to store and organize the information.

The procedures proposed for the creation of data should not be considered a rigid approach that precludes scholars' receptiveness to inductive discoveries. As Yom states, research processes in social science are far from being deductive and linear; researchers commonly "move back and forth between theory and data in creating causal explanations."[28] Particularly in qualitative studies, scholars often refine their theories and hypotheses in iteration with fieldwork,[29] extracting "new ideas at close range."[30] When this occurs in an early phase of fieldwork, researchers may need to amend their qualitative DMPs to reflect, for instance, additions to the data-collecting protocols, for example, new questions in an interview protocol, or changes to the list of people to be interviewed, among other modifications.

In my own research on the adoption of legal abortion laws in Latin America, my original hypothesis stated that these laws required two jointly necessary conditions: women's mobilization and a majoritarian left-wing party in Congress. When I was planning my fieldwork, I recorded the initial data requirements of my hypothesis as well as the possible data sources. Yet after conducting five or six interviews in Argentina with women legislators, I realized that, under Latin American presidential democracies, presidents should be systematically integrated into the analysis. Women representatives told me over and over how Peronist president Cristina Fernández had hindered the negotiations in Congress to pass the law. They told me that, in a vertical party structure such as that of Peronism, if a president were against a reform, Peronist legislators would not act to pass it, regardless of their own position on the issue.

As a result of this iteration, I understood I needed to modify my theory and hypothesis to incorporate the role of presidents as another relevant condition in the mechanisms that led to my outcome of interest (laws legalizing abortion). Thus, I modified the data requirements for my hypothesis, and I revised my interview protocol to ask about the role of presidents in my cases. I registered these changes in my DMP as part of an iterative process with fieldwork. When researchers record these types of changes, they can be more transparent when writing their manuscripts, specifying that their theories were not solely derived from deductive processes.

Step 2: Organizing and Storing Data

The second step of a DMP entails designing a system for organizing and storing the data collected. A researcher should do this before entering the field, otherwise they may reach the end of the fieldwork stage with a large volume of disorganized information and no real plan for managing it. This can make it difficult to work with the data in future stages of the project. Your data management system may change as you begin to collect data. When this occurs, you can modify your DMP to better adjust it to the data produced. By defining your data storage plan before starting fieldwork, you will at the very least lay the groundwork for organizing your data as you collect it. The devising of a system to organize and store information depends on the type of data to be gathered; however, it should generally consider at least four aspects: a suitable and sufficient space to store the raw data, a system to archive the information, a systematic production of metadata, and a method to update files.

Many of the archives generated during qualitative fieldwork (e.g., audio files, video files, scanned documents, and photos) take up a lot of space. Therefore, at the start of the project, scholars would be better off considering data storage needs and the possibility of expanding their capacity by, for example, purchasing cloud storage. If during fieldwork activities, researchers gather sensitive data, they should also specify the way it will be protected (e.g., restricting access by assigning access codes to some files).

In reference to archiving, researchers avoid shortcut solutions, such as storing their files in a folder called "Fieldwork" full of indiscriminate and unidentified archives. This option may seem convenient in the short term, but it might prove incredibly inefficient in later phases of the project, such as during data analysis or manuscript writing. Instead, scholars should employ a method of archiving that allows them to classify and distinguish data. For instance, when collecting data from different sources, one can create folders by type of sources, such as labeling the different sources "Interviews," "Field notes," "Parliamentary verbatim records," and so on.

A critical element when scholars organize data is to anticipate protocols that enable metadata generation. The production of metadata implies briefly documenting information that describes, contextualizes, and easily identifies the data, providing information about how, when, and where it was collected.[31] Researchers should design metadata for all data they generate, both raw and processed. For instance, the metadata of a set of interviews can contain a brief description of the sample and a list of interviewees in which you specify each of their names, positions (e.g., former minister of economy), and the date and place of each interview. When a project involves sensitive information, or you do not have consent to reveal the identity of the interviewees, the metadata should distinguish the information that only the main researcher (or their team) will have access to from data which will be anonymized to be shared in publications, repositories, or appendices.[32] Your metadata should also specify which interviews were planned but could not be conducted (or which documents or press articles you had planned to revise but did not have access to). Metadata generation is critical for sharing data in publications' appendices or institutional repositories (see below).

Finally, a crucial issue when managing data is establishing a straightforward method to update files. A sound strategy is to label files with consecutive numbers each time they are modified (e.g., "Metadata In-depth Interviews_v1"; "Metadata In-depth Interviews_v2"). This strategy can help researchers organize their data and avoid losing information, as it allows backtracking whenever necessary. Although this updating strategy may produce many versions of the same file, researchers can always eliminate the old ones at the end of the project. Scholars should avoid file labels such as "Final version," since a final version of a file is never actually achieved. Additionally, one should avoid labeling files by date, because a scholar might make several important updates to a file.[33]

Step 3: Transforming and Processing Data

When planning the procedures to manage qualitative data, researchers ought to anticipate the ways the information retrieved from fieldwork will be transformed and processed for analysis. These procedures should be aligned with the methodological strategy pursued by the project and with the procedures proposed in the data creation stage of the DMP. For instance, in the case of research based on process tracing analysis, a plan for transforming and processing data means considering the causal process observations (CPOs) that should be extracted from the raw information collected (see also Chapter 34). A researcher may need to transcribe the interview's audio files to extract quotes representing CPOs of the proposed sequences or mechanisms. One may also need to use process tracing tests to justify the strength of the CPOs to evaluate the project's hypothesis. In other cases, researchers may need to code their large volume of qualitative data, developing clear coding protocols.

As part of the process of transforming and processing data, scholars should consider the need to anonymize sensitive information so it may be quoted in manuscripts or appendices or, eventually, shared in institutional repositories (see below). In this scenario, researchers should design de-identification protocols, determining which elements they will eliminate from the transcripts (e.g., personal names, specific personal affiliations of interviewees, place of residence).[34]

Step 4: Data Sharing

Data sharing (or data access) involves improving the availability of the data to other scholars. Data sharing is an increasingly debated issue in qualitative studies and a good practice to increase transparency (see Chapters 38 and 39). There are multiple ways of doing this.[35] Although one can decide on this subject when the research ends, it could be useful to make this decision at the very beginning of the project, because this could affect how one produces metadata during the research or how one transforms the raw data. Furthermore, considering in advance how data will be shared will help researchers to better plan their budgets since some data-sharing formats are costly.

While sharing data entails several decisions, it often implies at least three main types of consideration. First, one should decide what data to share and where to do this. The strategies might be multiple. Scholars may simply decide to share the data they used to make their inferences or interpretations. For example, Fairfield showed in an appendix the pieces of evidence she used (quotes from interviews, excerpts of press articles or documents) in her process tracing analysis to disentangle the strategies of President Lagos's government to tax the rich in Chile.[36] The use of appendices allows researchers to increase the transparency of their work, particularly analytic transparency, by making explicit the observations employed to draw and present their inferences in the limited number of words academic journals generally allow.

Another alternative in qualitative studies is the use of appendices to provide further details about the data collection procedures based on the DMP records. Scholars can also use appendices to share their metadata to increase the transparency of the investigation, showing, for instance, who the interviewees are or which kind of press they reviewed. A good example of both practices is Barnes's[37] research on criminal territorial control in Brazil. In his paper's appendix, he provides detailed descriptions of the procedures used during his ethnographic fieldwork, then presents a list of interviews, including general information on each of his interviewees.

Researchers may wish to share extensive materials in institutional repositories or websites, such as the transcripts of the interviews, field notes, or sets of documents. This strategy not only increases transparency but also contributes to the replicability and reuse of data, as well as its preservation. While there are several institutional repositories for sharing information, a novel initiative that specializes in qualitative data is the QDR at Syracuse University.[38] Another helpful strategy for sharing data is to use annotations. In particular, the Annotation for Transparent Inquiry is an efficient tool that contributes both to analytic transparency and to the accessibility of the entire set of materials on which a given investigation is based.[39]

A final consideration when sharing data is ethical in nature. Sometimes researchers cannot share all the data they used because it is confidential or under copyright, difficult to anonymize, or simply because they consider that only those immersed in their cases can fully understand the contexts and interpret the data.[40] However, researchers should always consider sharing their metadata through appendices, institutional repositories, or even personal websites. This step is critical to allow other scholars to evaluate the quality of your research (see Figure 15.2).

Potential Problems

This chapter has argued that planning documentation procedures to manage vast volumes of information in the data lifecycle through a DMP is a critical element of qualitative research. A DMP represents a formal beginning for fieldwork. It allows for more efficient data collection in the field, enables a scholar to revisit a project so they can understand what was done many months before, and increases research transparency.

One might claim that the proposed approach entails potential problems or risks. For some, the recommended approach may be excessively time-consuming. Scholars may need to spend several months preparing for fieldwork and much time organizing data and cleaning and preparing materials to be shared. Unfortunately, there is no way around this; qualitative research is inherently time-consuming and labor-intensive. Yet a DMP design may mitigate some of these problems by allowing researchers to better track their progress during fieldwork and by enabling them to make the best use of available time in the field to collect reliable data. As stated above, by carefully recording the data requirements, a DMP helps qualitative researchers identify a saturation point in data collection or justify when to stop fieldwork. This is critical for scholars who can make only one trip to their fieldwork sites (particularly PhD students or researchers with few economic resources) or for scholars who cannot spend much time doing fieldwork due to job responsibilities or family obligations. Furthermore,

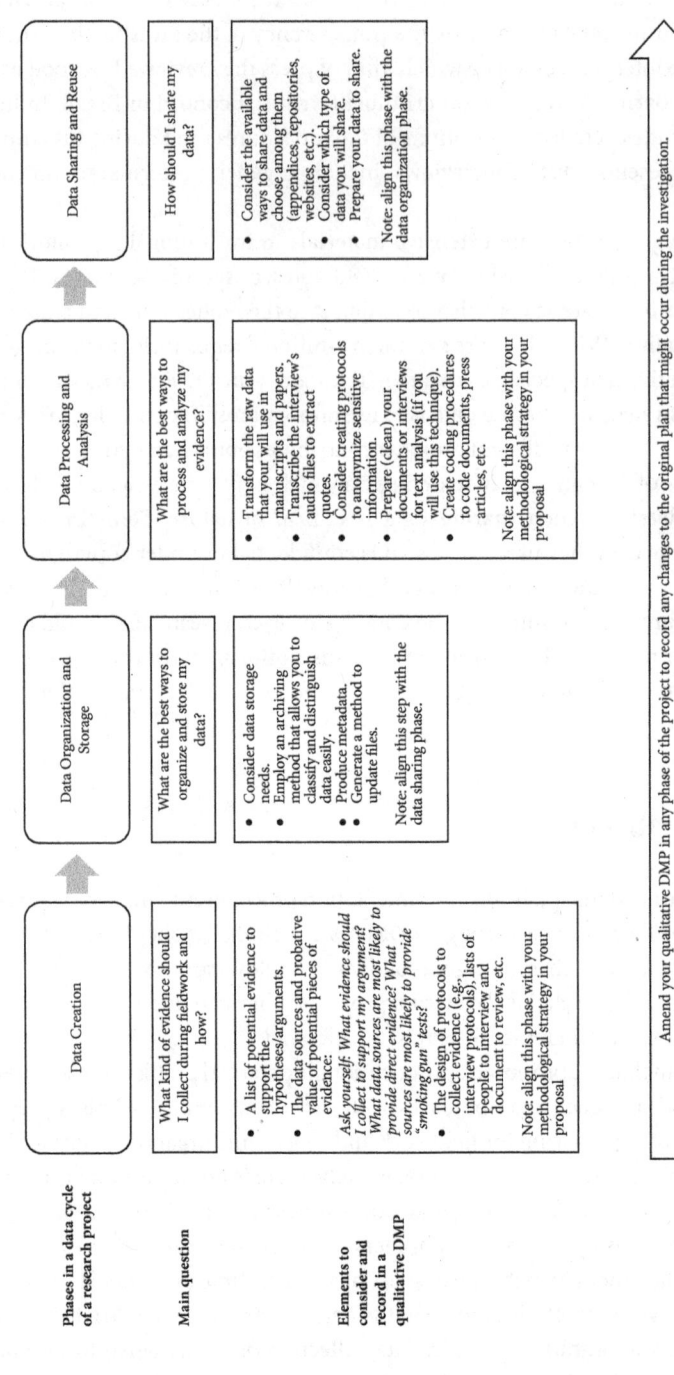

Phases in a data cycle of a research project	Data Creation	Data Organization and Storage	Data Processing and Analysis	Data Sharing and Reuse
Main question	What kind of evidence should I collect during fieldwork and how?	What are the best ways to organize and store my data?	What are the best ways to process and analyze my evidence?	How should I share my data?
Elements to consider and record in a qualitative DMP	• A list of potential evidence to support the hypotheses/arguments. • The data sources and probative value of potential pieces of evidence: *Ask yourself: What evidence should I collect to support my argument? What data sources are most likely to provide direct evidence? What sources are most likely to provide "smoking gun" tests?* • The design of protocols to collect evidence (e.g., interview protocols), lists of people to interview and document to review, etc. Note: align this phase with your methodological strategy in your proposal	• Consider data storage needs. • Employ an archiving method that allows you to classify and distinguish data easily. • Produce metadata. • Generate a method to update files. Note: align this step with the data sharing phase.	• Transform the raw data that your will use in manuscripts and papers. • Transcribe the interview's audio files to extract quotes. • Consider creating protocols to anonymize sensitive information. • Prepare (clean) your documents or interviews for text analysis (if you will use this technique). • Create coding procedures to code documents, press articles, etc. Note: align this phase with your methodological strategy in your proposal	• Consider the available ways to share data and choose among them (appendices, repositories, websites, etc.). • Consider which type of data you will share. • Prepare your data to share. Note: align this phase with the data organization phase.

Amend your qualitative DMP in any phase of the project to record any changes to the original plan that might occur during the investigation.

Figure 15.2 Summary of Main Elements in a Qualitative DMP.

as scholars carefully organize and document their procedures regarding how they deal with data during the research process, they are better prepared for the manuscript phase.

Second, some of the recommended procedures may be viewed as overly rigid. In particular, the procedures proposed in the first two phases of a qualitative DMP might not be the best options for researchers with minimal knowledge of their cases, who may need to conduct an exploratory stage before fieldwork. On the other hand, a benefit of thinking through a DMP is that it helps determine whether one is ready for fieldwork or needs more preparation. Additionally, some authors have criticized the practice of sharing interview transcripts or fieldwork notes because, in their view, only those immersed in a particular case can fully understand the contexts and interpret the data.[41]

Finally, scholars should consider the monetary costs of some of the procedures proposed for managing qualitative data. In particular, the transcription of interviews, the expansion of storage space, and the sharing of data in institutional repositories, all entail expenses that researchers should anticipate.

Notes

1. See, for instance, Beach and Pedersen, *Causal Case Study Methods*; Bennett and Checkel, *Process Tracing*; Brady and Collier, *Rethinking Social Inquiry*; Elman, Gerring, and Mahoney, *The Production of Knowledge*; Fairfield and Charman, *Social Inquiry and Bayesian Inference*; George and Bennett, *Case Studies and Theory Development in the Social Sciences*; Gerring, *Case Study Research*; King, Keohane, and Verba, *Designing Social Inquiry*.
2. See, for instance, Beach and Pedersen, *Causal Case Study Methods*; Boswell, Corbett, and Rhodes, *The Art and Craft of Comparison*; George and Bennett, *Case Studies and Theory Development in the Social Sciences*; Simmons and Smith, *Rethinking Comparison*.
3. Cyr, *Focus Groups for the Social Science Researcher*; Kapiszewski, MacLean, and Read, *Field Research in Political Science*; Koivu and Damman, "Qualitative Variations"; Mosley, *Interview Research in Political Science*.
4. Brady, "Data-Set Observations versus Causal-Process Observations"; Kapiszewski and Karcher, "Making Research Data Accessible."
5. Beach and Pedersen, *Causal Case Study Methods*; Bennett and Checkel, *Process Tracing*; Kapiszewski, MacLean, and Read, *Field Research in Political Science*.
6. Collier, "Data, Field Work, and Extracting New Ideas at Close Range"; Kapiszewski, MacLean, and Read, *Field Research in Political Science*; Mosley, "Introduction"; Seawright, *Multi-Method Social Science*.
7. Quoted in Munck and Snyder, *Passion, Craft, and Method in Comparative Politics*, 511.
8. Bennett and Checkel, *Process Tracing*; Kapiszewski, MacLean, and Read, *Field Research in Political Science*.
9. Kapiszewski, MacLean, and Read, *Field Research in Political Science*.
10. Lieberman, "Preparing for Field Research."
11. See, for instance, Jacobs et al., "The Qualitative Transparency Deliberations"; Kapiszewski, MacLean, and Read, *Field Research in Political Science*; Lieberman, "Preparing for Field Research"; Pérez Bentancur, Piñeiro Rodríguez, and Rosenblatt, "Using Pre-Analysis Plans in Qualitative Research."
12. Kapiszewski, MacLean, and Read, *Field Research in Political Science*.
13. See, for example, Purdue University, "Data Management Plan. SelfAssessment Questionnaire"; Van den Eynden et al., "Managing and Sharing Data."

14. Büthe and Jacobs, "Transparency in Qualitative and Multi-Method Research"; Elman and Kapiszewski, "Data Access and Research Transparency in the Qualitative Tradition"; Jacobs et al., "The Qualitative Transparency Deliberations"; Kapiszewski and Karcher, "Making Research Data Accessible"; Kapiszewski and Karcher, "Transparency in Practice in Qualitative Research"; Pérez Bentancur, Piñeiro Rodríguez, and Rosenblatt, "Unexplored Advantages of DART for Qualitative Research."
15. See, for instance, Stanford Libraries, "Data Management Plan"; Van den Eynden et al., "Managing and Sharing Data."
16. See: https://qdr.syr.edu/guidance/managing/dmp-checklist.
17. Kapiszewski and Karcher, "Making Research Data Accessible," 201.
18. Hall, "Aligning Ontology and Methodology in Comparative Research."
19. Bennett and Checkel, *Process Tracing*; Carsey, "Making DA-RT a Reality"; Jacobs et al., "The Qualitative Transparency Deliberations."
20. Kapiszewski, MacLean, and Read, *Field Research in Political Science*; Lieberman, "Preparing for Field Research."
21. Lieberman, "Preparing for Field Research."
22. Kapiszewski, MacLean, and Read, *Field Research in Political Science*.
23. Bennett and Checkel, *Process Tracing*; Kapiszewski, MacLean, and Read, *Field Research in Political Science*.
24. Pérez Bentancur, Piñeiro Rodríguez, and Rosenblatt, *How Party Activism Survives*.
25. As a matter of transparency, we preregistered our project's design, which includes the plan of data collection, through a pre-analysis plan in Evidence in Governance and Politics' online repository. See https://osf.io/q5fhx.
26. de Vries and Glawion, "Studying Insecurity from Relative Safety."
27. Mosley, "Introduction."
28. Yom, "From Methodology to Practice," 616.
29. Bennett and Checkel, *Process Tracing*; Yom, "From Methodology to Practice."
30. Collier, "Data, Field Work, and Extracting New Ideas at Close Range."
31. Carsey, "Making DA-RT a Reality."
32. It could be useful to assign a numerical code to each of the anonymized interviews
33. This strategy can be employed with any file that needs to be updated, including manuscripts drafts.
34. Kapiszewski and Karcher, "Transparency in Practice in Qualitative Research."
35. Lupia and Elman, "Openness in Political Science"; Jacobs et al., "The Qualitative Transparency Deliberations"; Kapiszewski and Karcher, "Making Research Data Accessible"; Kapiszewski and Karcher, "Transparency in Practice in Qualitative Research."
36. Fairfield, "Going Where the Money Is."
37. Barnes, "The Logic of Criminal Territorial Control."
38. See Kapiszewski and Karcher, "Transparency in Practice in Qualitative Research."
39. Kapiszewski and Karcher, "Transparency in Practice in Qualitative Research"; O'Mahoney, "A Practical Introduction to Annotating for Transparent Inquiry in Qualitative Research."
40. Cramer, "Transparent Explanations, Yes"; Yanow, "DA-RT and Its Crises."
41. Cramer, "Transparent Explanations, Yes"; Yanow, "DA-RT and Its Crises."

Recommended Readings

Kapiszewski, Diana, and Sebastian Karcher. "Making Research Data Accessible." In *The Production of Knowledge: Enhancing Progress in Social Science*, edited by Colin Elman, John Gerring, and James Mahoney 197–220. New York: Cambridge University Press, 2020.

This chapter discusses the steps scholars should take to share and preserve the data generated during an investigation. It highlights the value of "making the data meaningfully accessible" as a practice to produce more credible claims in social science, in both quantitative and qualitative studies. The chapter describes some of the infrastructure available for making data accessible and discusses the challenges scholars may face when sharing their data.

O'Mahoney, Joseph. "A Practical Introduction to Annotating for Transparent Inquiry in Qualitative Research." *Qualitative and Multi-Method Research* 19, no. 1 (2021): 19–23.

The article provides concrete steps and examples of the use of Annotation for Transparent Inquiry, a novel tool for sharing the extensive primary sources that social scientists commonly use to support their statements in published articles (e.g., archival documents, historical evidence). The paper extensively discusses the benefits and costs of this tool for enhancing transparency in qualitative inquiry.

Pérez Bentancur, Verónica, Rafael Piñeiro Rodríguez, and Fernando Rosenblatt. "Using Pre-Analysis Plans in Qualitative Research." *Qualitative and Multi-Method Research* 19, no. 1 (2021): 9–13.

This paper describes and provides examples of the use of qualitative pre-analysis plans as a systematic approach to fieldwork, to increase both efficacy and transparency in qualitative inquiry. The pre-analysis plan on which this paper is based represents a good example of the elements that researchers should consider in the phase of data creation of a qualitative DMP. It also provides examples of how to take into account the probative value of your pieces of evidence in advance.

de Vries, Lotje, and Tim Glawion. "Studying Insecurity from Relative Safety—Dealing with Methodological Blind Spots." *Qualitative Research* (2021), online first.

The authors describe the challenges of qualitative fieldwork in contexts of violence. Drawing on their fieldwork experiences in African countries, they state that researchers often do fieldwork in safety zones, for instance, conducting interviews with people who do not represent a risk. However, this fact affects the quality of the evidence collected. As a result, they propose a distinction between "inner" and "outer" circles as a practical guide for fieldwork in contexts of violence and as a way to evaluate the quality of the collected evidence. This paper represents a good example of how a qualitative scholar can consider the probative value of their evidence and the bias of their potential sources of information in advance.

Yanow, Dvora. "DA-RT and Its Crises." *Qualitative & Multi-Method Research* 16, no. 2 (2018): 1–9.

This article discusses the logic of interpretive qualitative research and then presents interpretive scholars' criticisms and concerns regarding the procedures proposed by positivist researchers in social science seeking to improve data access and research transparency in qualitative inquiry. The author argues against sharing interview transcriptions and fieldwork notes in public repositories and proposes other ways of improving transparency in qualitative studies, such as metadata sharing.

References

Barnes, Nicholas. "The Logic of Criminal Territorial Control: Military Intervention in Rio de Janeiro." *Comparative Political Studies* 55, no. 5 (2022): 789–831. https://doi.org/10.1177/00104140211036035.

Beach, Derek, and Rasmus Brun Pedersen. *Causal Case Study Methods: Foundations and Guidelines for Comparing, Matching, and Tracing*. Ann Arbor: University of Michigan Press, 2016.

Bennett, Andrew, and Jeffrey T. Checkel. *Process Tracing: From Metaphors to Analytic Tool*. New York: Cambridge University Press, 2015.

Bennett, Andrew, and Jeffrey T. Checkel. "Process Tracing: From Philosophical Roots to Best Practices." In *Process Tracing: From Metaphors to Analytic Tool*, edited by Andrew Bennett and Jeffrey T. Checkel, 3–37. New York: Cambridge University Press, 2015.

Boswell, John, Jack Corbett, and R. A. W. Rhodes. *The Art and Craft of Comparison*. Strategies for Social Inquiry. Cambridge: Cambridge University Press, 2019. https://doi.org/10.1017/9781108561563.

Boswell, John, Jack Corbett, and R. A. W. Rhodes, eds. *Process Tracing*. New York: Cambridge University Press, 2015.

Brady, Henry. "Data-Set Observations versus Causal-Process Observations: The 2000 U.S Presidential Election." In *Rethinking Social Inquiry. Diverse Tools, Shared Standards*, 2nd ed., edited by Henry Brady and David Collier, 237–242. Lanham, MD: Rowman & Littlefield, 2010.

Brady, Henry, and David Collier, eds. *Rethinking Social Inquiry: Diverse Tools, Shared Standards*. Lanham, MD: Rowman & Littlefield, 2010.

Büthe, Tim, and Alan M. Jacobs. "Transparency in Qualitative and Multi-Method Research: Introduction to the Symposium." *Qualitative & Multi-Method Research* 13, no. 1 (2015): 2–8.

Carsey, Thomas M. "Making DA-RT a Reality." *PS: Political Science & Politics* 47, no. 1 (2014): 72–77. https://doi.org/10.1017/S1049096513001753.

Collier, David. "Data, Field Work, and Extracting New Ideas at Close Range." *Newsletter of the American Political Science Association Organized Section in Comparative Politics* 10 (July 1999), 1–2, 4–6.

Cramer, Katherine. "Transparent Explanations, Yes. Public Transcripts and Fieldnotes, No: Ethnographic Research on Public Opinion." *Qualitative & Multi-Method Research* 13, no. 1 (2015): 17–20.

Cyr, Jennifer. *Focus Groups for the Social Science Researcher*. New York: Cambridge University Press, 2019.

de Vries, Lotje, and Tim Glawion. "Studying Insecurity from Relative Safety—Dealing with Methodological Blind Spots." *Qualitative Research* 23, no. 4 (2021): 883–899. https://doi.org/10.1177/14687941211061061https://doi.org/10.1177/14687941211061061.

Elman, Colin, John Gerring, and James Mahoney. *The Production of Knowledge: Enhancing Progress in Social Science*. Cambridge: Cambridge University Press, 2020.

Elman, Colin, and Diana Kapiszewski. "Data Access and Research Transparency in the Qualitative Tradition." *PS: Political Science & Politics* 47, no. 1 (2014): 43–47. https://doi.org/10.1017/S104909 6513001777.

Fairfield, Tasha. "Going Where the Money Is: Strategies for Taxing Economic Elites in Unequal Democracies." *World Development* 47 (July 2013): 42–57. https://doi.org/10.1016/j.worlddev.2013.02.011.

Fairfield, Tasha, and Andrew Charman. *Social Inquiry and Bayesian Inference: Rethinking Qualitative Research*. Strategies for Social Inquiry. Cambridge: Cambridge University Press, 2022.

George, Alexander L., and Andrew Bennett. *Case Studies and Theory Development in the Social Sciences*. Cambridge, MA: MIT Press, 2005.

Gerring, John. *Case Study Research: Principles and Practices*. 2nd ed. Strategies for Social Inquiry. Cambridge: Cambridge University Press, 2017.

Hall, Peter A. "Aligning Ontology and Methodology in Comparative Research." In *Comparative Historical Analysis in the Social Sciences*, edited by Dietrich Rueschemeyer and James Mahoney, 373–404. Cambridge Studies in Comparative Politics. New York: Cambridge University Press, 2003. https://doi.org/10.1017/CBO9780511803963.012.

Jacobs, Alan M., Tim Büthe, Ana Arjona, Leonardo R. Arriola, Eva Bellin, Andrew Bennett, Lisa Björkman, Erik Bleich, Zachary Elkins, Tasha Fairfield, Nikhar Gaikwad, Sheena Chestnut Greitens, Mary Hawkesworth, Veronica Herrera, Yoshiko M. Herrera, Kimberley S. Johnson, Ekrem Karakoç, Kendra Koivu, Marcus Kreuzer, Milli Lake, Timothy W. Luke, Lauren M. MacLean, Samantha Majic, Rahsaan Maxwell, Zachariah Mampilly, Robert Mickey, Kimberly J. Morgan, Sarah E. Parkinson, Craig Parsons, Wendy Pearlman, Mark A. Pollack, Elliot Posner, Rachel Beatty Riedl, Edward Schatz, Carsten Q. Schneider, Jillian Schwedler, Anastasia Shesterinina, Erica S. Simmons, Diane Singerman, Hillel David Soifer, Nicholas Rush Smith, Scott Spitzer, Jonas Tallberg, Susan Thomson, Antonio Y. Vázquez-Arroyo, Barbara Vis, Lisa Wedeen, Juliet A. Williams, Elisabeth Jean Wood and Deborah J. Yashar. "The Qualitative Transparency Deliberations: Insights and Implications." *Perspectives on Politics* 19, no. 1 (2021): 171–208. https://doi.org/10.1017/S1537592720001164.

Kapiszewski, Diana, and Sebastian Karcher. "Making Research Data Accessible." In *The Production of Knowledge. Enhancing Progress in Social Science*, edited by Colin Elman, John Gerring, and James Mahoney, 197–220. New York: Cambridge University Press, 2020.

Kapiszewski, Diana, and Sebastian Karcher. "Transparency in Practice in Qualitative Research." *PS: Political Science & Politics* 54, no. 2 (2021): 285–291. https://doi.org/10.1017/S1049096520000955.

Kapiszewski, Diana, Lauren M. MacLean, and Benjamin L. Read. *Field Research in Political Science*. Cambridge: Cambridge University Press, 2015.

King, Gary, Robert O. Keohane, and Sidney Verba. *Designing Social Inquiry: Scientific Inference in Qualitative Research*. Princeton, NJ: Princeton University Press, 1994.

Koivu, Kendra L., and Erin Kimball Damman. "Qualitative Variations: The Sources of Divergent Qualitative Methodological Approaches." *Quality & Quantity* 49, no. 6 (2015): 2617–2632. https://doi.org/10.1007/s11135-014-0131-7.

Lieberman, Evan S. "Preparing for Field Research." *Qualitative Methods* 2, no. 1 (2004): 3–7.

Lupia, Arthur, and Colin Elman. "Openness in Political Science: Data Access and Research Transparency: Introduction." *PS: Political Science & Politics* 47, no. 1 (2014): 19–42. https://doi.org/10.1017/S1049096513001716.

Mosley, Layna, ed. *Interview Research in Political Science*. Ithaca, NY: Cornell University Press, 2013.

Mosley, Layna. "Introduction: 'Just Talk to People'? Interviews in Contemporary Political Science." In *Interview Research in Political Science*, edited by Layna Mosley, 1–28. Ithaca, NY: Cornell University Press, 2013.

Munck, Gerardo L., and Richard Snyder, eds. *Passion, Craft, and Method in Comparative Politics*. Baltimore: Johns Hopkins University Press, 2007.

O'Mahoney, Joseph. "A Practical Introduction to Annotating for Transparent Inquiry in Qualitative Research." *Qualitative and Multi-Method Research* 19, no. 1 (2021): 19–23.

Piñeiro, Rafael, Verónica Pérez and Fernando Rosenblatt. "The Broad Front. A Mass-Based Leftist Party in Latin America. History, Organization and Resilience." Pre-Analysis Plan, 2016. https://osf.io/q5fhx.

Pérez Bentancur, Verónica, Rafael Piñeiro Rodríguez, and Fernando Rosenblatt. *How Party Activism Survives: Uruguay´s Frente Amplio*. New York: Cambridge University Press, 2020.

Pérez Bentancur, Verónica, Rafael Piñeiro Rodríguez, and Fernando Rosenblatt. "Unexplored Advantages of DART for Qualitative Research." *Qualitative & Multi-Method Research* 16, no. 2 (2018): 31–35. https://doi.org/10.5281/zenodo.3524354.

Pérez Bentancur, Verónica, Rafael Piñeiro Rodríguez, and Fernando Rosenblatt. "Using Pre-Analysis Plans in Qualitative Research." *Qualitative and Multi-Method Research* 19, no. 1 (2021): 9–13.

Purdue University. "Data Management Plan. SelfAssessment Questionnaire." https://www.purdue.edu/research/oevprp/docs/pdf/DMP_Self-Assess_14Feb2011.pdf

Qualitative Data Repository. "Data Management Plan (DMP) Checklist." Center of Qualitative and Multimethod Inquiry, Syracuse University. Accessed August 25, 2023. https://qdr.syr.edu/guidance/managing/dmp-checklist.

Schwartz-Shea, Peregrine, and Dvora Yanow. *Interpretive Research Design*. New York: Routledge, 2012.

Seawright, Jason. *Multi-Method Social Science: Combining Qualitative and Quantitative Tools*. New York: Cambridge University Press, 2016.

Simmons, Erica S., and Nicholas Rush Smith, eds. *Rethinking Comparison: Innovative Methods for Qualitative Political Inquiry*. New York: Cambridge University Press, 2021.

Van den Eynden, Veerle, Louise Corti, Matthew Woollard, Libby Bishop, and Laurence Horton. "Managing and Sharing Data: Best Practices for Researchers." UK Data Archive, University of Essex, 2011. https://dam.ukdataservice.ac.uk/media/622417/managingsharing.pdf

Yanow, Dvora. "DA-RT and Its Crises." *Qualitative & Multi-Method Research* 16, no. 2 (2018): 1–9.

Yom, Sean. "From Methodology to Practice: Inductive Iteration in Comparative Research." *Comparative Political Studies* 48, no. 5 (2015): 616–644. https://doi.org/10.1177/0010414014554685.

PART III
COLLECTING QUALITATIVE DATA

16
Interviewing Elites

Lantian Li

Introduction

Elites are people who have "vastly disproportionate control over or access to a resource."[1] When do we need to interview elites as a method? I suggest that there are two major scenarios. First, given elites' privileged positions in political, economic, or social realms, elite interviews can be very fruitful, or even necessary, if your purpose is to uncover the causes of social problems or the origins of public policies. After all, as opposed to vulnerable populations who, as Wendy Pearlman points out in Chapter 18 in this volume, have "diminished autonomy [that] renders them particularly susceptible to coercion, undue influence, mistreatment, or exploitation in research contexts," elites are the powerful minority who have the leverage to determine resource distribution and influence policymaking. By talking with elites, scholars can have a firsthand understanding of their roles in these processes. Second, in the cases where your research subjects are elites themselves, interviews can be a natural choice. For instance, to uncover gender differences in how entrepreneurs navigate the challenges of running companies, you may want to conduct in-depth interviews with entrepreneurs who have different gender identities, which is critical to arrive at a deep inquiry into their views and experiences.

But interviewing elites is a challenging art. Often the biggest challenge is the power asymmetry between elite interviewees and interviewers. Scholars, especially those who are still students in training, may need to approach elite interviewees who are much more resourceful or powerful than they. This can pose two unique challenges. First, it can be hard to gain access to these elites, who often have rather hectic schedules or simply have no interest in spending time with you. Second, even if you get to talk with them, the imbalanced power relation can make it hard for you to obtain high-quality testimonies. You may lose control of the conversation flow or fail to get them to open up and answer your questions in detail.

In this chapter, I will first review the state of the field, providing background information on elite interviewing practices. Then I will discuss the state of practice for addressing some of the previously mentioned challenges based on my own research experiences. I review five areas of practice for conducting elite-level interviews: sampling, gaining access (at both the national and local level), positioning strategies, power dynamics, and logistics. Last, I discuss potential risks and how to protect yourself from possibly traumatic experiences during the fieldwork.

Before I delve into the discussion, I would like to clarify that my views of elite interviews are shaped by my own position as a U.S.-based researcher studying China, an authoritarian country. I draw heavily on my own research experiences interviewing elites in the Chinese pharmaceutical sector at national and local levels, which can be very different from interviewing rural elites in America or government officials in India. You may want to use your contextual knowledge to gauge to what extent the lessons I discuss are applicable in your case.

Background

Conducting elite interviews is a prolific method used across the social sciences and has included financial actors in economic crises in Southeast Asia,[2] immigrant integration policymakers in Western Europe,[3] NATO staffers,[4] and political party officials and election commission workers in South Africa.[5] There has therefore also been a parallel literature on methodological best practices, including how to uncover useful insights through elite interviews while minimizing potential biases, how to access interview subjects, and how to accurately report one's interview findings. Layna Mosley's edited volume, *Interview Research in Political Science*, provides a comprehensive review of various aspects of elite interviews, covering topics from conducting interviews to the benefits and potential pitfalls of using them.[6] Work by William Harvey also offers practical advice and concrete strategies for planning and preparing in advance, including emphasizing that building rapport and trust is the key to interview success.[7]

These works provide useful, general knowledge for approaching and conducting elite-level interviews, and many of their recommendations transcend local and political contexts. However, reflections on elite interview methods tend to be rooted in the experiences of studying Anglo-American or Western topics, for example, interviewing healthcare corporate elites.[8] But as Ping-Chun Hsiung points out, we should challenge such a core-periphery knowledge divide based on locally grounded and globally informed qualitative research done in the Global South.[9] Yonatan Morse also discusses the unique challenges of interviewing elites in weak institutional environments of the developing world.[10]

It may be the case, and you might discover this in your own work, that some advice is useful in some contexts and not in others. For instance, Matthew Beckmann and Richard Hall usefully introduce the concept of "toehold" interviews, which refers to approaching the target elite or organization through a lower-level or more accessible individual.[11] While this bottom-up way of gaining access might be useful in some cases, my experience reveals how starting from the top may be a more effective strategy when contexts are more hierarchical. Indeed, context is crucial, and one should evaluate the utility of different interview tools as a function of the interviewee's political, economic, and professional background. Such variation in context may require nuanced adjustments of the researcher's positioning strategy when engaging the interviewees and building rapport with them in the conversation.

But we all want to produce interview data that is both valid and reliable. A concern that spans contexts is reducing the power imbalance as much as possible to build a more equal platform for conversation. This necessitates successful relationship building, which is critical to obtaining trust and navigating the power asymmetries between the researcher and interviewees. On this point, Lee Ann Fujii highlights in her book, *Interviewing in Social Science Research: A Relational Approach*, that researchers must be transparent about their research objectives and the use of the data collected.[12] Here, I suggest a series of tactics to achieve a fruitful working relationship with elites based on my fieldwork experience. I also highlight the importance of being sensitive to cultural differences and local dynamics, deriving my insights from a specific sector in pre-pandemic China. To be sure, the extent to which these insights are transferrable to other contexts will depend on the political, cultural, and organizational environments in which the target group is embedded.

State of Practice

This section presents strategies for conducting elite interviews. I begin with sample selection, discussing the best practice of sampling for two types of research questions: issue/problem/policy-oriented and elite experience–oriented questions. Next, I will reflect on how to gain access to elites according to their spheres of influence and compare the pros and cons of different referral approaches. Then I explain how we should adapt our positioning strategies according to the elite interviewee's identity (e.g., political, economic, professional). Building on this, I discuss how the power dynamics can be complicated by multiple structural and situational factors, and offer some suggestions for mitigating the power asymmetry. Moreover, I will review some logistical issues during elite interviews such as making contacts and obtaining consent.

Sampling

To begin with, you must identify who are the elites you need to interview through appropriate sampling methods. How can you choose the most efficient sampling method without introducing too much bias? I recommend selecting sampling methods according to the specific types of research questions you hope to answer. As mentioned earlier, there are two major types of research questions commonly addressed by elite interviews: one is problem/policy-oriented research, where elite interviews are used to uncover the causes of social problems or the origins of public policies; the other is elite experience–oriented research, where elites themselves are research subjects and understanding their personal experiences is essential to the study. For problem/policy-oriented research, nonprobability sampling methods such as purposive and snowball sampling would be most useful. For elite experience–oriented research, quasi-probability sampling is more appropriate.

First, for problem/policy-oriented research, I recommend purposive and snowball sampling to recruit elite interviewees. Through purposive and snowball sampling, researchers rely on their own judgment to select participants (purposive) and ask participants for referrals to expand participant pools (snowball). The priority is to find the most relevant and informative participants. In this case, you know the specific problem or policy you want to study, and there are certain groups of elites who are involved in the evolution of the problem/policy, so they are your recruitment targets. This is like solving a mystery, and your role is to be the investigator. You need to triangulate all the clues to identify who are the most informative people you should talk to (and can actually access). Take my dissertation research on the Chinese pharmaceutical industry as an example. My goal was to understand how government institutions and policies shaped the development trajectory of the pharmaceutical sector in China. To achieve it, I needed to identify the crucial institutional and policy reforms in the past decades, who initiated those reforms, what state organs were involved, how the reforms were carried out, what were the expected and unexpected consequences, and more. In addition to reviewing archival data, the best way to answer these questions was interviewing elites who engaged in or witnessed these reforms. But who exactly should I talk to?

I recommend starting with a pilot study, which is a small-scale preliminary study that allows you to build initial connections, test out your research plan (e.g., whether the interview script works or not), and gain a general sense of the feasibility of your project (e.g., tackle logistical challenges, if any). In my case, I planned to conduct at least 130 interviews in total, so I did around 20 interviews in my pilot study. From the pilot study, I learned a crucial fact that helped me plan for recruitment: professors at prestigious universities and research institutes were the most informative people for my purpose, because (1) they were deeply involved in the policymaking process in many crucial reforms as expert advisors, and (2) they were widely connected with and respected by officials from different state organs governing the sector as well as executives from different pharmaceutical firms who were industry leaders. Hence, these scholars were not only very knowledgeable about the substantive issues I tried to study but also were important gatekeepers of the field who could introduce me to the political, economic, and professional elites who were otherwise hard to reach. They knew who I should interview for a specific topic (e.g., who knew more about drug patent reform vs. pricing reform) and were more willing to help me given my academic background. It was with their help that I began to build my contact list through purposive and snowball sampling.

Second, for elite experience–oriented research, quasi-probability sampling is the preferred method. Quasi-probability sampling is not truly random sampling, but researchers will try to make it as representative as random sampling under certain conditions. In this case, representativeness and bias minimization are the priority. For instance, if you want to explore gender differences in how entrepreneurs navigate the challenges of running big corporations, you will need to make predetermined recruitment criteria for the sampling process: the entrepreneurs' gender identities; other demographic characteristics, such as age, race/ethnicity, and education; work experiences in their specific industry and firm; the characteristics of the industry and firm, such as size, revenue, and profitability. Depending on the scope of the study, you may choose to confine the sample to a specific industry or firm size. Since your focus is gender difference, ideally you would want to diversify the sample as much as possible along other dimensions so that your sample will be more representative. Fully random sampling is possible if you have enough resources to support recruitment (e.g., recruiting agencies with huge sampling pools).

But in reality, it is quite possible that you will face resource constraints (e.g., cannot get access to a full catalog of your research targets or hire recruiting agencies to do random sampling), or the elite field is simply too hard to characterize or break into. You may have to heavily rely on informal connections to understand who your potential interviewees are. In this case, quasi-probability sampling is more reasonable: you may need to combine stratified and snowball sampling for recruitment. For example, you may have an initial list of wine business owners from a local event, but you do not have a full list of all the owners in the state. Say you decide to recruit from three different age groups to diversify your sample. It could be difficult to break into the field in the first place, and once you somehow secure access to one age group, you may need their referrals to figure out who are in the other two age groups and how to reach out to them. In fact, fully random sampling is nearly impossible to do with any group of individuals, not to mention with elites. Hence, purposive and snowball sampling are usually more common. For research projects where representativeness matters, researchers may still end up having to solely rely on snowball sampling for recruitment. In this case, it is crucial for researchers to reflect on the limitations of the method and the findings.

Gaining Access

The most challenging part comes after sampling is done: now you know whom to contact, but how do you gain access to them successfully? I find that an elite interviewee's sphere of influence—national or local—is crucial to shaping how to best gain access because it determines the gatekeepers to the elite networks. In my research on the Chinese pharmaceutical sector, I wanted to uncover the origins, implementation, and consequences of crucial institutional and policy reforms, so I needed to interview both national and local elites. I found that national and local elite networks had very different nexuses: university professors and government officials, respectively. Obtaining their help turned out to be key to gaining solid and widespread access to elite informants.

At the *national level*, as mentioned above, those professors at prestigious universities and research institutes were very knowledgeable informants who had widespread connections with political, economic, and professional elites in the field. Sharing similar backgrounds with academic researchers, they were also the most accessible group, open to interview requests. Except for introducing my research topic, there was not much need to explain why I wanted to contact people for interviews, because they understood interviews as a method very well. Referrals from this group could be especially effective if they have already conducted research with your potential interviewees in the industry or government, who would treat your interview requests as a similar research effort.

This experience is not unique to the pharmaceutical sector or the Chinese context. If you are studying a sector at the national level and want to break into the field, you should search for media commentaries or existing literature written by national experts in this area and try to reach out to them with the help of your mentor or other academics you have worked with in the past. It is highly likely that you can find leading research institutions that host these national experts, who have established deep and widespread connections with a variety of key stakeholders in the field. Ask them for help, and then you can get exposure to their elite networks fairly quickly.

At the *local level*, however, elite networks have a very different dynamic. In my case, where there was a strong state, the local gatekeepers—the most resourceful and powerful local elites—were government officials. The lower the administrative level, the more important the role of government officials in bringing me to local elites. Compared to national elites, it was harder to identify the crucial local elite informants, which required a certain amount of "local knowledge" (e.g., less discernible from public sources). It was also more challenging to encourage local elites to open up and talk with me, since they were less frequently exposed to research through interviews. Government officials' referrals not only provided the necessary local knowledge, but they also helped boost the local elites' trust in my presence as an outsider. In some localities, especially at the village level, local elites may see you as the more privileged, government-affiliated researcher, and thus may pay you more respect and be more willing to cooperate.

Of course, the downside of this referral mode is that interviewees recruited in this way may be hesitant in commenting on specific topics, such as the state's action (e.g., what the state did right or wrong with the reforms). In fact, even in cases where the state is relatively weak and the local gatekeepers are other types of elites (e.g., community leaders), this problem of hesitation still exists if you seek their help for accessing the local elite networks. After all, given that it may be difficult for local elites to reject your interview requests through the gatekeepers' referral, it is even harder for them to speak ill of the government. A looming ethical question is that such requests may be more of a demand from the government. As the researcher, if you notice obvious hints that people are not really willing to speak with you, you may consider withdrawing your interview requests to respect their preference. Otherwise, you will need to think of strategies to reduce this bias, which I will discuss in more detail in the section on power dynamics.

One more thing to add is that you should certainly mobilize all sorts of networks you can resort to whenever convenient. While I find that informal ties through families and friends can be unstable for securing solid access to local elites, there is no harm in trying. During one of my trips, my informal ties were so strong that I was able to access multiple government officials as my gatekeepers, who later introduced me to all types of local elites I needed to talk to. Also, thanks to the informality of the connections, our mutual trust was high, so the elite interviewees were more willing to share their criticism about the government's action without much reservation. There were certainly cases where my informal ties were too weak to build such connections, but it did not compromise my other networking efforts. However, it is worth mentioning that I benefited from the fact that I have informal connections in the field site as a Chinese researcher, but this may not be the case for everyone. For researchers who are accessing a field site as a complete stranger, informal connections are not preexisting but may be built once you spend some time in the field.

Positioning Strategies

Now you finally get to sit down with the interviewees. How do you position yourself so that you can get the best quality testimonies out of the interviews? To begin with, you should read as much as you can about the elites you are going to interview to understand your interviewees' different interests and concerns. (Asking your referees about this is also a good approach.) Then, I advocate for different positioning strategies according to the elite interviewee's identity. I would like to discuss three strategies based on my experience: it is most rewarding to position yourself as a trustworthy, policy-oriented scholar in front of political elites; a neutral, nonprofit stakeholder in front of economic elites; and a perceptive, well-informed sociologist in front of professional elites. There can be other types of elites who require different positioning skills, but the key is to adapt according to their identities—in other words, their interests and concerns. Ask yourself: Why would they be interested in sharing their experiences with you? Can you give them the right incentives for opening up without provoking their concerns or losing control of the conversation?

1. A trustworthy, policy-oriented scholar in front of political elites.

Political elites are often most interested in seeing the policy implications of your research: how can your study be helpful in improving policies relevant to the problem at stake? In my pharmaceutical case, the government officials I interviewed were already embedded in an existing government-academia policy network, so it was not difficult for them to see the pragmatic value of my research. But I still highlighted the additional implications my project could bring from a fresh and more comprehensive perspective that had never been adopted by previous research, so that they would be more incentivized to open up.

In cases where such policy networks do not exist, however, more effort to showcase the policy relevance at the beginning of the interview will be necessary to provoke elites' interest. In particular, you may want to adapt framing strategies according to the political elite's specific position (e.g., relevance to drug patents or pricing policies). Another characteristic to highlight is your trustworthiness. Confidentiality protection is utterly important for political elites, who may get into trouble for sharing thoughts or experiences with you. This is especially true when your research topic is considered sensitive by the government and when the level of sensitivity may change over time. For instance, before the pandemic, pharmaceuticals and public health were among the "safe" topics in China, but they became highly politicized in the post-COVID era.

2. A neutral, nonprofit stakeholder in front of economic elites.

Compared to political elites, economic elites are more willing to share opinions about government policies; they are also happy to talk about general industry trends, but they can get secretive when it comes to their own firm's performance and strategies. Working for specific firms in specific roles, economic elites usually come with strong opinions when analyzing a policy or a problem. For instance, R&D (research and development) executives at foreign and domestic firms may have opposite judgments of the same policy due to their fundamentally different product strategies. Hence, you must clarify from the beginning that you are a 100% neutral, nonprofit stakeholder with no desire to make any business use of the conversation. Otherwise you may lose the economic elites' trust immediately, especially when they are CEOs of public companies who are always very cautious with what they share in interviews.

In general, it is easier to get testimonies about general industry knowledge (e.g., market trends, regulatory changes), but it is fairly challenging to learn about specific firm moves or stories. One strategy I find very useful is to inquire about their competitors' strengths and weaknesses, on which those opinionated economic elites are usually much more willing to comment. If you would like to learn about strategic moves or scandals about Firm A, go and talk to people at its neighboring competitor Firm B, and vice versa. You would be surprised at how much more you have learned once you triangulate their testimonies. In fact, this strategy can also be effective for interviewing political elites who come from different parties or factions; for example, you may get to the "real" story of Party A by talking to their competitors from Party B.

3. A perceptive, well-informed sociologist in front of professional elites.

Among all elite interviewees, professional elites tend to be highly educated with advanced degrees, so they are most interested in the unique academic contribution you can make to the field through your interviews. In many cases, they are also researchers themselves, so they pay special attention to how your research expertise overlaps with or differentiates from theirs. In my case, I was frequently asked two questions by these elites: Why would sociologists be interested in this topic? and How would sociology contribute to our understanding of the pharmaceutical sector? To tackle such challenges, I presented myself as a perceptive, well-informed sociologist (this is true for researchers with other disciplinary backgrounds as well, e.g., political scientist) who had done adequate homework on the sector and was highly aware of the different disciplinary takes on the topic.[13] This means doing as much background research as possible beforehand to demonstrate you are well-informed. If you are asking a question whose answer can be found on a ministry's website, you will risk being seen as an incompetent researcher who has not done your homework.

It was fairly easy to justify my sociological approach in front of those natural scientists and medical experts, whose lack of social science training made them feel the need to see more policy research. For social scientists who were trained in disciplines such as law and economics, it was also not difficult to emphasize the different perspective I adopted as a sociologist. What was challenging was when the interviewees had strong ideological preferences and wanted to see me siding with them (e.g., they may advocate for more or less government intervention in healthcare). I generally chose to agree with them to avoid inducing hostility, and I tried to reorient them back to more concrete questions. The strategy largely worked well, but in rare cases where the interviewees were aggressive or even hostile from the beginning due to deep-rooted bias, adjusting my own positioning was futile.

Power Dynamics

In this section, I would like to discuss how to navigate the power dynamics during the interview to improve its quality. The key is to mitigate the power imbalance between you and your interviewees. This is important to address because a more equal conversation can allow for more candid questions and answers. In my case, the major challenge was to boost my status and credibility in front of those national elites, most of whom were much more senior than me and with a higher social status.[14] As a young, female graduate student with little work experience, I needed to make extra efforts to convince them that I was a serious, qualified researcher. Several strategies were helpful: referring to the reputation of my alma mater in China, affiliated institutions, and referees; slightly "showing off" what I had learned about the topic during my probing questions; dressing in business casual attire with light makeup to appear professional and confident. Moreover, I found that male senior elite interviewees would become extraordinarily open when I impressed them with my expertise beyond their expectations. (By contrast, I do not recall any female senior elites I met being surprised by my expertise.) In some cases, I seized the opportunity to schedule additional interviews when I was able to challenge their stereotypical views of us young female researchers.

Another potential barrier occurred when I approached some local elites through government officials' referrals. Once they had the impression that I was somehow affiliated with the government, it added an unnecessary boost to my power status that could have alienated them. This was especially problematic when I tried to seek honest answers about the local impacts of government institutions and policies. To gain their trust, I would clarify that I was a researcher independent from the government, and that even the government referee was very candid when talking about the gains and losses of relevant reforms (which was true). I would also request one-on-one interviews, without the presence of any government people, when necessary. I believe these tactics helped buffer the negative side effects of government referrals for the local elite interviews.

Beyond this case, the power relations can be complicated by a lot of other factors, such as race/ethnicity, class, and nationality. For instance, if I needed to interview senior white male elites in the U.S. pharmaceutical sector as a young Asian female researcher, it may be even more difficult for me to alleviate the power imbalance between us. After all, the unique challenge of elite interviews is that the interviewees are often the powerholders, rather than the researchers. Any factor that can increase or reduce the power imbalance should be taken into consideration when adapting interview strategies. My experience suggests that it is critical to have the contextual or situational knowledge of whom you will be talking with beforehand. Be mindful of the subtleties that may affect the power dynamics, adapt accordingly, and think of the best way to mitigate the power asymmetry, if any. In some cases, you may even take physical surroundings into consideration to set up the conversation on a more equal ground. In my view, the rule of thumb is to boost your status when you may get looked down upon, and to add more humility when you may be seen as condescending. You may consider using any fact or hint that could serve as a signal to realize this purpose. In essence, it is about making the interviewees feel connected and respected at the same time.

Logistics

I would like to discuss some logistical issues during the fieldwork. First, elites in different cultural contexts may prefer different contact methods. In my case, the Chinese elites preferred text messages, phone calls, or WeChat for communication. This stands in sharp contrast to U.S. elites, who tend to prefer to receive formal interview requests via email. Second, I find that Chinese elites dislike written informed consent (you need to work with your institutional review board to get oral consent approval), which is similar to their Western counterparts.[15] Third, when I conducted interviews in the pre-pandemic era, it was much easier to gain trust and build rapport during in-person meetings compared to telephone interviews. But this might change dramatically in the post-pandemic era, as people have gotten very used to online work meetings. Still, one difficulty in the post-pandemic era is to ask for referrals during small talk after the interview when snowball sampling is the major recruitment method. During in-person interviews, it is usually much easier to have small talk before and after interviews, when researchers can easily seize the chance to build rapport and ask for referrals (e.g., talking while walking out of the building together). While online meetings still allow for formal interviews, researchers will find it difficult to chat informally with interviewees beyond the scheduled time frame. One strategy is to schedule more time than needed for formal interviews and use the last 5 to 10 minutes for more casual talk, so that the interviewees will not feel that you are running over time. Last, in terms of whether to share your findings with the elites after the interviews are done, my advice is no, unless explicitly requested by them, because it is highly likely that these elite interviewees have their own preferred answers to your research question due to their specific interests and concerns. It is impossible to make everyone satisfied, and it is not your job to provide a satisfactory answer for them after all.

Potential Problems

While I cannot discuss all potential problems related to elite interviews, I do want to highlight two major issues that you may want to be very cautious about. One is protecting your interviewees and yourself from potential censorship, especially when your research topic is considered politically sensitive. Confidentiality protection is crucial, and anonymization must be guaranteed. You also want to keep a low profile in any public sphere before and throughout the fieldwork. For instance, if you publish an op-ed in mainstream media about the topic and cite your interviewees' names (or even just anonymized testimonies) while you are still in the field, it may provoke unwanted attention that will discourage others from talking with you.

Another problem is about how to deal with your traumatic experiences during fieldwork. Since you are interviewing elites who may have much higher social status than you, it could be difficult to navigate situations that make you very uncomfortable. While most of my experiences were positive, in a rare case I was mansplained by explicitly hostile insults like "What you're doing/saying is nonsense/wrong" and dragged into hours-long one-way lecturing. But at that moment I dared not get too defensive or propose to end the conversation, since that interview was scheduled through a professor's referral, and I was afraid to jeopardize my connection with the referee and potentially the entire research network. That experience haunted me for a while. In retrospect, I should have ended the interview to protect myself before I got too uncomfortable. There have even been cases where the researchers' safety was threatened when the research subjects had an absolute power advantage. Self-protection is certainly a factor that one must keep in mind when planning for elite interviews in unfamiliar settings. A critical strategy to deal with this is to develop local support networks, such as by affiliating with local government or academic institutions, building communities with other researchers in the same area, and familiarizing yourself with channels for finding help during emergency situations.

Notes

1. Rahman Khan, "The Sociology of Elites."
2. Pepinsky, *Economic Crises and the Breakdown of Authoritarian Regimes.*
3. Goodman, *Immigration and Membership Politics in Western Europe.*
4. Hardt, *NATO's Lessons in Crisis.*
5. Wellman, "Emigrant Inclusion in Home Country Elections."

6. Mosley, *Interview Research in Political Science.*
7. Harvey, "Strategies for Conducting Elite Interviews."
8. Goldman and Swayze, "In-depth Interviewing with Healthcare Corporate Elites."
9. Hsiung, "Doing (Critical) Qualitative Research in China in a Global Era."
10. Morse, "Elite Interviews in the Developing World."
11. Beckmann and Hall, "Elite Interviewing in Washington, DC."
12. For a different epistemological perspective on transparency, see Bleich and Pekkanen, "How to Report Interview Data."
13. For more, see Li, "How to Tackle Variations in Elite Interviews: Access, Strategies, and Power Dynamics."
14. With regard to institutional affiliation, in my experience my alma mater in China worked better for entering social circles and securing interviews than my affiliation in the United States (Northwestern University). Seeking out a local affiliation may help someone new to the field build a network and obtain access to hard-to-reach individuals.
15. Harvey, "Methodological Approaches for Interviewing Elites."

Recommended Readings

Bogner, A., B. Littig, and W. Menz, eds. *Interviewing Experts*. New York: Palgrave Macmillan, 2009.
Fujii, L. A. *Interviewing in Social Science Research: A Relational Approach*. Routledge, 2017.
Mikecz, R. "Interviewing Elites: Addressing Methodological Issues." *Qualitative Inquiry* 18, no. 6 (2012): 482–493.
Mosley, Layna, ed. *Interview Research in Political Science*. Ithaca, NY: Cornell University Press, 2013.

References

Beckmann, M. N., and R. L. Hall. "Elite Interviewing in Washington, DC." In *Interview Research in Political Science*, edited by Layna Mosley. Ithaca, NY: Cornell University Press 2013.
Bleich, Erik, and Robert Pekkanen. "How to Report Interview Data." *Interview Research in Political Science* 1 (2013): 84–105.
Fujii, L. A. *Interviewing in Social Science Research: A Relational Approach*. Routledge, 2017.
Goldman, E. F., and S. Swayze. "In-depth Interviewing with Healthcare Corporate Elites: Strategies for Entry and Engagement." *International Journal of Qualitative Methods* 11, no. 3 (2012): 230–243.
Goodman, Sara Wallace. *Immigration and Membership Politics in Western Europe*. Cambridge University Press, 2014.
Hardt, Heidi. *NATO's Lessons in Crisis: Institutional Memory in International Organizations*. Oxford University Press, 2018.
Harvey, William S. "Methodological Approaches for Interviewing Elites." *Geography Compass* 4, no. 3 (2010): 193–205.
Harvey, William S. "Strategies for Conducting Elite Interviews." *Qualitative Research* 11, no. 4 (2011): 431–441.
Hsiung, P.-C. "Doing (Critical) Qualitative Research in China in a Global Era." *International Sociology* 30, no. 1 (2015): 86–102.
Li, Lantian. "How to Tackle Variations in Elite Interviews: Access, Strategies, and Power Dynamics." *Qualitative Research* (2021): 1468794121994475.
Morse, Yonatan L. "Elite Interviews in the Developing World: Finding Anchors in Weak Institutional Environments." *Qualitative Research* 19, no. 3 (2019): 277–229.

Mosley, Layna, ed. *Interview Research in Political Science*. Ithaca, NY: Cornell University Press, 2013.
Pepinsky, Thomas B. *Economic Crises and the Breakdown of Authoritarian Regimes: Indonesia and Malaysia in Comparative Perspective*. Cambridge University Press, 2009.
Rahman Khan, S. "The Sociology of Elites." *Annual Review of Sociology* 38, no. 1 (2012): 361–377.
Wellman, Elizabeth Iams. "Emigrant Inclusion in Home Country Elections: Theory and Evidence from Sub-Saharan Africa." *American Political Science Review* 115, no. 1 (2021): 82–96.

17
Interviewing and Listening to Ordinary People

Katherine J. Cramer

Descriptive Overview

Humans are constantly in the process of perceiving and making sense of their world. Listening to the way they talk can reveal so much about the type of person they think they are, what they think is appropriate in the present situation for a person like themselves, and what they value. Those identities and understandings are essential ingredients of political behavior. It is not surprising, then, that many political scientists find themselves drawn to listening methods.

Researchers do not often use the term "listening methods," but I use it here to refer to interviews of individuals or groups to emphasize the key value of talking with people as part of our work. Listening methods are quite distinct from surveys and other data gathering methods in their ability to uncover information we do not know we ought to look for and in the manner in which they often put us into relationship with the people we are studying.

I am a scholar of political behavior with a particular interest in individuals' understandings of their connections with other people and their governments. I use what I call "analytic listening" often. By analytic listening, I mean methods of data gathering that involve listening to the way people talk about public affairs, ideally in the venues they normally inhabit and with the people with whom they normally spend time, and comparing across such experiences to discover patterns in understandings and the resources people draw upon to create those understandings.[1]

My intent in this chapter is to give advice to researchers who want to study the understandings of ordinary people.[2] Much of this advice may be applicable to listening to political elites, but that work requires some additional considerations, such as unique strategies for gaining access, establishing credibility, and assessing the extent of spin being imposed, which I do not cover here. (By political elites, I mean people who spend a considerable amount of time, paid or otherwise, communicating with others about public affairs [e.g., elected and nonelected public officials, political consultants, journalists and bloggers, leaders of advocacy organizations, lobbyists, and social scientists who communicate often with the public at large]).

Analytic listening is not for everyone. You have to enter it with a good deal of courage and humility. It is not suited for people who are easily aggravated by other humans, do not like listening to other people, are uncomfortable introducing themselves to strangers, or do not see each human beings as inherently fascinating. You need to be able to be comfortable enough with yourself and your own views that you can set other people at ease, keep your mouth shut when people say things that you might find objectionable, and enter into every listening situation with a bit of wonder. Without those orientations, you may have difficulty gaining access to people, you will likely cause them to clam up, you may do damage to the reputation of social scientists in general, and you are likely to miss out on the main value of this approach, which is the experience of being made aware of perspectives much different from your own.

If you do choose to try analytic listening, you should do so with a deep understanding of the nature of public opinion data. Some people are skeptical that what people say in a one-on-one interview or small group conversation is a true reflection of their thoughts on a given issue. Such concerns convey a misunderstanding of the nature of public opinion. People do not have one true opinion on an issue. Instead, their opinions function more like a distribution around a central tendency.[3] As people communicate about a given political preference or attitude in different contexts, what they say varies. The extent of that variation will be broader the less they have thought about the topic and the less important it is to them. In other words, if people respond to a question in a survey one way, then say something else to you in an interview, both responses are true—they are true reflections of an underlying distribution. Your job as a researcher is to acknowledge this, explain how the context might have affected what people said, and provide enough detail to your readers so they can judge this variation for themselves. The fact that public opinion is context-dependent is all the more reason to use analytic listening. These listening methods enable us as researchers to study the lenses through which and the backgrounds from which people offer their opinions.

State of Practice

Listening to One Person versus Listening to People Talk in Groups

Most researchers who want to study the way people make sense of public affairs gravitate to one-on-one interviews. I encourage you to consider listening to people talk in groups, or what I have called "inviting yourself into the conversations of other people."[4] Because the expression of public opinion is context-dependent, who is in the room and to whom people are responding and trying to connect with are two things that matter for our understanding of the thoughts of members of the public. Think about what it must be like for someone to answer the questions of a social scientist, who is likely an employee of an institution of higher education, in a room alone with that person. Now think about what it must be like to talk with one's friends, family members, or coworkers with a social scientist whom you've all agreed to let into the conversation. It probably feels pretty different. The group context is probably one in which you feel more comfortable and a bit more in control in the situation. It is also likely a situation in which you can refer to and make use of your sense of the kind of person you are in the world, in other words your social identities. Now put yourself back in your shoes as a social scientist. If you are drawn to listening methods in part because you want to observe the work of social identities and the crucial role they play in political understanding and political behavior, it is in your interest to listen to people talking in a small group of people with whom they have chosen to spend time.[5]

These are not the same as focus groups. I repeat: I am not talking about using focus groups. I am talking about finding groups of people who already spend time with one another. Focus groups are created and convened by a researcher for the researcher's purposes. The participants typically come onto the researcher's turf to fulfill the researcher's goals. The group listening I am advocating involves the researcher asking permission to come onto the participants' turf to learn from them as they engage in interaction for whatever purpose they have already defined for themselves, from gathering just to visit, to gathering to engage in advocacy. The power, the agenda, and the connections between the participants are fundamentally different in this case than happens with focus groups.

I use this chapter to lay out advice for analytic listening through one-on-one interviews, as well as for listening via inviting yourself into small groups of people. I therefore refer to the people whom one might call research subjects as participants or informants rather than interviewees (and do not use the term "subjects" because of the dehumanizing nature of that term). I use the terms "listening session" or "conversation" as the umbrella terms for listening to individuals as well as groups.

Sampling and Case Selection

When you are designing whom to listen to in your analytic listening research, keep in mind what the point of sampling is in such a project. Unless you have a large research team or a long time horizon and large budget, you most likely will not be listening to people scientifically sampled from your population of interest (that is, sampled in a way that you know the probability of being sampled for everyone in your target population), which would allow you to generalize with a quantifiable degree of confidence from your sample to that broader population. Instead, listening methods are best suited for uncovering how particular people interpret and make sense of their world.[6] Obtaining insight on the way people understand public affairs illuminates the patterns we see in survey data can help generate hypotheses about such patterns, and can reveal insights about causal processes. Keeping that in mind will help you sample appropriately. It will help you choose people to listen to who provide sufficient variation on the characteristics that you expect to correspond with variations in understandings across people. This also is a reminder of the importance of a clear research plan before recruitment takes place, one that clearly identifies for you—the researcher— which characteristics need to be captured in sampling (see Chapter 10).

Recruitment and Gaining Access

In all of your interactions with the people you are studying, keep in mind that you are engaging in human relationships.[7] Treat the people you are studying with respect. You do not have to admire the people you are interviewing. Indeed, they may be people whose views you personally dislike. But admiration is not the same as respect. As researchers doing analytic listening, we are asking people to give part of themselves to us when we ask them for their thoughts. We need to treat those gifts as the precious things that they are regardless of who the speakers may be. Going into your research with such an attitude will help you in recruiting and gaining access.

Your institutional review board (IRB) will require you to inform the people you are studying of the purpose, risks, benefits, and safeguards of your study. In your recruitment and consent materials, I suggest using language you would use if asking such a person or group of people in person for the chance to listen to their thoughts, rather than the typical overly formal language of standard IRB materials. Analytic listening typically requires you to engage with humans directly. (An exception would be listening to prerecorded conversations.)[8] This means that you need to reach out to people with confidence, kindness, and clarity. You also need to demonstrate that you are aware you are asking them for their time, and that you are grateful for it. Explain why their time and effort is for a good cause.

Conducting the Listening

I think of analytic listening as a form of ethnography or deep immersion in a culture in order to understand a phenomenon from the point of view of people within that culture. I put it in its own category, though, because it involves temporary immersion in a series of cultures in order to compare across them. Some might call inviting oneself into the conversations of groups of people participant observation. I consider participant observation to also be a form of ethnography. I regard analytic listening as distinct from participant observation to acknowledge that the researcher is both observing and, at least in part, setting the agenda of the conversation.

You will set the agenda more in one-on-one interviews than when listening to groups of people. In both cases, however, you do want to, as much as possible, let the participants or interviewees raise topics and understandings on their own. Because you are listening to multiple people or groups, the limitations of time mean that you will need to introduce topics that allow you to study the phenomenon you are interested in.

You might want to consider gathering demographic data via a paper questionnaire that you can have informants fill out ahead of the listening sessions, while you are setting up, or at the end of the conversation as you are packing up. This will save precious conversation time and may also enable a bit more privacy for answering sensitive questions, such as questions about income. It will also help preserve as much as possible the conversational nature of your listening.

In general, you should aim to ask very open-ended questions that encourage your participants to tell you stories about their lives.[9] When people tell you their stories, they tell you what is important to them and show you how they piece together facts and values through the lenses of their identities.[10] One useful prompt for eliciting these stories is to ask something like "Can you give me an example from your life when you felt that way/experienced that?" In general, stories enable you to hear how people are making sense of their lives.

Your questions should invite your participants to reflect and elaborate on their responses. It is useful to have follow-up prompts in hand to encourage the people you are listening to to continue talking. Some of my favorites are "Say more," "Can you tell me more about that?," and "What's going through your mind when you think about that?" Some respondents will not need such encouragement, but many will, since they most likely are seldom asked about their opinions, hopes, and concerns regarding politics.

It may be easier to gather opinions using closed-ended questions, but it is advantageous to ask broader, open-ended questions to enable the people with whom you are engaging to draw your attention to things you were not looking for, things like the challenges they face on a daily basis, the people, organizations, or policies they blame for their circumstances, and the things that make them happy or that they wish were different in their lives. Your questions should strike a balance between being broad enough to elicit reflection and narratives and narrow enough that they enable you to investigate your research questions. Pilot-testing your questions with respondents who resemble your population of interest will be very useful in that respect.

Before you begin your listening sessions, prioritize your questions. You may not know precisely how much time you will have for a given session. Of course, you should estimate the time that you will need and give an upper bound to your informants, but things often happen that require you to cut a conversation short. Your participants may talk more in response to questions than you anticipate, or they may get a call that requires them to run off. Go into the conversation with a good sense of which questions you absolutely need responses to and which questions you may jettison without harming your research endeavor.

How many questions should you prepare to ask, and how long should the listening session be? This differs a bit depending on whether you are listening to a group or engaging with just one person. If you are listening to an individual, plan to hold the interview to about 60 to 90 minutes. People get pretty tired of talking after an hour, even if they are talking about themselves. I have interviewed some people who have really enjoyed talking about their lives and their thoughts and have had to end the conversation after two and a half hours because my own attention was waning. (I have also had people answer questions with the fewest words possible and therefore finished that same protocol in about 30 minutes.) For some research questions you may need several hours, and therefore should probably plan to talk with your respondents more than once. You should prepare to have about one main question with follow-up prompts for every 10 minutes of interview time. Build in time for introductions, signing consent forms, setting up recording equipment at the beginning, and wrapping up the interview at the end.

If you are inviting yourself into a conversation of a group of people, 60 to 90 minutes is still a reasonable timeframe, but you will need to be even more flexible about your list of questions. The larger the group, the fewer the questions you will get to. The 1-question-per-10-minute guideline is still a good rule of thumb, but you most likely won't know in advance how long the conversation will last. It is therefore useful to carefully prioritize which questions or topics you most want to hear answers to. Part of the value of the method is that you get to listen as people transition from one topic to the next, and it is in your interest to observe what people bring up themselves.

An important thing to consider to keep the conversation as natural as possible is the setting in which you listen. Always err on the side of listening to people in the places they normally spend time. This enables you to observe aspects of their lives that may not be obvious from the words they say, and also places some control in the hands of the people you are studying. If bringing people together requires food, it is best if you pay. If the people you are studying offer to feed you, you need to balance your presence as a researcher (and therefore minimize burdens on the people you are studying) with the practical reality that you are also a guest (and therefore abide by conventional norms of politeness, such as accepting their hospitality, and with gratitude).

Should you pay the people you are studying? If possible, yes, especially if the people you are studying are incurring an expense in order to let you listen to them. Logistically, this is easier to do when conducting one-on-one interviews and when you are collecting the identities of the people you are studying. For example, in a current in-depth interview project I am working on with political scientist Larry Bartels, we are paying our interviewees $100 for a conversation lasting approximately 90 minutes. However, my university requires that the people receiving this compensation provide their full names, addresses, and social security numbers on a W9 form. Some have declined the payment because they do not want to file this information with another government entity. As another example, in the group listening I conducted for my 2016 book, *The Politics of Resentment,* I did not compensate the people I spent time with in cash. When possible, I paid for their coffee or brought along a pan of brownies or other baked goods. The manner in which people came and left during a visit, my multiple visits, my desire to not collect personal information to protect their identities, the large number of people I spent time with, and my small research budget at the time made compensating people in cash not feasible.

How to Ask Questions

When people read my work in which I include portions of the transcripts of the analytic listening I've done with individuals as well as groups, they often remark that I say "Yeah" or "Okay" a lot. That is absolutely right. When I do analytic listening I participate with all of me: I use body language, eye contact, and also my voice, to let people know I am listening and trying hard to understand. I say small things like "Yeah" and "Okay" to let people know I am following what they are saying and I want them to continue. There is a fine line between listening supportively and agreeing with what people are saying. I try to show respect to all of the people I study regardless of their point of view. In other words, the way I conduct listening is much like a conversation in which I am a relatively silent but enthusiastic participant.

There are times when the people I am listening to ask for my own point of view. I try to avoid inserting that into the conversation as much as possible. I usually respond by saying some version of "I am not sure. What do you think?" There are times, though, when deflecting is not possible, and in those cases I always tell the truth about my views, and briefly. My experience has been that these questions arise after we have talked for a while and after I have had the opportunity to convey my respect for their perspectives. Therefore, sharing my own point of view has not stopped the conversation but has served as a point of comparison for their own thoughts.

Recording

If you are wondering whether or not you should record your listening sessions, the answer is yes, you should. In my first analytic listening project, I was studying the views of groups of people meeting regularly in Ann Arbor, Michigan, where I was in graduate school. For that project, I did not record most of the conversations. I thought it would be too intrusive to bring a recorder into the places where I was doing fieldwork (a corner store and a church). But reading *Sidewalk* by Mitch Duneier convinced me that if we want to grasp the way identity works in political understanding and enable our readers to almost come with us into our fieldwork to watch the interpretive process, it helps a great deal to have an exact transcript of what was said. In other words, recording is for me as much a matter of establishing trust with my reader as it is verifying that I heard things right. Therefore, in all of my subsequent work I have used a recorder. I have found that for the most part people do not mind. Also, placing a recorder prominently in the middle of the table has served as a useful reminder to me and to the people I am listening to that even though we are connecting as humans, I am there because I am conducting research.

Be sure to not just use one recorder. Always have at least two. There will be a time when your recorder malfunctions. I can guarantee it. And in that moment, you will want to have a backup. It always seems to be the case that as soon as I relax that strategy, my recorder fails and I am reminded that the small hassle of turning on another recorder and explaining why to the people I am spending time with is well worth it. There have been times when I have driven for hours, stayed overnight, witnessed an awesome, enlightening conversation, only to play back the recording and realize it is not there. Those are devastating moments. I encourage you to avoid them! These days, one of my recorders is a small handheld digital recorder, and the other is a smartphone with a high-quality microphone plugged into it.

Making Field Notes and Annotations on Your Transcripts

When you finish your listening session, as soon as is practical, check to see if at least one of your recordings worked. If neither of them have, record a memo as soon as possible on everything you can remember. Even if at least one recording is good, write or record a memo about the details of your experience. Give yourself notes on things like what you needed to do to find the location, what the setting was like (What kind of a room? What was on the walls? Any background sounds or smells?), the nature of the neighborhood, what the respondents looked like and what they were wearing, the way they smiled and laughed, their body language and manner of eye contact, what was said before and after your recorders were on, how you felt, as well as your general impressions of the interaction and what was said. It would also be helpful to give a brief summary of what occurred, which may or may not match up with your recollection once you relisten to the interview. All of this information will help you recall the nature of the interview when you revisit it for analysis. Your initial impressions help to capture the analysis you have already conducted while doing the interview. This is all data, and it is data that most likely will not appear in the transcript but will be very meaningful for understanding what people meant by the words they uttered. Another way of thinking about this is that human communication is about so much more than words, and at least at this point in time our digital recorders pick up only language, tone, and emphasis.

If you are able to transcribe the listening session yourself, you should do so. The act of transcription will push along your own processing of what you heard. However, transcribing is time-intensive. (It takes about three to four times as long as the length of the recording itself.) Not everyone can afford to take the time necessary to do their own transcriptions. If you are transcribing, insert notes about tone and laughter and body language that you recall. If you are using automated transcription or outsourcing transcription, read the transcription carefully while listening to your recording as soon as possible, to check for mistakes and to enable yourself to insert notes about pauses, tone, and other metadata.

Analysis

One of the most common questions that people new to listening methods ask is "How do I analyze all of this data?!" First, recognize that if you have already started to gather data, you have already started to analyze it. If you have proceeded rigorously, you will have started with good research questions that have then helped you craft good questions for your listening sessions. As you started your sessions, you probably noticed responses and things about the context that surprised you. Did the participants say things you did not expect? Were the answers to some of your questions so obvious to your participants that they thought the question was unnecessary or perhaps a bit ridiculous? Did the place where you met or were the people you talked with not what you expected? Noticing each of those types of things is the act of analysis. Questions that confuse your participants are the result of understandings you have that your interviewee does not share. Noticing that mismatch is also an act of analysis. Questions that seem unnecessary or ridiculous to your participants are about things that are central to their understandings of the world. Identifying those things is, again, analysis.

These types of analyses are greatly aided by knowing the relevant research literature. If your expectations are informed by the knowledge other scholars have built, your surprises and mismatches from your participants' understandings will likely be insights that are important contributions to the literature.

Analysis is far more, though, than your initial impressions. Often you may not notice things or be able to learn fully from your listening sessions until you listen to your recordings again when cleaning up your transcripts and conducting analyses. Generally, what you will need to do is remind yourself of your research questions and translate these into statements to yourself about what it is you are looking for in the listening session data. Some scholars like to think of this as a coding frame that you use to go back through your transcripts and code for the presence of certain topics, perspectives, or examples of certain types of narratives. There is a big difference, though, between quantifying how often a certain topic occurs and characterizing the understandings, perspectives, or interpretations your participants exhibit. While it is necessary to give yourself structure with which to analyze your listening session data (that is, clear questions about what it is that you are looking for), ideally this structure is broad and flexible enough that you can notice things you did not set out to observe.

Many people analyze their transcriptions with the use of qualitative software such as Nvivo. I prefer to use a different strategy that has proven to be more efficient for me. Once I have clearly identified the question I want to answer with my data, I open a Word document and read through my transcriptions (and often relisten to some of the recordings) while taking notes in this document about what each conversation or interview teaches me about that question. As I go through my transcriptions, I pause periodically to ask myself, "What am I learning? What more do I need to know? How do I know that what I think I am learning is an accurate reflection of what I have observed?"[11] Once I have gone through my transcriptions and have reflected on the patterns I think I am seeing, I continue the analyses with use of a spreadsheet. I create a row for each conversation or interview, and then a column for each characteristic that I think is important or relevant to the patterns I am observing. This enables me to look across the conversations and challenge myself about whether the patterns I think I am observing actually exist and how they vary across contexts or people. It also allows me to scrutinize and learn from the exceptions.[12]

This formal analysis of transcripts and field notes, as well as the analysis you do in your head as you are conducting fieldwork, often make it clear that you need to collect more data. I am continually asking myself, "How do I know what I think I know?," and the answer is often "I'm pretty confident in what I am concluding, but to be really confident I would see such understandings in X kind of group or Y kind of situation." For example, after a year of listening to informal groups around the state of Wisconsin, it seemed that I was hearing resentment toward cities and city people among people living in smaller and rural communities. I wanted to be more confident of that conclusion and better understand it, so I spent time in more rural areas, with a broader range of people in those communities, and asked more questions about the distribution of resources, attention, and respect in the state. Because that kind of adjustment is necessary when doing inductive work like this, it is important that you build in time to do additional listening as your study proceeds. It is also helpful, as well as a natural extension of treating your "subjects" like human beings, to maintain contact with the people you are studying.

Presenting Your Results

To provide a convincing presentation of your results, you should plan to provide an explanation of the patterns that you observed, specific excerpts of conversations or interviews that are typical of these patterns, as well as the exceptions and an explanation of why your conclusions are nevertheless justified. But the words alone are not enough. You need to provide enough information about the context of the situations in which you were listening that your reader can properly adjudicate the validity of your claims.[13] At a minimum, talk about the physical context in which the listening session took place (drawing on those detailed field notes you took immediately following your listening sessions). But you also need to explain why you listened to the people you did, how you recruited your participants, any resistance you received, what your initial research questions were and what you hoped to learn, and how those questions evolved over time. You also should provide details on the questions you asked and how you structured the interview or inserted questions into the group conversation, and whether and how the order of your questions and the wording shifted from listening session to listening session. As much as you can, enable your readers to come along with you into the listening.

Doing that kind of description and the presentation of conversation excerpts takes some space. You may find it helpful to provide a table that outlines whom you listened to and their characteristics. But for the most part, you will be presenting your data in the form of conversations or dialog, not figures or tables. Do not get discouraged about journal submission page limits. If you find it extremely difficult to fit into the page limits of a journal that you believe is a good placement for your work, communicate with the editors to see if they can make an exception at least for the initial round of reviews.

Conclusion

"Humans evolved to communicate in person. That is how many of us understand best and are best understood. So before drawing conclusions about any group of people, we should all strive to make sure we've talked with some of them face-to-face."[14] Conor Friedersdorf, a political journalist for *The Atlantic,* wrote those words while reflecting on the need for journalists, and all people, to not rely solely on impersonal (i.e., digital) communication to understand people. He was not necessarily talking to the discipline of political science, but he might as well have been. With our capacity to collect and analyze massive volumes of human language data, it seems increasingly rare for any of us to get out from behind our computers and listen to people in person. There is no substitute, however, for the deep understanding it can provide. I hope this chapter has provided a useful guide for you to begin that adventure.

Protocol for the Impact of Social and Political Change Interviews

September 2019

(This is the protocol I used in interviews for a project I am working on with Larry Bartels, in which we are reanalyzing the panel survey data from Kent Jennings and colleagues' Political Socialization Study [ICPSR Study #04037], and conducting in-depth interviews with the respondents, a nationally representative sample of people who were high school seniors in 1965. Prioritized questions are in bold. In practice, I insert additional transition phrases and slightly alter the wording and order of questions to fit with the flow of the conversation.)

Let's start with your childhood. What do you remember from your childhood that you think is important for the person you've become?

Let's turn now to politics specifically.
Was politics something that came up in your household growing up, over dinner perhaps? Could you describe what that was like?

How do you think politics in this country has changed over your lifetime?

Which party best represents the interests of people like you? Why? How has that changed over the course of your life? Have the parties changed over the course of your life?

Do you think the government pays much attention to people like you? Why do you think that is?

MAJOR EVENTS
Let's talk about some of the major events that have happened during your lifetime. I am very interested in your experiences and impressions during these times.

Let's start with the civil rights movement. What was it like to live during that time? How do you think growing up during that time affected you? What do you wish people living now remembered or knew about that time?

Next let's take the Vietnam War. [Take into account whether this person served in the military, and/or was an activist.] **What was it like for you during that time? How do you think growing up during that time affected you?** What do you wish people living now remembered or knew about that time?

How did you think about anti-war protestors at the time? How do you think about those protestors now?

How about Watergate—in what ways did Watergate change life in the United States? What kind of an impact do you think it had on you?

ROLE OF WOMEN
One of the major changes that has taken place across the course of your life is the changing role of women—how have you experienced that change?

During your lifetime, one of the issues that has received a great deal of attention is abortion. What are your personal feelings about this issue?

Another issue that has received a great deal of attention is gay marriage. What are your personal feelings about *this* issue?

RELIGION
Let's talk for awhile about religion—how would you describe the role that religion plays in your daily life? Do you think religion is more or less a part of your daily life than in the past? Why?

GOVERNMENT
Now I would like to have your help in understanding your views about government. Would you say that you can trust the government in Washington to do what is right? Why? How have your views about how much you can trust the federal government changed over time?

How about state government?

And how about local government?

What role *should* government play in our lives? Have we moved closer to that across the course of your life or farther away from that? [Take a moment to think of a particular event that sticks our in your mind as a time when government played the kind of role you think is best. Describe it to me.]

ECONOMICS
Many people talk about a growing gap between the haves and the have-nots in the United States. How do you think about that? [If person thinks a gap exists:] Do you experience it in your own life?

What do you think about the claim that the government has a responsibility to ensure that everyone has a decent standard of living?

NEWS
I would also like to hear your thoughts about the news media. Are there particular sources of news that you trust these days? Why?

If you want to find out about what is going on here in your local community, what news source do you use?

If you hear about state government or the governor, where are you usually hearing that from?

How has your news use changed over the course of your life? Do you think you pay more or less attention than 20 years ago? Why?

[If it has not already come up] How do you feel about Donald Trump? Hillary Clinton?

Which of the following two statements come closest to your view:[15]
1. Our lives are threatened by terrorists, criminals, and illegal immigrants and our priority should be to protect ourselves.
2. It's a big, beautiful world, mostly full of good people, and we must find a way to embrace each other and not allow ourselves to become isolated.

What advice would you give to a young person these days—say someone who is just starting their senior year of high school—to go on and have a happy, prosperous, fulfilling life?

How you would describe a good citizen in this country, that is, what things about a person are most important in showing that one is a good citizen?

If you could give a message to the entire country, not a high-pressure situation, but could somehow convey a message to the entire country, what message would you give? What would you want them to hear from you?

Notes

1. Cramer, "The Qualitative Study of Public Opinion."
2. By "ordinary people" I definitely do not mean boring, but merely the opposite of political elites.
3. Zaller, *The Nature and Origins of Mass Opinion*; Bartels and Jackman, "A Generational Model of Political Learning."
4. Cramer, *The Politics of Resentment*.
5. Cramer Walsh, *Talking about Politics*. There may be situations in which talking with groups of people is not feasible for practical or human subjects reasons, such as when you would like people to talk about sensitive topics or when you do not want the person you are listening to be distracted or influenced by the comments of others.
6. Schwartz-Shea and Yanow, *Interpretive Research Design*.
7. Fujii, *Interviewing in Social Science Research*.
8. For example, Cramer, "Deflecting from Racism."
9. Weiss, *Learning from Strangers*.
10. Cramer Walsh, *Talking about Race*.
11. Manna, "How Do I Know What I Say I Know?"
12. The process I describe is time-intensive and is much better suited to listening sessions in the dozens, not hundreds. I am in the process of trying to learn how to scale this process up without sacrificing attention to nuance, with my collaborator Deb Roy, other colleagues at the Center for Constructive Communication at the MIT Media Lab, and an associated nonprofit named Cortico.
13. Soss, "Talking Our Way to Meaningful Explanations."
14. Friedersdorf, "Pope Francis Is Right about My Profession."
15. This question was adopted from Hetherington and Weiler, *Prius or Pickup*.

Recommended Readings

Cramer, Katherine J. "A Method of Listening." In *The Politics of Resentment: Rural Consciousness in Wisconsin and the Rise of Scott Walker*, 26–44. Chicago: University of Chicago Press, 2016.
  This chapter describes how I applied these methods in the context of a particular study.
Fujii, Lee Ann. *Interviewing in Social Science Research: A Relational Approach*. New York: Routledge, 2017.
  This books teaches us how to treat our interviews as what they are: a human-to-human interaction in which we are sharing with each other.
Schwartz-Shea, Peregrine, and Dvora Yanow. *Interpretive Research Design: Concepts and Processes*. New York: Routledge, 2012.
  An essential text for understanding the distinctiveness of research that is oriented toward uncovering the understandings people use to navigate political life.
Soss, Joe. "Talking Our Way to Meaningful Explanations: A Practice-Centered View of Interviewing for Interpretive Research." In *Interpretation and Method: Empirical Research Methods and the Interpretive Turn*, edited by Dvora Yanow and Peregrine Schwartz-Shea, 2nd ed., 127–149. New York: M. E. Sharpe, 2014.
  An excellent how-to by one of the masters of listening methods.

References

Bartels, Larry M., and Simon Jackman. "A Generational Model of Political Learning." *Electoral Studies* 33 (2014): 7–18. https://doi.org/10.1016/j.electstud.2013.06.004.
Cramer, Katherine J. "Deflecting from Racism: Local Talk Radio Conversations about the Murder of George Floyd." In *Unequal Democracies: Public Policy, Responsiveness, and Redistribution in an Era of Rising Economic Inequality*, edited by Noam Lupu and Jonas Pontusson, 276–299. Cambridge: Cambridge University Press, 2024.
Cramer, Katherine J. *The Politics of Resentment: Rural Consciousness in Wisconsin and the Rise of Scott Walker*. Chicago: University of Chicago Press, 2016.
Cramer, Katherine J. "The Qualitative Study of Public Opinion." In *Oxford Handbook of Politics and Public Opinion*, edited by Thomas J. Rudolph, 41–53. Oxford University Press, 2022.
Cramer Walsh, Katherine. *Talking about Politics: Informal Groups and Social Identity in American Life*. Chicago: University of Chicago Press, 2004.
Cramer Walsh, Katherine. *Talking about Race: Community Dialogues and the Politics of Difference*. Chicago: University of Chicago Press, 2007.
Duneier, Mitchell. *Sidewalk*. New York: Farrar, Straus and Giroux, 1999.
Hetherington, Marc and Jonathan Weiler. *Prius or Pickup? How the Answers to Four Simple Questions Explain America's Great Divide*. Boston: Houghton Mifflin Harcourt, 2018.
Friedersdorf, Conor. "Pope Francis Is Right about My Profession." *The Atlantic*, November 2021.
Fujii, Lee Ann. *Interviewing in Social Science Research: A Relational Approach*. New York: Routledge, 2017.
Manna, Paul F. "How Do I Know What I Say I Know? Thinking about *Slim's Table* and Qualitative Methods." *Endarch: Journal of Black Political Research*, Spring (2000): 19–29.
Schwartz-Shea, Peregrine, and Dvora Yanow. *Interpretive Research Design: Concepts and Processes*. New York: Routledge, 2012.
Soss, Joe. "Talking Our Way to Meaningful Explanations: A Practice-Centered View of Interviewing for Interpretive Research." In *Interpretation and Method: Empirical Research Methods and the Interpretive Turn*, edited by Dvora Yanow and Peregrine Schwartz-Shea, 2nd ed., 127–149. New York: M. E. Sharpe, 2014.
Weiss, Robert S. *Learning from Strangers: The Art and Method of Qualitative Interview Studies*. New York: Free Press, 1995.
Zaller, John. *The Nature and Origins of Mass Opinion*. Cambridge: Cambridge University Press, 1992.

18
Interviewing Vulnerable Populations

Wendy Pearlman

Though both the definition of vulnerability and the utility of the concept are contested, researchers generally use "vulnerable populations"—also referred to as "disadvantaged," "marginalized," or "weakened"—to refer to research participants with characteristics or life circumstances that diminish their autonomy,[1] undermine their ability to make choices,[2] and thus render them particularly susceptible to coercive or undue influence[3] or to being mistreated or exploited in research contexts.[4] Concerns about vulnerable populations sometimes overlap with other kinds of research, such as research in war zones, conflict situations, and divided societies (see Chapter 24), or research on topics that are "sensitive" in the sense of being intimate, incriminating, or dangerous.[5]

While research ethics must govern all work with human subjects, many scholars insist that ethical research on vulnerable populations demands special scrutiny. At the same time, the question of vulnerable populations highlights the power of good qualitative research. Qualitative methods such as interviewing can help us hear from those who are often silenced by power and learn about their knowledge and experiences. With an eye to both the risks and the promise of interviewing vulnerable populations, this chapter begins with an overview of arguments in favor of distinguishing "vulnerable populations" as a category, as well as arguments against it. It then addresses practices for interviewing vulnerable populations and concludes with remaining questions. My discussion emphasizes the critical value of deep contextual knowledge of researched communities, as this is what allows researchers to understand situational nuances and read spoken and unspoken cues. That ability to perceive potential distress can critically help researchers assess when they might be asking too much, recognize when consent might be coerced, or identify other circumstances that could generate harm for vulnerable research participants. Throughout this discussion, I offer some examples from my own experience doing interviews with Syrians displaced by war, as well as with Palestinians in the West Bank and Gaza Strip about their experiences of occupation and violence.

Descriptive Overview

Seeking to prevent a recurrence of egregious violations, the National Commission for the Protection of Human Subjects of Biomedical and Behavioral Research's foundational "Belmont Report" recognizes that researchers have the capacity to harm any person recruited to participate in their studies.[6] It thus sets forth principles to guide ethical research with all human subjects, whether or not they are perceived to be particularly susceptible to coercion and exploitation. At the same time, the Report briefly nods to the need for special attention to groups for whom the potential for abuse appears especially salient. It mentions vulnerable persons with regard to each of the three key principles that it centers. "Respect for persons" requires researchers to acknowledge research participants' autonomy and protect those with diminished autonomy by ensuring that subjects give informed, voluntary consent. Here, researchers must attend to how vulnerability affects consent when inducements for participation become undue influence due to vulnerable people's dependent status or compromised capacity. "Beneficence" requires studies to maximize benefits and minimize harms. In this regard, researchers must justify involving vulnerable populations by systematically evaluating anticipated risks and benefits, as well as how vulnerability can affect both. "Justice" obliges researchers to distribute research benefits and burdens equally and treat subjects fairly. To this end, researchers must avoid continually recruiting vulnerable subjects only because they are readily available or "easy to manipulate."

The Belmont Report and other key ethics documents provide examples of vulnerable populations, such as pregnant women and institutionalized persons, but do not define the term.[7] Others have filled this definitional gap. Sieber and Tolich distinguish between risk, which refers to the significant possibility that research participation will cause harm, and vulnerability, which is the situation of persons who are not able to evaluate or refuse risk.[8] From a biomedical perspective, the Council for International Organizations of Medical Sciences views vulnerable people as those with "insufficient power, intelligence, education, resources, strength, or other needed attributes to protect their own interests."[9] Emphasizing structural contexts, Zion, Gillan, and Loff define vulnerable populations as those who lack foundational rights and liberties, without which one is not free to give genuinely voluntarily consent.[10] The American Political Science Association's "Principles and Guidance for Human Subjects Research" echoes this approach insofar as it refers to "low-power or vulnerable participants and communities" and advises researchers to be "especially careful to respect their autonomy, ensure that consent is informed and voluntary, protect them from harm, and treat them fairly."[11]

Kipnis digs deeper into the relationship between vulnerability and consent.[12] Everyday meanings of vulnerability, he argues, focus on some innate lack of capacity. By contrast, vulnerability in research contexts emerges from a disconnect between consent, in the sense of verbally permitting someone to do something, and permissibility, in the sense of its being ethical for another to do that thing even with consent. The vulnerabilities pertinent for research are research participants' special circumstances that demand a researcher to scrutinize whether, even with consent, research is permissible.[13] On this basis, Kipnis identifies six types of research vulnerability. "Cognitive vulnerability" encompasses impediments to the ability to absorb information and assess risks and benefits, such as immaturity, mental illness, trauma, or language barriers. "Vulnerability to authority" occurs when power relationships render it dangerous for one to refuse participation. "Deferential vulnerability" emerges when people's timidity or eagerness to please leaves them unable to express a desire to refuse participation. "Medical vulnerability" affects those whose illnesses push them to participate in research as a "last hope" for a cure. "Allocational vulnerability" applies to those who lack resources that they might obtain due to participation, rendering them liable to coercion. Finally, "infrastructural vulnerability" occurs when institutions lack means, such as funding, management, and technology, necessary to protect participants.

Not all qualitative researchers engage vulnerability as a concept. Fujii did pathbreaking research with populations typically considered to be vulnerable, such as people who experienced genocide. Her influential article "Research Ethics 101," however, mentions "vulnerable" only in quotation marks. She explains that she uses the term "with caution" to signal that these populations are not always weak or unknowing.[14] Her book on relational interviewing delves into principles often associated with vulnerable populations, such as treating interlocutors with dignity and regarding them as ends rather than means. Still, it does not invoke the term "vulnerable populations" at all.[15]

Others directly contest the "vulnerable populations" concept. While upholding the imperative of research ethics for all human subjects, these critics put forth several critiques of designating certain populations as particularly vulnerable and thus in need of special ethics scrutiny. First, some argue that institutional judgments about who is vulnerable are vague and arbitrary. Levine et al. regard the category "vulnerable populations" as simultaneously too broad (because it encompasses any group in need of "special consideration") and too narrow (because, in practice, it focuses on consent and neglects other sources of harm).[16] More adamantly, Van den Hoonaard dismisses vulnerability as an "invention" by institutional review boards (IRBs) that, developed primarily for biomedical research, are ill-equipped for social science.[17] Indeed, he and other critics charge, IRBs' main concern is not even research ethics as much as protecting universities from liability.

Second, critics posit that a priori specification of vulnerable traits or groups misses how vulnerability is dynamic, contingent, relational, and contextually dependent. For Macklin, researchers' positionality is key: when teams from powerful countries or entities carry out research in the developing world, their ability to coerce potential participants effectively renders whole communities or countries "vulnerable."[18] Research questions themselves also constitute vulnerability.[19] The entire population under an authoritarian regime is not typically regarded as vulnerable, but any citizen can be susceptible to harm when speaking to a researcher about politics.[20] Individuals' vulnerability can also change over time, including after a researcher has left the field site.[21] In conflict settings, for instance, a research participant may shift from the position of civilian to that of belligerent, refugee, survivor, or criminal—each of which carries different implications for how research participation can generate harm.[22]

Third, although classifying people as vulnerable is intended to reduce harm, it can itself do harm by reinforcing disrespectful or degrading stereotypes.[23] As Fujii suggests, it can unfairly cast as weak those who are actually strong, in part because the very hardships assumed to make people vulnerable can bring them to develop advanced coping strategies.[24] Labeling people as vulnerable might thus be seen as paternalistically emphasizing their insufficiencies rather than encouraging researchers to explore their capabilities.[25] If these labels create barriers to researching these populations, they can also impede the production of knowledge about their circumstances and thereby contribute to perpetuating their marginalization.[26]

Finally, classifications of vulnerable groups can have unnecessary and counterproductive chilling effects on research. Some argue that IRBs' wariness of research on vulnerable populations, like research on sensitive topics, overestimates the risks of talking about difficult experiences and underestimates its benefits, including self-awareness, solace, and empowerment.[27] Some people might want to participate in research precisely because they are vulnerable.[28] This can be especially the case for those who have endured violence or injustice and want to "speak their truths" as an act of agency, commitment, or desire to contest what they believe to be falsehoods.[29] Kostocicova and Knott suggest that denying such populations the opportunity to share their stories might itself be unethical.[30]

This discussion of critiques is not intended to dismiss concern about vulnerabilities, but rather to encourage serious attention to all research-induced harms, regardless of how we classify participants.[31] As Kottow insists, the fact that some people are predisposed to additional and compound forms of injury does not diminish the susceptibility of all humans and their need for equal protection.[32] Rather than asking only if research participants possess particular characteristics, therefore, researchers can focus on how their research projects themselves create or minimize research participant vulnerabilities.[33] Researchers can keep these debates in mind as they move forward designing and implementing thoughtful, sensitive, and ethical research practices.

State of Practice

While mindful of the above debates, I use the term "vulnerable" in the remainder of this chapter for the sake of communicative simplicity and in recognition of its widespread usage. Turning to research practice, I recognize that interviewing vulnerable people, like all ethical research, entails difficult trade-offs between multiple and sometimes contradictory priorities.[34] While in no way comprehensive, the following discussion builds on existing scholarship to offer some thoughts on navigating these challenges. It moves sequentially across the life course of a research project.

Initial Steps

From the very start of a project, researchers can think carefully about whether interviewing vulnerable populations is necessary or appropriate. At minimum, research must be designed such that it does not increase people's vulnerability.[35] Several scholars argue that this includes ensuring that published findings do not exacerbate discrimination, marginalization, or stereotyping of the researched population.[36] Putting to use deep knowledge about the community to be studied, researchers can thus think through possible harmful ramifications of research from its beginning stages. Beyond doing no harm, some hold that research with vulnerable populations is justified only if those research participants gain something from their participation.[37] For participants already susceptible to abuse, research must not be another kind of exploitation that treats them like objects by "stealing their stories."[38] Instead, research with vulnerable populations can be crafted to "give back," especially in ways that those populations themselves judge to be important.[39]

"Giving back" takes different forms in different contexts; the more that researchers know about the communities they research, and genuinely listen to what their interlocutors say, the more they can identify meaningful strategies to attain that goal. In my own work, for example, I have sought to "give back" by volunteering with Syrian- and Palestinian-led initiatives, writing expert affidavits for asylum cases, or offering a helping hand to interlocutors working on their own research or writing projects. More important, my research has helped me understand that, for both of these populations, the most valuable thing I can do with the information that I gather is to pass it along in ways that raise wider awareness and challenge misconceptions of their political struggles. I have thus tried to convey my research in public writing and speaking, showcasing the direct voices of my Syrian and Palestinian interviewees. I will never be able to "repay" these populations what their participation in my research has given me. However, I try to take the ultimate aspiration to "give back" as a requisite for my conducting this research in the first place.

Once researchers have developed a project that justifies interviewing vulnerable populations, they typically seek approval from their institution's ethics committee or IRB. As noted earlier, critiques of IRBs abound. I follow those scholars who urge us neither to dismiss IRB approval as a mere bureaucratic annoyance nor to exaggerate its authority as certification that a project is problem-free. Rather, they suggest, researchers can approach IRBs as one of many inputs in their ongoing reflections on research ethics.[40] Doing so, they can heed Sieber and Tolich's warning that even if an IRB—and indeed potential interviewees—believe that a study is safe, it might not be.[41] Again, Kipnis's distinction between consent and permissibility offers a useful rule of thumb as researchers navigate these complexities.

Recruitment

Vulnerable persons might be predisposed to distrust researchers and/or to fear the social, physical, or legal ramifications of being interviewed.[42] In this context, methods for identifying interviewees resonate with those discussed in Chapter 11 on sampling hard-to-reach populations. Liamputtong notes that the most common method is snowball sampling, which researchers typically initiate through some combination of efforts, including posting advertisements, spending time in places frequented by the population, or doing volunteer work at relevant organizations.[43] Researchers sometimes gain access by hiring research assistants from within or close to the community[44] or developing fuller community research partnerships of the kind discussed in Chapter 14. Each of these techniques brings its own methodological and ethical costs and benefits. This is particularly the case when researchers ask local leaders or nongovernmental organizations to introduce them to interviewees, as the power of these community "gatekeepers" can undermine the voluntariness of interviewees' consent.[45] Nuanced understandings of the research setting is critical for detecting and navigating these complexities.

In selecting interviewees, researchers should attend to the problem of "overresearched groups." Being repeatedly made the subject of research can itself generate excessive demands that increase populations' liability to emotional or other harms, including the feeling of being used.[46] Alternatively, being understudied can compound harm when it reinforces the neglect of populations by society and policymakers.[47]

Compensation of interviewees is the subject of considerable debate.[48] Some argue that paying vulnerable people for participation creates undue pressure, undermines free choice, and skews both recruitment and results. Others contest that it demonstrates respect for people's contribution, equalizes the power relationship between researcher and subject, or simply is necessary to recruit participation. Driscoll suggests that it is a Goldilocks problem: compensation must be sufficient to provide incentive but not so much that it is coercive.[49] I have approached this dilemma by taking cues from what I have learned to be socially customary in the communities that I research. In those contexts, I risk insulting interviewees if I offer to pay them in exchange for their speaking to me about their personal experiences of politics. This is particularly the case when those experiences are intertwined with values such as dignity, obligation, identity, and justice, which my interlocutors are likely to feel are denigrated by monetary compensation. Rather than payment, I therefore offer more symbolic tokens of appreciation. When I visit interlocutors in their homes, I bring small gifts, such as sweets, home decorations, or toys for children. When I meet interlocutors in cafés or restaurants, I fight for the bill and go to sometimes humorous lengths to insist upon paying. These are not perfect solutions to the tricky question of compensation. However, they are gestures authentic to the communities that I study. They are thus culturally appropriate, if very small, ways of communicating that I do not take interviewees for granted.

Logistics

Researchers should arrange interview logistics to protect vulnerable participants' physical, social, and emotional safety and well-being.[50] Cowles suggests that the choice of when to initiate contact with participants, the time allotted for research sessions, and the frequency of interviews or observations all have implications for the welfare of interviewer and interviewee alike.[51] Like timing, choices about location also require care.[52] Different places might have contradicting pros and cons; for example, interviewing people in their home might be where they feel most comfortable, but also might preclude confidentiality from family members. In addition, vulnerable persons might not want to be seen with researchers. This affects selection of the interview venue and might require that interviewer and interviewee arrive and depart separately. In my research, I communicate to interviewees that I am happy to meet them when and where they prefer, deferring to what they regard as in their best interests.

Consent

For political science research, challenges to the principle of informed, voluntary consent often stem from power asymmetries, whether within the community under study or between researchers and research participants. Bartolomei's reflection encourages pause: "When I go into a horrendous [refugee] camp situation as a white researcher, the people are so desperate for any form of assistance they would agree to anything just on the off-chance that I might be able to assist. It makes asking for permission ... a farce."[53] Approaching this dilemma, Lake, Majic, and Maxwell advocate a "dialogic" approach to consent in which researchers clearly articulate the risks and benefits of research participation, acknowledge their privilege, and work to redistribute power by encouraging participants to ask questions and challenge the researcher.[54]

Consent is perhaps best viewed not as a one-off prior to the interview but as an ongoing responsibility.[55] This is in part because neither researchers nor research participants might fully grasp potential risks and benefits before a study gets underway.[56] After beginning an interview, for example, I try to be vigilant in listening to my interviewees and reading their facial expressions and body language to discern whether they truly want to continue. I try to recurrently remind interviewees that it is genuinely no problem to forgo any part of the conversation, peppering our time together with interjections such as "Do you want to talk about this?" or "We only have to discuss that if you want to." These strategies do not resolve all the complexities entailed in informed and voluntary consent, but they have helped me intuit if an interviewee is not glad to be there; if they are not, I try to bring the interview to a quick end.

Nevertheless, the overwhelming majority of people whom I have interviewed about experiences of protest, violence, and displacement have genuinely seemed to want to tell their stories. For some, consistent with the findings cited earlier about the benefits of speaking about difficult topics, this is an act of agency or fulfillment of a sense of duty to friends, families, or a cause. For others, speaking offers some psychological relief or solace. More frequently than not, people thank me for inviting them to talk, for listening, or simply for paying attention to what their people suffer. That individuals would take time and energy to contribute to my work, recount often-painful experiences in the course of doing so, and then thank me for the opportunity continues to leave me deeply humbled about my privilege.

Conducting Interviews

Many works on vulnerable populations argue that it is fundamental, from the outset, for interviewers to establish "rapport," or a kind of harmonious interaction that demonstrates empathy and understanding and thereby helps interviewees feel comfortable speaking.[57] Critiquing notions of rapport, Fujii instead stresses the need for interviewer and interviewee to develop a working relationship on the basis of "mutually agreeable terms for interacting."[58] Duncombe and Jessop add that researchers can become skilled in "doing rapport" and "faking friendship"; these approaches are effective in getting others to talk, but they are insincere and thus ethically questionable.[59] In my research, the lines between "research participant," "person I feel lucky to get to sit with," and "new friend" often get blurred. These gray spaces are tricky and can create moments when researchers exploit a research participant's trust, perhaps even unintentionally. Though I am sure that I have made mistakes in my own research, I try to be always attentive to the potential for harm. I do my best to remember that my task is not to persuade others to divulge data but to create a space in which they can speak freely if they wish. My job is then to listen with the utmost care to whatever they decide to share.

There are different types of interviews and questions,[60] and researchers can think through which are appropriate given participant vulnerabilities. Many recommend not asking about sensitive topics directly but rather letting them emerge or not emerge, as participants' own comfort levels dictate.[61] Brannen argues that due to the power dynamics inherent in the "one-sided nature" of interviews, a researcher who is too directive will never get the full story.[62] Campbell's research with rape survivors offers a different perspective. "We ask about the rape early in the interview because it's like an elephant in the room," she writes. "We know they've been raped, they know we know; they assume correctly that we're going to ask about it. Many of the women ... acknowledged that they were glad to get it over with near the beginning."[63]

During the interview, the interviewer's core task is "active listening," which entails providing unconditional and nonjudgmental concentration, using verbal and nonverbal cues to communicate that one understands, and asking questions to encourage elaboration[64] (see Chapter 17). For Driscoll, the key to active listening is not only empathy but also "situational judgment of when it is time to stop."[65] This demands vigilance and care because, encouraged by a skilled listener, participants might disclose information in ways they later regret.[66]

While conducting interviews and subsequently analyzing them, researchers should be attentive not only to what interviewees say but also to the "metadata" of spoken and unspoken expressions that reveal interviewees' thoughts and feelings.[67] Without attention to these cues, especially pertinent where circumstances complicate frank answers, researchers risk missing or misunderstanding responses or increasing chances of participant harm. These cues are socially and culturally embedded and might be very different in the researched community than in the researcher's own home context. This is another reason why it is important for researchers to learn as much as they can about a vulnerable population before they set out to do interviews, and then never stop learning as they conduct that research.

Trauma and (Re)traumatization

A final issue deserves mention: the risk that involving vulnerable participants in research causes them trauma, defined as a state of disruption so severe that it hampers life-enhancing processes, or that research participation causes retraumatization, in the sense that it reactivates feelings associated with a past trauma.[68] Addressing this risk, the American Political Science Association encourages researchers to anticipate the potential for traumatization or retraumatization while designing a study; to regularly renew consent during a study by asking participants whether they wish to continue; to identify local resources to which participants might turn for help in addressing any resulting trauma; and, in scholarly publications and presentations, to report how they assessed and managed this risk of trauma.[69]

Given their relations to past or potential abuse, vulnerable populations might be at higher risk of (re)traumatization. As discussed earlier, however, they might instead be less prone to research-induced trauma because they have developed heightened abilities to cope with painful experiences or because they find meaning and comfort in talking through that pain.[70] In approaching questions of trauma, therefore, interviewers should not make assumptions but rather be vigilant in attending to each interviewee and employing deep knowledge about the contexts from which they come. Along the way, researchers must be careful to avoid acting as therapists unless they have requisite training.[71]

Potential Problems

This chapter cannot adequately address all the conceptual, methodological, and ethical issues involved in interviewing vulnerable populations. In closing, I highlight two questions that remain particularly outstanding. First, scholarship on vulnerable populations often implies that researchers are powerful vis-à-vis potential participants and that they sympathize with them. It offers less guidance on interviewees who themselves present a threat to researchers[72] or whose views researchers find loathsome.[73] Second, concern for participants' vulnerability ought not blind researchers to their own vulnerability and that of other research team members. With some important exceptions,[74] political science has given less attention to researcher distress than have other disciplines. These two problems, as well as others raised throughout this chapter, merit continued deliberation as qualitative researchers grapple with how to interview vulnerable populations in ways that are both effective and ethical.

Notes

1. Silva, *Ethical Guidelines in the Conduct, Dissemination, and Implementation of Nursing Research*.
2. Moore and Miller, "Initiating Research with Doubly Vulnerable Populations."
3. Stone, "The Invisible Vulnerable."
4. Levine et al., "Limitations of 'Vulnerability,'" 44.

5. Lee, "White-Knuckle Research."
6. National Commission for the Protection of Human Subjects of Biomedical and Behavioral Research, *The Belmont Report*.
7. Levine et al., "Limitations of 'Vulnerability,'" 45.
8. Sieber and Tolich, *Planning Ethically Responsible Research*.
9. Council for International Organizations of Medical Sciences and World Health Organization, *International Ethical Guidelines for Biomedical Research Involving Human Subjects*.
10. Zion, Gillam, and Loff, "The Declaration of Helsinki," 615.
11. American Political Science Association, "Principles and Guidance for Human Subjects Research," 3, 5.
12. Kipnis, "Vulnerability in Research Subjects."
13. Kipnis, "Vulnerability in Research Subjects," G-4.
14. Fujii, "Research Ethics 101," 722
15. Fujii, *Interviewing in Social Science Research*.
16. Levine et al., "Limitations of 'Vulnerability,'" 46.
17. van den Hoonaard, "The Vulnerability of Vulnerability," 306.
18. Macklin, "Bioethics, Vulnerability, and Protection," 472.
19. Lake, Majic, and Maxwell, "Research on Vulnerable and Marginalized Populations," 237.
20. Glasius et al., "Writing It Up," 100.
21. Knott, "Beyond the Field," 145.
22. Mazurana, Jacobsen, and Gale, *Research Methods in Conflict Settings*, 11.
23. Levine et al., "Limitations of 'Vulnerability,'" 47.
24. Clarke, "Research for Empowerment in Divided Cambodia," 98.
25. Ensign, "Ethical Issues in Qualitative Health Research with Homeless Youths," 46.
26. van Den Hoonaard, "The Vulnerability of Vulnerability," 317.
27. Buckle, Dwyer, and Jackson, "Qualitative Bereavement Research"; Finch, "'It's Great to Have Someone to Talk To'"; Wolgemuth et al., "Participants' Experiences of the Qualitative Interview."
28. Shaw et al., "Ethics and positionality," 2019, 288.
29. Lundy and McGovern, "Participation, Truth and Partiality"; Kostovicova and Knott, "Harm, Change and Unpredictability."
30. Kostovicova and Knott, "Harm, Change and Unpredictability," 12.
31. Levine et al., "Limitations of 'Vulnerability,'" 48.
32. Kottow, "The Vulnerable and the Susceptible," 463.
33. Lake, Majic, and Maxwell, "Research on Vulnerable and Marginalized Populations," 13; Levine et al., "Limitations of 'Vulnerability.'"
34. Fujiii, "Research Ethics 101"; Iphofen *Ethical Decision Making*; Wood, "The Ethical Challenges of Field Research in Conflict Zones."
35. Flaskerud and Winslow, "Conceptualizing Vulnerable Populations Health-Related Research"; Lee, "White-Knuckle Research"; see Liamputtong, *Researching the Vulnerable*, 33.
36. Flaskerud and Winslow, "Conceptualizing Vulnerable Populations Health-Related Research"; Dickson-Swift, James, and Kippen, "Do University Ethics Committees Adequately Protect Public Health Researchers?"; Paradis, "Feminist and Community Psychology Ethics in Research with Homeless Women," 854; cited in Liamputtong, *Researching the Vulnerable*, 27; also Pyett, "Innovation and Compromise," 109.
37. Liamputtong, *Researching the Vulnerable*, 57–59.
38. Pittaway, Bartolomei, and Hugman, "'Stop Stealing Our Stories,'" 236–237.
39. Zion, Gillam, and Loff, "The Declaration of Helsinki," 616.
40. Mosley, *Interview Research in Political Science*, 17; also see Driscoll, *Doing Global Fieldwork*, 13.
41. Sieber and Tolich, *Planning Ethically Responsible Research*, 3.
42. Liamputtong, *Researching the Vulnerable*, 50.

43. See Liamputtong, *Researching the Vulnerable*, 49–57.
44. Jenkins, "Assistants, Guides, Collaborators, Friends"; Mwambari, "Local Positionality in the Production of Knowledge in Northern Uganda."
45. Pittaway, Bartolomei, and Hugman, "'Stop Stealing Our Stories,'" 233.
46. Callaway, "San People Issue Research Code"; Iphofen, *Ethical Decision Making*; Omata, "'Over-researched' and 'Under-researched' Refugees."
47. Omata, "'Over-researched' and 'Under-researched' Refugees."
48. Liamputtong, *Researching the Vulnerable*, 62–65.
49. Driscoll, *Doing Global Fieldwork*, 14.
50. See Pearlman, "Emotional Sensibility."
51. Cowles, "Issues in Qualitative Research on Sensitive Topics," 164–167.
52. Liamputtong, *Researching the Vulnerable*, 41–42.
53. Pittaway, Bartolomei, and Hugman, "'Stop Stealing Our Stories,'" 234.
54. Lake, Majic, and Maxwell, "Research on Vulnerable and Marginalized Populations," 240.
55. Ensign, "Ethical Issues in Qualitative Health Research with Homeless Youths," 8.
56. Miller and Bell, "Consenting to What?"
57. Abbe and Brandon, "Building and Maintaining Rapport in Investigative Interviews," 208; Fontana and Frey, "Interviewing," 367; Liamputtong, *Researching the Vulnerable*, 34–37.
58. Fujii, *Interviewing in Social Science Research*, 12–15.
59. Duncombe and Jessop, "'Doing Rapport.'"
60. Roulston, *Reflective Interviewing*.
61. Brannen, "The Study of Sensitive Subjects"; Dempsey et al., "Sensitive Interviewing in Qualitative Research"; Luxardo, Colombo, and Iglesias, "Methodological and Ethical Dilemmas Encountered during Field Research of Family Violence Experienced by Adolescent Women in Buenos Aires"; Thomson, "Getting Close to Rwandans since the Genocide."
62. Brannen, "The Study of Sensitive Subjects," 555–556.
63. Campbell, *Emotionally Involved*, 5.
64. Weger, Castle, and Emmett, "Active Listening in Peer Interviews," 35.
65. Driscoll, *Doing Global Fieldwork*, 111.
66. Duncombe and Jessop 2012; Finch, "'It's Great to Have Someone to Talk To.'"
67. Fujii, "Shades of Truth and Lies."
68. See Pearlman, "Emotional Sensibility," 4.
69. American Political Science Association, "Principles and Guidance for Human Subjects Research," 10–11.
70. Buckle, Dwyer, and Jackson, "Qualitative Bereavement Research," 114–115; Wolgemuth et al., "Participants' experiences," 361
71. Driscoll, *Doing Global Fieldwork*, 119.
72. Malejacq and Mukhopadhyay, "The 'Tribal Politics' of Field Research."
73. Blee, "White-Knuckle Research"; Fujii, *Interviewing in Social Science Research*.
74. See, inter alia, Loyle and Simoni, "Researching Under Fire"; Shesterinina, "Ethics, Empathy, and Fear in Research on Violent Conflict"; Fujii, *Interviewing in Social Science Research*; Campbell, "Ethics of Research in Conflict Environments"; Mazurana, Jacobsen, and Gale, *Research Methods in Conflict Settings*.

Recommended Readings

Lake, Milli, Samantha Majic, and Rahsaan Maxwell. "Research on Vulnerable and Marginalized Populations." American Political Science Association Organized Section for Qualitative and

Multi-Method Research, Qualitative Transparency Deliberations, Working Group Final Reports, Report IV.3, 2018. https://papers.ssrn.com/sol3/papers.cfm?abstract_id=3333511.
> Noting that standard IRB categories of vulnerable populations do not cover the range of situations that political scientists encounter, the authors posit a fluid, context-dependent approach to vulnerability that attends to how relationships of power construct risk.

Lee, Raymond M. *Doing Research on Sensitive Topics*. London: Sage, 1993.
> This much-cited text offers a far-reaching probe into research on sensitive topics, a category of ethics concerns with many insights relevant for interviewing vulnerable populations.

Liamputtong, Pranee. *Researching the Vulnerable. A Guide to Sensitive Research Methods*. London: Sage, 2007.
> Rooted in the study of public health but pulling from existing scholarship and real-world examples across many disciplines, this comprehensive account delves into definitions of vulnerable populations, discussion of varied relevant ethical dilemmas, and practical applications for conducting research, including telephone interviews, interview by proxy, and conjoint interviews with multiple members of the same vulnerable group.

Sieber, Joan E., and Martin B. Tolich. *Planning Ethically Responsible Research*. Thousand Oaks, CA: Sage, 2015.
> The authors situate the question of vulnerable populations in an in-depth discussion of risk, building from the premise that risk is malleable and that calculating risks and benefits is an "art, not a science."

van den Hoonaard, Will C. "The Vulnerability of Vulnerability: Why Social Science Researchers Should Abandon the Doctrine of Vulnerability." In *The Sage Handbook of Qualitative Research Ethics*, edited by Ron Iphofen and Martin Tolich, 305–321. Thousand Oaks, CA: Sage, 2019.
> Critiquing overzealous IRBs for discouraging research that might benefit researched communities themselves, the author offers a spirited and thought-provoking challenge to the very concept of vulnerability for being vague, arbitrary, and difficult to operationalize.

References

Abbe, Allison, and Susan E. Brandon. "Building and Maintaining Rapport in Investigative Interviews." *Police Practice and Research* 15, no. 3 (2014): 207–220.

American Political Science Association. "Principles and Guidance for Human Subjects Research." 2020 Spring Council Meeting. https://www.apsanet.org/Portals/54/diversity and inclusionprgms/Ethics/FinalPrinciples with Guidance with intro.pdf?ver=2020-04-20-211740-153.

Blee, Kathleen M. "White-Knuckle Research: Emotional Dynamics in Fieldwork with Racist Activists." *Qualitative Sociology* 21, no. 4 (1998): 381–399.

Brannen, Julia. "The Study of Sensitive Subjects." *Sociological Review* 36, no. 3 (1988): 552–563.

Buckle, Jennifer L., Sonya Corbin Dwyer, and Marlene Jackson. "Qualitative Bereavement Research: Incongruity between the Perspectives of Participants and Research Ethics Boards." *International Journal of Social Research Methodology* 13, no. 2 (2010): 111–125.

Callaway, Ewen. "San People Issue Research Code." *Nature* 543 (2017): 475–476.

Campbell, Rebecca. *Emotionally Involved: The Impact of Researching Rape*. New York: Routledge, 2002.

Campbell, Susanna P. "Ethics of Research in Conflict Environments." *Journal of Global Security Studies* 2, no. 1 (2017): 89–101.

Ciuk, Sylwia, and Dominika Latusek. "Ethics in Qualitative Research." In *Qualitative Methodologies in Organization Studies. Vol. 1: Theories and New Approaches*, edited by Malgorzata Ciesielska and Dariusz Jemielniak, 195–213. Cham: Springer International, 2018.

Clarke, Helen Jenks. "Research for Empowerment in Divided Cambodia." In *Researching Violently Divided Societies: Ethical and Methodological Issues*, edited by Marie Smyth and Gillian Robinson, 92–105. London, Pluto Press, 2001.

Council for International Organizations of Medical Sciences and World Health Organization, eds. *International Ethical Guidelines for Biomedical Research Involving Human Subjects*. Geneva: CIOMS, 2002.

Cowles, Kathleen V. "Issues in Qualitative Research on Sensitive Topics." *Western Journal of Nursing Research* 10, no. 2 (1988): 163–179.

Dempsey, Laura, Maura Dowling, Philip Larkin, and Kathy Murphy. "Sensitive Interviewing in Qualitative Research." *Research in Nursing & Health* 39 (2016): 480–490.

Dickson-Swift, Virginia, Erica L. James, and Sandra Kippen. "Do University Ethics Committees Adequately Protect Public Health Researchers?" *Australian and New Zealand Journal of Public Health* 29, no. 6 (2005): 576–579.

Driscoll. Jesse. *Doing Global Fieldwork: A Social Scientist's Guide to Mixed-Methods Research Far from Home*. New York: Columbia University Press, 2021.

Duncombe, Jean, and Julie Jessop. "'Doing Rapport' and the Ethics of 'Faking Friendship.'" In *Ethics in Qualitative Research*, edited by Melanie Mauthner, Maxine Birch, Julie Jessop, and Tina Miller, 108–122. London: Sage, 2002.

Ensign, Josephine. "Ethical Issues in Qualitative Health Research with Homeless Youths." *Journal of Advanced Nursing* 43, no. 1 (2003): 43–50.

Finch, Janet. "'It's Great to Have Someone to Talk To': The Ethics and Politics of Interviewing Women." In *Social Researching: Politics, Problems, Practice*, edited by Collin Bell and Helen Roberts, 70–87. London: Routledge and Kegan Paul, 1984.

Flaskerud, Jacqueline H., and Betty J. Winslow. "Conceptualizing Vulnerable Populations Health-Related Research." *Nursing Research* 47, no. 2 (1998): 69–78.

Fontana, Andrea, and James H. Frey. "Interviewing: The Art of Science." In *The Handbook of Qualitative Research*, edited by N. Denzin and Y. Lincoln, 361–376. Thousand Oaks, CA: Sage, 1994.

Fujii, Lee Ann. *Interviewing in Social Science Research: A Relational Approach*. London: Routledge, 2017.

Fujii, Lee Ann. "Research Ethics 101: Dilemmas and Responsibilities," *PS: Political Science & Politics* 45, no. 4 (2012): 717–723.

Fujii, Lee Ann. "Shades of Truth and Lies: Interpreting Testimonies of War and Violence." *Journal of Peace Research* 47, no. 2 (2010): 231–241.

Glasius, Marlies, Meta de Lange, Jos Bartman, Emanuela Dalmasso, Aofei Lv, Adele Del Sordi, Marcus Michaelsen, and Kris Ruijgrok. "Writing It Up." In *Research, Ethics and Risk in the Authoritarian Field*, edited by Marlies Glasius, Meta de Lange, Jos Bartman, Emanuela Dalmasso, Aofei Lv, Adele Del Sordi, Marcus Michaelsen, and Kris Ruijgrok, 97–117. Cham: Springer International, 2018.

Iphofen, Ron. *Ethical Decision Making in Social Research: A Practical Guide*. New York: Palgrave Macmillan, 2009.

Jenkins, Sarah Ann. "Assistants, Guides, Collaborators, Friends: The Concealed Figures of Conflict Research." *Journal of Contemporary Ethnography* 47, no. 2 (2018): 143–170.

Kipnis, Kenneth. "Vulnerability in Research Subjects: A Bioethical Taxonomy." In *Ethical and Policy Issues in Research Involving Human Participants*, edited by National Bioethics Advisory Commission, G1–G13. Bethesda, MD: National Bioethics Advisory Commission, 2011. http://www.aapcho.org/wp/wp-content/uploads/2012/02/Kipnis-VulnerabilityinResearchSubjects.pdf

Knott, Eleanor. "Beyond the Field: Ethics after Fieldwork in Politically Dynamic Contexts." *Perspectives on Politics* 17, no. 1 (2019): 140–153.

Kostovicova, Denisa, and Eleanor Knott. "Harm, Change and Unpredictability: The Ethics of Interviews in Conflict Research." *Qualitative Research* 22, no. 1 (2020): 56–73.

Kottow, Michael H. "The Vulnerable and the Susceptible." *Bioethics* 17, nos. 5–6 (2003): 460–471.

Lake, Milli, Samantha Majic, and Rahsaan Maxwell. "Research on Vulnerable and Marginalized Populations." American Political Science Association Organized Section for Qualitative and Multi-Method Research, Qualitative Transparency Deliberations, Working Group Final Reports, Report IV.3, 2018. https://papers.ssrn.com/sol3/papers.cfm?abstract_id=3333511.

Lee, Raymond M. *Doing Research on Sensitive Topics*. London: Sage, 1993.

Levine Carol, Ruth Faden, Christine Grady, Dale Hammerschmidt, Lisa Eckenwiler, Jeremy Sugarman, and Consortium to Examine Clinical Research Ethics. "The Limitations of 'Vulnerability' as a Protection for Human Research Participants." *The American Journal of Bioethics* 4, no. 3 (2004): 44–49.

Liamputtong, Pranee. *Researching the Vulnerable: A Guide to Sensitive Research Methods*. London: Sage, 2007.

Loyle, Cyanne E., and Alicia Simoni. "Researching Under Fire: Political Science and Researcher Trauma." *PS: Political Science & Politics* 50, no. 1 (2017): 141–145.

Lundy, Patricia, and Mark McGovern. "Participation, Truth and Partiality: Participatory Action Research, Community-Based Truth-Telling and Post-Conflict Transition in Northern Ireland." *Sociology* 40, no. 1 (2006): 71–88.

Luxardo, Natalia, Graciela Colombo, and Gabriela Iglesias. "Methodological and Ethical Dilemmas Encountered during Field Research of Family Violence Experienced by Adolescent Women in Buenos Aires." *Qualitative Report* 16, no. 4 (2011): 984–1000.

Macklin, Ruth. "Bioethics, Vulnerability, and Protection." *Bioethics* 17, nos. 5–6 (2003): 472–486.

Malejacq, Romain, and Dipali Mukhopadhyay. "The 'Tribal Politics' of Field Research: A Reflection on Power and Partiality in 21st-Century Warzones." *Perspectives on Politics* 14, no. 4 (2016): 1011–1028.

Mazurana, Dyan E., Karen Jacobsen, and Lacey Andrews Gale, eds. *Research Methods in Conflict Settings: A View from Below*. New York: Cambridge University Press, 2013.

Miller, Tina, and Linda Bell. "Consenting to What? Issues of Access, Gate-keeping and Informed Consent." In *Ethics in Qualitative Research*, 2nd ed., edited by Tina Miller, Maxine Birch, Melanie Mauthner, and Julie Jessop, 61–75. London: Sage, 2012.

Moore, Linda Weaver, and Margaret Miller. "Initiating Research with Doubly Vulnerable Populations." *Journal of Advanced Nursing* 30, no. 5 (1999): 1034–1040.

Mosley, Layna, ed. *Interview Research in Political Science*. Ithaca, NY: Cornell University Press, 2013.

Mwambari, David. "Local Positionality in the Production of Knowledge in Northern Uganda." *International Journal of Qualitative Methods* 18 (2019): 1–12.

National Commission for the Protection of Human Subjects of Biomedical and Behavioral Research. *The Belmont Report: Ethical Principles and Guidelines for the Protection of Human Subjects of Research*. Washington, DC: U.S. Department of Health and Human Services, 1979. https://www.hhs.gov/ohrp/regulations-and-policy/belmont-report/read-the-belmont-report/index.html.

Omata, Naohiko. "'Over-researched' and 'Under-researched' Refugees." *Forced Migration Review* 61 (2019): 15–18.

Paradis, Emily K. "Feminist and Community Psychology Ethics in Research with Homeless Women." *American Journal of Community Psychology* 28, no. 6 (2000): 839–858.

Pearlman, Wendy. "Emotional Sensibility: Exploring the Methodological and Ethical Implications of Research Participants' Emotions." *American Political Science Review*, first published online, December 14, 2022.

Pittaway, Eileen, Linda Bartolomei, and Richard Hugman. "'Stop Stealing Our Stories': The Ethics of Research with Vulnerable Groups." *Journal of Human Rights Practice* 2, no. 2 (2010): 229–251.

Pyett, Priscilla Margaret. "Innovation and Compromise: Responsibility and Reflexivity in Research with Vulnerable Groups." In *Technologies and Health*, edited by Jeanne Daly, Marilys Guillemin, and Sophie Hill, 105–119. Oxford: Oxford University Press, 2001.

Roulston, Kathryn J. *Reflective Interviewing: A Guide to Theory and Practice*. London: Sage, 2010.

Shaw, Rhonda M., Julie Howe, Jonathan Beazer, and Toni Carr. "Ethics and Positionality in Qualitative Research with Vulnerable and Marginal Groups." *Qualitative Research* 20, no. 3 (2020): 277–293.

Shesterinina, Anastasia. "Ethics, Empathy, and Fear in Research on Violent Conflict." *Journal of Peace Research* 56, no. 2 (2018): 190–202.

Sieber, Joan E., and Martin B. Tolich. *Planning Ethically Responsible Research*. Thousand Oaks, CA: Sage, 2015.

Silva, Mary Cipriano. *Ethical Guidelines in the Conduct, Dissemination, and Implementation of Nursing Research*. Washington, DC: American Nurses Publishing, 1995.

Stone, T. Howard. "The Invisible Vulnerable: The Economically and Educationally Disadvantaged Subjects of Clinical Research." *Journal of Law, Medicine & Ethics* 31, no. 1 (2003): 149–153.

Thomson, Susan. "Getting Close to Rwandans since the Genocide: Studying Everyday Life in Highly Politicized Research Settings." *African Studies Review* 53, no. 3 (2010): 19–34.

van den Hoonaard, Will C. "The Vulnerability of Vulnerability: Why Social Science Researchers Should Abandon the Doctrine of Vulnerability." In *The Sage Handbook of Qualitative Research Ethics*, edited by Ron Iphofen and Martin Tolich, 305–321. Thousand Oaks, CA: Sage, 2019.

Weger, Harry, Gina R. Castle, and Melissa C. Emmett. "Active Listening in Peer Interviews: The Influence of Message Paraphrasing on Perceptions of Listening Skill." *International Journal of Listening* 24, no. 1 (2010): 34–49.

Wood, Elisabeth J. "The Ethical Challenges of Field Research in Conflict Zones." *Qualitative Sociology* 29 (2006): 373–386.

Wolgemuth, Jennifer R., Zeynep Erdil-Moody, Tara Opsal, Jennifer E. Cross, Tanya Kaanta, Ellyn M. Dickmann, and Soria Colomer. "Participants' Experiences of the Qualitative Interview: Considering the Importance of Research Paradigms." *Qualitative Research* 15, no. 3 (2015): 351–372.

Zion, Deborah, Lynn Gillam, and Bebe Loff. "The Declaration of Helsinki, CIOMS and the Ethics of Research on Vulnerable Populations." *Nature Medicine* 6, no. 6 (2000): 615–617.

19
Focus Groups

Jennifer Cyr

In *Duck! Rabbit!*, a rather quirky book for young kids, two protagonists argue over the extent to which a simple image represents the head of a duck or a rabbit.[1] The long rabbit ears, which are turned to the side and therefore parallel with the ground, might also be taken as the long, slightly open beak of a duck. Open to interpretation, the story teaches children about perspective, meaning-making, and the role of interaction and conversation in unveiling how people think.

Focus groups are useful when we think the issues or concepts we study, like the main storyline from *Duck! Rabbit!*, may be interpreted differently by different people. When these issues or concepts are discussed in a social setting—that is, in a focused, group conversation—rich, nuanced, and multilayered ideas about the topics of interest can emerge. Focus groups, as I suggest below, are incredibly useful for getting at different types of information. And, like all data collection methods, focus groups are well suited for certain types of research questions. In what follows, I seek to help you decide if focus groups are useful for your research project. I also provide tips on how to execute them, with an emphasis on moderating and the question protocol. Finally, I address some of the challenges commonly associated with focus groups.

An Overview of What Focus Groups Are and When to Use Them

Focus groups bring together a group of people to discuss a short set of questions associated with a research topic of interest. A moderator asks the questions with the hope of generating a conversation among participants. Data are produced by the answers the participants proffer and the discussion that unfolds as participants react to what others say.

Focus groups have certain qualities that, when taken together, make them uniquely suited for specific social science tasks. The first, and perhaps most notable, quality is that focus groups are a *social* data collection method. Data emerge from group conversations: participants share their thoughts with others. The focus group's social dynamic means that a researcher cannot separate what an individual might say in private from what they feel compelled, for whatever reason, to say in the public setting of the focus group. Nevertheless, the social nature of the focus group should be embraced and exploited—indeed, the method's inherently social method underpins many of the reasons why we should use focus groups in our research projects in the first place, as we see below.

Second, focus groups generate data that are emic in nature. Data are generated from the perspective of the focus group participant. Focus group moderators ask questions of participants, of course, but these are open in nature and are intended to let the participants answer as they prefer. (Etic data, by contrast, emerge from more "closed" formats, such as multiple-choice questions, where the specific goals of the researcher are privileged.) With an emic approach to data collection, researchers lose control over the kinds of responses proffered. But they gain in terms of the variety and breadth of those responses. As we will see, one does not organize a focus group to ask yes/no questions.

Finally, focus groups produce data at three levels of analysis.[2] You can solicit *individual-level* responses by asking participants to write down their answer to a question before sharing it with the group. By writing their answers before discussing them, participants are presumably less influenced by the social setting of the focus group. Data at the *group level* focus on how conversations unfold, the nuances that emerge, and the consensus that is forged (or not) as the conversation winds down. Finally, you can engage with *interactive-level* data by focusing on specific, discrete exchanges, where new or unexpected ideas may crop up.

These three noteworthy features of focus groups mean that the method is particularly apt for generating incredibly insightful information on specific types of research goals. In my work,[3] I identify six—a comprehensive but perhaps not exhaustive list of the kinds of research goals that focus groups can help address.

Assessing Group Processes. Why do some Venezuelans identify as *chavistas* (i.e., hard-core supporters of Hugo Chávez and his political movement) while others identify as anti-*chavistas* (i.e., rabid opponents of Chávez and his movement)? What does it mean to be anti-*chavista*? How do they view themselves? How do they view *chavistas*?

Focus groups are extremely useful when we want to understand how groups see themselves and the world around them. By bringing together a set of individuals who share an identity (due to partisanship, a shared religion, fanaticism for a sports team) or a similar experience (as single fathers, drug addicts, young immigrants) one can get at questions about those groups and how they think, make decisions, and view the world around them.

Addressing Intersubjective Phenomena. Some concepts, like power and peace, have complex, evolving, and highly contextualized meanings. An act of corruption in Vietnam is not the same as an act of corruption in the United States.[4] These kinds of phenomena are clearly important to study, but their meaning is complicated to capture in a survey question and difficult to assess in a one-on-one interview, precisely because how people understand them is a function of context, experience, and interaction with others.

Focus groups are well suited for discussing complex phenomena, like power, corruption, and peace, whose meaning is socially constructed—that is, acquired through processes over time, exposure, and interaction with others. On the one hand, focus groups allow a group of individuals to share the high-cognitive effort required to meaningfully discuss these kinds of complex topics. On the other, the focus group mimics the social setting in which individuals typically acquire meaning about these kinds of phenomena. Group discussions allow participants to work together to get at complicated ideas and offer their interpretations of those ideas. For example, focus groups revealed that individuals in conflict-laden areas do not define peace as the absence of violence, which is the most common indicator of peace used by conflict scholars. Instead, it occurs when, for instance, they are not scared of people standing near shops or when people can worship any religion they choose.[5]

Pursuing Proper Contextualization. Many of the phenomena we study represent ideas that are not universally shared. This is true of the intersubjective phenomena discussed previously. It is also true of other, everyday customs, acts, and perspectives upon which the reliable and valid interpretation of, say, a survey question can hinge. For example, if you want to measure the importance of the ritual of family dining in different settings, you might ask a U.S. citizen how often they eat dinner as a family or to describe a typical Sunday dinner. In Latin America, however, the analytical equivalent has historically been lunch. Asking Argentines in La Pampa about a "typical family dinner" may not effectively capture what you wish to measure.

Focus groups allow a researcher to measure the extent to which specific notions travel from one setting (e.g., a country or a generation) to another. By asking focus group participants to discuss how and when they eat as a family, a researcher can ascertain functional equivalents, such as the use of lunch versus dinner in a survey question, and derive the phrases and vernacular that would be appropriate to use in a survey in that country or for that generation. Often, just one or two focus groups are enough to develop valid indicators for a survey or experiment protocol. Focus groups, in this sense, can be excellent pretests in a mixed-method research design.[6]

Understanding Individuals in Social Settings. Focus groups are social in nature. Centering one's analysis on individual responses to focus group questions can be problematic. One cannot know for sure that what the individual says in the group setting is an accurate reflection of what they would have said in the absence of the (focus) group dynamic.[7] When you wish to access a person's private thoughts, individual interviews (see, e.g., Chapters 16, 17, and 18) may be more appropriate.

Nevertheless, sometimes we are interested in assessing how individuals act in social settings precisely because we suspect that their personal responses may change in the face of social pressures. This was the case for a project that sought to measure whether a radio program helped to shift a culture of deference in postgenocide Rwanda.[8] The project compared individual responses in a (one-on-one) interview to responses from a focus group to see if the social dynamics of the latter affected the extent to which a person might express dissent. For these kinds of moments, a focus group is ideal, since the social setting replicates the social dynamics in which we wish to see how individuals think, act, and talk.

The Study of Sensitive Topics and Vulnerable Groups. Some phenomena that are vital for understanding society and social behavior are also difficult to discuss. This may be because they are traumatic (e.g., domestic abuse) or illicit (e.g., drug trafficking), or because they underscore deep-seated, structural problems (e.g., racism or poverty). Focus groups are useful when we wish to study topics or events that are sensitive or taboo, or when we wish to understand something unique to vulnerable or marginalized groups. There are at least two reasons for this.

First, a focus group can be a safe space for discussing shared experiences.[9] A victim of domestic violence may not feel comfortable addressing their past in a one-on-one setting. When they are in a focus group with other victims, however, those experiences may be easier to share. Second, the emic nature of focus groups means that participants have the power to choose what they will and will not discuss. Focus groups, in this sense, are empowering for the participants.[10] Where the topics discussed are sensitive, or the groups participating are vulnerable, the empowering aspect of focus groups is especially significant, since it allows the participant to determine what they reveal (or not) about their experiences.

Exploration of New Ideas. Focus groups, finally, can be particularly illuminating when we wish to embark on a new research project or to learn about topics that have received little previous attention. How do citizens interpret different messages about an evolving pandemic? To answer this question, it may first be useful to know *which* messages different communities receive. In my work on anti-*chavistas*, focus groups were appropriate not only because

I wanted to study a group identity, but also because we knew so little, in general, about the individuals who self-identified as anti-*chavistas*.

Focus groups allowed me to learn about these individuals. They also helped me to identify the kinds of questions that would be salient to ask via other data collection strategies. Focus groups can produce new insights—in the form of an omitted variable or an unexpected interaction—that can help to improve our models or explain anomalies. Because data are generated via conversations, responses can be nonlinear, nuanced, even contradictory. This can make analysis more complicated. But it also leaves ample room for discovery.

How to Do Focus Groups

Let me start by saying that, in such a restricted space, it is hard to be comprehensive about every aspect of the focus group process, from start to finish. Happily, other literature exists to help you out, should you decide to incorporate focus groups into your research design.[11] Figure 19.1 provides a set of questions to consider as one plans to undertake focus groups.

Here, I want to focus on a few of these questions—specifically, 11 and 12—but I also want to emphasize one running theme that should stay in your mind from the time you sit down to write out a game plan to when you finish the last focus group you have set out to undertake.[12]

That running theme is the following: when undertaking focus groups *your participants come first; your research goals come second*. To be sure, your research goals are vital for determining with whom and about what you speak. But if your research goals may harm the people with whom you wish to speak, then those goals should be adjusted.

Once you know who will be a part of your focus group, then you can work to be as sensitive as possible to their needs as you decide how to recruit (Q4, Figure 19.1), where you will carry them out (Q6), the materials you should prepare and the recording method (Q7, Q8), the costs you might incur (Q9), and how consent will be obtained (Q10). For a great example of

Figure 19.1 Basic Questions about Focus Groups

1. How many focus groups should I carry out?
2. What is my sampling frame?
3. What should the composition of each focus group be?
4. How should I recruit participants?
5. Will I work with a research consultancy?
6. Where will the focus groups occur?
7. What materials should I prepare?
8. How will I record the conversation?
9. What costs should I expect?
10. Do I need consent?
11. Who will be my moderator?
12. What questions will I ask?

Source: Jennifer Cyr, *Focus Groups for the Social Science Researcher* (Cambridge: Cambridge University Press, 2017), 41, Table 3.1.

how many of these decisions are made and in some cases adapted, see Winslow, Honein, and Elzubeir's fascinating work on seeking out women's voices in the United Arab Emirates.[13]

Choosing a Moderator. Knowing your participants is also key to identifying an effective moderator. The moderator is the person who runs the focus group. They welcome participants, introduce the topic(s) of conversation, ask the questions, and ensure flow as the conversations unfold. This person is vital for executing the focus group, and so who you choose matters.

So, whom should you choose? One obvious choice is that you, the researcher, can be the moderator. There are plenty of good reasons for this. You know your research best, of course. You understand why you are asking the questions. You have a sense of what you think participants will say (or not). All of this sets you up for asking the questions, probing where necessary, and staying quiet to avoid *leading* your participants. The goal is to produce responses that are as unmediated as possible.

Knowing your project is an asset, to be sure. I nevertheless prefer to use a moderator rather than be one myself. The reasons for this are tied to my two goals of, first, privileging my participants and, second, working toward my research goals. Moderators are busy during a focus group, as mentioned. They set the tone for the session and ideally make the participants as comfortable as possible. Because of this, having a moderator that is relatable to the participants is ideal. Are you organizing focus groups of first-generation Muslim women college students in the United Arab Emirates? Ideally, your moderator will be just like them—or as close as possible and, at the very least (given the restricted gender dynamics in the context described), a woman.

A relatable moderator may also better know how and when to probe. They may more effectively and delicately engage with quiet participants and discourage dominant ones, keeping the flow of the conversation active and encouraging as many participants to speak as possible. Overall, moderators should perform their functions with a good knowledge of what is culturally and contextually appropriate. This will help facilitate the conversation and keep it as natural as possible. Where participants are more comfortable, a researcher can more credibly claim that the data generated emerged through more natural, and less forced, conversations.

A moderator must also be well informed about the project. The researcher should convey several things to their chosen moderator. For example, they should have a basic sense of what the research is about, as well as its goals. Do not reveal your hypotheses, of course. The more a moderator knows about what you think is going on, the greater the possibility that they will, consciously or not, lead focus group participants to express ideas that conform with those inklings. You also want the moderator to understand the questions and the goals behind them—again, without explaining what you think or hope the answers will be. Here, it can be helpful to point out any terms or ideas that, once voiced by the participants, you want the moderator to probe.

Finally, the researcher should identify and explain any phrases or concepts that the moderator must *not* say so as to avoid leading focus group participants toward a particular response or idea. For example, in my work on anti-*chavista* identifiers, it was important that the moderator not use the term "anti-*chavista*" before it was used by participants themselves. To credibly claim that this was an identity that mattered, I had to show that it was a term that participants used on their own volition. Once used, I invited the moderator to ask why participants used the term and what it meant to them.

So how does one identify a moderator? In my experience, the best choice is to start with interlocutors on the ground. Someone at a local university, consultancy, or particular community may be helpful for identifying an appropriate moderator. What do I mean by "appropriate"? The answer is highly contextual. Nevertheless, the key, I think, is empathy. An appropriate moderator can be knowledgeable—even trained and experienced in moderating focus groups—but above all else the person should have the capacity to make your participants comfortable. You want a moderator who can "read the room," to know, for example, when to ask for more and whom to gently prod. Empathy is especially vital when addressing sensitive or taboo topics. A moderator who can relate to participants may be better equipped to elicit conversations about difficult issues. Appropriate moderators tend to share certain sociodemographic traits or experiences with participants. Local networks can help to locate that person and put you in touch.

Asking the Right Questions. How does one go about devising focus group questions? My poorly worded subheading aside, I think there are no "right" focus group questions for a particular research project. Instead, different questions tap into distinct ideas and, consequently, yield different data.

The trick to elaborating a question protocol is to examine your goals and motivations. Why are you planning to do focus groups? What do you hope to get from them? Identify a few topics to prioritize in the session and build your questions around these. Ideally, you will ask about each topic more than once, so you can maximize coverage and breadth in the response. On this point, variety matters.[14] A diversity of questions—one that asks participants to write their answers first; another that encourages the group to work together on an activity like listing or ranking; one that engages with visual material of some kind; and "conventional" ones that simply invite conversation—will keep participants interested and can tap into different ideas.

In addition to being varied, focus group questions should be open, inviting participants to provide longer, more thoughtful responses. (A closed question offers only a few options, like multiple-choice or yes/no questions.) Questions should also be unidimensional; they should not include multiple parts or elements. You want to focus the conversation on a particular topic to the extent that you can. When questions have multiple parts (e.g., What does it mean to be an anti-*chavista*, and how do you utilize the term on a daily basis?), participants may be confused about how to answer, or they may focus on only one aspect of the question.

There are also practical matters to consider. A focus group should not last longer than 1.5–2 hours. Participants will get tired or lose enthusiasm. Moreover, you want each question to yield an extended conversation—something like 5–10 minutes in length, if not more. Finally you need to build in time for consenting, introductions, and wrapping up.

Overall, you really have time only for 8–10 questions. One of these will need to be an icebreaker, or a relatively easy introductory question to warm up the group. Another should introduce the group to the main topics at hand. One will conclude the conversation. Ultimately, 5–7 questions will be oriented toward your topics of interest. If you ask more than one question about each topic, you may reasonably cover only three topics. In sum, spending time on what you want to ask, and what you hope to get at, matters.

If it seems like I am putting a lot of pressure on question development, it is because I am. As with all question-based data collection methods, the protocol you generate for your focus groups will shape the data generated. Nevertheless, do not despair! Your chosen moderator, as well as other knowledgeable interlocutors, including local academics, can read through questions for appropriate syntax and interpretation.

Additionally, you can adjust your questions if, after one or two focus groups, you find that they are not having the impact you desired. I did this in my own work. In a set of focus groups on how citizens in Bolivia, Peru, and Venezuela spoke of formerly important political parties that had dropped out of national contention,[15] I showed participants images of each party's founding leader. They all easily identified each leader. This was an interesting data point for me: these men were recognizable and known. Nevertheless, I decided I could better use the time from that question on a different one that would helpfully generate more conversation and more varied, nuanced responses.

Finally, keep in mind that in the focus group participants control their own responses. They may, consequently, simply ignore the question asked and discuss something else. In the same set of focus groups referenced above, I asked Peruvian participants to provide their impressions of a political party (*Acción Popular*, for those interested) as a way to assess how relevant this historic but electorally weak party was in the present context. Rather than discuss the party, participants chose to talk about a particular deceased leader. Despite probing and returning to the question at hand, participants did not talk about AP. This occurred in more than one focus group. Their lack of a response about AP, and their discussion instead of the leader, indicated to me that what was meaningful about that party in the (then) current context was that person and not much else. A lack of direct response to a question is itself data.

In sum—and forgive me the rather forced metaphor—like a horse to a watering hole, you can bring your focus group participants to a certain set of questions, but you cannot force them to answer. What is thrilling about focus groups is that, in ceding some control over what your participants discuss, you gain immeasurably in terms of nuance and meaning-making.

One last point. As with most qualitative data collection methods, data saturation is a primary goal of focus groups. In the focus group setting, a general rule of thumb is that one does not need more than six focus groups.[16] At that point, the costs of the focus groups, in terms of money[17] but also with respect to time, energy, and resources, may outweigh the benefits. Ideally, you will find that answers across focus groups share common points or overlap in terms of the language used and ideas shared. This, again, was the case in Peru, when participants in different focus groups chose not to talk about AP. When this occurs, you can more credibly claim that those responses are not simply an expression of a unique conversation among a set of focus group participants. Cross–focus group responses likely tap into common understandings of a notion or topic, and you can discuss this in your analysis.[18]

Nevertheless, if generalizability is a goal of the project, focus groups will not be sufficient as a data collection method. Let's turn to this point now, as well as other challenges that are typically raised when one contemplates using focus groups for a project.

Potential Problems

Like all data collection methods, focus groups are not perfect, nor do they perfectly generate "objective" data that can be neutrally analyzed and slotted into one's project write-up. I want to mention different potential challenges that you may face when integrating focus groups into your research design.[19]

One common concern when it comes to focus groups is that the conversation will generate false consensus. Focus groups can include overly passive and also dominant participants. Rather than hash out distinct nuanced perspectives about a particular topic, some participants may prefer to stay quiet or feel pressure to acquiesce. This dynamic is called "groupthink," a "preference toward agreement" that may bias the data generated.[20] What is registered as agreement in the transcript can mask real differences that exist among your participants.

You may never know for certain if groupthink is operating, but you can work to mitigate the dynamic. For example, you can ask participants to write down answers to certain questions before discussing them, and later examine if what they said in the group differs from their original response. Additionally, you can instruct the moderator to watch for nonverbal communication, such as eye-rolling or head-shaking, that indicates disagreement and follow up with those persons. Finally—and perhaps most crucially—I'd remind readers that focus groups are *social* in nature. These kinds of group dynamics are to be expected. Groupthink and other dynamics, such as participant passivity/dominance and group silence, are normal parts of any social interaction. Focus groups "mimic the natural process of forming and expressing opinions";[21] this is why they are so well-suited for studying group behaviors.

A second challenge has to do with whether focus group data are generalizable. In general, the answer is no—and that's okay! Just as you likely would not carry out experiments to understand the causes of war, you wouldn't undertake focus groups to draw causal inferences on population-wide dynamics. It may, however, be possible to transfer certain insights gleaned from a set of focus groups comprised of individuals from a very particular context to others like them. For example, let's say that I undertook four focus groups with low-income parents from Flint, Michigan, about the difficulties of accessing clean water. If several shared challenges were expressed across those focus groups, a reasonable implication would be that these challenges reflect the kinds of concerns of other low-income families living in similar conditions of poor water quality. On this point, comparability of context is key.[22]

Finally, I would be remiss if I did not draw your attention to the power dynamics that can imbue a focus group setting. Focus groups are inherently social, and so asymmetrical power relations are inevitable. They may occur between the moderator (and/or researcher) and the participants; they may also take place among participants, as previously discussed. A moderator should know to gently push back against a dominant participant or invite a taciturn one to speak.

Researchers should also be aware of any deference or discomfort between the moderator and participants, and also between participants and the researcher. For one, the focus group should not create undue harm for any participant. Your institutional ethics review board should help you work through some of these potential concerns. Additionally, though, it is not good for your data if participants simply tell the moderator (or you) what they think you want to hear.

To mitigate the impact of relations of power, researchers should find a moderator who is as much like the participants as possible—someone who is knowable to them. All participants should sit in a circle to avoid any head-of-the-table hierarchy. You, as the researcher, should be visible and transparent. Introduce yourself; explain your role and your motivations for the focus groups (without, of course, revealing too much about your research and your expectations). As the focus group unfolds, you can observe the relational dynamics among participants and with the moderator. Do they treat the moderator differently? Do they count the moderator in the conversation? Are they willing to interject or speak over the moderator? These are clues that the group feels comfortable and safe. (For more on these concerns, see Chapter 12.)

Conclusion

Focus groups are an inherently social data collection method that generates emic data at multiple levels of analysis. These elements, when taken together, make focus groups extremely well suited for certain research questions and tasks. As with other people-centered data collection methods, you should organize focus groups by, first, prioritizing your participants and then prioritizing your research. This means choosing a moderator carefully and elaborating questions that are useful to your research and respectful of the group's time.

For more information on focus groups, as well as when and how to do them, please see the following texts.

Notes

1. Rosenthal and Lichtenheld, *Duck! Rabbit!*
2. Cyr, "The Pitfalls and Promise of Focus Groups as a Data Collection Method."
3. See, e.g., Cyr, *Focus Groups for the Social Science Researcher*.
4. Johnson, *The Struggle against Corruption*
5. Firchow and Ginty, "Measuring Peace."
6. Fuller et al., "Using Focus Groups to Adapt Survey Instruments to New Populations."
7. One can effectively tap into the individual point of view by asking focus group participants to write their answers before discussing them openly.
8. Paluck and Green, "Deference, Dissent, and Dispute Resolution."
9. Kitzinger, "The Methodology of Focus Groups."
10. Liamputtong. *Focus Group Methodology*.
11. Barbour, *Doing Focus Groups*; Cyr, *Focus Groups for the Social Science Research*; Krueger and Casey, *Focus Groups*.
12. By the way, writing out a game plan is a great idea before you begin a research project. It can serve as a kind of research "wish list." You write down everything you would do if you had unlimited resources, and then revise that list as your research unfolds. What could you do? What couldn't you? How did the (un)expected changes impact your research plan? Your findings? Your hypotheses? Make note of the changes and how they affect your research. Keep those notes, as they will be incredibly useful as you write up your findings and potentially revisit them well in the future. See Chapter 10 for more on this.
13. Winslow, Honein, and Elzubeir, "Seeking Emirati Women's Voices."
14. For excellent examples of different types of focus group questions, see Colucci, "'Focus Groups Can Be Fun.'"
15. Cyr, *The Fates of Political Parties*.
16. Morgan. "Focus Groups."
17. A focus group will ideally have six to eight participants, and so the budget for a set of focus groups can add up quickly. Do you need to rent a space, or can a local organization lend you a room with a table and chairs? Will you provide food and beverages? (You most certainly should.) Do you need pens, notebooks, paper, photocopies? Compensation is an additional cost. On this last point,

whether to compensate and how much to compensate can be tricky (see, e.g., Anderson, "A Proposal for Fair Compensation for Research Participants"). My take is that compensation is important and necessary, but it may not always be monetary. One can compensate with public transportation vouchers, for example, to offset the costs of travel. The key is to acknowledge participation without *inducing* it in the first place (see, e.g., Cyr, *Focus Groups for the Social Science Researcher*, 50).
18. Even a single focus group can produce meaningful, useful data. One need not assert that focus group data reflect ideas that are held by a larger group or population to actually engage with those data. After all, focus groups are settings where individuals engage in conversation, often about complicated or sensitive topics. The interactive nature of the group means that the process of meaning-making during that conversation is itself worthy of analysis.
19. For insight into other ethical challenges, see Sim and Waterfield, "Focus Group Methodology."
20. Viscek, "Issues in the Analysis of Focus Groups," 132.
21. Schutt, *Investigating the Social World*, 309.
22. Sim, "Collecting and Analysing Qualitative Data," 349.

Recommended Readings

Cyr, Jennifer. *Focus Groups for the Social Science Researcher*. Cambridge: Cambridge University Press, 2019.
    This book provides a set of guidelines on how to undertake focus groups, from start to finish, with an eye toward social scientists who may wish to integrate focus groups into their methodological, and perhaps even mixed-methods, toolkit.

Hennink, Monique M. *International Focus Group Research: A Handbook for the Health and Social Sciences*. Cambridge: Cambridge University Press, 2007.
    This book focuses on what one must take into consideration when undertaking focus groups in the Global South.

Hunter, Wendy and Natasha Borges Sugiyama. "Transforming Subjects into Citizens: Insights from Brazil's Bolsa Família." *Perspectives on Politics* 12, no. 4 (2014): 829–845.
    This article uses focus groups in the research design and is uncommonly thorough in explaining how focus group data are analyzed and written up.

References

Anderson, E. E. "A Proposal for Fair Compensation for Research Participants." *American Journal of Bioethics* 19, no. 9 (2019): 62–64.

Rosaline Barbour. *Doing Focus Groups*. 2nd ed. London: Sage, 2018.

Colucci, Erminia. "'Focus Groups Can Be Fun': The Use of Activity-Oriented Questions in Focus Group Discussions." *Qualitative Health Research* 17, no. 10 (2007): 1422–1433.

Jennifer Cyr. *The Fates of Political Parties: Institutional Crisis, Continuity, and Change in Latin America*. Cambridge: Cambridge University Press, 2017.

Jennifer Cyr. *Focus Groups for the Social Science Researcher*. Cambridge: Cambridge University Press, 2019.

Jennifer Cyr. "The Pitfalls and Promise of Focus Groups as a Data Collection Method." *Sociological Methods and Research* 45, no. 2 (2016): 231–259.

Firchow, Pamina, and Roger Mac Ginty. "Measuring Peace: Comparability, Commensurability, and Complementarity Using Bottom-Up Indicators." *International Studies Review* 19, no. 1 (2017): 6–27.

Fuller, Theodore D., John N. Edwards, Sairudee Vorakitphokatorn, and Santhat Sermsri. "Using Focus Groups to Adapt Survey Instruments to New Populations: Experience from a Developing Country." *Successful Focus Groups: Advancing the State of the Art* 156 (1993): 89–104.

Johnson, Roberta Ann. *The Struggle against Corruption: A Comparative Study.* New York: Palgrave Macmillan, 2004.

Kitzinger, Jenny. "The Methodology of Focus Groups: The Importance of Interaction between Research Participants." *Sociology of Health & Illness* 16, no. 1 (1994): 103–121.

Krueger, Richard A., and Mary Anne Casey. *Focus Groups: A Practical Guide for Applied Research.* 5th ed. Thousand Oaks, CA: Sage, 2015.

Liamputtong, Pranee. *Focus Group Methodology: Principles and Practice.* London: Sage, 2011.

Morgan, David. "Focus Groups." *Annual Review of Sociology* 22, no. 1 (1996): 129–152.

Paluck, Elizabeth Levy, and Donald P. Green. "Deference, Dissent, and Dispute Resolution: An Experimental Intervention Using Mass Media to Change Norms and Behavior in Rwanda." *American Political Science Review* 103, no. 4 (2009): 622–644.

Rosenthal, Amy Krouse, and Tom Lichtenheld. *Duck! Rabbit!* Clermont, FL: Bunny Books, 2009.

Schutt, Russell K. *Investigating the Social World: The Process and Practice of Research.* Thousand Oaks, CA: Sage, 2011.

Sim, Julius. "Collecting and Analysing Qualitative Data: Issues Raised by the Focus Group." *Journal of Advanced Nursing* 28, no. 2 (1998): 345–352.

Sim, Julius, and Jackie Waterfield. "Focus Group Methodology: Some Ethical Challenges." *Quality & Quantity* 53, no. 6 (2019): 3003–3022.

Viscek, Lilla. "Issues in the Analysis of Focus Groups: Generalisability, Quantifiability, Treatment of Context and Quotations." *Qualitative Report* 15 (2010): 122–141.

Winslow, Wendy Wilkins, Gladys Honein, and Margaret Ann Elzubeir. "Seeking Emirati Women's Voices: The Use of Focus Groups with an Arab Population." *Qualitative Health Research* 12, no. 4 (2002): 566–575.

20
Ethnography

Jessica Pisano

One way to think about ethnography is that it is research requiring a sustained commitment to trying to understand other people's lives, expressed as a willingness to let your interlocutors' activities determine how you spend your time in research. There's variation in what people think ethnography is and how to do it, with different approaches to thinking about its underlying epistemologies and intellectual purpose.[1] In this chapter, I argue that at its best, contemporary ethnography is a form of research in which you learn with and from other people, approaching others not as objects of inquiry but as fellow human beings whose ideas and ways of seeing things interest you. Noting that you'll want to consult a range of works on the subject, I provide some guidelines for how to prepare for and conduct ethnography, alert you to some challenges you might encounter, and highlight ways ethnography can be particularly well-suited for advancing our understanding of the world and one another.[2]

Overview: What Is Ethnography?

Sociologist Matthew Desmond describes ethnography as "what you do when you try to understand people by allowing their lives to mold your own as fully and genuinely as possible."[3] In addition to emphasizing immersion and a radical acceptance of others' habits and practices, some approaches also emphasize the importance of interest in how people understand their own lives and politics.[4] This latter element is often, though not exclusively, associated with interpretivist epistemological traditions, in which inquiry centers on how people understand and give meaning to things that happen in their lives, and not necessarily on what happened and why.

Ethnography can reveal how people frame their worlds and understand their politics, but it also can provide a granular view of causal processes. In my book *Staging Democracy*, I used ethnography for different purposes: to establish causality ("Why do people participate in performances of democratic institutions?"), to analyze the content of political concepts ("How do those performances change the meanings that attach to democratic participation?"), and to illuminate areas of our conceptual vocabulary that may require expansion ("What may regime-type concepts obscure about the ways people experience political coercion?").[5]

Ethnography can reveal things other methods may not. For example, in the early 2000s, research about Ukrainian politics often focused on electoral outcomes and emphasized societal division based on linguistic identity. Ukrainian society, the story went, was divided into a pro-Russia East and a pro-Europe West. Conducting ethnographic research in Ukraine's East in the 2000s and 2010s, though, it was clear that ostensibly pro-Russian voting behavior often was an expression not of identity but of economy—whether a result of Moscow's funding of housing and infrastructure projects in Luhansk or a product of the fact that Viktor

Yanukovych's Party of Regions was most effective manipulating votes in the large industrial towns and agricultural enterprises of the East. For many Ukrainians who spoke Russian in their everyday lives, apart from difficulties elders sometimes encountered deciphering instructions included with their medications, language politics usually barely registered as a concern. In this case, a ground-level view exposed a flaw in a widely-held interpretation.

What is required for doing ethnography? Ethnographic research requires presence and participation, an abiding openness to trying to understand how other people see the world, and a willingness and capacity to acquire the skills necessary to do the work.

Dominant definitions of ethnography emphasize participant-observation research. This is research in which you are not just watching people or talking with them—you're doing what they do. In my own research in rural Ukraine and Russia, this has meant activities ranging from accompanying land surveyors as a driver in Kharkiv to drawing water and harvesting walnuts near Uzhhorod, to participating in community gatherings like church services, "bench hour" in villages as the cows come home, and scores of other activities. Throughout, those activities have offered opportunities to notice details that could be observed only in the context of a daily routine and to participate in sustained dialogue.

Participant-observation research is an investment: it requires not just "being there" and taking part in things your interlocutors do, but also being able to communicate with people both about the details of their life or events and about how they think about those things. Sometimes the researcher needs to expend considerable effort acquiring enough skill in the activities of their interlocutors so that the researcher's presence, even as a learner of certain kinds of work, does not hinder those activities.

It bears noting that interactions with other people are a necessary condition for doing ethnographic research, but they are not a sufficient one. It might be tempting, for example, to imagine that extended conversations with taxi drivers and other people a researcher might encounter in the process of conducting in-situ interviews constitute ethnographic research. But conversations with taxi drivers are not ethnography unless you are studying taxi drivers, or unless that discussion is part of a much larger constellation of research conversations. Neither are structured interviews ethnography unless they are embedded in an investigation of local context. Ethnography requires understanding people's statements in context, and acquiring that knowledge of context requires sustained presence. Otherwise, you're doing interview research,[6] which has its own rules, advantages, and particularities (on this, also see Chapters 16–18).

Ethnography also requires a sincere effort to understand your interlocutors' subject positions and a genuine curiosity about how they experience the world. Critically engaging the realities of a community or place through your own eyes is not enough: ethnography requires ongoing reflexive analysis of the ways in which your theoretical and cultural baggage influences your perception as well as active engagement with other people's perceptions. Even traditions of autoethnography, which place the researcher's own embedded experience at the center of inquiry, require contextual understanding of surrounding relationships and meanings that help constitute individual experience. Regardless of your subject position or the epistemological tradition within which you locate your work, the best works of ethnography mean to illuminate the world by embracing and thinking about how different people say they experience it.

What other skills does ethnography require? An effort to understand how people say they see the world requires you be able to communicate in the language or languages your interlocutors use on a daily basis. If you must work through a translator, you're almost certainly doing interview research, not ethnography. If you're working in a multilingual environment, it can be important either at least to understand all the relevant languages or, short of that, to know enough about context to be able to ask questions about and try to figure out what is going on in conversations in the other languages. This is particularly important in postcolonial environments, where narratives delivered in different languages not only may vary in interpretation but also may cohere around different understandings of basic facts of history: Was land purchased or stolen? Were children given an education or robbed of their cultural heritage?

Additionally, you may find that in multilingual environments the very same individuals may tell one story about a particular event in one language and an entirely different story about the same event in another language. Or in another language, that same event may not exist in people's minds as a significant event—or even as an event at all.

To illustrate, while conducting research in southwestern Ukraine, where a large number of Hungarian-speaking people live, I usually tried to interact in Hungarian with people who spoke that language at home. I already spoke Ukrainian when I started research for that project, but in order to interact with Hungarian speakers in rural areas, I studied Hungarian over a period of 11 years while conducting fieldwork in the region. After Ukraine's Revolution of Dignity in 2013–2014, people who previously spoke to me only in Hungarian suddenly switched languages, expressing their criticism of the Yanukovych government in Ukrainian. Ukrainian had become the language of political critique and the space for expressing dissatisfaction with status quo politics. Without the acquired ability to communicate in both languages I would have missed important conversations—and I wouldn't have picked up on the fact that the same individuals who, when speaking Hungarian, seemed happy enough with certain politicians expressed a very different opinion in their whispered conversations in Ukrainian.

Amid substantial investments of language and other skill development, ethnography requires an extended time horizon, for contextual knowledge and skill in participant-observation research accrues over months and years. For this reason, it may not be practical to decide to treat ethnography as one of many different types of tools in your methodological toolbox.[7] But that need not be seen as a limitation. You can commit to ethnography as a method while exploring a vast range of research questions using it.

The era of the colonially inflected expectation that researchers spend an entire agricultural cycle in a single community has now passed, and the amount and intervals of time you spend conducting research may vary according to the project, but all ethnography involves a substantial investment of time and effort. For my book *The Post-Soviet Potemkin Village*, which analyzed changes in landownership in rural communities along each side of the Ukraine-Russia border, I first made a short exploratory trip to one of the regions where I would be working and then spent two years conducting field research. I returned in subsequent years for follow-up research. This approach worked well for that project because I was trying to gather, understand, and synthesize material about a large physical area where rural communities were spread out and, at the time, not always easily accessible.

Before I began that period of fieldwork, I had already spent substantial amounts of time in Ukraine and Russia, and I spoke both languages. Those skills required improvement, though. As I conducted research and my own speech came to reflect local variations, my Russian losing Moscow's long vowels and hard consonants, my Ukrainian acquiring lexical elements and constructions particular to Slobozhanshchyna, the region surrounding the city of Kharkiv, my interlocutors visibly warmed to our conversations, the content of discussions deepened, and I became able to ask questions that were more sensitive to the realities of my interlocutors than before.

Later, for a monograph about a single street in rural southwestern Ukraine, a different approach made better sense. I conducted research there over the course of a decade, visiting for several weeks or months most years. This model was adapted to the context of that small community. For one, it allowed me to conduct research over a period of years without, I hope, wearing out my welcome. More important, repeated shorter visits turned out to yield layered narratives that developed like sedimentary rock: each time I returned, I heard a new angle on or interpretation of the basic set of narratives people had related during my first visit. Figuring out what approach will be right for any given project requires some trial and error. Since this kind of experimentation will not be possible for all projects, depending on the costs of living where you do research, it's helpful to seek out as much personalized advice as possible before you begin your research.

How to Conduct Ethnography

Begin from an awareness of your subject position relative to the community or communities where you are working and an understanding that accumulation of localized knowledge takes time. In your intellectual preparations, take care to examine closely your own theoretical frameworks and cultural baggage. What are your expectations about the people with whom you interact? How do the beliefs you take with you into your research shape your observations?

Ethnographic research often quickly exposes flaws in theoretical frameworks and research questions. As you find out what is important to the people with whom you interact, it's likely your questions will change. This is one reason why it's a good idea, if you can, to conduct a few weeks or a month or two of preliminary in-situ research before completing a research proposal. It's not uncommon to discover that what your interlocutors actually care about, or the ways they understand their own politics, have little if anything to do with the way the literature in a given subfield or discipline treats the questions at hand. Although this may be frustrating, it is good for science: ethnography helps illuminate the frictions between theory and the dominant conceptual language, on the one hand, and people's lived realities, on the other.

When you choose the community of people with whom you want to learn, it's important to be reflexive and honest with yourself about your positionality. Reflexivity can result in greater transparency, more granular contextuality for your claims, more rigor, and more clarity about which observations can be used for what purposes. Ethnography requires deep knowledge of context, good training, and an ability to read the room. Yet reflexivity and knowledge aren't always enough: people do not have equal access to participant-observation as a research method in all contexts. In certain circumstances, depending on your positionality and research question, it can be difficult or dangerous or even impossible to do this work.

It can help to work with a community with which you are already familiar. But it would be a mistake to assume that outsider status itself is necessarily an impediment to collecting observations. Often, even as people may not want to open up to their neighbors, they'll be perfectly happy to share details of their lives with a researcher who is not permanently embedded in their community. As with the proverbial itinerant priest, people sometimes confess to a researcher precisely *because* of their outsider status.

However, just because people might speak freely to a researcher does not mean the researcher will understand precisely what they are saying. Here, I'm not referring only to the subtleties of language. I'm also referring to detailed knowledge of context, because hearing and listening are not the same as understanding: What are the cultural and historical references being invoked, the implicit touchstones and shades of meaning? When is speech ironic or indirect, when should you take it on face value, and how do you tell?

Further, how will you know when you have acquired enough contextual familiarity to confidently make such adjudications? There is no single answer to this last question, and each researcher must find their own way of developing and evaluating the cultural literacy needed to conduct any given project of ethnographic research. In my own case, early in my career I spent many hours watching televised improvisational comedy in places where I conducted research (and much later wrote about those shows),[8] reasoning that if I could understand jokes that drew on reservoirs of widely shared cultural knowledge, I could feel reasonably confident about my ability to discern verbal cues and catch references in other situations.

Investing in learning as much as you can before and during your research about the details of the lives of people in the communities you are interested in will help you better answer these questions. This includes historical knowledge. In her work on Moscow theater, anthropologist Alaina Lemon discussed differences in stage actors' training in Russia and the United States. If American method acting asks the performer to reach into their *own* experience to identify with a character, Russian approaches emphasized detailed knowledge of others' lives as a condition for the empathy needed to perform.[9] Unless you are writing autoethnography, the latter is a more helpful approach: when conducting research, it's important to take care not to assume that you and your interlocutors will experience, feel, or reflect on shared experiences in the same way. Especially if your research unfolds in a community under stress from war, disease, hyperinflation, or some other calamity and your home is somewhere else, it's important to remember that even a theoretical possibility of leaving shapes how a person sees things.

While conducting research, one important decision you will make—or others will make for you—is how you will inhabit social roles. Your main identity is as a researcher, but your participation in the activities of your interlocutors may end up depending in part on demographic categories to which you belong and to which people in the communities where you are doing research are socialized to respond in a particular way. Different social roles will expose you to different kinds of knowledge, so even as you seek to allow your interlocutors' realities to shape your activities, you will need to consider how the roles you inhabit align with the research questions you have asked.

For example, while conducting research in a rural borderlands community in southwestern Ukraine, I lived with my male partner in the home of a widowed grandmother. In that context, I was expected to perform work that belonged to women of the middle generation: drawing water, washing dishes, and whatever tasks were assigned to me by our host. I was not to cook—that was our host's job as the eldest woman in the household. My chores often were boring and lonely. But they led me into conversations by and with people who passed through the homestead enclosure. Meanwhile, my partner spent time with men of his age with livestock, in fields, and repairing machinery. He participated in an entirely different set of conversations. Between us, we learned not only about who said what to whom, but also how our different social roles defined the spaces of knowledge to which we were exposed—and how differently positioned interlocutors could interpret shared events in distinct, sometimes conflicting ways. We each took our own notes, discussing what we learned and comparing perspectives at the end of each day. We drew only on our own notes for individual publications, while our coauthored work drew on both sets of field notes. In both cases, our interpretations were informed by those conversations.

Depending on the context, finding people with whom to speak can be the easiest or hardest part of ethnographic research. Participating in community activities is a good way to meet people, and being willing to do a job can be one way to invite your inclusion. Participation also allows you first to learn and observe, then to seek out conversation. Acquiring knowledge of people's work also can be important and helpful in establishing connections, and a significant portion of your time conducting ethnographic research may be devoted to learning about context—even before you are able to formulate questions that both you and your interlocutors recognize as relevant. For example, conducting research on farms along the border between Russia and Ukraine for *The Post-Soviet Potemkin Village*, I wanted to know how agricultural land was, or was not, changing hands.[10] At the beginning, it was hard to make connections, and I went to Moscow and Kyiv to obtain letters of introduction from government officials who could open doors for me at the regional level. But my ability to find people with whom to initiate conversations changed as I made the effort to learn more about monoculture in the region: How far apart are seeds planted in rows of sunflower? What tool is used to thin sugar beet? How much acreage of pasture does a single cow need? And what were the differences between tractors manufactured in Kharkiv and in Minsk? As I learned these things, my ability to participate productively in conversations improved, and the people I wanted to meet became more interested in taking time to talk with me. This learning is one of the advantages of ethnographic fieldwork: conversations are iterative, and there are opportunities to correct mistakes, refine questions, and check findings—and to correct course when things don't go as planned.

When you identify people with whom you want to talk, asking questions and listening to answers is important, but it's also important to cultivate the ability to read and tolerate silence. Take care to avoid jumping into the breach. If you're a teacher as well as a researcher, use your classroom skills: after a question, wait a few beats past the onset of your own discomfort if there's no answer right away. Sometimes a revealing exchange can be ruined by an overeager attempt to keep the conversation moving just when someone is about to say something interesting.

Preparation for conversations is key. Practice taking notes. Although it may be technically possible in some situations to make audio recordings of certain conversations, this may not be advisable for a number of reasons. First and most obviously, people say different things in the presence of an active recording device than they do without one. Second, what people say is only one part of the story. Who else is in the room, as well as gestures, facial expressions, and other nonverbal communication, are important to note as well—and your understanding of what those details mean to your interlocutors may evolve as you conduct your research. Third, it's hard to say in advance which conversations will be most important for your research. When you are back at home, processing your notes, the fact of having memorialized a conversation through audio recording can lead it to take on an outsized significance compared to your other conversations. Fourth, it's unlikely you will ever have the time to listen to, never mind transcribe, that many hours of conversation—or to edit machine-produced transcription. Finally, and sometimes most important: as the eminent late social anthropologist F.G. Bailey emphasized in his fieldwork advice to graduate students, it's a good idea for people to see you taking notes. It reinforces your social role as a researcher, and openness about what you are doing can be very important to the people with whom you interact.

How should you take notes? In some circumstances (though certainly not all), it can be preferable, and sometimes even a responsibility, to keep notes on paper rather than electronically, or to keep indexes of people's names and pseudonyms on paper while storing notes electronically. If you upload notes to a server, knowing in what country that information is physically stored and the laws governing it may be important for protecting your interlocutors' anonymity: knowledge of context is necessary for evaluating risk.

In most cases, as Bailey recommended, it's helpful to type up and analyze your notes right away, ideally the same day. While this may not always be possible, doing so will prompt you to recall details you may not have written down during conversations, and this process will aid you in improving your skills of recall. If you're not able to do this soon after the conversations in question, you may be likely to forget key details or miss important connections by the time you do this work. By analyzing your notes as you do research, you will learn and notice things that will make each successive ethnographic conversation more productive. Above all, if you travel to conduct research, do not wait until you return home to organize and analyze your notes.

For this and other reasons, it's key not to discount the importance of physical stamina. Especially if you are conducting research in a language you do not otherwise use regularly in everyday life, ethnographic research can be one of the most physically challenging types of intellectual work you can do. After actively participating in conversations for several hours, sitting down to spend another several hours writing up your notes is often the very last thing you feel like doing.

Since pushing through day after day like this can be tiring, especially in the beginning, it's a good idea to prepare physically for research in the same way you might prepare for a road race or other athletic competition. It's also important to maintain your physical condition: if you are conducting research far from home for an extended period, be prepared for some people to delay seeing you until soon before you leave, and for your last weeks to be exceedingly busy for this reason.

The same goes for your mental health. As F.G. Bailey advised, if you are conducting research over a period of months or more in a place you do not normally live, it can be a good idea to take regular breaks, going somewhere else, even if just for a day or so nearby. This is especially the case if you are living in a small community in which you are both observing and being observed. For all the human interaction ethnography involves, this type of research can sometimes be a lonely business, so it makes sense to prepare accordingly.

A Few Caveats

Because ethnographic research is not reproducible—what's true on a given day for someone and revealed to and understood by one researcher may not be true, revealed to, or understood by another—some consider ethnography less useful for testing hypotheses than some other methods. Even if you're doing the kind of research that focuses on meaning-making, finding corroboration for a theory in the real world can be like finding evidence for any given political position in the Bible: if you know the text well enough, you'll likely be able to locate support in it for what you want to say, whatever that might be. For that reason, ethnographic research demands a high level of rigor, integrity, and transparency on the part of the researcher, as well as a commitment to understanding that transcends interest in making or testing a particular argument.

On the other hand, depending on the researcher's skill at navigating social landscapes and hierarchies, ethnography can be excellent for helping apprehend realities that interview and survey research—even using the latest tricks of the trade—may obscure. For example, list techniques in survey research can help begin to discern what people might think about a particular phenomenon even in authoritarian regimes. But what if the phenomenon in question is itself an exercise in deception? In some polities, a practice political technologists call "victim of the regime" involves opposition parties postering for their candidates, and then ripping down their own posters. This creates an impression of persecution by the powers that be, and that impression can help drum up opposition support for the candidates in question. Short of being present when people deface posters, without the kind of detailed local knowledge ethnographic research requires, it would be difficult to know that such practices exist—and difficult to correctly formulate questions about a landscape that includes such posters.

What about conducting research without traveling any distance, or even leaving your workspace? Can a commitment to understanding begin and end in virtual space, with digital ethnography? The availability of social media in communities across the globe can make research at a distance an attractive proposition. But caution is warranted: apart from the obvious challenges of source verification, knowledge of real-world context is always necessary for interpreting the stories people tell in any medium. Conducting research at a distance can work where you have an existing network of real-world relationships and shared experiences upon which to draw.[11] But diving into a context that is new for the researcher and doing only digital research may easily lead to interpretive errors. And without real-world knowledge of local context, those errors could go unnoticed by the researcher. Yet responsible shifts in the here-there spatial and social binaries that long have characterized ethnographic research are possible.[12]

Certain contexts, like war and postwar situations, require specialized advice (see, for instance, Chapters 17 and 24). And conducting ethnographic research in contexts with a certain kind of current or historical police apparatus can pose special challenges. In these cases, seek the counsel of experienced and reliable advisors: there are ways to parry some of those challenges.

Regardless of context, it's important to remain mindful that, while things change over time, responsibilities to your interlocutors do not. Given the usual timelines of academic publishing, by the time your work is published, the realities you encountered while conducting research may have shifted, perhaps dramatically. And the future of the past can be uncertain. For example, while doing fieldwork in Russian regions starting in the 1990s, some material that I obtained legally from local government offices came later to be classified as secret and its publication or transfer punishable. I decided not to use that material; even if I had not revealed where and from whom I had received it, state agents with knowledge of the communities where I had worked easily could have retraced my steps. Likewise, certain conversations with people in rural communities along Ukraine's borders in the 2000s and 2010s seemed unproblematic at the time they took place, but as Russia's war against Ukraine unfolded in its early years, I decided not to refer to them in my published work because the political situation had changed for my interlocutors.

The type of knowledge produced through ethnographic research both compels the researcher to take great care with the material they collect and can help them navigate the complexities of its use. For example, just as my book *Staging Democracy* went to press, the Russian Federation expanded the armed territorial conquest it had begun in 2014 and launched its full-scale invasion of Ukraine. Some rural communities in Ukraine where I had conducted research came under temporary occupation by Russian forces, who committed atrocities against people in those communities. In other communities where I had worked, homes, schools, and civilian infrastructure were destroyed by Russian artillery and ballistic missiles.

While writing that book, long-term relationships with my interlocutors had informed my decisions about what ethnographic detail to include. The local knowledge that filtered through those relationships had led me to imagine that, even as life in certain places seemed relatively stable, my interlocutors in Ukraine might one day collectively find themselves in mortal danger. I made decisions about my use and publication of research material based on those inferences. In the absence of the sustained engagement ethnography requires, I might not have known to withhold certain details from published work and might potentially have placed in even greater peril people who had trusted me with information about their lives. While it is impossible to predict the future, or to foresee all of the ways published research might be used, the deep contextual analysis involved in ethnographic work both demands and holds out the possibility of responsible research sensitive to its possible impacts on people involved in it.

Just as consideration for your interlocutors may sometimes limit what you write, the timeline required for ethnographic research does not always match well with professional incentives—at least if you want to tread the beaten path. On the one hand, ethnographic research involves building relationships and real-world social networks, and that takes time. It can take years to understand a subject and long periods of uninterrupted work to thoroughly analyze field notes. This means that there can be trade-offs between steady advancement along the traditional trajectories of academic careers and the production of quality work based on ethnographic research. On the other hand, ethnography can generate deep and lasting analysis, the kind that has a long shelf life and is worth investing in, as well as lifelong relationships that may develop alongside research but are not only *for* research.

But the long timeline for ethnographic research need not be a disadvantage; this kind of research can adapt well to some changing life circumstances and can be friendly to different stages of life, depending on what kinds of questions interest you. For some topics, and given the researcher's willingness to accept others' realities for their own family, ethnography can be more readily conducted with young children than can other types of research. I've conducted research in rural communities in Ukraine with children of different ages and also while, as a research interlocutor once delicately described my late third-trimester self, "a little bit pregnant." In almost all circumstances, research with family members was both more interesting and pleasant than it would have been alone. It was a positive experience for the young people. It also turned out to make for richer conversations with research interlocutors. Accompanied by children, I had more recognizably in common with my interlocutors, and family life placed us on some familiar shared terrain.

For example, trips in Ukraine with a young child in the summer of 2014 led to a different register of conversations with families displaced from areas of Ukraine temporarily occupied by Russian forces than otherwise would have been likely. As the children played together, long conversations turned around both everyday problems recognizable to parents everywhere, and to discussions of my interlocutors' situations. Of course, whether such a format for learning is possible or desirable depends on the research question and context. But it can be worth considering. And arguably, it can nudge the researcher toward questions that make visible a wider range of questions, interlocutors, and life situations than might otherwise suggest themselves.

The -graphy Part of Ethnography

Once you've done ethnographic research, how do you get from field notes to analysis? Much has been written about this topic, but here are a few key pieces of advice others gave me that I found to be most important and useful.

First, as noted, if you are going somewhere to conduct research, it's crucial to begin processing your fieldnotes before you return home: organize your own typed-up notes, read and think about them, and journal about them in context. When you return home, you will analyze the material again, but from a different situated perspective. Your notes will look different to you months later, and it's crucial to capture your own thoughts and observations about your research before you complete it.

Second, choose a method of organizing your notes and text and stick with it. Figure out what system works in the context in which you are conducting research and keep it simple. If you use software for organizing and storing notes, it can be a good idea to use an application that has been around for a while and will not require you to pay for regular updated versions to maintain access to your notes. I have used the same database program, formatted simply with a few text fields, for well over two decades. Because I have spent decades conducting research and have made dozens of extended trips, consolidating my notes in this way allows me to locate and use material regardless of the project for which I might have gathered it. Other researchers like to keep material for each project or research separate. The most important thing is to figure out what system works for you and use it consistently. Your midcareer self will thank you.

Third, regardless of the role of qualitative analysis software in your research analysis, the act of typing up your notes or even recopying them by hand can be immensely useful; as you recopy or enter your notes, you will recall contextual details you may not have recorded the first time, you'll make connections you did not register before, and you'll push your analysis forward. Later, holding and rereading a page of handwritten notes can unleash a flood of contextual recollection, like Proust's madeleine.

These points have to do with the mechanics of analyzing research material. But some might ask: How does a researcher write ethnography that is social science, as opposed to storytelling, which has its own heuristic value? The key is to engage in constant dialectic, examining your research question in light of what you have learned, and vice versa. Once you are satisfied that you have framed your question correctly in your emergent text, think about how your material helps you answer that question—not the question with which you may have begun your research. After all, from a certain point of view, the reason to do ethnography is not to confirm received wisdom about people's lives but to challenge and improve what we as researchers think we know.

Notes

1. Special thanks to members of the Decolonizing Eastern European Studies research group who commented on an earlier version of this chapter, and to participants in a cross-disciplinary political ethnography workshop at Yale University in December 2022. Lisa Wedeen provides a clear exposition of these debates in "Reflections on Ethnographic Work in Political Science."
2. A number of the recommendations presented here are informed by advice in a mimeographed handbook written by F. G. Bailey for his graduate students in social anthropology at the University of Sussex, handed down by James C. Scott to his PhD students in the 1990s.
3. Desmond, *Evicted*, 317–318.
4. Schatz, "Introduction."
5. Pisano, *Staging Democracy*.
6. Pisano, "How to Tell an Axe Murderer."
7. But see Bayard de Volo and Schatz, "From the Inside Out."
8. Pisano, "How Zelensky Has Changed Ukraine
9. Lemon, "Sympathy for the Weary State?"
10. Allina-Pisano, *The Post-Soviet Potemkin Village*.
11. Pisano, "Notes from Kharkiv."
12. Society for Cultural Anthropology, "A Manifesto for Patchwork Ethnography."

Recommended Readings

Here are a few examples of works whose quality and originality reflect the authors' deep engagement with and attentiveness to the people with and from whom they learn, and whose theoretical contributions arguably could not have been produced except through ethnography.

Berdahl, Daphne. *Where the World Ended: Re-unification and Identity in the German Borderland*. Berkeley: University of California Press, 1999.
Fujii, Lee Ann. *Killing Neighbors: Webs of Violence in Rwanda*. Ithaca, NY: Cornell University Press, 2009.
Hanser, Amy. *Service Encounters: Class, Gender, and the Mark for Social Distinction in Urban China*. Stanford, CA: Stanford University Press, 2008.
Wedeen, Lisa. *Authoritarian Apprehensions: Ideology, Judgement, and Mourning in Syria*. Chicago: University of Chicago Press, 2019.

References

Allina-Pisano, Jessica. *The Post-Soviet Potemkin Village: Politics and Property Rights in the Black Earth*. New York: Cambridge University Press, 2008.
Bayard de Volo, Lorraine, and Edward Schatz. "From the Inside Out: Ethnographic Methods in Political Research." *PS: Political Science and Politics* 37, no. 2 (April 2004): 267–271.
Desmond, Mathew. *Evicted: Poverty and Profit in the American City*. New York: Broadway Books, 2016.
Lemon, Alaina. "Sympathy for the Weary State? Cold War Chronotypes and Moscow Others." *Comparative Studies in Society and History* 51, no. 4 (2009): 832–864.
Pisano, Jessica. "How to Tell an Axe Murderer: An Essay on Ethnography, Truth, and Lies." In *Political Ethnography: What Immersion Contributes to the Study of Power*, edited by Edward Schatz, 53–73. Chicago: University of Chicago Press, 2009.
Pisano, Jessica. "How Zelensky Has Changed Ukraine." *Journal of Democracy* 33, no. 3 (July 2022): 5–13.

Pisano, Jessica. "Notes from Kharkiv: An Ethnographer Reflects on Communication in Wartime." *Public Seminar*, February 23, 2023. https://publicseminar.org/essays/notes-on-kharkiv/.

Pisano, Jessica. *Staging Democracy: Political Performance in Ukraine, Russia, and Beyond*. Ithaca, NY: Cornell University Press, 2022.

Schatz, Edward. "Introduction." In *Political Ethnography: What Immersion Contributes to the Study of Power*, edited by Edward Schatz, 1–22. Chicago: University of Chicago Press, 2009.

Society for Cultural Anthropology. "A Manifesto for Patchwork Ethnography." June 9, 2020. https://culanth.org/fieldsights/a-manifesto-for-patchwork-ethnography.

Wedeen, Lisa. "Reflections on Ethnographic Work in Political Science." *Annual Review of Political Science* 13 (2010): 255–272.

21
Supplementing Qualitative Work with Surveys, and Vice Versa

Emily Thorson and Emily M. Farris

Descriptive Overview

Surveys are an extraordinary tool for understanding aggregate patterns in public opinion, as they can provide insight into over-time trends and differences between groups. By design, the typical closed-ended survey question constrains what people are able to express into simplified and standardized responses. This method streamlines data collection, but it also inevitably misses critical nuances in measuring public opinion or political behavior. For example, a survey question that simply asks respondents how much they trust the news media ignores the fact that people have very different understandings of "trust" and "news media."[1] More traditional qualitative methods, such as interviews, may better capture the potential dynamics in respondents' choices but would likely be limited to a smaller number of respondents and a longer data collection process. We suggest that these challenges present opportunities for qualitative research and surveys to work together.

In this chapter, we show how surveys can be a useful component of and complement to qualitative research, as well as a novel source of qualitative data generation. Surveys can help solve some of the challenges of qualitative work. Open-ended questions, where respondents are not offered predefined answer choices, may be embedded in a survey to examine how a wide range of respondents think about a nuanced topic. By integrating survey research and qualitative approaches, researchers can combine multiple sources of data to answer their research questions more effectively.

We offer practical advice for how surveys can generate important qualitative data, as well as how qualitative research and survey data can improve, supplement, and contextualize each other. Our hope is that researchers increasingly pair qualitative and survey research rather than seeing them as mutually exclusive alternatives. We discuss practical approaches for bringing together qualitative and survey research and potential problems to consider in the practice, drawing on our own experiences (labeled by our initials when speaking in first person) and other scholars' work to help the reader navigate the practice.

State of Practice

Surveys enable social scientists to collect large amounts of data in a relatively short time and can be administered in person, online, or by mail or telephone. Surveys offer several advantages. The relative anonymity of some of these modes can be helpful when asking participants about potentially sensitive topics. In addition, data gathered from a larger (and potentially more representative) sample can allow for greater generalizability of results. However, while a well-designed survey instrument offers the benefit of standardized and reliable questions, it can also face challenges of validity and risks of inflexibility. Qualitative work can help to address these limitations, just as surveys can be a useful supplement to qualitative work.

There is a range of ways in which researchers might use survey and qualitative research to complement each other. Surveys with open-ended questions can generate qualitative data. Open-ended questions offer insight into participants' responses and provide important context for interpreting aggregate patterns. Researchers can also combine surveys and qualitative research to help clarify or contextualize trends or concepts and improve surveys. Qualitative research can improve surveys, and surveys can both enrich and produce qualitative data.

Using Surveys to Generate Qualitative Data

Open-ended survey questions allow researchers to collect larger numbers of respondents than may be possible with interviews or focus groups. Because open-ended questions do not include a set of response options, the respondents answer using their own words, either verbally or in writing. These questions may assess knowledge (e.g., asking them to name one of their elected representatives) or be used when there is an unknown or wide set of possible answers (e.g., asking them to articulate their concerns about a particular issue). Open-ended questions offer several advantages to the researcher: they can help researchers explore how respondents think about different concepts, shed light on the mechanisms driving experimental effects and observational associations, and generate new avenues of research.

First, open-ended questions can help researchers explore the considerations that participants have about a particular topic. For example, my coauthor and I (EF) used an open-ended question on a survey of U.S. county sheriffs to ask them about the top issues in their most recent election. This approach was a more inductive way of eliciting priorities than asking the sheriffs to choose from a list of potential issues. While we could have subsequently decided to apply a coding rule to this raw material to make it quantified and comparable, the open-ended question itself elicited interesting and useful qualitative data. Similarly, Ferrario and Stantcheva asked participants to respond to the broad question "What are your main considerations?" when thinking about income taxes, and then coded respondents' answers into topics such as distribution, fairness, and government spending.[2] By avoiding the risk of priming respondents, open-ended questions can capture participants' initial considerations of an issue. A disadvantage of this approach, discussed more in the following section, is that responses can vary widely and thus be challenging to analyze or code.

Open-ended questions can also be used as a dependent variable in an experiment by analyzing how responses vary depending on question wording or other prompts. In a study examining how news coverage of misinformation shapes attitudes, I (ET) showed respondents a headline about the issue of misinformation (e.g., "Google Announces Plan to Combat Spread of Misinformation"), and then asked them the open-ended question "What comes to mind when you see this headline?"[3] Half the respondents were randomly assigned to receive a version of the headline that used the word "misinformation," while the other half received a version that used the word "fake news." I then coded each response for whether it included a partisan reference, which allowed me to examine whether the term "fake news" elicited a more partisan response than "misinformation."

When asked after an experimental treatment is administered, open-ended questions can also help to shed light on potential mechanisms driving experimental effects. In one survey experiment, I (ET) tested the hypothesis that providing participants with information about *current* refugee policy would increase support for refugee-friendly policies more than providing them with information about refugee policy *outcomes*.[4] In addition to closed-ended measures of policy support, I included a posttreatment open-ended question asking people what came to mind when they thought about refugees. The quantitative analyses supported my hypothesis, and the coding of the open-ended responses suggested a potential mechanism: people who received the information about current policy were substantially more likely to mention the danger and persecution that refugees faced.

Finally, open-ended questions can help generate ideas for new research. In one survey on policy issues, I (ET) included an open-ended question that asked people to provide factual information about policies, such as "What is the major reason that Social Security is facing financial difficulties? If you're not sure of the answer, you can type 'not sure.'" By providing an explicit "not sure" option, I reduced the likelihood of people inventing reasons solely to satisfy the interviewer.[5] After collecting the information, I created a coding scheme that captured the most commonly given reasons, including (among others) demographic shifts (the correct answer), government misuse of funds (e.g., Social Security trust fund being used to fund the Affordable Care Act), and "scammers" taking advantage of the system. I then used these categories to inform a closed-ended question I included on a later survey. Another approach is to include an open-ended question at the end of a survey asking respondents what else they might like to tell the researcher, and then using these responses to help shape future data collection.

Practical Advice for Using Open-Ended Questions

For respondents, open-ended questions are more cognitively taxing and have a reputation for higher rates of nonresponse and lower response quality. They also increase survey completion time, which can drive up the cost of surveys (discussed in more detail later). Given these trade-offs, we recommend using open-ended questions sparingly, and below we offer a few design and analysis considerations to help maximize their usefulness.

First, as with all data collection, open-ended questions raise concerns about response bias: not all people are equally likely to take the time and effort to write a response.[6] However, offering a prompt (e.g., "It is important that you take your time and answer this question carefully") can help reduce nonresponse and differential quality. In addition, being specific about how much you want the respondent to write can be helpful in reducing the cognitive load of the question. For example, in a survey on policy attitudes, I (ET) wanted to investigate what people liked and disliked about a variety of policies. To do this, I asked each respondent two questions: "What is one thing you would change about [policy]" and "What is one thing you would keep the same about [policy]?" Explicitly asking respondents to identify only *one* thing in each category reduces the effort required to answer the questions.

If a survey is completed with a live interviewer, researchers should be aware of interviewer recording errors and provide clear training instructions to interviewers. Open-ended questions can be recorded by the interviewer in narrative, entering verbatim the respondents' answers, or summarized or field-coded by the interviewer. Another recent innovation involves using a chatbot, in lieu of a live interviewer, to engage respondents online and collect open-ended survey responses through automated dialog.[7] If responses can be recorded, then coders can also process them after the survey to improve accuracy and minimize interviewer error.[8]

After responses have been collected, a researcher may choose to code the responses. While this process can be expensive and time-consuming, we offer several suggestions to help streamline the process. One common approach is hiring research assistants; the coding of open-ended questions can be an excellent task for undergraduates. As an example of the time commitment required, I (ET) hired an undergraduate assistant to help with coding open-ended responses to the question "When you think of refugees who seek to come to the United States, what thoughts come to mind?" I created seven binary categories (e.g., "Terrorism," "Positive impact," and "Negative impact") based on a randomly selected subset of responses, and then provided the assistant with a coding sheet that included instructions for how to code each response. I opted for binary categories because it is often faster and more straightforward to simply code for the presence or absence of a particular element (e.g., coding responses for whether they mention partisanship) than to implement a more complex coding scheme (e.g., coding intensity of partisanship). For example, the instructions for the "Negative impact" category asked the coder to enter a 1 in the spreadsheet if the response had a reference to any negative impact that refugees might have on the United States, and a 0 otherwise. In the coding instructions, I included several examples from real responses to illustrate (e.g., "They are a burden to our society"). It took the research assistant a total of 16 hours to code 2,225 responses.

If the researcher can increase the number of coders, they can check for intercoder reliability. Regardless of how many coders are working on the project, we recommend checking in often with them and encouraging them to provide ongoing feedback (e.g., in a column marked "Notes") because often new categories or nuances can emerge during the coding process. In addition to human coders, there are also an increasing number of options and advancements in computer-aided text analysis that can be of use to researchers when analyzing data from open-ended survey questions.[9]

Finally, survey platforms can be used in a nontraditional way as a tool for assisting in *coding* qualitative data. While many scholars use qualitative data analysis software such as Dedoose or Nvivo to organize and analyze their data, survey tools can be more accessible for some, particularly undergraduate research assistants, to assist in the coding process. For instance, when I (EF) was working with a data set of images from news magazine stories dealing with U.S. immigration, my coauthor and I employed two undergraduate research assistants to code numerous components in each of the images.[10] To help facilitate and organize the research assistants, my coauthor and I created a survey on Qualtrics that the research assistants filled out for each image as they were analyzing it. The survey instrument was not a traditional survey distributed to a sample of respondents to collect information about themselves, but rather a tool to help guide the research assistants in recording their findings as they examined the visual data. Coding qualitative data can be a complex process, and survey platforms can streamline the steps required for researchers.

Using Qualitative Research and Survey Responses to Contextualize Each Other

Science is fundamentally an iterative process, a reality increasingly reflected in scholarly work. While a few decades ago, it was standard practice to publish a paper with only a single survey or data source, now scholars more regularly include multiple approaches within a single paper, such as replications of a particular finding or observational research supplemented by an experiment. For example, in "To Emerge? Breadwinning, Motherhood, and Women's Decisions to Run for Office," the authors employ a multimethod design to explore gendered candidate emergence among alumnae of a Democratic campaign training organization in the United States, drawing on participant observation, interviews, and a survey.[11] Mixed-methods approaches that combine qualitative and survey work are well suited for a variety of research questions (see also Chapter 7).

Qualitative research can be used in combination with surveys in various ways to explore potential explanations for observed patterns in quantitative data. In mixed-methods studies, this explanatory-sequential approach can be used through two phases of data collection, where data collection can run either sequentially or concurrently. This research approach can assist in understanding patterns across research designs, building on the strength of both quantitative and qualitative methodologies. The growing interest in integrating quantitative and qualitative research designs has led to productive debates among scholars on both its feasibility and its approach.[12]

In a sequential mixed-methods design, one data collection method follows the other. For instance, Simonsen uses a mixed-methods study that includes surveys in order to understand the role of political rhetoric in shaping immigrant political incorporation. The article combines content analysis of focus group discussions with immigrants in Denmark with survey data from 18 Western European countries across a 12-year period. As Simonsen explains in the introduction, the qualitative data and quantitative data build on each together to develop causal inference: "The quantitative part takes advantage of empirical variation in the salience of anti-immigrant political rhetoric across Europe to test theoretical hypotheses and patterns indicated in the qualitative part."[13]

One example of a concurrent design, where survey data and qualitative data are collected at the same time, is Bos et al.'s article examining gendered political socialization among children.[14] The authors used a mixed-methodological approach to collect their data from children in grades 1 through 6, either surveying or interviewing the children and asking them to draw a political leader. The authors interviewed some respondents in the study, based on the age and abilities of the respondent and availability of time with them. For some populations, interviews may be a more appropriate type of data collection and serve as a complement to a survey research design.

Surveys and qualitative work can be combined in one research design or as part of a larger research agenda over different projects. In our study on U.S. sheriffs, my coauthor and I (EF) have conducted two national surveys of sheriffs—the first in 2012 and the second in 2021.[15] One notable finding that emerged from the data in the first survey was the extent to which county sheriffs differ from the general public and even from other law enforcement officers on the issue of gun control and gun rights. To explore why sheriffs were such strong supporters of gun rights, my coauthor and I turned to both observational research on the Constitutional Sheriffs and Peace Officers Association (an organization which mobilized sheriffs to oppose Obama's gun reform measures following the deadly shooting in Sandy Hook, Connecticut, in 2012) and content analysis of sheriffs' public statements opposing gun reform efforts during that time. Similarly, we have used findings from the survey to generate ideas for future projects. For instance, future work could include in-depth interviews with sheriffs on issues such as the opioid and mental health crises, which sheriffs identified in open-ended responses on our survey when asked about top issues of concern for their counties.

Qualitative research can help inform and improve surveys, particularly in understudied populations. For instance, Thachil's 15 months of fieldwork among urban migrants in India informed the study's sampling protocols, with fieldwork revealing the circular mobility of migrant populations and showing that migrants' worksites, rather than traditional residences, would allow for a better arena of access.[16] Additionally, Thachil details how ethnography improved the construct validity of survey experiments, by designing more precise and accessible experimental vignettes. Thachil describes using language from informant quotes collected during his ethnographic fieldwork to help design his vignette experiment and operationalize a key concept in his study.

Qualitative methods can help us better understand how people conceptualize political concepts and process political information. For example, in a recent project, I (ET) sought to identify widespread misperceptions about public policy.[17] One approach would have been to draw on fact-checking websites, elite misinformation, or intuition to create a list of potential misperceptions, and then administer a survey measuring belief. However, this approach would inevitably be subject to selection bias and thus offer an incomplete picture of false beliefs. Instead, I identified potential misperceptions through an in-depth interview process that elicited factual beliefs as part of a larger discussion of politics and policy.[18] I posted an ad on randomly selected Craigslist message boards offering the potential to earn a gift card by participating in a phone interview and asking interested people to fill out a brief survey including a consent form, their contact information, and demographic information. From that group, I selected 40 interview participants. The 20-minute interviews focused on eliciting factual assertions as well as opinions about policy issues. Drawing on these interviews, I created a list of 12 closed-ended factual questions that I then asked on a representative survey. This bottom-up process enabled me to identify several widely held misperceptions that previous research had missed. For example, while the false belief that Temporary Assistance to Needy Families benefits are time-unlimited was mentioned by several interviewees and turned out to be held by more than half of survey respondents, it does not appear on fact-checking or "fake news" websites.

Drawing on qualitative research to inform the creation of survey questions can also pose challenges for researchers. Recording and transcribing interviews can be a helpful step, since it makes it easier to review the transcripts and identify patterns that can then be used to create closed-ended survey questions. It is also important to recognize that not all insights gleaned from interviews will translate into meaningful patterns in survey data. For example, in conducting interviews to identify common policy misperceptions, two people incorrectly stated that "Medicare" referred in part to a type of hospital. However, when I (ET) used this as the basis of a survey question on a representative sample, I found that fewer than 5% of Americans held that misperception. Conversely, other common misperceptions that I had previously identified via survey research did not show up in the interviews. Ultimately, however, the two approaches complemented each other: the survey filled in holes in the interview data just as the interviews enabled me to create a more complete survey instrument, together creating a more accurate and detailed picture of beliefs and attitudes.

Potential Problems

Using surveys as part of qualitative research can pose several problems for the researcher to navigate. The two major costs, money and time, challenge nearly all methodologies in different ways. In this final section, we discuss several of these issues specific to surveys and offer suggestions for potential solutions.

To start, surveys can be expensive. Depending on your sample and administrative needs, surveys can cost thousands of dollars. For example, for the 2022 Cooperative Election Study, a national survey of Americans fielded for each federal election and supported by the National Science Foundation, a team module (1,000 respondents for one team's content along with the common content) costs $13,000. Given inequities in research resources, scholars at many institutions may not have access to funds to support research without applying for grants, a process which itself can be an additional cost in time and resources. However, there are ways of procuring less expensive samples. Platforms like Lucid and Mechanical Turk allow researchers to conduct surveys at a lower cost than large survey vendors such as YouGov, albeit sometimes at the cost of representativeness. Some survey vendors also allow for researchers to add single questions onto existing omnibus surveys, which can be a less expensive option than paying for an entire survey. Another option is partnering with a researcher already conducting a survey to add a question or two at the end of the instrument. And of course, it is also possible to recruit a convenience sample (e.g., by providing undergraduate course credit for completing a survey or posting a survey link on social media).

There is an important cost of time for the researcher to consider, as creating a survey and analyzing the results may require learning a new method and skill set. Coauthoring with scholars trained in survey research methods may be a way to combine both resources and expertise to be able to include surveys in qualitative research. Many universities have access to survey platforms such as Qualtrics, which not only help build and host surveys but also include extensive tutorials. While there are free or cheaper ways to make online surveys, such as Google Forms, these tend to include fewer options for survey structuring and analysis.

Conclusion

Although surveys are typically thought of as only a component of quantitative research, we have shown how they may be a useful complement to qualitative research in a variety of ways. First, responses to open-ended questions on surveys can be a source of qualitative data. We offer advice on the use of open-ended questions and the coding of that data. Second, surveys can be a critical part of an iterative research agenda, both by generating new research ideas and by applying insights from qualitative data to a more representative sample. We hope researchers find surveys can improve qualitative research and vice versa.

Notes

1. Daniller et al., "Measuring Trust in the Press in a Changing Media Environment."
2. Ferrario and Stantcheva, "Eliciting People's First-Order Concerns."
3. Thorson, "How News Coverage of Misinformation Shapes Trust and Beliefs."
4. Thorson and Abdelaaty, "Misperceptions about Refugee Policy."
5. Thorson, *The Invented State*.
6. Miller and Dumford, "Open-Ended Survey Questions."
7. Xiao et al., "Tell Me about Yourself."
8. Smyth and Olson, "How Well Do Interviewers Record Responses to Numeric, Interviewer Field-Code, and Open-Ended Narrative Questions in Telephone Surveys?"
9. Roberts et al., "Structural Topic Models for Open-Ended Survey Responses."
10. Farris and Mohamed, "Picturing Immigration."
11. Bernhard, Shames, and Teele, "To Emerge?"
12. Brookes, "Introduction to Symposium."
13. Simonsen, "The Democratic Consequences of Anti-Immigrant Political Rhetoric," 145.
14. Bos et al., "This One's for the Boys."
15. Farris and Holman, "Public Officials and a 'Private' Matter."
16. Thachil, "Improving Surveys through Ethnography."
17. Thorson, *The Invented State*.
18. This process is different from the process of cognitive interviewing, an approach designed specifically to pretest an existing survey instrument by asking respondents to expand on their answers. Beatty and Willis, "Research Synthesis."

Recommended Readings

Chong, Dennis. "How People Think, Reason, and Feel about Rights and Liberties." *American Journal of Political Science* 37, no. 3 (1993): 867–899.
    Uses in-depth interviews to explore the way respondents think about controversial political issues and makes recommendations for designing survey questions to capture the complex structure of public opinion.

Dillman, Don A., Jolene D. Smyth, and Leah Melani Christian. *Internet, Phone, Mail, and Mixed-Mode Surveys: The Tailored Design Method*. Hoboken, NJ: Wiley, 2014.
    Textbook on survey research methods.

Haddock, Geoffrey, and Mark P. Zanna. "On the Use of Open-Ended Measures to Assess Attitudinal Components." *British Journal of Social Psychology* 37, no. 2 (1998): 129–149.
    Describes a range of ways that open-ended questions can be used to assess attitudes and includes a wide range of examples.

Smyth, Jolene D., Don A. Dillman, Leah Melani Christian, and Mallory Mcbride. "Open-Ended Questions in Web Surveys." *Public Opinion Quarterly* 73, no. 2 (2009): 325–337.
    Discusses strategies for improving response quality in open-ended questions in online surveys.

Singer, Eleanor, and Mick P. Couper. "Some Methodological Uses of Responses to Open Questions and Other Verbatim Comments in Quantitative Surveys." *Methods, Data, Analyses* 11, no. 2 (July 2017): 115–134.
    Reviews several methodological uses of open-ended questions on surveys.

References

Beatty, Paul C., and Gordon B. Willis. "Research Synthesis: The Practice of Cognitive Interviewing." *Public Opinion Quarterly* 71, no. 2 (2007): 287–311. https://doi.org/10.1093/poq/nfm006.

Bernhard, Rachel, Shauna Shames, and Dawn Langan Teele. "To Emerge? Breadwinning, Motherhood, and Women's Decisions to Run for Office." *American Political Science Review* 115, no. 2 (2021): 379–394. https://doi.org/10.1017/s0003055420000970.

Bos, Angela L., Jill S. Greenlee, Mirya R. Holman, Zoe M. Oxley, and J. Celeste Lay. "This One's for the Boys: How Gendered Political Socialization Limits Girls' Political Ambition and Interest." *American Political Science Review* 116, no. 2 (2022): 484–501.

Brookes, Marissa. "Introduction to Symposium: The Road Less Traveled: An Agenda for Mixed-Methods Research." *PS: Political Science & Politics* 50, no. 4 (2017): 1015–1018. https://doi.org/10.1017/S1049096517001196.

Chong, Dennis. "How People Think, Reason, and Feel about Rights and Liberties." *American Journal of Political Science* 37, no. 3 (1993): 867–899. https://doi.org/10.2307/2111577.

Daniller, Andrew, Douglas Allen, Ashley Tallevi, and Diana C. Mutz. "Measuring Trust in the Press in a Changing Media Environment." *Communication Methods and Measures* 11, no. 1 (2017): 76–85. https://doi.org/10.1080/19312458.2016.1271113.

Dillman, Don A., Jolene D. Smyth, and Leah Melani Christian. *Internet, Phone, Mail, and Mixed-Mode Surveys: The Tailored Design Method.* Hoboken, NJ: Wiley, 2014.

Farris, Emily M., and Mirya R. Holman. "Public Officials and a 'Private' Matter: Attitudes and Policies in the County Sheriff Office Regarding Violence against Women." *Social Science Quarterly* 96, no. 4 (2015): 1117–1135. https://doi.org/10.1111/ssqu.12182.

Farris, Emily M., and Heather Silber Mohamed. "Picturing Immigration: How the Media Criminalizes Immigrants." *Politics, Groups, and Identities* 6, no. 4 (2018): 814–824. https://doi.org/10.1080/21565503.2018.1484375.

Ferrario, Beatrice, and Stefanie Stantcheva. "Eliciting People's First-Order Concerns: Text Analysis of Open-Ended Survey Questions." AEA Papers and Proceedings, vol. 112, May 2022, 163–169. https://doi.org/10.3386/w29686.

Haddock, Geoffrey, and Mark P. Zanna. "On the Use of Open-Ended Measures to Assess Attitudinal Components." *British Journal of Social Psychology* 37, no. 2 (1998): 129–149. https://doi.org/10.1111/j.2044-8309.1998.tb01161.x.

Miller, Angie L., and Amber D. Dumford. "Open-Ended Survey Questions: Item Nonresponse Nightmare or Qualitative Data Dream?" *Survey Practice* 7, no. 5 (2014): 1–11. https://doi.org/10.29115/sp-2014-0024.

Roberts, Margaret E., Brandon M. Stewart, Dustin Tingley, Christopher Lucas, Jetson Leder-Luis, Shana Kushner Gadarian, Bethany Albertson, and David G. Rand. "Structural Topic Models for Open-Ended Survey Responses." *American Journal of Political Science* 58, no. 4 (2014): 1064–1082. https://doi.org/10.1111/ajps.12103.

Simonsen, Kristina Bakkær. "The Democratic Consequences of Anti-Immigrant Political Rhetoric: A Mixed Methods Study of Immigrants' Political Belonging." *Political Behavior* 43, no. 1 (2021): 143–174. https://doi.org/10.1007/s11109-019-09549-6.

Singer, Eleanor, and Mick P. Couper. "Some Methodological Uses of Responses to Open Questions and Other Verbatim Comments in Quantitative Surveys." *Methods, Data, Analyses: A Journal for Quantitative Methods and Survey Methodology (MDA)* 11, no. 2 (2017): 115–134. https://doi.org/10.12758/mda.2017.01.

Smyth, Jolene D., Don A. Dillman, Leah Melani Christian, and Mallory Mcbride. "Open-Ended Questions in Web Surveys." *Public Opinion Quarterly* 73, no. 2 (2009): 325–337. https://doi.org/10.1093/poq/nfp029.

Smyth, Jolene D., and Kristen Olson. "How Well Do Interviewers Record Responses to Numeric, Interviewer Field-Code, and Open-Ended Narrative Questions in Telephone Surveys?" *Field Methods* 32, no. 1 (2020): 89–104. https://doi.org/10.1177/1525822x19888707.

Thachil, Tariq. "Improving Surveys through Ethnography: Insights from India's Urban Periphery." *Studies in Comparative International Development* 53, no. 3 (2018): 281–299. https://doi.org/10.1007/s12116-018-9272-3.

Thorson, Emily. "How News Coverage of Misinformation Shapes Perceptions and Trust." Working paper. https://www.dropbox.com/scl/fi/u4wmg332bsrgynmgtowdz/elements.pdf?rlkey=hlcap4azlkvicsf3hpclpsxlo&dl=0

Thorson, Emily. *The Invented State*. Oxford: Oxford University Press, forthcoming.

Thorson, Emily, and Lamis Abdelaaty. "Misperceptions about Refugee Policy." *American Political Science Review* 117, no. 3 (2022): 1123–1129.

Xiao, Ziang, Michelle X. Zhou, Q. Vera Liao, Gloria Mark, Changyan Chi, Wenxi Chen, and Huahai Yang. "Tell Me about Yourself." *ACM Transactions on Computer-Human Interaction* 27, no. 3 (June 2020): 1–37. https://doi.org/10.1145/3381804.

22
Locating and Working with Historical Data

Diana S. Kim

Descriptive Overview

Qualitative research utilizing historical data is inextricably tied to the practice of archival research. Archives can enable researchers to revisit canonical theories with a fresh empirical eye. Declassified records of state agencies can hint at how formal institutions think and behave. Witness testimonies and legal depositions may yield insight into why social actors make certain choices. The sirens of archival research may also excite those animated by questions about longue durée causes, the (social) origins, (political and economic) foundations, and (ideological) roots of contemporary phenomena as well as lasting legacies (of empires and colonial rule, wars, or environmental crises, for instance). Beyond simply looking back in time, the many histories that reside in archives invite us to theorize the present.

This chapter introduces strategies for navigating archives that address analytical challenges that accompany the act of collecting records about the past and transforming them into evidence for qualitative analyses. I am invested in conveying how seductively exciting archival research can be, alongside reasons to be cautiously modest about the nature of historical data it can yield.

"Archive" can have several meanings. In a literal sense, the archive is a physical place where collections of records, both textual and nontextual, are kept for purposes of preservation. Imagine the physical building of the National Archives of Myanmar in Yangon (Figure 22.1). Or a corner room in the Kowloon branch of the Hongkong and Shanghai Banking Corporation (HSBC) in Hong Kong (Figure 22.2). An archive may also refer to a virtual repository of digitized records, which can be accessed remotely or on site. In its most abstract sense, an archive extends to nontangible embodiments of collective memory, past ideas, and experiences—some may conceive of an art festival, commemoration events, the human body itself or a spoken language as an archive of identity.[1]

Broadly speaking, there are two types of archives: those that collect their own records and those that serve as an external repository for the records of others. For instance, the HSBC keeps its own institutional records, while the National Archives of Myanmar receives records from other government agencies. Distinctions are also made between official and informal archives. Both the HSBC and National Archives of Myanmar fall under the former category as most of their records are produced and preserved by formal institutions, while informal archives refer to "unmapped, non-systematized collections of material kept by individuals and groups in areas under study."[2]

Two core issues that animate archival research concern *audience* and *preservation*: Why was a record created, and who decided to preserve it? "An archive presupposes an archivist, a hand that collects and classifies," writes Arlette Farge, the great social historian of France, reflecting on her practice of using the judicial archives of 18th-century Paris: police

256   Diana S. Kim

Figure 22.1 The Myanmar National Archives Building in Yangon. Photograph by author.

Figure 22.2 Entrance to the Archives of the Kowloon branch of HSBC in Hong Kong. Photograph by author.

interrogations, trials, case summaries, and court sentencings that contain vast information on the city's poorest inhabitants, vagrants, petty criminals and protestors.[3] There can be something thrilling about a wealth of fine-grained incident reports of urban disorder, which also contain testimonies by everyday people who seldom left records about themselves. At the same time, Farge reminds us, these types of records contain "the rough traces of lives that never asked to be told in the way they were, but were one day obliged to do so when confronted with the harsh reality of the police and repression."[4] The *audience* was a police officer; *preservation* happened thanks to an institution with a need for surveillance and punishment.

Every archive—whether official or informal, material or nontangible, direct or indirect—is riddled with biases created by issues of audience and preservation. For instance, Farge's archives, held at the Library of the Arsenal, a department of the French National Library and famed for holdings that include the Bastille prison archives, represent a site of captured speech, curated by the French police state. Reading society from the top down, these records likely give excess coherence to people's motivations for criminal behavior and overestimate the magnitude of urban disorder and threats to the state. Also, the voices of 18th-century Parisians who avoided or circumvented the state are absent from this type of archive. But then, among those who *do* appear, it is possible to discern gender differences in repertoires of illegal and contentious action by using different types of records. Farge finds women expressed themselves differently from men when testifying before the police, "preferring to speak loudly and forcefully"; this tendency appears in documents for filing complaints and petitions to the police but not in interrogation reports where the police asked formulaic questions to which people only responded.[5]

To be clear, biases in historical records are hardly a reason to dismiss them. Rather, they give reason to dig deeper, to relentlessly contextualize a record to understand when and why different biases occur, and to decide if and how such biases are likely to affect one's analysis. By way of doing so, it becomes possible to design research strategies that are creative about rather than apologetic for the analytical limitations of historical data; that are explicit about scope conditions and what inferences can (and cannot) be made from a truncated sample; and that thus constantly strive to balance fidelity to an archive's specificities with a desire to make generalizable arguments and tell abstract narratives.

State of Practice

It is imperative to first know basic archive terminology.[6] *Provenance* (also known as *respect des fonds*) is a type of principle for arranging records in a way that preserves their integrity based on how they originated, and informs the practice of *original order*, by which archives maintain records according to how creators arranged them originally. This is why records are not necessarily found chronologically, alphabetically, or according to geography. The organizing categories are those created by the individual, family, or agency from whom the archive acquired the documents.

Many archives follow a standard hierarchy for arranging records.[7] *Collections* are a general grouping of records that do not necessarily share the same provenance. Within a collection, the highest level of description is a *fonds* (record group), in which records share provenance. Fonds are subdivided into *series* (and *subseries*), which are further subdivided into *files*. The lowest level of the hierarchy is an *item*, which is a record that is indivisible. The item-level record is what we usually understand as an archival document—the piece(s) of paper for a surveillance file of an individual, a court proceedings' transcript, a tax record, a photograph.

Locating Historical Data

How does one even begin? A very pragmatic mind can be helpful. Try thinking like a detective who works backward from the information at hand. To figure out where to go, which archive to start from, consider browsing the last pages of an influential, rigorous, and inspiring history book or article on your topic and time period. Look at the primary sources that the author(s) consulted. Where is the physical (or digital) location of the archive(s)? What shelf numbers or box numbers are cited, for which item, which series and fonds? But before choosing that anchoring history, read widely. In order to know which specific book or article to glean clues from, it is necessary to know what are the already existing histories and historiographical debates on your topic and time period. They may reveal that some archives, certain records, are famously controversial. It is also possible that methodological challenges rooted in these primary sources, which may later haunt you, have already been well-addressed.[8]

The daunting first step into an archive can often be found by retracing already trodden paths. Graduate classes fully devoted to archival research are uncommon in political science, and few enter an archive with systematic training in archival studies.[9] It is not unusual to begin sheepishly, as an applied practitioner of archival methods and theory that one is not yet familiar with, and at once draw upon the acquired know-how of others and expand through one's own cumulative experience, in ways that can sound embarrassingly pedestrian when conveyed out loud but are in fact guided by nuanced logics of inquiry.

It is tempting to believe that historical data can be collected by "sampling" the archive, namely, identifying documents that are representative of a general universe of records, which capture an empirical historical reality. It seems straightforward. In practice, however, this approach is one of the most difficult ways to begin archival research. It is necessary to know where a document fits within a record hierarchy as well as the full scope of temporal and geographical coverage of its embedding file, series, and collection. Such knowledge, in turn, requires knowing how an archive—official or informal, large or small—acquired, appraised, preserved, organized, and/or cataloged records, not least because such decisions affect what is visible and accessible to the researcher. Professional archivists may spend years learning the infrastructure of a specific collection.

It can feel overwhelming. Almost paralyzing. At least, this was my feeling when I first approached the India Office Records (IOR) at the British Library in London, hoping to consult records on opium regulation in Burma under British colonial rule during the 19th and 20th centuries.[10] This is a vast collection of over 70,000 volumes of official publications and 105,000 manuscripts and printed maps produced by various government agencies comprising the British Empire since the 17th century that spans 14 kilometers of shelves, along with the private papers of employees.[11] It is an official archive with excellent catalogs down to item-level records, which are searchable online and accessible in person at the Asian and African Studies Reading Room at the British Library. This makes the IOR one of the easier collections to navigate and locate documents within, compared with, for instance, the National Archives of Myanmar (that has a less fine-grained catalog for searching records) or the personal papers of anti-opium reformers (which are held by family descendants in their private homes). Yet the more I learned about the scale and complexity of this collection, the idiosyncratic organization of its composite series and files, as well as how many existing records relating to British opium regulation in Burma it *did not* include, it seemed patently absurd to imagine ever approaching this archive systematically, let alone identify documents from which I could discern meaningful information, facts, or interpretations about the colonial state and opium regulation in British Burma.

Take a breath. Briefly suspend your belief in a knowable general universe of archival records and a linked empirical reality. Instead, presume that it is impossible to know the former's full size and scope, and that the link to the latter is always mediated by an archivist—that is, a human or institution with their own goals, interests, and reasons for making a document available.

From this perspective, there are strategies for exploring an archive's collections from the bottom up and making informed choices about how to consult documents selectively. One especially effective strategy is to repeatedly consult the metarecords: finding aids, indexes, and research guides.

A *finding aid* provides detailed inventories of specific collections, including information on provenance, a summary of contents and organization, administrative history and biographical notes, and size (e.g., number of boxes, linear feet of records).[12] An *index* (or *catalog*) is a list of records with shelf or call numbers. A collection such as the IOR do not have a single finding aid, in part because it is a vast and disparate collection without a centralized record hierarchy. Rather, there are numerous and disparate "local" finding aids or indexes, some produced by archivists or commissioned experts, while others are compiled by researchers. For instance, Figure 22.3 shows an index of itemized lists of documents in the British Colonial Office's series of records on reports, telegrams, and other forms of correspondence exchanged between London and the Straits Settlements (Singapore and parts of today's Malaysia), compiled by the historian Paul Kratoska and available as a published book.[13]

Finding aids and indexes are cryptic and not necessarily meant to be read from cover to cover but consulted selectively. Hidden within their flat prose is often invaluable contextual information. A quick glance through them can be enormously informative about a collection's chronological and geographical scope and how its records are organized, as well as help a researcher identify important keywords and proper nouns for locating documents.

Research guides are narrative explanations about how to navigate an archive's collections, which may also include descriptions of its institutional history, record-keeping practices, and

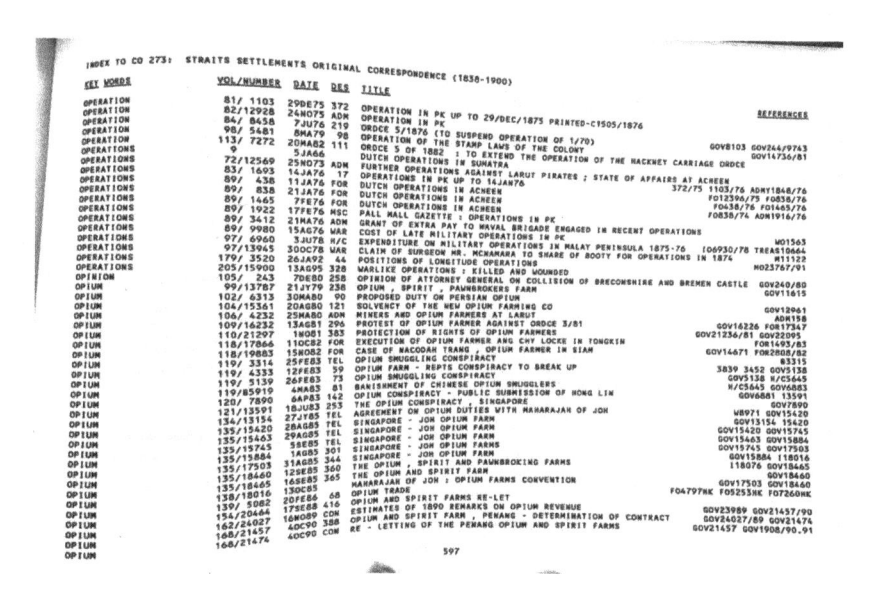

Figure 22.3 Index for Colonial Office Records, Series Number 273 (CO 273). The first entry for opium contains information on the file number (Volume 99) and item number (Number 13787) for a document entitled "Opium, Spirit, Pawnbrokers Farm" created on July 21, 1879. The citation for this record is CO 273/99/13787.

references to relevant secondary sources, often written by an archivist or subject specialist. Imagine a research guide as doing the storytelling that a person very familiar with an archive can reveal about its riches and quirks.[14] Compared with finding aids and indexes, research guides are often more reader-friendly but also must be consulted discerningly, as they are the products of another's interpretation of the archive.

Working with Historical Data

Scholars in pursuit of theory-driven evidence inevitably distort the original structure of an archive. Considerable time is spent curating one's own archive, transforming words and numbers found in documents into formats that follow best practices of analysis according to relevant standards for qualitative, quantitative, interpretive, and mixed-methods approaches.

How does a researcher assemble this archive-within-an-archive? First, chronology matters. She has found documents from 1889, 1890, and 1906 that are excise tax reports identified from an index of IOR documents relating to British colonial Burma. Skimming quickly through these records, she learns that the first two are about changes in Burma's territorial boundaries after the 1885 Third Anglo-Burman War, which does not seem directly relevant to her topic of interest: opium regulation. The third one, however, is clearly important: bureaucrats are exchanging correspondence about a pending colony-wide policy to restrict the availability of opium to Burmans.

The researcher begins to take notes. She opens an Excel spreadsheet and enters the years—1889, 1890, 1906—each annotated with a very short description of why it does (and does not) seem to matters for her research, along with identifying information (the file number and embedding series). Recording the nonrelevant observations of 1889 and 1890 is crucially important. For the 1906 document, she takes more detailed notes, perhaps even pauses to make digitized copies. An hour has passed. She is already elbow-deep in the nitty-gritty process of archival research. She has three data points for a timeline of events, which will soon be busily populated by many more dates, alongside facts, information, interpretations gleaned from more records. She might decide that a long run perspective is necessary (because she cares about if and how opium regulation shifts over time) and thus consult documents from earlier in the 1880s and later into the 1910s. Or perhaps she needs historical data on subnational variations (because she suspects that the colonial state was selective about the actual scope and targets of anti-opium reforms) and thus seek records produced around 1906 but specifically for the towns of Akyab, Rangoon, Moulmein, and Kengtung, which are geographically dispersed in the colony, or records that mention groups other than the Burmese, such as the Chinese, Indians, Shan, Karen, or Kachin.

This timeline of the researcher is different from the chronology of an archive. Later on, her timeline will prove essential for process tracing in a case study and identifying causal mechanisms, which rely on precise sequencing of events. (For more, see Chapter 33.) It also helps ward against accusations of "cherry-picking" evidence, because she has a running record of all documents consulted, which include irrelevant ones to her topic of interest, not just those that ended up in her final analysis. Her timeline will also prove useful for discerning negative events in the archives, that is, years when her favored theories of state-building would expect certain outcomes but none appear in the records. Absences, silences, and omissions in the archival record occur for many different reasons.[15] Later, she will reread research guides, consult secondary sources, or email an archivist directly to figure out whether this is a true negative event or a product of the archive's record-keeping.

Potential Challenges

Biases

There are at least five types of biases that researchers often encounter while doing archival research.[16] *Source bias* occurs at the level of record creation, which reflects the extent to which governments and the powerful tend to be the ones that produce records in the first place. *Survival bias* occurs at the level of record preservation, when records are missing and destroyed in a nonrandom way. *Reinforcement bias* occurs when researchers focus on collecting a subset of records that confirm their hypotheses without consulting other record groups. *Transfer bias* occurs when the records that an archive acquires ("accession") and catalogs reflect asymmetries of power, wealth, and privilege that favor certain agencies and individuals or the archive's own institutional interests. *Digitization bias* can amplify transfer bias when archives are selective about which records are digitized and made accessible remotely.

Promises and Pitfalls of Digitization

The digitization of records and evolving technologies have altered practices of archival research.[17] The online availability of digitized documents has reduced economies of scale for identifying, accessing, and collecting data in archives that once required significant time investment and country-specific and regional expertise. The full-text searchability of archival records and improved quality of optical character recognition enables multisite, multilanguage archival research. Such promises of a digital turn in archival research are accompanied by the pitfalls of abundance, namely, an excess availability of digitized records that are *too easily* accessed remotely. Readily available digitized sources and their remote accessibility make it difficult for researchers to learn the structure of archives while often amplifying biases.

Notes

1. Steedman, *Dust*; Stoler, *Along the Archival Grain*.
2. Auerbach, "Informal Archives," 345. Auerbach provides a lucid description of the making of informal archives by slum leaders in India who has avidly collected notes from community meetings, copies of petitions filed with the state, photographs of public events, as well as newspaper coverage of her own settlement and acts of leadership (353). On distinctions between formal and informal institutions, see Helmke and Levitsky, "Informal Institutions and Comparative Politics."
3. Farge, *Allure of the Archives*, 3.

4. Farge, Allure of the Archives, 6.
5. Farge, Allure of the Archives, 35.
6. This discussion of archive terminology is from Kim, "Taming Abundance," 2.
7. The ubiquity of this standardization reflects the birth of the modern archival sciences in Western Europe and histories of imperialism that diffused archival record-keeping practices to colonized territories. Schellenberg, "Principles of Arrangement"; Sweeney, "The Ambiguous Origins of the Archival Principle of 'Provenance.'"
8. See Lemercier and Zalc, *Quantitative Methods in the Humanities*.
9. For a lucid review of archival studies as a field of information studies that researchers can learn from, especially in the digital age, see Carbajal and Caswell, "Critical Digital Archives."
10. I wanted to understand the colonial state's reasons and rationales for prohibiting opium. I found prohibition puzzling because the drug had been a source of official tax revenue, which the British were abandoning, contrary to what most theories of the state said about revenue-maximizing behavior. How—under what conditions and through what mechanisms—did anti-opium reforms occur in British Burma? See Kim, *Empires of Vice*.
11. For a personal account of how this specific archive was navigated, the budget and travel itinerary, see Kim, "Navigating Multiple Archives across Southeast Asia." See Redman, *Historical Research in Archives* for a detailed step-by-step guide for designing an archival trip, from selecting a site to gaining access and choosing technologies for copying records.
12. See the Society of American Archivists' website for an example of an annotated finding aid, within a succinct and helpful discussion of effective ways to navigate archives by the archivist Laura Schmidt, available here: https://www2.archivists.org/usingarchives/appendix.
13. Kratoska, *Index to British Colonial Office Files Pertaining to British Malaya*.
14. Kim, "Taming Abundance," 3.
15. Trouillot, *Silencing the Past*; Stoler, *Along the Archival Grain*.
16. This discussion on biases in archival research is from Kim, "Taming Abundance," 2. For more detail, including the analytical consequences of such biases, see Lustick, "History, Historiography, and Political Science"; Cirone and Spirling, "Turning History into Data"; Lee, "The Library of Babel."
17. This discussion on digital archival research is from Kim, "Taming Abundance," 2. See Putnam, "The Transnational and the Text-Searchable" on how a transformational era for virtual reach and remote access to digitized records has decoupled data collection from place-based research. See Carbajal and Caswell, "Critical Digital Archives" on best practices for digital archival research from a historians' perspective.

Recommended Readings

Auerbach, Adam. "Informal Archives: Historical Narratives and the Preservation of Paper in India's Urban Slums." *Studies in Comparative International Development* 53 (2018): 343–364.
    Auerbach addresses how political scientists may collect and use informal archival materials, providing rich empirical examples drawing from the author's 20 months of fieldwork in India's urban slums.

Farge, Arlette. *The Allure of the Archives*. New Haven, CT: Yale University Press, 2013.
    This book explains the practice of archival research from the perspective of a social historian. It provides an intimate account of the physical experience of exploring 18th-century police records of Paris within the judicial archives of the Bastille at the Arsenal Library in France, and addresses more broadly how to read, think critically, and write about information encountered in official archives.

Kim, Diana. "Taming Abundance: Doing Digital Archival Research (as Political Scientists)." *PS: Political Science and Politics* 55, no. 3 (2022): 530–538.

> This article offers a practical guide to doing digital archival research as a political scientist seeking theory-driven evidence. It also explains when and why political scientists utilize archives and addresses the ethical implications to archival research as a type of field research.

Lemercier, Claire, and Claire Zalc. *Quantitative Methods in the Humanities: An Introduction.* Charlottesville: University of Virginia Press, 2020.

> This book surveys methods by historians for using quantitative data alongside textual sources and offers techniques for building a data set from historical sources, data visualization, sampling practices, and GIS/spatial analysis. It underscores how numbers and quantification, typically thought of as the domain of social scientists, matter for humanistic inquiry as well.

Putnam, Lara. "The Transnational and the Text-Searchable: Digitized Sources and the Shadows They Cast." *American Historical Review* 121, no. 2 (2016): 377–402.

> This article explains the impact on historians of the digitization of archival sources and technologies for web-enabled access. It identifies the promises and pitfalls of this digital turn and introduces "side glancing" as a method through which global, international, and transnational histories are increasingly being told.

References

Auerbach, Adam. "Informal Archives: Historical Narratives and the Preservation of Paper in India's Urban Slums." *Studies in Comparative International Development* 53 (2018): 343–364.

Carbajal, Itza, and Michelle Caswell. "Critical Digital Archives: A Review from Archival Studies." *American Historical Review* 126, no. 3 (2021): 1102–1120.

Cirone, Alexandra, and Arthur Spirling. "Turning History into Data: Data Collection, Measurement, and Inference in HPE." *Journal of Historical Political Economy* 1 (2021): 127–154.

Helmke, Gretchen, and Steven Levitsky. "Informal Institutions and Comparative Politics: A Research Agenda." *Perspectives in Politics* 2, no. 4 (2004): 725–740.

Kim, Diana-. *Empires of Vice: The Rise of Opium Prohibition across Southeast Asia*. Princeton, NJ: Princeton University Press, 2020.

Kim, Diana. "Navigating Multiple Archives across Southeast Asia: Three Questions I Wish I Had Known to Ask." *APSA-Comparative Democratization* 15, no. 3 (2017): 16–20.

Kim, Diana. "Taming Abundance: Doing Digital Archival Research (as Political Scientists)." *PS: Political Science and Politics* 55, no. 3 (2022): 530–538.

Kratoska, Paul. *Index to British Colonial Office Files Pertaining to British Malaya*. Kuala Lumpur: Arkib Negara Malaysia, 1990.

Lee, Alexander. "The Library of Babel: How (and How Not) to Use Archival Sources in Political Science." *Journal of Historical Political Economy* 2, no. 3 (2022): 499–526.

Lemercier, Claire, and Claire Zalc. *Quantitative Methods in the Humanities: An Introduction.* Charlottesville: University of Virginia Press, 2020.

Lustick, Ian. "History, Historiography, and Political Science: Multiple Historical Records and the Problem of Selection Bias." *American Political Science Review* 90, no. 3 (1996): 605–618.

Putnam, Lara. "The Transnational and the Text-Searchable: Digitized Sources and the Shadows They Cast." *American Historical Review* 121, no. 2 (2016): 377–402.

Redman, Samuel J. *Historical Research in Archives: A Practical Guide*. Washington, DC: American Historical Association, 2013.

Schellenberg, Theodore R. "Principles of Arrangement." Staff Information Paper Number 18. Washington, DC: National Archives and Records Administration, 1951.

Steedman, Carol. *Dust: The Archive and Cultural History*. New Brunswick, NJ: Rutgers University Press, 2002.

Stoler, Ann. *Along the Archival Grain: Epistemic Anxieties and Colonial Common Sense*. Princeton, NJ: Princeton University Press, 2009.

Sweeney, Shelley. "The Ambiguous Origins of the Archival Principle of 'Provenance.'" *Libraries & the Cultural Record* 43, no. 2 (2008): 193–213.

Trouillot, Michel Rolph. *Silencing the Past: Power and the Production of History*. Boston: Beacon Press, 1995.

23
Fieldwork in Fragile Contexts and with High-Risk Populations

Ethics, Relationships, and Rapport

Julie Chernov Hwang

Andrew Silke notes that much of what has been written about terrorism has been authored by individuals who have never actually talked to a terrorist.[1] It is also fair to say that many of those who write about political violence have never actually talked to current or former participants in that violence. Yet if one wants to understand motivations for joining an extremist group, a rebel movement, or a faction in a conflict, the pathways via which one joins, commitment to the group, role assignment, tactics, recruitment, terror cells, disengagement, reintegration, recidivism, or side switching, then talking to leaders, operatives, and rank-and-file members is important. Secondary sources can take one only so far. One gains unprecedented and direct perspective when one can ask questions of, clarify responses from, and follow up with those who were or are members of an extremist group or rebel group, rather than rely exclusively on data sets or journalistic accounts or neglect the individual level of research altogether.

Yet some dismiss the possibility of fieldwork in fragile and violent contexts out of fear. It may seem dangerous. They may assume that if they could convince a terrorist or a rebel to speak with them, they would inevitably be lied to, and so it's not worth the risk. However, there are ways to conduct this fieldwork safely and ethically, even in fragile or violent contexts and with high-risk populations. This chapter will detail the process of how one can go about conducting such fieldwork, focusing primarily on three components of the process: institutional review boards (IRBs), guides, and rapport-building. In so doing, it will highlight the importance of building relationships with interviewees over time, the role of trust and rapport, and the benefits that come from doing such interviews in terms of the quality of material gathered and the degree of understanding obtained. This is accomplished through iterated visits and empathetic, nonjudgmental listening.

It must be stated at the outset that one's experiences conducting such interviews may vary from country to country. The degree to which one can be systematic in sampling will also vary. In countries and cases where participation in interviews is at low risk and low cost, one may use a combination of purposive sampling, convenience sampling, and snowball sampling in order to identify respondents.[2] In countries where there may be higher risks associated with participation in interviews, an interviewer may rely more on convenience sampling.[3] In a democracy, the risks and costs to the interviewee for consenting to the interview are comparatively lower than in a more authoritarian country. Thus, it may be possible to identify interviewees through research and contacts (purposive sampling) as well as asking guides and longtime interviewees to recommend other potential respondents

Julie Chernov Hwang, *Fieldwork in Fragile Contexts and with High-Risk Populations* In: *Doing Good Qualitative Research.* Edited by: Jennifer Cyr and Sara Wallace Goodman, Oxford University Press. © Oxford University Press 2024. DOI: 10.1093/oso/9780197633137.003.0023

(snowball sampling).[4] Ideally, it is desirable to vary the dependent variable and include a control group.[5] For example, if one is writing on disengagement, one would include both former members of extremist groups who had ceased participation in acts of violence and a "control group" of individuals who remained active members. However, this is not always possible. The ability of a scholar to avoid "selecting on the dependent variable" will be shaped by (1) the fragile or violent context in which one researches, (2) the level of risk one is willing to take on, and (3) one's access within extremist communities.

Institutional Review Boards

Once one has decided to conduct fieldwork interviewing current and former members of rebel groups, extremist movements, terrorist groups, or other actors in political violence, the first step is to seek permission from one's IRB. The stated purpose of IRBs is to minimize risk to the extent possible in human subjects research. The IRB pushes interviewers to assess risk and cost to both the interviewees and interviewer and to take whatever steps are possible to minimize physical, psychological, and reputational harm.[6] Any proposal submitted to the IRB will be classified as exempt (not requiring review), expedited (reviewed by one or two committee members), or full board review (the entire board will review the proposal and collectively arrive at recommendations). If one intends to do research in fragile or conflict-prone regions, with current or former rebels, insurgents, extremists, or terrorists, one can typically assume that one will have to prepare for a full board review.

One common complaint regarding IRBs is that their members lack expertise in conflict and terrorism research.[7] Most often, this will be true. An IRB will constitute members of different university departments. They may come from education, sociology, psychology, political science, or anthropology. As a result of disciplinary training and personal concerns, each will have their own understanding of risk. A psychologist may assume risk of trauma in a way that an anthropologist, with training in ethnography, would not. A faculty member in the department of education may unintentionally infantilize interviewees because they are used to considering risks in terms of children and teenagers. Thus, while all involved, including those submitting the research proposal, will be seeking to minimize harm and risk, *how* one assesses risks will differ. Those who have experience researching only in the United States may bring U.S.-based assumptions regarding norms, rules, regulations, and state capacity that simply don't apply in the country in which one is researching. As a result, they may over-inflate or misdiagnose the risks of terrorism studies and conflict research.

This raises the question of how scholars should proceed to familiarize such an IRB committee with the appropriate measures for gauging risk and cost in the study of conflict and terrorism, especially in those cases where research is to be done in countries where norms and systems differ from those in the United States. The first step in this long and involved process is the research proposal. When one writes a research proposal for the IRB, one must be very deliberate in contextualizing the research and familiarizing the committee with the country, its political system, the issue which the proposal endeavors to study, why it matters, the conflict environment, and any pertinent information regarding the norms for conducting research in said country. This initial contextualization is important for framing risks. If one is researching in a democratic country, where citizens are free to advocate for an Islamic state, for example, the risks in interviewing members of a nonclandestine extremist group advocating for an Islamic state will be far less than in an authoritarian country, where such advocacy is banned. One should make special note, in this initial proposal, about how the IRB process is similar to and differs from that in one's home country. For example, if IRB committees are constituted only for natural science projects, it may not be possible to convene a local IRB to evaluate your project. It is important to highlight that systems differ across countries and *that should be expected.*

Second, a strong IRB proposal will clearly outline the project, its purpose, and why it is necessary to conduct such research in light of risks. The benefits of the project must be clearly stated, as this is a question the IRB will ponder, especially if the research is to be conducted with high-risk populations like extremists, terrorists, rebels, or insurgents. In describing the project, it is also important to highlight how one incorporates internal assessment or risk and cost into the program design. For example, are there certain groups one will exclude from an interview sample because the risk to their members or to the researcher is simply too high? Might one stipulate that one will not conduct interviews in prison out of concern the prisoners might be coerced into speaking with the researcher? Drawing boundaries around one's project is a way of conveying to the IRB that one is taking risk and cost seriously in the program design, and that one is taking precautions necessary to minimize undue harm. In doing so, one can convey that one is an active participant in the review process *with the IRB.*

In addition to contextualization and a clear articulation of the project, its goals, and its benefits, a strong IRB proposal should address five areas:[8]

1. Participants' rights, safety, and vulnerability.
2. Informed consent.
3. Confidentiality and anonymity.
4. The researcher's rights, safety, and vulnerability.
5. Data storage.

The first key point to convey in an IRB proposal is that when seeking an interview, you and, if pertinent, your guide will ensure potential interviewees understand that their participation is strictly voluntary. If a question makes them uncomfortable, they are under no obligation to answer it. If they request a response be "off the record," it will be. They can end the interview at any time. You should also stipulate that you will always ask permission to use a voice recorder and to quote any interviewee.

Second, you must apprise participants of the purpose and goals of the project, where you seek to publish, what the potential risks of their involvement could be, the steps you and your research team will take to protect their identity, and how any interview notes or recordings will be stored. This is termed "informed consent." Receiving informed consent from participants prior to the onset of any interview is vital, not only to the IRB but, more important, to the conduct of ethical research.[9] Traditionally, informed consent was obtained in writing, through a signed document detailing the specifics of the research and any potential risks that could be present.[10] However, in conducting research on terrorism or extremism and among high-risk populations, it is becoming far more common to obtain informed consent orally. The script for oral consent can be drafted by the researcher and amended by the IRB committee before being translated into the native language or languages where the research is taking place. The researcher, in conjunction with the IRB, can assess the risks and costs of recording oral consent, which may vary depending on the location of the research. The advantage of oral consent is twofold. First, a written record could adversely link the participants to the project and inadvertently expose their identities.[11] Dolnik cautions that in a war or conflict zone, it is best for the safety of any interviewees that they have plausible deniability of having been in contact with the researcher, as it could potentially lead to arrest or interrogation at the hands of government troops.[12] Even in cases where one is working in a nonconflict area, in a democratic country, the written consent document can have a chilling effect on one's ability to build rapport, as it could trigger fears of manipulation by outside forces.[13] Second, if the interviewees assume the signed documents will be turned over to an intelligence agency, that could endanger the researcher's safety.[14]

Third, the IRB will take a decided interest in how the researcher will take steps to ensure anonymity and confidentiality. A researcher may choose to create aliases for interviewees or ask the interviewee to either choose a general title or a pseudonym. If you request the interviewee select their own alias, it's important that this be a pseudonym specifically for this project and not an alias they used in the past, for which there might be an existing record. Additionally, in seeking to ensure anonymity and confidentiality to the best of your ability, you should eliminate any revealing details that might expose the identity of the participant. Alongside this, the IRB will likely express concern that the interviewee could reveal potentially incriminating details about illegal activities. While this is unlikely to happen, it is easily preempted by including a brief statement in the oral IRB informed consent script about not disclosing such information.[15]

Fourth, the IRB may seek assurances that the researcher is taking steps to ensure their own safety. In drafting the IRB proposal you should explain how steps like adequate prior preparation, oral informed consent, and working with guides can enable safe research. In the spirit of the IRB being a conversation, should the IRB committee make a recommendation that would put you at risk, you should push back against it. Moreover, you should also assess how your own positionality may affect your ability to conduct the research and your way of accessing interviewees.

Finally, data storage is another area of concern for the IRB and is also critical for ethical conduct of research. For those using a recording device, password-encoding your downloads, denoting interviews by numbers or aliases, and deleting recordings from the device at the end of each day are important to safeguarding the data. Ensuring that any transcribers or interview translators are familiar with IRB protocols regarding not sharing data is also critical. The IRB may request you put such guarantees (of nonsharing) in writing as part of a contract and wordsmith the language with the IRB.

Some IRBs may seek to circumvent their lack of knowledge on conflict and terrorism by bringing in an outside reviewer with knowledge of the country, conflict, or group. In my own dealings with IRBs, I have put the committee in touch with my guides, all of whom had obtained master's degrees or PhDs in either the United Kingdom or Australia and were therefore familiar with ethics protocols. The IRB at Goucher College invited a human rights activist specializing in South and Southeast Asia to give an independent assessment of my project and offer recommendations. Outside reviewers and contacts can be advantageous for a smooth IRB process, as outsiders can offer their expertise and encourage IRB members to revise any faulty assumptions to meet the actual circumstances on the ground.

In short, in order to interview in conflict zones and with high-risk populations (terrorists, extremists, rebels, insurgents), one will need to go through a full board IRB review. To increase your chances at success in that process, you should treat the IRB process as a conversation in which you, the researcher, educate the committee about the country in which you plan to work, its political system, the norms of research, and why this project is beneficial, given the risks of conducting it. A strong IRB proposal must also detail steps taken to ensure the participants' rights and safety, informed consent, confidentiality and anonymity, security of data storage, and the safety of the research team. In such a proposal the researcher conveys that they will take the necessary steps to avoid undue risk of harm to the participants. Should the IRB committee be unable to make appropriate recommendations, seeking the assistance of outside specialists is advisable.

Guides

As one is working to obtain approval from the IRB, it is important to begin planning the research trip itself. Some of the research trip will take shape once the researcher arrives in country. However, there's critical background research that can also be done as well as identification and recruitment of interviewees, and guides can be a good part of that. Some individuals may choose to go through professional fixers. A fixer's job is to arrange meetings. However, an alternative can be working through guides. Guides may work for nongovernmental organizations, terrorist rehabilitation organizations, or human rights groups. They may be academics, PhD candidates, or journalists. As a side job, they may agree to assist a foreign researcher for a few days, using their contacts and trust relationships to arrange meetings and to ensure the safety of the foreign researcher by accompanying them to meetings. One typically finds such guides via one's relationships with other international and local scholars, NGO activists, and journalists, who may recommend a specific person. It is advisable to work with several guides at the same time, budget permitting, because each may have a different trust network upon which to draw.

Guides facilitate greater variation in the kinds of sampling a researcher can employ. For example, in interviewing former members of terrorist groups and extremist groups without a guide, one may have to rely on convenience sampling at first, speaking to those former members who are most public and most available. However, in working with a guide, one can utilize a purposive sampling approach by requesting interviews with specific persons or with persons who took on a specific role while in the group. For example, if one is working on disengagement from terrorism, one can ask a guide to find members who are still persistent activists, still committed to the group, to offer a "control group." As a side note, this is something that researchers have to consider: to weigh the methodological benefits of having a control group against the risks of interviewing current members of terrorist groups, extremist movements, or rebel groups. Is it possible, given one's contacts and one's guides' contacts, to recruit a similar number of interviewees for the control group? Only the researcher can make that decision based on their understanding of possibility, risk, and safety. However, a guide can also provide critical advice in this regard.

In contracting with guides, one may choose to give the guide specific names of individuals, perhaps gleaned from think-tank reports or media accounts. One may also work collaboratively with guides by sharing certain parameters for interviews, such as individuals who worked in social media for extremist websites or who were tasked with recruitment. Then the guide would identify pertinent individuals. It is always best to work with more than one guide because some guides may have closer relationships with specific individuals of interest;

thus, by figuring out the nature of the relationships the guides have, one can see who would be best suited to set up the meeting. If the interviewee has a strong trust relationship with the guide, they may feel more comfortable opening up and answering questions.

It is important to build rapport with the guides with whom you work and to have open and honest conversations about the goals of and expectations for the research. For example, do you expect the guide to arrange the meetings or to take things a step further and accompany you to the meeting? How far in advance do you want to see a draft schedule of meetings? Do you want to have a prebrief in the morning to discuss the day's meetings? Do you want to debrief in the evening to discuss the day's interviews to compare observations? You should also be sure to discuss fees structures and bonuses with the guides. Typically, an experienced guide will have a set rate per day or per meeting. If they do not, it is useful to discuss rates with other experienced researchers to see what the average going rate is. It is advisable to stipulate all of this beforehand to avoid miscommunication.

If a guide lacks prior experience with IRB protocols they need to follow to arrange a meeting—ensuring any potential participants know their inclusion is strictly voluntary, making sure they know the purpose of the research so that they can make an informed decision—it is important for the researcher to apprise them. This is especially important in cases where research in prisons is required. If you expect that you will have a private space to interview in a prison and the guide is not aware of that, it may be nearly impossible to procure it in the moment. If a prison official wants to sit in on the interview and the guide is unaware that this is a deal-breaker, this could create tensions in the guide-researcher relationship. Thus, it is best to discuss all of this beforehand, if the guides don't have their own independent research experience with IRBs or their country's equivalent.

For female scholars, the guide can also function as an intermediary. Having a male guide accompany a female researcher may make the interviewee more comfortable, especially in very conservative circles where strict gender segregation is practiced. Moreover, the presence of the guide will likely reduce instances of sexual harassment, attempts at extortion, or intimidation by the occasional unscrupulous interviewee.

Trust and Rapport-Building

Once you have arrived in country to conduct fieldwork interviews, there are several key points to keep in mind. First, if information is available, do background research on each person you intend to interview via primary and secondary sources. Second, wordsmith your questions with your guides, especially if you are interviewing in a foreign language, to ensure that the language you are using is clear and appropriate. No matter how proficient you are in a foreign language, it can always help to have a native speaker who is familiar with the idioms used in the communities in which you plan to interview to edit your word choice. Third, it is always advisable to conduct the interview in the native language if you are proficient in that language rather than work with a translator. A guide may help here and there with a word or two, and you may hire a native speaker to transcribe interviews to ensure an accurate record of the interview. However, it is important for you to become proficient in the language and conduct your own interviews. It is exceedingly difficult to build rapport and trust independent of a guide if you are relying on the guide to communicate. Hiring out interviews is also problematic because you will lose key aspects, like tone of voice and body language, as well as the ability to ask in-the-moment follow-up questions, any chance to build rapport and trust, and any ability to ensure that informed consent is followed.

Fourth, it is likewise advisable to return to the same interviewees on multiple occasions in order to ask follow-up questions, seek clarification, and, above all, build trust independent of the guide. Interviewees may be understandably reluctant to be forthcoming when first meeting the researcher. These kinds of interviews are not easy conversations, especially if the researcher is asking personal questions about involvement, side-switching, roles, motivations, disengagement, and the like. Some interviewees may obfuscate, leaving out large chunks of their narratives. Others may have developed a standard story they devised specifically for researchers. Only when they come to trust you will they give you a fuller and more complete account. That can happen only with time and interaction.

Trust is best gained through iterated interviewing over months and even years. In an initial interview, a participant may give only superficial answers to questions. They may hesitate. In this meeting, the interviewee is making an initial assessment: Are you trustworthy? Why do you care about their story? Should they share their story with you? Trust is built slowly. When you return a few months or a year later on a subsequent trip, you may approach the interviewee again, but this time just for coffee and conversation, perhaps asking a few clarifying questions from the original interview. The purpose of that meeting is to show that you care and take an interest beyond the interview itself. When you return a third time, then you can request another interview, returning to those questions where you received only a general answer, to gain a fuller account of their experiences. There can even be a fourth and fifth interview as questions arise, as clarification becomes necessary. For example, in 2011, I had the opportunity to interview Yusuf, a former member of Jemaah Islamiyah. Many Western scholars had interviewed Yusuf before me. He had a pat story he would tell researchers. I could sense he was guarded when we spoke. I ran into him again in 2012 at my guide's house. At that time, we spoke generally about our families and I asked him a single clarifying question. Two years later, another guide I worked with hired Yusuf to drive for us. He seemed more at ease. That evening, I asked him to share his story with me again. He told me a vastly different story, one that connected him directly to JI as a member. When I asked him why he was sharing this version of his story, he answered, "Because I trust you now." Two years later, one of my co-researchers and I asked Yusuf to share details of his recruitment process, and he readily agreed. Yusuf became one of my most reliable contacts for understanding JI, until his death in 2022.

Through iterated interviewing, one learns more intimate, more personal details that round out a narrative. Repeat interviews can chart change, progress, and regression. One can see an interviewee join a rebel group, become active, take on various roles, and eventually disengage. Repeat interviews also enable the researcher to concentrate on specific topics, such as motivations and pathways to entry. The participant's role, jihad experiences, and so on. Over time, the researcher peels back the layers. People are like onions.

Not only are iterated interviews important for building trust; *how* one interviews is also key. One should be a nonjudgmental, empathetic, and engaged listener. (Please see Chapter 17 for further discussion on this subject.)[16] Nonjudgmental listening does not require you to sympathize with an interviewee's decision to participate in violence. However, you should be mindful of question wording, of body language, of facial expression, and of tone of voice so as not to convey judgment. Also important, you should make every effort to empathize with the interviewee. Again, this does not mean you approve of or sympathize with their choices;

you do not need to lie and pretend to sympathize. Instead, you should attempt to understand the emotions that undergirded their choices. To that end, you must practice perspective taking. For example, several interviewees in the district of Poso in Indonesia reported to me that they joined an extremist group after a dozen members of their family were killed in a massacre. A practiced field researcher should be able to hear narrative with empathy understanding the grief, anger, trauma, and horror underpinning the choice.

Additionally, one can build trust by adhering to an interviewee's wishes with regard to (1) use of a voice recorder; (2) keeping certain details off the record, when requested; (3) using pseudonyms or general titles; and (4) not disclosing the location of the interview. Showing one is willing to conform to dress norms is also a way of showing respect. Such actions—showing respect, deferring and adhering to the interviewee's wishes as they pertain to ethical concerns, sharing a coffee or a meal without a formal interview—are also ways to build rapport.

Conclusion

Fieldwork in fragile contexts and with high-risk populations can be done safely and ethically. This chapter highlighted three points to that end: the importance of building trust and rapport with those you seek to interview, the utility of guides, and the role of the IRB. In conducting fieldwork, trust and rapport are of paramount importance. In order for the interviewee to agree to share their narrative in all its color and depth, they first have to trust the researcher. For that to occur, the researcher needs to visit them on multiple occasions, and not only for interviews—sometimes just for coffee or a meal and conversation. While iterated interviewing is slow interviewing, it affords the researcher the opportunity to chart change—progress and setbacks—in a way that few other forms of research do. In so doing, there is tremendous opportunity for learning.

Working with guides and gatekeepers can help researchers because guides already have built trust and rapport within the communities you may seek to enter. Thus, they can vouch for you, and the interviewee will give you a chance on their word. In time, you may be able to establish rapport and trust independently of the guide, but at least initially you should draw upon the trust relationship between the guide and the interviewee. Moreover, guides are your intermediaries with government and prison officials. They can keep you safe and can facilitate effective communication between you and the interviewee.

Finally, a strong ethical compass is important when conducting fieldwork in fragile and violent contexts. Working with the IRB, you can develop an action plan to address participant rights, safety, and vulnerability; informed consent; confidentiality and anonymity; data storage; and ensuring you yourself are safe. Although the IRB may misdiagnose actual risks of research in violent and vulnerable contexts due to their lack of knowledge about research in conflict zones and with high-risk populations, treating the IRB as a conversation can assist in making it a productive process. You should not hesitate to politely push back if the IRB suggests a change that would put you or your interviewees at risk or, alternatively, insists on a change completely at odds with the possible in the country of research. In writing a proposal for the IRB, you should take care to specify in great detail and clear language the context in which you are working, the political system, the norms of the society, the capacities of the state, and how all of these may differ from the United States and how may impact assumptions with regard to the research. Bringing in outside evaluators with experience in the country and in fieldwork with high-risk populations can also be helpful. It can also help to sit on the IRB committee for a few terms to gain a greater understanding of how colleagues assess risk; then you can better tailor your proposal to the committee when you are ready to begin research.

Notes

1. Silke, "The Impact of 9/11 on Research on Terrorism," 77
2. See Bernard, *Research Methods in Anthropology*.
3. See Bernard, *Research Methods in Anthropology*.
4. See Kenney and Hwang, "'Should I Stay or Should I Go?'"
5. Khalil, "A Guide to Interviewing Violent Extremists," 3.
6. Morrison, Silke, and Bont, "The Development of the Framework for Research Ethics in Terrorism Studies," 273.
7. Morrison, Silke, and Bont, "The Development of the Framework for Research Ethics in Terrorism Studies," 276.
8. Morrison, Silke, and Bont, "The Development of the Framework for Research Ethics in Terrorism Studies," 274.
9. Morrison, Silke, and Bont, "The Development of the Framework for Research Ethics in Terrorism Studies," 277.
10. Morrison, Silke, and Bont, "The Development of the Framework for Research Ethics in Terrorism Studies," 277.
11. Wood. "The Ethical Challenges of Research in Conflict Zones," 380.
12. Dolnik, "Conducting Field Research on Terrorism," 9.
13. Dolnik, "Conducting Field Research on Terrorism," 9.
14. Dolnik, "Conducting Field Research on Terrorism," 9, 12.
15. Dolnik, "Conducting Field Research on Terrorism," 10.
16. Krause, "The Ethics of Ethnographic Methods in Conflict Zones," 330.

Recommended Readings

John Morrison, Andrew Silke, and Eke Bont. "The Development of the Framework for Research Ethics in Terrorism Studies (FRETS)." *Terrorism and Political Violence* 33, no. 2 (2021): 271–289.
    Offers a superb discussion of IRB design.
Adam Dolnik. "Conducting Field Research on Terrorism: A Brief Primer." *Perspectives on Terrorism* 5, no. 2 (May 2011).
    A useful primer.

References

Bernard, H. R. *Research Methods in Anthropology: Qualitative and Quantitative Approaches*. 5th ed. Lanham, MD: Altamira, 2011.
Dolnik, Adam. "Conducting Field Research on Terrorism: A Brief Primer." *Perspectives on Terrorism* 5, no. 2 (May 2011).

Kenney, Michael, and Julie Chernov Hwang. "'Should I Stay or Should I Go?' Understanding How British and Indonesian Islamist Extremists Disengage and Why They Don't." *Political Psychology*, December 10, 2020. https://doi.org/10.1111/pops.12713.

Khalil, James. "A Guide to Interviewing Violent Extremists." *Studies in Conflict and Terrorism* 4 (2019): 429–443.

Jana Krause, "The Ethics of Ethnographic Methods in Conflict Zones." *Journal of Peace Research* 48, no. 3 (2021): 271–289.

Morrison, John, Andrew Silke, and Eke Bont. "The Development of the Framework for Research Ethics in Terrorism Studies (FRETS)." *Terrorism and Political Violence* 33, no. 2 (2021).

Silke, Andrew. "The Impact of 9/11 on Research on Terrorism." In *Mapping Terrorism Research: State of the Art, Gaps, and Future Directions*, edited by Mangus Ranstorp. London: Routledge, 2007.

Wood, Elizabeth Jean. "The Ethical Challenges of Research in Conflict Zones." *Qualitative Sociology* 29 (2006): 373–386.

24
Studying Indigenous Peoples' Politics
Recommendations for Non-Indigenous Researchers

*Tulia G. Falleti**

Overview

I write this chapter for the non-Indigenous and non-anthropologist student or social scientist who is considering embarking on research *with* (maybe even *for*) Indigenous communities.[1] In particular, I write this for students and colleagues in political science who are non-Indigenous and who are considering researching Indigenous peoples' politics, by which I mean the politics of Indigenous collective rights and of Indigenous collective demand-making vis-à-vis the state.[2] The politics of Indigenous rights and demands are changing the international legal landscape and global order,[3] the territorial organization of nation-states,[4] the education systems and languages of the state,[5] the types and practice of democracy,[6] and the political economy of natural resource extraction[7] and of energy transitions,[8] just to mention some topics that are of interest to political scientists. Indigenous peoples' politics should be of paramount importance in political science, yet until recently it has remained largely understudied in our discipline.

From 1990 to 2020, only 10 research articles were published containing the word "Indigenous" or "Native" (as applied to Indigenous peoples) in either their title or abstract in the top three generalist political science journals (six articles in the *American Political Science Review*, one in the *American Journal of Political Science*, and three in the *Journal of Politics*). Expanding the search to include *World Politics*, a leading comparative politics journal, five more articles can be found in this 30-year period. Kennan Ferguson has powerfully denounced this disciplinary exclusion and has proposed 16 methodological, cognitive, and organizational changes to Indigenize our field.[9] There have been noteworthy exceptions, particularly in the comparative study of Indigenous politics in Latin America.[10] Indeed, this scholarship has set important research agendas upon which we can build our future research.

As collective identities acquire greater relevance to define legal rights and political demands, political scientists and sociologists are increasingly turning to the study of Indigenous nations and politics.[11] The qualitative research tools we use to study Indigenous politics are the same as those used to study other populations: in-depth interviews, open-ended surveys, focus groups, ethnographic fieldwork, shadowing of key informants, and participant observation, among others.[12] However, as non-Indigenous researchers we must ask ourselves: How do we do this in a way that is nonextractive and interculturally sensitive? Moreover, why would non-Indigenous researchers rather than Indigenous scholars themselves study Indigenous peoples' politics?

Anthropologists, especially cultural and linguistic anthropologists and archaeologists, have a long tradition of studying Indigenous peoples and cultures. Their methods and approaches have been the subject of debates and critiques regarding gendered, racist, and colonial practices, such as the extraction of knowledge and cultural heritage and the silencing or invisibilization of female Indigenous collaborators and coauthors.[13] Anthropologists have attempted to address and redress these colonial legacies and extractive tendencies, with deep reflexivity and transformative work.[14] Such debates are too expansive to discuss here, and anthropologists and archaeologists are better positioned to chart them. However, the ethical imperatives for non-Indigenous social scientists of working with Indigenous communities in a culturally sensitive and nonextractive way demand a careful discussion, separate from other considerations we may have when working with other vulnerable and marginalized populations.

In this chapter, I will argue that as non-Indigenous researchers conducting research with Indigenous communities or on Indigenous topics, our research and actions must be guided by the principles of *respect, reciprocity,* and a *decolonizing ambition*.[15] These attitudes and practices must be developed at the preparatory as well as the research and dissemination stages.

Preparatory Stage

More so than the study of other populations, researching *with* Indigenous communities requires a great deal of preparation. Indigenous communities constitute nations within nations, even if not recognized as such by the colonial powers or the republican nation-states. Indigenous nations are built on ancestral traditions, practices, and oral histories. They have their own languages, whether currently spoken or not. Moreover, Indigenous communities have their own ontology and epistemology, even if in some cases hybridized with colonial religions, ontologies, and epistemologies. Thus, much learning and preparation on their history and present are required prior to conducting qualitative research with Indigenous communities. This research may be developed in parallel with the preparation of an application to your university's institutional review board (IRB), which sees that research is conducted ethically, at least as defined by university administrations and reflecting current standards of the scientific community.

But unlike the histories of countries, for instance, that are readily available, the academic accounts of the history and political lives of Indigenous nations, which have relied mostly on oral tradition rather than written record, are either thin or missing. Moreover, Indigenous peoples were the subjects of assimilation, elimination, and genocide by the colonial powers first and the nation-states later on. Outside of anthropology, Native American and Indigenous studies, and some subfields in history, Indigenous nations have been largely invisible in academia. Furthermore, not only is the existing academic record on the histories of many Indigenous nations thin; until recently, it had been written by and from the perspective of the colonizer or those who sought to dispossess and dominate Indigenous peoples. Fortunately, as the number of Indigenous scholars grows, so does their scholarship on their histories, cultures, and societies, and their critiques of colonialism and racism.[16]

Thus, the initial two preparatory tasks for the non-Indigenous social scientist are, first, to learn the history of the Indigenous peoples who will be part of their research; second, find the Indigenous *voceros*, the relevant Indigenous voices and their own narratives. There are Indigenous nations, such as the Navajo and the Mapuche, for instance, who have their own members in the academy and in journalism, writing about their history and present. These are the authors and scholarship we must know before we delve into our field research. In the case of First Nations in Canada and Native peoples in the United States, the Indigenous self-production of knowledge is extensive, and members of these nations have found institutional homes in U.S. and Canadian universities—even if their representation in academia is still very low. In other cases, we must dig much deeper to learn about the relevant histories and narratives of the Indigenous peoples we are engaging with. This has been my experience in doing research with the Wichí people in the province of Salta in northern Argentina. The written record is thin. It is taking me several visits to the area, many conversations with local inhabitants, and access to the very localized production and distribution of knowledge, to gather some of the relevant history and context for the research. While not exclusively, I have found some relevant information in facsimile reports, locally published books, and locally gathered data. I found some of these documents in the town's church, the hospital, and nearby health clinics.[17] It is also worth highlighting that, as is the case with practically any collective group, Indigenous peoples and communities do not speak with a single voice. On occasions they might, but often the researcher must search, recognize, and become familiar with the multiple voices, viewpoints, and interpretations that narrate Indigenous nations' history and present struggles.

Third, just as the comparative political scientist or sociologist must learn the languages of the areas of the world or countries where they seek to conduct research, so too the non-Indigenous qualitative researcher should learn the languages of the Indigenous nations they work with, especially when the colonial language is not widely spoken. There is no substitute for the deep understanding of foreign cultures that familiarity with their language may afford. This is also the case with Indigenous cultures. In my research, I found a substantial and meaningful difference between the degree to which research and communication were successful when conducted in the Spanish language with Mapuche vis-à-vis Wichí communities. Whereas Spanish is widely spoken in the Wallmapu (the traditional ancestral territory of the Mapuche people in the south of what is nowadays Argentina and Chile), Spanish is a secondary and often rarely spoken language among Wichí households in the north of Argentina. While communication with Mapuche leaders and community members in Spanish was possible and effective, in both Argentina and Chile, communication in Spanish with Wichí women was very limited. When speaking through a Wichí interpreter, Wichí women were more talkative and forthcoming with information and experiences. But relying exclusively on the Wichí interpreter's mediation in our communication was a major impediment to fully grasping the meaning and deeply comprehending what the Wichí women were conveying. At times, for instance, long speeches in Wichí by the interviewed women would be reported back to me as one sentence in Spanish. Yet the educational materials and opportunities to learn the Wichí language are scarce; this is admittedly a pending task for me. Ideally, we would become fluent in the Indigenous language that is required for meaningful exchanges. If for reasons of access to educational materials or time such a goal is unattainable, we must be cognizant and explicit about the limitations of our research.

Fourth, Indigenous nations not only have different languages, but also *ontologies*, worldviews or conceptions about the physical and spiritual world and their multiple connections. Indigenous ontologies, transmitted orally through generations, often include religious and spiritual beliefs, which are also foreign to the non-Indigenous researcher. In my experience, understanding and respecting Indigenous ontologies has been the most challenging learning process I have encountered since studying Indigenous peoples' politics. Indigenous ontologies often present a spirituality that I cannot fully grasp or share. However, I must respect it. During the preparatory stage of our research, we should therefore seek, to the degree available or accessible to us, to comprehend the ontology of the Indigenous peoples we will engage with. At the same time, it is important to understand that Indigenous peoples have been impacted by the colonial encounter and the colonial experience. Indigenous ontologies may be permeated with new religions (evangelism in particular) and colonial cultures. In my experience, I have had to negotiate between my ontology and understanding of the world and that of the Indigenous communities or individuals that provide me with glimpses into their philosophy or interpretations of the human, nonhuman, and natural worlds. After several years interacting with Indigenous leaders and community members, I can better appreciate the boundaries and partial connections between my ontology and theirs. Where significant gaps emerge between my ontology (even if evolving) and theirs, I strive for respect and for not making value judgments. Interculturality, in my opinion, is rooted in this respect for what is different and to a large extent incommensurable, noncomparable, and nonanalogous to what is familiar to us. In other words, I have had to learn to recognize that there are certain beliefs, philosophies, or ontologies that I will not fully comprehend but that I must respect.[18]

Learning the Indigenous history, reading their authors, learning their language, and experiencing the process of understanding their ontology are the bases for a respectful relationship with our Indigenous partners and collaborators and the Indigenous leaders and community members with whom we seek to interact. Such interactions must be based on the Indigenous communities' choice to participate in research projects and to share their knowledge with researchers.

Fieldwork Research and Dissemination Stages

During the fieldwork experience, together with respect, reciprocity must guide our behavior and interactions. Reciprocity requires acknowledging our structural power and privilege, whenever existent, and employing strategies to minimize that power differential.[19] Among other attitudes and dispositions, this requires humility, the ability to listen and observe (even during long conversational silences), and a sincere disposition to learn—or unlearn. In our conversations and interviews with Indigenous people, we are there to learn. I recall an interview with a Mapuche *machi* (spiritual leader) in Chile, when she turned the tables and our interview started with 30 minutes of questions about me, my research, its significance and purpose. On few occasions have I felt so deeply examined as at the onset of that interview. When the machi felt satisfied with my answers, she agreed to give me the interview and answer my questions. What followed was an amazing conversation wherein I learned much more than I could ever teach my students.

But reciprocity is more than the capacity to observe, listen, and learn. It also entails giving back to the community or the individuals who open their doors and give unselfishly of their knowledge and time. There are easy and concrete ways to do this. For instance, when I have invited Indigenous leaders to speak at my university or in my courses, I have paid them honoraria, as I would do with scholars and distinguished guests. I recognize that traditional and ancestral knowledge—regardless of formal education or degrees—is at least as valuable to my learning community as the knowledge that is recognized with university degrees and scholarly publications.

Steps like this are part of the work I believe we must do to start decolonizing academia.[20] But we can do much more, of course. Many scholars are guided by the principle that no research on Indigenous communities should be conducted without their active participation and coauthorship. Indigenous communities say, "Nothing about us, without us." I am striving to make this a reality in the research I undertake, identifying Indigenous collaborators and making them coauthors in the research process and dissemination of materials. This may entail exploring other ways of disseminating information than the written journal articles or books we are used to. Video documentaries are a tool for dissemination of Indigenous knowledge and experiences, and Indigenous leaders and communities may use those video documentaries for their own purposes. The growing digital humanities units in our universities could be hubs for the dissemination of findings or materials coauthored with Indigenous communities. There is even a new platform, Mukurtu,[21] designed with Indigenous communities to manage and share their digital cultural heritage.

Finally, Indigenous politics does not happen in a vacuum. Studying Indigenous politics also implies fully appreciating the myriad ways in which colonialism, racism, and the nation-state have defined and shaped what are Indigenous identities, rights, demands, and politics. To date, national legislation and census categories shape and define Indigenous identities. National and subnational legislation define the rights of Indigenous peoples and nations. Colonialism, racism, and the dispossessions of territories, bodies, and cultural heritage have profoundly affected and shaped these Indigenous communities. At the same time, Indigenous communities have resisted and continue to do so. In the international, national, and local arenas, Indigenous rights and demands are progressing. Whether it is the right to an intercultural education, intercultural health, a plurinational state, their ancestral territory, or to free, prior, and informed consent, Indigenous communities are putting forward multiple alternatives to colonialism and colonial power. As non-Indigenous social science researchers, our more just reciprocity strategy should be to amplify those alternative futures and work to repair some of the historical and generational damage inflicted upon Indigenous peoples.

Why Should a Non-Indigenous Social Scientist Study Indigenous Politics?

As non-Indigenous researchers we should be acutely aware of our positionality as nonmembers of the Indigenous communities we are working with. I started studying Indigenous political demands and states' responses as a consequence of my research on local community participation, which developed from my previous interest in processes of decentralization of government. However, in researching Indigenous politics, as with no other previous research topic, I have repeatedly found myself asking whether as a non-Indigenous scholar I have the right to research Indigenous politics. Is it ethical? Of course, the IRB approval process at my university requires compliance with ethical research practices. But is that enough? Is it ethical or even productive for me, a non-Indigenous researcher, to study Indigenous politics? Never before had I thought that certain topics or questions could be outside of what I was morally or ethically "allowed" to research. Yet the extraction of Indigenous knowledge, territories, bodies, and cultural heritage, which has taken place over hundreds of years and has been perpetrated by white people like me, was a reason to ponder. Could I ever be entrusted with Indigenous knowledge?

I want to believe that, with time, it will be mostly Indigenous scholars who will write about the rights, demands, and politics of Indigenous peoples, as well as so many other aspects of their nations and cultures. At most, we should become strategic coauthors, called upon by Indigenous scholars when our particular expertise may be needed. I want to believe that, with time, it will be mostly Indigenous scholars who will communicate about Indigenous peoples' politics to wider audiences. This will imply, among other rights and opportunities, access to higher and postgraduate education and academic jobs. Yet these are rights and opportunities that unfortunately are scarcely available to many Indigenous communities, particularly in the Global South. Thus, I have come to terms with the idea that in the meantime, the scholarship of non-Indigenous social scientists is necessary to amplify the voices of Indigenous nations and their demands, to contribute to rectifying the historical and political record and to making progress on plurinationality and sovereignty claims as well as reparations and restorative justice measures, where Indigenous nations have called for them. In other words, I believe the non-Indigenous social scientists (me included) can be allies of Indigenous nations, but ultimately it should be up to Indigenous scholars to study Indigenous peoples' politics, and we should pave the way for this to happen. In the future, non-Indigenous scholars could instead focus their attention on interactions between Indigenous nations and other political entities such as states, corporations, or international organizations and complement the scholarship of Indigenous scholars.

In my experience, the position of allyship has required bridging cultures and communities. I have done so in my classroom, in particular in the course People of the Land: Indigeneity and Politics in Argentina and Chile,[22] as well as in the programming of the Center for Latin American and Latinx Studies (CLALS) that I have directed at the University of Pennsylvania (2016–2024), and of the Latin American Studies Association (LASA) Section of Center Directors that I have chaired (2021–2023). In my course, the students and I started reading mostly Indigenous and some non-Indigenous scholars on how to decolonize academia, and political science in particular. We also learned how to conduct in-depth interviews, particularly in situations of power asymmetry. During the second part of the course the students, working in pairs, interviewed Mapuche Indigenous leaders, who were paid honoraria as our course's distinguished guests. The course's collective final project was a 23-minute video documentary with selections of the interviews conducted, which was approved by and shared with our interviewees.[23] At CLALS and in collaboration with partners in a Just Futures Initiative grant from the Mellon Foundation, our team has brought Indigenous leaders to lecture at Penn, such as Glicérica Jesús da Silva[24] and Luiz Eloy Terena,[25] and has engaged with scholars, practitioners, and Indigenous communities in participatory research throughout Latin America. With the executive committee of the Section of Center Directors of LASA, we launched a series in the fall of 2021 entitled "Indigeneity, Afro-Descendants, and Other Marginalized Populations in Latin America." During the 2021–2022 academic year, seven events were organized by partnering centers from the United States, the United Kingdom, and Latin America, who engaged 26 speakers, the majority of whom were Indigenous or Afro-descendants. Finally, as a member of my university community, I strive to increase the number of Indigenous students and faculty who are part of our university.

Of course, the practice of allyship can take different actions and forms, depending on the researcher's positionality and the needs and desires of the Indigenous communities and members with whom we are involved or collaborate through research and education.

Why Does It Matter, and What Can You Do?

In my opinion, Indigenous politics holds the key to some of the most interesting problems and questions of our time. Studying Indigenous politics requires learning, measuring, understanding, and ultimately coming to terms with the consequences of colonialism and racism in our societies and countries. It brings complexity to the celebrated narratives of statehood and nation-state building, highlighting the processes of exclusion, forced removal, violence, even genocide that took place as the "us" of the modern nation-states were created. Indigenous knowledge, in some cases, also holds the key to sustainability and to better care for the planet we inhabit. In all the Indigenous ontologies I know of, nature, humans, and nonhumans are not separated but part of a single whole. Caring for humans, flora, animals, and the environment is all part of the same process. Indigenous politics has taught me that dispossessions of territory are intimately related to collective and individual health. And in my opinion, the best way to approach these topics and questions is through a qualitative methodology that pursues understanding, or *Verstehen*, as Max Weber wrote.[26]

Should you, as a non-Indigenous researcher, choose this path of study, my final recommendation is to escape the simple, reductionist, and easy binary classifications. As Silvia Rivera Cusicanqui has written, a world of gray is possible.[27] Studying Indigenous politics has taught me to avoid binary reductionist labels and to embrace hybridity instead. This does not mean that anything goes or that differences do not exist. There can be differences, in rights, demands, and politics in hybrid settings, depending, for example, on what aspects of the identity become more salient in different times and contexts. The nation-states and anthropologists have had a central role in defining some identities and communities, while at the same time invisibilizing or erasing others. In Latin America, for instance, for most of the 20th century Indigenous peoples were erased and then redefined as *campesinos*. Indigenous identities are nowadays made more visible and, alongside Indigenous languages, recuperated where they had been suppressed. To study with Indigenous peoples we should guide our practice with respect and reciprocity and strive to indigenize the academy and decolonize our own disciplinary knowledge.

Notes

* The author gratefully acknowledges the support of The Mellon Foundation *Just Futures* Initiative grant N-2009-09221 entitled "Dispossessions in the Americas: the Extraction of Bodies, Land, and Heritage from *la Conquista* to the Present," administered by the University of Pennsylvania, coordinated by Principal Investigator: Tulia G. Falleti, and with co-principal investigators Margaret Bruchac, Ricardo Castillo-Neyra, Ann Farnsworth-Alvear, Michael Hanchard, Jonathan D. Katz, Richard M. Leventhal, and Michael Z. Levy; as well as helpful comments from the editors, Daniela Alarcón, Catherine Bartch, Carew Boulding, Cristopher Carter, Jonathan Fox, Raymond Foxworth, José Antonio Lucero, Kristina Lyons, Thea Riofrancos, Maria Paula Saffón, and the participants of the 2022 REPAL Conference.

1. I capitalize the word "Indigenous" when referring to a person, community, or nation to distinguish it from the word "indigenous" as applied to nonhuman entities originary of a certain place (as an indigenous plant, for instance). In doing so, I follow the recommendations of the American Native Association of Journalists as well as the *New York Times* writing style. I recommend non-Indigenous researchers to capitalize the word "Indigenous" when applied to individuals, communities, or nations.
2. Cobo, JM. (1986). Study of the problem of discrimination against Indigenous populations. International Covenant on Civil and Political Rights Geneva: United Nations. Cited in Foxworth and Ellenwood (2023, 100).
3. Brysk, *From Tribal Village to Global Village*; Anaya, *Indigenous Peoples in International Law*; Lightfoot, *Global Indigenous Politics*.
4. Schavelzon, *El Nacimiento del Estado Plurinacional de Bolivia*; Cunha Filho, *Formacao do Estado e Horizonte Plurinacional na Bolívia*.
5. Gustafson, *New Languages of the State*.
6. Rivera Cusicanqui, "Liberal Democracy and Ayllu Democracy in Bolivia"; Bicas, "Democracia Aymara Andina."
7. Falleti and Riofrancos, "Endogenous Participation"; Wright and Tomaselli, *The Prior Consultation of Indigenous Peoples in Latin America*.
8. Velasco-Herrejón, Bauwens, and Friant, "Challenging Dominant Sustainability Worldviews on the Energy Transition."
9. Ferguson, "Why Does Political Science Hate American Indians?"
10. Yashar, *Contesting Citizenship in Latin America*; Van Cott, *From Movements to Parties in Latin America*; Lucero, *Struggles of Voice*; Rice, *The New Politics of Protest*; Trejo, *Popular Movements in Autocracies*; Eisenstadt, *Politics, Identity, and Mexico's Indigenous Rights Movements*; Madrid, *The Rise of Ethnic Politics in Latin America*; Jung, *The Moral Force of Indigenous Politics*; Brysk, *From Tribal Village to Global Village*.
11. Carter, "States of Extraction"; Unzueta, "Consensus and Conflict over Ethnic Classifications"; McMurry, Hiraldo, and Carter, "The Rise of Indigenous Recognition."
12. Among others, see the chapters by Cyr, Gellman, Pisano, and Pearlman in this volume.
13. Bruchac, *Savage Kin*; Panich and Gonzalez, *The Routledge Handbook of the Archaeology of Indigenous-Colonial Interaction in the Americas*.
14. I thank my anthropologist colleague Kristina Lyons for her related comment.
15. I use commonsense definitions for "respect" and "reciprocity." With regard to "decolonization" there is an ample literature and debate on the topic, which I cannot cover in the space afforded here. For an excellent introduction to what decolonization is and is not, see Tuck and Yang, "Decolonization Is Not a Metaphor." I thank Raymond Foxworth and José Antonio Lucero for recommending this article to me.
16. For example, Blackhawk, *Violence over the Land*; Rivera Cusicanqui, *Un Mundo Ch'ixi Es Positble*; Simpson, *Mohawk Interruptus*; Deloria, *Playing Indian*; Lightfoot, *Global Indigenous Politics*; Pairican Padilla, *Malon*; Estes, *Our History Is the Future*.
17. When information outside of the field sites is scarce, our "preparatory stage" for research continues through the iteration of multiple fieldwork research visits.
18. I have also found that I can respect Indigenous ontologies as long as they do not violate human rights. So far, I have learned that my cultural understanding and respect end where I suspect the possibility of a human rights violation (particularly in the case of Indigenous nations that are not untouched). I am, furthermore, cognizant that the human rights I uphold are temporally bound (i.e., defined by our historical time) and derived from the liberalism doctrine that is part of colonialism and of the Indigenous peoples' colonial experience. I acknowledge there is an unresolved tension in this position.

19. MacLean, "The Power of the Interviewer."
20. According to Tuck and Yang, "Decolonization Is Not a Metaphor," decolonizing the academy will remain an aspiration, or always a work-in-progress, given the history and legacies of settler colonial states, societies, and economies.
21. https://mukurtu.org/.
22. Link to syllabus: https://upenn.box.com/s/qvlg86dgt8kcfklprnfyt4t0ejegnra5.
23. Link to video: https://upenn.box.com/s/0ebbrhqplvlpuisto6iztinuov90swsp.
24. Also known as Célia Tupinambá, she is a well-known Indigenous leader, teacher, intellectual, and artist from the village of Serra do Padeiro, located in the Tupinambá de Olivença Indigenous Territory (southern Bahia, northeastern Brazil).
25. Dr. Luiz Eloy Terena has served as the general counsel for the Articulation of Indigenous Peoples of Brazil (APIB, Associação dos Povos Indígenas do Brasil).
26. Weber, *Economy and Society*.
27. Rivera Cusicanqui, *Un Mundo Ch'ixi Es Positble*.

Recommended Readings

De la Torre, Joely [Proudfit Joely]. "A Critical Look at the Isolation of American Indian Political Practices in the Nonempirical Social Science of Political Science." In *Indigenizing the Academy. Transforming Scholarship and Empowering Communities*, edited by D. A. Mihesuah and A. C. Wilson, 174–190. Lincoln: University of Nebraska Press, 2004.
    The author provides an American Indian perspective on the state of political science in U.S. academia. She invites readers to examine Native Americans as sovereign political entities and highlights the importance of understanding group rights and tribal culture, history, customs, and issues.

Kovach, Margaret. "Doing Indigenous Methodologies: A Letter to a Research Class." In *The Sage Handbook of Qualitative Research*, 5th ed., edited by N. K. Denzin and Y. S. Lincoln, 214–234. Los Angeles: Sage, 2018.
    Kovach invites her readers to do Indigenous methodologies, which are based on Indigenous epistemologies. According to Indigenous epistemology, knowledge is holistic (empirical, experiential, sensory, and metaphysical); arises from interconnectivity and interdependency, as well as from a multiplicity of sources, including nonhuman; and is animate and fluid.

Foxworth, Raymond, and Cheryl Ellenwood. "Indigenous Peoples and Third Sector Research: Indigenous Data Sovereignty as a Framework to Improve Research Practices." *Voluntas* 34, (February 2023): 100–107.
    Foxworth and Ellenwood propose Indigenous data sovereignty as "the right of Indigenous peoples and nations to govern the collection, ownership, and application of their own data" (100) and discuss a series of practices "to engage in research *with* and *for*—and not *on*—Indigenous communities" (107).

References

Anaya, S. James. *Indigenous Peoples in International Law*. 2nd ed. New York: Oxford University Press, 2004.

Bicas, Mara. "Democracia Aymara Andina: Taypi y Diversidad Deliberativa para una Democracia Intercultural." In *Estado Plurinacional y Democracias. Alice en Bolivia*, edited by Boaventura de Sousa Santos and José Luis Exeni Rodríguez. La Paz: Friedrich Ebert Stiftung, 201–228, 2019.

Blackhawk, Ned. *Violence over the Land. Indians and Empires in the Early American West*. Cambridge, MA: Haravard University Press, 2006.

Bruchac, Margaret M. *Savage Kin: Indigenous Informants and American Anthropologists.* Tucson: University of Arizona Press, 2018.
Brysk, Alison. *From Tribal Village to Global Village. Indian Rights and International Relations in Latin America.* Stanford, CA: Stanford University Press, 2000.
Carter, Christopher L. "States of Extraction: The Emergence of Indigenous Rights in Latin America." 2020. https://escholarship.org/uc/item/8pr3q6g8
Cunha Filho, Clayton Mendonca. *Formacao do Estado e Horizonte Plurinacional na Bolívia.* Brazil: Curitiba Editorial Appris, 2018.
Deloria, Philip J. *Playing Indian.* New Haven, CT: Yale University Press, 1998.
Eisenstadt, Todd A. *Politics, Identity, and Mexico's Indigenous Rights Movements.* New York: Cambridge University Press, 2011.
Estes, Nick. *Our History Is the Future: Standing Rock versus the Dakota Access Pipeline, and the Long Tradition of Indigenous Resistance.* London: Verso, 2019.
Falleti, Tulia G., and Thea N. Riofrancos. "Endogenous Participation: Strengthening Prior Consultation in Extractive Economies." *World Politics* 70, no. 1 (January 2018): 86–121.
Ferguson, Kennan. "Why Does Political Science Hate American Indians?" *Perspectives on Politics* 14, no. 4 (2016): 1029–1038.
Foxworth, Raymond, and Cheryl Ellenwood. "Indigenous Peoples and Third Sector Research: Indigenous Data Sovereignty as a Framework to Improve Research Practices." *Voluntas*, (February 2023): 100–107.
Gustafson, Bret. *New Languages of the State: Indigenous Resurgence and the Politics of Knowledge in Bolivia.* Durham, NC: Duke University Press, 2009.
Jung, Courtney. *The Moral Force of Indigenous Politics: Critical Liberalism and the Zapatistas.* New York: Cambridge University Press, 2008.
Lightfoot, Sheryl. *Global Indigenous Politics: A Subtle Revolution.* New York: Routledge, 2016.
Lucero, Antonio. *Struggles of Voice: The Politics of Indigenous Representation.* Pittsburgh, PA: University of Pittsburgh Press, 2008.
Lyons, Kristina M. *Vital Decomposition: Soil Practitioners and Life Politics.* Durham, NC: Duke University Press, 2020.
MacLean, Lauren M. "The Power of the Interviewer." In *Interview Research in Political Science*, edited by Layna Mosley, 67–83. Ithaca, NY: Cornell University Press, 2013.
Madrid, Raúl L. *The Rise of Ethnic Politics in Latin America.* New York: Cambridge University Press, 2012.
McMurry, Nina, Danielle Hiraldo, and Christopher L. Carter. "The Rise of Indigenous Recognition: Implications for Comparative Politics." *APSA-Comparative Politics Newsletter* 31, no. 1 (Spring 2021): 93–102.
Pairican Padilla, Fernando. *Malon: La Rebelión del Movimiento Mapuche, 1990–2013.* Santiago, Chile: Pehuén Editores, 2014.
Panich, Lee M., and Sara L. Gonzalez. *The Routledge Handbook of the Archaeology of Indigenous-Colonial Interaction in the Americas.* London: Routledge, 2021.
Rice, Roberta. *The New Politics of Protest: Indigenous Mobilization in Latin America's Neoliberal Era.* Tucson: University of Arizona Press, 2012.
Rivera Cusicanqui, Silvia. "Liberal Democracy and Ayllu Democracy in Bolivia: The Case of Northern Potosí." *Journal of Development Studies* 26, no. 4 (1990): 97–121.
Rivera Cusicanqui, Silvia. *Un Mundo Ch'ixi Es Positble: Ensayos desde un Presente en Crisis.* La Paz: Piedra Rota y Tinat Limón, 2020.
Schavelzon, Salvador. *El Nacimiento del Estado Plurinacional de Bolivia: Etnografía de una Asambela Constituyente.* La Paz: CEJIS and Plural Editores, 2012.
Simpson, Audra. *Mohawk Interruptus: Political Life across the Borders of Settler States.* Durham, NC: Duke University Press, 2014.
Trejo, Guillermo. *Popular Movements in Autocracies.* New York: Cambridge University Press, 2012.
Tuck, Eve, and K. Wayne Yang. "Decolonization Is Not a Metaphor." *Decolonization: Indigeneity, Education & Society* 1, no. 1 (2012): 1–40.

Unzueta, Maria Belén. "Consensus or Conflict over Ethnicracial Categories? Classificatory Systems in Chile and Bolivia." Unpublished manuscript, 2022.

Van Cott, Donna Lee. *From Movements to Parties in Latin America: The Evolution of Ethnic Politics.* New York: Cambridge University Press, 2005.

Velasco-Herrejón, Paola, Thomas Bauwens, and Martin Calisto Friant. "Challenging Dominant Sustainability Worldviews on the Energy Transition: Lessons from Indigenous Communities in Mexico and a Plea for Pluriversal Technologies." *World Development* 150 (2022): 105725.

Weber, Max. *Economy and Society: An Outline of Interpretive Sociology* (1922). Berkeley: University of California Press, 1978.

Wright, Claire, and Alexandra Tomaselli. *The Prior Consultation of Indigenous Peoples in Latin America: Inside the Implementation Gap.* New York: Routledge, 2019.

Yashar, Deborah J. *Contesting Citizenship in Latin America: The Rise of Indigenous Movements and the Postliberal Challenge.* New York: Cambridge University Press, 2005.

25
Qualitative Research as a Minoritized Scholar

Robin L. Turner

Overview

The distinct challenges, opportunities, and pitfalls minoritized scholars confront in undertaking qualitative research are often disregarded. Yet minoritization affects all aspects of the research process, from question development through research design, data generation and analysis, to reception of one's scholarship. This chapter defines minoritization, discusses the traits of scholars most likely to experience minoritization, describes how minoritization influences the research process, and offers strategies to address the particular opportunities and pitfalls minoritized scholars confront at each stage of the research process. The chapter focuses on those strategies available to minoritized individuals because those are most within the scholar's control, not because addressing it is their responsibility. Rather, minoritization is a structural disciplinary problem impeding scholarship and knowledge production.

At the outset, it is important to note that this chapter deliberately employs the term "minoritized scholars" rather than "minority scholars." Why? Minoritization is an imposed, power-laden status in which one is treated by dominant, sometimes hegemonic actors as different, unrepresentative, and less significant. Minoritization arises from individual behaviors, collective actions, and institutional practices that establish the normative characteristics of the ostensible majority and impose minority status upon those who do not fit those often unstated norms. Minoritized scholars are understood to comprise a small, unrepresentative share of the scholarly/epistemic community; they often experience marginalization; and their scholarship often is presumed to be inferior. Using the term "minority" reinforces these misperceptions, directs attention away from the forces producing minoritization, and often is inaccurate.

Minoritization is about positionality, one's "placement within a set of relations and practices."[1] Minoritization reflects how a scholar and their work are positioned, seen, and interacted with, in relation to how other, presumably more normative scholars and their work are positioned. Dominant perceptions locate minoritized scholars far from the perceived center of the field, the norm, or the majority. Positionality tends to be associated with fluidity because one's relative position is subject to change. Minoritization is fluid in principle but often stable in practice. Black, Indigenous, Latinx, and queer scholars have continued to experience minoritization in American political science even as disciplinary concerns, methods, and more or less accepted knowledge and theories have shifted.[2]

So which scholars are subject to minoritization? If minoritization denotes being perceived or treated as both different from the norm and less representative, then many scholars experience minoritization to some extent. Cisgender women scholars have been minoritized in the cis-male-dominated political science discipline, for example. Race, ethnicity, and caste are other important dimensions of minoritization. White supremacist policies and practices pervaded every aspect of early and mid-20th-century American society, and the discipline of political science in the United States was developed by heterosexual white men whose white supremacist perspectives shaped the questions they explored, the journals they created, and their embrace of putatively objective statistical approaches in a deeply racialized context.[3] Incisive contemporary critiques by W. E. B. Du Bois and Ralph Bunche failed to shift the discipline, these scholars' Blackness undoubtedly contributing to disciplinary disregard.

These examples highlight how scholarly minoritization tends to mirror and reproduce sociopolitical minoritization, as is particularly evident with racial, ethnic, caste, and global hierarchies. BIPOC, Roma, and Muslim scholars experience minoritization in contemporary Global North political science, in the academy more generally, and in society. Dalit and Adivasi scholars experience minoritization in South Asian universities and in society. Poor and working-class-origin people are minoritized in society and academia. The widespread treatment of Global North scholars and scholarship as universal and Global Majority/Global South scholars and scholarship as provincial reflects global power asymmetries. And the presumption that scholars can and will devote substantial, uninterrupted time to field research and data analysis rests on patriarchal, ableist, and classist social norms about bodily capacities, caregiving labor, familial obligations, and academic institution type.

Minoritized status is not tethered to objective indicators or demographic statistics. To illustrate, scholars of color and contingent faculty both are minoritized in the (U.S.) American academy, but people of color make up a small share of the political science discipline, while contingent faculty comprise more than 63% of the professoriate.[4] These overlapping groups have less individual and collective power in the academy than white tenured and tenure-track faculty, and their work, perspectives, and experiences often are treated as ancillary.

The separate treatment of these contributors to minoritization belies their mutually constitutive character. BIPOC, Roma, Dalit, and Adivasi scholars are more likely to be poor or have working-class origins; women and poor and working-class scholars are more likely to have caregiving and familial support responsibilities; women of color are more likely to be poorly paid contingent scholars; and women and scholars of color are more likely to employ qualitative methods. Minoritized scholars often find the quantitative methods environment hostile and study substantive questions less suited to quantification.[5] Race/ethnicity, gender, precarity, and qualitative approach jointly contribute to minoritization and cannot be readily disentangled. What's clear is that most methodological texts and other guidance are written as if their readers are white, able-bodied, heterosexual, cisgender male, middle/upper class, Anglo, Global North citizens with secure positions at research-intensive universities.

Minoritization matters throughout the research process. Minoritized scholars are likely to encounter greater skepticism about their competence and may have difficulty finding useful interlocutors as they develop research projects, share their ideas, and seek funding for their research. Minoritization also presents distinct data generation challenges and opportunities. For instance, while minoritized scholars might not receive the many research-facilitating privileges granted to nonminoritized scholars, these same scholars might be able to generate data that is unavailable or is less available to nonminoritized scholars. At the conclusion of their research, some minoritized scholars face a double bind in which their scholarship is subject to greater scrutiny but is less seriously engaged than comparable work by nonminoritized scholars.

Qualifiers such as "might," "may," "likely," and "often" recur throughout the remainder of this chapter for two reasons. First, minoritization is not a fixed state with uniform effects across scholars and projects but rather a relative status whose effects vary across higher education institutions and research contexts. The experiences of minoritized scholars whose research focuses on a polity or community to which they have strong ties and those who focus on polities or communities to which they lack such ties will differ, for instance. Second, qualitative research encompasses a wide range of positivist, interpretive, and critical approaches and methodologies. Epistemological and methodological differences affect how minoritized scholars understand their experiences and approach their research. The chapter does not attempt to identify best practices for each method addressed.

This chapter reviews how minoritization influences each stage of the research process and offers practical strategies for addressing these challenges and opportunities. I focus on the interpersonal aspects of qualitative research design, data generation, and analysis and write as if the scholar is the principal data generator or collector. The chapter relies principally on work by Black and Asian women scholars who work at Global North research universities. These scholars have made crucial interventions into research methods scholarship, but their work does not and cannot encompass the full scope of minoritization. Although these scholars experience raced-gendered intersectional marginalization, their working conditions are relatively conducive to publication in widely distributed journals and Global North university presses. Precariously employed scholars and those who work at Global Majority and teaching-focused institutions are underrepresented in the literature, as are Indigenous, Dalit, disabled, and queer scholars, among others. The chapter is impoverished by these absences.

State of Practice

This section walks through pragmatic, positional, and ethical considerations for the minoritized scholar at each stage of research. Minoritization presents opportunities and challenges as scholars craft questions, prepare for fieldwork, generate and analyze data, and write up their findings.

Research Question Development and Design Phase

Minoritization does not determine a researcher's epistemology, their research questions and concerns, or their methodological inclinations. Minoritized scholars might approach their research from positivist, interpretivist, or feminist standpoints; might seek to develop persuasive causal arguments that address the "big questions" in their field or to address putatively marginal questions; and might generate data from archival documents, interviews, or ethnography, for example. This section first considers the opportunities and challenges confronting minoritized scholars who adopt mainstream approaches and questions and then considers how attending to one's minoritization can generate innovative research questions and interventions.

Minoritized scholars whose research fits squarely into the center/mainstream of their discipline/subfield usually will encounter fewer challenges in this phase because nonminoritized scholars should have little difficulty understanding their questions and approaches.

These minoritized scholars are well-positioned to benefit from the ever-growing set of qualitative methods texts and workshops and from disciplinary conferences. The principal challenge is likely to be securing critical engagement and sponsorship from expert interlocutors. Adopting a mainstream approach does not insulate minoritized scholars from disregard, hostility, or discrimination, nor does it guarantee access to the networks through which some garner thorough feedback on work in progress and amplification of their publications by established scholars.[6] Black and Latinx graduate students in the United States, for example, report receiving little support from their advisors or mentoring from nonminoritized faculty.[7] These and other minoritized scholars often receive constructive critiques on their research projects at workshops and associations created to support minoritized scholars, such as Women in Legislative Studies, the (U.S.) Latino Caucus in Political Science/Sector Latino de Ciencia Politica, and the (U.S.) National Conference of Black Political Scientists.

Minoritization can sensitize scholars to weaknesses, gaps, and inappropriately universal claims in established scholarship, creating opportunities for distinctive interventions. As Patricia Hill Collins writes, "Where white males may take it as perfectly normal to generalize findings from studies of white males to other groups, Black women are more likely to see such a practice as problematic, as an anomaly. Similarly, when white feminists produce generalizations about 'women,' Black feminists routinely ask 'Which women do you mean?'"[8] An article by Pamela Paxton illustrates both points.[9] Noticing that several influential studies of democracy and democratization included universal adult suffrage in their definitions of democracy but then conflated universal suffrage with (white) male suffrage in their measures, thereby disregarding the enfranchisement of women like herself, Paxton recoded the data to include women in each suffrage measure. Doing so shifted the year of democratic transition in almost every case and showed there was little support for Huntington's contention that democratization occurred in waves with a women-inclusive measure.[10] Her recoding suffered from the conflation of white women's suffrage with women's suffrage, as is evident in the dating of the U.S. transition to democracy to 1920. Most white women gained the franchise that year when sex-based suffrage restrictions ended, but the disfranchisement of African Americans, Native Americans, and other minoritized citizens persisted until the 24th Amendment and the Voting Rights Act brought the country much closer to universal suffrage in the mid-1960s. This example highlights the utility and limitations of research questions focused solely on the exclusion of similarly minoritized people. Minoritized scholars may be particularly well suited to crafting research projects whose attention to exclusion advances the theoretical and empirical literature.

Other scholars depart from the mainstream by centering the experiences, perspectives, and actions of similarly minoritized people in their research. The work of Nadia Brown and Natasha Behl demonstrates the productive potential of this strategy and of feminist and interpretive approaches.[11] Brown studied the identities, experiences, and decision-making of Black women legislators to better understand legislative behavior, adopting a Black feminist ethnographic approach that attended to her experiences as a Black woman researching Black women throughout the research process. Behl's interpretive political ethnographic analysis of citizenship, democracy, and gendered violence centered the experiences and perspectives of Sikh people in Punjab, India, integrating consideration of her diasporic researcher positionality throughout. Intersectionally minoritized scholars often adopt nonpositivist research epistemologies, as these examples highlight, perhaps because their experiences conflict with the positivist premise that one's attributes can (or should) have no effect on one's interpersonal interactions.

This centering of minoritized experiences and research questions is not without cost. These projects and scholars are likely to find that some dismiss their projects as overly niche or biased "me-search." It may be helpful to keep in mind that all perspectives are partial—this work is no more biased than that focused on nonminoritized people—and it is essential to look elsewhere for guidance. These scholars should search for other scholarship by and about minoritized scholars or that is grounded in the same or a compatible epistemology for guidance. These publications may model how to frame and convey the importance of this work to diverse audiences. The methodological discussions in these publications can help the scholar address the design, data generation, and analytic issues that arise in "outsider-within," "native informant," and "diasporic" research neglected in standard methods texts. Scholars also should search for compatible scholarly communities within the minoritized scholars-focused networks discussed above and beyond their discipline.

Preparing to Generate Data

Minoritized scholars should critically engage with the guidance offered in research methods texts, by their colleagues and peers, and in exemplary prior texts because these often presume the people generating data are not minoritized or are minoritized along a single dimension, for instance as cisgender women. This guidance usually fails to address the data generation pitfalls and opportunities differently minoritized or intersectionally minoritized scholars encounter or gestures to these concerns without addressing them in depth. Most positivist qualitative methods texts are written as if scholars' attributes have or should have no effect, while interpretivist methods texts often approach positionality and reflexivity as if researchers have a degree of structural power that minoritized scholars may lack. I highlight potential data generation pitfalls, safety considerations, opportunities, and strategies in turn.

Minoritized scholars' plans should take into account the potential withholding of privileges regularly extended to nonminoritized scholars. Nonminoritized scholars may be granted easier access to field facilities, data archives, and research participants; often are subject to less stringent competence assessments; and are less likely to have their presence questioned. These affordances often are invisible to their normative nonminoritized beneficiaries. Failure to recognize the discretionary character of these research-facilitating privileges may leave minoritized scholars ill-prepared to be treated as "space invaders" or "bodies out of place" in some research contexts and locales.[12] For example, the African American scholar Francis Henderson had not anticipated that white racism might jeopardize her lodging in Maputo, Mozambique, but found she and her advisor's brother had to persuade the owners to honor her reservation.[13] Henderson directs blames at herself for not sending her local advisor and facilitators a photo before arrival.

Inadequate guidance based in presumed normativity can create other pitfalls. Enze Han and M. Brielle Harbin were surprised by the data generation problems they encountered as novice researchers. "Trained as a positivist political scientist" in the United States, Han had not anticipated his ethnicity would affect his field research but found his Han Chinese ethnicity presented a nearly insurmountable barrier to productive research interactions with Uyghur people despite their willingness to talk with white American researchers.[14] These "negative experiences colored [his] emotional reaction to them."[15] Harbin, a Black scholar, had similar difficulties in the United States, where she confronted a hostile environment in one West Virginia polling place and was entirely refused access to a New Jersey site.[16] Harbin was able to poll voters at a different West Virginia location but still encountered a starkly different climate than her white exit polling counterparts: "People stared at me as if I were confusing them or unexpected in their environment. Some bluntly blurted out, 'What's your business here?' People also were curious about my colleagues, but … they did not feel like they were under surveillance."[17] Although Harbin was gathering data for a quantitative project, similar problems can arise in attempting to gather qualitative data from gated archives, collections, and properties. Minoritized scholars may have little immediate recourse if gatekeepers refuse to respect their legal right to engage in an activity, as happened in New Jersey, or if they narrowly interpret and enforce formal rules more strictly, slow-walk archive and document requests, or simply refrain from sharing helpful information or courtesies, like the snacks and chairs offered to white polling team members.

There are strategies for anticipating and planning for hostile treatment that may reduce its harmful effects. Seeking out other minoritized people familiar with the research context can help to identify potential problems and develop strategies to address them. Preliminary visits to potential research sites also can be very helpful, if feasible. I benefited from conversations with other African Americans, graduate study in South Africa, and pre-dissertation research in South Africa and Uganda. These experiences prepared me for dissertation fieldwork on nature tourism and rural politics in southern Africa, where I correctly anticipated my race would heighten the substantial entry barriers to rural white-owned farms. These expectations led me to focus that project in and around state-owned lands where I could secure official access permission and help with contact details for other property owners, managers, and workers.

Of course, thoughtful preparation does not prevent all problems or harms. Harbin and her team leader had researched election laws, discussed her safety as a Black woman, and took that into account in choosing polling locations but did not realize that poll workers might simply disregard the law. She "was caught off guard, hurt, and angry" by these experiences.[18] Nor does preparation eradicate the emotional weight of differential treatment. "It is arduous to be treated as a racialized, foreign Other both in the field *and* at home" and to have to "to prove my credibility as a researcher," Sean Yom writes.[19] Returning to my experience in rural southern Africa, I divided my time between the rural data generation sites and a more welcoming city a few hours' drive away, and also talked with understanding friends and colleagues in that city and further away, to deal with occasional racist, sexist, and homophobic encounters in research locales.

There are a number of strategies available to minoritized scholars that may help in confronting unexpected pitfalls. Scholars might deploy other resources, such as academic credentials, Global North currency or citizenship, American- or British-accented English, or their "Western-ness or academic title," to shift gatekeepers' perception of their status.[20] Scholars might also search for a friendlier interlocutor by visiting the gated locale at different days and times. If that proves impossible, minoritized scholars might have a nonminoritized proxy access the gated resource on their behalf. Harbin could not generate sufficient exit polling data independently but was able to use team-generated data for her project.

Each strategy presents unfortunate trade-offs that vary across projects and individuals. Relying on proxies to access archival records is quite different from doing so for interviews or ethnography, although it's not ideal in either case. Melissa Harris-Perry used a male proxy to garner data about typical everyday Black male barbershop talk, a strategy that reflected not only access issues but also a desire to minimize observer effects that interpretivists do not share.[21] The personal costs of deploying Global North citizenship or other forms of strategic self-presentation are unfortunately similar to those minoritized scholars bear throughout the academy, as Yom points out. We often have to display credentials and amplify or mute particular aspects of our identities to be treated not quite as well as other nonminoritized individuals.

Minoritized scholars also need to take safety into account in developing data generation strategies, considering not only the harms to which all researchers (and sometimes all people) in their research sites are vulnerable but also those connected to their specific minoritization. Scholars who are minoritized in their data generation locales, who cannot count on observers and officials to act on their behalf if problems arise, or who are women, queer, trans, or disabled, or otherwise disproportionately subject to violence, need to take particular care. Many women scholars have sought to reduce risk by conforming to social norms with which they disagree. For example, Vasundhara Sirnate strategically presented herself as a traditional, "respectable," "homely girl" in need of protection to reduce the risk of predatory gendered personal violence in the Chhattisgarh, India context.[22] In other circumstances, risk reduction might entail forfeiting data generation opportunities. Yolande Bouka did not expand her field research from Rwanda to Goma because her physical similarity to local people made her more vulnerable to arrest and border difficulties than white researchers and because the Canadian embassy had disavowed responsibility for citizens traveling to the Democratic Republic of Congo.[23] Reminding scholars that native and minoritized scholars sometimes have few or no risk-reduction options, Bouka recounted the case of University of Toronto graduate student Alexander Sodiqov, who was arrested and detained shortly after beginning research. Sodiqov had little access to state protection or diplomatic assistance because his research was in Kazakhstan, his home country.

Despite the difficulties and potential pitfalls, minoritized scholars should consider minoritization-linked data generation opportunities in crafting research designs. Those who plan to generate most of their data from similarly minoritized people may have easier initial access to participants *if* they can demonstrate cultural competence and navigate gatekeeper and participant expectations. Nadia Brown writes, "As an African American woman interviewing African American women state legislators, I avoided the position of researcher-as-stranger."[24] Natasha Behl also details, "My prior knowledge, Punjabi language mastery, race/ethnicity, religion, and familial contacts enabled me to gain access in a way not available to other researchers."[25] Those of us who lack such close ties to our research contexts need to think carefully about whether and how minoritization in our home context might enhance our research and whether other attributes, such as our appearance, cultural background, or work history, might open doors. My Black woman-ness surprised many southern Africans with whom I first interacted by email; my name led most to expect a white English male. My racialization often eased building productive research relationships with South Africans who had experienced apartheid as (young) adults but did not have the same effect in Botswana or Uganda, places which were not subject to settler colonization.

Minoritized scholars should treat preparing to generate qualitative data with the same seriousness as other research design and methodological concerns. Gathering information about each data generation locale by reading broadly about each context and talking to a broad range of similarly minoritized, differently minoritized, and nonminoritized people can provide the foundation for the critical engagement with standard research texts and guidance recommended above. Seeking perspectives on key concerns from ordinary people, activists, volunteers, and missionaries who have spent time in the locale will help minoritized scholars have a sense of their potential reception, likely opportunities, potential pitfalls, and hazards. Conversations with an African American acquaintance prepared me for my frequent interpellation as "Coloured" before I first traveled to Cape Town, South Africa, in the late 1990s. His comments helped me connect my intellectual understanding of the racial landscape to the discomfiting experience of having easy access to places where darker-skinned people were unwelcome and hearing anti-Black discourse from people who seemed to presume I would find it unobjectionable. Attending to one's potential place in context-specific status hierarchies and along the insider-outsider spectrum can assist scholars to craft a data generation plan that is not only aligned to their research objectives but also is feasible and maximizes opportunities while reducing risks.

Data Generation

Once data generation and analysis begin, minoritized scholars have to figure out how to make good use of their preparation and planning without being blinkered by it. Anticipating how individuals in data generation locales are likely to perceive and respond is useful. However, scholars can never know how others perceive them, and those who hold too tightly to their preparatory preconceptions may miss opportunities or fail to learn from mistakes.[26] Talking through field impressions and interpretations with local research assistants, colleagues, and friends and documenting both in field notes can help scholars maintain or regain this delicate balance.

Effective data generation entails doing several things concurrently or recursively: implementing the research design and data generation plan and engaging in metacognitive observation and reflection about the data generation and the field experience more generally. From this perspective, data generation is a process in which the scholars are participant observers for whom both data generation—accessing archives, interviewing people, engaging in visual analysis, or ethnography—and the other experiences they have in research locales are data that can inform their subsequent actions in each field and sometimes contribute more directly to their analysis. Attending to "meta-data," such as rumors, inventions, and nonverbal behaviors, and engaging in "accidental ethnography" by "paying systematic attention to unplanned or 'accidental' moments in the field" can help scholars better understand research participants, the data generation context, and thus the data, and to navigate each locale in a way that minimizes risks to participants and to scholars.[27] Conversations at a local hair salon about America, hip-hop, and other matters helped Christian Davenport to connect with Rwandans, to better understand their perceptions of life before and after the war and (many years later) that "being an African American was [his] way in" to many fields.[28] Adopting a more intentional approach might be helpful. Recognizing that her "skinfolk connection [with Rwandans] at times offered great insights about respondents' understanding of violence" but "created confusion during the [other] interviews," when her questions concerned matters locals considered common knowledge, Yolande Bouka took care to ensure that hesitant respondents understood she was not Rwandan.[29]

Jessica Soedirgo and Aarie Glas offer guidance on "active reflexivity," the metacognitive aspect of data generation and analysis.[30] Active reflexivity is a recursive practice in which scholars document their expectations and assumptions as they prepare for data generation; record their observations, reflections, and tentative analysis after each encounter; seek others' perspectives on their encounters/reflections; update their expectations (and revise their strategy if needed); and then begin again, repeating the cycle until data generation is complete. Approaching data generation praxis in this way increases the likelihood that minoritized scholars will recognize opportunities and learn from surprises and mistakes; creates a set of records that can be integrated into analysis and cited in publications; and makes the praxis more transparent. Adopting this approach benefits positivist and nonpositivist minoritized researchers alike and ensures that analysis begins long before the scholar leaves the field.

I have taken an active reflexive approach to researching southern African women's involvement in the chieftaincy and other traditional institutions. My field notes document interactions with research participants, interlocutors, and assistants; event observations and context notes; and metadata about nonverbal behaviors along with preliminary interpretations. Asking research assistants and colleagues for their perspectives on shared field experiences has shaped and sometimes shifted my analysis. For instance, Mahlogonolo Rangata helped me understand repeated interview postponements might reflect the particularly fraught local political context in July 2018. Conversations with Mahlogonolo and other southern African Black women have helped me think through and navigate raced-gendered expectations arising from my skinfolk connection to research participants.[31]

Continuing Issues

Minoritized scholars have significant control over the research questions they pursue, the polities and people they study, the epistemology and methods they choose, and their data generation plans and praxis. Considering the issues discussed above and adopting the most relevant strategies can improve the research and research experiences of minoritized scholars. We have much less control over the reception of our research, however. Studies indicate that women are both underrepresented and undercited in "top" journals, that race and ethnic politics-focused scholarship often is treated as marginal, and that women of color faculty in the United States are frequently "presumed incompetent."[32] Minoritized scholars generally, and intersectionally minoritized scholars in particular, are likely to encounter numerous hindrances to publishing their work in the most prestigious outlets and to securing serious engagement with their work by other scholars. Exclusionary practices reduce the impact of our research. Minoritized scholars can, should, and have responded to these barriers by mentoring one another, creating new and more welcoming journals, and sometimes attempting to transform prestigious outlets. Scholars also have built intellectual communities that provide critical engagement and created initiatives such as Women Also Know Stuff, People of Color Also Know Stuff, and Cite Black Women to amplify our work. These initiatives are important but insufficient to remedy minoritization in the absence of action by more powerful, nonminoritized scholars to transform the discipline.

Notes

1. Anthias, Where Do I Belong?, 501.
2. Alexander-Floyd, "Women of Color, Space Invaders, and Political Science"; Michelson and Monforti, "Elusive Inclusion"; Restrepo Sanín, "'I Don't Belong Here.'"
3. Blatt, *Race and the Making of American Political Science*; McClain, "Crises, Race, Acknowledgement"; McClain et al., "Race, Power, and Knowledge."
4. American Association of University Professors, *The Annual Report on the Economic Status of the Profession*; American Political Science Association, "Data Dashboard Summary Update."
5. Shames and Wise, "Gender, Diversity, and Methods in Political Science."
6. I thank Sara Goodman for the network reminder.
7. Majic and Strolovitch, "Editors' Introduction"; Monforti and Michelson, "Diagnosing the Leaky Pipeline"; Jordan-Zachery, "Reflections on Mentoring."
8. Hill Collins, "Learning from the Outsider Within," 27.
9. Paxton, "Women's Suffrage in the Measurement of Democracy."
10. Paxton, "Women's Suffrage in the Measurement of Democracy," 100–102.
11. Brown, *Sisters in the Statehouse*; Behl, *Gendered Citizenship*; Brown, "Negotiating the Insider/Outsider Status"; Behl, "Diasporic researcher."
12. Alexander-Floyd, "Women of Color."
13. Henderson, "'We Thought You Would Be White.'"
14. Han, "Positionality and Subjectivity in Field Research," 235.
15. Han, "Positionality and Subjectivity in Field Research," 234.
16. Harbin, "Who's Able to Do Political Science Work?"
17. Harbin, "Who's Able to Do Political Science Work?," 145.
18. Harbin, "Who's Able to Do Political Science Work?," 144; Han, "Positionality and Subjectivity in Field Research," 234; Henderson, "We Thought You Would Be White," 291.
19. Yom, "Becoming Othered," 16.
20. Yom, "Becoming Othered," 17.
21. Harris-Perry, *Barbershops, Bibles, and BET*. Lee Ann Fujii emphasized this point in a personal communication on October 7, 2017.
22. Sirnate, "Positionality, Personal Insecurity, and Female Empathy in Security Studies Research."
23. Bouka, "Researching Violence in Africa as a Black Woman."
24. Brown, "Negotiating the Insider/Outsider Status," 21.
25. Behl, *Gendered Citizenship*, 121.
26. Fujii, *Interviewing in Social Science Research*.
27. Fujii, "Shades of Truth and Lies"; Fujii, "Five Stories of Accidental Ethnography."
28. Davenport, "Researching While Black."
29. Bouka, "Researching Violence."
30. Soedirgo and Glas, "Toward Active Reflexivity."
31. Turner, "Remembering Lee Ann in South Africa."
32. McClain et al., "Race, Power, and Knowledge"; Teele and Thelen, "Gender in the Journals"; Maliniak, Powers, and Walter, "The Gender Citation Gap in International Relations"; Gutiérrez y Muhs et al., *Presumed Incompetent*.

Recommended Readings

Behl, Natasha. "Diasporic Researcher: An Autoethnographic Analysis of Gender and Race in Political Science." *Politics, Groups, and Identities* 5, no. 4 (2017): 580-598. doi:10.1080/21565503.2016.1141104.

This article provides a critical reflexive account of how minoritization manifests in U.S. political science and in data generation sites.

Bouka, Yolande. "Researching Violence in Africa as a Black Woman: Notes from Rwanda." Conflict in Difficult Settings Working Paper Series. 2015. http://conflictfieldresearch.colgate.edu/wp-content/uploads/2015/05/Bouka_WorkingPaper-May2015.pdf

This nuanced account of preparing for and then generating data in a postconflict setting illustrates how minoritized scholars can attend to participant perceptions without becoming blinkered by their preconceptions.

Fujii, Lee Ann. *Interviewing in Social Science Research: A Relational Approach*. Routledge Series on Interpretive Methods. New York: Routledge, 2018.

The humane, ethical, and practical guidance offered in this book is useful for all minoritized scholars who generate data through interpersonal reactions, not solely the interpretivists to whom it is principally directed.

Hill Collins, Patricia. "Learning from the Outsider Within: The Sociological Significance of Black Feminist Thought." *Social Problems* 33, no. 6 (1986): S14–S32. doi:10.2307/800672.

This classic article describes the distinctive experiences of Black women and details how minoritized scholars' "outsider within" perspectives offer productive vantage points for generating knowledge when put to good use.

References

Alexander-Floyd, Nikol G. "Women of Color, Space Invaders, and Political Science: Practical Strategies for Transforming Institutional Practices." *PS: Political Science & Politics* 48, no. 3 (2015): 464–468. https://doi.org/10.1017/S1049096515000256.

American Association of University Professors. *The Annual Report on the Economic Status of the Profession, 2020–21*. July 2021. https://www.aaup.org/report/annual-report-economic-status-profession-2020-21.

American Political Science Association. "Data Dashboard Summary Update, July 2020." 2020. https://apsanet.org/Portals/54/diversity%20and%20inclusion%20prgms/DIV%20reports/APSA%20Dashboard%20Data%20report%20-%202020%20.pdf.

Anthias, Floya. "Where Do I Belong? Narrating Collective Identity and Translocational Positionality." *Ethnicities* 2, no. 4 (2002): 491–514.

Behl, Natasha. "Diasporic Researcher: An Autoethnographic Analysis of Gender and Race in Political Science." *Politics, Groups, and Identities* 5, no. 4 (2017): 580–598. https://doi.org/10.1080/21565503.2016.1141104.

Behl, Natasha. *Gendered Citizenship: Understanding Gendered Violence in Democratic India*. New York: Oxford University Press, 2019.

Blatt, Jessica. *Race and the Making of American Political Science*. American Governance: Politics, Policy, and Public Law. Philadelphia: University of Pennsylvania Press, 2018.

Bouka, Yolande. "Researching Violence in Africa as a Black Woman: Notes from Rwanda." Conflict in Difficult Settings Working Paper Series. May 2015.

Brown, Nadia E. "Negotiating the Insider/Outsider Status: Black Feminist Ethnography and Legislative Studies." *Journal of Feminist Scholarship*, no. 3 (2012): 19–34.

Brown, Nadia E. *Sisters in the Statehouse: Black Women and Legislative Decision Making*. New York: Oxford University Press, 2014.

Davenport, Christian, "Researching While Black: Why Conflict Research Needs More African Americans (Maybe)." *Political Violence at a Glance*, April 10, 2013. https://politicalviolenceataglance.org/2013/04/10/researching-while-black-why-conflict-research-needs-more-african-americans-maybe/.

Fujii, Lee Ann. "Five Stories of Accidental Ethnography: Turning Unplanned Moments in the Field into Data." *Qualitative Research* 15, no. 4 (2015): 525–539. https://doi.org/10.1177/1468794114548945.

Fujii, Lee Ann. *Interviewing in Social Science Research: A Relational Approach*. Routledge Series on Interpretive Methods. New York: Routledge, 2018.

Fujii, Lee Ann. "Shades of Truth and Lies: Interpreting Testimonies of War and Violence." *Journal of Peace Research* 47, no. 2 (March 2010): 231–241. https://doi.org/10.1177/0022343309353097.

Gutiérrez y Muhs, Gabriella, Yolanda Flores Niemann, Carmen G Gonzalez, and Angela P Harris, eds. *Presumed Incompetent: The Intersections of Race and Class for Women in Academia*. Boulder: University Press of Colorado, 2012.

Han, Enze. "Positionality and Subjectivity in Field Research." In *Stories from the Field: A Guide to Navigating Fieldwork in Political Science*, edited by Peter Krause and Ora Szekely, 232–237. New York: Columbia University Press, 2020.

Harbin, M. Brielle. "Who's Able to Do Political Science Work? My Experience with Exit Polling and What It Reveals about Issues of Race and Equity." *PS: Political Science & Politics* 54, no. 1 (2020): 144–146. https://doi.org/10.1017/S1049096520001080.

Harris-Perry, Melissa V. *Barbershops, Bibles, and BET: Everyday Talk and Black Political Thought*. Princeton, NJ: Princeton University Press, 2004.

Henderson, Frances B. "'We Thought You Would Be White': Race and Gender in Fieldwork." *PS: Political Science & Politics* 42, no. 2 (April 2009): 291–294.

Hill Collins, Patricia. "Learning from the Outsider Within: The Sociological Significance of Black Feminist Thought." *Social Problems* 33, no. 6 (1986): S14–S32. https://doi.org/10.2307/800672.

Jordan-Zachery, Julia S. "Reflections on Mentoring: Black Women and the Academy." *PS: Political Science & Politics* 37, no. 4 (2004): 875–877. https://doi.org/10.1017/S1049096504045317.

Majic, Samantha, and Dara Z. Strolovitch. "Editors' Introduction: Mentoring and Marginalization." *PS: Political Science & Politics* 53, no. 4 (2020): 763–769. https://doi.org/10.1017/S1049096520000773.

Maliniak, Daniel, Ryan Powers, and Barbara F. Walter. "The Gender Citation Gap in International Relations." *International Organization* 67, no. 4 (Fall 2013): 889–922. https://doi.org/10.1017/s0020818313000209.

McClain, Paula D. "Crises, Race, Acknowledgement: The Centrality of Race, Ethnicity, and Politics to the Future of Political Science." *Perspectives on Politics* 19, no. 1 (2021): 7–18. https://doi.org/10.1017/S1537592720004478.

McClain, Paula D., Gloria Y. A. Ayee, Taneisha N. Means, Alicia M. Reyes-Barrientez, and Nura A. Sediqe. "Race, Power, and Knowledge: Tracing the Roots of Exclusion in the Development of Political Science in the United States." *Politics Groups and Identities* 4, no. 3 (2016): 467–482. https://doi.org/10.1080/21565503.2016.1170704.

Michelson, Melissa R., and Jessica L. Lavariega Monforti. "Elusive Inclusion: Persistent Challenges Facing Women of Color in Political Science." *PS: Political Science & Politics* 54, no. 1 (2020): 152–157. https://doi.org/10.1017/S1049096520001079.

Monforti, Jessica Lavariega, and Melissa R. Michelson. "Diagnosing the Leaky Pipeline: Continuing Barriers to the Retention of Latinas and Latinos in Political Science." *PS: Political Science & Politics* 41, no. 1 (2017): 161–166. https://doi.org/10.1017/S1049096508080232.

Paxton, Pamela. "Women's Suffrage in the Measurement of Democracy: Problems of Operationalization." *Studies in Comparative International Development* 35, no. 3 (Fall 2000): 92–111.

Restrepo Sanín, Juliana. "'I Don't Belong Here': Understanding Hostile Spaces." *Journal of Women, Politics & Policy* 40, no. 1 (2019): 112–121. https://doi.org/10.1080/1554477X.2019.1563417.

Shames, Shauna L., and Tess Wise. "Gender, Diversity, and Methods in Political Science: A Theory of Selection and Survival Biases." *PS: Political Science & Politics* 50, no. 3 (2017): 811–823. https://doi.org/10.1017/S104909651700066X.

Sirnate, Vasundhara. "Positionality, Personal Insecurity, and Female Empathy in Security Studies Research." *PS: Political Science & Politics* 47, no. 2 (2014): 398–401. https://doi.org/doi:10.1017/S1049096514000286.

Soedirgo, Jessica, and Aarie Glas. "Toward Active Reflexivity: Positionality and Practice in the Production of Knowledge." *PS: Political Science & Politics* 53, no. 3 (2020): 527–531. https://doi.org/10.1017/S1049096519002233.

Teele, Dawn Langan, and Kathleen Thelen. "Gender in the Journals: Publication Patterns in Political Science." *PS: Political Science & Politics* 50, no. 2 (2017): 433–447. https://doi.org/10.1017/S1049096516002985.

Turner, Robin L. "Remembering Lee Ann in South Africa: Meta-Data and Reflexive Research Practice." *Qualitative and Multi-Method Research* 16, no. 1 (2018): 48–50. https://doi.org/10.5281/zenodo.2562288.

Yom, Sean. "Becoming Othered, Thrice: Race, Positionality, and Fieldwork." Paper presented at the Annual Meeting of the American Political Science Association, virtual/Seattle, WA, September 30–October 3, 2021.

26
Mental Health, Identity, and Fieldwork

Dana El Kurd and Calla Hummel

Descriptive Overview

Fieldwork is an invaluable part of the research process for scholars across all subfields within political science. The data collection that fieldwork affords enriches research findings and facilitates greater expertise. Such fieldwork can take place both near and far, at international destinations or within communities closer to the researcher's home. There are many resources on how to approach fieldwork with care, making sure to prepare properly, understand the power and positionality of the researcher before engaging with research subjects, and answering the ethical questions that fieldwork raises.[1] Part of this increased awareness includes the costs of undertaking such work on the researcher and their mental health.[2]

Academia comes with its own array of issues and can be uniquely harmful to mental health in ways other professions are not.[3] This is particularly the case for graduate students, who struggle with the precarity of their position on top of the other mental tolls that academia imposes.[4] Engaging in fieldwork can exacerbate these trends, as field researchers often leave their home support networks, try to gather data quickly and effectively, and grapple with the added pressure of publishing and showing value in an increasingly competitive academic environment.[5]

Fieldwork in violent or repressive contexts and recently active conflict zones poses particular challenges to mental health, but so does fieldwork in less intense or overtly dangerous environments. Danger, risks, and stressors can be reduced or magnified by the researcher's positionality and identity.[6] Research experiences can create secondary trauma, that is, trauma responses and stress from listening to or engaging with subjects who have themselves been the target of violence, repression, or exclusion.[7] Symptoms might include disturbing thoughts, issues with sleep, as well as clinical conditions such as depression.[8] This occurs for scholars even when they are able to maintain their own physical well-being and safety throughout the duration of their fieldwork stay. Research shows that one of the best ways to manage and resolve secondary trauma is to prepare for it and process the experiences when they happen.[9]

Fieldworkers need to carefully plan for and implement their projects with attention to their mental health. This means not only ensuring that the logistics of travel and accommodation and contacts are arranged but also having a clear understanding of the realities of fieldwork before research commences and the ways in which a researcher might face unique challenges given their background. Importantly, careful fieldwork means setting a plan for supporting the researcher's mental health when fieldwork issues inevitably arise.

The Mental Toll of Fieldwork

For just about every researcher, fieldwork will involve a degree of stress and isolation that the researcher must actively work to address in order to preserve their mental health and ensure successful fieldwork. Many people find it stressful and nerve-racking to be in a new place and engage with strangers, often while navigating a new cultural context. Researchers may develop burnout in addition to myriad mental health conditions such as depression and anxiety. Scholars who have preexisting mental health conditions may find their ability to manage them impeded by the logistics or added stress of fieldwork circumstances. In this section, we will address how mental health pertains to different types of data collection during fieldwork, the emotional toll of sensitive topics, and the positionality of the researcher.

First, it should be noted that qualitative research methods such as ethnography can be particularly grueling.[10] Not only do researchers come "face-to-face with people who have experienced trauma," but such methods also "require researchers to remain immersed in the data over lengthy periods, through the iterative processes of data collection, transcription, coding, analysis and paper writing."[11] These methods increase the likelihood that researchers will vicariously experience other people's trauma and develop secondary trauma through the course of research. This workplace exposure to trauma is similar to conditions that other professionals, like journalists, social workers, and teachers, face.[12]

Williamson et al. note that research which attempts to engage "with people" rather than be conducted "on people," lends itself to greater immersion as well as greater emotional entanglement in the field site.[13] It is for this reason that secondary trauma has been highlighted as a threat to mental health for researchers involved at all levels, from professors to graduate students and research team members.[14] This can happen both within what we traditionally think of as "difficult" field sites, that is, sites of active or recently active conflict or violence, as well as sites seen as safe or stable but where a researcher is studying a sensitive topic.

A topic's sensitivity also varies with the identity and position of the researcher. A researcher whose identity is related to their area of study might bear a greater emotional toll during fieldwork. Pearce suggests that such research might have more of a traumatic impact on the scholar than if their identity was not at risk or if their identity was not the topic of discussion.[15] Even doing fieldwork in one's own country or close to one's institution can take a toll on researcher mental health. Ansoms notes that "doing research 'at home' intensifies its emotional challenges" because "it mingles 'on duty' and 'off duty' situations, with (barely) any opportunity to escape from 'the field.'"[16] This makes the "emotional toll of research" more intense, given that the topic impacts the researcher's life directly or the lives of those they care about.

These issues are often not addressed directly in academia because in our profession we have a tendency to describe the researcher's role as "neutral" and flatten the distinctions as well as varying lived experiences of those with different identities. As Nobles notes, "whether we care to admit it or not," researchers "are participants, not detached observers."[17] A Black scholar studying a topic—even if not directly about Black politics or racism—will bring fresh perspective to the research. Studying one's own community or a topic of personal relevance has been found to yield "particularly robust scholarship," as a result of, rather than in spite of, the researcher's identity.[18] Nevertheless, marginalized scholars face different obstacles in the field than a white scholar would.

Researchers from historically excluded communities will likely experience more issues with access to the field site and to interlocutors, more doubt about research credentials, and microaggressions as well as more blatant forms of racism and prejudice.[19] For example, Christian Davenport notes that while he was working on cases of repression against African Americans, sending his white graduate student to American police stations for information yielded much more data than when he attempted to access information at the police stations himself as a Black professor.[20] Non-American white scholars studying American racism have found the opposite: that their positionality opened doors for them rather than restricted their access. While interlocutors might have been suspicious of the goals of American researchers, being an outsider "disarmed" their suspicion of the researcher most of the time.[21] Paradoxically, doing research on a scholar's own community—especially when a scholar is not white—is often denigrated as being less valid, rigorous, or objective than if a (white) outsider had implemented the same research.[22] This assumption is what NiCole Buchanan refers to as "epistemic exclusion," which can have the effect of leaving someone "bewildered by the difficulties" they experience, "unable to pinpoint the cause, internalizing the blame, and questioning (their) abilities."[23]

All of this can wear on a researcher, leading to burnout, unfavorable self-evaluation, increased stress, and an array of other mental and physical symptoms. Carter, writing on the traumatic impact of racism, notes that the "potentially cumulative nature of racism" means "a seemingly innocuous or minor event may trigger a stress reaction."[24] The literature on this is rich. One study finds "racial minority individuals may sustain a lasting psychological injury from a traumatic racial victimization,"[25] which includes a strong and direct correlation with clinical depression and negative affect.[26] There are many other studies in this vein that find corroborating evidence.[27]

One of the authors—El Kurd, an Arab American woman conducting research in the Arab world, often in Palestine, her country of origin, was already aware that her personal safety would be more compromised as a result of her identity. Her dissertation research examined the connections between the Israeli occupation, American intervention, and Palestinian protests and resistance. Fieldwork research entailed conducting interviews with the Palestinian security apparatus, running a public opinion poll within the Palestinian territories, and observing the activism and protests of Palestinian opposition parties and movements.

During fieldwork for this project, she realized that she would not have the privilege associated with American or Western citizenship, unlike her white colleagues conducting research at the same site. For instance, Israeli officials—within the Israeli army, border security, and those working within organizations tasked with monitoring Palestinians in Jerusalem—would treat her as an Arab, discounting her U.S. citizenship, and she was at greater risk of Israeli violence and repression. She also could not "get away" from the difficult conditions in the Palestinian territories and spend a few days on the beach or in the Tel Aviv bubble, as many of her white peers often did. There were clear differences between her experience and the experiences of white colleagues, even those studying similar topics.

But it came as a surprise to find that her identity would sometimes be an obstacle even with other Palestinians, members of her own community. She quickly realized that they were less likely to provide access to her than to white researchers working alongside her at the same time. Directors and senior members of research institutions and universities would be very friendly and personable with white researchers, while El Kurd found them difficult to contact. She would often have to meet with secretaries and more junior members of the organization to try to get the same information. Members of her own community occasionally doubted her intentions and questioned her credentials, making it considerably more difficult to engage with interlocutors or establish contacts with relevant people. Being a white researcher clearly implied importance, research rigor, and impact in a way that being Palestinian did not. Moreover, being plugged in to the community she was studying meant that her interlocutors sometimes assumed her political positions or motivations because they knew her family and/or background.

An added layer that played a role in fieldwork was her gender identity, which meant male research assistants were often treated with more respect than she was as a recently graduated PhD. While these issues were cropping up, it was difficult not to internalize these experiences and assume that they spoke to her value as a researcher, which led to negative self-evaluation, anxiety, and burnout.[28]

Mitigation Strategies

In order to mitigate these issues, researchers should take steps to safeguard their mental health prior to engaging in fieldwork and maintain check-ins throughout their fieldwork stay. We want to emphasize that while our focus in this chapter is on fieldwork, academia presents mental health challenges before, during, and after fieldwork. Developing proactive mental health practices during fieldwork can help researchers cope with academia in general.

Prior to fieldwork, we recommend that researchers establish a mental health plan, similar to what Hummel and El Kurd have outlined.[29] This entails creating a plan for how a researcher will access medication, therapy, and health professionals during fieldwork, and sharing that plan with people close to the researcher whom the researcher trusts. We recommend that researchers establish a relationship with a therapist if one does not already exist. There are a number of remote options that have made therapy cheaper and easier to access around the world.[30]

For example, one of the authors, Hummel, manages an anxiety disorder and is in recovery from alcohol abuse. When xy does research in other countries, xy takes several months of prescription medication (and checks current regulations about bringing medication into field sites with a prescription).[31] Xy also switches to biweekly telehealth sessions with a therapist. The author makes a list of activities that xy enjoys and that xy can do anywhere. Xy also tries to fill up xyr evenings because xy knows that isolation in the evening is a major trigger for xyr alcohol consumption. The author tells xyr partner and close friends about plans and checks in regularly to prevent relapse with alcohol abuse. The researcher also has a list of local health professionals, a dentist, a physical therapist, and a primary care doctor, which local colleagues have recommended in the past.

Second, having clear and manageable expectations for fieldwork—including a minimal list of goals as well as backup plans for contingencies—will help researchers avoid burnout. Researchers should plan frequent breaks during fieldwork and practice boundary-setting around weekends and vacations. In the case of graduate students, this is where mentors bear a responsibility for advising on what realistic expectations look like. Moreover, both the researcher and/or their advisors and mentors should facilitate success by reaching out to contacts in the field prior to travel, setting up institutional affiliations whenever possible, and providing as much structure as possible upon arrival.

The implications of identity on mental health should be discussed and planned for prior to fieldwork, preferably not by the researcher alone. Mentors and institutions have a responsibility to their graduate students and researchers to acknowledge that these disparities exist as well as to provide resources to mitigate them. These include trainings, support groups, equitable research funding, and advisors who understand how these issues might impact fieldwork productivity.

Third, peer support networks are key.[32] These include other researchers working on the same topic area, within the same field site, and local researchers or individuals with similar interests (not necessarily to the research itself; one author joined a rugby team at a field site). For junior researchers, we strongly recommend creating community with a graduate student cohort, especially with those engaging in fieldwork at the same time. These networks can act as a crucial support when fieldwork obstacles accumulate. These networks of like-minded scholars can also help to troubleshoot and problem-solve.

For instance, when preparing for dissertation fieldwork in La Paz, Bolivia, one of the authors—Hummel—asked for advice from xyr advisor, who had worked in La Paz years before, and a graduate student in another department who had recently returned from La Paz. The advisor provided a list of local academics, and the graduate student shared a contact at a local university that helped establish a visiting scholar affiliation. Both sets of contacts were central in establishing a social network of researchers, finding local lectures and events, and setting up useful resources, including research credentials and library access. These contacts and networks helped the author transition into fieldwork and develop lasting relationships with Bolivian academics.

Finally, local community support can be essential to successful fieldwork. If a researcher approaches their relationship with their interlocutors not as one of extraction but as one of partnership,[33] the researcher will likely be better supported in terms of maintaining both physical safety as well as mental health. Local colleagues can share tips and cultural expectations, as well as referrals to dentists, primary care doctors, physical therapists, pharmacists, and local hospitals.

Because of this network approach, one of the authors (El Kurd) was able to turn to community members within her field site when issues with documentation, and her legal status, arose. Community members also ensured her personal safety on a number of occasions, guiding her through checkpoints and transporting her to hard-to-access locations. These were not just occasions of logistic support but also helped ease a great deal of anxiety that came with being in an unfamiliar place.

Potential Problems

The premise itself—maintaining mental health while in the field—portends the potential problems at hand. Without a rigorous mental health plan, a system of support, and social contacts to assist in navigating a new place, researchers may become isolated and unproductive or slip into harmful coping strategies. We obviously want to avoid that.

Sometimes it is difficult to tell when your mental health condition is deteriorating. The researcher should reflect on how they are likely to respond to stress or isolation. Reflecting on personal responses can help a researcher pinpoint what actions (or lack thereof) indicate they are reaching a breaking point, or tip off their support network that intervention is necessary. This looks different for each person; some people might respond to the mental toll of fieldwork by withdrawing or neglecting responsibilities, while others might experience worsening anxiety and panic attacks. Either way, proactive planning and reflection on this point can help avoid this problem.

Local support can be particularly useful for maintaining accountability mechanisms regarding productivity and output, as well as providing a space to commiserate. Such community support can assist with issues of isolation as well as logistics, as previously outlined.

Conclusion

Mental health considerations should be a priority when planning and executing fieldwork. We can protect and preserve our mental health with tried and tested strategies, as we've described. We want to emphasize that it is the responsibility of mentors to normalize mental health concerns and strategies to mitigate risks. Institutions should provide resources to graduate students and faculty members who engage in fieldwork, including support groups and increased access to mental health professionals. We train researchers in research ethics, we provide methodological training, and we emphasize language acquisition; we should also train graduate students and each other to take mental health seriously in fieldwork preparation.

Notes

1. Kapiszewski, MacLean, and Read, *Field Research in Political Science*; Driscoll and Schuster, "Spies Like Us"; Cronin-Furman and Lake, "Ethics Abroad."
2. Hummel and El Kurd, "Mental Health and Fieldwork"; Loyle and Simoni, "Researching Under Fire."
3. Dutt-Ballerstadt, "Institutional Betrayals"; Grollman, "Trauma on Display."
4. Levecque et al., "Work Organization and Mental Health Problems in PhD Students"; Evans et al., "Evidence for a Mental Health Crisis in Graduate Education."
5. Driscoll and Schuster, "Spies Like Us."
6. Loyle and Simoni, "Researching Under Fire."
7. Browne, Evangeli, and Greenberg, "Trauma-Related Guilt and Post-Traumatic Stress among Journalists"; Cieslak et al., "A Meta-Analysis of the Relationship between Job Burnout and Secondary Traumatic Stress among Workers with Indirect Exposure to Trauma."
8. Warden, "Feet of Clay"; Pearce, "A Methodology for the Marginalised."
9. Hargrave, Scott, and McDowall, "To Resolve or Not to Resolve"; Trippany, White Kress, and Wilcoxon, "Preventing Vicarious Trauma."
10. See Chapter 20 in this volume.
11. Williamson et al., "Secondary Trauma."
12. Browne, Evangeli, and Greenberg, "Trauma-Related Guilt and Post-Traumatic Stress among Journalists"; van der Merwe and Hunt, "Secondary Trauma among Trauma Researchers"; Loyle and Simoni, "Researching Under Fire." It is important to note that the trauma mentioned here, faced by researchers, is different from the trauma that research subjects may face while participating in our fieldwork. Chapters 11 and 18 of this volume address the latter type directly.
13. Williamson et al., "Secondary Trauma."
14. Loyle and Simoni, "Researching Under Fire."
15. Pearce, "A Methodology for the Marginalised."

16. Ansoms, "Research in Times of Crisis."
17. Nobles, "Race and the Study of a Racial Democracy," 242.
18. See examples in Ayoub and Rose, "In Defense of 'Me' Studies."
19. See also Chapter 3.
20. Davenport, "Researching While Black."
21. King, "Race and the Study of a Racial Democracy," 245–246.
22. Ayoub and Rose, "In Defense of "Me" Studies"; Rivadulla and Luna, "Can I Pick Your Brain for a Minute?"
23. Buchanan, "Researching While Black (and Female)," 93.
24. Carter, "Racism and Psychological and Emotional Injury," cited in Okazaki, "Impact of Racism on Ethnic Minority Mental Health," 104–105.
25. Okazaki, "Impact of Racism on Ethnic Minority Mental Health," 104.
26. Nadal et al., "The Impact of Racial Microaggressions on Mental Health."
27. See the literature reviewed in Pearce, "A Methodology for the Marginalised" for more details.
28. Chapter 3 in this volume on positionality reviews these issues more thoroughly.
29. Hummel and El Kurd, "Mental Health and Fieldwork."
30. Chandrashekar, "Do Mental Health Mobile Apps Work."
31. Xy/xyr here are gender neutral pronouns, used by nonbinary or genderqueer individuals.
32. Cassese and Holman, "Writing Groups as Models for Peer Mentorship among Female Faculty in Political Science."
33. For more, see Chapter 14.

Recommended Readings

Advancing Research on Conflict (ARC) Consortium, "Vulnerability, Emotions, and Trauma" bibliography. https://advancingconflictresearch.com/vet
    This consortium compiles resources related to fieldwork in "fragile and violence-affected environments," including a bibliography on "Vulnerability, Emotions, and Trauma" research that can help scholars preserve their mental health.
Dart Center for Journalism and Trauma. "Working with Traumatic Imagery." August 12, 2014. https://dartcenter.org/content/working-with-traumatic-imagery.
    The Dart Center for Journalism and Trauma has created a resource for researchers who regularly work with disturbing imagery, with tips on how to reduce the "trauma load."
Krause, Peter, and Ora Szekely, eds. *Stories from the Field: A Guide to Navigating Fieldwork in Political Science*. New York: Columbia University Press, 2020.
    This edited volume contains a number of relevant chapters on the topic of mental health, identity, and how to navigate uncomfortable experiences during fieldwork.

References

Ansoms, An. "Research in Times of Crisis: Caring for Researchers' Mental Health in the Covid-19 Era." Insights from the Social Sciences. Social Science Research Council, May 21, 2020. https://items.ssrc.org/covid-19-and-the-social-sciences/social-research-and-insecurity/research-in-times-of-crisis-caring-for-researchers-mental-health-in-the-covid-19-era/.
Ayoub, Phillip, and Deondra Rose. "In Defense of 'Me' Studies." Inside Higher Ed, April 14, 2016, https://www.insidehighered.com/views/2016/04/14/scholarly-importance-studying-issues-related-ones-own-identity-essay?utm_source=Inside%2BHigher%2BEd&utm_campaign=379e943367-DNU20160414&utm_medium=email&utm_term=0_1fcbc04421-379e943367-197324337#.Vx8NS.

Browne, Tess, Michael Evangeli, and Neil Greenberg. "Trauma-Related Guilt and Post-Traumatic Stress among Journalists." *Journal of Traumatic Stress* 25, no 2 (2012): 207–210.

Buchanan, NiCole T. "Researching While Black (and Female)." *Women & Therapy* 43, nos. 1–2 (November 19, 2019): 91–111. https://doi.org/10.1080/02703149.2019.1684681.

Carter, Robert T. "Racism and Psychological and Emotional Injury: Recognizing and Assessing Race-Based Traumatic Stress." *Counseling Psychologist* 35, no. 1 (January 2007): 13–105. https://doi.org/10.1177/0011000006292033.

Cassese, Erin, and Mirya R. Holman. "Writing Groups as Models for Peer Mentorship among Female Faculty in Political Science." *PS: Political Science & Politics* 51, no 2 (2018): 401–405.

Chandrashekar, Pooja. "Do Mental Health Mobile Apps Work: Evidence and Recommendations for Designing High-Efficacy Mental Health Mobile Apps." *MHealth* 4 (2018): 1–4. https://doi.org/10.21037/mhealth.2018.03.02.

Cieslak, Roman, Kotaro Shoji, Allison Douglas, Erin Melville, Aleksandra Luszczynska, and Charles C. Benight. "A Meta-Analysis of the Relationship between Job Burnout and Secondary Traumatic Stress among Workers with Indirect Exposure to Trauma." *Psychological Services* 11, no 1 (2014): 75.

Cronin-Furman, Kate, and Milli Lake. "Ethics Abroad: Fieldwork in Fragile and Violent Contexts." *PS: Political Science & Politics* 51, no 3 (2018): 607–614.

Davenport, Christian. "Researching While Black: Why Conflict Research Needs More African Americans (Maybe)." Political Violence at a Glance, February 5, 2020. https://politicalviolenceataglance.org/2013/04/10/researching-while-black-why-conflict-research-needs-more-african-americans-maybe/.

Driscoll, Jesse, and Caroline Schuster. "Spies Like Us." *Ethnography* 19, no. 3 (2018): 411–430.

Dutt-Ballerstadt, Reshmi. "Institutional Betrayals: In Our Own Words." Inside Higher Ed, March 6 2020. www.insidehighered.com/advice/2020/03/06/Underrepresented-faculty-members-share-real-reasons-they-have-left-various.

Evans, Teresa M., Lindsay Bira, Jazmin Beltran Gastelum, L. Todd Weiss, and Nathan L. Vanderford. "Evidence for a Mental Health Crisis in Graduate Education." *Nature Biotechnology* 36, no. 3 (March 2018): 282–284. https://doi.org/10.1038/nbt.4089.

Grollman, Eric. "Trauma on Display." Inside Higher Ed, September 29, 2015. https://www.insidehighered.com/advice/2015/09/29/essay-trauma-associated-graduate-school.

Hargrave, Petrina, Kate M. Scott, and John McDowall. "To Resolve or Not to Resolve: Past Trauma and Secondary Traumatic Stress in Volunteer Crisis Workers." *Journal of Trauma Practice* 5, no 2 (2006): 37–55.

Hummel, Calla, and Dana El Kurd. "Mental Health and Fieldwork." *PS: Political Science & Politics* 54, no. 1 (2021): 121–125.

Kapiszewski, Diana, Lauren M. MacLean, and Benjamin L. Read. *Field Research in Political Science: Practices and Principles*. Cambridge: Cambridge University Press, 2015.

King, Desmond. "Studying Racial inequality in the United States from the Outside." In *Stories from the Field: A Guide to Navigating Fieldwork in Political Science*, edited by Peter Krause and Ora Szekely, 245–254. New York: Columbia University Press, 2020.

Levecque, Katia, Frederik Anseel, Alain De Beuckelaer, Johan Van der Heyden, and Lydia Gisle. "Work Organization and Mental Health Problems in PhD Students," *Research Policy* 46, no. 4 (2017): 868–879. https://doi.org/10.1016/j.respol.2017.02.008.

Loyle, Cyanne E., and Alicia Simoni. "Researching Under Fire: Political Science and Researcher Trauma." *PS: Political Science & Politics* 50, no. 1 (2017): 141–145.

Nadal, Kevin L., Katie E. Griffin, Yinglee Wong, Sahran Hamit, and Morgan Rasmus. "The Impact of Racial Microaggressions on Mental Health: Counseling Implications for Clients of Color." *Journal of Counseling & Development* 92, no. 1 (January 2014): 57–66. https://doi.org/10.1002/j.1556-6676.2014.00130.x.

Nobles, Melissa. "Race and the Study of a Racial Democracy," In *Stories from the Field: A Guide to Navigating Fieldwork in Political Science*, edited by Peter Krause and Ora Szekely, 238–244. New York: Columbia University Press, 2020.

Okazaki, Sumie. "Impact of Racism on Ethnic Minority Mental Health." *Perspectives on Psychological Science* 4, no. 1 (January 2009): 103–107.

Pearce, Ruth. "A Methodology for the Marginalised: Surviving Oppression and Traumatic Fieldwork in the Neoliberal Academy." *Sociology* 54, no. 4 (March 9, 2020): 806–824. https://doi.org/10.1177/0038038520904918.

Rivadulla, María José Alvarez, and Juan Pablo Luna. "Can I Pick Your Brain for a Minute?" Razones y personas: Repensando Uruguay, August 11, 2019. http://www.razonesypersonas.com/2019/08/can-i-pick-your-brain-for-minute.html.

Trippany, Robyn, Victoria E. White Kress, and S. Allen Wilcoxon. "Preventing Vicarious Trauma: What Counselors Should Know When Working with Trauma Survivors." *Journal of Counseling & Development* 82, no. 1 (2004): 31–37.

van der Merwe, Amelia, and Xanthe Hunt. "Secondary Trauma among Trauma Researchers: Lessons from the Field." *Psychological Trauma: Theory, Research, Practice, and Policy* 11, no 1 (2019): 10–18.

Warden, Tara. "Feet of Clay: Confronting Emotional Challenges in Ethnographic Experience." *Journal of Organizational Ethnography* 2, no. 2 (2013): 150–172. https://doi.org/10.1108/joe-09-2012-0037.

Williamson, Emma, Alison Gregory, Hilary Abrahams, Nadia Aghtaie, Sarah-Jane Walker, and Marianne Hester. "Secondary Trauma: Emotional Safety in Sensitive Research." *Journal of Academic Ethics* 18, no. 1 (July 2020): 58. https://doi.org/10.1007/s10805-019-09348-y.

27
Navigating Ethical Issues and Choices in the Field

Lauren Duquette-Rury

Most qualitative researchers in the social sciences would, I believe, affirm the importance of ethics to the overall quality of the work we do. Procedurally we must. Researchers working with human participants must adhere to the requirements of institutional review boards (IRBs) and relevant committees to proceed with data collection. But following the principles of procedural ethics does not preclude "ethics in practice" from happening—the ethical tensions, contradictions, and conflicts that emerge when doing research.[1] When observing people and making sense of their lifeworld, how do we recognize and react to discrete and polyvalent ethical issues when they surface during fieldwork? What informs our decisions when we are not sure what to do but we want to do right? To affirm our ethical selves and recognize our study participants' full humanity, I invite us to consider how a relational *ethics of care* practice may chart the course.

Building on principles of procedural ethics, including respect for persons, beneficence, and justice encased in the IRB process, I locate an ethics of care practice in reflexivity, context sensitivity, and the five pillars of relational care: attentiveness (caring about), responsibility (caring for), responsiveness (care receiving), competence (care giving), and solidarity (caring with).[2] When an ethics of care is rooted in relations and situations, the primary unit of moral concern is the self-in-relation to others. An ethics of care practice offers researchers a set of questions, strategies, and skills to help them navigate what Guillemin and Gillam call "ethically important moments," those difficult, often subtle, and usually unpredictable situations, relationships, and issues that arise when qualitative researchers are enmeshed in the recruitment, data collection, and analysis phase of their studies. These ethical moments appear after research studies have received the IRB stamp of approval. Ethics in practice are important because anticipating all ethical issues before fieldwork is a fool's errand and because specifying risks to participants in the planning stages of research puts the cart before the proverbial horse for some researchers. Grounded theory ethnographers, for example, rely on field observations to make sense of people's lived experiences, and these observations are what inform their risk assessments to study groups.[3] When there is no prescription for how we are to behave under circumstances of uncertainty, an ethics of care is a guide to traverse the bumpy, albeit enlivening terrain of qualitative research. As Reich argues, an ethic of care is not a new expectation of qualitative research; rather, "it identifies core tenets of the method done correctly."[4]

Regardless of the methodological approach we use and our awareness of ethical ambiguities afoot, ethical considerations are implicated in all kinds of empirical research, from seed idea to publication. Whether we study human behaviors as numerical tabulations in surveys, field experiments, and networks, as text on a screen and documents in archives, as attitudes or subjective experiences recounted in dialog, or as observations made in situ, what varies, Lee Ann Fujii observes, is the distance between researcher and participants.[5] It is not our normative commitment to ethical practice. Yet many researchers assume that ethics should and do matter more for qualitative researchers given the proximity we have to the people we learn from. I agree. After all, our presence in field sites and conversations with participants alters the interactional dynamics in their social worlds. Our presence introduces risk and, potentially, harm into their lives. But all methodologists should value care ethics because the practice improves the researcher-participant relationship. Care ethics also improves the reputation, trust, and value of academic institutional partnerships with community groups and organizations. Qualitative researchers should practice an ethics of care because it works to mitigate unwitting harm, distress, and the infliction of vicarious and secondary trauma to study participants and research team members. Adopting a relational care practice alerts us to our impulses to extract and misrepresent others' stories and reproduce inequalities in service of our own professional goals.

I am not the first to champion an ethics of care approach; it has been the methodological provenance of autoethnography, communication studies, and nursing. Relational care, for example, is the centerpiece of feminist ethics and a branch of moral philosophy. Relational care ethics recognizes the value of "mutual respect, dignity, and connectedness between researcher and researched," while situational ethics focuses on a specific context and the impact of our presence on communities we study.[6] An ethics of care practice is no magic wand for eliminating all blunders and ethical missteps in the field. But acting from the principles of care offers a set of tools to recognize and respond to ambiguous moments when they do arise. Even the most sensitive, present-oriented researchers experience challenging moments during fieldwork and need strategies to draw on accordingly.

Who am I to offer these questions and suggestions? I am writing this piece from a place of what sociologist Jodi O'Brien, invoking Gloria Anzaldúa, calls *academic nepantla*—the experience of being in between, inhabiting the liminal space between worlds, where "going inward" into uneasy territory allows for transformations and deeper understandings of the research we do on others and ourselves.[7] I offer these reflections from my position as an academic researcher who has conducted multisite fieldwork in Mexico with individuals and groups in which I am an outsider. I also collaborate with community-based organizations to collect data for mutual benefit and potential policy interventions. Finally, I write from my experiences as a study participant in research based on my membership in a vulnerable group: survivors of childhood abuse and trauma. Occupying the space of both researcher and "researched" has allowed me to consider and share some difficult choices I made in the field; it also informs my intention to support colleagues and students when they encounter their own "ethically ambiguous moments." By pushing us "to think what we are doing" in the practice of qualitative research, I am also, in a sense, trying to protect myself and others like me from unintentional harm that accompanies asking about and observing others' lives to produce knowledge.

I start by providing a brief overview of procedural ethics and how they differ from ethics in practice. Next, I describe how researchers lean on reflexivity and mindful awareness to inform their practice before turning to a discussion of how a relational ethics of care applies to qualitative methods. I then draw on my fieldwork experiences and collaborations with community-based organizations to show how a care practice provides a touchstone when ethical issues surface. Finally, I examine the limits of a relational care approach and suggest other avenues that may guide purposive action.

Procedural Ethics and Ethics in Practice

In a remarkably generative article, Marilys Guillemin and Lynn Gillam offer a framework that differentiates between *procedural ethics* and *ethics in practice*. Procedural ethics, also known as categorical ethics, refers to the ethical principles formulated for biomedical research (usually in the quantitative tradition) applied to qualitative social science. For research involving human subjects, researchers must convince relevant review committees that they will follow basic ethical principles, including respect for persons (acknowledge individual autonomy), beneficence (protect participants from harm), and justice (determine fairness in the distribution of benefits and burdens).[8] Incumbent on researchers in review protocols is a clear articulation of procedures for protecting, recruiting, and selecting participants fairly, ensuring their voluntary, informed consent and their confidentiality and privacy. I think it is fair to say, as Bosk and De Vries plainly do, that "none of us truly objects to the goals of the IRB research—we all wish our subjects to be treated with respect, protected from harm, and saved from embarrassing exposure,"[9] however onerous the review process may be.

What is clarifying about the Guillemin and Gillam piece is their exposition of the limits of formal ethical review. Their call for greater attention to and deeper exploration of what constitutes an ethical research practice is resonant since many of us have had little relevant training and mentorship beyond the IRB. Concentrating on ethics in practice is also necessary because procedural ethics focuses almost exclusively on individual human subjects, overlooking ethical considerations in situational or community contexts. When qualitative methodologists discuss the prickly, confusing ethical moments they encounter, it illuminates lurking risks of harm, power, representation, group vulnerabilities, inequalities, and the politics of knowledge production.[10]

Critical to researchers' ethical research practice is reflexive praxis at all stages of the research (see also Chapter 3). A reflexive researcher is aware of the consequences of their presence in communities, especially those in which they are conspicuous outsiders, and they commit to transparency in the reporting of their research engagement.[11] As Fine and coauthors discuss, staying attuned to who we are as we coproduce others' stories helps us be aware of how the public and policymakers may "receive, distort, and misread our data."[12] Misrepresentation happens when researchers center themselves and their proximity and intimacy with those they deem "dangerous" or "pitied," thereby stripping them of their agency and multidimensionality in service of professional ascent. These kinds of one-dimensional, often stereotypical portrayals of marginalized others fall prey to what Mario Small calls "rhetorical exploitation." Rhetorical exploitation occurs when researchers either purposely or unwittingly improve their own representation by worsening the representation of the other. It also involves reifying troubling tropes in the public imagination about communities that are already marginalized and vulnerable.[13]

Being reflexive and transparent about one's positionality helps avoid rhetorical exploitation. Sociologist and criminologist Reuben J. Miller offers a master class on presenting participants in all their complexity and full humanity. In his book *Halfway Home,* readers learn how abuse, poverty, and trauma often preceded participants' substance abuse, criminal offenses, and incarceration. Miller provides readers the full narrative arc of his participants' lives. Readers come to experience their joys, flaws, and frailties, their network of relationships and teams of care, the systems they are attached to, their agency, the calculus of their decision-making, and their rich and painful histories before, during, and after their prison sentences. Without sanitizing participants' lives or glorifying his "gift of proximity" to the carceral state, Miller describes and accepts his own vulnerabilities while sitting with others' joy and pain. Miller reflects on and checks his own interpretations of others' stories with care. He is but one example of many thoughtful scholars relying on reflexivity and care ethics (without naming it necessarily as such) to portray participants in their multivocality.[14]

Mindful awareness is another approach that researchers use to be present for and respond to ethical quandaries. González-López describes "mindful ethics" as a present-oriented attitude that makes researchers aware of how peering into and asking intimate questions about others' lives may cause them pain and suffering and, in turn, cause retraumatization and secondary trauma.[15] Mindful awareness helps researchers stay alert to participants' trauma responses; it helps research team members, too, who also bear the emotional and psychological heft of study relationships. In her research on sexual violence and incest in Mexico, for example, González-López's mindful ethics informed her field preparation and how she communicated with adult participants who experienced incestuous relationships. González-López had become a mother figure for interviewees, someone who listened to their stories with respect and compassion. A young woman who had gone to great lengths to be interviewed misrepresented her age because she wanted to share her untold story. Unable to interview the 16-year-old because of age restrictions in the study protocol, González-López faced an ethically ambiguous moment: should she interview the person anyway? Mindfully, she explained that she could not formally interview her because of the study's age restrictions, but she listened to her story off the record to prevent her additional pain. González-López's mindfulness attuned her to the distress that could be caused had she either misled the young woman and proceeded with the interview as if her story would be included or declined to speak with her at all. Instead, the exertion of care spared the young woman more discomfort.

González-López recounts other ways mindfulness made her more aware of her study participants' needs. For example, she engaged in pre-interviews so potential participants could personally assess whether her therapy training was sufficient to receive their stories with care. She volunteered with organizations of mental health professionals and women's rights advocates to not only build trust with the organizations that helped recruit participants but also to ensure that her research questions were in service of the communities' needs. She also formally shared the study results at workshops and seminars with her organizational partners and incorporated their experiential knowledge into the findings. A mindful, reflexive approach helped González-López resist the "intellectual colonization" that may occur when researchers enter and exit the field.

An Ethics of Care Practice

An ethics of care practice can guide our choices during "ethically important moments" during qualitative research. But what is it? And what does it mean to practice care? Care ethics is a relational ontology with roots in feminist thought. Psychologist Carol Gilligan's groundbreaking research on feminist ethics, Nel Noddings's on caring and moral education, and Sara Ruddick's moral care philosophy in the 1980s jump-started a vibrant research tradition on a relational ethic of care.[16] Care ethics focuses on the relationship between the care receiver and the care giver. Political theorist Jean Tronto describes it as an approach that starts from the reality that all human beings need care and give care to others.[17] Caring for others means one has a regard or inclination for them. Caring also means being charged with the welfare or protection of someone. Caring can be viewed as a manifestation of behavior (acts of showing care), carefully considered inaction, commitment (the potential for caring), and caring attitudes. Taken together, an ethics of care has five moral pillars: (1) attentiveness (caring about), (2) responsibility (caring for), (3) responsiveness (care receiving), (4) competence (care giving), and (5) solidarity (caring with).[18] Based on these principles, care ethics prioritizes active communication, including listening, feeling, identifying, and making connections with participants in our studies.[19]

When we are faced with ethical concerns while doing research, care principles work to displace our own interest and sit with the reality of the other. Care ethics help de-automate our thoughts and actions to make us more aware of potentially harmful situations. What we do when making ethical choices, Noddings says, depends on the constellation of conditions that are viewed through both the eyes of the one caring and the eyes of the cared for, since not everyone shares the same values.[20] Starting from a place of caring, Ellis says, informs "which questions we ask, which secrets to keep, and which truths are worth telling"[21] and orients us toward moral action. To be sure, caring is work. It feels awkward at times and can be mentally draining. There are limits to an ethic of care that I discuss shortly. But it is worth a reminder that conducting research with human participants is a privilege and not a right. It calls on us to be critically introspective, that is, sensitive to how our life experiences govern how we relate to and behave toward our participants. It asks us to imagine or at least anticipate how we would feel if we were on the receiving end of our own communications, actions, and questions.

An exhaustive list of ways of caring during fieldwork is impractical. But I do believe there is a strategy for practicing an ethics of care that is rooted in the five pillars. I derive the strategy from what psychologist George Bonanno and colleagues call the *flexibility sequence*.[22] Here's how it works: After we have done our homework and prepared for recruitment and data collection (stage 1), we engage in context sensitivity during fieldwork (stage 2)—decoding and staying present for contextual clues (verbal and nonverbal) during our face-to-face exchanges or observations in particular moments or situations. If we sense any tensions, red flags, or participants' concerns, we assess whether more information is needed, and then determine if we need to respond. Next, we consult our response repertoires (stage 3) to consider possible actions; in other words, we assess what we can do. The range of possible responses includes clarifying, reframing, or amending language; checking in with participants about levels of comfort; suppressing or expressing emotions; validating experiences; acknowledging discomfort; apologizing for unintentional behaviors or choices; extending resources; reminding participants they can terminate their engagement; and offering to discontinue dialogs or other types of conversation. After we consult our response repertoires, we engage in feedback monitoring (stage 4). In this step, we take stock and adjust our actions based on the feedback we receive and, if needed, revisit our response options and consult with our support systems for guidance. The final stage in the sequence (stage 5) invites practitioners to consider ethical ways of exiting the field. The key to the flexibility sequence is, well, to be flexible and receptive to feedback that may require us to change course. Informed by the pillars of relational care, I provide a set of questions for researchers to consider at different points in the flexibility sequence (Table 27.1) to make ways of caring more concrete and accessible.[23]

Peering into others' lives carries responsibility and the need for introspection. As Carolyn Ellis reminds us, there may be something disingenuous, maybe even unethical about "exploring the depths of another's life when you haven't opened up your own to the same" since our own self-exploration helps us understand others.[24] An ethics of care refocuses our attention on the needs of study individuals and gives us the resolve we need to make amends, discuss conflicts, and ask difficult questions of ourselves. And since not all moral issues are problems of reasoning or judgment, sometimes we might have to feel our way through. In the next section, I reflect on ethically important moments I have negotiated in the field and how a relational care practice informs my collaborations with organizational partners.

Ethically Important Moments during Fieldwork

Ethical moments surface in a variety of contexts and invoke different care principles. *Example 1*: I was encouraged to leave out key details of a participant's actions (a migrant) after a community conflict occurred in a field site; they also asked me to intervene in the conflict directly and use my position as an American outsider to tell the opposing faction how they were wrong. *Response 1*: Carefully considered inaction. I chose this strategy from my response repertoire because I also cared for other participants in the community whose story I was telling and did not want perceptions of power (my position as an American outsider) to affect the presentation of a key conflict. I included the most important details because they were germane to understanding the participant's political position and community disfavor, but I asked them to review and check me on any issues of interpretation before I left the field (reflexivity). Doing this last part proved a key moment, since it afforded us another opportunity to review how we each interpreted a situation, and I came to understand their action more clearly (caring for). *Example 2*: An interview participant became visibly emotional when she told me about domestic abuse. *Response 2*: Pausing the interview to check in with her and remind her we could move on to other topics (caring about). She was steadfast, however, and recounted how the abuse motivated her decision to naturalize because citizenship meant safety to leave her partner. I offered her my hand and a tissue during this part of our conversation because physical touch seemed appropriate, and she took both (caring for and care giving). Ethics of care invites us to step out of our own personal frame of reference and consider how caring about (attentiveness), caring for (responsibility), caring with (solidarity), care giving (competence), and care receiving (responsiveness) can inform our choices during fieldwork.[25]

A more pressing concern arose while I was conducting comparative fieldwork in Mexico between 2009 and 2011. The municipality in one of my field sites was implicated in criminal governance and was either willingly working with nefarious actors or being extorted by them. Ethically important moments are not easily operationalized because they run the gamut and are subjectively experienced. In my case, I discerned a series of contextual and relational cues, subtle changes that were clustered together and raised some alarms. The cues included changes in the level and kind of communication between me and community members, retreat of some community informants who were previously social, and participants' outward

Table 27.1 A Flexibility Strategy and Consideration for an Ethics of Care Qualitative Practice

Sequence	Prompts and Questions for Consideration
Stage 1. Preparing for the Field	• Does the study absolutely warrant first-person interviews or observations with vulnerable groups? Have I consulted others who have conducted similar research to discuss ethical challenges they faced and how they handled them? • Do I have the requisite training to probe participants about vulnerable subject matter? Do I have resources on hand to dispense to participants if and when it becomes necessary? • Have I provided the requisite training to research team members and organizational partners? • Have I asked vulnerable participants whether they would like to review the interview guide beforehand or asked them to verbally flag triggers or subjects that are off-limits for discussion? • Do I know how to identify potential trauma responses (e.g., disassociation) and what to do? Have I thought about what I will do if a participant becomes visibly emotional? Have I practiced any emotional care and response strategies (e.g., "I see that you are upset, would you like to take a moment?" "Should we move on from this subject matter?") • Have I offered participants to ask me or my team members any questions about our training to make respondents feel safer and in control of the interview process? • Who will I reach out to if I need to discuss ethical considerations in the course of my research? What systems of support do I have or need to put in place prior to fieldwork? • Do I have a data security plan? • What is the division of labor and responsibilities between me and any partnering organizations? How will the organization adhere to principles of confidentiality, informed and voluntary consent? Is a stakeholder meeting or memorandum of agreement warranted? What are the ground rules for governing the collaborative relationship, and how will we settle disputes? If responsibilities have shifted in the course of the research, have I effectively communicated this information to all the necessary parties?
Stage 2. Relational and Context Sensitivity	• What is happening here? What is bothering me about this situation/interaction/relationship? Is there a problem? What do I understand the problem to be? • What are the cues that I'm receiving? Have I intercepted any verbal or nonverbal clues that my presence in the community or the organization has created distress or potential harm for participants or community members? Is there a level of threat that I can perceive? How urgently is a response needed? How much control do I have over this situation? Do I feel safe? Are my research team members safe? Have they decoded any cues that I must be aware of and potentially respond to? • Do I have the tools in my repertoire to guide me? If not, what systems of support do I have access to that can help me negotiate a thoughtful, caring response? • Do I have the sense that there is academic research fatigue among the community? How widespread is it felt? Who have I talked to about this? Do I have a clear sense of why they feel this way and whether it is appropriate for me to proceed with planned activities, participant observations, interviewing, focus groups, etc.? If key informants or gatekeepers suggest we proceed, but proceed with caution, have I discussed how I can do better than the academics before me to mitigate trepidation? • How am I working to build trust with participants in communities in which I am perceived as an outsider? Am I offloading the perception of trust to my organizational contacts? Am I prioritizing relationships over rules, schedules, and rigid time frames? • Am I aware of how partnering organizations are communicating with others about my study? How are organizations/key informants representing the research and my role in it? What steps am I taking to share authority with study participants and organizational stakeholders? Am I valuing different forms of experiential knowledge, including accuracy, details, or in the production of coproducing a narrative, research report, data, and findings? • Have I received any requests for assistance that may have influenced participants' involvement in the study? Should I change how I recruit study participants from this point forward?

Navigating Ethical Issues and Choices in the Field 315

Table 27.1 Continued

Sequence	Prompts and Questions for Consideration
Stage 3. Response Repertoire	• What coping and emotional regulation skills are suitable in my response? Suppressing my emotions? Expressing emotion as an act of solidarity and genuine care or concern? Do I need to probe any emotional entanglements further? • If participants have become emotional or I perceive distress, have I offered breaks and reminded them about their voluntary participation and ability to discontinue, end, or skip a line of questioning? Do I need to clarify any aspect of the discussion/communication/actions with participants? • Is it necessary to end a study relationship? If so, what is the best course of action I should take to minimize potential harm? • Should I reframe or amend particular language to make it more accessible/culturally sensitive? Do my study participants understand what I am asking them and what the information they provide me is for? • Have I acknowledged awkward exchanges, the appearance of distress, the perception of slights, etc.? • Is it appropriate to validate participant responses or actions?
Stage 4. Assess and Adjust	• Is the response I've used working? Have I met the challenge? Do I need to try another strategy or response? • Have I checked in with my support network regarding this issue? • Have I provided assurances of responsibility to study participants in meaningful ways that I carry out? If responsibilities have shifted in the course of the research, have I effectively communicated this information to all necessary parties?
Stage 5. Exiting the Field	• How will I attend to any misgivings, tensions, or conflicts before I exit the field if I have not already? • What is my plan for communicating (physical) exit from the field? • Have I attributed credit to all who supported the project (research assistants, local informants/fixers, organizations, etc.)? • When working with organizational partners, what is the plan for establishing the end of the collaborative partnership? Who will "own" the data and findings, and how will data be shared? • Have I offered a multivocal lens of the participants in the community and/or organizations I study?

concern for my care and protection. Gentle probing of my most trusted informants revealed that a criminal organization, rumored to be hiding in a nearby town, was threatening locals.

I was unaware of the threat when I selected the field site, and informants did not disclose the security issues when I asked during a pilot trip.[26] A few weeks into my stay, though, I sensed something had changed. Locals became less inclined to speak with me or hurried me along from the street to inside their house to chat. While traveling to an outlying community, an informant driving the vehicle suddenly pushed my head down when we approached what seemed to be a military checkpoint, obscuring me, but not others, from their view. We were waved on. When we debriefed about the incident later, the driver said he could not make out if those at the checkpoint were military personnel or members of the criminal network who sometimes dressed in military garb and scoped out targets. He worried for my safety. I had made friends with the pastor at the Catholic church where I went to mass, and some of the parishioners invited me to eat with them regularly after services. When I mentioned to the small church group that the emotional energy had seemed to change and I recounted the checkpoint incident, the pastor confirmed that a criminal organization had been stoking fear in the community and episodes of violence were reported in a neighboring town. Especially troubling to them was the strong suspicion that the criminal organization was extorting members of their local government. They were relieved to hear the driver took extra precautions on my behalf.

Attention to these incidents and candid discussions suggested what I would now identify as an ethically important moment. Given what I had learned, should I stop my fieldwork and leave the site? I had to confront the fact that my conspicuous presence was contributing to locals' anxiety and the possibility that talking with me put them in danger. Every day I walked around with locals, visited their homes, shared meals in the plaza, and spoke with business owners. I could be putting those who spoke with me in harm's way. I also interviewed government officials and party operatives of the opposition and incumbent parties—how would locals perceive the fact that I had conversations with politicians who some of them feared for their unscrupulous connections? I am a light-skinned American woman who was living in a nearby hotel alone. Because care is relational, I was not only the one-who-cares in my capacity as a researcher; I was also receiving care from friends and acquaintances in the community. Leaving the field site posed a difficult challenge to the comparative framework and quality of data collection I aspired to work with. But caring about, for, and with others in the town meant the best course of action, in my view, was to leave. A relational ethics of care showed me that leaving the field was the most moral action I could take, even though I did not know I was using a care ethics at the time.

In my view, that case is the weakest in my first book because data collection was hampered. There are sometimes trade-offs when researchers act on care principles. Examples include the need to end study relationships, stop recruitment, leave field sites, take more time in the field to build trust and relationships, endure criticism, vulnerabilities, and expend emotional labor, and check our privilege and ego, which can be unpleasant. Although prioritizing care means we may lose data or alter our preferred design and study goals, we can identify creative ways to compensate for the loss. For example, I relied more on interviews with immigrants in the United States and Skype and telephone calls with locals back in Mexico to collect and triangulate data. Certainly the overreliance on migrant voices to understand the local context likely introduced bias into the analysis by giving more weight to migrants' interpretations needed to piece together the story. I was transparent in my accounting of the case in my book, while maintaining confidentiality, although I should have had more of a discussion on reflexivity and my positionality in the appendices.[27]

A lesson I carry forward with me and my network of students and colleagues is that an ethics of care calls on us to be human first and researchers second. We can conduct our research, interpret and write our findings honestly and transparently, with a level of objectivity and dispassion, but also prioritize care and participants' humanity. Emotional entanglements and care for our study communities, partners, and ourselves provides deeper insight into the human condition and social and political life.

An ethics of care also supports study relationships with communities and community-based organizations (CBOs). While I do not have space to fully engage the voluminous research on participatory action and community-based participatory research (CBPR), I will describe how CBPR "best practices" inform my current collaboration with a naturalization service provider in Detroit. I believe participatory methods, while not without their limitations, will help the organization and me conduct more impactful, meaningful, policy-oriented research.

First, a major element of a participatory approach is "knowledge for action," where data and research findings have a purpose beyond academic understanding. Second, the approach recognizes and adopts shared authority and power with community-based priorities, processes, and perspectives. As Cornwall and Jewkes describe, defining and determining the "who" of the research problem and process is paramount to a participatory approach: determining who collects, analyzes, represents, and owns the data and findings requires critical negotiations before and throughout the research partnership.[28] Finally, most participatory approaches have different modes of participation that move along a continuum from more "shallow" (researcher's control) to "deep" (locals'/CBO's control), which may change at different stages in the research process. Whether participation is more contractual, consultative, collaborative, or collegiate, a primary step in all participatory research is determining roles, responsibilities, and expectations between researcher and community partner. It is best if conversations occur early on and stay flexible to changing dynamics throughout the relationship. Some partnerships also formally document the terms of collaboration in a memorandum of understanding, especially if trust relationships are nascent.[29]

Recently I developed a partnership with a local CBO that has provided naturalization classes, legal advocacy, and other care services to the immigrant population in Detroit. I started by building a relationship with the director of the organization and learning about all facets of their mission, a time-intensive process, and inquiring about the outstanding needs of the organization. Before even discussing a potential research collaboration, I tried to find ways that I could be useful to the organization. What skills did I possess that fit the needs and goals of the organization? How could the research goals of my project benefit the organization, if at all? Were there any academic networks, funding agencies, or conferences that I knew about that I could connect the organization to? After consulting with their board, we identified one research project we would spearhead together, established an internship partnership between my university department and the organization, and sat on a panel together at a national conference held in Detroit to shed light on their local work. The research problem was not one of my direct goals, but it was close enough to my project and I was eager to learn the answer: How do communication strategies that emphasize different benefits of citizenship affect the propensity to naturalize? We decided on a division of labor in which I prepared grant proposals through various funding agencies that drew on reports they authored. The reports were based on their own research and experiential knowledge concerning what they saw as more and less successful strategies for attracting eligible-to-naturalize green card holders to one-on-one consulting, workshops, and clinics the CBO offered. While the global pandemic halted our efforts, we plan to test our collaborative hypotheses in a field experiment with qualitative interviews and focus groups. The ethics of care and CBPR principles of caring about, for, and with the organizational leaders and members has been my guide and made for a rewarding and instructive process to date.

Limits of Care and the Role of Emotion

Procedural ethics, reflexivity, and mindfulness will likely guide many qualitative researchers toward an ethical practice that grants study participants all the dimensionality, humanity, and protection they deserve. When ethical tensions have arisen during our research, I have offered a relational care approach as a lantern to guide the way. But an ethics anchored in care certainly has its limits. How would a relational ethics of care apply to study participants of hate groups, in which the researcher shares no ideological compatibility? Would a researcher's engagement with hostile study groups invite public reprisal, such as charges that the researcher sympathizes with group ideologies?

Consider the research of Kathleen Blee on self-defined racist and anti-Semitic women. Blee used life history interviews to make sense of how women activists in racist groups, for example the Ku Klux Klan, white power "skinheads," and neo-Nazi groups, adopted their racial convictions and activities. Care, in this context, seems hard to fathom and is also risky. What is at stake is that focusing solely on the "cared for" risks the potential that researcher becomes inadvertently complicit in loathsome political agendas, provides a platform for violent, racist propaganda, or becomes "numb to the horrors" they learn about while establishing rapport with respondents.[30] An ethics of care may be inappropriate in research with "unloved" groups. Instead, Blee suggests that articulating one's position with respect to group ideologies but promising an accurate portrayal of participants helps immensely. She promotes probing emotional entanglements throughout the data collection process as a way to explore the ethical dimensions of interpersonal relationships since "scholars and informants jointly shape knowledge in qualitative scholarship."[31] Blee identified how fear was wielded by her respondents to strategically influence the scope of her data collection and interpretation. Her awareness of this emotional manipulation helped her recognize how participants also used fear inside the racist organizations for social control.

Actively probing emotional dynamics during data collection is another companion or alternative to an ethics of care practice. Sociologist Leisy Abrego is astutely aware of how keeping the emotional well-being of her participants front and center and fostering community has led her to more honest, ethical, and rigorous research.[32] In her research on legal violence and Central American immigrant groups, Abrego describes her empirical practice as "research as accompaniment." Abrego writes:

> Academia presupposes a separation between intellectual and embodied pursuits and prioritizes what feminists and scholars of color critique as a false expectation of objectivity (Collins 1989). An uncritical emphasis on objectivity requires that researchers ignore the messiness of life to categorize people and experiences into dependent and independent variables. Good social science research, in this formulation, is "objective" because it will consistently lead to the same findings, regardless of scholars' social location or emotions. As an out-of-place scholar, I know this to be false and I welcome the grainy truths that arise in my embodied research and analysis. I navigate my social location and emotions in detail and at length at every stage of the research to serve the purpose of accompanying the very targets of violent laws. (p. 16)

The accompaniment framework centers emotions. Rather than expecting objectivity, Abrego adopts an embodied practice, one that is more precise because she remains open to emotional entanglements and what they reveal.

Competing forces that act on researchers make an ethics of care practice challenging, maybe even unnecessary in some contexts, and problematic at times. Academics face constraints on their emotional bandwidth. The time needed to anchor relational care into one's research practice is also a finite resource. Yet I am confident that even though it may be more time-consuming, once we adopt relational care principles, we are far more alert and able to respond ethically when academic self-interest collides with ambiguous moments in the field. Adopting an ethical care approach would stop us from asking one more question, scheduling one more interview, or staying in a field site because we "need" the observations for our dissertation, our next article, our book. An ethics of care would also help us recognize when we lack the professional training and ability to mobilize resources on behalf of our respondents, as González-López and Abrego do in their research practices. We sometimes tell ourselves that the tears we observe on our respondents' faces or the shakes and trembles that accompany their description of horrifying incidents are justified because they are part of untold stories that deserve a witness. We may even tell ourselves that we are helping respondents by giving them a safe space to process their emotions. All this may be true. But sometimes researchers have not a clue how to support trauma victims and their posttraumatic stress symptoms and need to stop causing additional harm. I have experienced this firsthand. Adopting a relational ethics of care would embolden us to prioritize attentiveness, responsibility, responsiveness, competence, and solidarity with our participants when ethical ambiguities arise.

Notes

1. Guillemin and Gillam, "Ethics, Reflexivity, and 'Ethically Important Moments' in Research"; Iphofen and Tolich, "Foundational Issues in Qualitative Research Ethics."
2. Noddings, *Caring*.
3. Bosk and DeVries 2004.
4. Reich, "Power, Positionality, and the Ethic of Care in Qualitative Research," 579.
5. Fujii, "Research Ethics 101," 717.
6. Ellis, "Telling Secrets, Revealing Lives," 4; Tracy, "Qualitative Quality."
7. O'Brien, "Sociology as an Epistemology of Contradiction." See also González-López, "Epistemologies of the Wound" and Anzaldúa and Keating (2002).
8. See, for example, National Commission for the Protection of Human Subjects of Biomedical and Behavioral Research, *The Belmont Report*.
9. Bosk and DeVries 2004: 256.
10. Davis and Holcombe, "'Whose Ethics?'"; Blee and Currier, "Ethics beyond the IRB"; Fujii, "Research Ethics 101"; Reich, "Power, Positionality, and the Ethic of Care in Qualitative Research."
11. Iphofen and Tolich, "Foundational Issues in Qualitative Research Ethics." See also Bloemraad and Menjívar, "Precarious Times, Professional Tensions."
12. Fine et al., "Qualitative Research," 127.
13. Small, "De-Exoticizing Ghetto Poverty," 353.
14. Moore, *Invisible Families*; Hoang, *Dealing in Desire*; Compton, Meadow, and Schilt, *Other, Please Specify*; Stuart, *Ballad of the Bullet*; Miller, *Halfway Home*.
15. González-López, "Mindful Ethics."
16. Gilligan 1982; Noddings, *Caring*.
17. Noddings, *Caring*.
18. Tronto, "An Ethic of Care"; Tronto, *Moral Boundaries*.
19. Way and Tracy, "Conceptualizing Compassion as Recognizing, Relating and (Re)Acting," 304.
20. Noddings, *Caring*.
21. Ellis, "Telling Secrets, Revealing Lives," 26.
22. Galatzer-Levy, Burton, and Bonanno, "Coping Flexibility, Potentially Traumatic Life Events, and Resilience."

23. See also Cronin-Furman and Lake, "Ethics Abroad" for a discussion of conducting fieldwork in violent and fragile contexts. Included is a comprehensive set of questions for researchers to consider before, during, and after research. The Advancing Research on Conflict consortium also has a bevy of resources on ethics and other themes. See https://advancingconflictresearch.com.
24. Ellis, "Compassionate Research," 8.
25. Readers may consider the selected examples and believe different responses were preferrable. They may be right. Two researchers acting from pillars of care may arrive at different responses. My concern is more in convincing readers of the value and importance of ethics in practice and adopting a relational care practice as a guide toward moral action and mutual understanding.
26. There are several possible reasons why I was unaware of security issues. It could have been that security issues were not yet or enough of a threat to warrant disclosure or that I did not ask the most knowledgeable sources in the community. It is also possible that informants withheld the information from me for various reasons or that I did not ask about security issues directly enough. I had been advised by several informants to discuss issues of criminal governance carefully, including the exclusive use of hand signals to refer to distinct criminal organizations. During my fieldwork, concerns about criminal networks and violence in the states where I was based (Zacatecas, Guanajuato, and Jalisco) were not yet as widespread as they were even two years later, when territorial disputes flared up. As I write this in 2022, the reality of the violence is regrettable and starkly different.
27. See chapter 4 of Duquette-Rury, *Exit and Voice*.
28. Cornwall and Jewkes, "What Is Participatory Research?," 1667. See also Ross et al., "The Challenges of Collaboration for Academic and Community Partners in a Research Partnership."
29. Biggs, "Resource-Poor Farmer Participation in Research."
30. Blee, "White-Knuckle Research," 392.
31. Blee, "White-Knuckle Research," 392.
32. Abrego, "Research as Accompaniment," 16.

Recommended Readings

Abrego, L. "Research as Accompaniment: Reflections on Objectivity, Ethics, and Emotions." In *Out of Place: Fieldwork and Positionality in Law and Society*, edited by Lynette Chua and Mark Massoud. Cambridge Studies in Law and Society, Cambridge: Cambridge University Press, 2024.
    Abrego adeptly shows how emotions, as a guiding research practice, are not anathema to rigorous, careful, "objective" qualitative research; instead, she convincingly argues it's just the opposite.

Blee, K. M. "White-Lnuckle Research: Emotional Dynamics in Fieldwork with Racist Activists." *Qualitative Sociology* 21, no. 4 (1998): 381–399.
    Blee vividly shows the limits of care and offers readers an alternative route: a sense of how probing emotional entanglements between researcher and participant can become a source of data in research with racist groups.

Compton, D. L., T. Meadow, and K. Schilt, eds. *Other, Please Specify: Queer Methods in Sociology*. Oakland: University of California Press, 2018.
    Essential reading for empirical social science praxis studying difference—ethnic, gender, sexuality, race—using an intersectional lens that embraces the challenge and promise of queer theory and methods in studying social life.

Guillemin, M., and L. Gillam. "Ethics, Reflexivity, and 'Ethically Important Moments' in Research." *Qualitative Inquiry* 10, no. 2 (2004): 261–280.
    A pioneering article that distinguishes procedural ethics from ethics in practice and the need for deeper exploration into ethically important moments that arise during research after the IRB is approved.

Miller, R. J. *Halfway Home: Race, Punishment, and the Afterlife of Mass Incarceration*. Boston: Little, Brown, 2021.

Although he doesn't explicitly use the language of care ethics, Miller's approach contains all the principles of relational and situational care in this breathtaking qualitative study of how the racialized U.S. carceral state system affects the lives of those who served prison sentences and their networks of support.

References

Abrego, L. "Research as Accompaniment: Reflections on Objectivity, Ethics, and Emotions." In *Out of Place: Fieldwork and Positionality in Law and Society*, edited by Lynette Chua and Mark Massoud. Cambridge Studies in Law and Society, Cambridge: Cambridge University Press, 2024.

Anzaldúa, G., and A. Keating. *This Bridge We Call Home: Radical Visions for Transformation*. New York: Routledge, 2002.

Biggs, S. D. "Resource-Poor Farmer Participation in Research: A Synthesis of Experiences from Nine National Agricultural Research Stations." Report no. 3 for the Special Series on the Organization and Management of On-Farm Client-Oriented Research, International Service for National Agricultural Research, 1989.

Blee, K. M. "White-Knuckle Research: Emotional Dynamics in Fieldwork with Racist Activists." *Qualitative Sociology* 21, no. 4 (1998): 381–399.

Blee, K. M., and A. Currier. "Ethics beyond the IRB: An Introductory Essay." *Qualitative Sociology* 34, no. 3 (2011): 401–413.

Bloemraad, I., and C. Menjívar. "Precarious Times, Professional Tensions: The Ethics of Migration Research and the Drive for Scientific Accountability." *International Migration Review* 56, no. 1 (2022): 4–32.

Bosk, C. L., and R. G. De Vries. "Bureaucracies of Mass Deception: Institutional Review Boards and the Ethics of Ethnographic Research." *Annals of the American Academy of Political and Social Science* 595, no. 1 (2004): 249–263.

Collins, P. H. "The Social Construction of Black Feminist Thought." *Signs: Journal of Women in Culture and Society* 14, no. 4 (1989): 745–773.

Compton, D. L., T. Meadow, and K. Schilt, eds. *Other, Please Specify: Queer Methods in Sociology*. Oakland: University of California Press, 2018.

Cornwall, A., and R. Jewkes. "What Is Participatory Research?" *Social Science & Medicine* 41 (1995): 1667–1676.

Cronin-Furman, K., and M. Lake. "Ethics Abroad: Fieldwork in Fragile and Violent Contexts." *PS: Political Science & Politics* 51, no. 3 (2018): 607–614.

Davis, M., and S. Holcombe. "'Whose Ethics?' Codifying and Enacting Ethics in Research Settings." *Australian Aboriginal Studies* 2 (2010): 1–9.

Duquette-Rury, L. *Exit and Voice: The Paradox of Cross-Border Politics in Mexico*. Oakland: University of California Press, 2020.

Ellis, C. "Telling Secrets, Revealing Lives: Relational Ethics in Research with Intimate Others." *Qualitative Inquiry* 13, no. 1 (2007): 3–29.

Ellis, C. "Compassionate Research: Interviewing and Storytelling from a Relational Ethics of Care." In *The Routledge International Handbook of Narrative Life History*, edited by I. Goodson, 431–445. New York: Routledge, 2016.

Fine, M., L. Weis, S. Weseen, and L. Wong. "Qualitative Research, Representations, and Social Responsibilities." In *Handbook of Qualitative Research*, edited by N. K. Denzin and Y. S. Lincoln, vol. 2: 107–131. Thousand Oaks, CA: Sage, 2000.

Fujii, Lee Ann. "Research Ethics 101: Dilemmas and Responsibilities." *PS: Political Science & Politics* 45, no. 4 (2012): 717–723.

Galatzer-Levy, I. R., C. L. Burton, and G. A. Bonanno. "Coping Flexibility, Potentially Traumatic Life Events, and Resilience: A Prospective Study of College Student Adjustment." *Journal of Social and Clinical Psychology* 31, no. 6 (2012): 542–567.

Gilligan, C. *In a Different Voice: Psychological Theory and Women's Development*. Cambridge, MA: Harvard University Press, 1982.

González-López, G. "Epistemologies of the Wound: Anzaldúan Theories and Sociological Research on Incest in Mexican Society." *Human Architecture: Journal of the Sociology of Self-Knowledge* 4 (2006): 17–24.

González-López, G. "Mindful Ethics: Comments on Informant-Centered Practices in Sociological Research." *Qualitative Sociology* 34, no 3 (2011): 447–461.

Guillemin, M., and L. Gillam. "Ethics, Reflexivity, and 'Ethically Important Moments' in Research." *Qualitative Inquiry* 10, no. 2 (2004): 261–280.

Hoang, K. K. *Dealing in Desire: Asian Ascendancy, Western Decline, and the Hidden Currencies of Global Sex Work*. Oakland: University of California Press, 2015.

Iphofen, R., and M. Tolich. "Foundational Issues in Qualitative Research Ethics." In *The Sage Handbook of Qualitative Research Ethics*, edited by R. Iphofen and M. Tolich, 1–18. London: Sage, 2018.

Miller, R. J. *Halfway Home: Race, Punishment, and the Afterlife of Mass Incarceration*. Boston: Little, Brown, 2021.

Moore, M. *Invisible Families: Gay Identities, Relationships, and Motherhood among Black Women*. Oakland: University of California Press, 2011.

National Commission for the Protection of Human Subjects of Biomedical and Behavioral Research. *The Belmont Report: Ethical Principles and Guidelines for the Protection of Human Subjects of Research*. [Bethesda, MD]: The Commission, 1978.

Noddings, Nel. *Caring: A Relational Approach to Ethics and Moral Education*. Berkeley: University of California Press, 2013.

O'Brien, J. "Sociology as an Epistemology of Contradiction." *Sociological Perspectives* 52, no. 1 (2009): 5–22.

Reich, J. A. "Power, Positionality, and the Ethic of Care in Qualitative Research." *Qualitative Sociology* 44, no. 4 (2021): 575–581.

Ross, L. F., A. Loup, R. M. Nelson, J. Botkin, R. Kost, G. R. Smith, and S. Gehlert. "The Challenges of Collaboration for Academic and Community Partners in a Research Partnership: Points to Consider." *Journal of Empirical Research on Human Research Ethics* 5, no. 1 (2010): 19–31.

Small, M. L. "De-Exoticizing Ghetto Poverty: On the Ethics of Representation in Urban Ethnography." *City & Community* 14, no. 4 (2015): 352–358.

Stuart, F. *Ballad of the Bullet: Gangs, Drill Music, and the Power of Online Infamy*. Princeton, NJ: Princeton University Press, 2020.

Tracy, S. J. "Qualitative Quality: Eight 'Big-Tent' Criteria for Excellent Qualitative Research." *Qualitative Inquiry* 16, no. 10 (2010): 837–851.

Tronto, J. C. "An Ethic of Care." *Generations: Journal of the American Society on Aging* 22, no. 3 (1998): 15–20.

Tronto, J. C. *Moral Boundaries: A Political Argument for an Ethic of Care*. New York: Routledge, 2020.

Way, D., and S. J. Tracy. "Conceptualizing Compassion as Recognizing, Relating and (Re)Acting: A Qualitative Study of Compassionate Communication at Hospice. *Communication Monographs* 79, no. 3 (2012): 292–315.

28
Digital Fieldwork
Opportunities and Challenges

Diana Kapiszewski, Lauren MacLean, and Lahra Smith

Overview

This chapter explores the long-standing and continually emerging methods of digital fieldwork.[1] "Digital fieldwork" refers to collecting and generating data and evidence in digital or computerized form, often remotely (i.e., removed from the dynamics or community of focus), using electronic technologies and platforms.[2] The chapter's first section discusses strategies for conducting digital fieldwork, and the second section considers motivations for doing so. While some scholars first adopted digital fieldwork when they were unable to conduct conventional fieldwork due to the 2020 pandemic, its practice precedes and will succeed that public health crisis; moreover, digital fieldwork has benefited and can benefit scholars well beyond those who *need* to conduct fieldwork digitally. In the third section, we show that conducting digital fieldwork in a way that generates novel insights and avoids exploitative research relationships requires drawing on many of the same principles and practices of conventional fieldwork. In particular, we argue that deep preparation and the systematic documentation of trade-offs are essential to navigate digital fieldwork. In the fourth section, we highlight the personal, operational, and ethical opportunities and challenges that digital fieldwork presents, consider the intellectual implications, and suggest how reflexivity and ethical engagement can help scholars to maximize the benefits and address the challenges. We conclude that digital fieldwork has the potential to expand fieldwork's inclusivity *if* the inequalities of digital access in our scholarly communities are simultaneously reduced; we also encourage open dialog about evolving fieldwork practices.

What Is Digital Fieldwork?

Digital fieldwork includes many strategies and can take many forms. For instance, researchers can conduct digital fieldwork when distanced from a particular context or population of interest, or while living in a field site. What makes fieldwork "digital" is the use of digital technologies to mediate interpersonal interactions and gather data. Technological advancements, increased access to and engagement with technology by individuals and organizations globally, and the digitization of information sources all over the world encourage and facilitate the conduct of digital fieldwork. Scholars might carry out interviews, and potentially record them, via telephone (e.g., using an Olympus Tp7 telephone or TapeACall on iPhone), a voice-over-IP service (e.g., Whatsapp or Viber), or a video-conferencing platform (e.g., Zoom, Skype, or Whereby). To conduct focus groups digitally, a scholar might

---

Diana Kapiszewski, Lauren MacLean, and Lahra Smith, *Digital Fieldwork* In: *Doing Good Qualitative Research*. Edited by: Jennifer Cyr and Sara Wallace Goodman, Oxford University Press. © Oxford University Press 2024. DOI: 10.1093/oso/9780197633137.003.0028

employ software that can track individual participants by voice (e.g., Otter.ai). Experiments and surveys may also be conducted online.[3] Over the past 10 years, scholars have even been developing strategies for carrying out more "site-intensive" methods (e.g., ethnography and participant observation) digitally (e.g., "digital ethnography").[4]

Beyond facilitating interaction with human participants, digital technologies can also help researchers collect and process data in other ways. For instance, many scholars have used digital cameras and mobile telephones to take pictures of people, places, and events, as well as documents and other textual material, in the field. As archives around the world are increasingly digitizing their holdings to preserve and increase access to them,[5] scholars can peruse those holdings from afar; in turn, voice and video technologies can facilitate discussions with archivists and curators. Web scraping is a newer, increasingly popular approach to data generation.[6] Scholars might also use satellite imagery or GPS (the Global Positioning System) to map and record digital locations, and GIS (the Geographic Information System) to link location data to phenomena of interest.[7]

Why Conduct Digital Fieldwork?

Scholars may choose to carry out digital rather than traditional fieldwork for many reasons. Some researchers conduct digital fieldwork because it is more efficient, allows them to access more information (e.g., by reaching more project participants), or helps them to gather data better suited to answering their research question or to the type of analysis they hope to conduct. Alternatively, researchers may not be able to travel due to a wide range of health and safety risks, as was the case during the COVID-19 pandemic, or because of a limited budget, travel or visa restrictions, or personal or family limitations.

Many scholars can benefit from conducting fieldwork using digital technologies. Often, collecting data using digital techniques requires many of the same skills as collecting data in person. For instance, carrying out interviews via a remote conferencing platform like Zoom is in many respects similar to in-person interviewing. Moreover, digital fieldwork has several advantages with regard to accessing people, places, and data, as we outline in this chapter's next section. Digital fieldwork may be particularly useful in certain contexts and for certain scholars. For instance, the COVID-19 pandemic that emerged in early 2020 restricted international travel and interpersonal contact in ways that precluded traditional, in-person fieldwork for many researchers, encouraging them to investigate and adopt digital fieldwork strategies. Also, digital fieldwork may be necessary for or appealing to scholars for whom conducting fieldwork in person is difficult, including researchers with disabilities, limited financial resources, substantial professional or family obligations, and/or visa barriers.

However, digital fieldwork may be easier for some scholars to conduct than for others. For example, scholars with deeper knowledge of the context they intend to research and who have already forged trusting relationships and connections during prior in-person fieldwork may be better equipped to navigate digital fieldwork than researchers who have never visited the places they are studying. Moreover, digital fieldwork is most available to scholars with good access to technology. For other researchers, particularly those from the Global South who struggle with unreliable access to electricity or the internet or lack adequate computers or telephones, conducting digital fieldwork may be challenging or even out of reach.

Preparing for and Documenting Digital Fieldwork

Preparing for, planning, and conducting digital fieldwork involve many choices and decisions.[8] Scholars who are used to carrying out in-person fieldwork—or may be conducting fieldwork digitally despite having planned to carry out in-person field research—should think carefully about the differences between these two modes of inquiry. For some scholars, digital fieldwork may mainly involve using familiar data gathering techniques in new ways (e.g., conducting human participant research via Zoom). Others may capitalize on the opportunities that emerging digital technologies provide to collect data using strategies that are completely new to them.[9]

Preparing for traditional fieldwork and preparing for digital fieldwork are similar in many senses, and preparation is absolutely critical for both types of inquiry. Scholars should learn as much as possible about the research topic and their anticipated field sites and incorporate that knowledge into the design of their projects (e.g., see Chapters 10 and 20). Developing relevant language expertise and gathering and reading locally produced material are critical, particularly if a scholar will be researching an unfamiliar context. Another good idea is building on-the-ground "virtual" networks, including people who can offer guidance and support.[10] Researchers might also establish research affiliations with local institutions, carefully considering how the people with whom they plan to interact will think about and interpret their affiliation choices. Making and cultivating such connections from afar can demonstrate commitment and help researchers continue learning about their field sites. Scholars conducting human participant research via online communication platforms should carefully consider the ethical issues doing so can raise and discuss those with their local institutional review board (IRB). Researchers should also identify and secure any formal and informal approvals they may need to carry out their research. It is also useful to develop a budget—considering how the costs of digital fieldwork may differ from those of traditional fieldwork—to inform funding proposals.

Identifying information sources and selecting data-generation strategies are important parts of planning any fieldwork. Some information a scholar would like to gather (e.g., statistics or documents) might already have been digitized by the organization that created it, or that organization might be willing to digitize it. Alternatively, a digital version of the information might be available from other scholars studying similar topics, an archive, the national library in the same or another country, or relevant university research or area studies centers. Scholars should select data-gathering strategies that they can use (or learn to use) expertly and that will be culturally acceptable and productive in the contexts of interest. Identifying both ideal and next-best information sources and strategies can be helpful in case the project does not proceed as planned. This is particularly likely when scholars use data-collection techniques that are new to them or use familiar approaches in new ways.[11]

Scholars should try to anticipate whether the individuals or organizations with whom they seek to interact will be willing and able to participate online, develop strategies to facilitate their participation, and consider the implications for their analysis of not being able to reach certain people or groups. For instance, if governments or other actors in the research context impose constraints on the use of particular technologies or platforms, researchers should investigate alternatives. Alternatively, scholars may anticipate that participants may not be comfortable with the technology they wish to use or able to afford to use it. In these cases, scholars can help participants to better understand the technology or identify ways to defray the costs of using it, perhaps including these costs in the budget of their funding proposal. Scholars will also need to carefully explore the safety, privacy, and confidentiality protocols of the data-gathering technologies they wish to use (e.g., how they store data and how safe the storage is from hacking). How scholars resolve these issues will affect how they conduct research and what they can promise to potential participants as they seek their informed consent to engage in the research. For instance, one of the authors doing a research study in Kenya offers her respondents the opportunity to choose from among a set of online phone platforms for phone interviews, and then arranges in advance to transfer phone credit to them.

Scholars conducting digital fieldwork remotely may also need to identify and engage a few trusted intermediaries based in their research settings to help them lay the groundwork for and carry out their projects. These might be individuals or organizations (or both) who are already familiar to the researcher, or people they get to know via their virtual network. Working with intermediaries may be particularly important for scholars researching topics they have not studied before or working in fieldsites they have not visited. Scholars who work with intermediaries need to carefully train and supervise them. Doing so at a distance can be challenging, but can also yield big research benefits, serve as an excellent opportunity to both teach and learn from these project partners, and result in fruitful and enduring collaborations.

Intermediaries might help researchers in many ways. They may serve as research assistants, facilitators, interpreters, or translators. They may provide key information about the field site, for instance, concerning which technologies work particularly well or are familiar or preferred. They might also assist with identifying research participants, coordinating focus groups or interviews, familiarizing respondents with the technology the researcher hopes to use to interact with them, or carrying out other data-collection tasks. Making these individuals substantive partners can transform digital fieldwork, facilitating access to places, documents, and people that would otherwise be unavailable.[12] Intermediaries should be acknowledged in publications and compensated appropriately. In some cases, they may even become coauthors.[13]

As scholars prepare for and conduct digital fieldwork, they should carefully document the research process. Indeed, while scholars may dismiss the notion of taking "field notes" if they are not in the field, doing so may be *more* important for scholars conducting digital fieldwork than for scholars researching in situ. With less exposure to the images, sounds, smells, tastes, and tactile feedback that form part of the traditional fieldwork experience, scholars may have more trouble remembering their observations, impressions, and insights. Chronicling their observations—even fleeting fragments of context—will help anchor their memories. In addition, the research design choices and changes that scholars make as they conduct digital fieldwork should be carefully described and justified, and the resulting documentation securely stored. Such documentation helps scholars to keep track of what they have done and still have to do and enables them to be open and transparent about their research down the line.

Opportunities and Challenges in Conducting Digital Fieldwork

Digital fieldwork provides a range of benefits and poses important challenges. We consider the trade-offs in three areas—personal, operational, and ethical—all of which have important intellectual implications for research.

Personal Opportunities and Challenges

A first set of opportunities and challenges is *personal*. One distinct advantage of digital fieldwork is that scholars do not have to put their life completely "on hold," as they often do when they engage in the intellectually, psychologically, emotionally, and indeed physically intense experience of traditional fieldwork. Instead, they can be present at home, engaged in family life, and in touch with their normal support systems. They can also remain active at their home institution, keeping at least one foot firmly planted in an academic setting, among colleagues (and dissertation committee members) with whom they can discuss and share emerging ideas and insights.[14] Distance from the field site may also help researchers to maintain better perspective on the topics and people they are learning about (i.e., avoid the "field goggles" that scholars who spend a lot of time immersed in the field can sometimes seem to wear).

In addition, for scholars whose research focuses on settings marked by authoritarian politics, political instability, conflict, crime, corruption, or violence, conducting research in person can be dangerous. In some contexts, that danger is exacerbated if one is of a minority identity status (e.g., belongs to a racial or ethnic minority or is LGBTQ+). Under these circumstances, researchers conducting traditional fieldwork can expend a great deal of time, effort, energy, and money simply staying safe. Conducting research at a distance using technology may protect the researcher's personal safety at far less cost. Doing so may also help scholars to elide the "minders" who keep tabs on academic researchers in some contexts and can impede or block their access to the people or places they would like to reach.

Yet remaining "at home" and/or close to one's home institution can also have downsides. Some researchers, particularly those used to the experience of "being there" and the intensity of in-person field research, may not *feel like* they are carrying out fieldwork when they use technology to connect with the people and places of study. It may be difficult to get and stay focused on field research when one remains immersed in (and potentially overwhelmed by) the obligations of one's home and work life. Also, staying put in one's usual setting can make it hard to define the points at which fieldwork begins and ends. When is a scholar "finished with" fieldwork if it is perpetually possible to contact one more archive or conduct one more interview?

To balance these trade-offs, scholars might impose some structure on the fieldwork they conduct remotely. Similar to traditional fieldwork, they might set aside specific blocks of time—particular times of the day, days, weeks, or even months—to conduct fieldwork, and seek to minimize the amount of other work they carry out simultaneously (including teaching and service). When feasible, identifying and consistently working from a particular physical space that is quiet and away from personal or other distractions can facilitate deeper engagement with participants, field sites, and data collected. Scholars should also seek advice and insights from others who have conducted digital fieldwork to see how they have navigated this terrain.

Operational Opportunities and Challenges

A second set of opportunities and challenges is *operational*. On the plus side, conducting fieldwork via digital technologies may provide flexibility in data gathering. Scholars may not need to plan data collection for or carry it out during a delimited amount of time. Instead, they may be able to proceed more slowly and incrementally with their work. This allows time for more frequent and critical reflection on what they are learning and discovering, for analyzing data as they are collected, and for integrating the resulting insights more thoughtfully and thoroughly into the ongoing design and conduct of the project. All of these steps produce clear intellectual benefits.[15]

Relatedly, conducting fieldwork digitally lowers or even eliminates the costs of travel and lodging, reducing the overall per-site cost of research and potentially allowing scholars to conduct research in more field sites. Also, researchers who conduct digital fieldwork can base their case selection decisions more fully on intellectual factors and less on budgets or logistics. In addition, research does not need to be completed in one site prior to commencing in another: a scholar could interview a senator in Mumbai at 8 a.m., a Supreme Court justice in Buenos Aires at 9 a.m., and an activist in Delhi at 10 a.m.[16] The same logic may operate within any particular field site: conducting fieldwork remotely using technology may allow researchers to work in more locations, collect documents in more archives, and interact with more people than they could during a short in-person fieldwork trip.[17] Traversing from one data-collection opportunity to the next—either around the world or across a city—can be stressful and time-consuming and is greatly facilitated with digital fieldwork.

In addition, some scholars may believe that the distanced interaction that technology makes possible helps minimize some forms of researcher bias. For example, in digital interviews (particularly but not only conducted without video), respondents' race, ethnicity, gender, and sexual orientation, or their height, weight, and disability status may be more difficult to discern. Without access to information on these features, some scholars may believe they are less prone to knowingly or unwittingly make assumptions about respondents. Similarly, when participants blur their background on video calls, some scholars may feel they are less likely to intentionally or unknowingly draw conclusions about them from what they view in their surroundings.

Yet digital fieldwork may also have operational downsides. For instance, facilitated data gathering may lead scholars to collect *too much* information rather than being more discerning and focusing on collecting the information they need to answer their research questions. Being able to engage in multiple back-to-back data-generating activities in a row, as digital fieldwork allows, may discourage scholars from taking time for thought and reflection while gathering information. Systematic respondent selection may be complicated when researchers are distant from field sites. Scholars interested in recruiting locally for survey respondents, for instance, may find it difficult to carry out random or representative sampling. Researchers who work with local enumerators may face challenges managing the selection process and ensuring its quality. Further, not being physically present may make it hard for researchers to establish credibility with, earn the trust of, and ultimately gain entrée to the people, organizations, and places they wish to engage and understand. Indeed, in order to evaluate and approve their study, some local institutions (e.g., government offices or IRBs) may require that researchers be physically present, offering original copies of paper documents.

Less cultural immersion may make it more difficult for researchers to "get a feel" for the places they wish to understand and to interpret the information they gather. Scholars' attenuated ability to assess research subjects' personal and professional attributes can complicate interacting with them, in particular making it harder to know how to pose sensitive questions. Researchers may also have a harder time interpreting the information participants convey and evaluating the evidentiary value of that information.

For all scholars, conducting research from a distance provides fewer opportunities for "serendipity": they may be less likely to "happen upon" data sources for which they were not intentionally looking, or unexpectedly come into contact with people who can inform their work. Likewise, formal interactions with respondents may be less prone to transitions to, or lead to invitations to, informal events where a researcher can meet additional people or where the respondent may feel more at ease to speak openly. As a result, the evidence gathered through digital fieldwork may more closely track official narratives or be more narrowly focused.

Digital fieldwork can also raise technical challenges. Technology can fail to work optimally (or at all): digital connections can be unstable, connectivity can lapse, and the accessibility of locations via online communication platforms can vary. Technical problems may arise unpredictably; they may result from equipment failures or be intentionally caused by powerful actors (e.g., authoritarian regimes). Moreover, not all technology works equally well with non-English languages or with heavily accented English.[18] Technology may be unavailable or alienating to some potential respondents and may thus hinder participation. While technology should become increasingly available and familiar and easier to use as the information revolution continues forward, in the short term some of these challenges will persist for many people.

The precise nature of these operational concerns and challenges, and how much and how they will affect the conduct of research, are highly project- and context-dependent. Addressing them requires deep knowledge of the settings of study. Scholars should learn as much as they can in advance about social, economic, and political developments in the contexts of interest, and keep learning as they conduct fieldwork. Likewise, they should seek good information about which technologies are effective and preferred in those settings—together with their practicality, efficiency, and security—so they can choose technology that will work optimally. Scholars reading well-regarded media and engaging with their virtual networks (including trusted intermediaries and researchers with experience working in the country, city, archive, or other location of interest) can help them gain this knowledge.

Ethical Questions

Finally, we highlight how conducting fieldwork digitally can both help to mitigate some of the ethical concerns that can attend traditional fieldwork (in particular research involving human participants) and pose new ethical challenges. One set of issues relates to the safety of the people involved in the research. In contexts where it could be risky for respondents and researchers to be seen together, interacting via technology may mitigate that risk, potentially allowing more people to more safely participate in the research. Likewise, using technology to interact with participants may help to ensure the privacy of research interactions, as respondents can engage from their preferred location (as long as the relevant communication technology can function there). The degree to which interacting via technology is safer than interacting in person is contingent upon the technology being used and its safety protocols, as well as site-specific factors. It bears repeating that researchers need to investigate and understand the details of the technologies they are using and to explain these nuances to the study participants.[19]

Digital fieldwork can also help to address ethical concerns related to positionality. Interacting via digital technology may decrease the salience of power differentials, subtly reducing pressure on respondents: the dynamics of two people speaking by phone can be very different from those of an in-person interaction in which a researcher occupies the physical space of their interlocutor. Indeed, digital technology may have a leveling effect on power differences, whether the researcher is "studying up or down." The distance may also reduce the likelihood of excessive quid-pro-quos in which respondents condition information provision on the researcher doing or providing something for them (e.g., a ride, cash, or medicine). Relieving these sorts of strains can facilitate effective field research, helping scholars to achieve their intellectual goals.

Yet digital fieldwork can also pose *new* ethical challenges.[20] For instance, assessing interlocutors' vulnerability to risks is critical to a scholar's decisions about how to interact with them and how to treat the information they convey. However, doing so at a distance without the ability to observe respondents' surroundings or context can be difficult. Respondents' reactions to sensitive, disturbing questions may also be harder to understand or effectively manage from a distance and when mediated by technology. Scholars may also find it more challenging to gauge whether they have caused harm and to consider how to redress it. Further, remoteness may make it more difficult for researchers to assess what would be fair and culturally appropriate compensation for participation in the research[21] and to provide that compensation, given geographic variation in the use of mobile payment platforms. Conversely, interacting remotely prevents respondents from taking in myriad cues they use, knowingly and unwittingly, to gauge a researcher's credibility. As a result, establishing the trust in researchers that respondents may want or need to consent to participate in a research interaction may be complicated. In aggregate, these concerns suggest that scholars who conduct research digitally need to be very transparent with participants about their work, goals, and motivations in order to gain and keep their trust.

A broader set of ethical concerns relates to how the conduct of research using technology inevitably directs our attention toward some places and people and away from others. Of course, accessing and including hard-to-reach populations has been a perennial issue for traditional fieldwork. Nonetheless, these challenges may be particularly acute in digital fieldwork: while it is uncontestable that more people in more locations have more access to better technology today than ever before, conducting research virtually could lead scholarly work to overemphasize people and field sites that are "on the grid."[22] What are the ethical implications of political scientists examining crucial institutions, dynamics, and challenges—and potentially contributing to addressing them—only in better-endowed parts of the world? Could conducting fieldwork digitally exacerbate inequalities? What ramifications does using technology to conduct fieldwork have for the accumulation of knowledge and the generalizability of our findings?

These questions have no ready answers. Nonetheless, continued conversation about digital fieldwork, and collaboration between researchers and local intermediaries, should help scholars to develop thoughtful, actionable responses. Scholars should engage with the IRB at their home institution and other ethics boards that issue or enforce regulations in their research site(s), discussing their specific ethical concerns and the challenges they foresee, and asking their help with identifying potential ethical pitfalls and devising and implementing proper participant protections.[23]

Scholars should also engage directly with study participants to learn about their ethical concerns. Ethical commitments extend beyond obtaining potential respondents' informed consent. It is both ethically important and practically useful to assess participants' comfort level with the technology to be used in advance of the research encounter and to resolve any questions or concerns that arise. One strategy is to make at least two technology options available to participants and ask them to make the final selection (e.g., between Zoom and WhatsApp for an interview). Further, scholars can inquire whether participants feel safe and comfortable as the research interaction commences and as it progresses, seeking to allay their fears as appropriate. Researchers should also follow up in a timely manner after their interaction with human participants to thank them and to provide them with anything they promised (e.g., research results, publications, or other compensation).

In short, given the thorny and context-sensitive nature of ethical challenges, scholars need to elicit feedback from diverse sources and perspectives. Nonetheless, the most profound step that scholars can take is to adopt intentionally reflexive approaches to navigating ethical challenges. Prior to beginning research, scholars should think carefully about their ethical commitments and what they imply for the conduct of research. While conducting digital fieldwork, they should continuously reflect on the ethical dimensions of their research choices. To offer a few examples, due to the challenges of conducting research in Afghanistan during the COVID crisis in early 2020, Isaqzadeh chose to carry out a phone survey that significantly reduced the risk of violence to enumerators.[24] In South Africa, partly as a result of the research topic and on-the-ground conditions, Backe decided to digitally collect white papers, podcasts, and policy briefs rather than do interviews.[25] Hirschel-Burns chose to cancel planned interviews in postconflict Colombia because they did not feel certain about participants' safety when using technologies such as WhatsApp.[26] Carefully reflecting on their ethical commitments and constructing strong ethical foundations for their research help scholars to navigate both the familiar and the unexpected challenges that will invariably arise as digital research progresses.

Conclusion

In this chapter, we considered some long-standing practices and some emerging techniques for conducting fieldwork from afar using digital technologies, and we discussed some of the opportunities and challenges associated with digital fieldwork. We hope we have demonstrated digital fieldwork's breadth, versatility, and utility. In doing so, we in no way seek to diminish the extraordinary value of traditional fieldwork or suggest that it remains anything but vital. Both modes of inquiry have strengths and weaknesses, both involve difficult personal, operational, and ethical choices, and both require trade-offs with important intellectual implications. The core differences lie in what factors impinge on those choices and define those trade-offs. Scholars being aware of and transparent about those choices and trade-offs will enrich their research and help others understand how they carried out their work, why they did what they did, and what they found. Used in tandem—by one researcher or a research community—both traditional and digital fieldwork helps scholars to answer critical questions about the world.

The use of digital technologies to conduct research can increase fieldwork's inclusivity. Conducting fieldwork at a distance using digital technologies may be particularly useful for scholars for whom traditional fieldwork has been or has become untenable due to personal, professional, or financial circumstances, visa restrictions, or conditions in the places they wish to study. Scholars later in their careers, with family responsibilities (including children or aging/ailing parents or partners) or other commitments at home, with ability/disability or health challenges, or at underresourced institutions, can greatly benefit from the opportunities that evolving technology creates. In turn, the increased use of technology to conduct research should augment the legitimacy of using digital techniques—independently or in tandem with in-person approaches—to learn about contexts that are remote from one's own setting geographically, culturally, or in other ways. Ultimately a virtuous cycle may emerge in which continued technological and intellectual innovations, and increasing acceptance of these modes of fieldwork, allow for the inclusion of more scholars in research communities whose scholarship draws on fieldwork. Further, the use of digital fieldwork could lead to new and innovative research collaborations in which scholars from different research institutions partner to explore topics of mutual interest.[27]

Yet, it is also important to acknowledge that digital technologies do not *automatically* democratize original data collection. Conducting digital fieldwork remains out of reach for many scholars who lack access to the technology or infrastructure it requires. More scholars reaping the benefits of digital fieldwork requires that we all intentionally work against the inequalities associated with digital access. Universities and professional associations should strongly advocate for research collaborations and funding mechanisms that support research partnerships across digital divides and that include scholars in less well-resourced areas such as the Global South. Building and funding these partnerships will broaden the scope of social science research and also address some of the technical and ethical questions that we raise here.

In sum, we hope this chapter contributes to ongoing conversations about digital fieldwork that ultimately expand to include diverse scholars all around the world. As ways of thinking about and accessing our research sites, participants, and materials evolve, scholars of all backgrounds and intellectual interests need to participate in a shared dialog about this emerging range of fieldwork practices. Doing so will help new—and seasoned—researchers to use new techniques to gain fresh insights into crucial political dynamics.

Notes

1. This chapter draws on conversations and collaboration with Michael Findley and Amy Liu, to whom the authors are indebted. We also appreciate the time and effort that three research assistants at Georgetown University—Jessica Hickle, Amanda Lin, and Daniel Solomon—invested in building the associated Digital Fieldwork website (www.digitalfieldwork.org; see recommended readings). We developed the site in hopes of encouraging discussion about digital fieldwork and advancing its practice, and we welcome your engagement and contributions. We are also grateful for feedback from the volume's co-editors, Jennifer Cyr and Sara Goodman.
2. While we focus our definition of digital fieldwork on collecting and generating data, we recognize that scholars engage in other research tasks as they carry out fieldwork, for example, analyzing collected data and designing aspects of their research (see Kapiszewski, MacLean, and Read,

"Dynamic Research Design"). The differences between digital fieldwork and traditional fieldwork, however, mainly relate to the practices that scholars use to collect and generate data.
3. See, e.g., Buskirk and Andres, "Smart Surveys for Smart Phones"; Chen and Konstan, "Online Field Experiments."
4. The term "digital ethnography" can be used to refer to the study of online worlds and virtual communities (see, e.g., Gruzd, "Online Communities") or the remote study of physical people and communities (see, e.g., Hjorth et al., *The Routledge Companion to Digital Ethnography*); we use the term here to refer to the latter.
5. See McCausland, "A Future without Mediation?" and Bak, "For the Record" for a note of caution.
6. Dogucu and Cetinkaya-Rundel, "Web Scraping in the Statistics and Data Science Curriculum."
7. See, e.g., Dobson, "Fieldwork in a Digital World"; Martini, "Using GPS and GIS to Enrich the Walk-Along Method."
8. The discussion here draws on Kapiszewski, MacLean, and Read, *Field Research in Political Science*, chs. 3 and 4.
9. Technological advances also allow scholars to keep digital data safe (e.g., using cloud services) and secure (e.g., via encryption) in new ways; to automate the transcription of recorded conversations (using, e.g., Zoom, Otter, Rev, Descript, Sonix, Voicerecord, Temi, Trint), and to use some of the same programs (e.g., Otter) or qualitative data analysis software (e.g., Nvivo, ATLAS.ti, Dedoose) to code those transcripts.
10. Examples might include scholars and practitioners at local academic institutions, think tanks, and nongovernmental organizations, embassy personnel and journalists, and/or actors and agents directly involved in the dynamics the researcher wishes to understand. As with in-person fieldwork, scholars can build such networks, for example, through snowball sampling from a few people who are knowledgeable about and/or relevant to their research topic, the field site they plan to study, or potential data sources.
11. See Kapiszewski, MacLean, and Read, *Field Research in Political Science*, ch. 3 on creating a "data collection plan."
12. See, e.g., Bouka, "Collaborative Research as Structural Violence"; Strohm, "Where Is 'the Field'?"; Tilley and Kalina, "'My Flight Arrives at 5 am."
13. See Asiamah, Awal, and MacLean, "Collaboration for Designing, Conceptualizing and (Possibly) Decolonizing Research in African Politics"; Coetzee, "Ethical?!"
14. Of course, communication technologies also allow those conducting in-person fieldwork to stay connected with such support structures.
15. See Kapiszewski, MacLean, and Read, "Dynamic Research Design."
16. Likewise, some of the people with whom a researcher would like to interact may find it easier to agree to a 20-minute meeting on Zoom in which they can participate while on the move, for example, than to a formal, sit-down, in-person interview.
17. An additional (minor) upside to "visiting" archives or conducting interviews virtually is that the researcher can better capitalize on the time they spend waiting for an archivist or respondent; options are more limited when the researcher is physically in an archive or a respondent's office. Of course, sometimes periods of time waiting in person in the field can reveal unexpected evidence and shape scholars' understanding of context.
18. Other challenges can arise if the interfaces (commands and options) of the online communication platforms a researcher would like to employ cannot be displayed in a language that participants speak.
19. As reflected on the Digital Fieldwork website, there is vibrant discussion in research circles about how technology platforms and safety protocols are evolving. Researchers are encouraged to carefully consider respondents' privacy and safety, in particular when investigating unstable contexts and/or sensitive topics.

20. See, e.g., van Baalen, "'Google Wants to Know Your Location'"; Gelinas et al., "Navigating the Ethics of Remote Research Data Collection."
21. Porisky and MacLean, "The Ethics of Compensation in Field Research."
22. Such tendencies might operate at multiple levels, leading scholars to select particular countries or cities to study or to overrepresent in sampling frames respondents with greater means who can pay for internet access.
23. See, e.g., Fujii, "Research Ethics 101." Also, during the COVID-19 pandemic that emerged in 2020, the IRBs at many U.S. universities issued statements on conducting human participants research remotely in ethical ways; see, e.g., guidance from Carnegie Mellon University (https://www.cmu.edu/research-office/communications/remote-hsr-guidance.pdf), New York University (https://www.nyu.edu/content/dam/nyu/research/documents/IRB/HUMAN%20RESEARCH%20DURING%20THE%20COVID-19%20PANDEMIC.pdf), and Iowa State University (https://www.compliance.iastate.edu/sites/default/files/imported/irb/guide/docs/working-remotely-with-HSR.pdf).
24. See Isaqzadeh, "Digital Fieldwork: Lessons Learned from Afghanistan."
25. See Backe, "Slow Research in Urgent Times: COVID-19, Gender-Based Violence and the Ethics of Crisis."
26. See Hirschel-Burns, "Choosing to Not Conduct Digital Fieldwork on Sensitive Topics."
27. Technology can also limit the resources scholars need to use or expend to conduct fieldwork: digital fieldwork may require relatively small amounts of increasingly scarce grant funding, and little travel, reducing researchers' carbon footprint.

Recommended Readings

Barratt, Monica J., and Alexia Maddox. "Active Engagement with Stigmatized Communities through Digital Ethnographies." *Qualitative Research* 16, no. 6 (2016): 701–719.
    The authors' research on a "dark-web drug-use community" represents a model for investigating digital environments where participants talk about sensitive and illicit activities; issues such as the safety and security of researchers, participants, and data are discussed.
Digital Fieldwork website, www.digitalfieldwork.org, especially the searchable "References" page: https://digitalfieldwork.iu.edu/bib-entry/.
    Built by researchers for researchers, this website offers references to scholarship about, resources for, and reflections on conducting field research using digital means, and provides a forum in which scholars interested in carrying out digital fieldwork can help each other to identify and capitalize on the data-gathering opportunities it offers and explore and address the data-gathering challenges it poses.
Forrestal, Sarah G., Angela Valdovinos D'Angelo, and Lisa Klein Vogel. "Considerations for and Lessons Learned from Online, Synchronous Focus Groups." *Survey Practice* 8, no. 3 (2015).
    The authors draw on their experiences conducting online, synchronous focus groups to offer lessons for their use and implementation.
Günel, Gökçe, Saiba Varma, and Chika Watanabe. "A Manifesto for Patchwork Ethnography." Member Voices, Fieldsights, June 9, 2020. https://culanth.org/fieldsights/a-manifesto-for-patchwork-ethnography.
    This piece conceptualizes and advocates for "a new methodological and theoretical approach to ethnography"—*patchwork ethnography*—which "refer[s] to ethnographic processes and protocols designed around short-term field visits, using fragmentary yet rigorous data, and other innovations that resist the fixity, holism, and certainty demanded in the publication process."
Rosenzweig, Leah, and Yang-Yang Zhou. "Team and Nation: Sports, Nationalism and Attitudes towards Refugees." *Comparative Political Studies* 54, no. 12 (2021): 2123–2153.

This article considers whether "by heightening nationalism ... victories also affect attitudes toward *foreign* out-groups, specifically refugees"; it draws on both "the 2019 Africa Cup football match between Kenya and Tanzania" and "an online survey experiment conducted with a panel of 2,647 respondents recruited through Facebook."

References

Asiamah, Gildfred, Mohammed Awal, and Lauren M. MacLean. "Collaboration for Designing, Conceptualizing and (Possibly) Decolonizing Research in African Politics." *PS: Political Science & Politics* 54, no. 3 (2021): 549–553. doi:https://doi.org/10.1017/S1049096521000226.

Backe, Emma Louise. "Slow Research in Urgent Times: COVID-19, Gender-Based Violence and the Ethics of Crisis." Digital Fieldwork, January 25, 2001. https://digitalfieldwork.iu.edu/slow-research-in-urgent-times-covid-19-gender-based-violence-and-the-ethics-of-crisis/.

Bak, Greg. "For the Record: Digitizing Archives Can Increase Access to Information but Compromise Privacy." *The Conversation*, February 28, 2021. https://theconversation.com/for-the-record-digitizing-archives-can-increase-access-to-information-but-compromise-privacy-155364.

Bouka, Yolanda. "Collaborative Research as Structural Violence." *Political Violence at a Glance*, July 18, 2018. https://politicalviolenceataglance.org/2018/07/12/collaborative-research-as-structural-violence/.

Buskirk, T.D., and C. Andres. "Smart Surveys for Smart Phones: Exploring Various Approaches for Conducting Online Mobile Surveys via Smartphones." *Survey Practice* 5, no. 1 (2012). https://doi.org/10.29115/SP-2012-0001.

Chen, Y., and J. Konstan. "Online Field Experiments: A Selective Survey of Methods." *Journal of the Economic Science Association* 1, no. 1 (2015): 29–42. https://doi.org/10.1007/s40881-015-0005-3.

Coetzee, Carli. "Ethical?! Collaboration?! Keywords for Our Contradictory Times." *Journal of African Cultural Studies* 31, no. 3 (2019): 257–295. https://doi.org/10.1080/13696815.2019.1635437.

Dobson, Jerome E. "Fieldwork in a Digital World." *Geographical Review* 91, nos. 1–2 (2001): 430–440. https://doi.org/10.2307/3250846.

Dogucu, Mine, and Mine Cetinkaya-Rundel. "Web Scraping in the Statistics and Data Science Curriculum: Challenges and Opportunities." *Journal of Statistics and Data Science Education* 29 (2021): S112–S122. https://doi.org/10.1080/10691898.2020.1787116.

Fujii, Lee Ann. "Research Ethics 101: Dilemmas and Responsibilities." *PS: Political Science & Politics* 45, no. 4 (2012): 717–723. doi:10.1017/S1049096512000819.

Gelinas, Luke, Walker Morrell, Sarah A. White, and Barbara E. Bierer. "Navigating the Ethics of Remote Research Data Collection." *Clinical Trials* 18, no. 5 (2021): 606–614. doi:10.1177/17407745211027245.

Gruzd, Anatoliy. "Online Communities." In *Encyclopedia of Social Network Analysis and Mining*, edited by Reda Alhajj and Jon Rokne, 1635–1645. New York: Springer, 2018. https://doi.org/10.1007/978-1-4939-7131-2_81.

Hirschel-Burns, Danny. "Choosing to Not Conduct Digital Fieldwork on Sensitive Topics." Digital Fieldwork, November 9, 2021. https://digitalfieldwork.iu.edu/choosing-to-not-conduct-digital-fieldwork-on-sensitive-topics/.

Hjorth, Larissa, Heather Horst, Anne Galloway, and Genevieve Bell. *The Routledge Companion to Digital Ethnography*. New York, NY: Routledge, 2017.

Isaqzadeh, Mohammad. "Digital Fieldwork: Lessons Learned from Afghanistan." Digital Fieldwork, March 28, 2022. https://digitalfieldwork.iu.edu/digital-fieldwork-lessons-learned-from-afghanistan/.

Kapiszewski, Diana, Lauren M. MacLean, and Benjamin L. Read. *Field Research in Political Science: Practices and Principles*. Cambridge: Cambridge University Press, 2015.

Kapiszewski, Diana, Lauren M. MacLean, and Benjamin L. Read-. "Dynamic Research Design: Iteration in Field-Based Research." *Comparative Politics* 54, no. 4 (2022): 645–670.

Martini, Natalia. "Using GPS and GIS to Enrich the Walk-Along Method." *Field Methods* 32, no. 2 (2020): 180–192. https://doi.org/10.1177/1525822X20905257.

McCausland, Sigrid. "A Future without Mediation? Online Access, Archivists, and the Future of Archival Research." *Australian Academic and Research Libraries* 42, no. 4 (2011): 309–319. https://doi.org/10.1080/00048623.2011.10722243.

Porisky, Alesha, and Lauren M. MacLean. "The Ethics of Compensation in Field Research." 2022.

Strohm, Rachel. "Where Is 'the Field'? Centering the Periphery in Kinshasa." *The Republic,* December 9, 2019. https://republic.com.ng/december-19-january-20/centring-the-periphery-in-kinshasa/.

Tilley, Elizabeth, and Marc Kalina. "'My Flight Arrives at 5 am, Can You Pick Me Up?' The Gatekeeping Burden of the African Academic." *Journal of African Cultural Studies* 33, no. 4 (2021): 538–548. https://doi.org/10.1080/13696815.2021.1884972.

van Baalen, Sebastian. "'Google Wants to Know Your Location': The Ethical Challenges of Fieldwork in the Digital Age." *Research Ethics* 14, no. 4 (2018): 1–17. https://doi.org/10.1177/1747016117750312.

PART IV
ANALYZING QUALITATIVE DATA

29
Reading Closely

Antje Ellermann

Introduction

Few social science graduate programs teach their students the skill of close reading. While reading closely may feature prominently in high school curricula, close reading is usually quickly discarded in graduate school, where reading loads and comprehensive exam reading lists make the adoption of speed-reading a matter of academic survival. Even when students embark on their own research, the ready availability of digital data, with its attendant challenge of information overload, makes reading closely a luxury few feel they can afford. Without denying the utility of speed-reading, this chapter makes a case for slowing down our reading in order to hone the skill of closely reading qualitative data.

Close reading has its origins in literary studies, where it contributed to the rise of literary criticism in the first half of the 20th century.[1] When literary studies expanded into cultural studies, close reading came to be applied to nonliterary texts as well. While to this day discussions of close reading are mostly situated in the humanities, this chapter argues that social scientists also stand to gain from the practice of reading closely.

What do we mean by "reading closely"? Reading closely is the text-based equivalent to "soaking and poking" in the field—the researcher's immersion in and active engagement with the phenomenon they seek to understand. Reading closely allows the reader to get intimately acquainted with a passage of text by reading it word-by-word or sentence-by-sentence. In doing so, the reader reads between the lines, breaks apart and then reassembles text in order to explore new interpretations and meanings. In the humanities, close reading describes an interpretive process that analyzes the *linguistic* properties of text, including syntax, grammar, and phonology. In the social sciences, by contrast, the practice of close reading describes a reading and rereading of text that pays close attention to *the ways in which arguments are constructed and supported.*

Of particular importance to reading closely in the social sciences is the identification of *frames*. Frames constitute simplified interpretations of reality that allow us to process and communicate in contexts marked by complexity. In other words, a frame is a cognitive lens that allows us to interpret the world around us. Importantly, any decision to adopt a frame is at the same time a decision against the use of alternative frames, with important implications for how issues are understood and communicated. Public opinion researchers have repeatedly shown the cognitive power of frames in shaping how individuals make sense of social and economic issues. For instance, in one study respondents were asked whether a hate group should be allowed to hold a political rally; twice as many respondents expressed support when the question was framed as one of freedom of speech ("Given the importance of free speech . . .") than when the issue was framed as one of public order ("Given the risk of violence . . .").[2] Similarly, individuals are significantly more likely to support public spending

---

Antje Ellermann, *Reading Closely* In: *Doing Good Qualitative Research*. Edited by: Jennifer Cyr and Sara Wallace Goodman, Oxford University Press. © Oxford University Press 2024. DOI: 10.1093/oso/9780197633137.003.0029

on income assistance when the issue is framed as "assistance to the poor" than when it is framed as "welfare."[3]

This chapter will proceed by arguing that reading closely is a crucial foundation for the critical and interpretive analysis of textual data. It offers four criteria for structuring close reading as a method of data analysis, whereby a researcher pays attention to context, positionality, frames, and alternatives. It illustrates the use of these criteria by taking the reader through a step-by-step exercise in reading closely, zooming in and zooming out of text excerpts from a Canadian government document on immigration. The chapter concludes by discussing cherry-picking text as a common pitfall of reading closely.

Why Read Closely

Close reading can serve a number of distinct purposes. Reading closely for informational purposes seeks to grasp the literal meaning of text and help us to comprehend and retain information. Without denying the importance of reading for information's sake, this chapter is motivated by a different purpose of close reading: *to critically analyze and interpret text*. Unlike informational reading, analyzing and interpreting text always requires us to read closely in order to understand how meaning is produced and communicated. Analytical and interpretive reading requires us to grapple with a speaker's choice of frame, with the context in which speech and text are situated, as well as with what remains unsaid. Close reading thus allows the reader to enter into a conversation with the text. It asks us to zoom in on the construction of frames, to ask questions, and to explore a range of interpretations and meanings. What, then, might this process of "interrupted reading"[4] look like in practice? How does a researcher engage in close reading in ways that facilitate their analysis and interpretation of text?

The Practice of Reading Closely

To read closely means to make multiple passes through text in order to capture its subtleties and nuances and explore the possible range of interpretations. We will now engage in an iterative process of zooming in and out in order to closely read text excerpts from a government document. I suggest four criteria for structuring a close reading: context, positionality, frames, and alternatives. The process begins with an overview establishing the *context* in which the text was spoken/written. Second, we zoom in on the author's *positionality*. Paying close attention to questions of positionality means identifying an author's location within social and organizational power hierarchies. By being mindful of an author's positionality, we recognize that identity cannot be separated from text because the act of speaking and writing is necessarily embedded within a person's social and institutional environment. Third, we zoom in further by focusing our reading on the *dominant frame*. When identifying a frame, we ask questions such as: What is the author's problem diagnosis? What are the proposed solutions? What evidence does the author draw on? What evidence is ignored? Fourth, we zoom out and situate the text in its broader discourse in order to identify *alternative frames* that are absent from the text. Structuring a close reading according to these four criteria enables a systematic collection of data.

We will now engage in close reading of a text excerpt from a regulatory impact assessment statement published by the Canadian government. Regulatory impact assessments are intended to improve the quality of regulatory decision-making by providing stakeholders with information about a proposed regulation and its implementation. They usually outline different regulatory options and provide evidence-based assessments of their expected impacts before making a case for a proposed regulatory change. The text we will examine was authored by Citizenship and Immigration Canada, Canada's immigration department (subsequently renamed Immigration, Refugees, and Citizenship Canada), prior to the coming into force of amendments to Canada's immigration regulations. It was published on May 18, 2013, in the *Canada Gazette,* a government publication of new statutes and government regulations.

Context: Since the 1980s, Canadian immigration policy has moved from a system dominated by family-sponsored admissions to one centered on economic immigration. In 2012, the Conservative government set in motion a new round of reforms targeting the admission of family-sponsored immigrants. In addition to restricting the immigration of elderly parents and grandparents, the regulatory reforms sought to limit the admission of immediate family members by lowering the immigration age threshold for dependent children from 22 to 19 years. The text of the regulatory impact assessment statement reads as follows (ellipses denote text that has been omitted for brevity's sake):[5]

Background:
Over the past four years, Canada has weathered the global recession well; however, economic stability remains fragile. Accordingly, emphasis on the objectives of IRPA [Immigration and Refugee Protection Act] to maximize the economic benefits of immigration and support the development of a strong and prosperous Canadian economy has become more central to the immigration agenda. Significant transformations to Canada's immigration system are still needed to sustain economic growth, job creation and prosperity. A key element of these transformations is an efficient and effective immigration system focused on Canada's economic and labour-force needs to attract immigrants who would contribute to the Canadian economy....

Issues and Objectives:
Dependent children of selected immigrants are admitted on the basis of their relationship to the principal applicant. Dependent children represent 30% of the overall immigrants admitted annually to Canada. Statistics demonstrate that older dependent children (those who arrive between the ages of 19 and 21) have lower economic outcomes than those who arrive in Canada at a younger age (between 15 and 18 years old).

Research (see footnote 2) has demonstrated that older immigrants have a more challenging time fully integrating into the Canadian labour market; this is more evident for immigrants who are not selected based on their own merits (e.g. dependent children)....

In other words, the current definition of a dependent child for immigration purposes is out of step with the Government of Canada's objective of selecting migrants who contribute best to Canada's economic growth and sustainability. Furthermore, this misalignment creates operational inefficiencies.

The primary objective of the proposed amendments is to enhance economic integration of immigrant dependent children to increase Canada's economic potential. This would be achieved by reducing the maximum age of dependent children to admit those dependent children who are more likely to successfully integrate into the labour market and contribute to the Canadian economy. To further ensure admittance of younger dependent children, the exception to the age limit of dependent children for full-time students would be removed.

This proposal would respond to Government priorities of having an immigration system focused on Canada's economic and labour force needs. Reducing the age of dependent children would support Canada's immigration priorities by placing more emphasis on younger immigrants, who integrate more rapidly into the labour market and who would spend a greater number of years contributing to the economy.[6]

Positionality. Reading the Regulatory Impact Analysis Statement, it is evident that we are not privy to the authors' social identity. While the end of the document (not included here) lists "Caroline Riverin Beaulieu" as "Assistant Director of Social Policy and Programs for Citizenship and Immigration Canada," this information is included for contact purposes only. All we can deduce about the authors is their organizational identity: the text was drafted and approved by federal immigration bureaucrats within the immigration department's Social Policy and Programs Branch. Yet it is precisely the reader's lack of knowledge of the authors' identities and social positioning that imbues the document with technocratic authority. The authors speak on behalf of the Government of Canada, referencing "the Government of Canada's objective" and "Government priorities." By retaining their anonymity, the authors project a Weberian legal-rational authority that rests on impersonal, technocratic decision-making. The authors' positionality as nameless federal civil servants thus legitimates claims of the impact assessment as objective, evidence-based, and reliant on technocratic expertise ("Statistics show," "Research (footnote 2) has demonstrated that"), rather than as expressive of partisan ideology or personal opinion.

While a close reading allows us to draw some inferences about the authors' positionality, it is important to recognize that the text in its published form is the product of an editorial process that the reader is not privy to. In order to understand the pressures bearing on the bureaucrats who drafted, reviewed, and redrafted the text, we would need to gain interview access to these actors to learn about the document's editorial process. Alternatively, a future generation of scholars might search the archives for earlier document drafts once the closure period for government records has passed.

Dominant frames. We will now zoom in and examine the text's dominant frame. The authors' choice of frame shapes not only problem diagnosis and definition of policy goals but even the very concept of the immigrant. The authors justify the government's proposal to narrow the immigration definition of dependent child as a solution to suboptimal labor market outcomes. The text begins with a general problem definition: the recent global recession has destabilized Canada's economy ("economic stability remains fragile"). The authors continue to employ this economic frame when asserting that the goals of immigration policy are to "maximize the economic benefits of immigration" and to prioritize those immigrants who "contribute best to Canada's economic growth and sustainability." In order to meet this goal, they argue, "significant transformations to Canada's immigration system" are necessary. Among the immigration policies that need to be "transformed" is the definition of dependent child. Introducing an immigration-specific problem diagnosis, the authors point to the "lower economic outcomes" of dependent children arriving between the ages of 19 and

21, compared to those arriving between the ages of 15 and 18. Lowering the age limit of dependent children, they reason, will increase the economic benefits of immigration.

By employing an economic frame, the authors conceive of immigrants as (potential) workers. For example, in a utilitarian economic calculation, the authors distinguish between age groups when calculating children's projected earnings. In a footnote (not cited here), the authors refer to government research that suggests that, by age 30, children who arrived in Canada at ages 15 to 18 earn approximately 20% more than those who immigrated at ages 19 to 21. In a second calculation, the authors compare differently aged immigrant children based on the projected number of years of labor market participation. Not surprisingly, younger dependent children "would spend a greater number of years contributing to the economy."

Analyzing frames is also an opportunity to simultaneously perform the fourth guideline: considering alternatives. What other way could this document frame immigration? For instance, immigration could also be framed as an issue of intergenerational care. The corresponding family frame would foreground the dependency of children past the age of majority; in a subsequent passage the authors assure the reader that "[t]he proposed definition of dependent child, based on the age of 19, is in line with most provincial, federal and international standards by which a child is considered to have reached the age of independence." A close reading of this sentence, however, prompts us to question whether this legal standard should be applied to the definition of dependent child for the purpose of immigration. Not only does the proposed definition violate some legal standards (as the authors acknowledge), but it is not obvious why a standard developed for the purpose of determining the age of majority—the authors reference the Criminal Code and voting rights—should be used to determine until what age a child can be expected to live with their parents. It is here that the absence of text stands out, as the authors choose not to draw on statistical data in making this assessment. Had they done so, they would likely note that, based on the 2011 Census, over 42% of young adults ages 20 to 29 years in Canada still lived with a parent, a proportion that is even higher (50%) in immigrant families. These omitted data suggest extending, rather than narrowing, the definition of dependent child under immigration law.

A close reading of text requires us to pay attention as much to what remains unsaid as to what is said. Regulatory impact assessment statements are intended to offer an evidence-informed discussion of a policy's costs *and* benefits. Looking at how the statement draws on empirical research, however, we find that of the nine research references, eight emphasize the economic costs of retaining the current age of dependence. Accordingly, younger immigrant children are presumed to fare better than their older counterparts when it comes to gaining "human capital skills specific to the Canadian labour market" and to "adjust[ing] to a new linguistic and cultural context" because "they receive a Canadian education and later obtain Canadian work experience." Only a single reference in the text touches on the regulatory change's impact on immigrant families, noting that, "at current processing levels, approximately 7,000 (see footnote 10) dependent children (ages 19 and above, from all immigration categories combined) would no longer be considered dependent children given the proposed amendment." Once again utilizing their economic frame, the authors turn to the impact on different immigration streams and note that the proposed amendments "would not have a significant impact on the overall economic stream as dependent children aged 19 and over account for less than 3% of all approved persons in the economic programs."

Significantly, the authors choose not to address the question of how the denial of sponsorship rights for children ages 19 to 22 would affect their families. By framing immigration exclusively in economic terms, the consideration of impact is limited to, first, the (positive) labor market implications of lowering the age of dependence and, second, the assurance that economic immigration programs will not be adversely affected by the amendment. The authors implicitly recognize that parents will not want to be separated from their young adult children by stating that those children may decide to come to Canada as international students. If such international students acquire Canadian work experience after graduation and meet other applicable requirements, they may apply for immigration under the Canadian Experience Class (CEC), which to date has yielded positive economic and labor market outcomes. Others may decide to apply to come to Canada on their own merit through various economic programs. This would help Canada attract and retain qualified immigrants who have the skills and experience required to contribute to Canada's overall economic growth.

By applying an economic frame to the question of family dependents, the authors consider young adult children as independent bearers of human capital who may come to Canada not as family dependents, but rather "on their own merits," conditional on their ability to demonstrate that they will enhance economic growth. Alternatively, adult children may enter Canada as international students, once again putting the onus on the adult child to demonstrate academic "merit." Significantly, the authors fail to acknowledge the enormous financial costs imposed on immigrant parents who would have to pay the steep price of international student tuition for the sake of family unity.

Regulatory impact assessment statements are designed to provide a measured cost-benefit analysis of regulatory change. By zooming in on this document, we have shown that the authors' decision to employ a single frame has skewed their consideration of the costs and benefits of narrowing the definition of dependent child. By employing an economic frame, the authors limit their cost-benefit analysis to labor market considerations, conceiving of immigrants and their children exclusively as bearers of human capital and disregarding the corresponding impact on immigrant parents and their adult children. It is this analysis that—combined with the close reading of other texts—elsewhere allowed me to construct the concept of "human-capital citizenship" as a qualitatively new understanding of membership in contemporary liberal democracies.[7] In order to better understand the implications of frame *absence*, we will now zoom out and examine the use of an alternative family frame in previous policy reform.

Absent frames. As mentioned, the analysis of frames provides an opportunity to simultaneously consider both present and alternative frames. As stated in Canada's Immigration and Refugee Protection Act, the objectives of Canadian immigration policy are manifold and extend well beyond economic considerations. In addition to the support of economic prosperity, they include the pursuit of social, cultural, and economic benefits of immigration, enrichment of the "social and cultural fabric of Canadian society," family reunification, immigrant integration, and the promotion of international justice and human rights.

Historically, the admission of family dependents to Canada has been justified under the family frame. This frame prioritizes the right of individuals to live with members of their family (however narrowly defined) over their economic contributions to society. The text of the regulatory impact analysis statement itself implies this logic by noting that, under the policy status quo, dependents "are not selected on the basis of their own merits" but rather on the basis of their close relationship to a principal applicant.

Canada's 1976 Immigration Act, which set the foundation of the country's skills-based immigration system, affirmed the moral imperative of an inclusive, largely unconditional family immigration policy, which extended to the children, elderly parents, and grandparents of principal applicants.[8] We will now read two text passages from the 1960s and 1970s that speak to the family frame's relevance. The first excerpt is taken from the Green Paper that preceded the 1976 Immigration Act:

> When Canada accepts immigrants, we consider ourselves duty-bound also to accept those close relatives who would normally be dependent on them in a society such as our own.[9]

The second text is excerpted from a speech by Prime Minister Lester Pearson in 1967, the year when the major reforms of the 1976 Immigration Act—including the point system—were first passed in the form of regulation:

> I do not think that we should require, for this kind of [parent and grandparent] sponsorship, any financial evidence of ability to support the sponsored immigrant. To impose financial standards smacks of paternalism. If a man wants to take his old grandmother into his house, it is not for government to say that he doesn't have room or can't afford it.... [I]n my view the unity of the dependent family ought not to be set aside because it can result, in a few cases, in the community having to bear extra welfare costs.[10]

Comparing these statements with the 2013 regulatory impact assessment statement, the contrast between the family frame and the economic frame is stark. Rather than conceiving of family members as carriers of varying amounts of human capital, the earlier texts treat the family as an intergenerational unit marked by interdependence. Not only is interdependence among family members naturalized rather than problematized, but the texts further assert a duty of the state to respect familial interdependence by not erecting unnecessary hurdles to family unification, even when this results in greater welfare costs to the state.

The step of zooming out by reading earlier texts on family sponsorship has brought into sharp relief the distinctly novel interpretation of family immigration by the authors of the regulatory impact assessment statement. By applying an exclusively economic frame to the regulation of family sponsorship, the authors reject not only a family frame but also the conception of immigration policy as a *balancing* act between competing goals. Instead, economic considerations are given primacy over alternative policy goals, even to the point of defining the dependent child age threshold in economic terms. To cite the text once more, "[T]he primary objective of the proposed amendments is to enhance economic integration of immigrant dependent children to increase Canada's economic potential."

Potential Problems of Reading Closely

We will now turn to a potential pitfall of reading closely: the cherry-picking of text. Cherry-picking text describes the picking and choosing of text passages that are congruent with an existing, or preferred, frame, while disregarding text that does not fit the frame. It can also take the form of relying on selective texts where a researcher may not know the "universe" of potential texts. Alongside a regulatory impact assessment, for instance, there may be draft reports available online, or memoranda of understanding that might be shared by a government contact. Alternatively, there may be statements by the stakeholders submitted to the department which may offer useful contextualization.

Cherry-picking within a text can result from either time pressure or reader bias. Because reading closely takes time, it can be tempting to skim text rather than closely reading a document in its entirety. Without having read a document from beginning to end, however, we cannot draw firm conclusions about its framing. By limiting close reading to shorter excerpts, for instance, we might miss the use of a nondominant frame. Reading closely for the purpose of data analysis and interpretation thus requires us to commit time to allow for the close reading of a text in its entirety.

Cherry-picking text can also result from the reader's confirmation bias—people's tendency to seek out information that is congruent with their values and beliefs. It is tempting to pick text passages that confirm a preferred interpretation while disregarding those that do not conform to a favored frame. Yet without reading closely for alternative interpretations, our analysis lacks validity. Close reading requires us to systematically read and reread text with an eye to alternative interpretations. When using ellipses to denote the omission of text, for instance, we need to take care that the omitted passages do not entail rival interpretations. The close reading of text should thus be guided by questions such as: What are alternative interpretations of a given passage? If a different reader were to read this text, what is the likelihood that they would follow our interpretation? Cultivating the practice of asking these questions will significantly reduce the risk of cherry-picking and strengthen the validity of our analysis.

Finally, while the space constraints of academic publishing leave us with little choice but to be selective in the textual evidence we include, there are additional steps we can take to persuade the reader that we were careful not to cherry-pick our evidence. Returning to our earlier discussion of the shift in immigration discourse from a family to an economic frame, we could include additional passages of the regulatory impact assessment statement in an appendix or add evidence for the adoption of economic frames in other documents (such as legislative transcripts). Alternatively, we could reference scholarship that identifies the adoption of economic frames in social policy other than immigration, or incorporate data from interviews with government officials or from biographies of party leaders that give insight into policymakers' values and beliefs. While recognizing that we are rarely (if ever) able to closely read all available and relevant sources of text, approaching our reading with an awareness of the temptation of cherry-picking is the first, and most important, step in guarding against confirmation bias when collecting text-based data.

Conclusion

In this chapter, I have made the case for honing the skill of close reading of text. Using the example of a Canadian government document, the chapter took the reader through a four-step process of close reading focused on identifying the *context* in which the document was written, the *positionality* of its authors, the dominant *frame* employed by the authors, and the identification of *alternative* frames that could have been, but ultimately were not, adopted. Doing so allowed for the kind of in-depth analysis and interpretation of text-based data that is inaccessible to the cursory reader. We concluded with a discussion of cherry-picking as a common pitfall of reading closely, and identified some strategies for guarding against the use of cherry-picked evidence.

Notes

1. Long, "Re(Reading) Close Reading."
2. Sniderman and Theriault, "The Structure of Political Argument and the Logic of Issue Framing."
3. Rasinski, "The Effect of Question Wording on Public Support for Government Spending."
4. Watson, "Making Sense of the Stories of Experience," 142.
5. Some of this discussion draws on Ellermann, "Human-Capital Citizenship and the Changing Logic of Immigrant Admissions."
6. Government of Canada, "Regulations Amending the Immigration and Refugee Protection Regulations."
7. Ellermann, "Human-Capital Citizenship and the Changing Logic of Immigrant Admissions."
8. See Ellermann, "Human-Capital Citizenship and the Changing Logic of Immigrant Admissions."
9. Department of Manpower and Immigration Canada, *Immigration Program*, 52.
10. Cited in Elrick, "From Intimate Relationships to Market Relationships," 52.

Recommended Readings

Watson, Jinx Stapleton. "Making Sense of the Stories of Experience: Methodology for Research and Teaching." *Journal of Education for Library and Information Science* 42, no. 2 (2001): 137–148.
    In exploring the ways professionals construct the meaning of work, the author takes the reader through a step-by-step exercise of closely reading these interview transcripts.
Ellermann, Antje. "Human-Capital Citizenship and the Changing Logic of Immigrant Admissions." *Journal of Ethnic and Migration Studies* 46, no. 12 (2020): 2515–2532.
    Referenced throughout this chapter, this comparative analysis examines the shift from a family frame to an economic frame in the making of family immigration policy in Canada and Germany.
Hinchman, Kathleen A., and David W. Moore. "Close Reading: A Cautionary Interpretation." *Journal of Adolescent & Adult Literacy* 56, no. 6 (2013): 441–450.
    This article discusses the practice of close reading (grounding in the humanities) in relation to comprehension and retention as well as analysis and interpretation.
Bonjour, Saskia. "Speaking of Rights: The Influence of Law and Courts on the Making of Family Migration Policies in Germany." *Law & Policy* 38 (2016): 328–348.
    This article demonstrates a close reading of federal judicial rulings on family unification in Germany between 1975 and 1990.
Beaman, Jean. *Citizen Outsider: Children of North African Immigrants in France*. Berkeley: University of California Press, 2017.
    Based on a close reading of in-depth interviews with middle-class children of North African immigrants in France, the author examines the ways in which upwardly mobile immigrants experience cultural exclusion based on ethnic origin.

References

Department of Manpower and Immigration Canada. *Immigration Program: Green Paper on Immigration*. Vol. 2. Ottawa: Information Canada, 1974.

Ellermann, Antje. "Human-Capital Citizenship and the Changing Logic of Immigrant Admissions." *Journal of Ethnic and Migration Studies* 46, no. 12 (2020): 2515–2532.

Elrick, Jennifer. "From Intimate Relationships to Market Relationships: Legal Definitions of Immigrant Families and the Changing Social Contexts behind the Demise of Settler Societies." Unpublished manuscript, 2018.

Government of Canada. "Regulations Amending the Immigration and Refugee Protection Regulations." *Canada Gazette*, part 1, 147, no. 20 (May 18, 2013). https://gazette.gc.ca/rp-pr/p1/2013/2013-05-18/html/reg1-eng.html.

Long, Mark C. "Re(Reading) Close Reading." *The Far Field* (blog). October 12, 2020. https://thefarfield.org/reading-and-writing/reading-close-reading/.

Rasinski, Kenneth A. "The Effect of Question Wording on Public Support for Government Spending." *Public Opinion Quarterly* 53, no. 3 (1989): 388–394.

Sniderman, Paul M., and Sean M. Theriault. "The Structure of Political Argument and the Logic of Issue Framing." In *Studies in Public Opinion*, edited by Willem E. Saris and Paul M. Sniderman, 133–165. Princeton, NJ: Princeton University Press, 2004.

Watson, Jinx Stapleton. "Making Sense of the Stories of Experience: Methodology for Research and Teaching." *Journal of Education for Library and Information Science* 42, no. 2 (2001): 137–148.

30
The Role of Description

Deborah Avant

Introduction

Looking at the world often reveals patterns that are surprising to conventional wisdom. Take Anne-Marie Slaughter's description of global governance.[1] While theorists bemoaned the lack of global governance, looking for it as had been conventionally understood in agreements or treaties among states, she examined what was unfolding around particular issues on the ground. In the wake of 9/11, for instance, she saw collaboration in networks of financial regulators, law enforcement officials, and intelligence operatives. Describing their efforts demonstrated a different pattern of governance. Global governance was there, Slaughter's description demonstrated, just not where scholars were looking. John Ruggie's depiction of the interaction between companies and civil society actors around the UN Global Compact and HIV/AIDS treatment programs similarly both revealed something that was there (actors and practices many scholars were not examining) and generated a different way to think about them—not as "private" actors but as participants in what he called a new public domain.[2] Peter Andreas's description of the siege of Sarajevo made legible the business of survival in war. His description allowed for a new appreciation of the interrelation between licit and illicit activities and the dark side of globalization that has become a critical area of research.[3]

These highly influential arguments did not grow out of law-like claims about the relationship between *a* and *b*, but out of descriptions of patterns they see in the world. They told it like it was. Though description is often maligned in political science and journals regularly profess reluctance to publish "merely" descriptive work,[4] description plays a vital role in both noticing problems with established theories and generating theoretical advances. Description can also be an end in itself. Much of the value of social network analysis is in its description of associations we might not otherwise see.[5]

So, what are descriptive arguments? How does description contribute to political analysis? What makes these, and other descriptive arguments like them, persuasive or good? How can new researchers practice good description?

An Overview of Description

Many analyses of description contrast it with explanation. In a thoughtful example of this, John Gerring explains that it is primarily about the question a researcher is asking. Description "aims to answer *what* questions (e.g., *when, whom, out of what, in what manner*) about a phenomenon or a set of phenomena."[6] Gerring claims that description is interested in the who, what, when, where, and how questions associated with good journalism. Description can focus on particular individual accounts, but it can also aim toward indicators that allow one to generalize, associations that one claims among different dimensions of a phenomenon, syntheses, and typologies.[7] Gerring contrasts this with the *why* questions that animate causal accounts. He claims that these should be understood as different forms of argumentation.[8]

In some instances that may be true—understanding what January 6, 2021, was (a protest, an insurrection, or a self-coup?), who participated (right-wing militants? white supremacists? Trump supporters?), and how it happened (spontaneous or planned violence?) entail descriptive analysis. Understanding why it happened (the product of democratic backsliding? factionalization? the politics of resentment?) is a causal story.[9] Barbara Walter's book, though, titled *How Civil Wars Start*, is very much a causal story. There is a lot of "why" behind the "how." Similarly, to justify describing January 6 as a self-coup, Pion-Berlin, Bruneau, and Goetze use claims about why it occurred—often the product of democratic backsliding—to appropriately categorize it.[10] In practice, the lines between description and explanation are not clear; there is often explanatory logic behind description and description in explanation—the why and the how are intertwined.

Even though the distinction between explanation and description is not always clear, Gerring's overarching claim that description is important on its own terms remains important. As he puts it, describing only in the quest for causal inference will leave us with less knowledge and knowledge that is "less, precise, less reliable, and perhaps subject to systematic bias."[11] Focusing on *what* questions, even if they cannot be entirely separated from *why*, primes scholars to understand more about social and political interactions. This generates greater openness to seeing the patterns that disrupt conventional wisdom—be they relations among substate governors, business and civil society organizations, or smugglers and peacekeepers. Noticing new patterns can also foster creative ways to think about them. Attention to description on its own terms helps scholars guard against trapping themselves in models that are inadequate for solving problems in the world.

How description is understood and practiced varies with analysts' epistemological and methodological commitments. By its very nature, though, as Amartya Sen put it years ago, description is choice.[12] Description has an aim and thus promises to shape the world it describes.

Positivist or Not?

Gerring's argument is speaking to the social science mainstream, animated by positivist notions of truth. In this logic, it is common to aim descriptive accounts toward unbiased or neutral facts.[13] These facts are useful for uncovering systematic categories or general universal relationships. There is a truth "out there," and it is the job of social scientists to uncover it, get it right, and reveal the general patterns it can elucidate. Take the Correlates of War (COW) as an example. Like many data projects, it defined a phenomenon, war, and specified variables related to it to make possible the systematic study of war over space and time.[14] Its categories, including national capability, alliances, geography, polarity, status, and battle deaths, represent the dominant views about war and its causes in the 1970s.[15] According to this project, World War I is a "war" with over 9 million battle deaths and involving nine countries divided between the Central Powers (Germany, Austria-Hungary, and Turkey) and the Allies (France, Great Britain, Russia, Italy, Japan, and, later, the United States).

Feminist, constructivist, critical, and pragmatic approaches, on the other hand, are skeptical of claims about the neutrality or universality of facts. These approaches encourage attention to less visible *whos* or *whats* and claim that different vantage points generate different stories about what happened. For instance, enterprises such as the COW are embedded in a canon dominated by white male leaders from Western imperial powers.[16] How might the view change if one considered the perspectives of more peripheral subjects? For one, it might disrupt the logic of looking at World War I through the lens of countries. Looking at U.S. behavior through the eyes of Black intellectuals in the United States, for instance, tells us that the U.S. decision to enter World War I was not only action to protect U.S. interests, or the Allies but also an effort to preserve white hegemony *within* the United States as well as abroad.[17] Similarly, women from many different countries worked to promote peace against what Jane Addams called "a tribal form of patriotism."[18] Lauren Wilcox demonstrates that counting battle deaths is only one of many ways to think of the interaction between bodies and violence.[19] Rather than aiming to account for facts "out there," these approaches urge awareness of how "facts" and their worthiness for study are influenced by one's perspective. Differently situated people may see and experience phenomena in different ways. By attending to whose viewpoint is included (or not), one might get a very different narrative.

Thick or Thin?

Description can be thin or thick. Thin description is sometimes described as superficial.[20] Related to positivist assumptions, it is often informed by "facts" and established theoretical categories about who and what matter. It asks questions about when and where events happened. The answers to these questions are often assumed to hold regardless of place or time. Many data projects, such as the COW, are aimed at this type of description. Important insights can be generated from this kind of inquiry. Using the COW data, for instance, John Vasquez has argued that power politics behavior does not avoid war but brings states close to it.[21]

Thick description, on the other hand, explores the underlying meanings that make sense to participants. It is more sensitive to history, culture, and practices. As Clifford Geertz writes, "[I]t is not in our interest to bleach human behavior of the very properties that interest us before we begin to examine it."[22] This perspective has us pay great attention to *how* questions. From this view, describing the World War I case that went into the COW data set requires that we go beyond thinking of it as "a war" by virtue of what it was (a violent interaction resulting in a specified number of "battle deaths") and who was involved (nation-states). We could consider it instead a particularly tragic conflict—a war no one wanted that nonetheless caused unfathomable devastation.[23] We could also find important the individual plotting related to failed diplomacy and beliefs about the advantage of the offensive that shaped strategies of the protagonists, the erosion of civilian control, and brinksmanship.[24] All of this is important to understanding how these particular events unfolded. Thick description and thin description tell us different things about the same happenings.

Description's Creative and Normative Side

Description is often contrasted not just with explanation but also with experimental approaches (that intervene to create a treatment) or normative accounts (that tell how things *should* happen).[25] But description does not merely represent, accurately or not, what has "happened."[26] The act of describing also shapes how we think about what has happened. It can make even those involved in a process see themselves, their roles, or others differently than they did as things were happening. Vitalis argues, for instance, that international relations scholars in the United States in the middle of the 20th century actively constructed a narrative of states, state power, the state system, and the scientific study of states to obscure the concerns with race and race subjugation that drove policy earlier in the century.[27] Fortna used sophisticated statistical methods to generate a more nuanced description of peacekeeping, taking account of the relative difficulty of various violent situations, which revealed a different picture of peacekeepers' impact.[28] Autesserre's portrayal of peace challenges the dominant scholarly view of what peace is and how it unfolds.[29] Description is creative. Through talk we make vivid something about social interaction. Our language not only reflects but also shapes the facts we see.

The act of describing also centers narratives, people, and understandings that reflect values and impact power dynamics. Many traditional theories in the political science canon reproduce Western dominance and white privilege, obscure the role of women, and are built on logics that emphasize masculine and belittle feminine traits.[30] Describing what is obvious and taking commonsense categories as given reinforce dominant values. Efforts to unsettle these accounts are often more self-conscious of their normative frame and seek to dislodge rather than reinforce dominant values. Both, though, have potential normative impact.

As is likely clear by now, my own style is skeptical of positivist claims. I often endeavor to describe in a thicker manner, and I am attentive to the creative and normative impact of my work. Regardless of whether your orientation is similar to or different from mine, though, there are some agreed-on best practices for good description. Next I explain strategies that help generate persuasive description regardless of your ontological, epistemological, or methodological style.

Doing Good Description

Ask who, what, when, where, and how questions. Even though it is not always possible to separate *why* questions from *who, what, when, where,* and *how,* Gerring's suggestion is a good place to start. Examine things that actually happened. Who did what? Anne-Marie Slaughter examined actual government officials—police investigators, financial regulators, judges, and legislators—and what they were doing: exchanging information and coordinating activity across national borders. This activity is how they worked to tackle crime, terrorism, and a variety of other international problems. Her description was important in and of itself, but also became the basis for a causal argument about how networks of substate officials could be an additional and sometimes more effective source of global governance.

Acknowledge your assumptions. What you set out to describe is inevitably informed by the categories in your mind. Rather than ignoring this or assuming your mind is just like everyone else's, good description often follows when the author is aware of their frame of reference. A descriptive account that makes clear its starting point and associated expectations is better poised to notice anomalies. What is leading you to look at an instance—what do you anticipate seeing? Who do you expect to act? What do you think will happen? When? Where? How do you think things will unfold? Thinking through what you expect, and making your implicit assumptions explicit, allows you to separate your expectations from your observations. Gelman and Basbøll argue that stories are most likely to be impactful when they represent aspects of life that are not explained by existing models.[31] This is what Dewey argued was the difference between blind reacting and a scientific method.[32] It allows you to learn—to generate new concepts or new ways to think about old concepts.

Consider Stathis Kalyvas's description of the Greek Civil War. Clarifying commonly held assumptions about war that were based around macro-accounts, including those coded by the COW, allowed him to notice that activity outside of these assumptions was consequential for violence in the Greek Civil War.[33] This ultimately led him to describe individual, more micro rationales for violence that many had ignored. His insight generated a different description of the Greek Civil War than was commonly accepted. By self-consciously unsettling the macronarratives researchers had taken for granted, Kalyvas's argument influenced a wide array of research looking at microdynamics in violent encounters. This has included investigations around popular participation in violence, more or less productive peacebuilding practices, and even how nonviolent activities might affect the dynamics of violence.[34] His new assumptions were also fundamental for building a causal argument about violence related to territorial control, but his careful unveiling and disruption of common assumptions was, arguably, even more important for generating important new thinking—descriptive and causal—about the world.

Look broadly at your phenomena. What is happening all around the issue you care about? How does it look in specific instances? What is the general texture of political and social relations around your concern? As King, Keohane, and Verba recount, Richard Fenno's deep study—often referred to as "soaking and poking"—of Congress and the behavior of Congress members allowed American politics researchers to frame better questions.[35] In Gerring's words, "[I]f an evidence-gathering mission is conceptualized as descriptive rather than causal (which is to say, no single causal theory guides the research), it is more likely to produce a broad range of evidence that will be applicable to a broad range of questions, both descriptive and causal."[36] Descriptive efforts require knowledge that allows the analyst to paint a vivid picture for the reader. They thus do not shy away from complexity and detail.

Specific techniques might include reading histories and memoires, looking at documents, and scouring secondary sources. There are many other ways to gather data, including ethnography, field research, interviews, focus groups, and participant observation. Creating timelines and knowing the actors involved can be important. Establishing coding rules, exploring content analysis, or using factor analysis can also play roles in descriptive efforts. Persuasive descriptive accounts often rely on a combination of these to bring the story to life and demonstrate its integrity. Being able to write a good description commonly requires the author to know a tremendous amount of background information and context, much more than they will ever fit in the pages of their work.

Conveying deep knowledge about a specific instance or a phenomenon can help convince others of the value of one's account. Extensive knowledge of the issues Ruggie addressed and ability to explain who was doing what, when, and how were key to much of his work, from his analysis of embedded liberalism as an ordering principle, to the disjuncture between the study and practice of international organizations, to his argument about new public actors in global governance.[37] This deep exploration can also result in fruitful pathways you may not have expected. While she was reading widely to gather context and texture as she began work on what became *Before the West*, Ayse Zarakol stumbled upon the story of Ibn Battuta.[38] She hadn't expected to write about him but realized that "this is a person like me." Even though he lived in the 13th century, the degree to which his life paralleled the life of an academic in the 21st century was a vivid illustration of just how connected the world had been much earlier than we commonly assume.[39]

Among the most prominent and purposeful examples of the connection between broad understanding and fruitful description can be found in feminist international relations. Consider Cynthia Enloe's *Bananas, Beaches, and Bases*.[40] Even her early work on ethnicity's role in the military and police reveals curiosity about what she was seeing on the ground and how it mattered to different people, including women. Centering women's experiences led her to describe military bases in much greater detail than had been the case before. Rather than seeing them only as a strategic decision with impacts on the sovereignty of the host, she described them as larger phenomena, with impacts on the shape of local economies, race relations, crime, the lives of sex workers, and more. Enloe's work demonstrates the worth of exploration. Looking beyond the strategic decisions of states and the associated view of the world that highlights masculine elements of the human condition led Enloe to attend to a more holistic view that incorporates feminine features as well.[41] In so doing, she practiced good description and also generated considerable theoretical insights.

Compare. Structured, focused comparison can be its own method, but it also can be useful in generating a narrative.[42] Comparing what you think of as similar instances can push you to discover important details and to check your narrative. If a comparison with apparently similar instances reveals different processes, it can sharpen your description by alerting you to what is not happening and thus enhancing attention to paths not taken. As Keck and Sikkink ask in their preface, "Why did this event [a military slaughter of student demonstrators in Mexico], a 1968 version of China's 1989 Tiananmen Square massacre, not inspire an international response?"[43] Thinking through the two events side by side generated attention to a set of actors many might have ignored in Tiananmen Square: transnational networks. A comparative frame led to both better (more detailed, complex, and compelling) description of the Tiananmen Square incident as well as new causal hypotheses. Subsequent analysis generated an explanation of how these networks could both elevate human rights consciousness globally and restrict the ability of governments to suppress information. Noticing similarities among what are assumed to be different situations can also be productive. Susan Sell and Aseem Prakash found similarities in the strategies of what were assumed to be very different actions by businesses and NGOs.[44] This led them to examine each side by side, which again led to better description that detailed normative claims by business and material concerns among NGOs, and also a novel explanation.

Take account of "inconvenient facts." Related is Max Weber's observation that a key criterion for the scientific vocation is its willingness to take account of "inconvenient facts." "Inconvenient facts" are specifics that go against one's personal or political views. Weber wrote about inconvenient facts in his essay on science as a vocation as fundamental to the academic enterprise.[45] Unlike the politician whose inner conviction is so strong that nothing can shake it, scientists are persons of knowledge and aim for understanding that accounts for inconvenient facts.[46] Being able to support the importance of United Nations activities in Sarajevo while still acknowledging that they were not possible without black markets, as Peter Andreas did, is one example. Different epistemological positions do this in different ways. Those assuming the potential for objectivity endeavor to keep themselves at a distance. Those skeptical of objectivity strive to make their positionality clear. Awareness of one's positionality and the epistemology (and related values) that drive one's account portends a kind of distance not completely unlike efforts to be objective in more positivist traditions. Both stances encourage an openness to evidence—even evidence that is uncomfortable.

Take note of your subjects' views. Researchers are well served by attending to how descriptions are understood by research subjects. Latour urged scholars to follow the actors and chart their experience as it made sense to them as the best that scholars could do.[47] Even if one is working toward systematic and universal statements, checking how these statements resonate with those involved gives researchers critical information. The use of focus groups to design improved survey questions is one example of this insight in practice.[48] So is ethnography, which, as Fu and Simmons argue, offers great insights into arguments about contentious politics.[49] Another is knowing the actors involved by reading their memoires or other firsthand accounts and conducting interviews. All these can help you understand how those you are researching understood what unfolded. How one does this should be attentive to various pitfalls. Research subjects can outright lie or strategically construe their experiences. Participants can also recount what they think researchers want to hear rather than explain how they actually felt as they lived through events.[50]

Triangulate among perspectives. Triangulation can be important for ferreting out lies or strategic constructions. Even if they are being honest, though, participants in the same interaction often see things differently. Triangulating among perspectives and tools can thus also be useful for gaining a more complete picture—including one that recognizes how participants experienced the same event differently.[51] Dancing between participant views and theoretical or "outsider" perspectives (such as those encouraged by a positivist perspective) can also generate important descriptive understandings. Playing back events to those who participated can engender new angles that, if they resonate, generate creative insights. I experienced this personally as I tried to make sense of the impact of the Swiss Initiative (a coordinated effort between the Swiss government and the International Committee of the Red Cross) on private security governance. The meetings leading to the Montreux Document gained acceptance, in part, due to the assertion that the two parties would simply take stock of existing arrangements and introduce "nothing new." But by pulling the private military and security industry into international humanitarian and human rights law, the process, in fact, created new norms for the industry. Based on interviews and participant observation, I depicted events in ways that participants saw as accurate but also situated these in a pragmatic argument. In so doing, I highlighted the creative new practices that had developed even as participants claimed they were doing nothing new. My description shifted the way some involved in the process thought about both their past interactions and the potential for future governance in this arena.[52]

Be open to surprise. Its tendency to notice phenomena that are surprising is a critical part of what makes description so important for both understanding the world and contributing to theories about it. Martha Finnemore's experience provides a useful example here. Curious about the increasing talk of "humanitarian" intervention in the 1990s, Finnemore set a research assistant on the task of reading history on past interventions and how they were justified. The very astute research assistant (Andreas Katsouris) identified and returned interventions in the early and mid-20th century and even the late 19th century, but as he got further back in time, he found no more talk of interventions. Instead, he reported, people spoke not of intervention but of war. A more positivist research strategy might have led a research assistant to define "interventions" in an abstract way as violent phenomena, no matter how participants spoke of them. Acknowledging the meaning participants assigned to the phenomena, though, led Finnemore to describe intervention as historically bound—and with meaning that has shifted over time with changes in international society.[53] Different traditions place various values on definitions that are stable across time versus those more open to participant meaning, but all gain from being open to the potential that data can produce surprises.

Be clear about how you came to your description. What did you do to acquire the information in your description? What did you read? Who did you survey or interview? What did you ask them? How did you collect the data in your data sets (and from what sources)? Transparency about what led you to your description is important for replicability, critique, and complementary innovation.

Dilemmas in Description

Inferring from the above, good description asks questions beyond why. It looks at events that actually happened, acknowledges its assumptions, looks broadly at phenomena, takes account of inconvenient facts, takes note of its subjects' views, triangulates among perspectives, is open to surprise, and is clear about how it created a narrative that is vivid and compelling. It is not, however, without dilemmas.

Striking a balance between persuasiveness and humility is the first. The notion that description simply "tells it like it is" implies certainty about a range of "facts." The importance Gelman and Basbøll attach to a story's immutability implies a search for clarity and certainty.[54] And yet there is more and more evidence that connection and turbulence in the contemporary world—and perhaps historically as well—generates deep uncertainty that is rarely overcome.[55] How to craft descriptions that are persuasive and useful but also open to correction and resistant to misplaced certainty is a critical dilemma. Scholars are often driven to cast their arguments as more certain than they are to convince a skeptical field that "merely" descriptive work is nonetheless valuable. But such efforts can stymie creativity among academics and practitioners alike.

A related second dilemma surrounds the potential for self-fulfilling prophesies. If our descriptions also shape the social world, there is the possibility that describing dangers can make them more likely. Concerns in the wake of the January 6 U.S. insurrection are a case in point. Describing events in the United States with reference to various established arguments about the potential for civil war have led Walter and others to raise flags about the risk the country faces.[56] Others, though, have pointed to the way in which talking about the risks could actually inflame them.[57] Similar concerns have been leveled in the past about claims of inevitable war—which played into arguments about the cult of the offensive that some claim made World War I more likely.[58]

In sum, description both reveals and creates. It is critical to assessing and producing theory, and it helps us make sense of the world around us. Though it is hard to separate from explanatory accounts in practice, valuing description on its own can generate appreciation of the complexity and detail that often encourages creativity. The good descriptive practices described above are applicable across epistemological perspectives and can be important for understanding, explaining, and shaping social interactions.

Notes

1. Slaughter, *A New World Order*.
2. Ruggie, "Reconstituting the Global Public Domain."
3. Andreas, *Blue Helmuts and Black Markets*.
4. Gerring, "Mere Description," 729–730.
5. Scott, *Social Network Analysis*.
6. Gerring, "Mere Description," 722.
7. See Gerring, "Mere Description," 725.
8. Gerring, "Mere Description," 724.
9. Walter, *How Civil Wars Start*.
10. Pion-Berlin, Bruneau, and Goetze, "The Trump Self-Coup Attempt."
11. Gerring, "Mere Description," 733.
12. Sen, "Description as Choice."
13. King, Keohane, and Verba, *Designing Social Inquiry*, 56–59.
14. https://correlatesofwar.org/.
15. https://correlatesofwar.org/history.
16. Shilliam, *Decolonizing Politics*, 15–18.
17. Vitalis, *White World Order*, 1–2.
18. Tickner and True, "A Century of International Relations Feminism"; Addams, "Passing of the War Virtues," 216 (cited in Tickner and True).
19. Wilcox, *Bodies of Violence*.
20. Holloway, *Basic Concepts for Qualitative Research*, 154.
21. Vasquez, "The Steps to War."
22. Geertz, *The Interpretation of Cultures*, 17.
23. Tuchman, *Guns of August*.
24. Tuckman, *Guns of August*; Van Evera, "The Cult of the Offensive and the Origins of the First World War"; Snyder, "Civil-Military Relations and the Cult of the Offensive."
25. It is not always clear that the separation is tenable (Hollis and Smith, *Explaining and Understanding International Relations*).
26. Latour, *Reassembling the Social*.
27. Vitalis, *White World Order*, 1.
28. Fortna, "Does Peacekeeping Keep the Peace?"
29. Autesserre, *Frontlines of Peace*.
30. Anievas, Manchanda, and Shilliam, *Race and Racism in International Relations*; Zvobgo and Loken, *Why Race Matters in International Relations*; Shilliam, *Decolonizing Politics*; Elshtain 1981; Tickner, *Gendering World Politics*; Parashar, Tickner, and True, *Revisiting Gendered States*.
31. Gelman and Basbøll, "When Do Stories Work?"
32. Dewey, *Democracy and Education*, 210.
33. Kalyvas, *The Logic of Violence in Civil War*.
34. Fujii, *Killing Neighbors*; Fujii, *Showtime*; Autesserre, *Peaceland*; Avant et al., *Civil Action and the Dynamics of Conflict*.
35. King, Keohane, and Verba 1994, p. *Designing Social Inquiry* 38.
36. Gerring, "Mere Description," 734.

37. Ruggie, "International Regimes, Transactions, and Change"; Kratochwil and Ruggie, "The State of the Art on the Art of the State"; Ruggie, "Reconstituting the Global Public Domain," respectively.
38. Zarakol, *Before the West*.
39. Denvir, "Before the West with Ayşe Zarakol."
40. Enloe, *Bananas, Beaches and Bases*.
41. Tickner, *Gendering World Politics*; Parashar, Tickner, and True, *Revisiting Gendered States*.
42. George and Bennett, *Case Studies and Theory Development in the Social Sciences*.
43. Keck and Sikkink, *Activists Beyond Borders*, ix.
44. Sell and Prakash, "Using Ideas Strategically."
45. Weber, "Science as a Vocation," 22.
46. Strong, "Weber and Freud."
47. Latour, *Reassembling the Social*.
48. O'Brien, "Improving Survey Questionnaires through Focus Groups"; Cyr, "The Unique Utility of Focus Groups for Mixed Method Research."
49. Fu and Simmons, "Ethnographic Approaches to Contentious Politics."
50. Parkinson, "(Dis)courtesy Bias."
51. Latour, *Reassembling the Social*.
52. Avant, "Pragmatic Networks and Global Governance."
53. Finnemore, *The Purpose of Intervention*.
54. Gelman and Basbøll, "When Do Stories Work?"
55. Kay and King, *Radical Uncertainty*; Katzenstein and Seybert, *Protean Power*.
56. Walter, *How Civil Wars Start*.
57. O'Toole, "Beware Prophesies of Civil War."
58. Van Evera, "The Cult of the Offensive and the Origins of the First World War"; Snyder, "Civil-Military Relations and the Cult of the Offensive."

Thanks to Sara Goodman and Jen Cyr for terrific edits and suggestions. Thanks also to the organizers (Michelle Jurkovich, Meg Guliford, Carolyn Holmes, and Mary Ann Mendoza) and participants (too many to list) involved in "Just Telling It Like It Is: Descriptive Work and Social Science Research." The very productive conversation at that workshop improved my thinking and this chapter.

Recommended Readings

Gerring, John. "Mere Description." *British Journal of Political Science* 42 (2012): 721–746.
    A good overview of description and the value of thinking of it on its own. Though pitched to a positivist audience, its analysis is useful beyond that.
Gelman, Andrew, and Thomas Basbøll. "When Do Stories Work? Evidence and Illustration in the Social Sciences." *Sociological Methods and Research* 43, no. 4 (2014): 547–570.
    Good tips on what makes a persuasive descriptive argument.
Latour, Bruno. *Reassembling the Social*. Oxford: Oxford University Press, 2005.
    An introduction to actor-network theory and a strong pitch for centering description based in network theory and relational ontology.
Parkinson, Sarah. "(Dis)courtesy Bias: 'Methodological Cognates,' Data Validity, and Ethics in Violence-Adjacent Research." *Comparative Political Studies* 55, no. 3 (2021): 351–385.
    Important insights on pitfalls in interview strategies.
Shilliam, Robbie. *Decolonizing Politics: An Introduction*. Cambridge, UK: Polity Press, 2021.
    An astute analysis of how Western and colonial assumptions shape a good portion of "normal" political science and what can be gained by attending to a broader array of experiences.

References

Addams, Jane. "Passing of the War Virtues." In *Newer Ideals of Peace*, 209–238. New York: MacMillan, 1907.

Andreas, Peter. *Blue Helmuts and Black Markets: The Business of Survival in the Siege of Sarajevo*. Ithaca, NY: Cornell University Press, 2011.

Anievas, Alex, Nivi Manchanda, and Robbie Shilliam. *Race and Racism in International Relations: Confronting the Global Colour Line*. London: Routledge, 2014.

Autesserre, Severine. *Peaceland: Conflict Resolution and the Everyday Politics of International Intervention*. Cambridge: Cambridge University Press, 2014.

Autessere, Severine. *Frontlines of Peace: An Insider's Guide to Changing the World*. New York: Oxford University Press, 2021.

Avant, Deborah. "Pragmatic Networks and Global Governance: Explaining Governance Gains in Private Military and Security Services." *International Studies Quarterly* 60, no. 2 (2016): 330–342.

Avant, Deborah, Marie Berry, Erica Chenoweth, Rachel Epstein, Cullen Hendrix, Oliver Kaplan, and Timothy Sisk. *Civil Action and the Dynamics of Conflict*. Oxford: Oxford University Press, 2019.

Cyr, Jennifer. "The Unique Utility of Focus Groups for Mixed Method Research." *PS: Political Science and Politics* 50, no. 4 (2017): 1038–1042.

Denvir, Daniel. "Before the West with Ayşe Zarakol." *The Dig* (blog), April 28, 2022. https://www.thedigradio.com/podcast/before-the-west-w-ayse-zarakol/?s=09.

Dewey, John. *Democracy and Education*. New York: MacMillan, 2016.

Elshtain, Jean Bethke. *Public Man, Private Woman*. Princeton: Princeton University Press, 1981.

Enloe, Cynthia. *Bananas, Beaches, and Bases: Making Feminist Sense of International Politics*. Berkeley: University of California Press, 1990.

Finnemore, Martha. *National Interests in International Society*. Ithaca, NY: Cornell University Press, 1996.

Finnemore, Martha. *The Purpose of Intervention*. Ithaca: Cornell University Press, 2003.

Fortna, Virginia Page. "Does Peacekeeping Keep the Peace? International Intervention and the Duration of Peace after Civil War." *International Studies Quarterly* 48, no. 2 (2004): 269–292.

Fu, Diana, and Erica S. Simmons. "Ethnographic Approaches to Contentious Politics: I What, How, and Why." *Comparative Political Studies* 54, no. 1 (2021): 1695–1721.

Fujii, Lee Ann. *Killing Neighbors*. Ithaca, NY: Cornell University Press, 2009.

Fujii, Lee Ann. *Show Time: The Logic and Power of Violent Display*. Ithaca, NY: Cornell University Press, 2021.

Geertz, Clifford. *The Interpretation of Cultures*. New York: Basic Books, 1973.

Gelman, Andrew, and Thomas Basbøll. "When Do Stories Work? Evidence and Illustration in the Social Sciences." *Sociological Methods and Research* 43, no. 4 (2014): 547–570.

George, Alexander, and Andrew Bennett. *Case Studies and Theory Development in the Social Sciences*. Cambridge, MIT Press, 2004.

Gerring, John. "Mere Description." *British Journal of Political Science* 42 (2012): 721–746.

Hollis, Martin, and Steve Smith. *Explaining and Understanding International Relations*. Oxford: Oxford University Press, 1990.

Holloway, I. *Basic Concepts for Qualitative Research*. London: Blackwell Science, 1997.

Kalyvas, Stathis. *The Logic of Violence in Civil War*. Cambridge: Cambridge University Press, 2009.

Katzenstein, Peter J., and Lucia A. Seybert, eds. *Protean Power: Exploring the Uncertain and Unexpected in World Politics*. Cambridge: Cambridge University Press, 2018.

Kay, John, and Mervyn King. *Radical Uncertainty: Decision-Making beyond the Numbers*. New York: W. W. Norton, forthcoming.

Keck, Margaret, and Katherine Sikkink. *Activists Beyond Boarders: Advocacy Networks in International Politics*. Ithaca: Cornell University Press, 1998.

King, Gary, Robert O. Keohane, and Sidney Verba. *Designing Social Inquiry: Scientific Inference in Qualitative Research*. Princeton, NJ: Princeton University Press, 1994.

Kratochwil, Frederich, and John G. Ruggie. "The State of the Art on the Art of the State." *International Organization* 40, no. 4 (1986): 753–775.

Latour, Bruno. *Reassembling the Social*. Oxford: Oxford University Press, 2005.

O'Brien. Kerth. "Improving Survey Questionnaires through Focus Groups." In *Successful Focus Groups: Advancing the State of the Art*, edited by David Morgan, 105–117. New York: Sage, 1993.

O'Toole, Finton. "Beware Prophesies of Civil War." *The Atlantic*. December 16, 2021.

Pion-Berlin, David, Thomas Bruneau, and Richard B. Goetze Jr. "The Trump Self-Coup Attempt: Comparisons and Civil-Military Relations." *Government and Opposition* (2022): 1–18.

Parashar, Swati, J. Ann Tickner, and Jacqui True. *Revisiting Gendered States: Feminist Imaginings of the State in International Relations*. Oxford: Oxford University Press, 2018.

Parkinson, Sarah. "(Dis)courtesy Bias: 'Methodological Cognates,' Data Validity, and Ethics in Violence-Adjacent Research." *Comparative Political Studies* 55, no. 3 (2021): 351–385.

Ruggie, John G. "International Regimes, Transactions, and Change: Embedded Liberalism in the Postwar Economic Order." *International Organization* 36, no. 2 (1982): 379–415.

Ruggie, John G. "Reconstituting the Global Public Domain—Issues, Actors, and Practices." *European Journal of International Relations* 10, no. 4 (2004): 499–531.

Scott, John. *Social Network Analysis*. 3rd ed. New York: Sage, 2013.

Sell, Susan, and Aseem Prakash. "Using Ideas Strategically: The Contest between Business and NGO Networks in Intellectual Property Rights." *International Studies Quarterly* 48, no. 1 (2004): 143–175.

Sen, Amartya. "Description as Choice." *Oxford Economic Papers* 32, no. 3 (1980): 353–369.

Shilliam, Robbie. *Decolonizing Politics: An Introduction*. Cambridge, UK: Polity Press, 2021.

Slaughter, Anne-Marie. *A New World Order*. Princeton, NJ: Princeton University Press, 2004.

Snyder, Jack. "Civil-Military Relations and the Cult of the Offensive, 1914 and 1984." *International Security* 9, no. 1 (1984): 108–146.

Strong, Tracy. "Weber and Freud: Vocation and Self-Acknowledgement." *Canadian Journal of Sociology* 10, no. 4 (1985): 391–409.

Tickner, J. Ann. *Gendering World Politics: Issues and Approaches in the Post–Cold War Era*. New York: Columbia University Press, 2001.

Tickner, J. Ann, and Jacqui True. "A Century of International Relations Feminism: From World War I Women's Peace Pragmatism to the Women, Peace and Security Agenda." *International Studies Quarterly* 62, no. 2 (2018): 221–233.

Tuchman, Barbara W. *The Guns of August*. New York: Ballantine Books, 1962.

Van Evera, Stephen. "The Cult of the Offensive and the Origins of the First World War." *International Security* 9, no. 1 (1984): 58–107.

Vasquez, John. "The Steps to War: Towards a Scientific Explanation of Correlates of War Findkings." *World Politics* 40, no. 1 (2011): 108–145.

Walter, Barbara, F. *How Civil Wars Start*. New York: Crown, 2022.

Weber, Max. "Science as a Vocation" (1919). In *From Max Weber: Essays in Sociology*, edited and translated by H. H. Gerth and C. Wright Mills, 129–156. New York: Oxford University Press, 1958.

Vitalis, Robert. *White World Order, Black Power Politics: The Birtch of American International Relations*. Ithaca: Cornell University Press, 2015.

Zarakol, Ayşe. *Before the West: The Rise and Fall of Eastern World Orders*. Cambridge: Cambridge University Press, 2022.

Zvobgo, Kelebogile, and Meredith Loken. "Why Race Matters in International Relations." *Foreign Policy* 237 (2020): 11–13.

31
Content Analysis

Zawadi Rucks-Ahidiana

Descriptive Overview

The term "content analysis" is used in two distinct ways in methodological discourse. The first defines the term broadly as analyzing qualitative data sources, as in "analyzing content." The second definition is a specific approach to qualitative data analysis that uses word and term searches to identify patterns in language use in qualitative data sources. This chapter will focus on the latter approach, sometimes also called "text analysis," to uncover meaning behind the use of language.

This form of content analysis is often used to identify linguistic patterns in qualitative data sources of all kinds, from interview transcripts to letters and tweets. Language is usually of interest to social science researchers not only because of what words mean but because of what words signal. Specific words and phrases signal a direct engagement with a topic, group, or idea. But they can also signal indirect references to values, stereotypes, and assumptions.

For example, the press can describe someone as an "immigrant," "recent arrival," "illegal immigrant," "undocumented immigrant," "refugee," or "alien resident." Each of these descriptions signals (1) an engagement with different types of immigration and (2) a value judgment of whether immigration is "good" or "bad." Describing someone as an "illegal immigrant" focuses on how they immigrated to a country. It signals that they did not arrive by legal means and thus suggests they engaged in a criminal activity to immigrate, presenting their immigration negatively. In contrast, the term "undocumented immigrant" focuses on citizenship rather than immigration. The term identifies an individual as not a citizen, without referencing how they entered the country, presenting their immigration more neutrally. Through content analysis, researchers can identify when and how language is used across documents and whether it varies by important subgroups within a data set such as a region or the race and gender of respondents.

Content analysis can also address a practical challenge: tackling large quantities of qualitative data. With smaller samples of qualitative data sources, researchers can apply different approaches of hand coding in a reasonable amount of time. Once qualitative data sources begin to approach hundreds or even thousands of documents, it is more challenging to conduct hand coding of all documents even with a team of researchers. With content analysis, a researcher can conduct a targeted analysis of a large set of documents. Using search terms can isolate the focus of the analysis to specific sections of each document and even eliminate some documents as irrelevant.

There are three approaches researchers tend to use for text analysis. Researchers searching for specific language in qualitative sources can use simple text searches to search for the words or phrases of interest. A second approach is pairing text searches and coding in a qualitative data analysis (QDA) software package, which allows the researcher to combine traditional qualitative coding techniques with text analysis.[1] Last, researchers can apply dictionary searches with computational tools like R or Python, which allows researchers to combine text analysis searches with statistical methods.[2] While all three approaches overlap in how they are applied, the last option requires advanced coding skills in R or Python.[3] Because of this, I focus here on using text searches in Word, Adobe Acrobat, or a QDA software package.

Regardless of the approach they choose, researchers must think carefully about the words and phrases to include in their searches, how to clean the results, how to deal with documents that use more than one search term, how to connect search terms with the context in which they were used, and what software to use to implement the method. As I detail below, each of these decisions has implications for what kinds of questions researchers can answer.

Throughout the chapter, I refer to my own research using content analysis. The research project I describe answers the question: How does the news media connect race to gentrification?[4] In the study, I use newspaper articles from the two most circulated newspapers in Baltimore and San Francisco, which I analyze with a combination of text analysis and hand coding, as I describe further below.

State of Practice

If you're interested in language and how it's used or are navigating a large data set and need an approach that will help you locate a relevant subset of documents for your analyses, content analysis may be the approach for you. Content analysis allows the researcher to analyze when, where, and how language is used in their source documents. Before getting started, though, there are five decisions that researchers should make before they engage with content analysis: (1) what software to use to apply the method, (2) which terms to search for, (3) what references to search terms are irrelevant, (4) how to analyze overlap between search terms, and (5) how to connect the search terms to the context in which they were used. The decision of what software to use is best made with answers from the other questions. So in the following section, I review these four core decisions and then turn to choosing a software package to guide you through developing an analysis plan. I pair software package selection with a discussion of how to implement your decisions in the software of your choosing to illustrate how to implement your analysis plan.

Which Search Terms?

To implement content analysis, you need to construct a dictionary of terms that you will search for in your documents. You may already have some ideas of the kind of language you need to look for, in which case you can construct a list of those terms. Be sure to include derivatives of the terms to capture relevant variations. For example, I study how news articles about gentrification discuss race, which includes multiple terms for each racial category. So instead of just searching for references to "Black," I also search for references to "African American," "African," "Caribbean," and "West Indian."

If you are not sure about the language you need to search for, look through 5 to 10 of your documents to better understand which words and phrases are used in reference to your topic. These documents can be the first 5 to 10, randomly selected, or a set of documents you know are representative of other documents in your sample. Read through carefully and keep a running list of what you find. Keeping that list in Word or Excel will allow for easy sorting to identify and remove repeated terms.

Reviewing your data for language is particularly important for less systematically formatted documents and topics. While a policy or legal form might be structured to include specific information with clearly defined terms, most documents, including interviews, focus group transcripts, and newspaper articles, do not have a specific format with clearly defined responses. Even within some formatted documents, you might be interested in content that is not compiled systematically. For example, you could easily construct a list of government policies by name and number without ever consulting your policy documents, but if you were interested in how these policy documents talk about poverty, you would likely need to review some examples. Poverty could be referenced with descriptions such as "poor," "low-income," or "poverty," but may also appear in other ways, such as "food insecure," "living paycheck to paycheck," or "struggling to make ends meet." Thus, even if you have a good idea of what terms you need, you may find it useful to look at your data sources to check that your search terms broadly cover your topic.

When I used content analysis in my research on how the news media connects race to gentrification, I looked for references to race in newspaper articles that mention gentrification.[5] I knew I needed to search for broad, umbrella race terms like Asian, African American, Black, Hispanic, Latina, Latino, Native American, American Indian, and White. However, I also knew that race would be signaled with references to specific nationalities and that the nationalities mentioned would vary between Baltimore and San Francisco. I read about each city's immigration history and reviewed newspaper articles from both cities to develop a list of specific nationalities within each racial category. In reviewing some examples, I also realized that newspaper articles might signal race in more indirect ways, with phrases like "diverse" or "people of color." By the time my codebook of search terms was completed, I had gone through about four versions of the list: (1) a list of umbrella terms, (2) a list that included site-specific nationalities associated with immigration, (3) a list with references found in my review of a subset of articles, and (4) a final list that incorporated a small number of additions that I found while hand-coding for the context of references to race (described below). As shown in Table 31.1, the final list of search terms included racial terms found on the census, nationalities, and colloquial references. While your compilation process may not take four iterations, the point is that you can expect to create multiple iterations of the list as you gain insight into how your documents talk about the topics you are studying.

When Are Search Terms Irrelevant?

Inevitably, your list of search terms will pick up references to something that is *not* what you are interested in capturing. For my research project, the search terms "Black" and "White" picked up references to black and white as colors, such as "black jeans" and "white picket fence." I also found that some words appeared in the middle of other words that affected the coding. For instance, the search term "Asia" picked up "Caucasian," which would have categorized a term associated with the White category with the Asian category.

You may also find that there are uses of your search terms that are not aligned with your research interests. For instance, I found lots of search terms used in reference to food such as

Table 31.1 Race Search Terms

Race/Ethnicity Category	Search Terms
Asian	Asia, China, Chinese, India, Japan, Korea, Vietnam, Filipino, Philippines
Black	Black, Africa, Caribbean, Jamaica, "West Indian," "West Indies"
Latino	Hispanic, Latino, Dominican, Mexican, Mexico, "Puerto Rican," "Puerto Rico," "El Salvador," "Central America," Guatemala, Nicaragua
Biracial	Biracial, "mixed race," multiracial
Native American	"Native American," "American Indian"
White	White, Europe, French, France, German, Irish, Ireland, Italian, Italy, wasp, Caucasian, Polish, Poland, Greek, Greece
Unclear	Diversity, multicultural, minorities, "people of color"

Note: There are quotation marks around search phrases that had to appear together. Some search terms captured more than one relevant reference to nationality. For example, searches for "Asia" also captured "Asian" and "Asian American," thus I did not need to search for all three phrases.

"French" with "fries" or "Italian" with "sausage." While I was interested in when there was a French or Italian restaurant referenced in the articles, food descriptions like these were not relevant on their own.

As you identify your search terms, think about alternative ways the words and phrases may be used in your data. This could be slang uses of the term, the use of a word as an adjective instead of a verb or noun, or the use of a word in a specific phrase. You will be able to identify some of these issues before conducting your searches, as with "Black" and "White" being used as color words. However, others will emerge as you clean the results of your search for your list of relevant terms. Be sure to keep notes in a document or codebook of what references you chose to omit from the sample. Following the sample codebook in Table 31.1, you could add an "Exclusions" column to keep notes about the kinds of references that weren't applicable to your study for each search term.

How Will You Analyze Overlap between Search Terms?

To plan your analysis of the search results, you will need to consider how to deal with overlap and interrelationships between your search terms. Many times, more than one of the specific words that researchers are interested in appear in the same document. Figure 31.1 shows an example of a newspaper article from my study on coverage of gentrification that references both Black and White actors. In fact, there are four references to race using the search terms in the third paragraph of the article alone.

For my analysis, I focused on how many articles referenced a racial category at least once. I looked at the presence or absence of race in articles by counting any reference to race as the presence of the mention of race. But I also considered which racial categories were referenced in each article. The article shown in Figure 31.1 would be coded as mentioning race, as well as referencing Black and White racial categories.

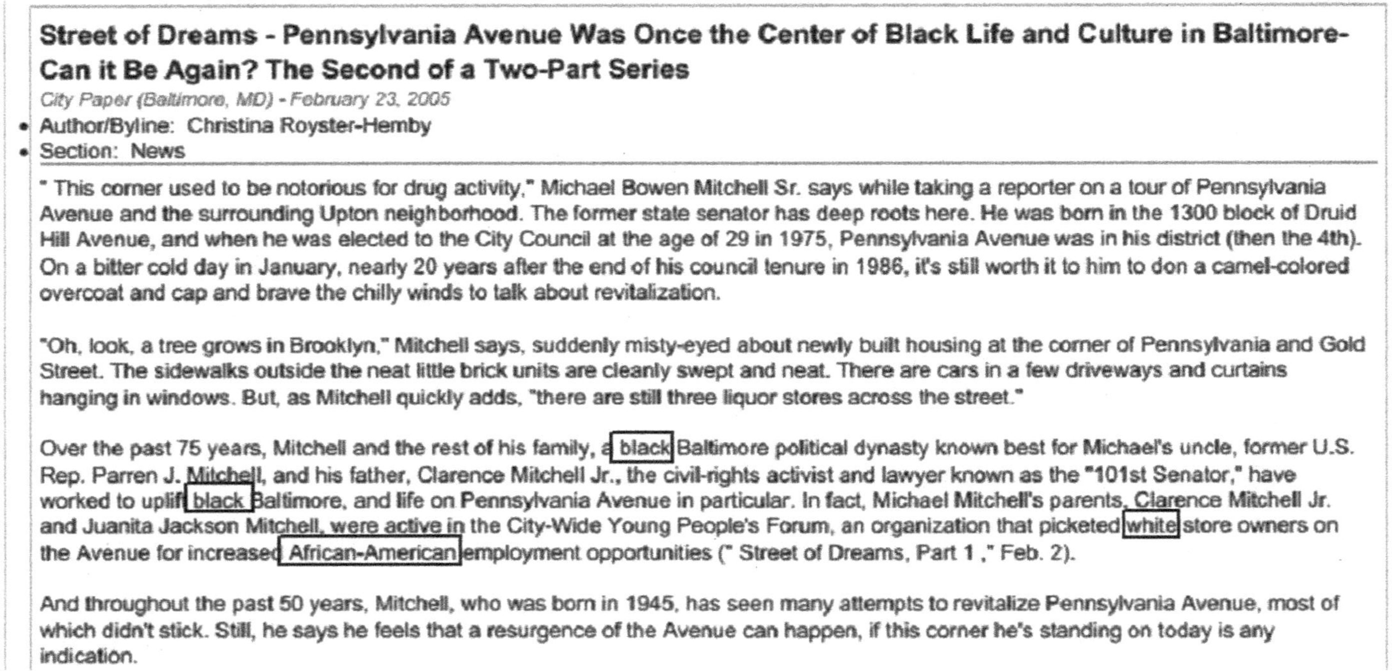

Street of Dreams - Pennsylvania Avenue Was Once the Center of Black Life and Culture in Baltimore- Can it Be Again? The Second of a Two-Part Series

- *City Paper (Baltimore, MD) - February 23, 2005*
- Author/Byline: Christina Royster-Hemby
- Section: News

"This corner used to be notorious for drug activity," Michael Bowen Mitchell Sr. says while taking a reporter on a tour of Pennsylvania Avenue and the surrounding Upton neighborhood. The former state senator has deep roots here. He was born in the 1300 block of Druid Hill Avenue, and when he was elected to the City Council at the age of 29 in 1975, Pennsylvania Avenue was in his district (then the 4th). On a bitter cold day in January, nearly 20 years after the end of his council tenure in 1986, it's still worth it to him to don a camel-colored overcoat and cap and brave the chilly winds to talk about revitalization.

"Oh, look, a tree grows in Brooklyn," Mitchell says, suddenly misty-eyed about newly built housing at the corner of Pennsylvania and Gold Street. The sidewalks outside the neat little brick units are cleanly swept and neat. There are cars in a few driveways and curtains hanging in windows. But, as Mitchell quickly adds, "there are still three liquor stores across the street."

Over the past 75 years, Mitchell and the rest of his family, a black Baltimore political dynasty known best for Michael's uncle, former U.S. Rep. Parren J. Mitchell, and his father, Clarence Mitchell Jr., the civil-rights activist and lawyer known as the "101st Senator," have worked to uplift black Baltimore, and life on Pennsylvania Avenue in particular. In fact, Michael Mitchell's parents, Clarence Mitchell Jr. and Juanita Jackson Mitchell, were active in the City-Wide Young People's Forum, an organization that picketed white store owners on the Avenue for increased African-American employment opportunities ("Street of Dreams, Part 1," Feb. 2).

And throughout the past 50 years, Mitchell, who was born in 1945, has seen many attempts to revitalize Pennsylvania Avenue, most of which didn't stick. Still, he says he feels that a resurgence of the Avenue can happen, if this corner he's standing on today is any indication.

Figure 31.1 Sample Article.

This approach is analyzing the presence or absence of each search term in a document. One alternative is to analyze for the relative use of each term. To do that, I would look at how many references there were to Black relative to White in the article in Figure 31.1. I could analyze the number of references to each racial group or calculate a ratio of references to each racial category (e.g., Asian-Black, Asian-Latinx, Asian–Native American, Asian-White). This paired with an analysis of to what extent each racial category overlapped in the articles would tell me about the relative discussion of racial groups.

One additional option is to analyze which terms are used most often in each document. For example, the article in Figure 31.1 mentions the Black community most often, with three references to Black and only one to White. Making similar calculations for each article would give me one racial category per article rather than several, as in the other two options. This would tell me what racial group readers would most likely remember after reading an article.

To narrow down which analytical approach is best for your project, return to the empirical questions you want to answer. Based on those questions, select the analysis that will best provide answers. Keep in mind that using a combination of these analyses could be most useful, particularly for preliminary analyses to identify the main themes in your findings. For my own project, the approach of looking at how many articles mentioned race at least once and what races articles mentioned let me identify whether the news media connected race to gentrification and, when they did, how.

How Will You Connect Search Terms to Context?

Finally, researchers have to decide how to connect the words and phrases they search for in documents with the context in which they were used. This analysis will reveal (1) how the search words and phrases were connected to people, places, or things in your documents. But it can also be used to understand (2) when the search terms surface in the data sources.

I used the first approach in my study of race in news articles on gentrification to identify whom racial terms were used to describe. As shown in Table 31.2, this included whether the racial descriptions were used to identify businesses, recent in-movers to a neighborhood, community organizations, neighborhood residents, or some other actors.

However, *when* a term or phrase is brought up in a document may be more relevant to your research questions. To capture this, you might plan to code for what topics came up prior to the use of the term or phrase, in the paragraph where the word or term was used, or in the broader document itself. For interview data, that could include what question the term or phrase came up in response to. Regardless of which questions you aim to answer, this part of the work will involve doing additional coding of your documents, as I discuss further below.

What Software Will You Use? How Will You Apply Your Decisions?

Once you make preliminary decisions about the four questions above to define your analysis plan, you can determine how best to implement your plan. I focus here on two approaches that provide the easiest means to analyze your results across documents. The first approach uses manual searches in Word or Adobe and compiles the results in a spreadsheet, building

Table 31.2 Actor Codes

Code	Subcodes	Explanation
Actors		
	Businesses	Captures relevant business actors
	In-movers	New residents of the neighborhood. Includes description of "recent" and "new" as well as any people who have moved in three or fewer years at the time the article was written.
	Community organizations	Includes nonprofits, advocates, organizers, and other community organizations
	Residents	Captures all non-recent residents, including older residents of the neighborhood. Includes descriptions of "old," "long standing," and "raised," as well as anyone who has lived in the neighborhood for more than three years. Also used to capture historical references to neighborhood composition.
	Other	Captures any actors not captured in the subcodes for this chapter (e.g., developer, politicians, etc.), as well as actors that won't be captured in other subcodes (e.g., police, social workers, etc.).

off the Contextual Text Coding approach.[6] The second approach uses a QDA software package, which I explain with the example of MaxQDA.

With the manual method, you will use the search function (e.g., control + F on a conventional U.S. keyboard) to search your documents for each term.[7] You can highlight each search term with a color as you find it so that you can easily locate them later, or simply review the results to compile information into a spreadsheet. The spreadsheet should include the file name of the document in the first column,[8] followed by a column for each of your search terms or categories. For instance, I could have a column for each racial category (e.g., Asian, Black, Latinx, Native American, White, Unclear) or for each specific search term (e.g., Asia, China, Chinese, India, Japan, Korea, Vietnam, Filipino, Philippines). The former is best if you only need to know a document referenced a category that includes a number of search terms, and the latter is best if you need to know what specific term was used to reference a category. One option to condense the number of columns you work with is to create columns for each category and enter the specific search terms that were found in the document in the cells.[9] With either approach, you can also identify which documents do not reference a category by leaving cells blank. In the spreadsheet, you will mark off either which categories or search terms each document in your data set referenced *or* how many references there were for each category of the search term, depending on your decision about how to analyze the use of terms. This includes an omission of your search terms with either a blank cell for the lack of reference to a search term or a zero for the number of references to a search term.

Because you will see each hit as the search finds it, you can omit irrelevant references to the search term as you go. As you view the search term in use, you will decide whether or not to highlight it as a relevant use of the term. Similarly, you can code for context as you go, adding columns to your spreadsheets of the contextual codes that you wish to capture, as well as a column for quotations to easily access examples during the writing process.

Depending on the size of your project and your budget, you might approach this process as the one and only coder, or with a group.[10] The manual method is a no- or low-cost option for conducting content analysis, and can be particularly useful when working with a team to reduce costs. In fact, with a tool like Google Forms, you can construct a data entry form that auto-populates a spreadsheet to capture all the information you need for analysis.

To analyze the results, you can calculate statistics manually or use Pivot Tables[11] in your spreadsheet program. If I wanted to know how often Black search terms were referenced relative to White search terms, I could use a simple equation with division to look at the ratio of the references of Black to White. To capture whether more than one race category was referenced, I could use the Sum function or a Pivot Table to identify those documents that have more than one race mentioned. Finally, if I wanted to look at the largest number of references to race, I could use the functions Lookup and Max, as I demonstrate in the note, to identify the largest quantity of references to race.[12] In most spreadsheet programs, you can also use conditional formatting to highlight columns with specific values or a range of values to visually identify which documents meet certain characteristics, such as highlighting the articles in my data that use the Latinx search terms. Using these approaches will give you a sense of how many documents you have in each of your categories or search terms and provide the means to compare the use of terms across your documents.

The alternative is the QDA approach. QDA packages require licenses, which are often quite costly. However, the expense can be worth their ability to facilitate the process of text search, coding, and analysis, particularly with large-scale projects. I use MaxQDA for content analysis because their "lexical search" tools simplify the process, as I describe below. Other software options include Atlas.TI, Dedoose, and NVivo.

To complete the content analysis of references to race in my articles about gentrification, I ran an extended lexical search in MaxQDA for each racial category. Each search included all of the search terms, which produced a screen of search results like that shown in Figure 31.2. Each search term was shown in context of the words before and after, as seen under "Preview." This allowed me to clean the search results, looking for uses of the search terms that did not align with the references to race I was hoping to find. For example, the results in Figure 31.2, which show the search I conducted for all Asian search terms, include "asia" in "Caucasian" and references to "Asian-style slaw." Since the former is incorrect and the latter is in reference to food, I flagged them as irrelevant (the circle with a line through it). After I reviewed and cleaned the full list of search results, I was able to automatically code the remaining results with the code "Asian." Doing this tagged each relevant search term use in the original document, making it easy to relocate the search term results without rerunning the extended lexical search.

After doing this for each racial category, I opened each document and coded for context. Again, I was specifically interested in who the references to race were used to describe. For each coded reference to race, I added a code to indicate which actor the article was describing from the codes shown in Table 31.2.

To analyze the results of the coding for search terms, I used two tools in the software to find out (1) what racial groups were referenced in the articles and (2) whose race they were used to describe to answer my questions about how and when the newspapers connected race to the process of gentrification. To address the first, I converted my content analysis

Search results

ANY: Asia China Chinese India Japan Korea Vietnam Filipino Philippines

	Preview	Beginning	Document group	Document name	End	Search item
①	were an all-girl, multiracial, mostly queer, mostly novice movie crew setting out to compete in a mostly male, mostly Caucasian, mostly	2: 1243	Baltimore City Paper	B 2004-07-21 CP kin...	2: 1246	asia
‖	Rick Sussman say the Pennsylvania Avenue corridor boasts a racially diverse mix of merchants, including whites, African-Americans, and Koreans. But	5: 1392	Baltimore City Paper	B 2005-02-23 CP str...	5: 1396	Korea
‖	I was having a great Korean barbecue dinner in "lower" Charles Village with friends and, after reading Mike Peters' letter	1: 3763	Baltimore City Paper	B 2005-10-12 CP be...	1: 3767	Korea
‖	Just like North Vietnam used our words to divide us, the terrorists do, too	2: 2399	Baltimore City Paper	B 2005-11-30 CP cat...	2: 2405	Vietnam
‖	visiting Japanese internment camps, POW camps, Katrina relief camps, boot camps for juvenile offenders, to compare and contrast them with	1: 1040	Baltimore City Paper	B 2006-07-26 CP uni...	1: 1044	Japan
‖	who marshaled the neighborhood forces when such controversies as the current rezoning battle occurred: Steve Bunker, owner of the China Sea	4: 2629	Baltimore City Paper	B 2007-03-21 CP po...	4: 2633	China
‖	as well as in Europe and South Korea. O	1: 4757	Baltimore City Paper	B 2007-11-28 CP ou...	1: 4761	Korea
‖	finds itself home to newer immigrant populations--the neighborhood is home to a burgeoning Latino community, as well as Indians, Koreans	2: 178	Baltimore City Paper	B 2008-04-16 CP gr...	2: 182	India
‖	itself home to newer immigrant populations--the neighborhood is home to a burgeoning Latino community, as well as Indians, Koreans, and	2: 187	Baltimore City Paper	B 2008-04-16 CP gr...	2: 191	Korea
‖	I mean, China? India	2: 2426	Baltimore City Paper	B 2009-07-29 CP so...	2: 2430	China
‖	China? India? We	2: 2433	Baltimore City Paper	B 2009-07-29 CP so...	2: 2437	India
‖	pollution? India has all of these tanneries, and there are kids working them, kids are just dying	2: 2565	Baltimore City Paper	B 2009-07-29 CP so...	2: 2569	India
‖	It also had enough bathrooms and a porch with a bench overlooking a Japanese maple	1: 4433	Baltimore City Paper	B 2009-12-23 CP in ...	1: 4437	Japan
①	rub, comes either in sandwich form ($10) or on a plate, served with Brussels sprouts—this time tossed in Asian-style slaw	1: 3220	Baltimore City Paper	B 2014-09-02 CP ge...	1: 3223	Asia
①	rub, comes either in sandwich form ($10) or on a plate, served with Brussels sprouts—this time tossed in Asian-style slaw	1: 3220	Baltimore City Paper	B 2014-09-02 CP ge...	1: 3223	Asia

Figure 31.2 Search Results for Asian Search Terms in MaxQDA.

coding into "document variables," which tagged each newspaper article as including references to a racial group or not.[13] I then looked at descriptive statistics of how many documents referenced each racial category with the tool Document Variable Statistics.

To analyze whose race terms were used to describe, I used the Code Relations Browser to review how the content analysis codes for references to race overlapped with codes for specific actors. This tool produces a table with a count of the number of times the codes overlapped across all documents. The table can also be reproduced for a specific subset of documents, to look at, for instance, differences across articles from my two study sites.

Reviewing these reports allowed me to identify the trends in references to race in the articles. These trends provided answers to whether the newspaper coverage associated race with gentrification, what racial groups it associated with gentrification, and which stakeholders' race it identified in covering gentrification. This included expected results; for instance, Baltimore articles rarely mentioned Asian or Latinx stakeholders, while San Francisco articles were more likely to. But it also revealed unexpected differences between the sites, such as that Baltimore articles were less likely to include mentions of race than San Francisco articles. It also allowed me to identify a specific subset of articles to revisit for qualitative examples of how these references appeared in the news.

Regardless of whether you use content analysis with a manual or a QDA approach, you will finish the process with counts and descriptive statistics to identify the trends in your data. You can use that information to present quantitative trends with graphs, but also identify specific qualitative examples to illustrate those trends as you write up your results.

Potential Problems

Qualitative researchers often critique content analysis in two ways. First, it introduces counting to qualitative methods, which is sometimes viewed negatively as applying quantitative methods to qualitative data. For example, some qualitative researchers prefer to use qualifiers like "some," "most," and "many" to describe their results rather than a precise figure like 63%. Counting may not be a traditional tool for most qualitative approaches, but there is a time and a place to leverage the tools of our quantitative colleagues to serve our needs in qualitative research. This is particularly the case with large-scale qualitative projects that may be quite hard to analyze without considering counts based on qualitative coding.

Second, qualitative researchers often see content analysis as removing words from their context (the broader documents in which the words are used). These critiques are particularly relevant for studies that focus on quantitative counts of search terms only. The approach that I document here specifically includes coding for context of when and how the search terms are used; doing so helps avoid this problem. Even if researchers using this approach present only quantitative trends in their results, they should also have results from the contextual codes and sample quotations to explain when and how their search terms appeared in the documents.

Thus, despite these potential issues, content analysis is a viable method to understand language, analyze a large number of qualitative sources, and even connect analyses across different types of documents. It is not well suited for understanding more nuanced topics, particularly ones in which there is no common vocabulary. However, content analysis is well suited to answer research questions about language and meaning in many areas of social science research.

Notes

1. See for example, Brown-Saracino and Rumpf, "Diverse Imageries of Gentrification."
2. See for example, Nelson, "Cycles of Conflict, a Century of Continuity."
3. See the recommended readings for a source on this approach.
4. Gentrification is the process of a neighborhood changing from predominantly low-income residents to predominantly middle-class.
5. This included derivatives of the term "gentrification" such as "gentrify," "gentrified," "gentrifying," and "gentrifier."
6. Lichtenstein and Rucks-Ahidiana, "Contextual Text Coding."
7. This assumes your documents are all searchable or have been converted through optical character recognition.
8. This means that each row in the spreadsheet will be associated with one data source.
9. For more discussion on how to set up a spreadsheet approach to coding, see Lichtenstein and Rucks-Ahidiana, "Contextual Text Coding."
10. Working with a team of coders can help spread out the work but does often require additional funds or some other way to compensate your coders. Some universities offer opportunities for faculty to hire undergraduate students for course credit to compensate them for their contributions to a research project.
11. Pivot Tables is available in most spreadsheet programs to calculate descriptive statistics.
12. Combining the lookup and max functions can display the column headers in a cell. For instance, typing this equation in Microsoft Excel "=LOOKUP(MAX(A2:D2), A2:D2, A1:D1)" will prompt Excel to look for the maximum value in cells A2 through D2 (the number of references to a category or search term) and then display the value of the corresponding cell for that column in row 1 (the labels).
13. This type of document variable is in the Boolean format indicating a presence or absence, but the software also allows the option of including an "integer" or the total count of the number of times a code is used in a document.

Recommended Readings

Brown-Saracino, Japonica, and Cesraea Rumpf. "Diverse Imageries of Gentrification: Evidence from Newspaper Coverage in Seven U.S. Cities, 1986-2006." *Journal of Urban Affairs* 33, no. 3 (2011): 289–315.
    An example that combines content analysis with qualitative coding. Given the large sample of their data, they use a sampling strategy for the qualitative coding to reduce the workload, something researchers working with large quantities of data should consider.

Nelson, Laura K., Derek Burk, Marcel Knudsen, and Leslie McCall. "The Future of Coding: A Comparison of Hand-Coding and Three Types of Computer-Assisted Text Analysis Methods." *Sociological Methods & Research* 50, no. 1 (2021): 202–237.
    Provides a review of computational text analysis techniques that use more technology. Readers considering learning R or Python to implement content analysis should read this article.

Sandelowski, Margarete, Corrine I. Voils, and George Knafl. "On Quantitizing." *Journal of Mixed Methods Research* 3, no. 3 (2009): 208–222.
    Defends the utility of counting in qualitative research, a core component of content analysis.

Ferree, Myra Marx. *Shaping Abortion Discourse: Democracy and the Public Sphere in Germany and the United States.* Cambridge, UK: Cambridge University Press, 2002.
    Provides an example of content analysis with newspaper data, including a detailed description of their approach.

Firman, Ruth L., Kelsey A. Bonfils, Lauren Luther, Kyle S. Minor, and Michelle P. Salyers. "Using Text-Analysis Computer Software and Thematic Analysis on the Same Qualitative Data: A Case Example." *Qualitative Psychology* 4, no. 3 (2017): 201–210.

Demonstrates a technique similar to the one described in this chapter of combining content analysis with thematic analysis to analyze interview data.

References

Brown-Saracino, Japonica, and Cesraea Rumpf. "Diverse Imageries of Gentrification: Evidence from Newspaper Coverage in Seven U.S. Cities, 1986–2006." *Journal of Urban Affairs* 33, no. 3 (2011): 289–315.

Lichtenstein, Matty, and Zawadi Rucks-Ahidiana. "Contextual Text Coding: A Mixed-Methods Approach for Large-Scale Textual Data." *Sociological Methods & Research* 52, no. 2 (2023): 606–641.

Nelson, Laura K. "Cycles of Conflict, a Century of Continuity." *American Journal of Sociology* 127, no. 1 (2021): 1–59.

32
Qualitative Social Network Analysis

Jennifer Spindel

Overview: What Are Networks, and What Are They Good For?

At the broadest level, qualitative social network analysis (QSNA) allows scholars to have a more nuanced and accurate picture of politics by centering relationships as the unit of analysis.[1] Different types of relationships create networks, and political actors are situated within multiple, overlapping networks. Each relationship and resulting network affects their interests and their behavior, and actors' behavior can in turn affect relationships and the structure of the network.[2] Therefore, QSNA is particularly well-suited for studying the interplay between actors and structure, and often highlights types of power that can go unnoticed by other approaches. By emphasizing roles (like brokers or bridges) and network characteristics (such as centrality or embeddedness), network analysis alerts us to the ways that power is infused in and reflected through relationships.[3]

QSNA shares some similarities with its quantitative relative. Both are interested in the types of ties or relationships between actors, why those ties form, and the effects of those ties. The primary difference between the two is in how they analyze connections between actors. Quantitative network analysis leverages big-N data to focus on structure and tends to abstract from the actual complexity of social and political systems.[4] One of the more common uses of quantitative network analysis is to incorporate node-level characteristics into standard statistical models by, for example, including a variable measuring each actor's connections (its density) or a variable that measures its importance to the overall network (its centrality).[5] Because our usual statistical models are anathema to interdependence of observations, inserting network measures into standard regressions often loses the dynamism, nuance, and meaning of the connections between actors. Quantitative network analysis uses statistical measures to identify actor importance and precisely where the actors sits in the broader network; these network statistics are often incorporated into regression analyses and are not the primary focus of the scholar's research. This use of quantitative analysis is thus better suited for a macro perspective and for studying static structures.[6] For example, scholars studying legislative networks within the U.S. Congress incorporate network concepts like weak ties or centrality into statistical models to predict how connections between members of Congress affect outcomes in different congressional classes.[7]

In an attempt to capture more of the dynamism and movement between individual level and structures, recent quantitative network analysis has turned to exponential random graph models (ERGMs) and temporal exponential random graph models (TERGMs). These are statistical models designed to account for interdependence of observations that can explain both when ties are likely to develop and structural properties of the network.[8] ERGMs and TERGMs are quite able to account for relational effects like friend-of-friend

Jennifer Spindel, *Qualitative Social Network Analysis* In: *Doing Good Qualitative Research*. Edited by: Jennifer Cyr and Sara Wallace Goodman, Oxford University Press. © Oxford University Press 2024. DOI: 10.1093/oso/9780197633137.003.0032

and enemy-of-friend dynamics that affect outcomes of interest like war initiation. While the models are a more accurate quantitative use of network data, the barrier to entry is high in terms of data collection, statistical knowledge, and programming knowledge required to use the models.[9] Further, the insights produced by ERGMs and TERGMs are often quite familiar to qualitative scholars, such as the fact that alliances are interdependent networks and that the actions and views of one (or more) states can rebound through the alliance network.[10]

QSNA, on the other hand, helps us identify specific mechanisms responsible for observed outcomes (e.g., did this individual vote because their friends voted, or because everyone at their office voted?) and holds on to the interplay between individual and structure. QSNA puts much greater emphasis on the content and meaning of the ties that connect actors. It is well suited for identifying change over time, for identifying informal connections between actors, and for linking micro and macro perspectives.[11] Unlike quantitative network analysis, QSNA is more commonly employed on its own rather than as an input for other methods. QSNA helps us understand the types of ties that led to that powerful actor's rise, and how different types of ties (e.g., shared alliance membership, familial ties, enmity) explain the actor's behavior. Where quantitative social network analysis often uses network statistics as one step in a bigger quantitative project, QSNA more directly and centrally focuses on the types and quality of relationships between actors.

Making relations between actors the unit of analysis means that QSNA picks up types of power that go beyond purely material or ideational. Seen as part of a network, actors can be powerful based on the structural position or characteristics of the role that they occupy.[12] While some power positions are correlated with material power, this is not always the case. One measure of power is an actor's centrality, or the degree to which they are connected to other actors. The more central, or the more connections, an actor has, the more influence they should have over the network.[13] Actors who serve as bridges, by connecting one subgroup to another subgroup, also have power. They can act as gatekeepers by moderating the information or contacts between the groups,[14] or they can act as a crucial tie for bringing the subgroups together.[15] International relations during the Cold War is a useful illustration of these points. We could construct a global network based on alliance/friendship ties and economic ties. It would show two distinct clusters, one with the United States at its center, connected to the NATO allies and many states in the Americas. The other cluster would have the Soviet Union as most central, connected to the Warsaw Pact countries, China, and many of the pro-Communist states. Then there would be places of overlapping ties, where the two superpowers were vying for influence. We would see competing ties in Egypt, Jordan, and Lebanon, for example, as well as in Vietnam and Afghanistan.

But there would be a third, smaller, but no less important cluster. Led by Egypt and Yugoslavia, the Non-Aligned Movement would not be as dense or as large a cluster, but the friendship and economic ties would reveal this important third bloc. This brings us to another type of structural phenomenon: the clique. As in the movie *Mean Girls*, actors are often part of exclusive subgroups and derive power from admitting or excluding other actors from the clique. One of the promises of QSNA is that it can identify power based on the position of actors in a network rather than based just on that actor's capabilities.[16]

Relationships are not static, and just because an actor occupies a powerful position at one point in time does not mean that they will always be there. QSNA is very good at depicting social reality in dynamic, continuous, and processual terms.[17] Changes in relationships between actors can open up network holes—places where a broker or gatekeeper *could* be but that no one has yet filled. An actor's ability to move into key network holes—by establishing new or modifying existing relationships—can give that actor significant political power.[18] QSNA is one of the few methodologies equipped to incorporate the dynamism of changing relationships; it does not take the unit of analysis (be it the state, the organization, the individual, or the ideas) for granted, and instead seeks to understand how changes in relationship affect actors and structure.

Because the relationship is the unit of analysis in QSNA, it is not just the *fact* of a tie between two actors that matters, but the *content* and *strength* of that tie. Consider the Cold War example again. We would expect the ties between the NATO allies to be qualitatively different from the ties between a NATO and a non-NATO ally, even if the latter pair were generally friendly. A major strength of QSNA is that it can differentiate between types of ties: kinship ties are different from ties created through economic interactions, which are different from ties that are created by the spread of information. The strength of the tie would differentiate between close (marriage) and more distant (third cousins twice removed) kinship ties, the degree of economic interaction, and the amount of contact between nodes that share information. The directionality of the tie also matters. Is a state exporting to or importing from another state? Did both actors pledge to defend one another, or is the defense treaty protectionist rather than mutual? Knowing how and why actors are connected is often more useful than knowing that actors are connected.[19] Figure 32.1 is a stylized visual representation of networks showing different tie strength, content, and directionality.

Relatedly, knowing the strength and content of ties helps us identify opportunities to exercise leverage. This relational power is based on network positions and characteristics and might not be picked up by other methodologies. Figure 32.1a, for example, would suggest that A has relational pressure over B, because A exports more to B than B sends to A. Threatening to cut economic ties should therefore hurt B more than it would hurt A.

Finally, a major benefit of QSNA is that it can link micro- and macro-level analyses and provides a framework for study meso-level phenomena in and of themselves.[20] One way it does this is by looking at the relationship between formal and informal networks. Individual-level interpersonal relationships can affect more formal relationships, like membership in

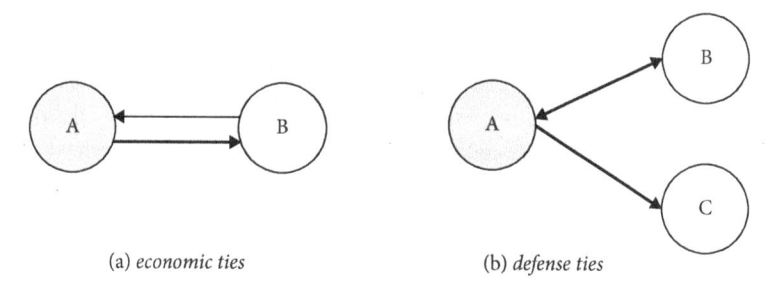

(a) *economic ties*   (b) *defense ties*

Figure 32.1 Networks Showing Weight and Types of Ties. (a) shows imports to node A from node B and exports from node A to node B. Note the direction of the ties. The ties are weighted by amount, showing that A exports more to B than it imports. In network (b) the dual direction of the ties between A and B represents a mutual defense treaty; A and B each pledge to come to the other's defense. The tie between A and C is directional, with A pledged to come to C's aid, but not the reverse.

a group, which can in turn have significant effects on outcomes of interest. For example, Parkinson found that informal discursive practices such as jokes and gossip were related to organizational ruptures within militant organizations.[21] The spread of jokes and gossip is an informal connection between actors, but she found these informal practices crucial to explaining factions within Fatah. This linking of individual interests to broader macro-level phenomena is one of the strengths of QSNA and helps explain why QSNA has found use in nearly all subfields of political science.

Linking micro- and macro-level analyses can also mean looking at the interactions between domestic and international politics. Keck and Sikkink's boomerang model is one example that explains how transnational networks interact with domestic networks to produce policy change.[22] In this model, ideas from transnational networks are adopted into domestic policies. Once developed, those domestic policies "boomerang" out to the transnational network, in turn reproducing and sometimes modifying the ideas circulating transnationally. QSNA can identify change over time, even in something as diffuse as ideas or norms. Analyzing networks (including network membership, characteristics, and structure) as well as actor attributes (such as centrality and what positions actors occupy) can help us understand how relationships change over time, and how those changes are related to different outcomes. One difficulty, however, is that identifying change and making inferences about its effects often depends on knowing the entirety of the network. As I discuss below, this is not always possible. Nonetheless, QSNA has the possibility of identifying sources and effects of changes in relationships over time.

Doing QSNA

As a methodological approach, QSNA is most appropriate for questions about the relationships that connect actors and the structures—both formal and informal—that result. Doing good QSNA often lies in knowing what type of evidence to collect to construct a network, how to find that data, and what to do once you have assembled a network. But how do you know if you potentially have or need network data?

Almost all political data could be constructed as a network, but not every political research question requires QSNA. For example, members of the U.S. Congress share ties if they served in the same congressional sessions. But unless there is a *relationship* at the center of the study, QSNA is not needed. Unless you think that shared congressional sessions affect voting behavior, create informal information networks, or have a different effect, you don't need to use QSNA. As another example, arms sale data is implicitly relational. A buys from B and sells to C. A nonrelational study could look at A's sales-to-purchase ratio, or the import-export ratio of the actors. A relational study using QSNA would ask *who* A sells to and receives weapons from, and the *type* of weapons it sells and receives. QSNA could be used to construct a network of tank sales, and compare that to the network of fighter jet sales; ties would be weighted by the number of weapons, and the nodes would be states. Another QSNA application might be less granular, looking at the network created by any arms sale rather than by type. In either case, the research would study the reasons for arms sales (why is a tie created here?) and/or the consequences of arms sales (how does this tie affect the relationship between the nodes?). QSNA is an appropriate method when a scholar wants to study relationships and structure.

While there are some existing data sets that can be used to construct and analyze networks, many scholars will have to collect new evidence to use social network analysis. Therefore, QSNA often starts from a descriptive point of view: scholars seek to describe how actors are situated in different networks based on relationships. Only then can we move to explanation and inference.

In terms of existing data sets, anything that captures relationships can be useful for QSNA. For example, the Correlates of War project includes information about alliances; the data set could be used to examine how alliances (or alliances with a specific country) have changed over time.[23] But there is no one right way to use this existing data set for social network analysis. The alliance data set includes information on alliance membership and type of alliance for each year an alliance exists. Some scholars might be interested in how alliance relationships affect trade relationships and could use a dichotomous yes/no conceptualization of an alliance relationship. Others might be interested in the consequences of different types of alliance relationships and could weight ties based on the type of alliance, with mutual defense pacts receiving more emphasis than weaker consultation pacts. The network analysis could reveal structural information about multi-alliance membership and differentiate between closer allies (mutual defense pacts) and weaker alignments. Comparative QSNA might address the different structures of rebel groups, or the community ties that make it more likely individuals will join a rebellion. In American politics, QSNA could look at how different types of relationships (kinship, job-related, neighborhood/geographic) affect voter turnout. Scholars should make their data and network decisions based on the types of relationships that they think matter for their research questions.

For those scholars seeking to collect new evidence, one of the first questions they need to consider is what types of relationships matter and how they can find evidence of those relationships. For example, we might be interested in why individuals join organizations or movements. Kinship ties might be one explanation,[24] or actors might join a movement because a salient relationship has been activated, such as ethnicity relations.[25] Because actors are embedded in multiple, overlapping networks, it is often the case that scholars need to collect data on more than one type of network, which can necessitate using multiple data collection strategies. In my own work on international weapons sales, I began with existing data from the Stockholm International Peace Research Institute to establish which states (nodes) were selling what types of weapons (ties) to other states. I then conducted original research in the U.S. national archives to determine which weapons types were perceived as more prestigious than others, and conceptually weighted ties based on prestige. With this new data set, I was able to identify networks of prestigious arms transfers and determine how prestige weapons sales shaped the depth of political relationships between states, including formal alliance relationships and less formal friendship ties.[26]

Collecting data on overlapping networks is especially important when there is reason to believe there is interaction between the networks, such as when formal and informal networks interact. Scholars need to think about the multiple types of relationships that are potentially relevant for their inquiries. For example, Hundman and Parkinson found that informal intramilitary networks overlap with formal military command structures, and that these overlaps help explain when individual officers disobeyed orders.[27] Understanding how actors are embedded in multiple types of relations is no small task: to identify these relevant networks, Hundman and Parkinson used archival materials, interviews, and memoirs. Similarly, Carpenter et al. used focus groups, interviews, surveys, hyperlink analyses, and website content analysis to identify gatekeepers in the human security network and understand how those gatekeepers affect issue adoption.[28] Collecting data on information networks, such as the ways gossip or rumors travel among a group, will require in-depth fieldwork and the trust of interlocutors.[29] Again, the evidence collection method needs to match the type of relationship being studied. The flexibility of QSNA means that there is no one "right" network, and scholars should instead think about the types of ties and the structures that become visible when different types of networks are created.

Because collecting evidence about a network can be labor-intensive, scholars might want to first think about cases within the network they want to study. One crucial difference between cases in QSNA and cases in other methodologies is that QSNA should be thought of as cases of relations. A short example will help illustrate the idea of cases of relations.

Actors exist in social and political relationships with one another, so scholars can choose a set of cases based on those relationships. For instance, Figure 32.2 shows the evolution of a rivalry relationship between India and Pakistan in the first part of the Cold War. Note that the ties are differentiated by type (friendly vs. rivalry) and weight (core vs. peripheral ally/rival). While initially the United States was friendly with Pakistan, this changed over time; China and India fought a border war in 1962, leading the United States to explore friendship ties with India. The tensions in the network—the United States was trying to be friends with both Pakistan *and* India (Pakistan's rival)—were too unstable. After India and Pakistan fought a war in Kashmir in 1965, the ties in the network became more balanced, as the United States effectively cut ties with Pakistan and pursued a weaker friendship with India. What does all of this tell us? One way to identify cases is to think about the types of relationships that matter. In this example, the casing began with the rivalry between Pakistan and India. Similar cases of regional rivalry (Egypt and Israel, for example) could flesh out a comparative network case study. Once cases of relations are chosen, scholars can think about additional ties that matter and map these other variables of interest onto the cases of relations. Arms sales, for example, would represent a different type of tie between the states in the case. Because QSNA differentiates ties based on content, it would then be possible to understand how the sale of tanks affected the political ties between the United States and Pakistan, or how the sale of planes affected U.S.-India relations.

I have talked a lot about "creating" a network based on the evidence collected. But what does that mean? Many scholars assume that doing QSNA requires creating a visualization of the network. While visualizing the network can be helpful—and there are numerous tools to

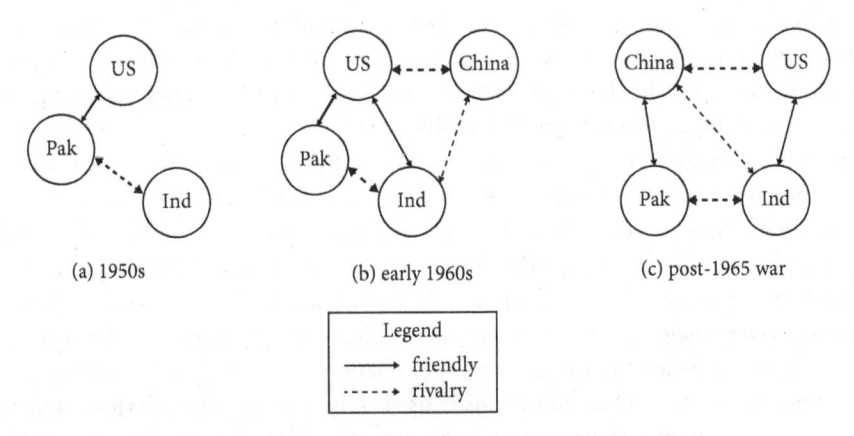

Figure 32.2 Friendship and Rivalry Ties, Indian Subcontinent, 1950s–1965.

help scholars do this—visualizing the network is not always necessary and can at times serve as a distraction. Many scholars use computer algorithms, generally in R, to actually "draw" their networks, which involves coding the qualitative network data and formatting it to be read by one of the various network programs. Having computers draw networks is particularly useful for large networks where scholars are interested in structural properties and characteristics of specific nodes, like brokerage or centrality, and for identifying substructures, like cliques.[30] Depending on the size of the network and the types of cases analyzed, it is also possible to draw smaller networks by hand and see how actors are linked to one another. Egocentric networks—or the study of the connections of one particular node—can certainly be done without the assistance of computer programs.[31]

Padgett and Ansell's study of Florentine elite families is an example of qualitative network evidence fed into algorithms. Studying the rise of the Medici, Padgett and Ansell used detailed biographical descriptions to identify nine types of relevant relationships, including kinship relations; multiple types of economic relations; political relationships, including patronage and personal loans; and personal friendship relationships.[32] With this qualitative evidence in hand, they constructed networks of family structure and organization in Florence using algorithms.[33]

Whether or not statistical programs are necessary depends on the type of network and the case(s) within it being studied. Heath, Fuller, and Johnston used interviews to construct egocentric networks to understand the socially embedded nature of educational decision-making. Through interviews, they were able to draw networks that show the ties their ego—the primary node they studied—had to others. Because their data set of family and friendship ties was small, they were able to manually create the network, with the ego at the center and ties radiating out from the ego.[34]

In some cases, a visual representation of the network is not even needed. Sometimes scholars are studying a part of a network or actors that are in specific roles. It is often possible to determine what parts of the network will be studied or which actor is in which role without a visual creation of the data. For example, Cooley and Nexon studied the network of U.S. overseas military bases to show it shared the hub-and-spoke structure of empires.[35] The evidence they used to construct the network came from treaties, including bilateral basing agreements, mutual defense pacts and security agreements, and status of forces agreements.[36] After examining these agreements, they were able to draw an abstract representation of the network, showing how the United States (the central hub) was connected to leadership and/or local actors in the host countries.[37] In this case, a visual re-creation of the exact network was not necessary, since Cooley and Nexon's data collection process revealed a series of bilateral agreements, placing the United States at the center of the network, and because the authors were interested in ideal-type networks rather than exactly reconstructing the overseas basing network.

Overall, then, doing good QSNA requires identifying the types of relationships that the scholar thinks matters, developing a research design to collect evidence about those relationships, and selecting cases of relations to focus on in depth.

Potential Problems

As with any method, QSNA is not without its potential problems and complications. One set of problems concerns the decisions that scholars make when using QSNA. For example, how do you know that you've collected relevant tie information for your research question? Who should draw the boundaries around the network: the scholar or the network nodes?[38] This question matters, because an externally imposed boundary might make sense for the scholar but could overlook crucial ties that members of the network think are important. On the other hand, allowing the network boundary to be drawn by the nodes could lead to too much extraneous information. Scholars need to find the balance between defining the boundaries of the network analytically and being open to expanding that definition based on what members of the network indicate. Similarly, because QSNA is flexible, how do you know which relationships matter? It is very possible to start a project believing that only formal alliance ties matter, only to determine later that less formalized friendship ties are equally important. To address these issues, scholars need to think carefully about criteria for including nodes in a network, and the types of relationships that are potentially important.

Defining the boundaries of the network is particularly difficult when members of the network cannot speak to the researcher. In these, most common cases, how can a researcher know they have tapped into the "right" networks and identified the proper network boundaries? Researchers should continue reading, with an eye to identifying actors or ties that the network members reference. For instance, in archival research, are there certain actors, locations, or ideas that are frequently mentioned in telegrams, conversations, or memoranda? The researcher should seek additional information on those items to understand how they link up with their existing network. Alternatively, a researcher might have to impose boundaries based on existing research, for example, looking at the kinship ties of a rebel group leader rather than trying to identify kinship ties for a majority of rebel group members. This process, though daunting, is not dissimilar to other boundary-drawing processes, such as counting as "war" only a conflict that has at least 1,000 battle-related deaths per calendar year.[39] Researchers should consider the boundary-drawing process iterative and be willing to update (either by adding or removing network information) their boundaries as their research continues.

A second set of problems concerns the practicalities of using QSNA. Scholars often get tempted by visual representations of a network, but this can lead to an emphasis on the visuals rather than understanding relations within the network. It can be tempting to draw the network, but unless there is a clear reason for visualizing the network scholars can be left with what looks like a ball of yarn: a messy, interconnected sphere of ties and nodes that does not make much analytical or explanatory sense. Not all networks need to be visualized. Scholars interested in network structure and position might find it more advantageous to visualize the network. But it also might be possible to visualize part of the network—as in Figure 32.2—and focus on types of relationships or part of the network that is relevant for the study at hand. The recommended readings below present different examples of visualized networks and networks that did not need to be visually represented. Determining whether or not to construct a network is a judgment call, and scholars might find that their visualization needs change as their project progresses. Nonetheless, it is important not to get distracted by the possibility of visually representing the network and instead to consider what, if anything, is analytically necessary.

Finally, QSNA has been criticized for remaining in the descriptive rather than the explanatory realm.[40] However, as the recommended readings show, it is possible to use QSNA to make causal and inferential arguments. Further, it's not clear why "being descriptive" should be levied as a criticism against QSNA. The method's explicitly relational approach—highlighting structure and actors and agency—often recovers mechanisms and dynamics that are missed with other approaches. In these cases, description is a necessary first step and must come before explanation. Scholars do need to be careful, though, in assessing causality. QSNA is, in many ways, a study of multicausality, which means that determining cause and effect is not necessarily linear or straightforward. An actor's position in multiple networks, or the structure of two networks, might explain outcomes. Distilling this down to the parsimonious explanations we are accustomed to is not an easy task, and means that scholars using QSNA will often have to triangulate onto causal processes.[41] Determining causality can be more complex, but this should not be a deterrent for scholars interested in using QSNA.

Notes

1. Victor, Montgomery, and Lubell, "Introduction."
2. Emirbayer, "Manifesto for a Relational Sociology," 294; Hafner-Burton, Kahler, and Montgomery, "Network Analysis for International Relations," 571; Hadden, *Networks in Contention*, 8. See also Wasserman and Faust, *Social Network Analysis*, 4.
3. Emirbayer, "Manifesto for a Relational Sociology"; Podolny, "Networks as the Pipes and Prisms of the Market."
4. Schipper and Spekkink, "Balancing the Quantitative and Qualitative Aspects of Social Network Analysis to Study Complex Social Systems." For a notable exception, see Gade, Hafez, and Gabbay, "Fratricide in Rebel Movements."
5. Ward, Stovel, and Sacks, "Network Analysis and Political Science," 250.
6. Froehlich, Van Waes, and Schäfer, "Linking Quantitative and Qualitative Network Approaches."
7. See, for example, Kirkland, "The Relational Determinants of Legislative Outcomes"; Kirkland and Gross, "Measurement and Theory in Legislative Networks"; Ward, Stovel, and Sacks, "Network Analysis and Political Science," 251.
8. Cranmer and Desmarais 2011. For use of ERGM and TERGM see Cranmer, Desmarais, and Menninga, "Complex Dependencies in the Alliance Network" on alliances; Pauls and Cranmer, "Affinity Communities in United Nations Voting."
9. The R package used to calculate ERGM is TERGM is called "Btergm," developed by Leifeld, Cranmer, and Desmarais. See Leifeld, Cranmer, Desmarais 2018.
10. Cranmer, Desmarais, and Menninga, "Complex Dependencies in the Alliance Network." For qualitative insights, see George and Smoke 1974; Schelling, *Arms and Influence*; and more recently Krebs and Spindel 2018; Spindel, "Arms for Influence?"
11. Ahrens, "Qualitative Network Analysis"; Crossley, "The Social World of the Network."
12. Hafner-Burton, Kahler, and Montgomery, "Network Analysis for International Relations"; Montgomery, "Proliferation Networks in Theory and Practice," 32.
13. Hafner-Burton, Kahler, and Montgomery, "Network Analysis for International Relations," 563; Wasserman and Faust, *Social Network Analysis*, ch. 5.
14. Carpenter et al., "Explaining the Advocacy Agenda."
15. Granovetter, "The Strength of Weak Ties," 1364.
16. Hafner-Burton, Kahler, and Montgomery, "Network Analysis for International Relations."
17. Emirbayer, "Manifesto for a Relational Sociology," 281.
18. Padgett and Ansell, "Robust Action and the Rise of the Medici."
19. Granovetter, "The Strength of Weak Ties," 1374.
20. Victor, Montgomery, and Lubell, "Introduction," 8; Granovetter, "The Strength of Weak Ties"; Heath, Fuller, and Johnston, "Chasing Shadows," 649.
21. Parkinson, "Money Talks."

22. Keck and Sikkink, *Activists beyond Borders*. See also Teater, "Using Transnational Advocacy Networks to Challenge Restrictions on Religion."
23. Gibler, *International Military Alliances*.
24. Parkinson, "Organizing Rebellion"; Larson and Lewis, "Rumors, Kinship Networks, and Rebel Group Formation."
25. Fox, "Strings of Traitors"; Larson and Lewis, "Ethnic Networks."
26. Spindel, "Beyond Military Power"; Spindel, "Policy Series 2021–38."
27. Hundman and Parkinson, "Rogues, Degenerates, and Heroes."
28. Carpenter et al., "Explaining the Advocacy Agenda."
29. Parkinson, "Money Talks"; Larson and Lewis, "Rumors, Kinship Networks, and Rebel Group Formation."
30. There are a number of packages in R that are useful for network analysis, including *iGraph*, *SNA*, and *networks*. Network evidence is often formatted as a three-column set, known as an edge list: Actor A, Actor B, and weight of the tie between them. These ties are generally called "edges," and actors are referred to as "vertices." For an introduction into using these packages in R, see Sadler, "Introduction to Network Analysis with R"; Ognyanove, "Network Analysis and Visualization with R and igraph."
31. For a description of egocentric networks, see Heath, Fuller, and Johnston, "Chasing Shadows," 648.
32. Padgett and Ansell, "Robust Action and the Rise of the Medici," 1265.
33. Padgett and Ansell, "Robust Action and the Rise of the Medici," 1274–1277. Unless a scholar is using existing data sets or is looking at a network where ties are quantitative (e.g., trading networks), most quantitative network analysis will also begin with qualitative data.
34. Heath, Fuller, and Johnston, "Chasing Shadows," 656; Knoke and Yang, *Network Fundamentals*, 15.
35. Cooley and Nexon, "'The Empire Will Compensate You.'"
36. Cooley and Nexon, "'The Empire Will Compensate You,'" 1037.
37. Cooley and Nexon, "'The Empire Will Compensate You,'" 1038.
38. Heath, Fuller, and Johnston, "Chasing Shadows."
39. This is the definition the Upsala Conflict Data Program (UCDP) uses to differentiate War from minor-intensity-level state-based conflict. See "UCDP Definitions," https://www.pcr.uu.se/research/ucdp/definitions/.
40. Fowler et al., "Causality in Political Networks"; Kahler, "Networked Politics."
41. Fowler et al., "Causality in Political Networks," 466.

Recommended Readings

Staniland, Paul. *Networks of Rebellion: Explaining Insurgent Cohesion and Collapse*. Cornell Studies in Security Affairs. Ithaca, NY: Cornell University Press, 2014.
> Staniland clearly lays out his empirical strategy (fieldwork, interviews, historical information) to demonstrate the horizontal and vertical ties that matter for insurgent networks.

Hundman, Eric, and Sarah E. Parkinson. "Rogues, Degenerates, and Heroes: Disobedience as Politics in Military Organizations." *European Journal of International Relations* 25, no. 3 (2019): 645–671.
> Hundman and Parkinson provide an excellent explanation of how to conceptualize multiple, overlapping networks and how to assemble and select "cases of relations."

Hadden, Jennifer. *Networks in Contention: The Divisive Politics of Climate Change*. Cambridge Studies in Contentious Politics. Cambridge: Cambridge University Press, 2015.
> Hadden's clear and precise discussion of social network theory and how she selected different sources of evidence to test her theory are an outstanding example of the use and application of social network analysis, showing how relational ties can structure the repertoire of possibility.

Heath, Sue, Alison Fuller, and Brenda Johnston. "Chasing Shadows: Defining Network Boundaries in Qualitative Social Network Analysis." *Qualitative Research* 9, no. 5 (2009): 645–661.
> The authors provide an extremely clear explanation of how they used interviews to understand the scope of their networks of interest, and the potential problem of a "shadow network," or missing network members that the researcher does not know about or does not have access to.

Carpenter, Charli, Sirin Duygulu, Alexander H. Montgomery, and Anna Rapp. "Explaining the Advocacy Agenda: Insights from the Human Security Network." *International Organization* 68, no. 2 (2014): 449–470.
> This article uses focus groups, interviews, surveys, hyperlink analyses, and website content to construct and visualize the human security advocacy network, revealing the crucial gatekeeper network position.

References

Ahrens, Petra. "Qualitative Network Analysis: A Useful Tool for Investigating Policy Networks in Transnational Settings?" *Methodological Innovations* 11, no. 1 (2018): 2059799118769816. https://doi.org/10.1177/2059799118769816.

Carpenter, Charli, Sirin Duygulu, Alexander H. Montgomery, and Anna Rapp. "Explaining the Advocacy Agenda: Insights from the Human Security Network." *International Organization* 68, no. 2 (2014): 449–470. https://doi.org/10.1017/S0020818313000453.

Cheng, Huimin, Ye Wang, Ping Ma, and Amanda Murdie. "Communities and Brokers: How the Transnational Advocacy Network Simultaneously Provides Social Power and Exacerbates Global Inequalities." *International Studies Quarterly* 65, no. 3 (2021): 724–738. https://doi.org/10.1093/isq/sqab037.

Cooley, Alexander, and Daniel H. Nexon. "'The Empire Will Compensate You': The Structural Dynamics of the US Overseas Basing Network." *Perspectives on Politics* 11, no. 4 (2013): 1034–1050.

Cranmer, Skyler J., and Bruce A. Desmarais. "Inferential Network Analysis with Exponential Random Graph Models." *Political Analysis* 19 (2011): 66–86. http://doi.org/10.1093/pan/mpq037.

Cranmer, Skyler J., Bruce A. Desmarais, and Elizabeth J. Menninga. "Complex Dependencies in the Alliance Network." *Conflict Management and Peace Science* 29, no. 3 (2012): 279–313. http://doi.org/10.1177/0738894212443446.

Crossley, Nick. "The Social World of the Network: Combining Qualitative and Quantitative Elements in Social Network Analysis." *Sociologica* 1 (2010): 1–34. https://doi.org/10.2383/32049.

Emirbayer, Mustafa. "Manifesto for a Relational Sociology." *American Journal of Sociology* 103, no. 2 (1997): 281–317. https://doi.org/10.1086/231209.

Fowler, James H., Michael T. Heaney, David W. Nickerson, John F. Padgett, and Betsy Sinclair. "Causality in Political Networks." *American Politics Research* 39, no. 2 (2011): 437–480. https://doi.org/10.1177/1532673X10396310.

Fox, Andrew. "Strings of Traitors: Social Networks and the Organizational Trajectory of the Khmer Rouge." May 2019. https://shareok.org/handle/11244/319601.

Froehlich, Dominik E., Sara Van Waes, and Hannah Schäfer. "Linking Quantitative and Qualitative Network Approaches: A Review of Mixed Methods Social Network Analysis in Education Research." *Review of Research in Education* 44, no. 1 (2020): 244–268. https://doi.org/10.3102/0091732X20903311.

Gade, Emily, Mohammed M. Hafez, and Michael Gabbay. "Fratricide in Rebel Movements: A Network Analysis of Syrian Militant Infighting." *Journal of Peace Research* 56, no. 3 (2019): 321–335. https://doi.org/10.1177/0022343318806940.

George, Alexander, and Richard Smoke. *Deterrence in American Foreign Policy: Theory and Practice*. New York: Columbia University Press, 1974.

Gibler, Douglas M. *International Military Alliances, 1648–2008*. Washington, DC: CQ Press, 2009.

Granovetter, Mark. "The Strength of Weak Ties." *American Journal of Sociology* 78, no. 6 (1973): 1360–1380.

Hadden, Jennifer. *Networks in Contention: The Divisive Politics of Climate Change*. Cambridge Studies in Contentious Politics. Cambridge: Cambridge University Press, 2015.

Hafner-Burton, Emilie M., Miles Kahler, and Alexander H. Montgomery. "Network Analysis for International Relations." *International Organization* 63, no. 3 (2009): 559–592.

Heath, Sue, Alison Fuller, and Brenda Johnston. "Chasing Shadows: Defining Network Boundaries in Qualitative Social Network Analysis." *Qualitative Research* 9, no. 5 (2009): 645–661. https://doi.org/10.1177/1468794109343631.

Hundman, Eric, and Sarah E. Parkinson. "Rogues, Degenerates, and Heroes: Disobedience as Politics in Military Organizations." *European Journal of International Relations* 25, no. 3 (2019): 645–671. https://doi.org/10.1177/1354066118823891.

Kahler, Miles. *Networked Politics: Agency, Power, and Governance*. Ithaca: Cornell University Press, 2009.

Keck, Margaret E., and Kathryn Sikkink. *Activists beyond Borders: Advocacy Networks in International Politics*. Ithaca, NY: Cornell University Press, 1998.

Kirkland, Justin H. "The Relational Determinants of Legislative Outcomes: Strong and Weak Ties between Legislators." *Journal of Politics* 73, no. 3 (2011): 887–898. https://doi.org/10.1017/S0022381611000533.

Kirkland, Justin H., and Justin H. Gross. "Measurement and Theory in Legislative Networks: The Evolving Topology of Congressional Collaboration." *Social Networks* 36 (2014): 97–109. https://doi.org/10.1016/j.socnet.2012.11.001.

Knoke, David, and Song Yang. *Network Fundamentals*. SAGE Publications, 2008.

Krebs, Ronald R., and Jennifer Spindel. "Divided Priorities: Why and When Allies Differ over Military Intervention." *Security Studies* 27, no. 4 (2018): 575–606.

Larson, Jennifer M., and Janet I. Lewis. "Ethnic Networks." *American Journal of Political Science* 61, no. 2 (2017): 350–364. https://doi.org/10.1111/ajps.12282.

Larson, Jennifer M., and Janet I. Lewis. "Rumors, Kinship Networks, and Rebel Group Formation." *International Organization* 72, no. 4 (2018): 871–903. https://doi.org/10.1017/S0020818318000243.

Leifeld, Philip, Skyler J. Cranmer, and Bruce A. Desmarais. "Temporal Exponential Random Graph Models with btergm: Estimation and Bootstrap Confidence Intervals." *Journal of Statistical Software* 83, no. 6 (2018): 1–36. https://doi.org/10.18637/jss.v083.i06.

Montgomery, Alexander H. "Proliferation Networks in Theory and Practice." In *Globalization and WMD Proliferation*, edited by James A. Russell and James J. Wirtz, 28–39. Routledge Global Security Studies. New York: Routledge, 2008.

Ognyanove, Katherine. "Network Analysis and Visualization with R and igraph." 2016. https://kateto.net/netscix2016.html.

Padgett, John F., and Christopher K. Ansell. "Robust Action and the Rise of the Medici, 1400–1434." *American Journal of Sociology* 98, no. 6 (1993): 1259–1319.

Parkinson, Sarah E. "Money Talks: Discourse, Networks, and Structure in Militant Organizations." *Perspectives on Politics* 14, no. 4 (2016): 976–994.

Parkinson, Sarah E. "Organizing Rebellion: Rethinking High-Risk Mobilization and Social Networks in War." *American Political Science Review* 107, no. 3 (2013): 418–432. https://doi.org/10.1017/S0003055413000208.

Pauls, Scott D., and Skyler J. Cranmer. "Affinity Communities in United Nations Voting: Implications for Democracy, Cooperation, and Conflict." *Physica A: Statistical Mechanics and its Applications* 484 (2017): 428–439.

Podolny, Joel M. "Networks as the Pipes and Prisms of the Market." *American Journal of Sociology* 107, no. 1 (2001): 33–60.

Sadler, Jesse. "Introduction to Network Analysis with R." October 25, 2017. https://www.jessesadler.com/post/network-analysis-with-r/.

Schelling, Thomas. *Arms and Influence*. Westport, CT: Greenwood Press, 1996.

Schipper, Danny, and Wouter Spekkink. "Balancing the Quantitative and Qualitative Aspects of Social Network Analysis to Study Complex Social Systems." *Complexity, Governance & Networks* 2, no. 1 (2015): 5–22. https://doi.org/10.7564/15-CGN23.

Spindel, Jennifer. "Arms for Influence? The Limits of Great Power Leverage." *European Journal of International Security* 8, no. 3 (2023): 395–412. https://doi.org/10.1017/eis.2023.3.

Spindel, Jennifer. "Beyond Military Power: The Symbolic Politics of Conventional Weapons Transfers." PhD diss., University of Minnesota, 2018.

Spindel, Jennifer. "Policy Series 2021-38: Trump's Transactional Follies: The Consequences of Treating the Arms Trade like a Business." *H-Diplo | ISSF* (blog), June 10, 2021. https://issforum.org/roundtables/policy/ps2021-38.

Teater, Kristina M. "Using Transnational Advocacy Networks to Challenge Restrictions on Religion: Christian Minorities in Malaysia and India." University of Cincinnati, 2019. http://rave.ohiolink.edu/etdc/view?acc_num=ucin156327356791683.

Victor, Jennifer Nicoll, Alexander H. Montgomery, and Mark Lubell. "Introduction: The Emergence of the Study of Networks in Politics." In *Oxford Handbook of Political Networks*, edited by Jennifer Nicoll Victor, Alexander H. Montgomery, and Mark Lubell, 3–57. Oxford: Oxford University Press, 2018.

Ward, Michael D., Katherine Stovel, and Audrey Sacks. "Network Analysis and Political Science." *Annual Review of Political Science* 14 (2011): 245–264. https://doi.org/10.1146/annurev.polisci.12.040907.115949.

Wasserman, Stanley, and Katherine Faust. *Social Network Analysis: Methods and Applications*. Cambridge: Cambridge University Press, 1994.

33
Process Tracing

Amy H. Liu

Descriptive Overview

Despite the popularity of using process tracing to explore a range of political phenomena—economic development,[1] opposition mobilization,[2] state formation,[3] party politics[4]—we have few instructions on how to employ this method. It remains very much a "tool [that] is neither well understood nor rigorously applied."[5] As a point of contrast, consider the detailed guidelines for choosing which statistical estimators to use for which data distribution, for how to design randomized controlled trials, and for how to model topical semantics. This is by no means a quantitative-qualitative distinction. We see similar rigor in other areas of qualitative methods, such as concept development and variable measurement,[6] typological constructions,[7] and case selection.[8] With a few exceptions,[9] the process tracing literature justifies the use of the tool but offers little instruction for its application. References are made to historical analyses and theoretical guidance, but these recommendations are of little use sans elaboration. The resulting inchoate understanding leads to poor implementation of process tracing research designs and deters outsiders from accessing and applying it. This chapter aims to offer one solution to rectify this disparity: a checklist.

While much of the recent attention is on causal mechanisms, process tracing is useful for identifying new variables. In scenarios where the causal effect is uncertain, process tracing can help identify the relevant independent variables.[10] Process tracing can be useful for concept development. When researchers observe something that cannot yet be adequately explained, process tracing a case study can be effective.[11] Process tracing can also be used in conjunction with other methods. For example, while game-theoretic models are often criticized for not being tied to political problems, the use of process tracing here can give context to the models.[12] Likewise, combining process tracing with a comparative case approach can diminish some of the disadvantages of small-N analyses, such as omitted variables, interaction effects, and few degrees of freedom.[13]

A caveat, however, warrants discussion. One reason for the current limitations on process tracing is precisely this multifunctionality. This very diversity means advocates of process tracing often speak past each other. Thus in this chapter, I target one particular subset of practitioners by focusing strictly on the use of process tracing for (1) theory-testing[14] through (2) a positivist lens.[15] Specifically, I am concerned with *the systematic study of the link between an outcome of interest and an explanation based on the rigorous assessing and weighting of evidence for and against causal inference.* By situating process tracing in positivist terms, I emphasize the role of theory and the empirical testing of hypotheses to identify causality.

State of Practice

I offer a seven-point checklist for how to conduct process tracing (see Figure 33.1). Note that while process tracing is technically a method for analysis, to execute it well requires a holistic approach, one that requires setting the stage at each step of the research process. Steps 1 through 5 are in the first row and are all at the research design stage and precede data collection. Steps 6 and 7 are the data collection and data analysis stage—for each hypothesis. While I use an example with two hypotheses in this chapter, the process need not be confined to two. I discuss each step in turn and, for each step, I offer a companion case study—explaining the development in Thai party politics—as an illustration for how to apply each step.

In principle, deep background knowledge, while helpful, is not necessary up to this point. Instead, Steps 1 through 5 are activities that should precede any fieldwork, from visiting archives to conducting interviews, from administering surveys to doing participant observations. They are essential for theory testing: they establish expectations about what researchers should encounter during their data-collection process. However, in practice, as process tracing is often iterative, researchers will likely revisit these steps throughout the project—especially in light of new data. But an initial plan for data collection should be designed based on the first five steps—without assuming any background knowledge.

Step 1: Identify Hypotheses

Good process tracing starts with a theoretically guided research design. In this first step, we need to establish testable hypotheses—much like other attempts at causal inference. There is, however, one important distinction. In process tracing, the burden of evidence is not for the concerned theory; instead, it is necessary to juxtapose rival explanations for testing.[16] The checklist is structured to allow for the testing of multiple—as many as required—rival hypotheses. These theoretical expectations should be plainly laid out prior to moving on to Step 2. These are "best practices" for any research design (for more, see Chapter 8) but vital for testing in process tracing.

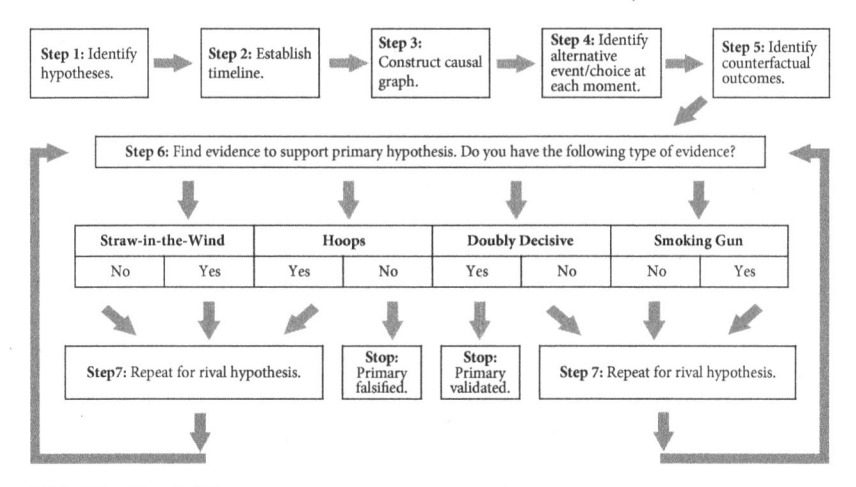

Figure 33.1 The Checklist.

To illustrate, we look at party politics in Thailand. We consider two explanations for why Thai Rak Thai (TRT) became dominant. Prior to 2001, Thailand's party system was characterized by party fragmentation and short-lived government coalitions. Yet in 2001, Thaksin Shinawatra's TRT would win 248 out of 500 seats—the first time a single party outright dominated an election. Thaksin would go on to become the first prime minister to complete a full term—and then win reelection in 2005 with an even bigger margin.

One common explanation for this dominance focuses on the individual, Thaksin.[17] TRT's success can be traced to Thaksin's wealth and power—a man "unrivaled in ... his sheer political energy, determination, vision, professionalism, ruthlessness, and network-building capacity, not to mention the incredible financial resources at his personal disposal."[18] Another explanation focuses on the institutions.[19] The 1997 Constitution changed the electoral arena. Previous constitutions perpetuated a system dominated by local elites who frequently party-switched. In contrast, the new Constitution called for greater accountability of elected officials. It stipulated that parties had to field candidates for at least 25–50% of the nationwide seats; it also constrained the practice of party-switching. This in turn forced (1) the death of many parties and, (2) for those that survived, a national orientation. In this chapter, I consider these two explanations as the two competing hypotheses: the primary hypothesis emphasizes Thaksin as an individual; the rival hypothesis focuses on the institutions.

Step 2: Establish Timeline

The next step is to sequence events. Timelines should be bookended according to theoretical expectations. The timeline ends at or shortly after the outcome of interest—that is, the dependent variable. The challenge is then to identify when the timeline starts. Good timelines should begin with the emergence of the theorized causal variable. Timelines offer multiple purposes. First, they help clarify the thought process. Second, they establish temporal precedence. Third, timelines provide what can be constituted as a "face validity" test for the argument. If the argument is that a constitutional change is what allowed TRT to dominate, the Constitution itself must then have changed *before* TRT's political rise. Timelines help establish this sequencing of events. If we find instead that the Constitution changed *after* Thaksin consolidated power (which we do not), this suggests inconsistency in our argument. Fourth, timelines help identify major events that could have shaped the outcome of interest—for example, a new Constitution in Thailand. This allows us to revisit our hypotheses and to check whether we might be missing an obvious probable cause.

Although timelines rarely find their way into published works, they are an imperative step in the research process. See Figure 33.2 for an example. I end with TRT's electoral win in 2005, and I start with the creation of the Constitutional Drafting Assembly in 1996. I chose the particular starting point given the relevance of the 1997 Constitution for the rival hypothesis. I could not have started later—for example, the 2005 TRT reelection victory—because it would have left-hand censored the explanatory variable (i.e., there was an institutional change). I could, however, have started even earlier, for example, the democratic transition in 1992. But the downside of choosing a timeline that begins too early is that it forces the researcher to have to identify an exponential number of counterfactual cases (more below in Steps 4 and 5).

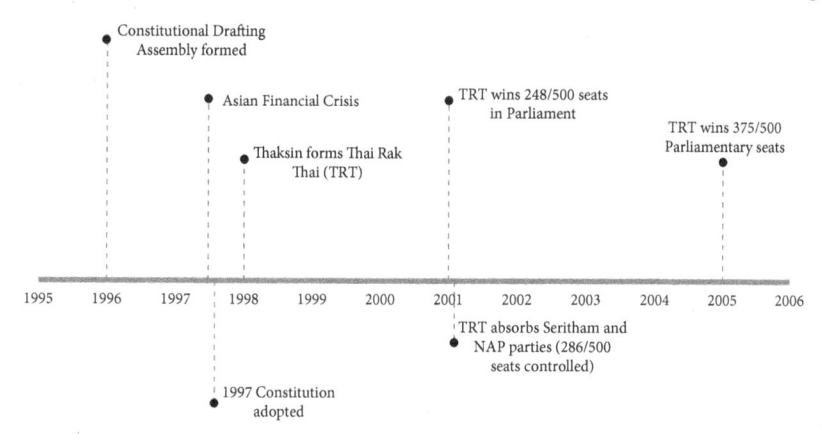

Figure 33.2 Example of a Timeline.

Step 3: Construct Causal Graph

After sequencing the timeline, we need to construct a causal graph, one per hypothesis. Such graphs identify the independent variable(s) of interest. It is possible that variables that are believed to be important but are in fact spurious end up being included on the graph. For now, that is okay. Causal graphs also provide structure, allowing us to focus on the link between the explanation and the concerned outcome. They visually depict the causal process through which X causes Y. With causal graphs, we can identify all moments when the concerned actor made a choice which *could have* affected the result. Note that this endogenous choice need not be contentious, but it does need to be theoretically relevant.

Two caveats warrant mention. First, just as not all choices are relevant moments, not all relevant moments are choices. They can also be exogenous events, such as financial crises. Put differently, we must allow for both agency and contingency in the causal graph.[20] Second, causal graphs can potentially include events that do not fit clearly into the causal process being identified but are believed to be of possible relevance. Again, for now, it is okay to include events that may be irrelevant. To distinguish this, I use dashed lines. Conversely, the causal process remains outlined with solid lines. This highlights and clarifies that not all interesting events are variables of interest.

Figure 33.3 shows how to construct a causal graph and how it physically differs from a descriptive timeline. Note that both graphs have the same set of events. Where they differ is in the dashed versus solid lines. In the top graph—using dashed lines—the TRT's continued dominance is not a necessary component of the explanatory story. The top graph also

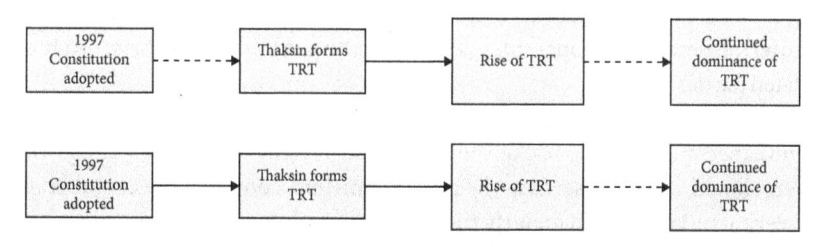

Figure 33.3 Example of a Causal Graph.

highlights that the 1997 Constitution is not part of the primary hypothesis; that is, Thaksin is the source of TRT's rise. This too is identified via a dashed line. In the bottom graph—using solid lines—TRT's formation is part of the causal process and not the ultimate explanation for the party's rise. Put differently, the formation of TRT is on the causal path, but it is not causal itself.

Step 4: Identify Alternative Choice/Event

At each relevant moment in the causal graph, a different choice could have been made or another event could have happened. For each moment, identify these alternative(s). It is important, though, that these alternatives are theoretically grounded. There must be some reason that the choice could have been made in another way or that the event could have manifested differently. In the Thai example, the alternative choices available would have included (1) the exclusion of the electoral rule changes and institutions by the constitution drafters in 1997 and (2) the choice by Thaksin to not create TRT. This is also where we see the challenges of having a timeline that starts too early, as it increases the number of alternative choices exponentially. If it seems that there are too many alternative choices in the timeline, it may be worth revisiting Step 2 to identify whether some of the earlier choices are essential for the causal graph in Step 3.

Step 5: Identify Counterfactual Outcomes

Next, for each moment identify the counterfactual outcome that would have happened if the alternative choice had been taken or the alternative event had transpired. This is where process tracing is different—almost dogmatically so—from other analytical methods. Counterfactuals are vital to process tracing, especially when no alternative cases are considered. When treating hypothetical predictions, it is imperative that some other outcome was possible. If there is no plausible theory-informed alternative outcome, then no real choice or event has taken place. Thus, the link between the inputs and the outcome was predetermined, and hence, process tracing provides us with little value-added. Note that Steps 4 and 5 are closely linked.

For instance, in the Thai example, we can imagine two alternative events. In the first, Constitution drafts exclude electoral rule changes in 1997. In this counterfactual, the prior Thai electoral rules would have continued spreading votes across multiple smaller parties. Without changes, barriers to party-switching (i.e., abandoning TRT) would have been low. Thus, in this alternate universe, coalition governments like those of the 1990s would have remained common occurrences. In the second event, an alternative choice would be Thaksin choosing to not create TRT. Per this counterfactual, in the absence of one ultra-wealthy political figure, the new institutional rules (1997 Constitution) would still have produced more consolidated parties.

As noted before, Steps 1 through 5 should in theory be conducted prior to data collection. There is no expectation of deep background knowledge. Armed with competing hypotheses, researchers should study a case: map the general timeline, construct the causal graph, identify the relevant moments, and identify the counterfactuals without the use of proper nouns. But of course, since process tracing is an iterative process, and since researchers rarely pick their cases at random, Steps 1 through 5 often do end up being shaped by some familiarity with the case.

Step 6: From Research Design to Data Collection: Finding Evidence for the Primary Hypothesis

This is the stage for data collection. Note that not all evidence types are the same. Here, I draw on Collier's four types of evidence, as summarized in Table 33.1, where each type is characterized by whether the evidence is necessary and/or sufficient (neither necessary nor sufficient: *straw-in-the-wind*), necessary but not sufficient (*hoops*), not necessary but sufficient (*smoking guns*), and necessary and sufficient (*doubly decisive*).[21]

It is important to think carefully about the evidence types collected since *most* information gathered will be of the straw-in-the-wind variety. While a great deal of data gathered might offer weak support for—or at least not negate—one hypothesis, it is not the most useful for testing purposes.[22] The causal graph is particularly useful at this point: it identifies the links that must be made between the concerned variables to establish causation. For instance, certain evidence types are necessary but not sufficient (hoops); for example, Thaksin was a man of wealth. This hoops evidence on its own cannot validate either hypothesis. However, the failure to find such evidence can allow us to eliminate one hypothesis. If it turns out (hypothetically) that Thaksin was actually a poor man, we would not be able to find any evidence to support the primary hypothesis, thereby allowing us to falsify it.

In contrast, smoking-guns evidence is sufficient but not necessary. If we find evidence of another individual just as wealthy and influential as Thaksin who failed to consolidate their party, this would be a smoking gun and validate the primary hypothesis. However, failure to find such evidence does not falsify it either. Finally, there are certain evidence types that can simultaneously support one proposed hypothesis *and* eliminate a rival one: the *doubly decisive*. If such a datum is found, then this concludes the process tracing effort. Unfortunately, such cases are rare, and thus we must increase the evidence pool to demonstrate that the working hypothesis is the best possible explanation.

Table 33.2 identifies the different types of data collected for each evidence type for our case study of Thai politics; it shows how to leverage the interpretation to test the primary hypothesis (i.e., it is about Thaksin the individual). The results show that while Thaksin was undoubtedly influential to TRT's survival, the evidence in aggregate fails to confirm—or falsify—the hypothesis. There is no doubly decisive evidence, and as such, the process tracing effort must continue to our rival hypothesis (i.e., it is about the institutions).

Table 33.1 Types of Evidence

		Necessary to Establish Causation (Certain Conditions)	
		No	Yes
Sufficient to Establish Causation (Unique Predictions)	No	Straw-in-the-Wind	Hoops
	Yes	Smoking Gun	Doubly Decisive

Step 7: Find Evidence for Rival Hypothesis

The final step is to repeat Step 6; at each choice node the focus should now be on the alternative explanations. As the two hypotheses are constructed to be rivalrous, any evidence gathered to support the alternative hypothesis must by design also be considered evidence to dismiss the primary hypothesis (and vice versa). Whether a piece of evidence is supportive (and dismissive)—and the extent of it—depends on its evidence type. For example, for a rival hypothesis, a hoops test evidence type is arguably the most important. Hoops evidence, if absent, can eliminate a hypothesis from consideration. If the hypothesized variable was not even present when the event happened, then it can be used to dismiss the rival hypothesis—and therefore support the primary hypothesis. If the rival explanation cannot be easily discarded, we must collect other data types. Wherever possible, look for opportunities to dismiss the rival hypothesis. (Alternatively, support it such that it eliminates the primary hypothesis.) Table 33.3 shows the different evidence type needed for the rival institutional hypothesis.

The evidence taken together provides strong support for the institutional hypothesis as an explanation for TRT's dominance. In a different world, where Thaksin tried to rise to power in the absence of the 1997 electoral reforms, there would still have been a stronger reliance on coalitions and faction politics as characterized the 1990s. While this evidence is not exactly doubly decisive, it does cast doubt on the primary hypothesis, which focuses strictly on the individual. Although Thaksin was personally influential, the evidence weighs more heavily in favor of the 1997 Constitution as the explanation for TRT's rise and success.

Potential Problems

While process tracing brings context to the case, it places a substantial burden on the researcher to find the different pieces of evidence for each hypothesis. Consider what happens when there is missing evidence: Is it missing because it does not exist, or because the researcher has not looked in the right places? Conversely, assume the researcher has identified smoking gun evidence to support the hypothesis; there is then the challenge to demonstrate that the researcher did not look only for evidence to support this hypothesis (i.e., ignoring all other evidence that would suggest otherwise). In short, while some people may find the evidence-hunting aspect of process tracing fun, the compounding challenges with each piece of evidence can make the method somewhat inaccessible for researchers with limited resources.

Process tracing can also place a substantial burden on how evidence is interpreted. This chapter focused on the use of process tracing for theory testing through a positivist framework. It requires we find the doubly decisive evidence—or a bundle of evidence that collectively functions as such. This can be a formidable barrier. One alternative is to employ formal Bayesian thinking. With Bayesian logic, researchers assume all pieces of evidence have some likelihood under each explanation. The probative power or explanatory weight of each piece of evidence is a function of its relative likelihood under the alternative hypotheses or explanations.[23]

Additionally, process tracing is not always about deductive theory testing. It can be interpretivist.[24] Likewise, process tracing is not always deductive; it can also be inductive.[25]

Table 33.2 Finding Evidence for Hypothesis 1

Individual Hypothesis: TRT's success can be traced to Thaksin.

Straw-in-the-Wind: *Personal assets and leadership are important for Thai politics.*

Indeed, Thai politics has been characterized by elites looking to bolster their status and accumulate wealth. Note that this data, however, suggests only that personalities are important, not that Thaksin was.

Hoops: *Thaksin was a man of wealth and leadership.*

Prior to his political career, in 1986 Thaksin owned the largest mobile carrier in Thailand. In the mid-1990s, Thaksin entered politics and joined the Palang Dharma Party (PDP). His first major position was foreign minister. He later assumed the PDP presidency—all suggesting Thaksin was a man of assets and capabilities.

Smoking Gun: *Thaksin was sufficient for TRT's dominance.*

There is no direct evidence for this; there is, however, counterfactual evidence. First, could another elite have established a TRT-like party? The evidence suggests no. There have been other wealthy and influential politicians who have tried but failed.

Doubly Decisive: *Thaksin was both necessary and sufficient for TRT's dominance.*

While Thaksin was sufficient, could he have done it without the new Constitution? Could the rise and success of TRT have happened prior to 1997? Available information suggests no. Recall, TRT was not Thaksin's first stint as a party leader. His stint as PDP leader (1995) was short-lived and ended with factionalism. While other factors were at play in PDP's failure, it seems Thaksin's personal charisma and wealth were not sufficient in the face of factional quarrels.

Table 33.3 Finding Evidence for Rival Hypothesis

Institutional Hypothesis: TRT's success can be traced to changes in the electoral rules in the 1997 Constitution.

Straw-in-the-Wind: *Constitutions affect institutions in Thailand.*

Pre-1997 electoral rules favored provincial politicians and did not discourage party-switching. Given these incentives, there was (1) a proliferation of parties contesting elections; (2) many parties in the national assembly; (3) oversized government coalitions; and (4) short-tenured governments. Consequently, governments were short-lived. In fact, no elected prime minister in the democratic era has served out their complete term—until Thaksin.

Hoops: *The 1997 Constitution was adopted before Thaksin rose to political prominence.*

While this fact does not validate the institutional hypothesis, it does ensure the hypothesis is not falsified. Consider if TRT's rise predated the constitutional reform. If true, logic would dictate that the Constitution cannot account for TRT's electoral dominance.

Smoking Gun: *The 1997 Constitution created incentives for politicians to consolidate into larger parties.*

Prior to the reform, 7.2 effective parties contested the national elections; after the reform, this number dropped to 3.8 in 2001 and then 2.6 in 2005. Moreover, for the 2001 election, TRT brought several political leaders and their supporters into its fold.

Doubly Decisive: *The Constitution—and not Thaksin—was necessary and sufficient for TRT's dominance.*

This is where the counterfactual is useful. In a universe where electoral reforms had not been included in the 1997 Constitution, would TRT still have been so dominant? The answer is no. As noted in Step 6, TRT was not Thaksin's first rodeo. It was, however, the first time he led a party in the postreform era. Thaksin's prior work with PDP ended in failure—suggesting limits to his personal capacity. Additionally, there is evidence that some factions would have abandoned TRT if it had not been locked into the party by constitutional rules.

Source: Vatikiotis and Tasker, "Prickly Premier."

Process tracing can be useful when we have no theory or little prior knowledge about the case. Such approaches appeal to "soaking and poking" to build theories or explain a phenomenon. Whether the purpose is to develop a generalizable explanation or to "craft a minimally sufficient explanation for a puzzling outcome,"[26] the checklist in this chapter—particularly Steps 6 and 7—may have limited utility. While this limited application is potentially a problem, it also highlights the very diversity—and thus the potential—of process tracing.

Despite the popularity of process tracing in empirical research, discussions on how to process trace have been largely absent in political science. There is frequent disjuncture between theoretically driven research designs and rigorously evaluated empirics. This has resulted in critics dismissing process tracing as nothing more than "reading history closely" and as being ineffective in explaining political phenomena beyond a singular case—if even that. Yet this chapter demonstrates one way that process tracing can be done rigorously and with structure—with theoretical implications beyond a singular case.

Notes

1. Doner, *The Politics of Uneven Development*; Ricks, "Agents, Principals, or Something in Between?"
2. Slater, "Party Cartelization, Indonesian-Style"; Weiss, *The Roots of Resilience*.
3. Huang and Kang, "State Formation in Korea and Japan"; Zarakol, *After Defeat*.
4. Hicken, "Party Fabrication"; Morgenbesser, "Cambodia's Transition to Hegemonic Authoritarianism"; Nelson, "Institutional Incentives and Informal Local Political Groups (Phuak) in Thailand."
5. Collier, "Understanding Process-Tracing," 823.
6. Adcock and Collier, "Measurement Validity."
7. Collier, LaPorte, and Seawright, "Putting Typologies to Work."
8. Lieberman, "Nested Analysis as a Mixed-Method Strategy for Comparative Research"; Seawright and Gerring, "Case Selection Techniques in Case Study Research."
9. Fairfield and Charman 2022; Zaks, "Relationships among Rivals."
10. Huang and Kang, "State Formation in Korea and Japan."
11. Johnson 1981.
12. Bates et al., *Analytical Narratives*.
13. Slater, "Party Cartelization, Indonesian-Style."
14. For other types of process tracing (e.g., inductive, theory developing), see Beach and Pedersen, *Process-Tracing Methods*; Bennett and Checkel 2015.
15. See van Meegdenburg, "Process Tracing" for an example of theory testing with process tracing using more interpretivist methods.
16. Rohlfing, "Comparative Hypothesis Testing via Process Tracing"; Zaks, "Relationships among Rivals."
17. McCargo and Pathmanand, *The Thaksinization of Thailand*; Pasuk and Baker, *Thaksin*.
18. Nelson, "Institutional Incentives and Informal Local Political Groups (Phuak) in Thailand," 126.
19. Hicken, "Party Fabrication."
20. van Meegdenburg, "Process Tracing," 405.
21. Collier, "Understanding Process-Tracing," 825.
22. Fairfield 2015.
23. Fairfield and Charman, *Social Inquiry and Bayesian Inference*.
24. van Meegdenburg, "Process Tracing."

25. For examples, see Huang and Kang, "State Formation in Korea and Japan"; Doner, *The Politics of Uneven Development*; Weiss, *The Roots of Resilience*.
26. Beach and Pedersen, *Process-Tracing Methods*, 3.

Recommended Readings

Ricks, Jacob I., and Amy H. Liu. "Process-Tracing Research Designs: A Practical Guide." *PS: Political Science & Politics* 51, no. 4 (2018): 842–846.
   An extended discussion of the checklist with more examples: emergence of the Japanese developmental state, TRT's dominance, English standardization in Singapore, and adoption of irrigation reforms in the Philippines.
Hicken, Allen. "Party Fabrication: Constitutional Reform and the Rise of Thai Rak Thai." *Journal of East Asian Studies* 6 (2006): 381–407.
   An example of theory-testing process tracing in practice. Argues TRT's rise is because of the constitutional change, and not because of Thaksin. The discussion and evidence for the rival hypothesis in this chapter draw heavily on this paper.
Huang, Chin-Hao, and David C. Kang. "State Formation in Korea and Japan, 400–800 CE." *International Organization* 76, no. 1 (2022): 1–31.
   An example of theory-generating process tracing in practice. Identifies the Korean and Japanese state institutions developed not because of war but because of emulation of the Chinese.
Ricks, Jacob I. "Agents, Principals, or Something in Between? Bureaucrats and Policy Control in Thailand." *Journal of East Asian Studies* 18, no. 3 (2018): 321–344.
   An example of theory-testing process tracing in practice. Calls attention to the role of bureaucrats in Thailand in effecting policy change.
Slater, Dan. "Party Cartelization, Indonesian-Style." *Journal of East Asian Studies* 18, no. 1 (2018): 23–46.
   An example of theory-testing process tracing in practice. Argues the nature of presidential power-sharing in Indonesia has stunted the nature of conventional identifiable oppositions.
Weiss, Meredith L. *The Roots of Resilience*. Ithaca, NY: Cornell University Press, 2020.
   An example of theory-generating process tracing in practice. Explains why electoral turnover is not sufficient for substantive regime change in either Malaysia or Singapore.

References

Adcock, Robert, and David Collier. "Measurement Validity." *American Political Science Review* 95 (2001): 529–546.
Bates, Robert H., Avner Greif, Margaret Levi, Jean-Laurent Rosenthal, and Barry Weingast. *Analytical Narratives*. Princeton, NJ: Princeton University Press, 1998.
Beach, Derek, and Rasmus Brun Pedersen. *Process-Tracing Methods*. Ann Arbor: University of Michigan Press, 2019.
Bennett, Andrew, and Jeffrey T. Checkel. *Process Tracing*. New York: Cambridge University Press, 2015.
Bennett, Andrew, and Jeffrey T. Checkel, eds. *Process tracing*. Cambridge University Press, 2015.
Collier, David. "Understanding Process-Tracing." *PS: Political Science & Politics* 44 (2011): 823–830.
Collier, David, Jody LaPorte, and Jason Seawright. "Putting Typologies to Work." *Political Research Quarterly* 65 (2012): 217–232.
Doner, Richard F. *The Politics of Uneven Development*. New York: Cambridge University Press, 2009.
Fairfield, Tasha. "Reflections on analytic transparency in process tracing research." *Qualitative and Multi-Method Research* 13.1 (2015): 47–51.
Fairfield, Tasha, and Andrew E. Charman. *Social Inquiry and Bayesian Inference: Rethinking Qualitative Research*. New York: Cambridge University Press, 2022.
Hicken, Allen. "Party Fabrication: Constitutional Reform and the Rise of Thai Rak Thai." *Journal of East Asian Studies* 6 (2006): 381–407.

Huang, Chin-Hao, and David C. Kang. "State Formation in Korea and Japan, 400–800 CE." *International Organization* 76, no. 1 (2022): 1–31.

Johnson, Chalmers. *MITI and the Japanese Miracle*. Stanford, CA: Stanford University Press, 1982.

Johnson, David W. "Student-student interaction: The neglected variable in education." *Educational researcher* 10.1 (1981): 5–10.

Lieberman, Evan S. "Nested Analysis as a Mixed-Method Strategy for Comparative Research." *American Political Science Review* 99 (2005): 435–452.

McCargo, Duncan, and Ukrist Pathmanand. *The Thaksinization of Thailand*. Copenhagen: Nordic Institute of Asian Studies, 2005.

Morgenbesser, Lee. "Cambodia's Transition to Hegemonic Authoritarianism." *Journal of Democracy* 30, no. 1 (2019): 158–171.

Nelson, Michael H. "Institutional Incentives and Informal Local Political Groups (Phuak) in Thailand." *Journal of East Asian Studies* 7 (2007): 125–147.

Pasuk Phongpaichit and Chris Baker. *Thaksin*. Chiang Mai: Silkworm, 2009.

Ricks, Jacob I. "Agents, Principals, or Something in Between? Bureaucrats and Policy Control in Thailand." *Journal of East Asian Studies* 18, no. 3 (2018): 321–344.

Rohlfing, Ingo. "Comparative Hypothesis Testing via Process Tracing." *Sociological Methods & Research* 43, no. 4 (2014): 606–642.

Seawright, Jason, and John Gerring. "Case Selection Techniques in Case Study Research." *Political Science Quarterly* 61 (2008): 294–308.

Slater, Dan. "Party Cartelization, Indonesian-Style." *Journal of East Asian Studies* 18, no. 1 (2018): 23–46.

van Meegdenburg, Hilde. "Process Tracing: An Analyticist Approach." In *Routledge Handbook of Foreign Policy Analysis Methods*, edited by Patrick A. Mello and Falk Ostermann, 405–420. London: Routledge, 2023.

Vatikiotis, Michael, and Rodney Tasker. "Prickly Premier." *Far Eastern Economic Review* 165, no. 14 (2002): 14–18.

Weiss, Meredith L. *The Roots of Resilience*. Ithaca, NY: Cornell University Press, 2020.

Zaks, Sherry. "Relationships among Rivals (RAR): A Framework for Analyzing Contending Hypotheses in Process-Tracing." *Political Analysis* 25, no. 3 (2017): 344–362.

Zarakol, Ayse. *After Defeat*. Cambridge: Cambridge University Press, 2010.

34
Comparative Historical Analysis

Prerna Singh*

Introduction

Comparative historical analysis (CHA) is a long-standing, enormously generative research tradition from which have emerged some of the foundational texts of political science and sociology[1] as well as more contemporary 20th-century "classics."[2] CHA has continued, even against the gustiest methodological headwinds, to chart a steady course forward for scholarship anchored to formulating new theories to explain big, substantively important questions.

CHA's outputs span the subfields of comparative politics, international relations and American politics. Within comparative politics, which will be the focus of this chapter, CHA has generated a steady stream of influential works on key topics, including regime types and transitions, state-building, war and peace, revolutions, social movements, economic development, welfare states and social policy, inequality, citizenship, ethnic and racial politics, and nationalism. Further, the method itself has been the subject of a substantial and sophisticated scholarship. In this chapter, I first delineate the core features that both define CHA and distinguish it from other methods. Following this overview, I bring these elements into active dialog with my own and other comparative historical work within comparative politics, with the goal of proposing some pointers for "how to do CHA."

What Is CHA (and What Is It Not)?

Rather than attempting to specify a single definition of CHA, in this section I draw on the rich corpus of writing on CHA, especially by scholars such as Dietrich Rueschemeyer, James Mahoney, Kathleen Thelen, Tulia Faletti, Daniel Ritter, Theda Skocpol, Edwin Amenta, and Mathew Lange, toward distilling a set of core elements that most frequently characterize and may thus be seen as constitutive of the tradition.[3] From its earliest, influential progenitors CHA is distinguished by a focus, first off, on the *asking of large, weighty questions* that "draw people to study social life in the first place, and that are constantly raised anew in the minds of non-specialists."[4] Why do countries witness social revolutions? What explains variations in regime types, transitions, and resilience? Why do some political parties survive, while others collapse? Why do political units vary in their economic development, welfare policies, criminality, or level of decentralization? Why do political identities persist despite social, political, and economic upheaval? Even as the current emphasis on causal inference draws the discipline into ever more narrowly specified questions, comparative historicists remain steadfastly committed to taking on complex empirical puzzles that other approaches are likely to either entirely miss[5] or deem, and dismiss, as too ambitious and intractable.

Following from the method's focus on large-scale, macropolitical outcomes, CHA features a range and occasionally combination of *different units of analysis*, traditionally nation-states but increasingly a range of subnational units, social and political movements, and even empires, and civilizations and world systems.[6]

The *number of cases is usually small*, often chosen to be sufficiently similar or different, or especially noteworthy instances of a phenomenon, to permit *systematic in-depth case study comparisons*. From these in-depth case comparisons emerge *novel theoretical frameworks*, a hallmark of CHA. CHA is not opposed to testing the predictions of established theoretical frameworks. Yet comparative historicists have rarely been content with assessing the relative veracity of an established set of explanations. They have more often been at the front lines of advancing theories that problematize and *push beyond conventional wisdom*. (See examples of this in the next section.)

In doing so CHA *deepens our understanding of established and encourages the development of new concepts*. To explain the differences in industrialization across South Korea, Brazil, India, and Nigeria during the 20th century, for example, Kohli develops a tripartite ideal-typical typology of state authority in the postcolonial world as either neopatrimonial, fragmented-multiclass, or cohesive-capitalist states.[7] Lieberman proposes the concept of "boundary institutions" to explain variations in AIDS policies in Brazil, South Africa, and India,[8] and I develop the concept of "subnationalism" to explain variations in social welfare policies and outcomes across Indian states.[9]

In contrast to the correlational logic of regression-based observational analyses, CHA is underpinned by a commitment to *establishing causality over long periods of time*, a goal that at first glance aligns it with historical political economy (HPE).[10] Yet there are fundamental differences. Where HPE tends to focus on examining the impact of a single variable in one particular case, CHA examines how a *combination of multiple factors* unfolds and influences their outcome of interest *within and across their chosen cases*. In CHA such *influence is temporally specific*. Unlike HPE, where the effect of the explanatory variable is assumed to be uniform across the swath of time over which it is estimated, CHA acknowledges and analyzes how *the degree to, and way in which, any one or combination of variables influences an outcome can vary through time*.

Where HPE privileges the identification of causality, CHA prioritizes *historical narratives that explicitly and meticulously detail the sequence and ways in which a configuration of factors influences their chosen outcome*. CHA moves beyond establishing a relationship between its explanatory and outcome variables to also unpacking the mechanisms through which this occurs. Thus where HPE's engagement with cases is focused on and often does not extend beyond establishing the as-if random assignment to a treatment variable that allows for a claim to valid causal inference, CHA's *configurational, mechanism-based approach* necessitates a knowledge of *context, both spatial and temporal*. A *deep knowledge of cases and their history* is essential to identifying the relevant configuration of causal variables (for more on this, see Chapter 6 on case selection) and the scope conditions under and mechanisms by which they operate.

CHA's commitment to showing the *how* of causality is most often realized through the tool of process tracing (see Chapter 33). The use of process tracing is not limited to CHA, but it is a particularly popular tool for comparative historicists and is used to highlight both points of transformation (critical junctures) and processes of persistence (path dependence).

Here it is useful to point out that there is some debate about the sources used in process tracing and CHA, some suggesting a "division of labor in which historians work for social scientists."[11] By this view historians and area specialists analyze primary data that CHA draws on and synthesizes with accounts of diplomats and journalists, on the one hand, and the secondary scholarship within sociology, political science, anthropology, and psychology, on the other, to craft their case studies.[12] The objective, by this account, is not to discover new facts but to shed "new light" through "old" evidence.[13] Others point out that comparative historical scholars frequently gather new information and supplement historiography with their own original archival research.[14]

This is in some ways a decision to be taken on a case-by-case basis, and dependent as much on the proclivities of individual researchers as the richness of the secondary scholarship on the research question(s). In my book, *How Solidarity Works for Welfare: Subnationalism and Social Development in India*, for example, I draw on a range of secondary sources to break down and analyze social expenditures and indicators in India. Yet, while there was a wealth of data and secondary research on the outcome that I was explaining (social welfare), there was a relative dearth of published material around my primary explanatory variable of subnationalism. This led me to archival research and a deep engagement with primary texts, such as the records of the States Reorganization Commission, appointed to analyze the demands for linguistic states in India in the 1950s. In any event, comparative historical analysis neither necessitates engagement with primary sources nor precludes it. The collation and analysis of "new" historical material can add to CHA inasmuch as it can strengthen the empirical substantiation of its theoretical framework. It is, however, rarely the sole or primary contribution of a comparative historical study.

A final point about the *methodological eclecticism* that characterizes CHA. CHA draws on evidence gleaned from a range of qualitative methods, such as archival analysis, ethnography, elite interviews, and focus groups; it frequently and powerfully uses the tool of process tracing to clearly and systematically delineate the historical sequence in, and mechanisms through, which its explanatory variables influence the outcomes it is explaining. But it also frequently includes descriptive statistics. For example, in my book I present a wide array of data from a range of sources to show the limits of alternative explanations as well as to trace the historical sequence by which subnationalism generates social development. CHA also combines well, as will be discussed in the next section, with regression analyses and other quantitative approaches.

How to (Decide to) Do CHA

Having delineated the key elements of CHA, I next provide some practical pointers for "doing" CHA. Here it is important to note that, to a greater extent than other methods, conducting CHA is a dynamic process that is characterized by the contemporaneousness and iterative nature, rather than a strict sequencing, of key tasks. This section will focus on four key tasks of setting up a CHA: first, developing a *why*-driven research question; second, selecting cases; third, identifying and engaging with alternative explanations toward, fourth, developing and empirically substantiating one's own theoretical framework. These tasks are presented in an order. Yet it is important to emphasize again that CHA necessarily entails going back and forth between, rather than beginning, completing, and moving forward to the next task in a neat succession.

But first, is CHA right for you and your project? In recognition of the necessarily open-ended and flexible nature of the research process and in line with my own inclination for the use of multiple methods, I see this not so much as a decisive decision to anoint CHA as "the" chosen method but more as a consideration about whether it might be in contention as a potential, perhaps (but not necessarily) the primary method for a project. Here, harking back to CHA's first foundational feature, a touchstone might be, to paraphrase Skocpol, whether you are "passionately engaged" with "big," burning, "first-order" questions. The research question is a necessary starting point for CHA. But it is, as I will point out, intimately and inextricably linked to case selection, which in turn requires a knowledge of and engagement with the rival explanations emphasized by the existing scholarship. This in turn unfolds into the generation of new theoretical perspectives through close-range research across and within cases.

CHA begins and builds up from a clearly specified research question. Following on from CHA's aim to establish causal connections, this is usually, though not always, framed as a *why*. It focuses on an outcome that (a comparative historicist must explicitly show) holds substantive and normative significance for both scholars and the lay public alike.

How do you pick a question? This decision is likely to be arrived at via a strong interest in a topic (say, democratization or federalism or social policy) and, within that, an investment in the study of a specific empirical puzzle. (For more on choosing a research question, see Chapter 2.) A comparative historicist can also focus on well-known outcomes, cast in a new theoretical light or framework. For example, Kohli reframes the question of variations in economic growth in terms of the differential role of the state in industrialization.[15] Equally CHA can conceptualize and center new phenomena. Against dominant descriptions of Latin America as characterized by weak ethnic cleavages, Yashar highlights and uncovers the causes for the variations in the unprecedented political mobilization of Indigenous people across the region in the late decades of the 20th century.[16] More recently, she draws our attention to the presence of and variation in what she terms "homicidical ecologies" across Latin America.[17] Naseemullah brings to light and seeks to explain the highly spatially differentiated patterns of violence across South Asian states.[18]

CHA's puzzles can be and indeed frequently are framed in general terms shorn of proper nouns: Why do some states institute federal while others put in place unitary systems? Why are some developing countries able to create stable democracies while others have slid into instability and authoritarianism? Indeed their amenability to being stated in such abstraction is part of their appeal and contribution.

Yet it is useful for potential CHA users to keep in mind that for most scholars who work within the tradition, these questions emerge from an engagement with and are rooted *in particular cases* at *specific times*. The question for Ziblatt, for example, is why, despite political, economic, and cultural similarities, Germany and Italy adopted federal versus unitary systems during their almost concomitant unification process in the 19th century.[19] For Tudor, the question is why, upon the 1947 Partition of British India, India was able to establish a stable democracy while Pakistan created an unstable autocracy.[20]

The puzzles studied by Ziblatt and Tudor, as for many other comparative historicists, are "historic," in that they focus on phenomena located in the past.[21] But this need not be the case. There are many influential instances of scholarship that have sought to identify the deep origins of contemporary outcomes. This can be the case because a comparative historicist might from the inception of a project be explicitly interested in locating the historical roots of a present-day phenomenon. This appears to have been the case for Gryzmala-Busse's analysis of why churches in some democratic countries wield far greater political power than others.[22] Alternatively, this could happen more serendipitously during the research process. For instance, it was his realization of the insufficiency of contemporary variables to explain the differences in the tax systems of South Africa and Brazil that pushed Lieberman back to the turn of the 20th century and to an emphasis on the variations in how the national political community was defined in the two states. Similarly, in my book *How Solidarity Works for Welfare: Subnationalism and Social Development in India*, I sought to explore a question that I had been struck by when traveling to and growing up in different parts of India. Why, within a single country, were Indian states characterized by such starkly divergent levels of social welfare? Early in my research I became aware of the over-century-long provenance and, relatedly, the need to uncover the historic roots of these contemporary social inequalities.

CHA, as you will recall, privileges historical timing and sequencing. Because of this, a comparative historicist can focus on decisive events at specific points, like the occurrence of a revolution or the passing of a constitution[23] or a clearly demarcated period, for example, the interwar years for Luebbert and for Cappocia[24] or the period of popular mobilization in Latin America for Collier and Collier.[25] They can analyze patterns that unfold over time, such as state formation,[26] capitalist development,[27] regime stability and durability,[28] as also the legacy of key events such as colonialism[29] and Communism.[30]

By now it should be clear that because research puzzles are formulated about cases (cases are spatially and temporally "built in" to CHA's research questions), case selection needs to be tackled in tandem. Yet the simultaneity of this task should not be mistaken for subordination. As will be discussed briefly in the next section, case selection has been a site of criticism of CHA, and it deserves attention on its own terms. Here a useful resource is the important scholarship within qualitative methods that lays out a rich repertoire of case selection strategies.[31]

Most and least similar designs have historically been two of the most commonly deployed case selection strategies. Many scholars try to understand why cases similar in many ways exhibit such variation, whether it be regarding party systems or the ability to achieve equitable development.[32] Other scholars focus on why cases that are quite different exhibit the same outcomes, whether it be successful revolutions,[33] "insurgent transitions" that institute robust popular democracies,[34] or competitive authoritarianism.[35]

Key dimensions along which cases are chosen to be most similar or different are those that correspond to the theoretical orthodoxy about the phenomenon in question. Gryzmala-Busse,[36] for example, chose her case comparisons to be able to "control," among other factors, for levels of religiosity and alliance with political parties, which are prominent rival explanations for the power of the church in a Christian democratic state. In my own work I emphasize the value of a subnational comparison of Indian states as it allows me to hold constant factors such as regime type and the constitutional structure that have been theorized to influence social welfare.

Case selection is cocooned within and proceeds conjointly with the third major task of CHA, a comprehensive grasp of and critical engagement with the established scholarship on a phenomenon. Here it is important to make explicit another instance of the iterative nature of key tasks within CHA. This is that the dialoging with alternative explanations in turn opens the door to and continues apace with the formulation of one's own distinctive thesis. Skocpol terms this an "intrinsically argumentative" way in which CHA unfolds.[37]

CHA theories emerge through deep and wide knowledge of particular cases. Yet even as comparative historicists are steeping themselves in histories, anthropological and sociological accounts, political science scholarship, and also novels, movies, conversations about, and often, if possible, physically inhabiting their cases, they are also sharpening their learning by knocking and (re)shaping it against the reigning rival explanations. Where experimental researchers begin with a specification (and preregistration) of the hypotheses that they are hoping to find evidence for, as a comparative historicist you are likely to have a sense of who/what you are arguing against before you have (more than) a hunch of what you are arguing for.

As an example of how a new theoretical perspective in CHA takes shape through a dissatisfaction and duel with conventional understandings of a phenomenon, I turn again to my book. Even after controlling for economic development, a prominent explanation that remained a contender for explaining variations in subnational social welfare across my cases was the presence of social democratic parties.[38] Among my five cases, Kerala was the only one with a history of Communist governments and (because of this, according to the influential theories of scholars like Heller and Frank and Chasin)[39] by far the best performing. Yet despite the hefty intellectual provenance of this theory, I was unconvinced. After all, West Bengal, a case with a longer history of democratically elected Communist governments, did not have anything close to Kerala's social indicators. It was my wrestling with this reigning dominant explanation that prompted me to begin my field and archival research in Kerala.[40]

Arguments emerge inductively and cumulatively in CHA by breaking cases into historical sequences. This process tracing can expose cracks in the established explanatory architecture that allow for the glimmerings of a new theoretical perspective. Schickler and Feinstein and Stickler,[41] for example, find that the Democrat and Republican parties' realignment on civil rights occurred much before the events of 1964, which have traditionally been credited with causing the realignment. Similarly in my research I found that Kerala's relative social gains were visible *prior* to the Communist Party's ascent to political power. They were also maintained apace *even in the periods when it was out of office*. Further, I found that, despite its name, the Communist Party's embrace of Malayali subnationalism was at least as intense and enthusiastic as and arguably more than its espousal of Communism. My archival research, specially of the biographies, memoirs, and writings of key Communist leaders, brought out how it was this subnational solidarity that underpinned the progressive social agenda of the Communists in Kerala, as also the more explicitly subnationalist parties in neighboring Tamil Nadu.

CHA theories rely heavily on and thus need to carefully consider how to structure their diachronic evidence. Here Lieberman's four potential periodization strategies that identify key points of variation in explanatory variables to test their influence on the dependent variable provide a useful entry point.[42] The temporal analyses of the cases in my book, for example, are structured around the "institutional origins" design,[43] in which an explanatory variable X (in my case, a powerful subnationalism) is demonstrated to cause an outcome of interest Y (higher social development) by showing that Y was not already in place prior to the emergence of X. I therefore dissect and analyze the historical record of all five states in terms of periods prior to and subsequent to the emergence of elite and mass subnationalism. For instance, I use the 1890s and 1950s as the two demarcations to structure the "within-case" historical process tracing of developmental expenditures and outcomes in Kerala. Up until the 1890s Kerala had not witnessed the emergence of a subnational solidarity. It also consequently performed no better than other Indian states in terms of most measures of social welfare. I show that subnational solidarity emerged and drove the institution of progressive social policy beginning in the 1890s. The 1950s saw a second decisive turning point with the emergence of mass subnationalism, which helped Kerala realize its now famous social achievements. Such chronological narratives are powerful tools for establishing causal inference, even more so when accompanied by visualizations, such as timelines.[44]

As noted in the previous section, CHA can rely on either secondary or some combination of secondary and primary documents. It incorporates diverse qualitative methods and statistical descriptions and associations. In my book, for example, I combine archival analyses of government documents from the colonial and postcolonial periods (especially the records of the States Reorganization Commission, appointed in the 1950s), newspapers, legislative assembly debates, as well as field research, including structured, open-ended elite interviews, focus group meetings, and participant observation at political party offices, schools, and health centers.

Finally, it is useful to flag and recommend the use of visualizations as an important heuristic in CHA. Comparative historicists frequently use maps, figures, and tables to show how their cases vary in terms of their outcomes of interest.[45] They also effectively use tables to list and to show the inability of established explanations of the variation in their cases,[46] thus prompting the popular designation of their research question as a "puzzle."

Pitfalls and Possibilities

CHA is not without its drawbacks. Many of the charges against it come from a quantitatively grounded ontology that privileges randomization (in selection, assignment, etc.). For instance, CHA purposefully "selects on the dependent variable," and readily acknowledges that it does so. Some hold this inherently problematic.[47] The selection of cases is rarely random and has thus been criticized for its vulnerability to bias.[48] Moreover, CHA is based on observational data. There is usually no identification strategy that permits the demonstration of "clean" causality. Theory is derived inductively from and thus potentially restricted to those places and times.

But CHA also offers unmatched advantages for understanding political and social problems. I propose a strategy of the four C's for thinking through these trade-offs associated with CHA (as indeed other methods): cognizance, commitment, combination, and collaboration.

First, it is essential for researchers to be *cognizant* and up front about the shortcomings associated with the method(s) they deploy. Together with this cognizance of what a method can do less well, or simply can't do, should be a *commitment* to doing well what it can. CHA, for example, stands out from other research traditions for its opening up of new research agendas. It is distinctive for its encouragement of the tackling of weighty questions, refining and developing new concepts and theory with particular attention to time and "slow-moving processes," and to a careful diachronic delineation of causal mechanisms. CHA analysts should take care that their work exemplifies these strengths.

Third, to the extent feasible, researchers could consider *combining* multiple methods toward maximizing analytical leverage and compensating for the pitfalls of a particular method. Inasmuch as CHA is "splendidly open to synergy and innovation,"[49] it offers specially rich opportunities for multimethod research. Lieberman's nested research design has proven to be a popular guide for how statistical analysis can set up and select cases for and test the broader validity of hypotheses uncovered by CHA.[50] In my book, *How Solidarity Works for Welfare*, following Rohlfing,[51] I use a (modified version of) Lieberman's off-the-line case selection strategy to systematically select Indian states for CHA. Toward the end of the book I use a cross-sectional, temporal regression analysis of all Indian states to show the generalizability of the subnationalism argument.[52] CHA can also, against the reservations of scholars like Mahoney and Thelen,[53] be effectively combined with experimental work, if we believe that the microfoundations of the theory discovered through CHA might hold across cases and over time.[54]

Combination also opens the door to the final C: collaboration. Time and skills impose real constraints on the conduct of multimethod research. As such, CHA researchers, if so inclined, could consider joining forces with scholars (better) trained in experimental research to conduct experiments to test the microlinks that lead to their macro-outcomes. As a last example from my own work, I teamed up with Volha Charnysh and Chris Lucas to conduct survey experiments to test the underlying causal mechanism about how place-based solidarities encourage prosocial behavior. In my book I had theorized about how subnational solidarity encouraged elites to prioritize collective welfare and push for public goods provision. In an ideal world I would have conducted an experiment with Indian political leaders to test this precise mechanism. Logistical constraints limited us to an online survey of Indian citizens. But as my theory predicted we did find that increasing the salience of national identity heightened altruism toward non-coethnic fellow nationals.[55]

Conclusion

CHA offers unparalleled insight into big, weighty questions that really matter but that other methods tend to shy away from. Despite high start-up costs (including deep, often cross-regional knowledge), it generates theoretically innovative frameworks rooted in careful historical research that are essential to understanding the political and social world.

Notes

* Acknowledgements: Thank you to Debora Duque and Tara Acharya for excellent research assistance, and to Dann Naseemullah for comments.
1. Weber, *The Protestant Ethic and the Spirit of Capitalism*; Tocqueville, *Democracy in America*.
2. Skocpol, *States and Social Revolution*; Moore, *Social Origins of Dictatorship and Democracy*.
3. Mahoney and Rueschemeyer, *Comparative Historical Analysis on the Social Sciences*.
4. Rule, *Theory and Progress in Social Sciences*, 46, cited in Skocpol, "Doubly Engaged Social Science," 409.
5. Ziblatt, *Conservative Parties and the Birth of Democracy*, 12. Ziblatt argues that just as aerial photography exposed settlements undetected by archaeologists working on the ground, CHA's long-run view that places single events within a larger time frame creates "temporal distance" that makes visible social-political patterns, in his case patterns of democratization, that would remain invisible to "snap shot" analyses.
6. Thelen and Mahoney, "Comparative Historical Analysis in Contemporary Political Science."

7. Kohli, *State-Directed Development*.
8. Lieberman, *Boundaries of Contagion*.
9. Singh, *How Solidarity Works for Social Welfare*.
10. Cirone and Pepinsky, "Historical Persistence."
11. Amenta, "What We Know about the Development of Social Policy," 97.
12. Ritter, "Comparative Historical Analysis"; Skocpol, *States and Social Revolution*.
13. Skocpol, *States and Social Revolution*, xi.
14. Amenta, "What We Know about the Development of Social Policy," 97.
15. Kohli, *State-Directed Development*, 5.
16. Yashar, *Contesting Citizenship in Latin America*.
17. Yashar, *Homicidal Ecologies*.
18. Naseemullah, *The Historical Roots of International Conflict and Competition in South Asia*.
19. Ziblatt, *Structuring the State*.
20. Tudor, *The Promise of Power*.
21. See also Skocpol, *States and Social Revolution*; Moore, *Social Origins of Dictatorship and Democracy*; Cappoccia and Keleman, "The Study of Critical Junctures."
22. Gryzmala-Busse, "The Difficulty with Doctrine."
23. Skocpol, *States and Social Revolution*; Ziblatt, *Structuring the State*; Tudor, *The Promise of Power*.
24. Luebbert, *Liberalism, Fascism or Social Democracy*; Cappocia, *Defending Democracy*
25. Collier and Collier, *Shaping the Political Arena*.
26. Tilly, *Coercion, Capital and European States*; Ertman, *Birth of the Leviathan*.
27. Polanyi, *The Great Transformation*; Rueschemeyer, Huber Stephens, and Stephens, *Capitalist Development and Democracy*.
28. Slater, *Ordering Power*.
29. Mahoney, "Path-Dependent Explanations of Regime Change"; Lange, *Comparative Historical Methods*.
30. Wittenberg, *Crucibles of Political Loyalty*; Gryzmala-Busse, "Political Competition and the Politicization of the State in East Central Europe"; Beissinger, *Nationalist Mobilization and the Collapse of the Soviet State*; Peisakhin, "Is Transparency an Effective Anti-corruption Strategy?"
31. Collier and Hoeffler, "Greed and Grievance in Civil War"; George and Bennet, *Case Studies and Theory Development in the Social Sciences*; Gerring, *Case Study Research*; Slater and Ziblatt, "The Enduring Indispensability of Controlled Comparison."
32. Reidl, *Authoritarian Origins of Democratic Party Systems in Africa*; Kuhonta, *The Institutional Imperative*.
33. Skocpol, *States and Social Revolution*.
34. Wood, *Forging Democracy from Below*.
35. Levitsk and Way, *Competitive Authoritarianism*.
36. Gryzmala-Busse, "The Difficulty with Doctrine."
37. Skocpol, "Doubly Engaged Social Science," 411.
38. Singh, *How Solidarity Works for Social Welfare*, 46–48, 112–146.
39. Heller, "Reinventing Public Power in the Age of Globalization"; Franke and Chasin, *Kerala*.
40. Singh, "We-ness and Welfare."
41. Schickler, *Racial Realignment*; Feinstein and Schickler, "Platforms and Partners," cited in Galvin, "Let's Not Conflate APD with Political History."
42. Lieberman, "Causal Inference in Historical Institutional Analysis."
43. Lieberman, "Causal Inference in Historical Institutional Analysis."
44. Singh, *How Solidarity Works for Social Welfare*, 68.
45. Singh, *How Solidarity Works for Social Welfare*, 6–20. In my book I use shaded maps (Figures 1.1 and 1.2) as well as graphs (Figures 1.3–1.7) to show the differences in social welfare across all Indian and my case study states, respectively.

46. Ziblatt, *Structuring the State*, 9; Slater, *Ordering Power*, 10; Singh, *How Solidarity Works for Social Welfare*, 6. In my book in Tables 1.1–1.3, I show how variations in social welfare outcomes are not predicted by key demographic and socioeconomic indicators, economic development, and colonial legacies, respectively.
47. King, Keohane, and Verba, *Designing Social Inquiry*.
48. Geddes, "How the Cases You Choose Affect the Answers You Get."
49. Skocpol, "Doubly Engaged Social Sciences," 419.
50. Lieberman, *Race and Regionalism in the Politics of Taxation in Brazil and South Africa*, 437; Lieberman, "Nested Analysis as a Mixed-Method Strategy for Comparative Research"; Lieberman, *Boundaries of Contagion*, 20; Singh, *How Solidarity Works for Social Welfare*, 18–20.
51. Rohlfing, "What You See and What You Get."
52. Singh, *How Solidarity Works for Social Welfare*, 197–242. The synergistic value of statistical analysis and CHA is further brought out by how it can help rule out rival explanations (for example, the presence of social democratic parties but also electoral competition). And how the need to develop a measure to include regressions can deepen conceptualizations, for example, of my key explanatory variable of subnational solidarity.
53. Scholars like Thelen and Mahoney.
54. Galvin, "Let's Not Conflate APD with Political History."
55. Charnysh, Lucas, and Singh, "The Ties That Bind."

Recommended Readings

Influential overviews by foundational thinkers about the comparative historical method:
Mahoney, James, and Dietrich Rueschemeyer, eds. *Comparative Historical Analysis on the Social Sciences*. Cambridge: Cambridge University Press, 2003.
Thelen, Kathleen, and James Mahoney, eds. *Advances in Contemporary-Historical Analysis*. Cambridge: Cambridge University Press, 2015.
A classic example:
Skocpol, Theda. *States and Social Revolution: A Comparative Analysis of France, Russia and China*. Cambridge: Cambridge University Press, 1979.
A contemporary example:
Singh, Prerna. *How Solidarity Works for Social Welfare: Subnationalism and Social Development in India*. Cambridge: Cambridge University Press, 2015.

References

Amenta, Edwin. "What We Know about the Development of Social Policy: Comparative and Historical Research in Comparative and Historical perspective." In *Comparative Historical Analysis in the Social Sciences*, edited by James Mahoney and Dietrich Rueschemeyer, 91–130. Cambridge: Cambridge University Press, 2003.
Beissinger, Mark. *Nationalist Mobilization and the Collapse of the Soviet State*. Cambridge: Cambridge University Press, 2002.
Bernhard, Michael, and Daniel O'Neill. "Comparative Historical Analysis." *Perspectives on Politics* 19 (2021): 699–704.
Cappocia, Giovanni. *Defending Democracy: Reactions to Extremism in Interwar Europe*. Baltimore: Johns Hopkins University Press, 2005.
Cappocia, Giovanni, and R. Daniel Keleman. "The Study of Critical Junctures: Theory, Narrative and Counterfactuals in Historical Institutionalism." *World Politics* 59 (2007): 341–369.

Charnysh, Volha, Christopher Lucas, and Prerna Singh. "The Ties That Bind: National Identity Salience and Pro-Social Behavior toward the Ethnic Other." *Comparative Political Studies* 48 (2014): 267–300.

Cirone, Alexandra, and Thomas B. Pepinsky. "Historical Persistence." *Annual Review of Political Science* 25 (2021): 241–259.

Collier, David. "Understanding Process Tracing." *PS: Political Science and Politics* 44 (2011): 823–830.

Collier, Paul, and Anke Hoeffler. "Greed and Grievance in Civil War." *Oxford Economic Papers* 56 (2004): 563–595.

Collier, Ruth Berins, and David Collier. *Shaping the Political Arena: Critical Junctures, the Labour Movement and Regime Dynamics in Latin America.* Notre Dame, IN: Notre Dame University Press, 2002.

Ertman, Thomas. *Birth of the Leviathan: Building States and Regimes in Medieval and Early Modern Europe.* Cambridge: Cambridge University Press, 1997.

Falleti, Tulia G., and Julia F. Lynch. "Context and Causal Mechanisms in Political Analysis." *Comparative Political Studies* 42 (2009): 1143–1166.

Feinstein, Brian, and Eric Schickler. "Platforms and Partners: The Civil Rights Realignment Reconsidered." *Studies in American Political Development* 22 (2008): 1–31.

Franke, Richard W., and Barbara H. Chasin. *Kerala: Radical Reform as Development in an Indian State.* San Francisco: Institute for Food and Development Policy, 1999.

Galvin, Daniel. "Let's Not Conflate APD with Political History and Other Reflections on 'Causal Inference and American Political Development.'" *Public Choice* 185 (2020): 485–500.

Geddes, Barbara. "How the Cases You Choose Affect the Answers You Get: Selection Bias in Comparative Politics." *Political Analysis* 2 (1990): 131–150.

George, Alexander L., and Andrew Bennet. *Case Studies and Theory Development in the Social Sciences.* Cambridge, MA: MIT Press, 2005.

Gerring, John. *Case Study Research: Principles and Practices.* Cambridge: Cambridge University Press, 2006.

Goldstone, Jack. "Comparative Historical Analysis and Knowledge Accumulation in the Study of Revolutions." In *Comparative Historical Analysis in the Social Sciences*, edited by James Mahoney and Dietrich Rueschemeyer, 41–90. Cambridge: Cambridge University Press, 2003.

Gryzmala-Busse, Anna. "The Difficulty with Doctrine: How Churches Can Influence Politics." *Government and Opposition* 51 (2016): 327–350.

Gryzmala-Busse, Anna. "Political Competition and the Politicization of the State in East Central Europe." *Comparative Political Studies* 36 (2003): 1123–1147.

Heller, Patrick. 2005. "Reinventing Public Power in the Age of Globalization: Decentralization and the Transformation of Movement Politics in Kerala." In *Social Movements in India: Poverty, Power and Politics,* edited by Ray Raka and Mary Fainson Katzenstein, 79–106. New York: Rowman & Littlefield, 2005.

King, Gary, Robert O. Keohane, and Sidney Verba. *Designing Social Inquiry: Scientific Inference in Qualitative Research.* Princeton, NJ: Princeton University Press, 1994.

Kohli, Atul. *State-Directed Development: Political Power and Industrialization in the Global Periphery.* Cambridge: Cambridge University Press, 2004.

Kuhonta, Erik. *The Institutional Imperative: The Politics of Equitable Development in South East Asia.* Stanford, CA: Stanford University Press, 2011.

Levitsky, Stevan, and Lucan Way. *Competitive Authoritarianism: Hybrid Regimes after the Cold War.* Cambridge: Cambridge University Press, 2010.

Lange, Matthew. *Comparative Historical Methods.* London: Sage, 2012.

Lieberman, Evan S. *Boundaries of Contagion: How Ethnic Politics Have Shaped Government Responses to AIDS.* Princeton, NJ: Princeton University Press, 2009.

Lieberman, Evan S. "Causal Inference in Historical Institutional Analysis: A Specification of Periodization Strategies." *Comparative Political Studies* 34 (2001): 1011–1035.

Lieberman, Evan S. "Nested Analysis as a Mixed-Method Strategy for Comparative Research." *American Political Science Review* 99 (2005): 435–452.

Lieberman, Evan S. *Race and Regionalism in the Politics of Taxation in Brazil and South Africa.* Cambridge: Cambridge University Press, 2003.

Luebbert, Gregory. *Liberalism, Fascism, or Social Democracy: Social Classes and the Political Origins of Regimes in Interwar Europe.* Oxford: Oxford University Press, 1991.

Mahoney, James. "Path-Dependent Explanations of Regime Change: Central America in Comparative Perspective." *Studies in Comparative International Development* 36 (2001): 111–141.

Mahoney, James, and Dietrich Rueschemeyer. "Comparative Historical Analysis: Achievements and Agendas." In *Comparative Historical Analysis on the Social Sciences,* edited by James Mahoney and Dietrich Rueschemeyer, 3–40. Cambridge: Cambridge University Press, 2003.

Moore, Barrington. *Social Origins of Dictatorship and Democracy: Lord and Peasant in the Making of the Modern World.* Boston: Beacon Press, 1966.

Naseemullah, Adnan. *The Historical Roots of International Conflict and Competition in South Asia.* Cambridge: Cambridge University Press, 2022.

Peisakhin, Leonid. "Is Transparency an Effective Anti-corruption Strategy? Evidence from a Field Experiment in India." *Regulation and Governance* 4 (2010): 261–280.

Polanyi, Karl. *The Great Transformation: The Political and Economic Origins of Our Time.* Boston: Beacon Press, 1945.

Reidl, Rachel B. *Authoritarian Origins of Democratic Party Systems in Africa.* Cambridge: Cambridge University Press, 2014.

Ritter, Daniel P. "Comparative Historical Analysis." In *Methodological Practices in Social Movement Research,* edited by Donatella della Porta, 97–116. Oxford: Oxford University Press, 2014.

Rohlfing, Ingo. "What You See and What You Get: Pitfalls and Principles of Nested Analysis in Comparative Research." *Comparative Political Studies* 41 (2008): 1492–1514.

Rueschemeyer, Dietrich, Evelyne Huber Stephens, and John D. Stephens. *Capitalist Development and Democracy.* Chicago: University of Chicago Press, 1992.

Rule, James. *Theory and Progress in Social Sciences.* Cambridge: Cambridge University Press, 1997.

Schickler, Eric. *Racial Realignment: The Transformation of American Liberalism, 1932–1965.* Princeton, NJ: Princeton University Press, 2016.

Singh, Prerna. *How Solidarity Works for Social Welfare: Subnationalism and Social Development in India.* Cambridge: Cambridge University Press, 2015.

Singh, Prerna. "We-ness and Welfare: A Longitudinal Analysis of Social Development in Kerala, India." *World Development* 39 (2011): 282–293.

Skocpol, Theda. "Doubly Engaged Social Science." In *Comparative Historical Analysis in the Social Sciences,* edited by James Mahoney and Dietrich Rueschemeyer, 407–428. Cambridge: Cambridge University Press, 2003.

Skocpol, Theda. *States and Social Revolution: A Comparative Analysis of France, Russia and China.* Cambridge: Cambridge University Press, 1979.

Slater, Dan. *Ordering Power: Contentious Politics and Authoritarian Leviathans in Southeast Asia.* Cambridge: Cambridge University Press, 2010.

Slater, Dan, and Daniel Ziblatt. "The Enduring Indispensability of the Controlled Comparison." *Comparative Political Studies* 46 (2013): 1301–1327.

Thelen, Kathleen, and James Mahoney. "Comparative-Historical Analysis in Contemporary Political Science." In *Advances in Contemporary-Historical Analysis,* edited by Kathleen Thelen and James Mahoney, 3–36. Cambridge: Cambridge University Press, 2015.

Tilly, Charles. *Coercion, Capital and European States, AD 990–1990.* Oxford: Blackwell, 1990.

Tocqueville, Alexis de. *Democracy in America.* London: Saunders and Otley, 1835.

Tudor, Maya. *The Promise of Power: The Origins of Democracy in India and Autocracy in Punjab.* Cambridge: Cambridge University Press, 2013.

Waldner, David. "Process Tracing and Causal Mechanisms." In *Handbook of Philosophy of Social Science,* edited by Harold Kincaid, 65–84. Oxford: Oxford University Press, 2012.

Weber, Max. *The Protestant Ethic and the Spirit of Capitalism.* London: Unwin Hyman, 1930.

Wittenberg, Jason. *Crucibles of Political Loyalty: Church Institutions and Electoral Continuity in Hungary.* Cambridge: Cambridge University Press, 2006.

Wood, Elisabeth Jean. *Forging Democracy from Below: Insurgent Transitions in South Africa and El Salvador.* Cambridge: Cambridge University Press, 2000.

Yashar, Deborah J. *Contesting Citizenship in Latin America: The Rise of Indigenous Movements.* Cambridge: Cambridge University Press, 2005.

Yashar, Deborah J. *Homicidal Ecologies: Illicit Economies and Complicit States in Latin America.* Cambridge: Cambridge University Press, 2018.

Ziblatt, Daniel. *Conservative Parties and the Birth of Democracy.* Cambridge: Cambridge University Press, 2017.

Ziblatt, Daniel. *Structuring the State: The Formation of Italy and Germany and the Puzzle of Federalism.* Princeton, NJ: Princeton University Press, 2008.

35
Discourse Analysis

Tania Islas Weinstein

The term "discourse analysis" is a capacious, elastic, and contested one. A quick browse through textbooks and scholarly articles about the topic points to over 50 varieties of discourse analysis, each of which requires deploying very different quantitative and qualitative research techniques and strategies. Accordingly, rather than defining it as a research method, it is perhaps best to define "discourse analysis" as an interdisciplinary *field* of research, one that studies verbal and nonverbal language and other semiotic practices and systems.[1] One way of navigating the different definitions and approaches to discourse analysis is via the epistemological commitments and schools of thought that encompass them. This chapter focuses on those that are based on interpretive epistemological commitments and draws heavily on two types of discourse analysis which are commonly referred to as Foucauldian discourse analysis (FDA) and critical discourse analysis (CDA).

Interpretivism is an approach to social science that—while it itself also encompasses a wide variety of epistemological, methodological, and political commitments—is rooted in the assumption that knowledge is historically situated and entangled in power relationships and that there is no unmediated or objective meaning of the world independent of how people conceive and speak of it (for more, see Chapter 4).[2] Even as there is no single blueprint or definition of discourse analysis or of its constituent parts—including the very concept of discourse—researchers who conduct discourse analysis from an interpretivist view are united by a similar goal: understanding how people make sense of the social world around them, including how they construct, disseminate, resist, and negotiate meanings about the political world.

Descriptive Overview

The term "discourse" encompasses both the *substantive* content of ideas and the interactive *processes* by which ideas are conveyed.[3] Researchers often use the term "discourse" to indicate language, and particularly spoken and written words. As linguist Norman Fairclough contends, "[O]ne of the distinguishing features of a discourse [is] likely to be features of vocabulary—discourses 'word' or 'lexicalize' the world in particular ways."[4] Following this view, conducting discourse analysis entails analyzing what people write and talk *about, how* they talk and write, and the political *effects* that these words may have. This is precisely why, as Vivian A. Schmidt puts it, "discourse is not just ideas or 'text' (what is said) but also context (where, when, how, and why it was said). The term refers not only to structure (what is said, or where and how) but also to agency (who said what to whom)."[5] But, of course, given that a crucial way of communicating is through nonverbal language, conducting discourse analysis can also entail analyzing symbols and images, including cartoons, photographs, films, and advertisements, as well as artworks and three-dimensional objects such as buildings and monuments. Discourses, in short, articulate and represent ideas and meanings about the world, including those that encompass political thought and that can, therefore, open (and foreclose) specific conceptions and imaginings about social life and political action.

But there is an even more encompassing definition of discourse, one that comes closer to how Michel Foucault deployed the concept.[6] This broader definition is one that requires looking *beyond* words and images. Rather than simply analyzing what people say (be it in speech, written, visual, or graphic form), researchers also need to pay attention to people's actions, behaviors, habits, and other semiotic practices. Semiotic practices—such as using money, kneeling during the national anthem, voting, attending a protest, or getting married—shape the way people navigate and give meaning to the world around them.[7] They communicate ideas to others and to themselves. Words and symbols that might never have been "put to paper"[8] are, nonetheless, very often inscribed into people's concrete actions, which, moreover, produce observable political effects.

To recapitulate: discourses include not simply the words and images people use to convey ideas about the world but also the "widely held and repeated interpretations of social conduct that produce and affirm behaviors."[9] Which of these researchers choose to analyze, including whether or not they decide to focus exclusively on visual and written texts rather than on semiotic practices more generally, will depend on the issues they seek to study.

In an attempt to keep things manageable when conducting discourse analysis, one approach is to delimit the spaces, actors, and events where one looks for discourses.[10] Indeed, much of the discursive analysis conducted by political scientists includes studying the usual suspects, like political speeches and debates,[11] congressional and parliamentary records,[12] protests and social mobilizations,[13] campaign propaganda,[14] and constitutional rights and legal records,[15] to name a few. These are crucial sites for the production and reception of political discourses and are, therefore, central to discourse analysis for political science. It is, however, important to remember that there is no right place to search for political discourses. Where one looks depends on the research question one wants to address. Some of the most provocative and stimulating discursive analyses being done in the discipline include work by scholars who are trying to find them in unexpected places, including art biennials,[16] Christian and Islamic religious sounds,[17] slaughterhouses,[18] social science journals,[19] coffee shops,[20] and television comedies.[21]

That the definition of discourse is extensive does not, however, mean that individual discourses don't have boundaries. The opposite is true: each discourse has a clear limit which is reached when ideas and representations of the world related to that discourse begin to seem "unintelligible" or "irrational" to people.[22] Discourses, in other words, make specific types of speech and behavior possible and others not and, therefore, rule some meanings in and others out.[23] For example, the discipline of political science discursively delimits what counts as "political." Analyzing political science as a discourse or discursive field does not, therefore, entail analyzing it as the study of predetermined political actors, institutions, and events. Instead, it requires examining why and how certain actors, institutions, and events *become* or *emerge* as subjects and objects of study of "political science" and others do not. Doing so requires that we pay attention to the ideas and arguments put forth by scholars of the discipline and to the concepts they deploy when doing so (including what they mean by words like "political" and "science"), as well as to the institutions and funding bodies (e.g., universities, journals, book publishers, associations, grants, prizes) that both enable and limit who gets hired as a political scientist, who graduates with a political science diploma, and what work gets published, labeled, and circulated as political science scholarship.

Discourses are often dismissed as being "mere idle chatter" and "window dressing" for material factors that are unduly assumed to be the "real substance and key drivers of politics."[24] For example, someone might say that a Canadian prime minister's references to Indigenous sovereignty are hollow given the Canadian government's commitment to exploiting Indigenous lands for extractive industries. But this simple dismissal misses the reasons why the prime minster might be making such references, the effects they have on different audiences, and what the relationship is of such utterances to policies that might materially go against them. This dismissal might also lead the researcher to miss the fact that while the prime minister deploys the word "sovereignty," he avoids words like "land" and "dispossession." Such dismissal of discourse, therefore, neglects the possibility that, as Lisa Wedeen argues, material interests are not necessarily objective criteria but are instead themselves "discursively produced: in other words, what counts as material interest is mediated through our language about what 'interest' means and what the material is."[25] Take, for instance, one of the case studies developed by Erica Simmons in her book *Meaningful Resistance*. Simmons shows how an increase in corn prices in Mexico in the early 2000s led to unprecedented mass protests. The reason why people mobilized to stop this increase in prices was not simply because corn is a commodity with tangible (material) nutritional value but because it had been *discursively* framed as representing ideas of family and the Mexican nation. The rise in corn prices was seen by many as a threat to their identity and worldviews and prompted them to mobilize. In short, the material and the discursive cannot be cleanly disentangled from one another: just like material interests are discursively constituted, so too are discourses shaped by material factors.

The goal of conducting discourse analysis through an interpretive lens is to understand how people make sense of and navigate the social and political world around them. By analyzing how people talk and act, we can lay bare how certain ideas, concepts, and conventions (e.g., political science, American, Indigenous, queer, woman, using money, getting married, voting) can come to seem natural rather than manufactured. Discourse analysis can, therefore, help to stimulate reflection about how people are ideologically interpellated and how power and social domination are reproduced *and* contested.[26] As the following section will explain in more detail, conducting this type of analysis requires analyzing the content of these meanings, the forms they take, and the context in which they become effective, dominant, and, at times, unreflexively taken for granted.

While both FDA and CDA analyze the ways discourses reproduce power, domination, and oppression, FDA conceives of power as being productive and generative in addition to limiting and disciplining, whereas CDA focuses exclusively on the latter and centers around questions of injustice. Accordingly, CDA is usually considered to be a "problem-oriented approach to research"[27] in the sense that it judges what is right and wrong and seeks to address "social wrongs in their discursive aspects and possible ways of righting or mitigating them."[28] I would argue, however, that while FDA is neither normative nor programmatic in the same way as CDA, it can indirectly be used to mitigate power injustices because it invites us to become aware of them.

State of Practice

While there are no clear guidelines that one must follow to successfully conduct discourse analysis and even as a wide range of techniques and methods can be used in the service of conducting this type of analysis—including, among others, archival research, participant observation, interviews, visual analysis, coding, and quantifying—a good place to start is to "stand back" from whatever "text"[29] one seeks to interpret and interrogate one's preconceived assumptions and ideas about it so that one can "render the familiar strange."[30] To do this, one must have a thorough understanding—"a sensitive, if not empathic, understanding"[31]—of the context under which the discourse emerges, circulates, and has effects. This can involve analyzing a discourse's underlying assumptions, as well as the concepts, classifications, and conventions that undergird it. All this is commonly referred to by scholars as following a "genealogical" approach to discourse, namely as identifying the conditions (social, political, economic, cultural, etc.) under which discourses arise, as well as their kinship and affiliation with other ideas and its relationship with specific actors and institutions.[32] This information is usually—or at least should be—included in the written analysis, but the details of course depend on the author and the type of output that is being produced.

If one chooses to focus, as many political scientists do, on the verbal language aspect of a discourse, then one would need to examine both *what* people talk about and *how* they talk. This requires analyzing the "content" of the discourse, including the issues and ideas that are discussed and the arguments that are made, as well as how they are logically structured and philosophically justified. It will also entail examining the explicit and implicit rhetorical strategies and techniques that are deployed, including the narrative structure, the lexicon and syntax, and the metaphors, analogies, and emotive language which can help indicate the tone of the speech. In some cases, the volume, pitch, and intonation of the speakers should also be noted. If the words are written rather than spoken, one would need to analyze the graphics to see how, if at all, these shape the meaning of the text (e.g., the use of headlines and the images that accompany the text, as well as its layout).[33] One must also, crucially, pay attention to what is *not* said, including the issues, arguments, and concepts that are omitted when discussing certain topics.[34] One must also identify other types of "metadata," defined by Lee Ann Fujii as "the spoken and *unspoken* expressions about people's interior thoughts and feelings, which they do not always articulate," and which, in addition to silences, can include rumors, inventions, denials, and evasions.[35] Metadata are a testament to the complexity and ambiguity that characterize the way people talk and behave.

It is not enough, in other words, to analyze the issues that politicians or activists put on the table; it is also necessary to analyze the ways in which they do so. For instance, in their book *The Changing Voice of the Anti-Abortion Movement*, Kelly Gordon and Paul Saurette argue that, in recent years, in an attempt to gain followers, the anti-abortion movement in Canada has appropriated a variety of classic feminist issues in order to appeal to a more progressive demographic but also that it has begun to use a "nurturant parent" tone (as opposed to a "strict father" tone).[36] A nurturant parent tone is one based on the assumption that individuals respond best to being positively encouraged rather than being made to feel guilt and shame. Without delving deeper into Gordon and Saurette's conclusions, the point here is that analyzing the issues promulgated by the anti-abortion movement needs to be done in conjunction with analyzing the way these issues are framed and the reasons for such framing.

Interpretivists assume that people's perceptions and observations about the world are mediated by words and language, which is why one of the tools that they use when conducting discourse analysis is to analyze specific concepts. While the potential for disagreement about the meaning of concepts is always present, it tends to become even more stark when studying concepts like "democracy," "justice," and "freedom" that are both descriptive *and* normative.[37] For example, even if everyone in a community agrees that the most important value to be defended is "freedom" and that it is the community's (or society's or government's) duty to ensure "freedom," they might, nonetheless, disagree about what freedom means. Freedom could be interpreted as the freedom from interference by other people (which would simply require restricting individuals from acting in ways that might impinge on others' ability to act a certain way), but it could also be interpreted as the possibility of doing certain things and acting in certain ways (which might require not simply restricting others from preventing individuals from doing and acting in those ways but also providing everyone with the necessary resources and conditions to do those things they seek to do). For instance, "freedom" might be seen as the freedom to own and carry guns or as the freedom to live in a society where gun ownership and the attendant risk from gun violence are minimized.

Disagreement also tends to be exacerbated when studying concepts cross-culturally and when the researcher is trying to compare their use in different languages. Frederic Schaffer draws from the work of ordinary language philosophers Ludwig Wittgenstein and J. L. Austin to provide a language-centered approach to analyze concepts.[38] One of the concepts that Schaffer has consistently analyzed in his work is the term "democracy." To do so he examines how people *use* this concept (or roughly equivalent concepts in other languages) in *all* its ordinary contexts, both political and nonpolitical. Schaffer finds, for instance, that in different places in the United States, "democracy" is used to index the existence not simply of free and fair elections but also of distributive equality, inclusive participation in a collective activity, the opportunity to take one's turn in the limelight, and a range of consumer choice.[39] In the Philippines, he instead finds that most people associate the concept *demokrasya* with the word *kalayaan*, which can mean peace, self-restraint, indulgent caring, the power to have one's demands acted upon, and the freedom to do or say what one wants.[40] Demonstrating this conceptual diversity allows Schaffer to question the widely held belief that people around the world conceive of the political world in the same or similar ways. This finding, in turn, allows him to trouble the logic behind liberal democracy promotion projects, ranging from research initiatives like the Global Barometer, which wrongly assume fixed definitions about democracy and other concepts as their basis for analysis and policy recommendations, including military interventions like the failed attempt by the United States to install liberal democracy in Iraq.

While the substantive content, rhetorical strategies, and ordinary use of particular concepts are all important features that one can examine when conducting discourse analysis, it is also very important to examine *who* does the speaking and communicating and in what context. In other words, it is important to distinguish—again following Austin[41]—the constative (or descriptive) aspects of an utterance from its performative aspects. Constative utterances are those that describe or report on something and which can, therefore, be true or false. Examples of constative utterances are "I am an American citizen" and "It is cold." Performative utterances, on the other hand, are those that *do* something and can be neither true nor false in the sense that they do not describe a reality. Rather than making a statement about the world, when one issues a performative utterance, one is performing an action.

Saying things like "You are under arrest" or "You're fired!" does not merely describe reality; it can also change it.

But for utterances to have this kind of power, it is not the intention of the speaker that matters but rather the accepted conventions surrounding the utterance. If these are in place, the performative will succeed regardless of the intention of the speaker.[42] In the simplest terms, "You are under arrest!" means something completely different if it is being said by a police officer than by a friend (unless, that is, your friend is a police officer). Literary critic and language philosopher Mikhail Bakhtin famously coined the term "authoritative discourse" to denote those verbal and written statements that are "backed up" or "indissolubly fused" with authority, namely those utterances that "stand and fall together" with the authority figure or institution that utters or supports them, be it a political or religious leader, a teacher, or even a parent.[43] When conducting discourse analysis, then, words, images, and semiotic practices *must* be analyzed in light of the way different authority figures, institutions, and sets of rules (e.g., aesthetic, scientific, legal, economic) shape and frame them.[44] In other words, the constative aspect of a text will not necessarily be the most relevant when determining its political significance.

It is often by analyzing how a specific utterance or argument is received and interpreted, and what its political effects are, that we can get a sense of the hierarchies of class, gender, race, education, nationality, and generation that are at play in specific places and moments. In her book *On Being Included,* Sara Ahmed analyzes the way that the utterance "Our university is diverse," when pronounced by certain authority figures within the institution and when enough people repeat it, might gain force and lead students, faculty, and staff to transform structural barriers that prevent students from certain ethnic and racial backgrounds from being admitted to a university or from graduating if they are admitted.[45] The same utterance, however, can help keep a university's existing racist values in place because it can lead to the illusion that the claim is describing an institution that is already racially diverse, which can generate complacency and disincentivize taking specific steps to actually tackle structural forms of oppression.[46] Conducting an analysis of the discourse of diversity in universities, therefore, requires analyzing more than just the content of the written documents, speeches, and mission statements. It might also necessitate conducting participant observation or archival research with an "ethnographic sensibility"[47] so as to get a better sense of the effects that certain utterances have, including on the actions taken by the university.

Another key aspect to keep in mind when conducting discourse analysis is the possibility of discourses traveling beyond their intended audiences and their potential redeployment for purposes other than those imagined by their authors (when and if those can even be identified). In other words, discourses do not develop in uninterrupted, continuous ways but, instead, are commonly susceptible to constant ruptures and transformations. A work of art, for example, can be preserved intact for decades or even centuries, and while its physical traits might remain completely unchanged, its meaning and political effect are likely to fluctuate significantly. In my work, for instance, I analyze what makes works of art politically transgressive. To do so, I cannot simply focus on an artwork's content and formal aesthetic traits. While, of course, these aspects matter significantly, it is also very important to pay attention to the funding structures, the organizations that house the artworks, and the public that has access to them at different points in time. I have found that while the content, the form, and the artist's intended message—which can be assessed through interviews with the artist, reviews of the work by art critics and theorists, and even my own interpretation of the piece—can be regarded as being provocative and transgressive, this will not necessarily be how members of the public, the state, or the ruling class might interpret the piece.

For example, in my article "A Eulogy for the *Coloso*," I discursively analyze a monument to shed light on Mexico's contemporary political zeitgeist.[48] The *Coloso* is an eight-ton, 66-foot-tall statue of a man with a prominent mustache and sideburns who holds a broken sword. It was commissioned by the state in 2010 to celebrate the country's 200 years of independence and 100 years of revolution. Both the artist and the state officials who commissioned the piece intended the statue to resonate with and represent "the Mexican people." But rather than identifying themselves with the statue, people stridently mocked it and maintained that instead of representing them it resembled specific figures, including a notoriously corrupt ex-president, a patron saint of the country's drug traffickers, and a famous *ranchero* folk singer. Many people also claimed that the *Coloso* was reminiscent of the thousands of anonymous bodies that began to appear in mass graves following the so-called war on drugs launched by the state in 2007.

My analysis included conducting participant observation and talking to people during the parade where the *Coloso* was first publicly displayed to get a sense of their opinions on the statue, including the rumors, silences, and other metadata that emerged in response to the statue. I also engaged in a thorough review of the mass and social media coverage of the *Coloso*, including television and radio broadcasts of the parade as well as articles, reviews, and analysis about these events published in newspapers and magazines. Additionally, I analyzed declarations and speeches by government officials about the commemorations and conducted a formal analysis of the aesthetics of the *Coloso*, which included researching its production process and the artist's views on the piece. However, had I focused only on these aspects without paying attention to the political context in which the statue was displayed and to the public's reaction, I would have missed the ways in which the statue evidenced the state's inability to shape national narratives and imaginaries about the country's political future and people's growing disappointment with the country's recent "democratic transition."

In summary, conducting discourse analysis can include analyzing the content of an utterance, a written document, an image, or a semiotic practice, as well as examining the social conventions, the institutions, and the power relations at play, namely paying attention to who speaks and performs an action and how it is received and interpreted.

As a way to conclude this section on how to conduct discourse analysis, I invite readers to remember that quantitative analysis and tools can also be deployed when conducting discourse analysis. These can help to measure the *frequency* of the use of words and concepts, phrases, and specific rhetorical strategies across a given discourse and can be used to code other types of text and data such as the researcher's interview transcripts, field notes, and archival documents, all of which can, in turn, help to interpret and analyze discourses.[49] Deploying quantitative techniques usually requires assembling data sets of specific words, phrases, or discourses; creating a coding book or dictionary designed to track a variety of definitions, meanings, rhetorical strategies, and the like; and then coding the data set, which entails assigning attributes to specific units of analysis, whether words, concepts, sentences, or topics. Computer software exists to conduct this type of analysis, although each of these steps can also be conducted manually (on this, see Chapter 32). One can follow an interpretivist epistemological tradition when using quantitative strategies and techniques because deciding how to categorize and code certain words, concepts, and ideas requires that the researcher understand the context in which these are uttered and interpret their meaning to decide on how to code them.[50]

Potential Limitations and Issues to Keep in Mind

Given the multiplicity of ways in which the term "discourse" is defined—ranging from words, rhetoric, and semiotic practices through to ideology, habitus, and worldview—simply claiming to conduct "discourse analysis" can be an empty signifier that does not tell the reader very much. The concept's capaciousness is certainly helpful in the sense that it indicates the vast range of strategies and techniques that a researcher can deploy when conducting discourse analysis and the many spaces and places that might require investigation. But in order to avoid confusion and speculation, researchers should always provide a precise description of the research techniques that they will be deploying (e.g., participant observation, archival research, visual analysis, interviews) when conducting discourse analysis and be as specific as possible about the places and spaces where they will do so (e.g., institutions, media, artworks).

An issue that researchers might encounter when conducting discourse analysis is that because they are dealing with ideas, meanings, and beliefs which are intangible and can be difficult to grasp, they might face questions of credibility.[51] Can researchers actually claim to get into people's heads? How can they really know what people think or when they are telling the truth? It is important to remember that claiming to understand people's real or truthful intentions and thoughts is not the goal of conducting discourse analysis, in part because people might not always or ever fully know why they think or act in certain ways. Instead of trying to access people's conscious or unconscious thoughts, conducting discourse analysis entails analyzing their words and actions—which are observable and recordable—and the tangible effects that these have in the world. To put it differently, this entails regarding discourse not as "ontologically distinct from or epiphenomenal of 'reality' but rather [taking] discourse to be the linguistic mediation of social relations and the concrete medium through which we reflect upon, make, and remake our social worlds."[52] But it is therefore important that researchers are clear that it is *this* and not people's "true" thoughts or feeling that they are studying.

Finally, researchers should avoid assuming that discourses will work as fixed, contained, and discrete independent (or dependent) variables. While it is possible for discourses to operate as variables that can transform the social context (or that are, themselves, transformed by such context), this will not necessarily be the case. Institutions, for instance, can produce and help circulate certain discourses, which, in turn, can help make certain political ideas thinkable and certain political goals reachable.[53] But discourses can also, simultaneously, be shaping institutions such that separating discourses and institutions into dependent and independent variables becomes untenable.[54] The point is that researchers who engage in discourse analysis need to learn to identify and to tell stories about the world that are not monocausal and do not follow strong causal trends.

Notes

1. Fairclough, Mulderring, and Wodak, "Critical Discourse Analysis."
2. Wedeen, "Ethnography as Interpretive Enterprise." See also Yanow and Schwartz-Shea, *Interpretation and Method*.
3. Schmidt, "Discursive Institutionalism."

4. Fairclough, *Analysing Discourse*, 129.
5. Schmidt, "Discursive Institutionalism," 305.
6. Foucault, "Politics and the Study of Discourse."
7. Wedeen, "Conceptualizing Culture," 714.
8. Parkinson, "Organizing Rebellion," 420.
9. Fischer, *Reframing Public Policy*, ch. 4.
10. Van Dijk, "What Is Political Discourse Analysis?"
11. Pugh. "Universal Citizenship through the Discourse and Policy of Rafael Correa."
12. Lerner, "Blurring the Boundaries of War."
13. Hayat, "Unrepresentative Claims."
14. Kolmasova and Krulisova, "Legitimizing Military Action through 'Rape-as-a-Weapon' Discourse in Libya."
15. Riofrancos, *Resource Radicals*.
16. Garnsey, *The Justice of Visual Art*.
17. Weitzel, "Common Sense Politics."
18. Pachirat, *Every Twelve Seconds*.
19. Bernhardt and Pin, "Engaging with Identity Politics in Canadian Political Science."
20. Walsh, "Putting Inequality in Its Place."
21. Wedeen, *Authoritarian Apprehensions*.
22. Weldes, "High Politics and Low Data," 230.
23. Fischer, *Reframing Public Policy*, ch. 4.
24. Saurette and Gordon, *The Changing Voice of the Anti-abortion Movement*, 18.
25. Wedeen, *Peripheral Visions*, 183.
26. Björkman et al., "Interpretive Methods."
27. Wodak and Meyer, "Critical Discourse Analysis," 3.
28. Norman Fairclough quoted in Catalano and Waugh, *Critical Discourse Analysis*, 2.
29. The word "text" in its broadest definition, which can include written documents, speeches, and images, but also events, institutions, concepts, and conventions.
30. Bacchi, "Why Study Problematizations?," 5.
31. Wedeen, "Ethnography as Interpretive Enterprise," 82.
32. Dreyfus and Rabinow, *Michel Foucault*, 104–125.
33. Van Dijk, "What Is Political Discourse Analysis?"
34. Foucault, *The History of Sexuality Vol. 1*.
35. Fujii, "Shades of Truth and Lies," 232.
36. Saurette and Gordon, *The Changing Voice of the Anti-abortion Movement*, 272–273.
37. Connolly, *The Terms of Political Discourse*.
38. Schaffer, *Democracy in Translation*, 9.
39. Schaffer, *Democracy in Translation*, 11–12.
40. Schaffer, "Thin Descriptions."
41. Austin, *How to Do Things with Words*, 6.
42. For an excellent account of the way conventions change the meaning of utterances, see Yurchak, *Everything Was Forever until It Was No More*.
43. Bakhtin, *The Dialogic Imagination*, 345–346.
44. Fischer, *Reframing Public Policy*, ch. 2.
45. Ahmed, *On Being Included*, 57.
46. Ahmed, *On Being Included*, 53–55.
47. Zacka et al., "Political Theory with an Ethnographic Sensibility."
48. Weinstein, "A Eulogy for the *Coloso*."
49. Political sociologist Tianna Paschel, for instance, used Tams Analyzer and NVivo software to code ethnoracial terminology used in debates and legislation (*Becoming Black Political Subjects*, 247).

50. Another software program that can be used to code text is QDA miner. See, for instance, Paulus and Lester, "ATLAS.ti for Conversation and Discourse Analysis Studies."
51. Wedeen, *Authoritarian Apprehensions*, 6.
52. Riofrancos, *Resource Radicals*, 16.
53. For a helpful example of the creative and productive dimensions of policymaking, including how gender mainstreaming discourses construct "gender experts," see Paterson's "What's the Problem with Gender-Based Analysis?" Thanks to Alex Hammond for pointing me to this reference.
54. Wedeen, *Peripheral Visions*, 217.

Recommended Readings

Mahmood, Saba. *Politics of Piety. The Islamic Revival and the Feminist Subject*. Princeton, NJ: Princeton University Press, 2005.
> Mahmood's sophisticated analysis deploys ethnographic methods to attend to the words, concepts, and practices that constitute the discourse of piety, and shows how it does not fit the binary terms of resistance and subordination. The book also demonstrates how academic liberal discourses have become taken from granted in the scholarship on gender.

Riofrancos, Thea. *Resource Radicals: From Petro-Nationalism to Post-Extractivism in Ecuador*. Durham, NC: Duke University Press, 2020.
> Riofrancos's discursive analysis of the politicization of resource extraction in Ecuador is a helpful example of how to identify interactions observed in protests, public events, meetings, interviews, texts, and radio and television broadcasts as discursively mediated. The book models how to conduct a Foucauldian genealogic study in the tradition of anthropologist James Ferguson's classic *The Antipolitics Machine: Development, Depoliticization, and Bureaucratic Power in Lesotho* (Minneapolis: University of Minnesota Press, 1994).

Wedeen, Lisa. *Peripheral Visions: Publics, Power, and Performance in Yemen*. Chicago: University of Chicago Press, 2009.
> By meticulously distinguishing discourses that are nationalist, democratic, and pious in *content* (e.g., the use of words and abstract concepts that index these ideas) from other ways in which national, democratic, and pious imaginings and attachments happen independently of this rhetoric (e.g., people's ordinary activities and everyday practices), Wedeen's book helps us identify the performative logics of discourses.

References

Ahmed, Sara. *On Being Included: Racism and Diversity in Institutional Life*. Durham, NC: Duke University Press, 2012.

Austin, J. L. *How to Do Things with Words*. Cambridge, MA: Harvard University Press, 1975.

Bacchi, Carol. "Why Study Problematizations? Making Politics Visible." *Open Journal of Political Science* 2, no. 1 (2012): 1–8.

Bakhtin, Michael. *The Dialogic Imagination: Four Essays*. Austin: University of Texas Press, 1981.

Bernhardt, Nicole, and Laura Pin. "Engaging with Identity Politics in Canadian Political Science." *Canadian Journal of Political Science* 51, no. 4 (2018): 771–794.

Björkman, Lisa, Lisa Wedeen, Juliet Williams, and Mary Hawkesworth. "Interpretive Methods." American Political Science Association organized section for Qualitative and Multi-Method Research, Qualitative Transparency Deliberations, Working Group Final Reports, Report III.2. January 2019. https://ssrn.com/abstract=3333411 or http://dx.doi.org/10.2139/ssrn.3333411.

Catalano, Theresa, and Linda R. Waugh. *Critical Discourse Analysis, Critical Discourse Studies and Beyond*. Cham: Springer, 2020.

Connolly, William. *The Terms of Political Discourse*. Oxford: Blackwell, 1993.
Dreyfus, Hubert, and Paul Rabinow. *Michel Foucault: Beyond Structuralism and Hermeneutics*. Chicago: University of Chicago Press, 1983.
Fairclough, Norman. *Analysing Discourse*. London: Routledge, 2003.
Fairclough, Norman, Jane Mulderring, and Ruth Wodak. "Critical Discourse Analysis." In *Discourse Studies: A Multidisciplinary Introduction*, edited by Teun A. Van Dijk, 357–378. London: Sage, 2011.
Fischer, Frank. *Reframing Public Policy: Discursive Politics and Deliberative Practices*. Oxford: Oxford Scholarship, 2003. Kindle.
Foucault, Michel. *The History of Sexuality Vol. 1*. New York: Penguin Random House, 1991.
Foucault, Michel. "Politics and the Study of Discourse." In *The Foucault Effect*, edited by Graham Burchell, Colin Gordon, and Peter Miller, 53–72. Chicago: University of Chicago Press, 1991.
Fujii, Lee Ann. "Shades of Truth and Lies: Interpreting Testimonies of War and Violence." *Journal of Peace Research* 47, no. 2 (2010): 231–241.
Garnsey, Eliza. *The Justice of Visual Art: Creative State-Building in Times of Political Transition*. Cambridge: Cambridge University Press, 2019.
Hayat, Samuel. "Unrepresentative Claims: Speaking for Oneself in a Social Movement." *American Political Science Review* 95, no. 1 (2021): 1–13.
Kolmasova, Sarka, and Katerina Krulisova. "Legitimizing Military Action through 'Rape-as-a-Weapon' Discourse in Libya: Critical Feminist Analysis." *Politics and Gender* 15, no. 1 (2019): 130–150.
Lerner, Adam B. "Blurring the Boundaries of War: PTSD in American Foreign Policy Discourse." *Perspectives on Politics* 21, no. 2 (2020): 1–18. https://doi.org/10.1017/S1537592720004223.
Pachirat, Timothy. *Every Twelve Seconds: Industrialized Slaughter and the Politics of Sight*. New Haven, CT: Yale University Press, 2011.
Parkinson, Sarah. "Organizing Rebellion: Rethinking High-Risk Mobilization and Social Networks in War." *American Political Science Review* 107, no. 3 (July 2013): 418–432.
Paschel, Tianna. *Becoming Black Political Subjects: Movements and Ethno-racial Rights in Colombia and Brazil*. Princeton, NJ: Princeton University Press, 2018.
Paterson, Stephanie. "What's the Problem with Gender-Based Analysis? Gender Mainstreaming Policy and Practice in Canada." *Canada Public Administration* 53, no. 4 (2010): 395–416.
Paulus, T. M., and J. N. Lester. "ATLAS.ti for Conversation and Discourse Analysis Studies." *International Journal of Social Research Methodology*, 19, no. 4 (2016): 405–428.
Pugh, Jeffrey D. "Universal Citizenship through the Discourse and Policy of Rafael Correa." *Latin American Politics and Society* 59, no. 3 (2017): 98–121.
Riofrancos, Thea. *Resource Radicals. From Petro-Nationalism to Post-Extractivism in Ecuador*. Durham, NC: Duke University Press, 2020.
Saurette, Paul, and Kelly Gordon. *The Changing Voice of the Anti-abortion Movement*. Toronto: University of Toronto Press, 2016.
Schaffer, Fredrich. *Democracy in Translation: Understanding Politics in an Unfamiliar Culture*. Ithaca, NY: Cornell University Press, 2018.
Schaffer, Fredrich. "Thin Descriptions: The Limits of Survey Research on the Meaning of Democracy." *Polity* 46, no. 3 (July 2014): 303–330.
Schmidt, Vivien A. "Discursive Institutionalism: The Explanatory Power of Ideas and Discourse." *Annual Review of Political Science* 11, no. 1 (2008): 303–326.
Simmons, Erica. *Meaningful Resistance: Market Reforms and the Roots of Social Protest in Latin America*. Cambridge: Cambridge University Press, 2016.
van Dijk, Teun A. "What Is Political Discourse Analysis?" *Belgian Journal of Linguistics* 11, no. 1 (January 1997): 11–52.
Walsh, Katherine Cramer. "Putting Inequality in Its Place: Rural Consciousness and the Power of Perspective." *American Political Science Review* 106, no. 3 (2012): 517–532.
Wedeen, Lisa. *Authoritarian Apprehensions: Ideology, Judgment, and Mourning in Syria*. Chicago: University of Chicago Press, 2019.
Wedeen, Lisa. "Conceptualizing Culture: Possibilities for Political Science." *American Political Science Review* 96, no. 4 (December 2002): 713–728.

Wedeen, Lisa. "Ethnography as Interpretive Enterprise." In *Political Ethnography: What Immersion Contributes to the Study of Power*, edited by Edward Schatz, 75–94. Chicago: University of Chicago Press, 2009.

Wedeen, Lisa. *Peripheral Visions: Publics, Power, and Performance in Yemen*. Chicago: University of Chicago Press, 2009.

Weinstein, Tania Islas. "A Eulogy for the *Coloso:* The Politics of Commemoration in Calderón's Mexico." *Journal of Latin American Cultural Studies* 24, no. 4 (2016): 475–499.

Weitzel, Michelle D. "Common Sense Politics: Religion and Belonging in French Public Space." *French Politics* 18, no. 4 (2020): 380–404.

Weldes, Jutta. "High Politics and Low Data: Globalization Discourses and Popular Culture." In *Interpretation and Method*, edited by Dvora Yanow and Peregrine Schwartz-Shea, 228–238. New York: Routledge, 2015.

Wodak, Ruth, and Michael Meyer. "Critical Discourse Analysis: History, Agenda, Theory, and Methodology." In *Methods of Critical Discourse Analysis*, edited by Ruth Wodak and Michael Meyer, 1–22. London: Sage, 2009.

Yanow, Dvora, and Peregrine Schwartz-Shea. *Interpretation and Method: Empirical Research Methods and the Interpretive Turn*. Abingdon: Routledge, 2015.

Yurchak, Alexei. *Everything Was Forever until It Was No More: The Last Soviet Generation*. Princeton, NJ: Princeton University Press, 2006.

Zacka, Bernardo, Brooke Ackerly, Jakob Elster, Signy Gutnick Allen, Humeira Iqtidar, Matthew Longo, and Paul Sagar. "Political Theory with an Ethnographic Sensibility." *Contemporary Political Theory* 20, no. 2 (2021): 385–418.

36
Qualitative Comparative Analysis
Ioana-Elena Oana

What Qualitative Comparative Analysis Is and When to Use It

Qualitative comparative analysis (QCA) is a set-theoretic comparative method aimed at identifying relations of necessity and sufficiency between conditions and an outcome of interest, with a focus on modeling causal complexity and an orientation toward explaining outcomes. While a relatively young method, since its beginnings in the late 1980s,[1] QCA has established itself as a main methodological tool in the social sciences and beyond. On par with its spread across disciplines in terms of application, the methodology behind QCA has also continued to develop and became more robust and sophisticated. Analytic protocols for QCA are continually refined and new analytic steps are proposed, especially as software solutions for QCA become more flexible, sophisticated, and readily available. This chapter provides an overview of the basic building blocks of what QCA is and when to use it, and how QCA works in practice; it also points the reader to state-of-the-art developments for building a solid QCA that goes beyond these basic analytic steps.

The first distinguishing feature of QCA is its *set-theoretic* nature. This means that the social phenomena analyzed, and the concepts used for capturing them, are understood and measured in terms of *sets to which cases belong or not*. Sets are a collection of cases that share a common property. As such, sets not only measure the extent to which a certain case exhibits a certain property but also establish qualitative differences between types of cases. For example, in a QCA one would analyze the set of "tall persons" by establishing a qualitative difference between "tall persons" and "not-tall persons" rather than just studying "height" (i.e., the measured property). For measuring concepts as sets, QCA can rely on both qualitative (e.g., interviews, expert reports) and quantitative (e.g., any kind of numerical data, irrespective of their level of measurement) data that undergoes a process of calibration, as described in the next section. QCA's foundations are in Boolean algebra, which means sets can be combined using basic *logical operators*: the logical AND (denoted with a *; all sets combined need to be present in the resulting set), the logical OR (denoted with a +; any of the sets combined can to be present in the resulting set), and the logical NOT (denoted with a ~; members of the set become nonmembers in the resulting set). As we think of cases as members in different sets, the core goal of set-theoretic methods is to investigate relations between such sets. In other words, we inquire into whether specific sets of cases are subsets or supersets of other sets of cases. These *set relations* directly translate into relations of *necessity* and *sufficiency* between various conditions and an outcome. For example, if the set of students who are active in class is a superset (contains all or more cases) of the set of students who obtain good grades, we can say that being active in class is a necessary condition for obtaining good grades.

Ioana-Elena Oana, *Qualitative Comparative Analysis* In: *Doing Good Qualitative Research*. Edited by: Jennifer Cyr and Sara Wallace Goodman, Oxford University Press. © Oxford University Press 2024. DOI: 10.1093/oso/9780197633137.003.0036

The second distinguishing feature of QCA, stemming from its set-theoretic nature, is its focus on *causal complexity*. Thus, with QCA we can model the presence of three core elements of causal complexity: *conjunctural causation, equifinality,* and *asymmetry*. QCA acknowledges that we can rarely understand social phenomena by focusing on the role of a single factor on its own. Instead, complex combinations of conditions usually bring about a certain outcome. Conjunctural causation, therefore, means that conditions are expected to often exert their impact in combination rather than in isolation from one another. Equifinality means there can be different, mutually nonexclusive explanations of the same phenomenon. In order words, there can be different (combinations of) conditions explaining an outcome of interest across various cases. Last, the occurrence of a social phenomenon may have different explanations than its nonoccurrence. This refers to asymmetric causation, which in QCA translates to performing separate analyses for the (combinations of) conditions explaining the presence of an outcome of interest and its absence.

The third distinguishing feature of QCA is its *orientation toward explaining outcomes*. This means that rather than being interested in the single, net effect of a specific variable in isolation across all cases, we are interested in how an outcome comes about through the complex interplay of different factors across different groups of cases. QCA, therefore, helps us address so-called *causes-of-effects* types of research questions that ask for the reasons why certain phenomena occur, hence with an orientation toward explaining outcomes.[2] Conversely, we would not use QCA for a "effects-of-causes" question asking about the magnitude of the effect of a single factor in isolation, hence with an orientation toward explaining the net effect of an independent variable.

Initially QCA was developed as a method combining the best features of both qualitative and quantitative methods, enabling formalized comparison with a strong focus on cases. Because of this, QCA is often perceived as the go-to method when one has a small or medium number of cases. However, QCA's analytic protocol lends itself to analyzing almost any number of cases, from relatively small (as a rule of thumb, more than 10 to enable comparison)[3] to very large numbers of cases. QCA can, therefore, be case-oriented or condition-oriented, depending on whether it integrates case knowledge and whether its focus is on obtaining a faithful representation of individual cases or just gaining conceptual knowledge about types of cases and obtaining robust solutions of how conditions relate to an outcome at the cross-case level.[4] Independent of the number of cases in the analysis, QCA can maintain its case-orientation to a certain degree as researchers can rely on within-case inferences to complement the cross-case QCA inferences in a systematic manner by integrating knowledge and analyses of individual cases at various steps. We return to this point in the last section of this chapter.

Given these features of QCA, the number of cases itself is not a good reason for choosing it. Instead, the choice for QCA as the suitable empirical research method for a particular research question depends on whether the social phenomenon under study is best conceived in terms of sets and sets' relations and on the orientation of that research question. In summary, the use QCA is advised when research questions are outcome-oriented and ask for the causes of a given effect, when the social phenomena under study are best represented in terms of sets and the relations between them, and when we assume that these empirical relations are complex. For example, studying the conditions under which democratic breakdowns occur[5] is a good candidate for QCA as an outcome-oriented question on phenomena that are well represented as sets. (Arguably, having a democratic breakdown indicates a different qualitative state than not having a breakdown, rather than being simply a matter of degree.) By contrast, being interested in the net effect of an increase in COVID infections on the number of street demonstrations in a particular state is not a good candidate, as a condition-oriented research question on phenomena that are arguably better represented as continuous properties in this particular research setup.

The Basics of QCA in Practice

In the previous section we explained the general goal and motivation for using QCA; we now turn to the basics of QCA in practice. We will give a brief overview of the different analytic steps involved in a basic QCA. Following Oana, Schneider, and Thomann,[6] we split these steps into stages *before* and *during the analytic moment*, before turning to enhancements to QCA, for example, robustness tests, cluster analyses, and follow-up cases, that can be done *after the analytic moment* in the next section.

Before the Analytic Moment

QCA begins like any other research project, where researchers face a series of research design decisions before embarking on the actual data analysis. These steps include *model specification*, that is, the definition and conceptualization of the outcome and conditions to be included in the analysis; the definition of the *scope conditions* within which the phenomenon of interest applies; the definition and selection of *cases* to be included into the analysis; and the *measurement* of the conditions and the outcome across the selected cases using qualitative and/or quantitative empirical information (for more, see the chapters in Part I).

Once these steps are clarified, and after data collection, any QCA must also include a data *calibration* step before proceeding to the actual data analysis. As mentioned, QCA is a set-theoretic method in that it conceives of the conditions and the outcome under analysis as sets that establish qualitative differences between different types of cases. Hence, the calibration process consists of transforming the available "raw" data gathered for the conditions and the outcome into set-membership scores reflecting whether (and how much) cases belong to each of these sets. In practice, this is done via the selection of various qualitative anchors (i.e., thresholds imposed on the data following qualitative criteria for creating [sub]sets) depending on the type of sets we want to calibrate.

For example, *crisp sets* are dichotomous and distinguish only between members and nonmembers of a set; hence they establish only a qualitative *difference-in-kind* between cases. Because of this, the calibration of a crisp set includes a single qualitative anchor, that is, the empirical threshold below which cases are defined as nonmembers (and receive a set-membership score of 0 in the set) and above which cases are defined as members of the set (and receive a set-membership score of 1 in the set). For example, Kuehn et al. calibrate the set of "direct military co-operation with the US" by using yearly data on the presence of U.S. military troops and counting those cases with presence of military troops in at least half the years under investigation as part of the set (crisp score of 1), and the rest as out of the set (crisp score of 0).[7] Nevertheless, more often than not, we are also interested in more fine-grained *differences-in-degree* between cases. To this end, *fuzzy sets* allow us to capture not only differences-in-kind through the qualitative anchors we define during calibration, but also differences-in-degree between cases of the same kind. Fuzzy sets always range from 0 (full nonmembership anchor) to 1 (full membership anchor), with the 0.5 value being the crossover point that establishes the qualitative difference-in-kind. Hence, cases with set-membership scores calibrated between 0.5 and 1 are more or less in the set to various degrees, whereas cases between 0 and 0.5 are more or less out of the set to various degrees. For example, Guzman-Concha calibrates the set of "high youth unemployment" in Western European cities using OECD data on unemployment rates and applying the following calibration anchors: 10%, full exclusion; 15%, crossover; and 20%, full inclusion.[8] Following this calibration strategy, for example, London, with a youth unemployment rate of 17%, obtained a 0.77 score in the set of "high youth unemployment," indicating that this is a case which qualitatively has youth unemployment (above 0.5), but to a certain degree.[9]

During the Analytic Moment

After having calibrated the conditions and the outcome into sets, one can proceed to the analysis of the relations between these sets. Hence, the core of QCA consists of investigating which (combinations of) conditions are subsets and/or supersets of the outcome, which translate into relations of necessity and sufficiency. We describe each of these relations and how to analyze them.

Necessary conditions are supersets of the outcome of interest. For example, we could observe that all students in a class who have good grades (set Y) are highly engaged in class discussions (set X). On the one hand, there are no students with good grades who are not highly engaged in discussions. On the other hand, there are some students who are highly engaged in discussions who do not have good grades. This can be translated into saying that being highly engaged in class discussions is a *necessary condition* for having good grades (set X is a superset of set Y). A relationship of necessity is denoted in QCA with a left-pointing arrow, for example, X ← Y, to be read as "the outcome set Y implies the condition set X." (In our example, having good grades implies being highly engaged.)

Since necessary conditions are supersets of the outcome (hence larger sets), the analysis of necessary conditions in QCA proceeds by testing whether any single conditions chosen fulfills the superset requirement before passing on to logical OR combinations of such conditions. The logical OR operator combines two conditions sets by creating a larger resulting set, as any of the two conditions can be present in the resulting set. Hence a logical OR combination of conditions, being a larger set, might pass the bar of the superset requirement. For example, being highly engaged in class discussions might not be a superset of the set of hiving good grades alone, but the combination of being highly engaged in class discussions OR engaging in teamwork might be, as it requires only one of the two requirements to be fulfilled. We call such conditions combined with the logical OR in the analysis of necessity SUIN[10] conditions, and they are one of the examples of how causal complexity is modeled in QCA. Finally, beyond empirically finding supersets of the outcome, be they in isolation or in a logical OR combination, any necessary conditions need to also be conceptually meaningful. In other words, we need to be able to specify a theoretically plausible mechanism linking the necessary (combination of) conditions to the outcome.[11]

Having performed the analysis of necessity, the next step in a QCA consists of the analysis of sufficiency. In terms of set relations, sufficiency is just the reverse side of the coin of necessity; hence a sufficient condition is a subset of an outcome of interest. For example, we could notice that all students in a class that pass the final exam (set X) pass the course (set Y). This relationship of sufficiency is denoted in QCA with a right-pointing arrow, for example, X → Y, to be read as "the condition set X implies the outcome set Y." (In our example, passing the final exam implies passing the course.) Notice that this relationship of sufficiency does not imply that a student can pass the course only by passing the final exam, but that those who do pass the final exam also pass the course. In other words, in the analysis of sufficiency we focus on (combinations of) conditions that always lead to the outcome, without excluding equifinality, hence other ways to reach this outcome.

Since the analysis of sufficiency is focused on subsets of the outcome, hence smaller sets, this analysis proceeds differently from the analysis of necessity. To analyze sufficiency, we start by looking at all possible combinations of conditions using a logical AND operator which combines conditions sets by creating their smaller, intersection sets. For example, the set of students who both pass the final exam AND write a good final paper is smaller than both of its composing sets and, by virtue of this, more likely to be a subset of the outcome of choice, passing the course. We call such conditions combined with a logical AND operator in the analysis of sufficiency INUS conditions.[12] They are another example of how causal complexity is modeled in QCA, exhibiting conjunctural causation.

To reveal all logically possible logical AND configurations of conditions and test their sufficiency, in QCA we use an analytic tool called a *truth table*. Each row of such a truth table represents a specific combination of conditions, while all truth table rows together display all the possible AND combinations of conditions. After building such a truth table, we evaluate whether each of the AND combinations of conditions in turn is a subset (hence sufficient) for the outcome. Finally, the last step in the analysis of sufficiency consists of *logically minimizing* all these sufficient combinations. This step is needed because some sets in these combinations might end up being redundant or irrelevant and their inclusion would make the final sufficient solution cumbersome to interpret. In practice this means using Boolean algebra rules to arrive at simpler ways of expressing the multitude of combinations of conditions that ended up being subsets of the outcome. In other words, the goal of truth table analysis is to find the shortest possible expressions of those combinations of conditions that are sufficient for the outcome.

The result of truth table analysis usually points to sufficient solutions that exhibit all features of causal complexity sketched above. For example, such a result could take the form $A + B*\sim C \rightarrow Y$, which we read as "either the presence of A on its own OR the combination of the presence of B AND the absence of C are sufficient for the outcome Y." We can notice that this result presents *equifinality* in that there is more than one way to obtain outcome Y. This result also presents *conjunctural causation*, in that in one of the sufficient paths to outcome Y ($B*\sim C$) we have a combination of conditions. Finally, *asymmetry* presents itself in two ways. First, we have asymmetry as we look at the causal role of a given qualitative state of a condition (its presence or its absence). Second, importantly, another feature of asymmetry comes through as analyses of necessity and sufficiency are performed separately for each qualitative state of an outcome, that is, its presence and its absence, with different results for each analysis.

Having sketched the major steps in the analysis of necessity and sufficiency in principle, in practice, especially when working with social science data, these analyses are usually less neat, as superset and subset relationships are rarely perfect and our data is usually limited in its diversity. To tackle the first issue of less than perfect superset-subset relationships we allow for small deviations from perfect patterns of necessity and sufficiency. For this purpose, there are several *parameters of fit* for necessity and sufficiency that allow quantifying the extent to which these set relations deviate from being "perfect," with more sophisticated parameters of fit being continuously developed. While an explanation of each of these parameters of fit exceeds the scope of this chapter, we want to mention the standard ones that any QCA should engage with and report. These are the consistency and coverage of sufficiency and necessity, the Relevance of Necessity (RoN), and the Proportional Reduction in Inconsistency (PRI) in the analysis of sufficiency.[13]

The second issue, *limited diversity*, presents itself in the analysis of sufficiency as not all of the logically possible combinations of conditions in a truth table might be observed in reality. In other words, not all configurations are present in our cases. We call these unobserved combinations *logical remainders*, and we deal with them in QCA using a variety of strategies. One such strategy is to perform our analysis only on the empirically observed combinations; the result of this strategy is obtaining a *conservative sufficient solution*. A second strategy is to engage with these unobserved combinations and select among them those that help in making our solution simpler via the logical minimization procedure. The result of this strategy is obtaining a so-called *most parsimonious sufficient solution*. Yet another strategy is to engage with logical remainders, but rather than select them solely based on parsimony, to use also theoretically guided criteria for their selection. The resulting solution is called an *intermediate sufficient solution*. On top of these three strategies, there are other guiding principles for dealing with the issue of limited diversity which further take into account the nature of these logical remainders and their analytic and theoretical plausibility. For studying these strategies, we point the reader to the literature on (enhanced) standard analysis, well-documented in several of the readings recommended below.[14]

Further Refining a QCA beyond the Analytic Moment

Having sketched the basics of how to perform a standard QCA and identifying necessary and sufficient (combinations of) conditions for the outcome, we now turn to ways in which researchers can enhance their QCAs beyond the analytic moment. These procedures help in building a more solid analysis by increasing researchers' confidence in their results, by bringing back a case-orientation that enables using within-case inferences to complement the cross-case QCA inferences, and by helping researchers to draw better theoretical conclusions.

First, as is apparent from the analytic steps detailed above, QCA requires researcher input at various stages in the analysis (when calibrating the sets to be included in the analysis, when evaluating less-than-perfect set relations through parameters of fit, etc.), with some decisions being more discretionary than others. If in the early days of QCA robustness and diagnostic tools to assess the consequences of such discretionary decisions were underdeveloped, manual, and cumbersome, the methodology behind QCA is being continually refined and now makes available a variety of tools for this purpose. Among these, we mention protocols for assessing the sensitivity and robustness of discretionary analytic decisions such as the one developed by Oana and Schneider,[15] but also diagnostic tools for clustered data (temporally, geographically, or otherwise) such as the one described in García-Castro and Arino.[16] We advise researchers embarking on a QCA to always perform these diagnostics with the goal of increasing confidence in their results.

Second, while QCA offers powerful tools for uncovering patterns at the cross-case level, we advise complementing these analyses with within-case studies. Hence, after the basic analytic steps described above, one should strive to bring individual cases back to the forefront. This can be done not only by using visualization tools of how patterns of sufficiency and necessity hold across cases and the identification of deviations to these patterns, but also by engaging in purposeful case studies. The goal of this process is not simply maintaining QCA's initial case orientation but strengthening the quality of causal inferences by combining findings on cross-case relations, with within-case findings on the mechanisms behind such relations. For this purpose, researchers have at their disposal a sophisticated literature on set-theoretic multimethod research (SMMR) that is focused specifically on protocols of combining QCA with qualitative case studies and process tracing.[17] For example, using the criteria provided by this literature, researchers can select the best available typical cases for a particular pattern of sufficiency with the goal of identifying or testing a hypothesized within-case mechanism linking the sufficient condition(s) identified via QCA and the outcome. The SMMR literature provides tools for the identification of a variety of types of cases (typical cases, deviant cases, individually irrelevant cases, etc.) that can be studied alone or in combination for specific analytic goals.

Third, due to QCA's close affinity with qualitative methods that often involve theoretical input at various steps in the analysis and, hence, a process of going back and forth between theory and evidence,[18] its logic is less compatible with standard hypothesis testing than those of quantitative methods. In light of this, rather than testing their hypotheses with the goal of confirming or disconfirming them in the standard way, we advise researchers undertaking QCA to engage in formal theory evaluation.[19] In practice, formal theory evaluation uses Boolean algebra to compare theories formulated in Boolean terms with the results generated by QCA. Rather than simply confirming or disconfirming theories, the goal of this process is reassessing theoretical hunches by identifying elements of a theory that are supported or not by empirical evidence and, hence, highlighting ways of expanding or contracting such theories. For example, say a theory suggests that media visibility is sufficient for street demonstrations to have an impact, but the QCA results indicate that it is not media visibility alone but only combined with the large number of participants that is sufficient for such success. This empirical result neither confirms nor fully rejects the initial theory, but rather indicates an amendment to it by the addition of the "large number of participants" condition. Similar ways of employing theory evaluation for more complex theories and QCA results can be applied using these tools.

To sum up, in this section we highlighted the fact that a solid QCA does not end with the analytic moment. After gaining an understanding of the basic steps involved in performing a basic QCA, from designing their research to performing the analysis of necessary and sufficient conditions, researchers should strive for solidifying, enhancing, and refining these analyses further. Engaging with a QCA after the analytic moment is an essential part of the method's iterative nature of going back and forth between theory and evidence. For example, robustness and diagnostic tests can reveal insights about calibration and threshold selection; post-QCA case studies might indicate the need for a different model specification; and theory evaluation can help with further building the theoretical hunches used at the start of the analysis. As these tools are becoming further refined and more readily available in the software solutions put at researchers' disposal, we hope they become part of the standard QCA toolkit. Software solutions for QCA include a number of traditional point-and-click programs (e.g., fs/QCA[20] and Tosmana[21]) that allow performing the basics steps outlined earlier. However, many of the state-of-the-art methodological innovations mentioned in this section are available only through dedicated packages (i.e., QCA[22] and SetMethods[23]) in the R command line software environment, which, beyond access to these innovations, also offers increased flexibility, replicability, and transparency.

The standard QCA toolkit, together with the more recent innovations in the field put forward in this section, offer researchers powerful analytical and computational tools for studying set-theoretic research questions on relations of necessity and sufficiency involving causal complexity. Given its relative novelty and continual development, QCA is not yet a "mainstream" method. While it is primarily applied in the fields of political science, sociology, and business and management, we believe its increasing robustness and sophistication make it an attractive tool beyond these fields. While this increased computational sophistication that QCA has been undergoing might come with practical hurdles for the qualitative-minded researcher, ever more resources are being created to facilitate the learning process. We list some of these below.

Notes

1. Ragin, *The Comparative Method*.
2. Goertz and Mahoney, *A Tale of Two Cultures*.
3. Oana, Schneider, and Thomann, *Qualitative Comparative Analysis Using R*.
4. Thomann, Ege, and Paustyan, "Approaches to Qualitative Comparative Analysis and good practices: A systematic review"; Thomann and Maggetti, "Designing Research with Qualitative Comparative Analysis (QCA)."
5. Tomini and Wagemann, "Varieties of Contemporary Democratic Breakdown and Regression: A Comparative Analysis."
6. Oana, Schneider, and Thomann, *Qualitative Comparative Analysis Using R*.
7. Kuehn et al., "Conditions of Civilian Control in New Democracies."
8. Guzman-Concha, "Radical Social Movements in Western Europe."
9. Beyond crisp and fuzzy sets, one could also calibrate multi-value sets that capture qualitative differences of more than one kind, but these are relatively less common (see Cronqvist and Berg-Schlosser, "Multi-value QCA (mvQCA)"; Haesebrouck, "The Added Value of Multi-value Qualitative Comparative Analysis"; Dusa, *QCA with R*).
10. Sufficient but Unnecessary parts of an Insufficient but Necessary condition.
11. Schneider, "Realists and Idealists in QCA."
12. Insufficient but Necessary parts of an Unnecessary but Sufficient condition.
13. Oana, Schneider, and Thomann, *Qualitative Comparative Analysis Using R*; Schneider and Wagemann, *Set-Theoretic Methods for the Social Sciences: A Guide to Qualitative Comparative Analysis*.
14. Oana, Schneider, and Thomann, *Qualitative Comparative Analysis Using R*; Schneider and Wagemann, *Set-Theoretic Methods for the Social Sciences: A Guide to Qualitative Comparative Analysis*.

15. Oana and Schneider, "A Robustness Test Protocol for Applied QCA." For more on robustness of applied QCA results, also see Emmenegger, Schraff, and Walter, "QCA, the Truth Table Analysis and Large-N Survey Data"; Schneider and Wagemann, *Set-Theoretic Methods for the Social Sciences: A Guide to Qualitative Comparative Analysis*; Skaaning, "Assessing the Robustness of Crisp-Set and Fuzzy-Set QCA Results"; Rutten, "Applying and Assessing Large-N QCA: Causality and Robustness From a Critical Realist Perspective." While we acknowledge that there is also a literature engaging with the question of how robust QCA as a method is, this wider methodological debate exceeds the scope of this chapter, as here we refer to the more applied issue of how robust specific QCA results are.
16. García-Castro and Arino, "A General Approach to Panel Data Set-Theoretic Research." For the software implementation of cluster diagnostic tests, see Oana and Schneider, "SetMethods"; Oana, Schneider, and Thomann, *Qualitative Comparative Analysis Using R*.
17. For SMMR, see Schneider and Rohlfing, "Case Studies Nested in Fuzzy-Set QCA on Sufficiency"; Schneider and Rohlfing, "Combining QCA and Process Tracing in Set Theoretic Multi-Method Research"; Schneider and Rohlfing, "Set-Theoretic Multimethod Research"; Schneider, *Set-Theoretic Multi-Method Research*; Rohlfing and Schneider, "Improving Research on Necessary Conditions"; Rohlfing and Schneider, "A Unifying Framework for Causal Analysis in Set-Theoretic Multi-Method Research." For its software implementation, see Oana and Schenider, "SetMethods"; Oana, Schneider, and Thomann, *Qualitative Comparative Analysis Using R*.
18. Ragin, *Fuzzy-set Social Science*.
19. For formal theory evaluation in QCA, see Ragin, *The Comparative Method: Moving beyond Qualitative and Quantitative Strategies*; Schneider and Wagemann, *Set-Theoretic Methods for the Social Sciences: A Guide to Qualitative Comparative Analysis*; For its software implementation see Oana and Schenider, "SetMethods."
20. Ragin and Davey, *Fuzzy-Set/Qualitative Comparative Analysis 4.0*.
21. Cronqvist, *Tosmana 1.61*.
22. Dusa, *QCA with R*.
23. Oana and Schneider, "SetMethods."

Recommended Readings

Oana, Ioana-Elena, Carsten Q. Schneider, and Eva Thomann. *Qualitative Comparative Analysis Using R: A Beginner's Guide*. Cambridge: Cambridge University Press, 2021.
   A comprehensive guide, complete with state-of-the-art software implementation guidelines on using QCA with R, for R novices and experts alike.
Schneider, Carsten Q., and Claudius Wagemann. *Set-Theoretic Methods for the Social Sciences: A Guide to Qualitative Comparative Analysis*. Cambridge: Cambridge University Press, 2012.
   An in-depth theoretical discussion of many of the issues surrounding QCA, including pitfalls in the analyses of necessity and sufficiency.
Rihoux, Benoît, and Charles C. Ragin. *Configurational Comparative Methods: Qualitative Comparative Analysis (QCA) and Related Techniques*. Thousand Oaks: Sage Publications, Inc., 2009.
   A broad introduction to the configurational comparative approach more generally.
Ragin, Charles C. *Redesigning Social Inquiry: Fuzzy Sets and Beyond*. Chicago: University of Chicago Press, 2008.
   Focuses on the differences between sets and variables and correlational and configurational based analyses.
Dusa, Adrian. *QCA with R: A Comprehensive Resource*. New York: Springer International Publishing, 2018.
   A more advanced treatment of using R in QCA for R experts.

References

Cronqvist, Lasse. *Tosmana [Version 1.61]*. University of Trier, 2019.
Cronqvist, Lasse, and Dirk Berg-Schlosser. "Multi-value QCA (mvQCA)." In *Configurational Comparative Methods: Qualitative Comparative Analysis (QCA) and Related Techniques,* edited by Benoit Rihoux and Charles C. Ragin, 69–86. Thousand Oaks, CA: Sage, 2009.
Dusa, Adrian. *QCA with R: A Comprehensive Resource*. New York: Springer International Publishing, 2018.
Emmenegger, Patrick, Dominik Schraff, and André Walter. "QCA, the Truth Table Analysis and Large-N Survey Data: The Benefits of Calibration and the Importance of Robustness Tests." COMPASSS Working Paper 2014-79 (2014).
García-Castro, Roberto, and Miguel A. Arino. "A General Approach to Panel Data Set-Theoretic Research." *Journal of Advances in Management Sciences & Information Systems* 2 (2016): 63–76.
Goertz, Gary, and James Mahoney. *A Tale of Two Cultures: Qualitative and Quantitative Research in the Social Sciences*. Princeton, NJ: Princeton University Press, 2012.
Guzman-Concha, Cesar. "Radical Social Movements in Western Europe: A Configurational Analysis." *Social Movement Studies* 14, no. 6 (2015): 668–691.
Haesebrouck, Tim. "The Added Value of Multi-value Qualitative Comparative Analysis." *Forum Qualitative Sozialforschung / Forum: Qualitative Social Research*. 17, no. 1 (2015).
Kuehn, David, Aurel Croissant, Jil Kamerling, Hans Lueders, and André Strecker. "Conditions of Civilian Control in New Democracies: An Empirical Analysis of 28 'Third Wave' Democracies." *European Political Science Review* 9, no. 3 (2017): 425–447.
Oana, Ioana-Elena, and Carsten Q. Schneider. "A Robustness Test Protocol for Applied QCA: Theory and R Software Application." *Sociological Methods & Research* 1, no. 32 (2021). https://journals.sagepub.com/doi/10.1177/00491241211036158
Oana, Ioana-Elena, and Carsten Q. Schneider. "SetMethods: An Add-on R Package for Advanced QCA." *The R Journal* 10, no. 1 (2018): 507–533.
Oana, Ioana-Elena, Carsten Q. Schneider, and Eva Thomann. *Qualitative Comparative Analysis Using R: A Beginner's Guide*. Cambridge: Cambridge University Press, 2021.
Ragin, Charles C. *The Comparative Method: Moving beyond Qualitative and Quantitative Strategies*. Berkeley: University of California Press, 1987.
Ragin, Charles C. *Redesigning Social Inquiry: Fuzzy Sets and Beyond*. Chicago: University of Chicago Press, 2008.
Ragin, Charles C. *Fuzzy-set Social Science*. Chicago: University of Chicago Press, 2000.
Ragin, Charles C., and Sean Davey. *Fuzzy-Set/Qualitative Comparative Analysis 4.0*. Irvine, California: Department of Sociology, University of California, 2022. https://sites.socsci.uci.edu/~cragin/fsQCA/citing.shtml
Rihoux, Benoît, and Charles C. Ragin. *Configurational Comparative Methods: Qualitative Comparative Analysis (QCA) and Related Techniques*. Thousand Oaks: Sage Publications, Inc., 2009.
Rohlfing, Ingo, and Carsten Q. Schneider. "Improving Research on Necessary Conditions: Formalized Case Selection for Process Tracing after QCA." *Political Research Quarterly* 66, no. 1 (2013): 220–235.
Rohlfing, Ingo, and Carsten Q. Schneider. "A Unifying Framework for Causal Analysis in Set-Theoretic Multi-Method Research." *Sociological Methods & Research* 47, no. 1 (2018): 37–63.
Rutten, Roel. "Applying and Assessing Large-N QCA: Causality and Robustness From a Critical Realist Perspective." *Sociological Methods & Research* 51, no. 3 (2022): 1211–1243.
Schneider, Carsten Q. "Realists and Idealists in QCA." *Political Analysis* 26 (2018): 246–254.
Schneider, Carsten Q. *Set-Theoretic Multi-Method Research: A Guide to Combining QCA and Case Studies*. Cambridge: Cambridge University Press, forthcoming.
Schneider, Carsten Q., and Ingo Rohlfing. "Case Studies Nested in Fuzzy-Set QCA on Sufficiency: Formalizing Case Selection and Causal Inference." *Sociological Methods & Research* 45, no. 3 (2016): 526–568.
Schneider, Carsten Q., and Ingo Rohlfing. "Combining QCA and Process Tracing in Set Theoretic Multi-Method Research." *Sociological Methods & Research* 42, no. 4 (2013): 559–597.

Schneider, Carsten Q., and Ingo Rohlfing. "Set-Theoretic Multimethod Research: The Role of Test Corridors and Conjunctions for Case Selection." *Swiss Political Science Review* 25, no. 3 (2019): 253–275.

Schneider, Carsten Q., and Claudius Wagemann. *Set-Theoretic Methods for the Social Sciences: A Guide to Qualitative Comparative Analysis*. Cambridge: Cambridge University Press, 2012.

Skaaning, Svend-Erik. "Assessing the Robustness of Crisp-Set and Fuzzy-Set QCA Results." *Sociological Methods & Research* 40, no. 2 (2011): 391–408.

Thomann, Eva, Jörn Ege, and Ekaterina Paustyan. "Approaches to Qualitative Comparative Analysis and good practices: A systematic review." *Swiss Political Science Review* 28 (2022): 557–580.

Thomann, Eva, and Martino Maggetti. "Designing Research with Qualitative Comparative Analysis (QCA)." *Sociological Methods & Research* 49, no. 2 (2020): 356–386.

Tomini, Luca, and Claudius Wagemann. "Varieties of Contemporary Democratic Breakdown and Regression: A Comparative Analysis." *European Journal of Political Research* 57 (2018): 687–716.

PART V
PUBLISHING QUALITATIVE RESEARCH

37
Research Transparency in Qualitative Inquiry

Diana Kapiszewski

Descriptive Overview

Research transparency is an essential attribute of rigorous social science inquiry.[1] Being transparent in presentations and publications associated with a study entails clearly stating how one gathered the information and evidence underlying the study's claims and conclusions; discussing how one interpreted and analyzed that information and evidence in order to arrive at those claims and conclusions; and making that information and evidence accessible to others. Research transparency can and should be pursued to different degrees and in different ways in different research projects. To what extent and how scholars pursue transparency depends on many factors, including the nature of their research and evidence, the audiences they have in mind, their epistemological commitments, and ethical and legal obligations.

Making one's scholarship transparent produces a range of benefits: transparent research is understood to be more fundable, comprehensible, evaluable, and publishable. Public and private foundations (e.g., the National Science Foundation, the Ford Foundation, and the Gates Foundation) and other entities that support social science research increasingly expect grantees to make funded scholarship transparent. Indeed, some funding organizations require that proposals include a data management plan (DMP) outlining how the prospective grantee will handle and potentially disseminate the data their work generates.[2] Scholars providing a robust DMP and carefully outlining in their proposals the steps they will take to make the intended research transparent (responsibly and as epistemologically appropriate) can strengthen their applications. In addition, scholars making their work as transparent as possible, and clearly describing any constraints on transparency, help others to understand their analysis and findings and enable more careful and accurate assessment of their work. Likewise, submitting transparent manuscripts to journals enables authors to meet journals' emerging expectations for openness in qualitative scholarship and can facilitate the review process.[3]

Scholars being transparent about their research practices, in particular sharing the information that underlies their scholarship, also has broader upsides. This clarity encourages good research procedures. It also helps researchers to see potential synergies between their work and that of other scholars, encouraging the creation or reinforcement of epistemic communities, fueling collaboration, and fostering inclusivity. Scholars making the data underlying a study available for other researchers to use in their own work decreases redundancy, speeds discovery, and expands knowledge. Shared data can also be used in qualitative methods instruction, allowing students to practice using the methods they are learning;[4] adopting

---

Diana Kapiszewski, *Research Transparency in Qualitative Inquiry* In: *Doing Good Qualitative Research*. Edited by: Jennifer Cyr and Sara Wallace Goodman, Oxford University Press. © Oxford University Press 2024. DOI: 10.1093/oso/9780197633137.003.0037

this approach should enhance skills acquisition given strong evidence of the effectiveness of "active learning."[5] Also, other scholars can replicate transparent scholarship (i.e., they can collect new data from the same population that was engaged in the original study, analyze those data using the same methods employed in that study, and see if the same substantive conclusions emerge),[6] helping us to establish, or leading us to question, the credibility of the original study's claims, again building knowledge.[7]

This chapter's goal is to provide information to encourage and empower scholars who use qualitative methods to make their work more transparent in more ways, as epistemologically appropriate and within ethical and legal limits. The next section discusses a few of the established and emerging practices that scholars can use to increase the openness of their scholarship. The third section considers ongoing debates about transparency, identifying potential concerns about and challenges to pursuing transparency and suggesting ways to address those issues. The concluding section elucidates the ethical bases of openness and encourages political scientists to contribute to discussions about transparency.

Transparency Practices

There is no "state of the art" or single "best practice" for making qualitative social inquiry transparent: the heterogeneity of such inquiry requires the adoption of diverse approaches to achieving transparency. As discussed in more depth in the next section, which technique or techniques will be most useful depends on multiple parameters of a research project (topic, setting, and sensitivity, for instance), practical considerations, the "audiences" scholars have in mind when pursuing transparency,[8] their epistemological commitments, and ethical and legal obligations.[9] Fortunately, social scientists and information scientists are continually developing new strategies to address the varied transparency needs of scholars who employ qualitative data and methods. This short piece highlights four that should be useful to scholars who generate and analyze qualitative data: preregistration, research appendices, annotation for transparent inquiry (ATI), and data sharing.[10]

Preregistration emerged in the early 2010s as a practice among political scientists who conduct experimental research.[11] While preregistration "means different things to different people,"[12] in general it entails publicly articulating aspects of the design of a research project, in particular specifying hypotheses and outlining plans for data analysis, prior to initiating the project. Creating and registering a pre-analysis plan both helps scholars to achieve transparency objectives and holds them accountable.

Some scholars who employ forms of inquiry in which some key aspects of research design can evolve as projects progress,[13] including some who use qualitative data and methods, discount the utility of preregistration as both a transparency technique and an accountability device. Yet from the start, those advocating for preregistration have recognized the importance of flexibility, understanding that deviations from initial research plans can be intellectually justifiable, and simply emphasizing the importance of documenting them.[14] Scholars are increasingly discussing how qualitative research can be preregistered and creating guidelines and tools to help researchers who use qualitative methods to capitalize on this powerful transparency technique.[15]

Research appendices comprise material that is not essential to the core text of an article or book but rather supplements and enhances the text. Such appendices may offer details on data sources or research processes or include material that is too unwieldy to be placed in the body of the text. The goal of creating such appendices is generally to facilitate comprehension or increase credibility by augmenting transparency. The material incorporated in such appendices generally does not count against the length limits that journals establish for published work. Often hosted by academic publishers, research appendices are frequently referenced in and linked to from the first footnote of a research article, making identifying them straightforward for readers.

Such appendices can take myriad forms. While they are practically de rigueur for quantitative work,[16] they are also increasingly employed in qualitative work, and are equally useful for enhancing its transparency. Some appendices mainly aim to shed light on the processes an author employed to generate data. For instance, Bleich and Pekkanen have developed an excellent template for detailing how interview data were produced, capturing in a single table key dimensions of the process as well as attributes of respondents.[17] Other appendices focus on illuminating how data were analyzed, for instance, specifying process tracing tests,[18] while still others discuss both data generation and analysis.[19]

ATI, an emerging approach for pursuing transparency in qualitative and multimethod research, empowers scholars to "annotate" specific passages in digitally published scholarship; ATI annotations appear on the same publisher web page (or PDF) as the text of the piece with which they are associated.[20] Authors can use annotations to clarify and expand on points or passages or offer details on how they collected or analyzed the data underlying inferences and interpretations. Annotations might also include excerpts from data sources that underlie an author's analysis (and citations to those sources) and/or links to the digitized sources themselves. Annotations and the data sources that underlie them can be curated and preserved by a data repository. Easily accessible to readers, annotations elucidate and enrich published research without increasing word count.[21]

Scholars might also share the data underlying their scholarship, perhaps in tandem with employing another transparency technique. They may share just the data mentioned or cited in a manuscript, or a broader swath of the data associated with a study; doing the latter helps readers to contextualize and interpret the cited data and facilitates secondary analysis. Best practice is to share research data in institutionalized venues developed and designed to publish and preserve digital data, such as self-service repositories like figshare, Zenodo, and Harvard Dataverse; institutional repositories managed by universities or other research entities; or domain repositories offering services tailored to the kinds of data typically employed by a discipline or group of disciplines.[22] Sharing data in institutionalized venues facilitates ethical data sharing. For instance, authors can impose "access controls" on the data they deposit in such venues, limiting others' ability to view the data.

It should be strongly emphasized that how scholars design and implement a research study greatly influences what strategies they will be able to use to make the resulting scholarship transparent, and how transparent they will be able to make that scholarship. Accordingly, scholars should start to consider intellectually appropriate and responsible strategies for making their work transparent from the very early stages of a research project. Of course, scholars' intellectual goals should drive how they design and execute their research. Nonetheless, creating a DMP, systematically documenting choices and decisions made while designing and conducting research, and carefully organizing data and keeping them safe and secure can facilitate both the effective execution of a research project *and* the pursuit of transparency.

Ongoing Debates, Potential Challenges, Suggested Solutions

The value and practices of research transparency have been a topic of debate in the social sciences for decades.[23] Discussions were reenergized in the early 2010s when it came to light that some social scientists were engaging in practices such as "p-hacking" in an effort to generate statistically significant results, in part due to a bias among social science journals toward publishing positive findings.[24] Relatedly, evidence was emerging that many published research claims in various social science fields could not be replicated.[25] Greater research openness and the evaluation it facilitates were considered important strategies for addressing these problems.

To help induce openness, various government agencies created policies and proposals calling for transparency in academic and other research.[26] In turn, as mentioned earlier, foundations and other funders of social science research, as well as academic journals, began to introduce guidelines for increasing the transparency of the research they fund and publish.

At the time that discussions about research transparency in political science were gaining new energy and urgency and broadening to include more voices,[27] few political scientists who collect and analyze qualitative data had practical experience with transparency. This lack of familiarity, as well as some scholars' impressions that their concerns about the epistemological and ethical limitations to pursuing transparency in qualitative work were not being recognized,[28] generated anxiety in some scholarly communities. The celerity with which disciplinary discussions advanced, and the initial steps taken by some journal editors to introduce openness expectations into their submission and publication guidelines,[29] compounded that unease among some scholars who generate and analyze qualitative data. To consider these concerns about transparency, beginning in 2015 at the behest of the Qualitative and Multi-Method Research section of APSA, hundreds of political scientists participated in the Qualitative Transparency Deliberations (QTD).[30] Ultimately the deliberations produced 14 working group reports examining different facets of transparency.[31]

Of course, pursuing transparency in *any* scholarship can raise concerns and pose challenges. Considering to what degree each challenge affects one's work can inform which transparency approach(es) to employ. Many of these challenges can be grouped into four categories: epistemological, practical-intellectual, professional, and ethical.

Identifying epistemologically appropriate transparency practices can present an initial difficulty. How scholars pursue transparency is significantly impacted by how they believe knowledge is generated and how they generate knowledge. Political scientists who use qualitative data and methods vary greatly in this regard: they are trained in diverse research traditions, adopt contrasting approaches to examining political phenomena, and use an array of methods to generate and analyze data. The techniques that will best reveal and showcase the intellectual foundations of different types of qualitative research vary concomitantly.[32] For instance, "sharing data" may be perfectly intelligible and achievable for some scholars whose research involves the collection of concrete evidence on which they draw to generate truth claims. Yet for scholars for whom the information generated in a research project is co-created through encounters with participants involving meaning-making, and thus in part reflects those scholars' own particular experiences, frameworks, and interpretations, the idea of sharing those empirical underpinnings may seem pointless or misguided.[33]

The best way to address this challenge is for scholars in different research traditions to continue actively thinking about and working together to develop and establish epistemologically apposite norms for openness. Small workshops at disciplinary meetings could be excellent venues for such conversations. Such norms should be direct derivatives of the logics that underpin the procedures scholars follow to arrive at findings and demonstrate their validity. Consequently, developing such norms could *also* help scholars to further develop and systematize the methods they employ.

A second set of challenges could be classified as practical-intellectual and stem from the nature of qualitative data and analysis. In quantitative analysis, with some exceptions, numerical data underlying a study are analyzed in aggregate; their analysis is presented in a table in the associated manuscript; and the aggregate data and code are shared as supplementary materials. With qualitative analysis, the data pertaining to a research project are often analyzed individually or in small groups, with references to them laced throughout the text of the associated manuscript. Making qualitative inquiry with these characteristics transparent thus requires introducing evidence and discussing its generation and analysis at multiple points in a manuscript. Moreover, some types of qualitative data—large posters, music recordings, or the vibrancy of ceremonial garb, for instance—can be difficult to "capture" and deploy in a manuscript. And even when qualitative data are textual (e.g., an excerpt from a document or interview transcript) and thus easier to integrate into a manuscript, including them can cause the length of the manuscript to exceed limits established by journals and publishers.

Fortunately, several of the techniques mentioned previously for making qualitative scholarship more transparent can help scholars address these challenges. ATI is specifically designed to allow scholars to deploy transparency-enhancing information, including links to relevant data, at exactly the points in a manuscript at which they are useful or invoked.[34] Importantly, ATI puts that information at a reader's fingertips (rather than in an appendix including all of the supplementary material accompanying an article) without overburdening the article text. ATI annotations can include links to forms of qualitative data that would be logistically challenging to integrate into article texts, and these can be curated and safely preserved in a data repository. As with methodological appendices, the material and clarifications in ATI annotations do not count against publication word-count caps.

A third set of concerns relates to academic advancement. Increasing the transparency of any form of inquiry can be time-consuming. Scholars may wonder if the opportunity costs of pursuing transparency (e.g., delay in initiating a new project or drafting another manuscript) may outweigh the benefits, particularly given that augmenting openness has no immediate professional payoff. Here scholars should keep in mind how pursuing transparency can facilitate securing funding for and publishing their work (as discussed previously). They should also consider how to capitalize on increasing the transparency of their work in ways that could advance their career, for instance, listing on their CV an original data set that they shared. More broadly, given that the "transparency revolution"—which extends far beyond the social sciences and academia[35]—is very unlikely to be reversed, scholars should spark and participate in disciplinary discussions about how to develop metrics for gauging and strategies for rewarding transparency (e.g., in evaluations of graduate students' progress and review and tenure processes).[36]

A final set of critical challenges and concerns pertains to pursuing and achieving transparency ethically and legally. These issues are broad and multifaceted. However, they may arise most often in research with human participants[37] and relate most closely to sharing research data. Any researcher who engages with human beings and uses information communicated via those interactions in their work is ethically bound to solicit research participants' informed consent to the researcher's proposed mode of interaction, topics of discussion, and approaches to managing, storing, deploying in research products, and disseminating the information produced through the interaction. Researchers are ethically obliged to amend their proposed procedures if asked to do so by participants (as long as the amended procedures remain within the bounds of what their institutional review board [IRB] approved)[38] and to adhere strictly to the agreements they reach with participants. Participants requiring anonymity or confidentiality, or researchers feeling that protecting participants requires them to redact or keep private the information participants convey, can—*and should*—impact how scholars can make their work transparent. Likewise, when data are under copyright or proprietary, they often cannot be freely disseminated.

Fortunately, some IRBs have begun to consider more carefully the intersections between research transparency and the protection of human subjects in the social sciences. These IRBs are increasingly developing options for and advice on how researchers can discuss with human participants, and help them to understand, the possibility and details of sharing the information participants convey in research encounters.[39] Engaging productively with the IRBs that have jurisdiction over scholars' research can be extremely helpful as scholars develop strategies for pursuing transparency.[40] Furthermore, some funders' proposal procedures and journal submission and publication guidelines clearly state that scholars may be exempted from sharing data when protecting human participants, or adhering to intellectual property law requires limiting the dissemination of data.[41] Consulting with personnel from and becoming familiar with the policies of all of these organizations from the early moments of a research project can help scholars to achieve transparency in epistemologically appropriate, ethical, and legal ways.

Conclusion

A key goal of social science scholarship is to produce information and results that are relevant to pressing political and social concerns and problems. Social scientists examine and elucidate a vast range of critical issues and challenges, from hunger to hostility, from corruption to climate change, from insecurity to inequality. We owe it to those experiencing these dynamics or their consequences to produce and provide accurate, intelligible, actionable information. Because social science is a collective, cumulative endeavor, we are best able to advance knowledge when we listen to and learn from each other. Showing each other how we generated and analyzed data, and sharing those data responsibly, empower intellectual progress and knowledge accumulation. Doing so also renders our work more understandable and thus more useful to society.[42]

The ethical conduct of research requires openness.[43] Accordingly, how to pursue and achieve research transparency responsibly will be a topic of discussion and debate in the discipline of political science into the future. Ongoing and focused conversation will enable us to continue creating strategies that help political scientists to capitalize on the broad range of benefits that pursuing research in a transparent way produces and to address the concerns and challenges that doing so can present. By working independently and together to develop,

Research Transparency in Qualitative Inquiry

discuss, and refine norms for openness, the multiple research traditions and epistemic communities that comprise our rich and heterogeneous discipline will devise epistemologically appropriate strategies for making all kinds of inquiry more transparent.

Notes

1. This chapter draws significantly on collaboration and work coauthored with Colin Elman and Sebastian Karcher; both were disqualified from coauthoring the chapter by the volume editors' decision to exclude male authors.
2. See, e.g., National Science Foundation, "Dissemination and Sharing of Research Results"; National Science Foundation, "Dear Colleague Letter"; National Institutes of Health, "NIH Data Sharing Policy and Implementation Guidance"; National Institutes of Health, "Request for Public Comments."
3. See e.g., the *American Journal of Political Science*'s "Guidelines for Preparing Replication Files" (4–8), https://ajps.org/wp-content/uploads/2018/05/ajps_replication-guidelines-2-1.pdf.
4. See, e.g., Jacobs, Kapiszewski, and Karcher, "Using Annotation for Transparent Inquiry (ATI) to Teach Qualitative Research Methods."
5. See, e.g., Rehak and Hmelo-Silver, "Active Learning."
6. See Gerring, "Coordinating Reappraisals" on types of "reappraisal."
7. The Center for Open Science advances and substantiates many of these claims; see their website (www.cos.io).
8. Discussions of research transparency often focus on transparency vis-à-vis one's research community, as this piece does; other audiences scholars might have in mind when seeking to make their research more open include research partners, individuals or groups they involve in their studies, or the policy community.
9. On the foundations of variation in transparency practices, see also Kapiszewski and Wood, "Ethics, Epistemology, Ethics, and Openness in Research with Human Participants."
10. See also Kapiszewski and Karcher, "Empowering Transparency."
11. See, e.g., Miguel et al., "Promoting Transparency in Social Science Research."
12. Ryan, "What Is Pre-registration For."
13. See, e.g., Yom, "From Methodology to Practice"; Kapiszewski, MacLean, and Read, "Dynamic Research Design."
14. See, e.g., Humphreys, Sanchez de la Sierra, and van der Windt, "Fishing, Commitment, and Communication."
15. See, e.g., Kern and Gleditsch, "Exploring Pre-registration and Pre-analysis Plans for Qualitative Inference"; Haven et al., "Preregistering Qualitative Research"; Jacobs, "Pre-Registration and Results-Free Review in Observational and Qualitative Research"; Pérez Bentancur, Piñeiro Rodríguez, and Rosenblatt, "Using Pre-Analysis Plans in Qualitative Research."
16. See Grossman and Pedahzur, "Can We Do Better?"
17. See Bleich and Pekkanen, "How to Report Interview Data."
18. For example, the appendix accompanying Fairfield, "Going Where the Money Is."
19. For example, the appendix accompanying Shesterinina, "Collective Threat Framing and Mobilization in Civil War."
20. ATI builds on "active citation," a transparency technique developed and advanced by Moravcsik, "Active Citation"; Moravcsik, "Active Citation and Qualitative Political Science." Developed by the Qualitative Data Repository (QDR) and the software nonprofit Hypothesis, ATI employs open-web annotation to enable the creation, sharing, and discovery of digital annotations across the web. See various webpages discussing ATI on the QDR website (https://qdr.syr.edu/ati) as well as Kapiszewski and Karcher, "Transparency in Practice in Qualitative Research."

21. For a series of revealing accounts of and pointers for using ATI, see the symposium on the technique in *PS: Political Science and Politics Political Science & Politics* 54, no. 3 (2021): 473–499.
22. See also Kapiszewski and Karcher, "Making Research Data Accessible." To view examples of qualitative data collections, visit the Qualitative Data Repository (www.qdr.org).
23. See, e.g., King, "Replication, Replication," including his citations to scholarship published in the 1980s in various social science disciplines considering data sharing and transparency.
24. See, e.g., Gerber and Malhotra, "Do Statistical Reporting Standards Affect What Is Published?"
25. See, e.g., Ioannidis, "Why Most Published Research Findings Are False" and Camerer et al., "Evaluating the Replicability of Social Science Experiments in *Nature* and *Science* between 2010 and 2015" on this so-called "replication crisis."
26. See, e.g., Holdren, "Increasing Access to the Results of Federally Funded Scientific Research"; Office of Science and Technology Policy, "Request for Public Comment."
27. For instance, in 2011 the American Political Science Association (APSA) developed the "Data Access and Research Transparency" (DA-RT) initiative, charging two working groups (one focused on quantitative inquiry and one on qualitative inquiry) to recommend clarifications to the transparency principles outlined in APSA's *Guide to Professional Ethics* (Lupia and Elman, "Openness in Political Science"). Between 2017 and 2020 an APSA Ad Hoc Committee on Human Subjects Research drafted new "Principles and Guidance" on ethics, which the APSA Council approved in April 2020.
28. See, e.g., Fujii, "Research Ethics 101"; Schwartz-Shea and Yanow, "Legitimizing Political Science or Splitting the Discipline?"; and the symposia on transparency published in the Spring 2015 issue (13, no. 1) of *Qualitative and Multi-Method Research* (the publication of the Qualitative and Multi-Method Research section of APSA) and the Spring 2016 issue (26, no. 1) of the *Comparative Politics Newsletter* (published by the Comparative Politics section of APSA).
29. Twenty-seven editors signing the "Journal Editors Transparency Statement" between 2014 and 2015 (https://www.dartstatement.org/2014-journal-editors-statement-jets) emerged as a major point of contention. In November 2015 nearly 1,200 political scientists signed a public petition (https://dialogueondartdotorg.files.wordpress.com/2015/11/petition-from-concerned-scholars-nov-12-2015-complete.pdf) calling on journal editors to delay implementing new transparency guidelines, and in January 2016, 20 former, present, and future APSA presidents sent a public letter (https://politicalsciencenow.com/letter-from-distinguished-political-scientists-urging-nuanced-journal-interpretation-of-jets-policy-guidelines/) to the journals that had signed the original Statement voicing concern about the language in the Statement and calling on editors to clarify how it would be interpreted.
30. See https://www.qualtd.net/.
31. The QTD's findings, together with summaries of working group reports, were published as a symposium: see Jacobs et al., "The Qualitative Transparency Deliberations."
32. See again the reports from the QTD working groups, which consider in detail the epistemological appropriateness of different transparency techniques for different types of inquiry (Jacobs et al., "The Qualitative Transparency Deliberations").
33. See Kapiszewski and Wood, "Epistemology, Ethics, and Openness in Human Participants Research," 4 for a related discussion.
34. For examples, see again the symposium on ATI in *PS: Political Science and Politics Political Science & Politics* 54, no. 3 (2021): 473–499.
35. See, e.g., Pera, "The Transparency Revolution and Why Business Is About to Change" and U.K. Department for International Development, "UK Leading Transparency Revolution for Empowerment and Growth" on transparency in business and government respectively.
36. "Open Research Badges"—awarded by certain journals to acknowledge that article authors used open science practices—while debated, are one option; see the Center for Open Science, https://www.cos.io/initiatives/badges.

37. The term "human participant," as used here, refers to any individuals or groups a scholar involves in their work, rather than only to "human subjects" as defined and regulated by the U.S. government's "Common Rule" (U.S. Government, Code of Federal Regulations).
38. IRBs are the ethics offices at universities and other institutions that approve scholars' plans for conducting research with human subjects.
39. Kirilova, Zhang, and Kapiszewski, "Data Sharing in the Social Sciences."
40. The data librarians in campus libraries can also be excellent sources of information and advice, as can data repositories such as ICPSR (https://www.icpsr.umich.edu) and the Qualitative Data Repository (www.qdr.org).
41. The policy articulated in the National Science Foundation's "Proposal and Award Policies and Procedures Guide" (see Chapter XI, Section D, Part 4) and the policies of two of the top journals in the discipline, the *American Journal of Political Science* (https://ajps.org/wp-content/uploads/2018/05/ajps_replication-guidelines-2-1.pdf) and the *American Political Science Review* (https://www.apsanet.org/APSR-Submission-Guidelines), are good examples.
42. This paragraph is inspired, in part, by the compelling points made in Lupia, "Practical and Ethical Reasons for Pursuing a More Open Science."
43. See, e.g., the statements on and codes of ethics of various social science disciplinary associations (e.g., the American Anthropology Association [2012] and the American Sociology Association [2018]), as well as those of the National Academies of Science (2019), all of which encourage research openness.

Recommended Readings

"Varieties of Transparency in Qualitative Research." *QMMR (Qualitative and Multi-Method Research)* 19, no. 1 (2021): 6–32, various contributions.
   This collection gathers short descriptions of the practical use, benefits, and challenges of a core set of techniques for making qualitative inquiry transparent.
"Annotation for Transparent Inquiry (ATI): Transparency in Practice in Qualitative and Multi-Method Research." *PS: Political Science and Politics* 54, no. 3 (2021): 473–499, various contributions.
   This collection includes brief articles by some of the political scientists who have pioneered the use of ATI, an emerging approach for making qualitative and multimethod research transparent, highlighting advantages, difficulties, costs, and best practices.
Jacobs, Alan M., Tim Büthe, Ana Arjona, Leonardo R. Arriola, Eva Bellin, Andrwe Bennett,... and Deborah J. Yashar. "The Qualitative Transparency Deliberations: Insights and Implications." *Perspectives on Politics* 19, no. 1 (2021): 171–208. https://doi.org/10.1017/S1537592720001164.
   This symposium summarizes the findings of the QTD (https://www.qualtd.net/); between 2015 and 2018, at the behest of the Qualitative and Multi-Method Research section of APSA, the QTD examined multiple issues related to making qualitative inquiry more open.
King, Gary. "Replication, Replication." *PS: Political Science and Politics* 28 (1995): 444–452. doi:10.2307/420301.
   Published nearly three decades ago, this piece offers a set of recommendations to facilitate "replicating" (or perhaps "reproducing") the findings and conclusions in political science scholarship.

References

Bleich, Erik, and Pekkanen, Robert. "How to Report Interview Data." In *Interview Research in Political Science*, edited by Layna Mosley, 84–108. Ithaca, NY: Cornell University Press, 2013. https://doi.org/10.7591/9780801467974-007.

Camerer, Colin F., Anna Dreber, Felix Holzmeister,... and Hang Wu. "Evaluating the Replicability of Social Science Experiments in *Nature* and *Science* between 2010 and 2015." *Nature Human Behavior* 2 (2018): 637–644. https://doi.org/10.1038/s41562-018-0399-z.

Fairfield, Tasha. "Going Where the Money Is: Strategies for Taxing Economic Elites in Unequal Democracies." *World Development* 47 (2013): 42–57. https://doi.org/10.1016/j.worlddev.2013.02.011.

Fujii, Lee Ann. "Research Ethics 101: Dilemmas and Responsibilities." *PS: Political Science & Politics* 45, no. 4 (2012): 717–723. doi:10.1017/S1049096512000819.

Gerber, Alan, and Neil Malhotra. "Do Statistical Reporting Standards Affect What Is Published? Publication Bias in Two Leading Political Science Journals." *Quarterly Journal of Political Science* 3, no. 3 (2008): 313–326. http://dx.doi.org/10.1561/100.00008024.

Gerring, John. "Coordinating Reappraisals." In *The Production of Knowledge: Enhancing Progress in Social Science*, edited by Colin Elman, John Gerring, and James Mahoney, 334–353. New York: Cambridge University Press, 2020. doi:10.1017/9781108762519.013.

Grossman, Jonathan, and Ami Pedahzur. "Can We Do Better? Replication and Online Appendices in Political Science." *PS: Political Science and Politics* 19, no. 3 (2020): 906–911. doi:10.1017/S1537592720001206.

Haven, Tamarinde L., Timothy M. Errington, Kristian Skrede Gleditsch, Leonie van Grootel, Alan M. Jacobs, Florian G. Kern, Rafael Piñeiro, Fernando Rosenblatt, and Lidwine B. Mokkink. "Preregistering Qualitative Research: A Delphi Study." *International Journal of Qualitative Methods* 19 (2020): 1–13. https://doi.org/10.1177/1609406920976417.

Holdren, J. P. "Increasing Access to the Results of Federally Funded Scientific Research." White House, 2013. https://obamawhitehouse.archives.gov/sites/default/files/microsites/ostp/ostp_public_access_memo_2013.pdf.

Humphreys, Macartan, Raul Sanchez de la Sierra, and Peter van der Windt. "Fishing, Commitment, and Communication: A Proposal for Comprehensive Nonbinding Research Registration." *Political Analysis* 21, no. 1 (2013): 11. doi:10.1093/pan/mps021.

Ioannidis, John. "Why Most Published Research Findings Are False." *PLoS Med* 2, no. 8 (2005): e124. https://doi.org/10.1371/journal.pmed.0020124.

Jacobs, Alan M. "Pre-Registration and Results-Free Review in Observational and Qualitative Research." In *The Production of Knowledge: Enhancing Progress in Social Science*, edited by Colin Elman, John Gerring, and James Mahoney, 221–264. Cambridge: Cambridge University Press, 2020. doi:10.1017/9781108762519.009.

Jacobs, Alan M., Tim Büthe, Ana Arjona, Leonardo R. Arriola, Eva Bellin, Andrwe Bennett,... and Deborah J. Yashar. "The Qualitative Transparency Deliberations: Insights and Implications." *Perspectives on Politics* 19, no. 1 (2021): 171–208. https://doi.org/10.1017/S1537592720001164.

Jacobs, Alan M., Diana Kapiszewski, and Sebastian Karcher. "Using Annotation for Transparent Inquiry (ATI) to Teach Qualitative Research Methods." *PS: Political Science and Politics* 55, no. 1 (2022): 216–220. https://www.doi.org/10.1017/S1049096521001335.

Kapiszewski, Diana, and Sebastian Karcher. "Empowering Transparency: Annotation for Transparent Inquiry (ATI)." *PS: Political Science & Politics* 54, no. 3 (2021): 473–478. doi:10.1017/S1049096521000287.

Kapiszewski, Diana, and Sebastian Karcher. "Making Research Data Accessible." In *The Production of Knowledge: Enhancing Progress in Social Science*, edited by Colin Elman, John Gerring, and James Mahoney, 197–220. New York: Cambridge University Press, 2020. doi:10.1017/9781108762519.008.

Kapiszewski, Diana, and Sebastian Karcher. "Transparency in Practice in Qualitative Research." *PS: Political Science and Politics* 54, no. 2 (2021): 285–291. https://doi.org/10.1017/S1049096520000955.

Kapiszewski, Diana, Lauren M. MacLean, and Benjamin L. Read. "Dynamic Research Design: Iteration in Field-Based Inquiry." *Comparative Politics* 54, no. 4 (2022): 645–670.

Kapiszewski, Diana, and Elisabeth Jean Wood. "Ethics, Epistemology, Ethics, and Openness in Research with Human Participants." *Perspectives on Politics* 20, no. 3 (2021): 948–964. doi:10.1017/S1537592720004703.

Kern, Florian G., and Kristian Skrede Gleditsch. "Exploring Pre-registration and Pre-analysis Plans for Qualitative Inference." Working paper, University of Essex, 2017. DOI:10.13140/RG.2.2.14428.69769.

King, Gary. "Replication, Replication." *PS: Political Science and Politics* 28 (1995): 444–452. doi:10.2307/420301.

Kirilova, Dessislava, Ying Zhang, and Diana Kapiszewski. "Data Sharing in the Social Sciences: An Empirical Study of IRB Guidance." Unpublished manuscript.

Lupia, Arthur. "Practical and Ethical Reasons for Pursuing a More Open Science." *PS: Political Science and Politics* 54, no. 2 (2021): 301–304. doi:10.1017/S1049096520000979.

Lupia, Arthur, and Colin Elman. "Openness in Political Science: Data Access and Research Transparency." *PS: Political Science and Politics* 47, no. 1 (2014): 19–42. doi:10.1017/S1049096513001716.

Miguel, Edward, et al. "Promoting Transparency in Social Science Research." *Science* 343 (2014): 30–31. doi:10.1126/science.1245317.

Moravcsik, Andrew. "Active Citation and Qualitative Political Science." *Qualitative & Multi-Method Research* 10, no. 1 (2012): 33–37. https://zenodo.org/badge/DOI/10.5281/zenodo.917652.svg.

Moravcsik, Andrew. "Active Citation: A Precondition for Replicable Qualitative Research." *PS: Political Science and Politics* 43, no. 1 (2010): 29–35. https://doi.org/10.1017/S1049096510990781.

Moravcsik, Andrew. "Transparency: The Revolution in Qualitative Research. *PS: Political Science & Politics* 47, no. 1 (2014): 48–53. doi:10.1017/S1049096513001789.

National Institutes of Health. "NIH Data Sharing Policy and Implementation Guidance." 2003. https://grants.nih.gov/grants/policy/data_sharing/data_sharing_guidance.htm.

National Institutes of Health. "Request for Public Comments on a DRAFT NIH Policy for Data Management and Sharing and Supplemental DRAFT Guidance." *Federal Register* 84, no. 217 (2019): 60398–60402.

National Science Foundation. "Dear Colleague Letter: Effective Practices for Data." NSF 19-069. May 20, 2019. https://www.nsf.gov/pubs/2019/nsf19069/nsf19069.jsp.

National Science Foundation. "Dissemination and Sharing of Research Results." 2011. http://www.nsf.gov/bfa/dias/policy/dmp.jsp.

National Science Foundation. "Proposal and Award Policies and Procedures Guide." 2020. https://www.nsf.gov/pubs/policydocs/pappg20_1/pappg_11.jsp#XID4.

Office of Science and Technology Policy. "Request for Public Comment on Draft Desirable Characteristics of Repositories for Managing and Sharing Data Resulting from Federally Funded Research." *Federal Register* 85, no. 12 (2020): 3085–3087.

Pera, Robert. "The Transparency Revolution and Why Business Is About to Change." LinkedIn, 2013. https://www.linkedin.com/pulse/20130617175247-1533676-the-transparency-revolution-and-why-business-is-about-to-change/.

Pérez Bentancur, Verónica, Rafael Piñeiro Rodríguez, and Fernando Rosenblatt. "Using Pre-Analysis Plans in Qualitative Research." *QMMR (Qualitative and Multi-Method Research)* 19, no. 1 (2021): 9–13. https://doi.org/10.5281/zenodo.5495552.

Rehak, Andi M., and Cindy E. Hmelo-Silver. "Active Learning." In *The Sage Encyclopedia of Out-of-School Learning*, edited by K. Peppler, 5–9. New York: Sage, 2017.

Ryan, Timothy J. "What Is Pre-registration For." 2021. https://timryan.web.unc.edu/2021/01/16/what-is-pre-registration-for/.

Schwartz-Shea, Peregrine, and Dvora Yanow. "Legitimizing Political Science or Splitting the Discipline? Reflections on DA-RT and the Policy-making Role of a Professional Association." *Politics & Gender* 12, no. 3 (2016): E11. doi:10.1017/S1743923X16000428.

Shesterinina, Anastasia. "Collective Threat Framing and Mobilization in Civil War." *American Political Science Review* 110, no. 3 (2016): 411–427. https://doi.org/10.1017/S0003055416000277.

U.K. Department for International Development. "UK Leading Transparency Revolution for Empowerment and Growth." Government of the United Kingdom, 2018. https://www.gov.uk/government/news/uk-leading-transparency-revolution-for-empowerment-and-growth.

U.S. Government. Code of Federal Regulations Title 45, Subtitle A, Subchapter A, Part 46, 1–35, 2018.

Yom, Sean. "From Methodology to Practice: Inductive Iteration in Comparative Research." *Comparative Political Studies* 48, no. 5 (2015): 616–644. https://doi.org/10.1177/0010414014554685.

38
Ethics of Transparency and Data Sharing

Samantha Majic

In December 2014, the journal *Science* published an article titled "When Contact Changes Minds: An Experiment on Transmission of Support for Gay Equality." Authored by Donald Green, a renowned experimentalist in political science at Columbia University, and Michael LaCour, then a graduate student in political science at UCLA, the study argued that gay canvassers—more so than straight canvassers—were powerfully persuasive with people who had voted against same-sex marriage. These findings were significant and promising for supporters of LGBTQ+ rights, as they challenged broader scholarly and social wisdom about social persuasion—namely, that people tend *not* to change their minds when presented with contrasting information. However, excitement about the study was short-lived: on May 26, 2015, the *New York Times*, among many other news outlets, reported that Green and LaCour's article misrepresented the study's methods and lacked evidence in support of its claims. Because LaCour failed to produce for Green (or anyone else) his original data, Green asked the journal to retract the study, which it did two days later, on May 28.[1]

The Green and LaCour scandal raised a number of questions in political science regarding research transparency (RT), defined broadly as "the obligation to make data, analysis, methods, and interpretive choices underlying their claims visible in a way that allows others to evaluate them."[2] While most political scientists support RT in principle, they remain conflicted about how to operationalize it in practice. As someone who has used qualitative methods of data collection—namely, interviews, participant observation, and visual materials—to conduct research about political activism and public policy related to the sex industry in the United States, I consider in this chapter the ethical and mechanical challenges of RT for qualitative researchers.[3] Drawing from my research experience and participation in the Qualitative Transparency Deliberations (QTD) process, I take a critical view of RT and data sharing, by which I mean that I do not see these as coherent and normatively agreed-upon practices. Instead, I hold that a variety of factors, including, but not limited to, the research project's epistemological orientation, the context and vulnerability of participants, and labor demands must shape how one understands and operationalizes them. As a result, I hold that debates about RT in political science remain—and should remain—unsettled, and I show how their recent manifestations in the discipline have generated many productive guidelines for scholars, reviewers, and editors alike as they conduct and review qualitative research. To illustrate, I begin with a brief overview of the discussions and debates about RT in political science, followed by a review of best and/or current practices here and suggestions for further reading.

Descriptive Overview

RT has long been central to political science research; after all, as Nancy Hirschmann writes, "[l]iving in a democracy, we tend to think of transparency as the highest good. It is the primary safeguard against corruption and abuse of power."[4] Yet, Hirschmann adds, transparency does not mean the same thing for all researchers. Debates about RT escalated as political science entered a "late methodological moment"[5] that followed the roiling methodological debates occasioned, in part, by the 1994 publication of King, Keohane, and Verba's *Designing Social Inquiry* and the 2000 Perestroika email. At this time, there were many efforts to promote and incorporate more qualitative research in the discipline, as indicated by, among other things, the 2003 founding of the Qualitative Methods section of the American Political Science Association (APSA). Yet this late methodological moment is also at a critical juncture, as advances in computing and other technologies have led field experiments and so-called big data collection and analysis to become "the newest enthusiasms that may increasingly occupy space in graduate curricula and scholarly journals."[6] Furthermore, archiving infrastructure for qualitative and quantitative data has expanded, and journals, publishers, and funders have adopted data management, archiving, and replication policies.[7]

Altogether, these developments raised questions in the discipline about the merits of qualitative and quantitative research and the limits, possibilities, and acceptable "extent" of RT in these traditions. Among the many efforts to advance RT in political science, few were more provocative than the Data Access and Research Transparency (DA-RT) initiative (see Chapter 38) and the associated Journal Editors' Transparency Statement (JETS), which the editors of 27 political science journals had signed as of March 2019.[8] Presented in 2014 as a policy endorsed by APSA, the DA-RT initiative would require "scholars not only to cite the data they generate in making claims, but also to provide other scholars with access to these data by depositing them in a 'trusted digital repository,' per JETS."[9] The only exception here was for so-called restricted data—for example, that which is classified, obtained under non-disclosure constraints, and/or must remain confidential under institutional review board (IRB) requirements. Authors must notify the journal editor about such data at the time of submission, and then the editor will decide whether to review the article or grant an exemption in line with their journal's policy.[10]

However, the problems that the DA-RT initiative was meant to solve were never addressed. While the Green and LaCour scandal indicated that data fabrication may occur in political science research, this was the exception and not the rule.[11] Fraud was the first-order concern; data availability was secondary. Not surprisingly, then, the DA-RT initiative soon sparked an avalanche of responses; at the 2015 APSA meetings in San Francisco alone, there were at least five meetings devoted to DA-RT, and a petition signed by over 1,100 political scientists called for delaying JETS's implementation.[12] Among the scholars who responded to DA-RT, those who conduct qualitative research— a category that "itself encompasses a vast range of logics of knowledge-production, methodologies, forms of evidence, and research settings"[13]— raised the most significant concerns. As Alan Jacobs et al. write, since "qualitative scholars have long taken an interest in making their research open, reflexive, and systematic, [DA-RT] provoked serious concern within qualitative research communities and raised fundamental questions about the meaning, value, costs, and intellectual relevance of transparency for qualitative inquiry."[14]

Although it is beyond the scope of this chapter to enumerate all of these concerns, the following are worth mentioning. Epistemologically, as Jeffrey Isaac wrote, the DA-RT initiative signaled "a resurgent neo-positivism within the discipline,"[15] which further privileges quantitative work, while pushing qualitative and theoretical work further to the margins.[16] Moreover, the DA-RT initiative's emphasis on RT for the purposes of "replication" ignored how this has been problematic in the natural and physical sciences, and that qualitative research is often not conducive to replication, particularly in the more interpretive tradition, given the importance of context, temporality, and researcher positionality here.[17]

Furthermore, debates about RT in the context of the DA-RT initiative raised a number of ethical and labor concerns. Regarding the former, many researchers who work with human participants inform and assure them that no one else will have access to their interview transcripts and other field notes (and often, university IRBs require these measures). These assurances are especially important for research participants who are at risk and/or marginalized as a result of their status, activities, and/or location, including their immigration status, engagement in criminalized labor, or location in a repressive regime (to name just some examples). For these participants, releasing their full interview transcripts and other materials documenting their activities and locations heightens their vulnerability to any number of consequences, ranging from deportation to incarceration. While DA-RT proponents indicated that such data may be classified as "restricted," this is often done at the journal editor's discretion, which raised alarms for scholars who were now reluctant to submit their work to various JETS-signatory journals.

Regarding labor, qualitative scholars also noted that their research is often incredibly time-consuming, as they must often develop relationships with various stakeholders and community members in order to facilitate access. These concerns resonated with me, from my research with sex worker rights activists and, later, with "john school" programs (where men arrested for prostitution solicitation may pay a fine and attend a day of classes to learn about the consequences of their actions in lieu of prosecution). Here I had to expend a significant amount of "sweat equity" to develop the relationships and trust needed to access my research sites and collect the data contained in my interview and other field notes. How is it fair to me, then, for another scholar to access my notes—which I would also have to spend additional time anonymizing and de-identifying for the purpose of data sharing—when they have done none of the (often frustrating and time-consuming) relationship-building work? Furthermore, I also offered labor in exchange for access, such as when I wrote grants for the community-based sex worker organizations I was studying in the San Francisco Bay Area. Could I guarantee that other researchers who may access my data will *also* offer something to the community/organization studied in return?[18]

State of Practice

In the context of these debates about RT, in 2015 APSA's organized section for Qualitative and Multi-Method Research (QMMR) initiated the QTD "as a venue within which qualitative scholars could deliberate the role, contribution, costs, and limitations of transparency in qualitative research ... [to] illuminat[e] areas of shared and divergent understanding across the discipline."[19] Altogether, several hundred political scientists took part in the QTD process, first through online forums, and then through 13 working groups. (I was part of Working Group IV.3, Research with Marginalized and Vulnerable Populations.) The working groups' final reports provide the most comprehensive guidance to date about how qualitative researchers may "do" RT, and I draw from these reports to outline a number of concrete practices below.

Altogether, the QTD deliberations offered a substantially more expansive understanding of "research transparency" than implied by the DA-RT discussions, which "focused almost exclusively on data sharing, transparency about evidence-generation, and transparency of analytic process." Instead, the "QTD reports point to a far wider array of features of the research process about which scholars might usefully share information with both research audiences and research participants."[20] These features are informed by the following broad principles, about which a strong consensus emerged in the QTD process. First, there exists no single "meta-standard" of RT that can operate coherently across all logics of qualitative inquiry. Second, uniform and maximalist data-sharing requirements would be highly problematic for ethical, practical, and epistemological reasons. And third, researchers' ethical obligations to protect human participants and their communities ought to take priority over the sharing of information with research consumers.[21]

In light of these principles, the QTD reports offer a number of ways that qualitative researchers may engage in RT in their presentations and publications, the first of which is being **explicit about their research project and process.** They may do this by specifying and explaining their *research goals*, such as their intellectual, political, and social objectives; their *processes of generating evidence*, such as the sites where they collected data, the locations of their sources, and the criteria upon which they selected their sources, among other things; and the *analytic processes* they used to draw conclusions from the evidence.[22] To illustrate, Renée Cramer's example from her qualitative-interpretive research with midwives in the United States is instructive:

> I should be clear, in my work, about how many field sites I had, how many hours I spent in them, how many interviews I did, and how many informal conversations in which I participated. You should know which archives I visited and where the archival and web data I found can be accessed. I should be clear about how many pages of field notes and transcripts I worked from, and how those field notes and interviews contributed to the way I searched archival material. And, as a key part of a transparent process, I should be clear about how I analyzed and interpreted those notes, transcripts, and other data.[23]

In short, as Cramer indicates, sharing details about one's research project and process in any published work offers readers access to the researcher's way of thinking and analyzing, as opposed to those who participated in the research. This insight is particularly valuable for scholars who study marginalized and/or vulnerable populations and/or do research around sensitive questions because, first and foremost, this research "can neither be replicated, nor reproduced, because it relies on *relationships*," that is, the researcher's expertise, their showing up, and their trust and capacity to share.[24] And second, direct access to interview and other notes may, as noted, compromise participants' identities and violate promises of anonymity and confidentiality, which may lead to other ethical risks, most notably exposure to potential harms, such as social stigmatization, loss of livelihood, imprisonment, torture, and even death (especially in violent or repressive political contexts).[25]

Next, as feminist scholars have long advocated and practiced,[26] qualitative researchers may be **explicit about themselves** by sharing details about their own *positionality* (for more, see Chapter 3). For example, they may reflect on how their location within power structures, especially vis-à-vis other research participants, influenced the evidence they gathered and their interpretations of it. As well, researchers may discuss their own *subjectivity* by explaining how their life experiences and individual characteristics may, for example, have influenced their data collection and analysis. These practices were very important in my research with sex workers. In my published work, I was explicit about my own position as a white, cisgender woman who, at the time, was a graduate student at an Ivy League school (and then, later, a professor) who had never engaged in sex work; this contrasted greatly with my research participants, many of whom were persons of color, transgender, economically marginalized, and engaged in criminalized activities such as prostitution. Here my position of privilege, in relation to my participants, may have shaped my data collection and analyses by, for example, potentially biasing my interpretations. However, I attempted to mitigate potential power differentials and biases by, for example, conducting interviews in locations that were comfortable for participants and by sharing my interpretations and writings with many of them.[27]

Third, qualitative researchers may detail the **risks and conflicts in their research** by discussing the *risks to human participants/communities* that their research may pose and how they managed these risks in the course of the project. They may also explain their *conflicts of interest*, including any vested interest in project outcomes, the sources of project funding, and relevant personal affiliations.[28] To illustrate the challenges and strategies here, the report from the QTD Working Group IV.2, Research in Violent or Post-Conflict Political Settings, is especially instructive. Because their research may include a range of phenomena and settings "in which the use, threat, or legacy of physical coercion imbues struggles over power, resources, and meaning, including violence by organized criminal groups," as well as research that is "conducted in contexts characterized by conflicts of these sorts," total data transparency may put research participants in danger, even unintentionally.[29] Here, for example, publishing full transcripts (even when anonymized) presents risks to interviewees themselves, as they may identify an individual or group that could cause them harm. Most violence researchers are thus wary of across-the-board transparency requirements, preferring instead to offer carefully selected quoted statements from interviewees, among other measures that err on the side of caution (for more, see Chapter 18).[30]

In addition to detailing these aspects of the research process, qualitative researchers may, in the end, decide that it is ethical, practical, and epistemologically important to engage in "full" data sharing by, for example, making available "raw" source materials such as interview transcripts. As Diana Kapiszewski and Sebastian Karcher show in their discussion of RT in practice, there are now more examples wherein qualitative scholars have successfully made their data available, such as Edwin Camp and Thad Dunning, who shared de-identified transcripts of interviews with political brokers in Argentina; they described the general region but not the specific location where the data were collected, and they restricted data access to researchers with clearly specified research plans.[31] Such examples indicate that, in making the decision to fully share data, it is essential for researchers to evaluate ethical risks. This must go beyond merely asking whether full data sharing will violate any agreements they have with the IRB and/or promises made to individual participants. The process of ethical evaluation must thoroughly consider the extent to which full data sharing may compromise the participants' anonymity and confidentiality and the potential risks that come with this. And if the participants have consented to share their identity and the full details of their research engagement (and even encouraged this sharing), the researcher must carefully consider whether and how this may harm participants in the long run, in unanticipated ways.

Altogether, the outcomes of the researcher's ethical assessment should determine whether data sharing may be maximalist, in that it shares complete material (e.g., an interview transcript), or more limited, in that it involves sharing only extended excerpts from a source text. Such sharing may occur within the body of a book or article, via a digital annotation, and/or in a posting on a digital platform or repository.[32] Furthermore, when deciding to fully share data, researchers should not ignore or minimize the potential costs that they may incur. For example, if a researcher decides to share their full interview transcripts, they will potentially have to translate/transcribe and anonymize them in preparation for sharing. And this labor is all the more onerous if the researcher is a junior faculty member facing the pressure of the tenure clock or a scholar at an institution with few or no resources to support this additional work.

Potential Problems

Even as the QTD working groups provide the most thoughtful and comprehensive suggestions for "doing" RT to date, potential trade-offs and pitfalls remain, and in this section I outline the most significant of these and offer suggestions for how to potentially engage and address them.

Among the RT practices detailed in the previous section, "full" data sharing remains the most hotly debated and contested, for many of the reasons I noted. For one, while providing readers with access to parts of the underlying evidentiary record is beneficial to assessing qualitative approaches such as content analysis, "the idea of sharing one's 'data' is not an intellectually coherent notion for ethnographers or practitioners of other interpretive methods."[33] Second, and more significant, fully sharing data may pose risks to human participants, for all of the reasons noted earlier. And third, full data sharing may have a number of potentially negative effects for researchers, including undermining the quality of the data that researchers are able to collect (e.g., requiring participants to consent to the public release of interview transcripts may introduce biases in their responses) and increasing their workload by requiring particularly labor-intensive practices such as the digitization of source materials.[34]

In light of these concerns, then, qualitative researchers must think carefully about "full" transparency. In short, as Jacobs et al. write, differentiated judgment is essential in the decision to share data as a researcher or to require this as an editor, reviewer, or funder. Namely, one must clarify here what, precisely "would be gained by asking an author to share their source materials; how much needs to be shared in order to reap these gains; what risks such sharing might pose to those whom the researcher may have an ethical obligation to protect; and how time-consuming and costly it would be for the author to make the source materials meaningfully accessible to others."[35] Of course—and especially for junior scholars—negotiating this decision with a journal editor may be challenging, given the power differentials, so editors must be sensitive to this.

Should researchers not fully share data and engage instead in the other RT practices noted above, they must be aware of other potential pitfalls and trade-offs—most notably, and seemingly mundanely, that of page limits. In short, being transparent about one's process of data collection and analysis, risks to participants, conflicts of interest, and positionality and subjectivity takes up space, which is often strictly limited in many political science journals. And space constraints are particularly challenging for qualitative researchers, who often include extensive methodological discussions and thick descriptions of their data to begin with. Altogether, qualitative researchers' potential need for longer page limits may limit where they publish in political science by forcing them to look to journals with longer page limits, as opposed to journals where their work may be a better fit and/or have a broader reach.

To address this issue, Hirschmann writes that one potential solution is "to say 'to heck with political science; we will publish in other journals,' and many political theorists, as well as qualitative comparativists, have decided to do just that."[36] However, she adds, this withdrawal "simply concedes more and more ground until there is too little left. Publication in non–political science journals reinforces the prejudice that we [theorists, and by extension qualitative researchers] are not part of the discipline, further reducing the numbers of faculty lines."[37] In response, I encourage scholars to submit their qualitative work to the growing number of highly regarded disciplinary journals that are open to it *and* do not have onerous RT requirements. For example, *Perspectives on Politics* is open to qualitative research, and it calls for manuscripts that engage a broad range of topics and methodological approaches; it was also a fitting place for my research about sex workers' civic engagement and social movement activism, which was based on interview and participant observation research, because the editor did not require me to submit all of my data and potentially compromise my participants' safety and confidentiality.[38] The *American Political Science Review*, under collective leadership at the time of writing, is also open to qualitative research, and its word limit (12,000) is more conducive to qualitative research submissions.

Of course, another solution for qualitative scholars is to simply avoid journals and their page limits and publish books instead. After all, "[t]he long-form monograph is ideal for publishing research that involves rich, descriptive ethnographic data, which is often more difficult to condense within the strict page limits of many journals."[39] And indeed, there are many books that present qualitative research that is persuasive, instructive, and thought-provoking *without* full data sharing. Some superb examples are Timothy Pachirat's ethnography *Every Twelve Seconds: Industrialized Slaughter and the Politics of Sight*; Kathy Cramer's *The Politics of Resentment: Rural Consciousness in Wisconsin and the Rise of Scott Walker*, which relies heavily on interview-based research; and Keisha Lindsay's *In a Classroom of Their Own: The Intersection of Race and Feminist Politics in All-Black Male Schools*, which offers an extensive discourse analysis of policy, news, and other documents.

But while publishing one's qualitative research in book form may be a compelling option for many scholars, this is easier said than done for many reasons. For one, the scholarly book market is also constrained by the fact that university libraries are now buying half as many academic books as they did in the 1980s.[40] And for another, the pressure in many departments to publish quickly and frequently may make book publishing challenging, particularly for junior scholars working to secure tenure and promotion.[41] However, these developments should not discourage qualitative scholars from attempting to publish books: many prestigious university presses remain extremely open to qualitative research, and if book publishing is not feasible for those early in their career, it may be an option later on.

Notes

1. Carey and Belluck, "Doubts about Study of Gay Canvassers Rattle the Field."
2. Moravcsik, "Transparency in Qualitative Research," n.p.
3. See, e.g., Majic, "'I'm Just a Woman'"; "Real Men Set Norms?"; and *Sex Work Politics*.
4. Hirschmann, "Data, Transparency, and Political Theory," 27.
5. Schwartz-Shea and Majic, "Introduction," 97.
6. Schwartz-Shea and Majic, "Introduction," 97.
7. Jacobs et al., "The Qualitative Transparency Deliberations," 172.
8. On DA-RT, see Lupia and Elman, "Openness in Political Science."
9. Schwartz-Shea and Majic, "Introduction," 98–99.
10. For more on the history of DA-RT and JETS, see Yanow, "DA-RT and Its Crises."
11. Yanow, "DA-RT and Its Crises." See also Schwartz-Shea and Majic, "Introduction."
12. Schwartz-Shea and Majic, "Introduction," 99; Jacobs et al., "The Qualitative Transparency Deliberations," 172.
13. Jacobs et al., "The Qualitative Transparency Deliberations," 173.
14. Jacobs et al., "The Qualitative Transparency Deliberations," 171.
15. Isaac, "For a More Public Political Science," 269.
16. Hirschmann, "Data, Transparency, and Political Theory," 28.
17. Yanow, "DA-RT and Its Crises," 3.
18. Majic, "Participating, Observing, Publishing," 104.
19. Jacobs et al., "The Qualitative Transparency Deliberations," 173.
20. Jacobs et al., "The Qualitative Transparency Deliberations," 177.
21. Jacobs et al., "The Qualitative Transparency Deliberations," 173–174.
22. Jacobs et al., "The Qualitative Transparency Deliberations," 176.
23. Cramer, "Trust, Transparency, and Process," 11.
24. Cramer, "Trust, Transparency, and Process," 11.
25. Jacobs et al., "The Qualitative Transparency Deliberations," 179.
26. See, for example, hooks, *Feminist Theory*.
27. Majic, *Sex Work Politics*, Methodological Appendix.
28. Jacobs et al., "The Qualitative Transparency Deliberations," 177.
29. Ana Arjona, Zachariah Mampilly, and Wendy Pearlman, "Research in Violent or Post-Conflict Political Settings (Working Group IV.2)," in Jacobs et al., "The Qualitative Transparency Deliberations," 200.
30. Ana Arjona, Zachariah Mampilly, and Wendy Pearlman, "Research in Violent or Post-Conflict Political Settings (Working Group IV.2)," in Jacobs et al., "The Qualitative Transparency Deliberations," 201.
31. See Edwin Camp and Thad Dunning, "Brokers, Voters, and Clientelism: The Puzzle of Distributive Politics," in Qualitative Data Repository (2015), doi:10.5064/F6Z60KZB, cited in Kapiszewski and Karcher, "Transparency in Practice in Qualitative Research," 288–289.
32. Jacobs et al., "The Qualitative Transparency Deliberations," 177.
33. Jacobs et al., "The Qualitative Transparency Deliberations," 185.
34. Jacobs et al., "The Qualitative Transparency Deliberations," 179–180.
35. Jacobs et al., "The Qualitative Transparency Deliberations," 185.
36. Hirschmann, "Data, Transparency, and Political Theory," 28.
37. Hirschmann, "Data, Transparency, and Political Theory," 28.
38. Majic, "Participating, Observing, Publishing," 107.
39. Schwartz-Shea and Majic, "Introduction," 99.
40. Lambert, "The 'Wild West' of Academic Publishing."
41. Schwartz-Shea and Majic, "Introduction," 99.

Recommended Readings

Jacobs, Alan M., Tim Büthe, Ana Arjona, Leonardo R. Arriola, Eva Bellin, Andrew Bennett, Lisa Björkman, Erik Bleich, Zachary Elkins, Tasha Fairfield, Nikhar Gaikwad, Sheena Chestnut Greitens, Mary Hawkesworth, Veronica Herrera, Yoshiko M. Herrera, Kimberley S. Johnson, Ekrem Karakoç, Kendra Koivu, Marcus Kreuzer, Milli Lake, Timothy W. Luke, Lauren M. MacLean, Samantha Majic, Rahsaan Maxwell, Zachariah Mampilly, Robert Mickey, Kimberly J. Morgan, Sarah E. Parkinson, Craig Parsons, Wendy Pearlman, Mark A. Pollack, Elliot Posner, Rachel Beatty Riedl, Edward Schatz, Carsten Q. Schneider, Jillian Schwedler, Anastasia Shesterinina, Erica S. Simmons, Diane Singerman, Hillel David Soifer, Nicholas Rush Smith, Scott Spitzer, Jonas Tallberg, Susan Thomson, Antonio Y. Vázquez-Arroyo, Barbara Vis, Lisa Wedeen, Juliet A. Williams, Elisabeth Jean Wood, and Deborah J. Yasha. "The Qualitative Transparency Deliberations: Insights and Implications," *Perspectives on Politics* 19, no. 1 (2021): 171–208.
  Instructive for scholars who want to learn more about the various dimensions of and approaches to RT in qualitative research.
QTD Working Group reports, available at the Harvard Dataverse, https://dataverse.harvard.edu/dataset.xhtml?persistentId=doi:10.7910/DVN/SWVFV8.
  Offers an up-to-date, detailed, and thoughtful discussion about RT and political science.
Isaac, Jeffrey. "For a More Public Political Science." *Perspectives on Politics* 13, no. 2 (2015): 269–283.
  Outlines the history of RT in the discipline, particularly in the context of the DA-RT initiative.
QMMR Newsletter 16, no. 2 (Fall 2018).
  Discusses DA-RT and the promises and limits of its conception of RT.

References

Carey, Benedict, and Pam Belluck. "Doubts about Study of Gay Canvassers Rattle the Field." *New York Times*, May 26, 2015. https://www.nytimes.com/2015/05/26/science/maligned-study-on-gay-marriage-is-shaking-trust.html.
Cramer, Kathy. *The Politics of Resentment: Rural Consciousness in Wisconsin and the Rise of Scott Walker*. Chicago, IL: University of Chicago Press, 2016.
Cramer, Renee. "Trust, Transparency, and Process." *QMMR: Newsletter of the American Political Science Association Organized Section for Qualitative and Multi-Method Research* 16, no. 2 (2018): 10–13.
Hirschmann, Nancy. "Data, Transparency, and Political Theory." *QMMR: Newsletter of the American Political Science Association Organized Section for Qualitative and Multi-Method Research* 16, no. 2 (2018): 27–30.
hooks, bell. *Feminist Theory: From Margin to Center*. Cambridge, MA: South End Press, 1999.
Isaac, Jeffrey C. "For a More Public Political Science." *Perspectives on Politics* 13, no. 2 (2015): 269–283.
Jacobs, Alan M., Tim Büthe, Ana Arjona, Leonardo R. Arriola, Eva Bellin, Andrew Bennett, Lisa Björkman, Erik Bleich, Zachary Elkins, Tasha Fairfield, Nikhar Gaikwad, Sheena Chestnut Greitens, Mary Hawkesworth, Veronica Herrera, Yoshiko M. Herrera, Kimberley S. Johnson, Ekrem Karakoç, Kendra Koivu, Marcus Kreuzer, Milli Lake, Timothy W. Luke, Lauren M. MacLean, Samantha Majic, Rahsaan Maxwell, Zachariah Mampilly, Robert Mickey, Kimberly J. Morgan, Sarah E. Parkinson, Craig Parsons, Wendy Pearlman, Mark A. Pollack, Elliot Posner, Rachel Beatty Riedl, Edward Schatz, Carsten Q. Schneider, Jillian Schwedler, Anastasia Shesterinina, Erica S. Simmons, Diane Singerman, Hillel David Soifer, Nicholas Rush Smith, Scott Spitzer, Jonas Tallberg, Susan Thomson, Antonio Y. Vázquez-Arroyo, Barbara Vis, Lisa Wedeen, Juliet A. Williams, Elisabeth Jean Wood and Deborah J. Yasha. "The Qualitative Transparency Deliberations: Insights and Implications." *Perspectives on Politics* 19, no. 1 (2021): 171–208.
Kapiszewski, Diana, and Sebastian Karcher. 2020. "Transparency in Practice in Qualitative Research." *PS: Political Science & Politics* 54, no. 2 (2020): 285–291.
King, Gary, Robert O. Keohane, and Sidney Verba. *Designing Social Inquiry: Scientific Inference in Qualitative Research*. Princeton, NJ: Princeton University Press, 1994.

Lambert, Craig. "The 'Wild West' of Academic Publishing." *Harvard Magazine*, January–February 2015. https://www.harvardmagazine.com/2015/01/the-wild-west-of-academic-publishing.

Lindsay, Keisha. *In a Classroom of Their Own: The Intersection of Race and Feminist Politics in All-Black Male Schools*. Urbana, IL: University of Illinois Press, 2018.

Lupia, Arthur, and Colin Elman. "Openness in Political Science: Data Access and Research Transparency." *PS: Political Science & Politics* 47, no. 1 (2013): 19–42.

Majic, Samantha. "'I'm Just a Woman. But I've Never Been a Victim': Re-Conceptualizing Prostitution Policy through the Complex Narrative." *Journal of Women, Politics and Policy* 36, no. 4 (2015): 365–387.

Majic, Samantha. "Participating, Observing, Publishing: Lessons from the Field." *PS: Political Science & Politics* 50, no. 1 (2017): 103–108.

Majic, Samantha. "Real Men Set Norms? Anti-Trafficking Campaigns and the Limits of Celebrity Norm Entrepreneurship." *Crime, Media, Culture* 14, no. 2 (2018): 289–309.

Majic, Samantha. *Sex Work Politics: From Protest to Service Provision*. Philadelphia, PA: University of Pennsylvania Press, 2013.

Moravcsik, Andrew. "Transparency in Qualitative Research." In *Sage Research Methods Foundations*. London: Sage, 2019. https://www.princeton.edu/~amoravcs/library/TransparencyinQualitativeResearch.pdf.

Perestroika. 2000. Email from Mr. Perstroika, October 17. Available at https://www.uvm.edu/~dguber/POLS293/articles/mrperestroika.pdf

Pachirat, Timothy. *Every Twelve Seconds: Industrialized Slaughter and the Politics of Sight*. New Haven, CT: Yale University Press, 2011.

Schwartz-Shea, Peregrine, and Samantha Majic. "Introduction." *PS: Political Science & Politics* 50, no. 1 (2017): 97–102.

Yanow, Dvora. "DA-RT and Its Crises." *QMMR: Newsletter of the American Political Science Association Organized Section for Qualitative and Multi-Method Research* 16, no. 2 (2018): 1–9.

39
Strategizing Fit and Legibility

Shantel Gabrieal Buggs and Jennifer Patrice Sims

Introduction

One of the more difficult parts of publishing research that does not tend to be readily apparent to junior scholars is the work of determining appropriate outlets. What does it mean to find the right "fit," and what does it mean to write legibly for different audiences, or even to be "legible" as a scholar? Often, "fit" refers to being qualified and being similar to others or having a sense of belonging with others[1] in an academic or workplace context. When referring to where to publish your research, this can mean accounting for which outlets will be receptive to your methods, your data, and/or your topic(s), or possibly the format of how your findings should be presented. Fit also asks us to consider what else is being published and talked about in either our own subfield(s) or elsewhere. As an exclusively qualitative methodologist (Buggs) and a mixed-methods researcher (Sims), we are familiar with a wide variety of publishing contexts and challenges. In this chapter, we utilize our experiences to provide a brief overview of the major aspects of fit and legibility that all scholars, but particularly qualitative scholars, should consider when making decisions on *where* and *how* to publish their findings.

Descriptive Overview

We break down the variety of ways that scholars conceptualize "fit" into three types: *methodological, topical,* and *genre*. By *methodological* fit, we mean alignment with an outlet's practice of publishing quantitative or qualitative work broadly as well as alignment with specific data collection methods (e.g., experimental, ethnographic, interview). By *topical* fit we mean the alignment of the subfield, keywords, theoretical framing, and so on of the paper with an outlet's stated focus on or observable history of publishing them. What we call *genre* fit refers to the alignment of the form of publication (e.g., article, book, opinion piece) with the structure, language, and word choice appropriate for that form.

Achieving good fit is also about knowing how to write "legibly" for different audiences. Effectively situating one's work in relation to prior literature or effectively presenting one's findings depends not just on clarity of methods and topic but also on the typical audience of a given genre of publication. To be "legible" as a scholar in the broader sense means to adeptly write about your work in ways in which your various intended audiences can understand and enjoy.

Legibility also can refer to perception of one as a topic expert, which can be helpful when publishing public works as well as books. In order to be invited to write for public outlets or to (convince) book publishers, you have to be visible as someone who has the topic and methodological expertise needed for that publication. For some scholars this is eased by their connections to prestigious institutions or receipt of fellowships and awards; however, emerging scholars and those with fewer academic resources do not have to be shut out of the process. In the following sections, we discuss the different types of fit and legibility, offering implementable suggestions based on our own publishing experiences, and then we identify what we see as potential problems and ways to navigate them.

State of Practice

Our priority for this chapter is to provide advice for qualitative researchers, but we recognize that "qualitative researchers" range from mixed-methods researchers to ethnographers, each of whom has particular challenges when it comes to deciding how to present findings. In addition, while we mainly focus on the genre of academic journal articles, we recognize that some methods and topics are more often presented as books and that all work has the potential to be legible as public-facing op-eds or podcasts. We include commentary on these types of publication, too, throughout the chapter as appropriate.

Methodological Fit

Probably the trickiest part to navigate with regard to fit for qualitative scholars is determining what type of outlet is best suited for the qualitative method that was used. While quantitative research can be published in just about any academic journal (and frequently also makes appearances in journalistic articles, books, policy reports, and court proceedings), qualitative research is not as broadly welcomed (for more, see Chapter 41) and thus can be more difficult to place. For example, scholars who use ethnography are often encouraged (pigeonholed) to write monographs, not articles. Ostensibly, this is to facilitate fleshing out all of their participant observation experiences in addition to any interviews and other data collected for the project. Most academic journals' word limit prevents the type of in-depth narrative presentation and theoretical development from the data that make ethnography so insightful and impactful. However, this view of methodological fit also stems from the perception among some scholars, as expressed in a review one author received, that "studies based on small, non-representative 'samples' … often amount to bad journalism and are more ideologically based than theoretically based. Nonetheless, such studies have a market that book publishers would like to serve." Despite this view, we can speak to methodological fit considerations for publishing ethnographic work in standard academic journal format. By "standard," we refer to the normative social scientific format of introduction, literature review and theory, methods, findings, discussion, and conclusion.

Buggs's first publication[2] was an autoethnographic study of her experience as a mixed-race woman who received familial pressure via social media to modify her racial presentation of herself due to blowback over an antiracist social media post. Though there are several formats for how the data of an autoethnography can be presented—vignettes of memories over time or journal entries, for example—the basic principles of reporting participant-observer data still apply (e.g., using thick description), with the addition of the author's feelings and internal narrative. When Buggs was writing the paper as a graduate student, she was aware of the need to make it seem "scientific," that is, being data-heavy rather than relying primarily on journalistic narrative. This was a significant reason why she included the text of dozens of social media posts for analysis in addition to her memories of conversations, so that there was recognizable "data" as the focus of the paper.

Of course, reactions from mentors and academic journals were mixed. In a graduate publishing class, the feedback Buggs received claimed the paper read "more like a *New Yorker* essay" than social science. When the article was submitted to *Qualitative Sociology*—a journal selected because of its prestige and the fact that it had published autoethnographic work before—reviewers suggested that the biographical material be scrapped and that the author should collect data on multiracial people living in white neighborhoods. The editor of the journal even stated that the paper did not make any significant contribution to autoethnography nor the study of race. While the article was accepted at the next journal Buggs submitted to—*Identities*, selected because of its interdisciplinary focus and critical approach to race scholarship—she used the reaction from that first submission to strengthen the section justifying the legitimacy of autoethnography as method. In citing 13 different autoethnographic articles, Buggs intended to make her methodological choices so well-defended that reviewers would not have grounds to dismiss it. In short, when trying to publish qualitative work, authors may need to use strategies such as "over-"citing to establish to reviewers and future readers that the work is legitimate. In addition, Buggs's experience points to the fact that even when publishing in outlets specializing in qualitative research, one may still need to justify methodological choices to establish "fit."

Topical Fit

Regarding interview studies, despite statistical generalization not being the goal in most qualitative work, sample size matters for fit. Content analysis in our discipline of sociology found that interview studies with large-N samples are the ones that most frequently appear in top "generalist" journals.[3] In our experience, though, topic matters too. Due to narrow assumptions about not only what counts as rigorous methodology but also what topics are of broad "general" interest, small-N interview-based work on nondominant populations are more frequently seen as having better methodological and topical fit with regional journals, subfield journals, and qualitative-methods-specific journals. One approach to assessing whether your work has topical fit with a target outlet is to determine whether your work would be "in conversation" with what has been published there. For books, this means looking at the recent publications in your discipline to see what topics the publisher covers, and then noting this in conversations with editors or in one's book proposal.

For journal articles, it is important to look at *where* and *which* scholars are publishing work on your topic right now. Journals are a key location of replies, rebuttals, challenges, and biting critiques, so we can think of publication as joining a conversation about a topic or as going to speak where people are currently discussing that topic. One way to identify this location is to take note of which journals' articles you are citing in your literature review. Aiming to publish in a journal that you frequently cite serves two purposes. First, it allows you to contribute to an in-progress scholarly conversation on your topic. Second, it is utilitarian because peer reviewers often expect that a manuscript submission will cite works from the journal as a means of "proving" the author is engaging with what has been published in that journal already.

Since any given paper has multiple topical angles, which one a scholar focuses on for fit is best directed by the literature. For example, Sims was working on a paper[4] about queer mixed-race people's views on parental consent requirements for minors versus older teens being allowed to consent for themselves. While reviewing the literature, though, she and her coauthor found little work in race journals that had previously published articles on mixed-race people; however, they kept finding amazing work studying the efficacy of various forms of consent for minors published from a specialty journal devoted to empirical research on human subjects. Though this journal had never published anything on the topic of queer mixed-race people, it was nonetheless a place where conversations about minors and consent were taking place. Thus, topically, the journal was a perfect fit. In sum, sometimes methodological fit should (or has to) be prioritized; at other times, finding where conversations on your topic are occurring—be that in a generalist, subfield, or even niche topic journal, or in a publisher's catalog—will result in an even better fit.

Genre Fit

In determining fit for qualitative work, it is important to align one's writing elements—that is, the written structure, tone, and language choice—with what is appropriate or typical for the desired form of publication (e.g., article, book, opinion piece). We call this "genre fit." When assessing genre fit between one's work and a target academic journal, one should consider how qualitative results are typically, or are required to be, presented in a given journal. There are two main ways qualitative results seem to be written up. One reports thematic findings in quantified terms, such as the percentage of interviewees who manifested a given theme or of the number of times a given code appeared in the data. Another discusses thematic findings in unquantified terms like "Many interviewees explained that...."

Some academic journals publish both styles, while others have preferences. The journal *Sociology of Race and Ethnicity* is an example of the former. Both authors have published qualitative articles in *SRE*, albeit with different styles. Sims's 2016 article[5] draws on interviews with mixed-race people in the United States and United Kingdom to assess the incidence and identity impact of being seen as racially ambiguous. Though she includes quotes from interviewees and later discusses the meaning of their experiences vis-à-vis extant theories of social experiences' impact on identity, she writes her thematic findings thus: "The majority (70 percent) of the interviewees in this sample reported frequently being asked about their race" and "When in the United States, two thirds of interviewees were frequently perceived to be Latino."[6]

By contrast, Buggs's 2017 article in *SRE*[7] does not use quantified language. Drawing on interviews with mixed-race women online daters, Buggs finds that the Black Lives Matter movement is used as a rhetorical frame to discuss race, gender, and racism. She includes quotes from interviews and later discusses how the women's experiences ultimately demonstrate how far the logics of colorblindness and anti-Blackness extend into everyday life. In presenting her results, Buggs focuses less on exactly quantifying the prevalence of given phenomena, as Sims did, and instead presents her results in language such as "few women explicitly stated" and "more white-skinned respondents had...." In sum, despite being written in different styles, both authors' qualitative articles were published in *SRE*, and based on citation and download metrics, both are being read and engaged with by scholars in the subfield.

Other journals, however, have a stated or de facto style preference regarding qualitative work that must be considered if one's work is to have genre fit there. In 2014, the editors of the journal *Addiction* (the official journal for the Society for the Study of Addiction) published a statement establishing that they prefer qualitative work to avoid "terms that have a specific quantitative meaning."[8] On the other hand, journals such as the *Journal of Marriage and Family* do not have overt editorial statements, though they nonetheless prefer to "see the numbers" in qualitative work. In Buggs's experience,[9] *JMF* reviewers indicated concern about the lack of Ns and a desire to see the prevalence of certain claims made clear; they also determined that "a sample of 30 interviews seems reasonable by qualitative standards."

To be clear, this concern from reviewers for methodological rigor is of course appropriate. However, due to the frequent privileging of quantitative over qualitative methods, qualitative journal submissions are sometimes assumed to be in unique need of being held to high standards. For example, the editors of the *American Political Science Review* recently offered comments on publishing qualitative work as part of their stated commitment to increasing qualitative submissions to the journal.[10] We see their comments as a welcome and positive step forward in decentering hegemonic quantitative logics. For instance, in their blog post they acknowledge that "some approaches do not emphasize generalizability, privileging instead the development of a deep understanding of an important phenomenon."[11] Though other common issues they describe reviewers having with qualitative submissions (such as weakness of evidence, theoretical development, and validity, or lack of transparency in concept definition and case selection) can be applied to all methodological approaches, not just qualitative ones, it is nonetheless helpful to see an editorial team provide guidance to facilitate more acceptances, not just more submissions.

For genre fit with such journals, a qualitative scholar using a small sample must take extra steps to ensure their work is seen as "sufficiently developed," a vague rigor standard that large-N work is automatically assumed to have achieved. The journal *Gender & Society* offers an example. In May 2021, they became the focus of academic criticism when they were accused of bias against small sample sizes. The editorial team attempted to clarify by publishing a statement: "Papers with exclusively interview data and fewer than 35 cases are *scrutinized carefully* to ensure there is good reason for the sample size, and *appropriate evidence* for the analytic argument" (emphasis added).[12]

Thus, genre fit for qualitative scholars means paying extra attention to what aspects of one's work (e.g., presentation of results, how sample size is framed) will be "scrutinized carefully" for "sufficient development." Even though journals may not define what these terms mean, the quantitative bias in publishing suggests that they may hold qualitative work to a standard that benefits only those with the resources (e.g., research assistants and funding to amass large sample sizes), implying such resources are evidence of scientific rigor.[13] The trade-off, then, may be that those with smaller sample sizes should clearly state the strengths and weakness of their approach and make a strong case for theoretical saturation.[14] Additionally, to be direct, one may need to avoid journals that have a reputation for being hostile to certain types of qualitative work.

As evidenced by the reviewer quoted above who likened qualitative research to "bad journalism" and opined that book publishers serve that market, there is a perception that scientific standards are loosened when it comes to publishing qualitative research in book format. However, this view ignores the rigor of academic presses' review process as well as the benefits of books having generous word limits. Sims's book proposals to Emerald Publishing,

Oxford University Press, and Polity Press all went through anonymous peer review prior to her being offered contracts to write the full manuscripts. Book proposal reviewers requested methodological revisions, such as providing more detail and clarification of the research, and theoretical revisions, such as engagement with additional literatures. Unlike reviewers of academic journal articles, however, the reviewers of Sims's book proposals, and later the full manuscript, were more knowledgeable about and less antagonistic to qualitative work. Reviewers of her proposals provided constructive criticism that helped her improve the description of her methods and her theoretical arguments. Moreover, the extended word length of books means that qualitative scholars can engage with reviewers' helpful suggestions more in depth than is typically possible in articles. Regarding requests for additional methodological transparency, it is very common for qualitative books to have a whole chapter or an appendix devoted entirely to an in-depth, reflective, and robust discussion of the author's methodology. Additionally, without the typical constraints of word limits, authors are able to go beyond tacking on a few extra citations in response to reviewers' suggestions of additional literature. For example, Sims and Njaka's book proposal for *Mixed-Race in the US and UK: Comparing the Past, Present, and Future* originally framed the book as adding to theories of the transatlanticness of mixedness; however, an anonymous reviewer commented that details on how "this work contributes to the building of global theory would be useful." With an 80,000-word limit, the authors comfortably expanded several chapters in order to engage with and demonstrate how their work fits into the global canon of mixed-race literature. In short, academic publishers' review process and books' longer word length together can facilitate the publication of qualitative research that meets and conveys hegemonic standards of scientific rigor.

For scholars who want to experiment with form or content outside of the bounds of hegemonic standards, however, there are academic book presses that will publish such work. The key is to find book series or presses that explicitly call for texts that incorporate alternative forms of presenting data or knowledge. For example, Buggs and Hoppe's 2023 edited volume, *Unsafe Words: Queering Consent in the #MeToo Era*, includes traditional academic essays, more personal essays informed by theory, and photo essays. The book was developed with the intention of speaking to academic *and* nonacademic audiences. This flexible format and even the inclusion of practitioners and activists—people who are not always socialized into academic writing—was possible due to the book series explicitly calling for such a book even though it is with a university press. Publishing qualitative work as a book, therefore, is a great genre fit for scholars who want space to flesh out complex ideas, discuss the "nuts and bolts" details of qualitative methodologies, and/or produce new and counterhegemonic forms of knowledge.

Writing qualitative pieces for audiences outside of academia includes but is not limited to writing for news outlets, online magazines, op-ed opinion pieces, and policy reports as well as newer outlets like blogging, podcasting, social media, and more. In terms of genre fit, though, public-facing writing is not conducive to the ways academics typically analyze or present qualitative data. In order to be legible to a nonacademic audience, public writing style typically uses fewer citations and less jargon and does not rely on large blocks of quotes from field notes or interviewees to illustrate a point.

Timing also diverges in academic and public writing styles. Academic genres of writing usually are initiated by scholars and are produced on their timeline with their agendas driving the focus. Publications directed toward public, nonacademic audiences tend to be related to some event that has recently occurred. For instance, both Buggs and Sims have written about multiracial people for public-facing outlets on multiple occasions. However, their self-driven research agendas, on multiracial women's online dating experiences and cultural differences in the perception of mixed-race people, respectively, are not the entry point of those public-facing publications. Instead, it was events of social and political interest which prominently featured a mixed-race person, such as U.S. Vice President Kamala Harris and Duchess Meghan Markle, that prompted public-facing venues to invite analysis of contemporary issues of personal identity, public perception, how race, gender, class, and sexuality inform identification of the self and of others, and how all of those are similar or different by cultural context. Emphasizing this current-events entry point is key when making a pitch to a public-facing outlet because if your proposed piece does not have some relevance to the current social political moment, a public outlet will likely pass.

Legibility

The different concerns regarding fit for academic and public-facing publications reminds us that a large part of all types of fit is writing legibly for the target audience. In our qualitative writing, we pay attention to both our word choice and how we connect the themes presented in the piece in order to make it legible for the intended audience. In publications for academic audiences, this looks like using succinct words and sentences to deliver a maximum amount of information in as few words as possible. Single transition words like "furthermore" communicate the same message as wordy clauses like "In addition to [topic] just discussed above." Likewise (see what we did there?), introductory sentences such as "This interview-based study examined [topic]" deliver the same amount of information as wordier ones like "In this study, interviews with participants were conducted in order to examine [topic]" yet use half of the words. While succinct writing is important for legibility in all publications because it aids readability, it is particularly important for articles because most academic journals have constraining word limits. "Short and sweet" legibility for public scholarship, by contrast, means using language that is "skim-able." For example, the editor of a public-facing online publication once changed Sims's use of the word "apoplectic" to "enraged." This was not about "dumbing down" the writing for the public but rather because legibility for public writing is more about rapid digestibility than academic work is.

In addition, we see legible qualitative work as making the interconnectedness of the findings clear to the audience. In academic writing, we use iterative language that ties parts of the piece together, for example, "as referenced above" (article) or "as stated in previous chapters" (book). Highly legible public writing, the type that online venues will accept when pitched or expect when invited, typically does not do this. Readers of public pieces, especially expert op-eds on current social or political events, are reading for information, not necessarily for connecting ideas or for theorizing. Thus, legibility for this audience involves presenting introduced topics sequentially versus circling back to earlier points; this makes the piece "flow" as one literally scrolls down the text.

Regardless of the audience, one constant regarding being legible is clearly articulating that you are an expert on your method, topic, findings, and conclusions. In academic writing this is straightforward, as there is always an author bio section as well as the legitimacy granted by virtue of being published in an academic outlet. Regarding public-facing publications, though, other methods are needed. For example, to demonstrate knowledge of the field, rather than a literature review section one should weave in references to research when appropriate, but not to the extent that a reader cannot grasp your main points by only skimming your piece. Typically, these will be included as hyperlinks, not as in-text citations. While being legible as an expert is key to successful pitching, being invited to write on your topic for the public requires having an established expertise on the subject.

Increasingly, many scholars are getting their names out as relevant experts via social media, personal blogs, podcasts, and more. Some scholars use public writing (or podcasts) as a way to further promote a recently published academic article. Others use public work as a way to make timely commentary on social issues in their area of expertise. Both approaches are effective, though it is important to note that some scholars avoid doing the latter unless they have an academic publication for fear of having concepts "scooped." Therefore, in choosing between academic and public-facing works one must consider what audiences you want to reach and your level of comfort with wider engagement with your ideas.

Potential Problems

In addition to the above-discussed issues surrounding fit regarding one's own scholarly work and goals, one potential problem is constraints due to institutional expectations. It is a pesky reality for many tenure-track and other full-time faculty (and to be honest, also for contingent faculty) that they must publish in "generalist" journals to illustrate how their work has relevance beyond their small(er) subfields. Qualitative research can be difficult to place in a generalist journal, however, for a number of reasons. Primarily, one must consider that not every "generalist" journal assumes the same "general" reader, and what subfields/topics have the most appeal to a "general" audience is neither consistent nor transparent across journals. For example, in our experience, some generalist journals want empirical articles to have a large amount of data and deep engagement with theory. The top journal in our field, *American Sociological Review*, is this type of generalist journal. Other generalist journals prefer work that is applied and/or policy-relevant, while still others favor specific subfields or regions. Moreover, all of this can change depending on the editorial team. Public writing is not prioritized in most academic disciplines, but it is increasingly becoming something scholars are encouraged to do in the interest of breaking down the barriers academic journals have introduced as a means of gatekeeping knowledge. Of course, opinion pieces for newspapers, blogs, podcasts, and newsletters[15] are not the extent of outlets for crafting content for the public.

In practice, scholars seeking to determine fit should consider both institutional expectations as well as their own goals for their work. What counts as productivity varies by institution, and thus informs how a scholar thinks about and prioritizes which outlets to submit to. Depending on the level of research activity of your university, scholarly activity can include anything from conference presentations to public writing, as well as traditional peer-reviewed journal articles or books. Expectations also vary among funding entities; some grants require projects to have policy or commercial applications.

All of these problems illustrate the trade-offs that must be navigated when publishing qualitative work. Some may experience a serious tension between the expectations of generalist journals and their own epistemological commitments. We are not suggesting that qualitative scholars avoid doing the research that moves them; however, one must balance publishing in the "expected" ways and pushing disciplinary boundaries. Many scholars are already doing this. For example, sociologists Ruha Benjamin and Tressie McMillan Cottom both published traditional academic monographs (Benjamin 2013; McMillan Cottom 2017) that met institutional expectations for tenure and promotion and then followed those books with "trade" books that, while not less rigorous, nonetheless provide a more personal and public-facing social analysis (Benjamin 2019, 2022; McMillan Cottom 2019). Ultimately, qualitative scholars should prioritize doing good work. The format that work takes—and where it fits—however, can and should vary.

Notes

1. Bean, "Nine Themes of College Student Retention."
2. Buggs, "'Your Momma Is Day Glow White.'"
3. Deterding and Waters, "Flexible Coding of In-Depth Interviews."
4. Sims and Nolen, "'I Wouldn't Trust the Parents to "Do No Harm" to a Queer Kid.'"
5. Sims, "Reevaluation of the Influence of Appearance and Reflected Appraisals for Mixed-Race Identity."
6. Sims, "Reevaluation of the Influence of Appearance and Reflected Appraisals for Mixed-Race Identity," 574, 577.
7. Buggs, "Dating in the Time of #BlackLivesMatter."
8. Neale, Miller, and West, "Reporting Quantitative Information in Qualitative Research," 175.
9. Buggs, "Color, Culture, Cousin?"
10. Austin and Dion, "Notes from the Editors."
11. Austin and Dion, "Publishing your Qualitative Manuscript in the APSR."
12. Gender and Society (@Gend_Soc), "The editorial team at Gender & Society has clarified our procedure and submission guidelines. They can be found at....," Twitter, May 27, 2021, https://twitter.com/Gend_Soc/status/1397956456897466375?s=20.
13. Gaither and Sims, "How Cross-Discipline Understanding and Communication Can Improve Research on Multiracial Populations."
14. Small, "'How Many Cases Do I Need?'"
15. For examples, look to the *New York Times* newsletter of sociologist Tressie McMillan Cottom or the cultural studies work of Anne Helen Petersen through *Vox* and her own subscription newsletter via the platform Substack.

Recommended Readings

Gerson, Kathleen, and Sarah Damaske. *The Art and Science of Interviewing*. New York: Oxford University Press, 2020.
    In the final chapter of this interviewing guidebook, "Pulling It All Together: Telling Your Story and Making Your Case," Gerson and Damaske provide information and tips on how to write up qualitative findings.

Golden-Biddle, Karen, and Karen Locke. "The Style and Practice of Our Academic Writing." In *Composing Qualitative Research*, 2nd ed., 9–24. Thousand Oaks, CA: Sage, 2006.
    This chapter (and the whole book) notes the importance of scientific writing embracing storytelling; the authors lay out a brief history and sensibility for traditional scientific writing.

Neale, Joanne, Peter Miller, and Robert West. "Reporting Quantitative Information in Qualitative Research: Guidance for Authors and Reviewers." *Addiction* 109 (2014): 175–176.
    In this editorial note, the editorial team of the journal *Addiction* provides their style expectations for qualitative submissions to their journal. Prior to doing so, the note acknowledges and discusses the conflicting views on the appropriateness and different ways of using quantified language in reporting results from qualitative work. As such, it can serve as a resource for qualitative scholars who are considering the style they may wish to use in their own work.

Reay, Trish, Asma Zafar, Pedro Monteiro, and Vern Glaser. "Presenting Findings from Qualitative Research: One Size Does Not Fit All!" In *The Production of Managerial Knowledge and Organizational Theory: New Approaches to Writing, Producing and Consuming Theory*, vol. 59, edited by Tammar B. Zilber, John M. Amis, and Johanna Mair, 201–216. Bingley, UK: Emerald, 2019.
    This chapter goes in depth regarding the different ways in which qualitative results can be presented in academic publications. While we discussed the level of quantification, since that is what academic publishers have focused on, Reay et al. detail additional facets of presenting results that scholars can consider.

References

Austin, Sharon Wright, and Michelle L. Dion. "Notes from the Editors: Increasing Qualitative Submissions." *American Political Science Review* 116, no. 2 (2022): v–vi. doi:10.1017/S0003055422000120.

Austin, Sharon Wright, and Michelle L. Dion. "Publishing Your Qualitative Manuscript in the APSR." *Cambridge Core Blog*, March 3, 2022. https://www.cambridge.org/core/blog/2022/03/03/publishing-your-qualitative-manuscript-in-the-apsr/.

Bean, John. P. "Nine Themes of College Student Retention." In *College Student Retention: Formula for Student Success*, edited by A. Seidman, 215–243. Westport, CT: Praeger, 2005.

Benjamin, Ruha. *People's Science: Bodies and Rights on the Stem Cell Frontier*. Stanford, CA: Stanford University Press, 2013.

Benjamin, Ruha. *Race After Technology: Abolitionist Tools for the New Jim Code*. Cambridge, UK: Polity, 2019.

Benjamin, Ruha. *Viral Justice: How We Grow the World We Want*. Princeton, NJ: Princeton University Press, 2022.

Buggs, Shantel Gabrieal. "Color, Culture, Cousin? Multiracial Americans and Framing Boundaries in Interracial Relationships." *Journal of Marriage and Family*, 81, no. 5 (2019): 1221–1236.

Buggs, Shantel Gabrieal. "Dating in the Time of #BlackLivesMatter: Exploring Mixed-Race Women's Discourses on Race and Racism." *Sociology of Race and Ethnicity* 3, no. 4 (2017): 538–551.

Buggs, Shantel Gabrieal. "'Your Momma Is Day Glow White': Questioning the Politics of Racial Identity, Loyalty, and Obligation." *Identities: Global Studies in Culture and Power* 24, no. 4 (2017): 379–397.

Buggs, Shantel Gabrieal, and Trevor Hoppe, eds. *Unsafe Words: Queering Consent in the #MeToo Era*. New Brunswick, NJ: Rutgers University Press, 2023.

Deterding, Nicole M., and Mary C. Waters. "Flexible Coding of In-Depth Interviews: A Twenty-First-Century Approach." *Sociological Methods & Research* 50, no. 2 (2021): 708–739.

Gaither, Sarah E., and Jennifer Patrice Sims. "How Cross-Discipline Understanding and Communication Can Improve Research on Multiracial Populations." *Social Sciences* 11, no. 3 (2022): 90. https://doi.org/10.3390/socsci11030090.

McMillan Cottom, Tressie. *Lower Ed: The Troubling Rise of For-Profit Colleges in the New Economy*. New York: The New Press, 2017.

McMillan Cottom, Tressie. *Thick: And Other Essays*. New York: The New Press, 2019.

Neale, Joanne, Peter Miller, and Robert West. "Reporting Quantitative Information in Qualitative Research: Guidance for Authors and Reviewers." *Addiction* 109 (2014): 175–176.

Sims, Jennifer Patrice. "Reevaluation of the Influence of Appearance and Reflected Appraisals for Mixed-Race Identity: The Role of Consistent Inconsistent Racial Perception." *Sociology of Race and Ethnicity* 2, no. 4 (2016): 569–583.

Sims, Jennifer Patrice, and Chinelo L. Njaka. *Mixed-Race in the US and the UK: Comparing the Past, Present, and Future*. Bingley, UK: Emerald, 2020.

Sims, Jennifer Patrice, and Cassandra Nolen. "'I Wouldn't Trust the Parents to "Do No Harm" to a Queer Kid': Rethinking Parental Permission Requirements for Youth Participation in Social Science Research." *Journal of Empirical Research on Human Research Ethics* 16, nos. 1–2 (2021): 35–45.

Small, Mario Luis. "'How Many Cases Do I Need?' On Science and the Logic of Case Selection in Field-Based Research." *Ethnography* 10, no. 1 (2009): 5–38.

40
Publishing Qualitative Research

Sara Wallace Goodman and Jennifer Cyr

Introduction

The last—but certainly not least—task a researcher faces in doing good qualitative research is publication. You did the hard, meticulous work. You formulated an interesting research question, you've collected data, you've analyzed data, you've written up your results. How do you get it published? Unfortunately, the answer is not straightforward. Qualitative work may always find a home in book publishing, but placing qualitative work in peer-reviewed journals has become increasingly difficult. The decline of qualitative studies in peer-reviewed journals can be attributed to a variety of reasons that range from methodological fads to the incentive structures that facilitate "fast research," as well as limited training in qualitative methods compared to quantitative methods.[1]

The answer to "how" to publish qualitative work in journals is also contingent on "where." Some considerations that researchers prioritize when submitting work include fit (perhaps you're submitting to a thematic or regionally oriented journal), reputation and prestige (relying on impact factor or other ranking systems), and networks (perhaps you know the editor; we need not pretend the review process is free from bias). But once you decide where to submit your manuscript and hit the "submit" button, the process is out of your hands. The *likelihood* of publication is determined by a whole host of factors: the expertise of reviewers, their disposition[2] on any given day, as well as editorial preferences.[3] Almost all these factors are outside of your control, but the choice of *where* you submit can affect your odds of success.

This chapter discusses how to publish qualitative work. In contrast to the previous chapters in this book, we reposition the lens of analysis away from the researcher (you) and move to the editors and reviewers, that is, the individuals who handle your work and determine whether good qualitative work gets published or not. We surveyed editors from a variety of political science journals,[4] asking them to share their perspectives on how reviewers handle qualitative submissions, how their journals think about qualitative work in general, and to describe what good qualitative work looks like. What we find is that standards of good qualitative work generally converge across journal type. Specifically, reviewers identify qualitative work as "good" when it identifies a general problem, makes a clear theoretical contribution, provides an explicit research design with convincing case selection, and speaks to generality and implications of findings. Some journals place a greater emphasis on causal mechanisms than others do (which may be more accommodating to descriptive work). The general impression from this editor sample suggests the decline in publishing qualitative work is on the supply side, while also recognizing the importance of having a reviewer pool that can evaluate and advocate for good qualitative work.

Before analyzing in more detail what journal practices tend to be, it is important to note that, while standards of good qualitative work generally converge across journals, there also seems to be a clear bias regarding how editors define qualitative work. Specifically, most editors we surveyed appeared to adopt a primarily positivist logic for articulating what publishable qualitative work looks like. We asked editors what types of qualitative methods they typically see in journal submissions. Some of the most frequently reported examples include cases studies, comparative historical analysis, causal and social mechanisms, and archival work. We also included interpretivism as an explicitly post-positivist item.[5] Only 8 out of 37 unique journal titles (21.6%) report "typically seeing" interpretivist submissions. These include comparative (*Government & Opposition, Journal of Common Market Studies*) and international relations (*International Organization, Security Studies, Review of International Political Economy*) journals, as well as *Perspectives on Politics*. We include this as a caveat before we proceed with an analysis of the evidence.

The Decline in Publishing Qualitative Research

Publishing qualitative work is difficult. Alan Jacobs, in drawing on data from "Mapping Methods in Contemporary Political Science Research" by Tranae Hardy, Diana Kapiszewski, and Daniel Solomon, writes, "[Q]ualitative methods have lost ground in political science's most visible outlets."[6] In looking at type of methods employed in a random sample of articles from top-10 journals between 2000 and 2009, the data, as Jacobs analyzes, reveal only 16.9% of single-method articles employ qualitative methods (inclusive of both small-N analysis and interpretive approaches). Moreover, between 2010 and 2018 this figure drops to 9.4% (mixed-method work that includes qualitative methods at 5.5%).

Journal editors are not blind to this decline. In 2010, then-editor of the *American Political Science Review*, Ron Rogowski, wrote about "getting qualitative research back into the APSR."[7] Despite this acknowledgment, and various efforts at encouraging more qualitative submissions,[8] by 2021 only "5.9% of our submissions have included only qualitative evidence, 7.9% include both qualitative and quantitative evidence." However, under the new editorial team (beginning in 2020), accepted articles that draw on qualitative methods almost doubled, from "11.7% of acceptances under the previous team to 21.5%." *American Political Science Review* editors attribute this jump to scholars "increasingly warming up to the idea that they can entrust their best qualitative work to the APSR."[9] Put simply, both reputation and editorial priorities shape where an author chooses to submit their work.

No matter what type of manuscript you have, submitting it to a peer-review journal is a significant time investment. Provided a manuscript passes desk review—where editors may choose to reject a manuscript for fit or quality or send it out for review—it can take months (sometimes a year or more!) for three reviewers (at least) to review a manuscript and return their reviews to the journal editor, and for an editor or editorial team to decide on the manuscript. And if the manuscript gets an invitation to "revise and resubmit" (R&R), you're looking at even more time. There is insufficient space here to discuss all the considerations that go into the strategy of choosing a journal for submission (scholars have a range of priorities—some want the most prestigious journal possible, some want quick review time, some want to address a specific audience, etc.), but we focus on method as a dimension of fit.

To gain a better understanding of what journals are looking for—and how reviewers evaluate qualitative work given the preponderance of quantitative work—we reached out to 74 political science journals in April 2022.[10] Our convenience sample draws from top generalist journals (*American Political Science Review, American Journal of Political Science*) to subfield (*Comparative Political Studies, International Organization*), thematic (*Political Behavior, Journal of Ethnic and Migration Studies*), and regional/area studies journals (*Journal of European Public Policy*). We received responses from 37 (yielding a 50% response rate).[11] A full list of participating journals is available in Appendix A at the end of this chapter.

We asked editors a series of questions that fall into three categories: *description* (how much qualitative work appears in a journal, whether this status quo is a priority, and if editors record submission by method), *editorial perspective* (what does good qualitative work look like, what kinds of mistakes do qualitative authors typically make), and *reviewer practices* (how do reviewers treat qualitative work compared to quantitative work). We examine each category in turn.

How "Qualitative" Are Political Science Journals?

Not all journals keep track of submissions by method type. *Comparative Political Studies, International Studies Quarterly, International Organization, Governance, Journal of Peace Research, Review of the International Political Economy,* and *PS: Political Science and Politics* were the only journals in our sample that reported that they do. (*American Political Science Review* keeps track but did not participate in the study.) We asked all editors to make an educated guess of what percentage of submissions to their journal they would characterize as using qualitative methods (as opposed to quantitative or formal methods). *Political Behavior* reports the lowest submission rate (5%), *American Journal of Political Science* and *Comparative Political Studies* were on the low end of the spectrum (15% and 18%, respectively), while some of the highest submission estimates were by *Security Studies* (80%) and *Journal of Politics in Latin America* (71%).

Given the range of journal types in our sample, we wanted to see if there was a pattern between number of qualitative submissions and journal type, depicted in Figure 40.1. We coded journal type as either general, thematic, or regional. All journals are general unless they exclusively publish on one topic (e.g., democracy, political economy) or they publish on only one region of the world (coding available in Appendix A). We see a clear pattern: the percentage of qualitative work is much higher in regional journals than in general or thematic journals, where the median hovers just above and below 30%, respectively. And though the size of our regional journal response is small, the difference is statistically significant (for nonresponse, see Appendix B).

We also asked editors whether these self-reported estimates or measures (if they record method type) of qualitative submissions represent the status quo. Put another way, have the number of qualitative submissions increased, decreased, or stayed the same in the past few years? Seven journals in our sample reported an increase in submissions in recent years: *Civil War, Europe-Asia Studies, International Studies Quarterly, Journal of Women, Politics & Policy, Social Science Quarterly,* and *Terrorism and Political Violence.* The modal response is that submission figures stayed the same, including at journals with high qualitative submission estimates (*Publius,* at 77%) and low (*Party Politics,* at 20%). Several editors reported submission declines, including *Comparative Political Studies, Governance, Government & Opposition, International Organization,* and *Perspectives on Politics.* The preponderance of outlets for comparative politics work here is notable, given the general decline of qualitative methods in comparative politics.[12]

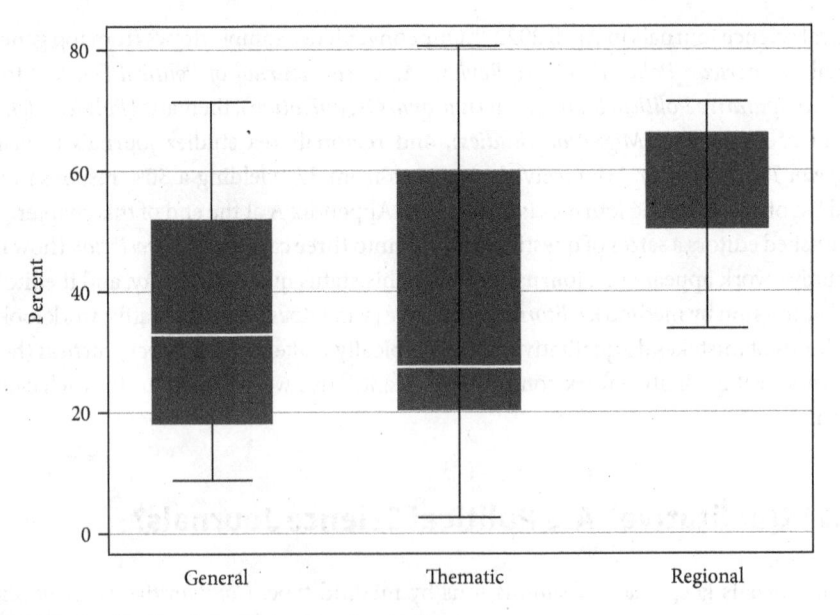

Figure 40.1 Qualitative Submissions by Journal Type.

Given the generally low submission rates of qualitative work at most journals, some editors indicated an expressed interest to offset this trend and increase submissions. These include *American Journal of Political Science, Comparative Politics, European Journal of Political Research, Perspectives on Politics, Public Opinion Quarterly,* and *Social Science Quarterly.* And, as the *American Political Science Review* example illustrates, editorial signaling can be decisive in reversing the tide.

To summarize, knowing the prevalence of qualitative work already published in a given journal as well as editorial preferences to increase qualitative submissions or not can be helpful information in determining where qualitative research is welcome. Moreover, there is a clear pattern that regional/area journals are more likely to receive qualitative submissions. These outlets are typically outside the scope of "top-10" journals (according to Hardy, Kapiszewski, and Solomon) and have lower impact factors. It is also, however, where journals appear to have a better reputation for receiving qualitative research and may be where the qualitative research "action" is. Familiarity with the type of work a journal publishes is a useful predictor for what kind of work they may be inclined to publish in the future, but a prospective author can always reach out to an editor before submission to see if their manuscript would be a good fit. Some journals also have high desk rejection rates,[13] which is another way for editors to signal potential journal fit as well as likelihood to survive the review process. While potentially stinging, *Comparative Political Studies* editors argue this quick decision respects and saves the author's time.[14]

The Editor's Perspective

What do editors define as good qualitative research? Many of our editor respondents echo the sentiments of *American Journal of Political Science* editors Kathleen Dolan and Jennifer Lawless: "We are agnostic to method. We are looking for papers that ask interesting questions and employ appropriate methods in a rigorous manner to answer those questions." In fact, several editors wrote that they perceived quantitative and qualitative work similarly, emphasizing that rigor and rules of transparency (*Public Opinion Quarterly, Politics & Gender, Journal of Common Market Studies*) apply to good work in all positivist approaches. Editors at *Journal of Peace Research, Political Behavior,* and *Journal of Conflict Resolution* all echo the emphasis on causal mechanisms, with the last writing, "Careful process tracing of causal mechanisms in select cases to illustrate and assess quantitative or experimental findings." An editor at *Governance* contextualizes this emphasis by writing that research should contain "[w]ell structured research design, clarity of causal mechanisms and sound sources of information." Related, an editor at *State Politics and Policy Quarterly* writes that " 'high-qualitative' research will address an important question (often a policy-related one) in a rigorous fashion." In general, where editors responded to the question, they typically underlined the importance of matching the method to the research question at hand, being explicit about the approaches and design choices, and rigorous testing.

Few editors called out specific attributes of qualitative research that would distinguish its quality from quantitative submissions. An editor at *Comparative Politics* emphasizes the importance of "original research—use of extensive fieldwork, interviews, participant observations. Clear theory." Nevertheless, some factors may be systematically different in qualitative work. An editor at *Security Studies* writes specifically about how word count can be a factor in shaping even the possibility of qualitative work getting published, especially for certain kinds of qualitative methods: "Because we permit rather long articles, it is a rare journal in our field that has the space to publish detailed archival research. However, we also get excellent work based on field research and interviews." Drawing from my (Goodman) own experience of publishing archive work, the use of appropriate and consistent citation style for referencing archive boxes and documents ate up most of my word count, requiring an exemption from the editor for publication.[15] To wit, an editor at *International Studies Quarterly* writes, "One disadvantage for qualitative work is that it frequently requires more writing, which can be difficult when working with a maximum word count. This means that much of the actual qualitative work—not just the summary or analysis—is put into an online appendix and not part of the published article."

Given that the definition of quality work is ambivalent to method type, we asked about features of qualitative work a second way. We asked editors to respond to the question "What are some of the mistakes that you find qualitative scholars commonly make in the articles they send in for review?" Many editors pointed to "insufficient level of details regarding case selection, interviews, etc." (*Governance*) or not "enough justification for the selection of a certain qualitative method for the purpose of testing a theory/hypotheses" (*International Studies Quarterly*). An editor at *Comparative Politics* gives examples, like "vague methodological approach; reference to 'original interviews' without any discussion of how these interviews were done (how interviewees were chosen, how interviews were conducted, etc.)." An editor at *Journal of Ethnic and Migration Studies* writes that "the main weakness in qualitative research is usually a lack of precision in method," using the example "Sometimes qual researchers think it is OK to just say I did ethnography, without offering specific details, whereas the burden of proof for methods should actually be as high as it is for all research." To use a concrete example, if an author does not provide a reviewer with information on how interviewees are selected, or what accounts for the number of interviews, for instance, a reader may be unable to determine whether a saturation point was reached in data collection and hypothesis testing. Put another way, "lack of description of each step" (*International Political Science Review*) and "insufficient attention to how data is gathered and analyzed" (*West European Politics*) are the most common mistakes qualitative researchers make in submitting manuscripts. This observation triangulates the previously mentioned emphasis on rigor and transparency. Other editors mentioned the lack of considering alternative explanations (*Political Studies Quarterly*) and overgeneralizing (*Political Studies Review, PS: Political Science and Politics*).

If we were to summarize the editors' perspective here, we can identify several common mistakes that might serve to build a sort of pre-submission checklist. Awareness of these pitfalls may increase the likelihood of success for qualitative manuscripts. These, of course, are good standards of practice for any type of research. They include articulating a clear and well-focused research question; supporting that question with a well-articulated research design; presenting a carefully developed theoretical argument; providing explicit, precise, and detailed discussion of methodology, including a clear justification of case selection; and discussion of findings in a broader context of larger questions (i.e., the "So what?").

Evaluating Qualitative Work

Recall that we did not survey reviewers, but we were able to ask editors how they read reviewer comments on qualitative articles, including what strengths and weaknesses reviewers typically point out. Editors read a lot of reviews and are also, of course, reviewers themselves, so we are confident these comments are reliable proxies. As such, a lot of comments about what they think reviewers pick up on echo their sentiments as editors. By and large, editors agree that reviewers see the strength of qualitative work as its empirical richness. As a weakness, they mostly identify reviewers focusing on questions of research design, including appropriateness of case selection (i.e., issues of selection bias, generalizability concerns, ability to test alternative hypotheses) as well as details of and precision in methods. An editor at *ISQ* highlights how reviewers pick up on design correspondence, that is, "whether the specific qualitative work (case studies, content analysis) pursued is the most appropriate for the analysis, as well as the depth and rigor of the work." An editor at *POP* describes this succinctly as "logic of argument, fit of evidence." Meanwhile, an editor at the *Journal of Common Market Studies* offers, "My sense is that with qualitative research the whole is examined more which gives depth to the review. Quantitative evaluations get more bogged down by the minutiae."

On this note, we asked editors to consider whether—from their perspective—the standards for reviewing articles that use qualitative methods are different from those that utilize other methods. As an editor at *Political Science Research and Methods* carefully notes, it is a difficult comparison "since the quantitative and qualitative reviewer pools don't overlap all that much." Still, we solicited editor opinions based on what they see, to build a general picture of reviewer expectations in reading qualitative manuscripts. Table 40.1 arranges editor responses by journal, sorted by whether qualitative and quantitative works are reviewed by similar standards (*left*) or different standards (*right*). For different standards, we quote editors or explain the difference when an answer is provided.

We see an even distribution in our sample between journal editors who see similarities and differences in review standards. Among those who identified different standards, some focus on the specifics of reviewing a specific methodological approach (e.g., robustness checks on quantitative analysis), while others focus on the ability of reviews to assess or advocate for good qualitative work. One particular concern worth flagging is that reviewers may not have "precise" standards for assessing qualitative work (in the words of an editor at *Governance*).

Table 40.1 Identifying Similarities and Differences in Review Evaluation, by Journal

Similar standards	*American Journal of Political Science*
	Comparative Political Studies
	International Political Science Review
	Journal of Ethnic and Migration Studies
	Journal of Conflict Resolution
	Journal of Peace Research
	Party Politics
	Political Studies Review
	PS: Political Science and Politics
	Public Opinion Quarterly
	Publius
	Research & Politics
	Security Studies
	Terrorism and Political Violence
	The Review of the International Political Economy
Different standards	*Civil Wars*: qual reviewed at higher standard
	Comparative Politics: "Reviewers reviewing qualitative manuscripts seem to focus less on methods and more on case studies themselves and theory."
	Governance: "reviewing standards [for qualitative work] are sometimes less precise
	Government & Opposition: "I have never seen a qualitative paper asked to include additional controls or robustness checks."
	International Studies Quarterly: "It's much easier to assess the validity and appropriateness of using certain quantitative methods to test certain hypotheses, while it's harder to assess the best qualitative methods for the same purpose."
	Journal of Women, Politics & Policy: "We have fewer reviewers who can assess qualitative manuscripts accurately and appropriately."
	POP: "Less abstruse methodological criticism in qualitative methods reviews."
	Political Behavior
	Political Science Quarterly: "They are different in that quantitative articles have different formal methodological requirements in evaluating the evidence."
	Politics & Gender: "Well-designed qualitative studies are well-received by reviewers, particularly when the author(s) explains their methods with sufficient detail"
	Social Science Quarterly: greater emphasis on theory and hypothesis development in qualitative work
	State Politics and Policy Quarterly: "more attention and emphasis tends to get placed on the theoretical contribution(s) of the manuscript and less so on the empirical contribution(s)."
	West European Politics: qualitative work subjected to more uneven standards

This brings us full circle to an observation presented at the beginning of the chapter: there are limited opportunities to receive qualitative training and, due to the decline in qualitative publications overall, a decreasing number of examples that reviewers not familiar with reading or producing qualitative work can learn from as a template for reviewing new work.

Getting to Submission

So what can you do to publish your good qualitative work? This chapter has indicated that a lot about the last stage of the research process—publication—is not entirely up to you. Nevertheless, there are certain things you can do to increase the likelihood that your good, qualitative work finds a home.

For one, you can embark on the submission process with an awareness of which journals publish work like yours. This is not simply thematic or regional matching but also a matching of methods, submitting with an eye toward editors' practices and preferences. Past publishing practices are not always the best predictor of future publishing intentions. Has the journal made explicit overtures to increase qualitative work? Are you seeing more and more qualitative work come out in a journal that does not have a reputation for methodological pluralism? If you don't know if your manuscript is a good fit for a given journal, ask. (If you're a graduate student, start by asking your advisor or a trusted professor.)

Next, if you determine that a particular venue is amenable to qualitative work, run through the checklist of "easy pitfalls to avoid." Is your research question clear? Have you been explicit about how the research design and data collection methods answer this question? Have you justified your case selection choices? Have you considered alternative explanations, where applicable? Have you addressed the larger implications of your work? Have you explicitly articulated and justified the approach your work takes? Can you cite work similar to yours to demonstrate precedent and publishability? None of these questions guarantees publishing success, but they will make your research clearer and more accessible, which may increase your odds.

You can also help your manuscript along by suggesting potential reviewers. Many editors remarked at the challenges of finding qualified reviewers. You can make the editors' job much easier by recommending your own reviewers—and many of them! Ethical standards require that you not identify colleagues with whom you work closely, but often senior scholars will signal that they are happy to review work like yours. Recommend them, and often! Who else do you know who has published work like yours? Recommend them! Who do you cite or admire as a scholar? Recommend them! On the other hand, who have you heard is generally unfair or a figurative "Reviewer 2"?[16] Leave them off the list. You can increase the publishing odds by recommending reviewers who will look favorably upon your work. Sometimes the submission software will invite you to list reviewers; sometimes this is information you'll want to include in your cover letter.

Finally, publishing good qualitative work, like all of the stages in the process of doing good qualitative work, requires strategy and perspective. Are you striving for perfection before you hit "Send" on your article? Recall that the publishing stage can be extended and even take years. And, although we know that you (yes, you!) can do good qualitative work, we strongly recommend that you resist the urge to make your paper as perfect as possible. Knowledge construction is subjective, and what you may think the article needs before it is "ready" to send off to the publisher may not accord entirely with what the reviewers think. You should strive to make your article the best it can be, to be sure. Doing *too much*, alternatively, can be a waste of your precious time.

So how to know when an article is ready? It is always helpful to share your work with others before sending it off. Conferences, working groups, peer-based writing exercises, trusted advisors—these are all excellent venues for workshopping your article. Next, you must assess the kind of feedback that you are receiving. Do the comments, generally speaking, reflect the "pitfalls to avoid" questions elucidated above? If so, your article likely needs more work. Or are the comments mainly positive, even if they are critical? More directly, do your informal peer reviewers think your work is ready to be reviewed? If so, then it may be time to set your own criticisms aside and send it off.

Finally, your peer networks will be vital for navigating the publishing waters. Share with them your publishing experiences, no matter how awful. Tell your friends and advisors what happened, even if (especially if!) you were rejected. We all have horror stories when it comes to the kind of feedback a negative review can entail. Sharing these stories can be remarkably cathartic. It also normalizes one of the most common and most difficult aspects of doing good qualitative research: rejection. Perhaps most strategically, these exchanges with colleagues are incredibly informative. Which journals are quick in turning around a review? Which ones are less responsive? Are the editors generally helpful? Acquiring this knowledge can increase your odds of a favorable review process in the future.

In the end, a lot of success in publishing good qualitative research comes down to luck. Several editors, for example, point to the importance of matching reviewers by methodological expertise (as opposed to simply subject matter). For example, the editor of *Perspective on Politics* writes, "In reviewing and publishing quality qualitative research it is important to choose high quality qualitative readers and readers from other traditions who are not methodologically imperialist. There are still some people who still dismiss rigorous well-designed qualitative work out of hand." An editor of *Review of International Political Economy* concurs, noting that because the journal predominantly publishes qualitative work, they "tend to seek reviews from predominantly qualitative reviewers who are able to assess the strengths and weaknesses of qualitative work." In short, the odds of receiving an appropriate reviewer for your manuscript requires a careful and committed editor, but this is not always going to be the case. Oftentimes your success is a matter of chance. To be sure, if you offer up suggestions of reviewers, as we recommended, you increase the likelihood of a good "match" between your article and your (eventual) reviewers.

So let's save our consternation and dedicate our energy to the things we have control over. The aim of this book was to help you produce good qualitative work. We have sought to cover—to the extent possible—the full arc of the research process, from developing a research question to, finally, finding a venue that will project your findings out into the world. The contributors have harnessed their extensive experience and knowledge to articulate myriad actionable steps that you can take to maximize each of the phases of the process. In sum, we have sought to help you produce high-quality, qualitative work while taking into account ethics, positionality, and strategy.

Ultimately, research is about producing and/or constructing knowledge. It is about adding to what we can know about the world around us. As we close this last chapter of the book, we would implore that you not lose sight of this goal. It is remarkably easy to get lost in the sometimes arduous tasks of selecting cases or sites, talking with others, actively observing, deriving an argument, making meaning, analyzing, thinking, writing. As you set off to do your own good qualitative research, remember that our primary task as researchers is to help humanity *know more*. Our work will be important, meaningful, and potentially impactful if we can keep that task in sight.

Appendix A

Appendix A Participating Journals, by Type

Journal Type (1= general; 2 = thematic; 3 = regional)	Journals
General (1)	American Journal of Political Science
	Comparative Political Studies
	Comparative Politics
	Current History
	European Journal of Political Research
	Governance
	Government & Opposition
	International Feminist Journal of Politics
	International Organization
	International Political Science Review
	International Studies Quarterly
	Perspectives on Politics
	Political Science Quarterly
	Political Science Research and Methods
	Political Studies Review
	PS: Political Science and Politics
	Research & Politics
	Social Science Quarterly
Thematic (2)	Civil Wars
	Journal of Conflict Resolution
	Journal of Ethnic and Migration Studies
	Journal of Peace Research
	Journal of Women, Politics & Policy
	Party Politics
	Political Behavior
	Politics & Gender
	Public Opinion Quarterly
	Publius
	Security Studies
	State Politics and Policy Quarterly
	Terrorism and Political Violence
	The Review of the International Political Economy
Regional (3)	Europe-Asia Studies
	Journal of Common Market Studies
	Journal of European Public Policy
	Journal of Politics in Latin America
	West European Politics

Appendix B

Journals That Did Not Respond to the Survey

African Affairs, American Politics Research, American Political Science Review, Asian Survey, BJPIR, BJPS, Canadian JPS, China Quarterly, Democratization, Electoral Studies, European Union Politics, European Journal of International Relations, Human Rights Quarterly, International Affairs, International Interactions, International Journal of Middle Eastern Studies, International Relations, ISR, JEPOP, Journal of Politics, Journal of East Asian Studies, Journal of Modern African Studies, Latin American Perspectives, Latin American Politics & Society, Latin American Research Review, Legislative Studies Quarterly, Middle Eastern Studies, Policy Studies Journal, Political Communication, Political Psychology, Political Research Quarterly, Political Studies, Politics and Society, Post-Soviet Affairs, Presidential Studies Quarterly, Studies in American Political Development, Studies in Comparative International Development.

Notes

1. Emmons and Moravcsik, "Graduate Qualitative Methods Training in Political Science."
2. And there is evidence that men review work by women more harshly. See Krawczyk and Smyk, "Author's Gender Affects Rating of Academic Articles."
3. Beyond subject matter, there is evidence that women authors experience more representation in journals edited or coedited by women (representing 52% of contributors, compared to 15% of female authors represented in journals edited by men) (Mathews and Andersen, "A Gender Gap in Publishing?").
4. We limited our scope to political science, as we view adjacent social science disciplines, like sociology and anthropology, as more accommodating to qualitative work.
5. We also included discourse analysis, but we believe this is a noisy signal. While qualitative methodologists predominantly understand this method of analysis to be post-positivist (see Chapter 35), we do not assume journal editors see it the same way. To wit, 48% (18 out of 37 unique journals) report receiving discourse analysis submissions.
6. Jacobs, "Letter from the Section President," ii.
7. Rogowski, "Getting Qualitative Research Back into the APSR," 2.
8. Rogowski, "Getting Qualitative Research Back into the APSR," 2. See also Elman, "Give Pieces a Chance."
9. "Notes from the Editors," v–vi.
10. This project qualifies as an Exempt Self-Determination status according to University of California, Irvine's IRB protocols. IRB #1143 (approval March 18, 2022).
11. There are hundreds, if not thousands of political science journals. As a convenience sample, we acknowledge the inferential limitations of a nonrepresentative sample.
12. Pepinsky, "The Return of the Single-Country Study."
13. Garand and Harman, "Journal Desk-Rejection Practices in Political Science."
14. Specifically, they find "the majority of papers that we desk reject are not published after more than six years, appear in journals with a lower impact factor than CPS, and/or obtain fewer citations" (Ansell and Samuels, "Desk Rejecting," 689).
15. Goodman, "'Good American Citizens.'"

16. The so-called "Reviewer 2" has gained infamy for writing the harshest and perhaps least fair or justified comments among what are typically three reviewers. Being a "Reviewer 2" means that, for whatever reason (lack of time or interest, ego, intellectual fragility, etc.), a person comes off as unusually harsh in their comments. Having knowledge of these kinds of reviewers can be crucial to setting the reviewer odds more in your favor, although it is often harder to identify the harsh reviewers than it is the more generous, fair ones.

References

Ansell, Ben W., and David J. Samuels. "Desk Rejecting: A Better Use of Your Time." *PS: Political Science & Politics* 54, no. 4 (2021): 686–689.

Elman, Colin. "Give Pieces a Chance: Submitting Manuscripts to the APSR." *Qualitative and Multi-Method Research* 8, no. 2 (Fall 2010): 3–4.

Emmons, Cassandra V., and Andrew M. Moravcsik. "Graduate Qualitative Methods Training in Political Science: A Disciplinary Crisis." *PS: Political Science & Politics* 53, no. 2 (2020): 258–264.

Garand, James C., and Moriah Harman. "Journal Desk-Rejection Practices in Political Science: Bringing Data to Bear on What Journals Do." *PS: Political Science & Politics* 54, no. 4 (2021): 676–681.

Goodman, Sara Wallace. "'Good American Citizens': A Text-as-Data Analysis of Citizenship Manuals for Immigrants, 1921–1996." *Journal of Ethnic and Migration Studies* 47, no. 7 (2020): 1–24. doi:10.1080/1369183X.2020.1785852.

Jacobs, Alan. "Letter from the Section President." *Qualitative and Multi-Method Research* 19, no. 2 (Fall 2021–Spring 2022): ii.

Krawczyk, Michał, and Magdalena Smyk. "Author's Gender Affects Rating of Academic Articles: Evidence from an Incentivized, Deception-Free Laboratory Experiment." *European Economic Review* 90 (2016): 326–335.

Mathews, A. Lanethea, and Kristi Andersen. "A Gender Gap in Publishing? Women's Representation in Edited Political Science Books." *PS: Political Science & Politics* 34, no. 1 (2001): 143–147.

"Notes from the Editors: Increasing Qualitative Submissions." *American Political Science Review* 116, no. 2 (2022): v–vi. doi:10.1017/S0003055422000120.

Pepinsky, Thomas B. "The Return of the Single-Country Study." *Annual Review of Political Science* 22, no. 1 (2019): 187–203. doi:10.1146/annurev-polisci-051017-113314.

Rogowski, Ronald. "Getting Qualitative Research Back into the APSR." *Qualitative and Multi-Method Research* 8, no. 2 (Fall 2010): 2–3.

Index

For the benefit of digital users, indexed terms that span two pages (e.g., 52–53) may, on occasion, appear on only one of those pages.

Tables, figures and boxes are indicated by *t*, *f* and *b* following the page number

Abdelaaty, Lamis, 64
abductive reasoning, 96–97, 98, 102–3, 111
Abrego, Leisy, 318–19
abstraction, 75
access, accessibility, 3, 6–7, 173, 437
   from below, 124
   digital technology and, 323–24, 330, 332
   direct, 126
   to elites, 184, 187–88
   to field, 114–15
   participant, 138
   proxy, 126
   to research populations, 122–28, 195–96, 197–98, 211, 212
   risk and, 126–28, 183
   trust and, 124, 125–26
accompaniment, 318
accountability, 118, 157, 436
ACLED (data set), 75–76
action, transformative, 26
activism, 26–27, 28, 157
Addams, Jane, 351
Adobe Acrobat, 366–67
affect, 16–17, 20–21, 21n.14
agency, 53, 54, 55, 56, 210, 213, 389. *See also* knowledge, knowledge production
agreement, 89
Ahmed, Sara, 26–27, 415
Albrecht, Holger, 125
alignment, 4, 5
alliances, 377
allyship, 280
ambiguity, 135, 148, 308–9, 311, 318–19, 413
Amenta, Edwin, 397
American Political Science Association (APSA), 215
   Data Access and Research Transparency (DA-RT) initiative, 447–48
   "Principles and Guidance for Human Subjects Research," 209
   Qualitative and Multi-Methods Research (section), 2–3, 438, 448–49
   Qualitative Transparency Deliberations (QTD), 438, 448–51
Andreas, Peter, 349, 354–55
Annotation for Transparent Inquiry (ATI), 173, 437, 439

anonymity, 172, 192, 245–46, 267, 268, 439–40, 449, 450–51
Ansell, Christopher K., 379
Ansoms, An, 300
anthropology, 25, 266, 399, 402
   fieldwork and, 112–13
   Indigenous peoples and, 275–76, 281
   researcher and, 27
   See also ethnography
anticolonial scholarship, 25, 26–27
antiracist scholar-activism, 26–27
Anzaldúa, Gloria, 309
appendices, 436–37
appropriateness, 65, 66
arbitrariness, 79
archive, archival analysis, 63, 80, 81, 151–52, 171, 255–57, 399, 415, 468
   challenges of, 261
   collections, 257
   digital access, 261, 324
   as field site, 114, 117
   finding aids, 259
   indexes, 259, 259*f*
   navigating, 257–61
   provenance, 257
   research guides, 259–60
Arieli, Tamar, 124
Arino, Miguel A., 427–28
Arnold, Matthew, 39
associations, 74–75
assumptions, 72, 74, 81
Atlas.TI, 368
attentiveness, 308, 311–12, 313, 318–19
audience, 462
Austin, J. L., 414–15
Autesserre, Severine, 352
autoethnography, 113–14, 234, 309, 457–58. *See also* ethnography

Backe, Emma Louise, 331
Bakhtin, Mikhail, 415
Banks Protest data/CNTS Data Archive, 75–76
Barnes, Nicholas, 173
Bartels, Larry, 199–200
Bartolomei, Linda, 213
Basbøll, Thomas, 352–53, 356

Index

Bates, Robert, 38–39, 166
Bayesian logic, 42–43, 392
Beckmann, Matthew, 184
behavioral turn, 1–2
Behl, Natasha, 289–90, 292
Ben-Ari, Adital, 139
Benjamin, Ruha, 463–64
Bennett, Andrew, 61
Berg, Christian, 44
bias, 1–2, 158, 316
   archives and, 256–57, 261
   in comparative historical analysis, 403
   during data collection, 127, 148, 149
   digitization, 261
   false consensus, 229
   in interviews, 184, 185–87, 188, 190
   minimizing, 328
   in minoritized research, 290, 301
   nonresponse, 123
   open-ended questions, 247
   p-hacking and, 438
   power and, 133
   quantitative, 459–61, 468
   reinforcement, 261
   sampling, 126
   selection, 123, 125
   source, 261
   survival, 261
   systemic, 81
   transfer, 261
Black feminism, 24, 25, 28–30, 289
Black radical scholarship, 25
Blatter, Joachim, 64
Blee, Kathleen, 318
Bleich, Erik, 437
Bonanno, George, 312–13
Boolean algebra, 422, 426, 428
Bos, Angela L., 249
Bosk, C. L., 310
Bouka, Yolande, 292, 293–94
boundaries, 136–37
Bourdieu, Pierre, 132–33, 137–38
Brady, Henry E., 2
Brannen, Julia, 214
broker, 139
Brown, Nadia, 289–90, 292
Bruneau, Thomas, 350
Brunner, Claudia, 138
Buchanan, NiCole, 301
Buggs, Shantel Gabrieal, 457–58, 459–60, 461–62
Bunche, W. E. B., 286–87
burnout, 300, 301, 302

Camp, Edgwin, 450–51
Campbell, David, 54
Campbell, Rebecca, 214
care, 139, 308
Carpenter, Charli, 377–78
Carter, Robert T., 301
case, case study, 2, 4, 42, 61, 72, 76–77, 77t, 468

   appropriateness, 65, 66
   case selection, 61, 63–68, 79–80, 89, 147, 197, 386, 400–2, 403
   comparative, 72, 76, 386, 398
   counterfactuals, 79
   cross-case comparison, 43, 45, 63–64, 88
   feasibility, 65–67, 68
   formal modeling and, 81
   generalizations and, 75–76
   identifying, 62
   inference and, 62–63, 68
   interest and, 65, 67–68
   iteration and, 401–2
   logic of, 149–50
   observational study and, 78–80
   qualitative comparative analysis (QCA) and, 422, 423, 424–25
   sequencing and, 402
   sets and, 422, 424–25
   size of, 61–62, 66
   temporal analysis of, 402–3
   types, 63–64
   within-case study, 42, 43, 45, 428
causality, 62, 63–64, 72
   asymmetry and, 423, 426
   in case study, 81
   causal graph, 389–90, 389f, 391
   causal mechanism, 38, 40–45, 63, 79, 81, 88, 146, 386, 468
   chronology and, 78
   complexity and, 422, 423, 425
   conjunctural causation, 423, 426
   constitutive, 96–97
   context conditionality, 40–41, 42
   description and, 349–50, 353
   discourse and, 417
   equifinality and, 423, 426
   experiment and, 74, 75
   granular view of, 233
   hypothesis and, 88–89
   inductive reasoning and, 403
   inference and, 68, 76, 397, 428
   interpretivism and, 96–97
   over long periods of time, 398
   multicausality, 380–81
   outcomes and, 400–1, 423, 424
   in observational studies, 74–75
   research design and, 85–93
   as unidirectional, 103
casual process observations (CPOs), 2, 172
censorship, 192
Center of Qualitative and Multimethod Inquiry (Syracuse University), 167
Charnysh, Volha, 404
chronology, 78
Cite Black Women, 294
clarity, 65, 91, 103, 197–98, 236, 356, 435–36, 456
class, 28, 41–42
   minoritization and, 286–88
   power and, 191

classification, 38
close reading, 2, 43–44, 45, 339–47, 394
   cherry picking and, 345–46
cognizance, 403
Cohen, Dara Kay, 74–75
Cohen, Nissim, 124
Cojocaru, Lee, 64
Coleridge, Samuel Taylor, 39
collaboration, collaborative methodology, 156–58, 162, 309, 404, 435–36
   benefits, 162
   positionality and, 158
   research design and, 158–60
   trade-offs, 160–62
Collier, David, 2, 76, 391
Collier, Ruth Berins, 76
Collins, Patricia Hill, 289
colonialism, 25, 27, 138, 159, 162, 279
   intellectual, 311
   labor and, 27
commitment, 5, 16–17, 118, 134–36, 156–57, 161, 210, 233, 234, 239–40, 308–9, 311–12, 325, 331, 332, 398, 403, 410, 435, 436. *See also* ethics; rigor
communication, 311–12
communication networks, 117
communication studies, 309
community, 303, 435–36
   community-based organizations, 316–17
   community-based participatory research, 316–17
   insiders and outsiders, 139
   meaning-making and, 111
comparative historical analysis (CHA), 2–3, 74, 76–77, 77t, 397–404, 468
   experiment and, 80
   observational study and, 78–80
comparative politics, 401
comparison, 62, 63–64, 66, 72, 74, 76, 78, 89, 354, 422–24
compatibility, 72, 81–82, 89, 158, 160, 290, 317–18, 428
competence, 308, 311–12, 313, 318–19
complexity, 42, 63, 223, 353–54, 373, 413, 422–23, 425
complicity, 318
concept, concept analysis, 2–3, 52, 61, 63, 76, 87–88, 250
   development, 146, 386
   discourse and, 414–15
   formation, 2, 100, 102
   mismatched, 79
   stretching, 76
conditions
   INUS, 426
   SUIN, 425
confession, 26–27, 30
confidentiality, 192, 267, 268, 439–40, 449, 450–51
configurative approach, 76
conflict, 41, 42, 51, 148, 289–90, 302, 308. *See also* collaboration
conflict of interest, 450
conflict research, 123, 124–25, 127–28, 160, 208, 210, 266–69, 272–73, 299, 300

consent, 138–39, 171, 197–98, 208–9, 213, 215, 265–66, 439–40
   informed, 267–68
   oral, 267–68
constructivism, 38, 111–12, 116, 351
content analysis, 43, 56–57, 111, 149, 361–70
context, contextualization, 40–41, 42, 50, 74, 100, 146, 210, 223–24, 234–35, 236, 237, 240, 266–67, 279, 370, 398
   close reading and, 340, 341–42
   discourse and, 410–11, 413–16
   of fieldwork, 112
   in interviews, 184
   sensitivity, 308
Contextual Text Coding, 366–67
contingency, 50, 91, 210, 389, 467
contradictions, 99, 102, 146, 148, 211, 225, 308
control group, 265–66, 269
conversation, 102, 117, 126, 146, 183, 184–85, 190, 191, 196, 197, 198, 199–200, 202, 203, 222, 223, 226, 227, 229, 231n.18, 234, 237–39, 268–69, 270, 271, 272–73, 308–9, 317, 340, 458–59
Cooley, Alexander, 379
Cornwall, Andrea, 317
Correlates of War, 350–49, 377
correlation, 43–44, 74–75
counterfactuals, 390–91
COVID-19 pandemic, 91, 104, 113, 114–15, 323, 324, 331
Cramer, Katherine, 158
Cramer, Renée, 449
creativity, 352, 356
credibility, 328, 330, 417, 435–37
culture, 37, 39–40, 41–42, 43–44, 45

data, data collection, 2, 90–91, 135–37, 145–48, 152, 166–67, 168–70, 168f, 223, 386
   accessibility of, 173
   anonymizing, 172, 267, 268
   bias and, 148, 149
   big data, 361–62, 447
   calibration, 424
   case study and, 149–50
   causality and, 40–41, 45
   coding, 172, 248
   data management plan (DMP), 166–75, 435, 437
   descriptive, 80
   digital collections and, 323–32
   emic approach, 222–23, 224
   ethics and, 437
   extraction, 114
   fabrication, 446, 447
   fieldwork and, 112–13, 114
   "framing data," 112–13
   generalizing, 148–49
   generating, 293–94b
   historical, 255–61
   induction and, 38–39, 40
   interpreting, 137–38, 148–49
   as intimate, 111

data, data collection (*cont.*)
　iteration and, 146–47, 170, 249–52, 265, 271
　limitations of, 149
　as messy and contradictory, 148
　metadata, 171, 173, 214–15, 293–94, 413
　modular, 150–51
　money and, 151–52, 175
　networks and, 376–81
　objectivity and, 90
　observational, 403
　organizing, 171–72
　positionality and, 149
　power and, 135–38
　processing, 172
　protecting, 171
　question-based, 227–28
　reflexivity and, 294
　sampling and, 149–50
　saturation, 127, 149–50, 228, 328
　sharing, 172–73, 203, 437, 438, 446–52
　"soaking and poking," 147–48
　social, 222, 224, 229
　sources, 72, 148–50
　stopping, 149–50
　storing, 116–17, 171–72, 267, 268
　strategies, 290–93
　text-based, 151–52
　"thick data," 111
　triangulating, 81, 148–49, 159
Data Access and Research Transparency (DA-RT), 157, 447–48
Davenport, Christian, 293–94, 301
D'Cruz, Heather, 25
de Vries, Lotje, 169–70, 310
decolonialism, 162, 279, 280, 281
Dedoose (software), 368
deductive reasoning, 75, 98, 170, 392–94
Defoe, Daniel, 39
depth, 76
description, 62, 76, 78–79, 80, 86, 349–57, 399
　assumptions, 352–53
　comparison and, 354
　complexity and, 353–54
　"inconvenient facts," 354–55
　participants and, 355
　perspective and, 355
　qualitative social network analysis (QSNA) and, 380–81
　surprise and, 355–56
　thick, 99, 100–1, 104, 351
　thin, 351
design, 85–93
　challenges and solutions, 92–93, 101–4
　competing explanations, 89–90
　contingency plans, 91
　core concept and variables, 87–88
　data collection and analysis, 90–91
　hypothesis, 88–89
　interpretive, 96–104
　methodology, 100
　question and, 86
　researcher and, 91
　stakes, 86–87
desire, 29
Desmond, Matthew, 233
Dewey, John, 352–53
Dickens, Charles, 41
digital, 113, 117, 118, 151, 203–4, 240, 261, 279, 323–32, 339, 437, 447, 451
Directed Acyclic Graphic, 76–77
disability, 286–88, 292
discourse, discourse analysis, 52–55, 56, 410–17
　authoritative, 415
　critical, 410, 412
　Foucauldian, 410, 412
　material domain and, 412
　quantitative analysis and, 416
　ruptures and transformations of, 415–16, 417
　sites of, 411
Disraeli, Benjamin, 44
dissertation, 13, 14–15, 17–18, 19
divergence, 72, 86, 148
diversity, 6, 25–26, 51–52, 64, 68, 166, 186–87, 227, 290, 331, 332, 427, 436
Dolan, Kathleen, 470–71
Dolnik, Adam, 267–68
domination, 26–27, 28, 29, 54, 133, 136–38, 140, 412. *See also* power
Doty, Roxanne, 96
Driscoll, Jesse, 210, 214–15
Du Bois, W. E. B., 286–87
Duffield, Mark, 126–27
Duncombe, Jean, 214
Duneier, Mitch, 200–1
Dunning, Thad, 450–51
dynamism, 75, 115, 119, 210, 373–75, 399–400

Eckstein, Harry, 38, 63–64
education, 37, 39, 41–42, 43–44, 45
El Kurd, Dana, 301–2, 303
elites, 183–92
　access to, 187–88
　economic, 189
　political, 189
　professional, 190
Ellis, Carolyn, 312, 313
Eloy Terena, Luiz, 280
Elzubeir, Margaret Ann, 225–26
embodiment, 28, 29–30, 137, 255, 318
emotion, 17, 124, 125, 132, 133, 212, 213, 271–72, 300, 311, 312–13, 314*t*, 316, 317–19, 327. *See also* burnout; passion; trust
endogeneity, 74–75
Enloe, Cynthia, 354
Enosh, Guy, 139
epistemology
　Eurocentric, 27
　hierarchies of, 27
　intepretivist approach to, 4
　power and, 25–26, 28–29, 30–31
　reflexivity and, 25, 28–29
　See also knowledge, knowledge production

Index **483**

ethics, 4, 6, 101, 122, 132, 133, 138, 160–61, 162
  of care practice, 308–10, 311–19
  of data sharing, 173, 437
  of digital fieldwork, 329–31
  of elite interviews, 188
  of fieldwork, 117–18, 127–28, 135–37, 138–39
  of interviewing vulnerable populations, 209, 210, 211–12, 213, 215, 267–68, 272–73
  mindful, 311, 317–18
  procedural, 308, 310–11
  situational, 309
  of transparency, 439–41, 446–52
  of working with Indigenous peoples, 275–76, 279–81
ethnicity, 56, 286–88, 290–91, 292, 294
ethnography, 14, 74, 75–76, 77t, 125–26, 149, 151–52, 233–42, 355, 399, 415
  accidental, 293–94
  analyzing, 242
  conducting, 236–39
  digital, 240
  experiment and, 78
  fieldwork and, 112–13
  generalizations and, 76
  grounded theory, 308
  limits of, 239–42
  listening and, 198, 233
  rapid assessment procedures, 112–13
  time requirements of, 235–36, 241
Eurocentrism, 27, 52
evidence, 168–70, 391–92
experiment, experimental study, 74, 75, 77t, 352, 403–4, 436
  comparative historical analysis and, 80
  ethnography and, 78
explanation, 64, 349–50
exploitation, 310–11
extractivism, 156, 159, 160–61, 162, 275–76, 279–80, 303

Fairclough, Norman, 410–11
Fairfield, Tasha, 172–73
Falleti, Tulia, 40–41, 397
Farge, Arlette, 255–57
feasibility, 61, 65–67, 68
Feinstein, Brian, 402
feminism, 96, 101, 134, 157, 288, 289–90, 309, 311–12, 351, 354. *See also* Black feminism
Fenno, Richard, 353
Ferguson, Kennan, 275
Ferrario, Beatrice, 246
fetishization, 27
fieldwork, 23, 25–26, 111–12
  access and, 114–15, 122–26, 138
  accountability, 118
  considerations, 114–15
  costs of, 328
  data collection, 135–37, 145–51, 152, 166–75
  digital, 323–32
  emotions and, 317–19
  ethical issues of, 117–18, 127–28, 135–37, 308–19
  financial constraints, 119
  funding, 151–52
  "game plan," 115–16
  with high-risk populations, 265–73
  immersion and, 328–29
  inclusivity and, 332
  interviews and, 191–92
  iteration and, 146–47, 170, 265, 271
  local networks, 325
  mental health and, 299–304
  as minoritized researcher, 290–93
  nontraditional sites, 113–14
  notes, 326
  participants' rights, 267
  populations, 122–28
  positionality and, 111, 117, 118, 133–34, 330
  power and, 118, 132–40
  preparing for, 115–19, 133–35
  purpose statement, 115–16
  as relational, 112–13, 114–15, 117–18, 119, 132–37, 278
  safety and, 301–2, 329–30
  saturation signal, 116
  "soaking and poking," 147–48, 339, 353, 392–94
  space of, 112, 113–15, 117
  temporality of, 112–13, 114–15
  trauma and, 300
  vulnerability and, 330
figshare (data repository), 437
Finnemore, Martha, 355–56
flexibility, 4, 5, 91, 98–99, 102–3, 104, 135–36, 138–39, 151, 152, 245–46, 312–13, 314t, 327–28, 377–78, 379–80, 436
focus groups, 74, 196–97, 222–23, 225b, 225–26, 230, 355, 399
  challenges of, 228–30
  moderator, 226–27, 229–30
  questions, 227–28
  understanding groups, 223–25
formal models, 75, 76–77, 77t, 81
formal theory evaluation, 428
Fortna, Virginia Page, 352
Foucault, Michel, 51, 55–56, 132–33, 137–38, 411
frames, framing, 339–45
  absent, 340, 344–45
  discourse and, 413
  dominant, 340, 342–44
Freire, Paulo, 137–38
Fu, Diana, 355
Fujii, Lee Ann, 122, 184–85, 209–10, 214, 308–9, 413
Fuller, Alison, 379

game theory, 77t, 81, 386
García-Castro, Roberto, 427–28
Gaskell, Elizabeth, 41
gatekeepers, 15–16, 114–15, 122–23, 187–88, 212, 290–91
Gaventa, John, 132
gaze, 138. *See also* positionality; reflexivity
Geddes, Barbara, 17
Geertz, Clifford, 351
Gelman, Andrew, 352–53, 356

gender, 28, 137
    centering female-identified voices, 157
    knowledge construction and, 56
    minoritization and, 286–88, 292
    nonbinary/genderqueer, 6–7
    objectivity and, 157
    power and, 191
    in qualitative research, 6–7
    researcher, 270, 302
    systematic sexism, 138
genealogy, 24, 413
generalization, 44–45, 63, 72, 75–76, 87, 100, 148–49, 228, 229, 245–46
George, Alexander, 61
Gerring, John, 61, 62–63, 64, 65, 349–51, 352, 353
Gillam, Lynn, 209, 308, 310
Gilligan, Carol, 311–12
GIS (Geographic Information System), 324
Gissing, George, 41
Glas, Aarie, 294
Glawion, Tim, 169–70
Global South, 184, 280, 287, 324, 332
Goertz, Gary, 2–3, 65
Goetze, Richard B., Jr., 350
Golden, Anne, 24
González, Yanilda, 148–49
González-López, G., 311, 318–19
Gordon, Kelly, 413
GPS (Global Positioning System), 324
Green, Donald, 446, 447
grounded theory, 14
groupthink, 229
Grundtvig, Nicholai Frederik Severin, 39
Gryzmala-Busse, Anna, 400–1
guides, 265–66, 268, 269–70, 272
Guillemin, Marilys, 308, 310
Gyllembourg, Thomasine, 41

Hall, Richard, 184
Han, Enze, 290–91
Harbin, M. Brielle, 290–91
Hardy, Tranae, 468
harm, 111, 116, 118, 127, 208–9, 210–11, 212, 214–15, 225, 229, 267, 291, 292, 308–9, 310, 312, 314*t*, 330, 449, 450–51. *See also* ethics; risk
Harris-Perry, Melissa, 291–92
Harvard Dataverse, 437
Harvey, William, 184
Haverland, Markus, 64
Hayward, Clarissa, 135
Heath, Sue, 379
Henderson, Francis, 290
Herrera, Veronica, 150
Herron, Michael C., 64
Hirschel-Burns, Danny, 331
Hirschmann, Nancy, 447, 452
historical political economy, 398
history, 50, 55, 63, 80, 276–77. *See also* comparative historical analysis (CHA)
Hobson, John M., 52
Holberg, Ludvig, 39
Holland, Alisha, 64
Honein, Gladys, 225–26
Hoppe, Trevor, 461
Hsiung, Ping-Chun, 184
humility, 159, 356
Hummel, Calla, 302, 303
Hundman, Eric, 377–78
hypothesis, 38, 40–41, 42–43, 45, 63, 64, 74, 76, 88–89
    causality and, 88–89, 169
    description and, 169
    generating, 63–64
    identifying, 387–88
    interpretivism and, 98
    rejecting, 147
    revising, 170
    rival, 89–90, 392, 393*t*
    testing, 75, 79, 103, 146, 147, 169–70, 239–40, 391–92, 393*t*, 428

identity, 25–26, 300, 301–2
    classification, 28
    politics of, 25
    power and, 97, 191
    in research, 28, 97, 99–100, 117, 118, 158
    structural basis of, 24, 26, 29
    See also positionality
imagined community, 54
immersion, 38–39, 111, 112–13, 114, 198, 233, 300, 328–29, 339
imperialism, 27, 56
inclusion, 5, 6–7, 157, 435–36
Indigenous feminism, 30
Indigenous peoples, 275–81
    in academia, 276–77
    ontologies, 277–78
individualism, 26
inductive reasoning, 38–39, 40–41, 76, 81, 98, 170, 392–94, 402, 403
inference, 40, 42–43, 62–63, 68, 76, 80, 85, 380–81, 397, 428
Institute for Qualitative and Multi-Methods Research, 2–3
institutional review board (IRB), 114, 122, 124, 127, 138–39, 158, 159, 197–98, 210, 212, 265, 266–69, 270, 272–73, 276, 308, 325, 439–40
intermediary, 326
international relations
    comparative historical analysis and, 397
    construction of knowledge and, 52
    feminist, 354
    positivism and, 103
interpellation, 412
interpretation, interpretivism, 4, 56–57, 96–104, 111, 139, 146, 148–49, 233, 277, 288, 289–90, 339–40, 392–94, 410–16, 468
    abductive reasoning and, 96–97, 98
    causality and, 96–97
    challenges of, 101–4
    critical, 96, 101
    feminist, 96, 101
    flexibility and fluidity of, 102–3, 104

identity and, 97, 99–100
positionality and, 97
positivism and, 103
sharing research findings, 101
trustworthiness and, 99–101, 103
intersectionality, 134, 135, 289–90
interviews, 63, 80, 102, 111, 146, 149, 169–70, 355
  access and, 183, 184, 187–88, 195–96, 197–98, 211, 212
  analyzing, 201–3
  anonymizing, 192
  bias and, 184, 185–87, 188, 190
  compensation for, 199–200, 210
  elite, 183–92, 399
  ethics of, 208–9, 210, 211–12, 213, 215
  giving back, 211–12, 278–79, 311
  group, 196–97
  iteration and, 271
  listening and, 195–204, 214–15, 271–72
  metadata, 214–15
  positioning strategies, 188–90
  power and, 183, 184–85, 190–91, 209, 278
  preliminary, 146
  questions, 198–99, 200, 214
  recording, 200–1
  relational, 209–10, 214–15, 278
  resource constraints, 186–87
  setting, 199, 213
  sharing, 203
  time and, 150–51, 198, 199, 201, 213
  toehold, 184
  transcribing, 152, 201, 202
  with vulnerable populations, 208–15
intimacy, 40–41, 111, 112–13
Isaac, Jeffrey, 448
Isaqzadeh, Mohammad, 331
iteration, 61, 146–47, 170, 249–52, 265, 271, 401–2, 430. *See also under* fieldwork

Jacobs, Alan, 447, 451, 468
jargon, 146
Jessop, Julie, 214
Jesús da Silva, Glicéria, 280
Jewkes, R., 317
Johnston, Brenda, 379
Jones, Martyn, 25
Journal Editors' Transparency Statement (JETS), 447, 448
justice, 113, 138, 140, 156, 208–9, 210, 212–13, 280, 308, 310, 412

Kalyvas, Stathis, 353
Kapiszewski, Diana, 91, 92, 146–47, 450–51, 468
Karcher, Sebastian, 450–51
Karnieli-Miller, Orit, 136
Keck, Margaret E., 354, 376
Keohane, Robert O., 353, 447
King, Gary, 353, 447
Kipling, Rudyard, 44
Kipnis, Kenneth, 209, 212
Knott, Eleanor, 210

knowledge, knowledge production, 21n.13, 25, 72
  in action, 317
  agency and, 53, 54, 55, 56
  collaboration and, 156–57
  as constructed, 24, 49, 50–57
  core-periphery divide, 184
  decontextualized, 103
  as emancipatory, 101
  epistemic violence, 138
  epistemological location and, 133–35
  Eurocentrism and, 52
  expanding, 435–36
  gender and, 56
  Indigenous self-production of, 276–77, 279
  intepretation and, 56–57
  justice and, 138
  language and, 52–54, 55–56
  local, 104, 187–88
  marginalized and, 56, 57
  as mediated, 410
  objectivity and, 49–51, 55–56, 57n.9
  politics of, 310
  positionality and, 25, 28–29, 51–52
  power and, 28–29, 30–31, 51, 53–56, 410
  reflexivity and, 25
  self and, 20–21, 132
  as social, 132
Koehler, Kevin, 125
Kohli, Atul, 398, 400
Kostocicova, Denisa, 210
Kottow, Michael H., 210–11
Kuehn, David, 424–25

lab model, 2
LaCour, Michael, 446, 447
Lake, Milli, 213
Lange, Mathew, 397
language, 234–35
  academic, 159–60
  analyzing, 361, 362–70
  close reading, 339–40
  constantive utterances, 414–15
  discourse and, 410–11, 413–15
  Indigenous, 277
  in interviews, 270–71
  knowledge and, 52–54, 55–56
  performative utterances, 414–15
  as socially constructed, 96, 100
  veiled, 146
large-N study, 40, 43–44, 62–63, 64, 67, 68, 373, 458, 460
Latin American Studies Association (LASA), 280
Latino Caucus in Political Science (Sector Latino de Cienca Politica), 288–89
Latour, Bruno, 355
Lawless, Jennifer, 470–71
learning models, 43
legibility, 456–57, 462–63
Lemon, Alaina, 237
leverage, 18–20
Liamputtong, Pranee, 212
Lieberman, Evan S., 65, 398, 400–1, 402–4

Lijphard, Arend, 63–64
listening, 37, 40–41, 195–204, 214–15, 271–72, 278, 311–12
literature, 39–40, 41, 42, 43, 44, 45
literature review, 86–87, 458, 462–63
Loff, Bebe, 209
logical operators, 422
Lucas, Chris, 404
Lucid (platform), 251
Lukes, Steven, 132
Lynch, Julia, 40–41

Macklin, Ruth, 210
MacLean, Lauren M., 91, 92, 146–47
Mahoney, James, 2–3, 49, 397, 403–4
Majic, Samantha, 213
Malthus, Thomas, 41
mapping, 74
marginalization, 57, 123, 138, 156, 162, 210, 286, 310. *See also* minoritization
market, 16, 20, 21n.12
Markle, Meghan, 461–62
Masterson, Daniel, 127
Mawhinney, Janet, 26–27
MaxQDA (software), 366–67, 368–70
Maxwell, Rahsaan, 213
Mayka, Lindsay, 148–49, 150, 151–52
McClendon, Gwyneth H., 74, 80
McMillan Cottom, Tressie, 463–64
meaning, meaning-making, 45, 54, 55–56, 96, 102, 104, 111, 222, 355–56
  discourse and, 410–11
  interpreting, 339–47
  as social, 223
  underlying, 351
measurement, 2, 74
Mechanical Turk (platform), 251
mediator, 139
Meng, Anne, 75
mental health, 299–304
mentorship, 288–89, 294, 302–3, 304, 310
Microsoft Office, 362–63, 366–67
Mill, John Stuart, 63–64, 89
Miller, Reuben J., 310–11
minoritization, 286–94
mixed methods, 43, 44–45, 64, 72–77, 81–82, 249–51
  combinations, 78–81
  identifying level of analysis, 76
  purpose and, 76–77
modeling, 75
Moore, Barrington, 61–62
moral philosophy, 309
Morse, Yonatan, 184
Mosley, Layna, 184
motivation, 29, 146
Mourad, Lama, 127
Mukurtu (platform), 279

narrative, 63
Naseemullah, Adnan, 14, 400

nation, nation-state, 54–55, 56, 191, 279
National Commission for the Protection of Human Subjects of Biomedical and Behavioral Research, "Belmont Report," 208–9
National Conference of Black Political Scientists, 288–89
native informant, 27, 290
natural sciences, 25, 49
necessity, 422, 425, 426, 427, 428
network
  boomerang model of, 376
  boundaries of, 379–80
  relationships and, 373–81
  visualizing, 378–79, 380
neutrality. *See* objectivity
Nexon, Daniel H., 379
Nietzsche, Friedrich, 50, 51
Njaka, Chinelo L., 460–61
Nobles, Melissa, 300
Noddings, Nel, 311–12
norms, normativity, 5, 29, 50, 51, 52, 53, 62, 91, 101–2, 111–12, 116–17, 118, 137, 266–67, 286, 287, 292, 352, 439
notes, note-taking, 238–39, 242
nursing, 26, 309
NVivo (software), 202, 368

Oana, Ioana-Elena, 424, 427–28
objectification, 27
objectivity, 1–2, 23–24, 25–26, 40, 49–51, 55–56, 57n.9, 61, 90, 156–57, 158, 159, 350–51, 354–55, 410. *See also* bias; positivism
O'Brien, Jodi, 309
observation, observational study, 74–77, 77t, 85, 111, 151–52, 403, 414
  case study and, 78–80
  levels of, 76
  participant, 198, 234, 355, 415, 416
O'Donnell, Guillermo, 16
Ohl, Dorothy, 125
Omata, Naohiko, 127
oppression, 28–29, 137–38
oral history, 111
Orientalism, 53–54, 58n.41
outcomes, 17, 38–39, 40, 42, 62, 63–64, 74–75, 76–77, 79–80, 81, 85, 86, 87–88, 89, 92, 169–70, 373–74, 375–76, 386, 388, 389, 390, 400–1, 402–3, 422–26
outliers, 42, 79

Pachirat, Timothy, 126, 127–28, 158
Padgett, John F., 379
Parkinson, Sarah E., 127, 375–76, 377–78
participant observation, 198, 234, 355, 415, 416
participatory action research (PAR), 113, 157–58
passion, 16–17, 20–21
Patana, Pauliina, 76
patterns, 349, 361
Paxton, Pamela, 289
Pearce, Ruth, 300
Pearlman, Wendy, 124–25, 183

Pekkanen, Robert, 437
People of Color Also Know Stuff, 294
perception, 28–29, 53, 195, 234, 250–51, 286–87, 293, 314t, 414
performativity, 26–27, 54
persistence, 398
perspective, 146, 222, 265, 327, 351, 355
Pessach, Liat, 136
Pillow, Wanda S., 26–27
pilot study, 186
Pion-Berlin, David, 350
Pivot Table, 368
political science, 14
  behavior and, 1–2
  comparative historical analysis and, 397
  culture and, 45
  discourse analysis and, 411–12
  elision of researcher, 23–24, 25–26
  experimental research, 436
  Indigenous peoples and, 275–81
  interpretive turn, 2–3
  methodological approaches in, 73–81
  normativity and, 352
  political methodology, 2
  positivism and, 23–24
  positivism and, 103
  power and positionality in, 158
  Profession Symposium on Engaged Research, 158
  Profession Symposium on Quantitative and Qualitative Collaborative Methodologies, 158
  qualitative methods and, 1
  relationality and, 29
  research transparency and, 438, 440–41, 446–52
  single-country studies, 63
population
  hard-to-reach, 122–28
  involving, 124–25
  locating, 124
  sampling frame, 123
  vulnerable, 448, 449
positionality, 23–24, 25–26, 28–30, 31, 66, 97, 236–37, 279–81, 286, 290, 300, 301–2, 309, 310–11, 313, 318, 327, 330, 354–55, 450
  close reading, 340, 342
  in data collection, 149
  in fieldwork, 111, 117, 118, 133–34
  as intersectional, 134, 135
  knowledge and, 51–52
  power and, 25, 28, 29–30, 134–35, 157, 158, 191, 450
  vulnerability and, 210
  See also power
positivism, 4, 23–24, 96–97, 99, 103, 116, 288, 290, 350–51, 355–56, 386, 448, 468
postcolonialism, 52
power, 25, 26–27, 132–40, 156, 157, 160, 310, 330
  asymmetry, 183, 184–85, 190–91, 192, 229–30
  bias and, 133
  circulation of, 132–33, 136, 136t
  competition for, 133
  dilemma of, 122, 127–28

discourse and, 410, 412, 415
epistemology and, 25–26, 28–29, 30–31
exercising, 132
fieldwork and, 118, 132–40
flexibility and, 135–36, 138–39
identity and, 97
knowledge and, 28–29, 30–31, 51, 53–56, 410
marginalized communities and, 156, 157, 159, 278
minoritization and, 286–88
positionality and, 25, 28, 29–30, 134–35, 157, 158, 191, 450
qualitative social network analysis and, 373, 374–75
relationality and, 375
sharing, 317
silence and, 137–38
subjectivity and, 23, 24, 25–26, 27
vulnerability and, 209
See also positionality
power resources theory, 38
pragmatism, 68, 91, 351
Prakash, Aseem, 354
preregistration, 436
privacy, 329–30
privilege, 24, 26–27, 28, 157, 290
probative value, 169–70
process tracing, 5, 42, 44, 45, 63, 76, 79, 81, 169–70, 172, 386–91, 387f, 398, 399
proxy, 291–92
Przeworski, Adam, 61, 63–64, 87
public opinion, 40, 196–97, 245, 339–40
  decline of qualitative research, 468, 469–70
  fit and, 456–64, 467, 468, 470, 474
  genres, 459–62
  publishing, 73, 452, 467–75
  standards of, 467, 470–74
publishing, 73, 452, 467–75
  decline of qualitative research, 468, 469–70
  fit and, 456–64, 467, 468, 470, 474
  genres, 459–62
  standards of, 467, 470–74
Putnam, Robert, 61–62
puzzle, 17–18, 19–20, 403
Python, 361–62

qualitative comparative analysis (QCA), 422–29
qualitative data analysis (QDA) software, 361–62, 366–67, 368–70
Qualitative Data Repository (QDR), 173
  "Data Management Plan (DMP) Checklist," 167
qualitative research, 1–7, 72–73
  as aligned, 4, 5
  data collection and, 2
  decline in publishing, 468, 469–70
  ethics of, 4, 6, 132, 133, 138–39
  evaluating claims, 42–44
  experimental studies and, 74
  as flexible, 4, 5
  gender and, 6–7
  generalizability, 44–45
  in graduate student training, 2, 3, 9n.9, 13, 14–18

qualitative research (*cont.*)
   identifying causal mechanisms, 40–42, 45
   as inclusive, 5, 6–7, 138, 139
   interpretivist approach to, 4
   in leading journals, 44–45
   minoritized scholars and, 6–7
   modernity and, 138
   participants and, 138, 139
   positivist approach to, 4
   power and, 132–40
   as rigorous, 4, 5
   theorizing and, 37, 38–39
   trends in, 5
qualitative social network analysis (QSNA), 373–81
Qualtrics, 248, 251
quantitative research
   case studies and, 62–63, 64
   discourse analysis and, 416
   as "fast science," 2
   in graduate student training, 2
   identifying causal relationships, 40, 43, 44, 45
   minoritized scholars and, 287
   as more "scientific," 1–2
   reflexivity and, 23–24
question, 13–15
   adjusting, 146–47
   causality and, 86
   centering minoritized experiences, 289–90
   focus group, 227–28
   future work, 151
   gap-filling, 15, 19–20, 40
   knowledge and, 21n.13
   leverage and, 18–20
   market and, 15–16, 20, 21n.12
   methods and skills for answering, 15–16, 19–20
   open-ended, 245–52
   passion and, 16–17, 20–21
   problem-driven, 15, 19–20
   as puzzle, 17–18, 19–20, 72, 98
Quinn, Kevin M., 64

R (computational tool), 361–62, 378–79
race
   embodied Black political subjectivity, 29–30
   labor and, 27
   minoritization and, 286–88, 290–91, 292–93
   objectivity and, 25–26, 157
   in political science, 25–26
   power and, 29–30, 191
   racialization, 28
   racism, 138, 279
   in research, 23, 25, 27, 28
   as socially constructed, 50
   whiteness and, 25–26
randomization, 64, 74–75, 78
Rangata, Mahlogonolo, 294*b*
Rapid Ethnographic Assessment Procedure (REAP), 112–13
rapport. *See* trust
Rasmussen, Vilhelm, 42
Read, Benjamin L., 91, 92, 146–47

reciprocity, 278–79
recognition, 139
records, recording, 80, 111, 170, 200–1
redundancy, 435–36
reflexivity, 23–27, 97, 99–100, 103, 118, 126, 127–28, 133–35, 137, 157, 236–37, 290, 308, 310–11, 313, 317–18, 331
   active, 294, 294*b*
   individualism and, 26
   limitations of, 26–27
   as performative, 26–27
   relational, 24, 28–31
refugees, 127
regression analysis, 72, 77*t*, 79–80
regulatory impact assessment statement, 341–45
Reich, J. A., 308
Reiling, Carrie, 87–88, 96, 98–99, 100–1, 102–3, 104
relationality, 24, 28–29, 132–40, 197–98
   ethics and, 308–9, 311–19
   of fieldwork, 112–13, 114–15, 117–18, 119, 265, 278
   identity markers and, 117, 118
   in interviews, 209–10, 214–15
   necessity and, 425, 427
   networks and, 373–81
   to other academics, 146
   to participants, 113, 132–40, 156–58, 183, 184–85, 190–91, 197–98, 229–30, 236–39, 240–41, 303, 308–9, 310–19, 331, 448, 449
   power and, 375
   relationship building, 184–85
   in sampling, 124–26
   sets and, 422, 425–27
   sufficiency and, 426, 427
   types of, 375
religion, 56, 74, 286–88
replication, 448
representation, 52–54, 62–63, 186–87, 310
reputation, 161–62, 308–9
research assistant, 139
researcher
   access, 122
   autoethnography and, 113–14
   bias, 158
   cultivating change, 113
   disinvestment, 157
   embodiment, 137
   as focus group moderator, 226
   gender, 270
   identity and, 97, 99–100
   insider/outsider, 139
   interest and, 67–68
   knowledge construction and, 50, 51–57
   labor, 448, 451
   mental health, 299–304
   minoritized, 286–94, 300–2
   needs of, 116, 118–19, 136–37
   physical challenges of research, 239
   positionality, 279–81, 286, 290, 300, 301–2, 309, 310–11, 313, 318, 327, 330, 450
   power and, 27, 28, 133–35, 156, 157, 160, 184–85, 190–91, 192, 278
   privilege, 290

relation to other academics, 146
relation to participants, 113, 132–40, 156–58, 183, 184–85, 190–91, 197–98, 229–30, 236–39, 240–41, 303, 308–9, 310–19, 331, 448, 449
relation to research, 24–27, 28–30, 31
in research design, 91, 97
safety, 267, 268, 292, 301–2, 303, 313–16, 327
skills, 67
as storyteller, 138
transparency and, 449
vulnerability, 215
resources, 66, 73, 119, 161, 173–75
constraints on, 186–87
funding, 151–52
respect, 139
responsibility, 308, 311–12, 313, 318–19
responsive action plan, 157
responsiveness, 308, 311–12, 313, 318–19
revelation, 44. *See also* surprise
Rich, Jessica A. J., 147, 150–51
Riedl, Rachel Beatty, 74, 80
rigor, 1–2, 3, 4, 5, 157, 460–61
Riofrancos, Thea, 62
risk, 209, 265–69, 292, 308–9, 318, 329–30, 450
Ritter, Daniel, 397
Rivera Cusicanqui, Silvia, 281
Rodríguez, Rafael Piñeiro, 168–69
Rogowski, Ron, 468
Rosenblatt, Fernando, 168–69
Ruddick, Sara, 311–12
Rueschemeyer, Dietrich, 2–3, 397
Ruggie, John, 349, 353–54
Ryan, Louise, 24

Saarinen, Jaana, 136
safety, 127, 292, 313–16, 327, 329–30
Said, Edward, 51–52, 53–54, 55, 58n.41
sampling, 125–26
archives and, 258
convenience, 251, 265–66, 269
elites and, 185–87
frame, 78, 123
interviews and, 185–87, 197, 265–66
logic, 149–50
purposive, 125, 185–86, 265–66, 269
quasi-probability, 186–87
random or representative, 64, 328
sample size, 458, 460
snowball, 124–25, 185–86, 191–92, 212, 265–66
See also ethnography
Saurette, Paul, 413
Schaffer, Frederic, 414
Schickler, Eric, 402
Schmidt, Vivian A., 410–11
Schneider, Carsten Q., 424, 427–28
Schwartz-Shea, Peregrine, 2–3, 100
Schwarz, Tanya B., 96, 97, 98, 99, 103
scope conditions, 63
Scott, James C., 75–76
Seawright, Jason, 62–63, 64, 68
Sell, Susan, 354

semiotic practices, 410, 411
Sen, Amartya, 350
set, 422, 424, 425–27
crisp, 424–25
fuzzy, 424–25
set-theoretic multimethod research (SMMR), 428
See also case, case study
sexuality, sexualization, 28
minoritization and, 286–88, 292
in research, 28
Sieber, Joan E., 209, 212
Sikkink, Kathryn, 354, 376
silence, 137–38
Silke, Andrew, 265
Simmons, Erica S., 61, 355, 412
Simonsen, Kristina Bakkær, 249
Sims, Jennifer Patrice, 459, 460–63
Sirnate, Vasundhara, 292
site. *See* case, case study
Skocpol, Theda, 61–62, 397, 400, 401–2
Slater, Dan, 87
Slaughter, Anne-Marie, 349, 352
Sluka, Jeffrey Alan, 127
small-N (non-numeric) study, 1, 4, 62–63, 68, 386, 458, 468
Small, Mario, 310
Smith, Nicholas Rush, 61
social location, 23–24, 25, 28, 29, 133–34
social sciences
close reading and, 339–40
focus groups and, 222
graduate student training, 2
interpretivism and, 410
objectivity and, 49, 158
p-hacking, 438
qualitative comparative analysis (QCA) and, 422
qualitative methods and, 1–4
reflexivity and, 23–27
research transparency and, 435, 436, 440
social work, 26, 29
sociology, 1, 397
Sodiqov, Alexander, 292
Soedirgo, Jessica, 294
solidarity, 308, 311–12, 313, 318–19
Solomon, Daniel, 468
source, 90, 399, 403
Southwest Workshop on Mixed Methods Research, 2–3
space, 112, 113–15, 117. *See also* fieldwork
Spaniel, William, 81
Spivak, Gayatri, 27
stakeholder, 149, 156–57, 158, 159, 161–62
Stantcheva, Stefanie, 246
statistics, statistical analysis, 72, 78–80
cross-sectional, 74–75
description and, 78–79, 399
exponential random graph models (ERGMs), 373–74
models, 40
network analysis and, 373–74
regression analysis, 373
temporal exponential random graph models (TERGMs), 373–74
See also observation, observational study

stereotype, 210, 310
Stockholm International Peace Research Institute, 377
strategic reasoning, 75
Strier, Roni, 136
structure, 373–74, 376, 377
subjectivity, 25, 450
   as embodied, 29–30
   knowledge and, 24–25
   power and, 23, 24, 25–26, 27, 28
   researcher and, 56
   social location and, 23–24, 28, 29
sufficiency, 422, 426–27, 428
support network, 303
surprise, 170, 355–56
survey, surveying, 40, 56–57, 159–60, 169, 245–52, 404

terrorism, 52, 265–73
Teune, Henry, 61, 63–64, 87
text analysis. *See* content analysis
Thachil, Tariq, 250
Thelen, Kathleen, 38, 397, 403–4
theory
   building, 63–64, 78–79, 81
   development, 37–40, 63, 65
   strong, 76
   testing, 65, 75–76, 386
Thomann, Eva, 424
time
   analyzing, 76, 80, 402–3
   collaboration and, 161
   data collection and, 150–52, 173–75
   ethnography and, 235–36, 241
   of fieldwork, 112–13, 114–15
   for interviews, 150–51, 198, 199, 201, 213
   sequencing, 401, 402
   speed of research, 435–36
   surveys and, 251
   time-consuming, 73
   timelines, 388, 389*f*
Tolich, Martin B., 209, 212
topic, 13–14, 20. *See also* question
Tourangeau, Roger, 122
Townsend-Bell, Erica, 25–26
training
   active learning and, 435–36
   in archival research, 258
   graduate student, 23, 25–26, 103, 161, 258, 288–89, 310
   minoritized scholars and, 288–89
transcription, 152, 172, 201, 202
transformation, 398
translation, 270–71, 277
transparency, 5, 25, 157, 160–62, 172–73, 184–85, 236–37, 310–11, 316, 330, 435–41, 446–52

trauma, 300
   retraumatization, 215, 311
triangulation, 72, 81, 90, 148–49, 150, 159, 185–86, 189, 355, 356, 380–81, 471–72
Tronto, Jean, 311–12
trust, 99–101, 103, 124, 125–26, 184–85, 188–89, 191–92, 214, 265, 269–72, 308–9, 311, 330
truth table, 426. *See also* qualitative comparative analysis (QCA)
Tudor, Maya, 400
typological constructions, 386

Um, Su Jung, 134, 136
uncertainty, 42–43, 308, 356, 386

Vähäsantanen, Katja, 136
validity, 63, 72, 73, 81, 245–46, 250
   achieving, 76
   external, 74, 76, 80
value, 50, 56–57
van den Hoonaard, Will C., 210
variable, 87–88, 386
variation, 74–75, 78–79
Vasquez, John, 351
Verba, Sidney, 353, 447
violence, 138, 265
visualizing, 378–79, 380, 403, 428
vulnerability, 118, 123, 127, 208–15, 224, 267, 310, 330
   transparency and, 448
   types of, 209
   See also population

Walter, Barbara, 350, 356
Weber, Max, 281, 354–55
Wedeen, Lisa, 412
Wells, H. G., 41–42
Wilcox, Lauren, 351
Wilfahrt, Martha, 78–79
Williamson, Abigail, 64
Williamson, Emma, 300
Winslow, Wendy, 225–26
Wittgenstein, Ludwig, 414
Women Also Know Stuff, 294
Women in Legislative Studies, 288–89

Yanow, Dvora, 2–3, 100
Yashar, Deborah J., 400
Yom, Sean, 92, 291–92
YouGov, 251
Yuval-Davis, Nira, 134

Zarakol, Ayse, 353–54
Zenodo (repository), 437
Ziblatt, Daniel, 87, 400
Zion, Deborah, 209
Zoom, 324